YOUNG QUEENS

ALSO BY LEAH REDMOND CHANG

Portraits of the Queen Mother:
Polemics, Panegyrics, Letters (with Katherine Kong)

Into Print:
The Production of Female Authorship in Early Modern France

YOUNG
QUEENS

 · · ·

THREE RENAISSANCE WOMEN
AND THE PRICE OF POWER

Leah Redmond Chang

Farrar, Straus and Giroux
New York

Farrar, Straus and Giroux
120 Broadway, New York 10271

Copyright © 2023 by Leah Redmond Chang
All rights reserved
Printed in the United States of America
Originally published in 2023 by Bloomsbury, Great Britain
Published in the United States by Farrar, Straus and Giroux
First American edition, 2023

Image credits can be found on pages 490–91.

Library of Congress Cataloging-in-Publication Data
Names: Chang, Leah L., 1973– author.
Title: Young queens : three Renaissance women and the price of power /
    Leah Redmond Chang.
Other titles: Three Renaissance women and the price of power
Description: First American edition. | New York : Farrar, Straus and Giroux, 2023. |
    Includes bibliographical references and index.
Identifiers: LCCN 2023003433 | ISBN 9780374294489 (hardcover)
Subjects: LCSH: Queens—Europe—Biography. | Europe—Kings and rulers—Biography. |
    Europe—Politics and government—1492–1648.
Classification: LCC D107.3 .C43 2023 | DDC 940.0099—dc23/eng/20230310
LC record available at https://lccn.loc.gov/2023003433

Our books may be purchased in bulk for promotional, educational, or business use. Please contact
your local bookseller or the Macmillan Corporate and Premium Sales Department at 1-800-221-7945,
extension 5442, or by email at MacmillanSpecialMarkets@macmillan.com.

www.fsgbooks.com
www.twitter.com/fsgbooks • www.facebook.com/fsgbooks

1   3   5   7   9   10   8   6   4   2

CONTENTS

PART 2

PART 3

PART 4

CONTENTS

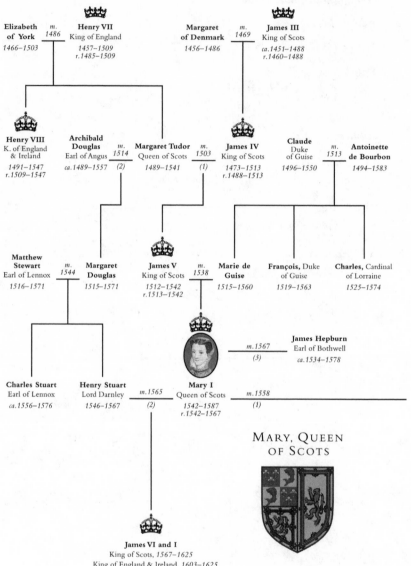

Elizabeth of York
1466–1503

m. 1486

Henry VII
King of England
1457–1509
r.1485–1509

Margaret of Denmark
1456–1486

m. 1469

James III
King of Scots
ca.1451–1488
r.1460–1488

Henry VIII
K. of England & Ireland
1491–1547
r.1509–1547

Archibald Douglas
Earl of Angus
ca.1489–1557

m. 1514
(2)

Margaret Tudor
Queen of Scots
1489–1541

m. 1503
(1)

James IV
King of Scots
1473–1513
r.1488–1513

Claude Duke of Guise
1496–1550

m. 1513

Antoinette de Bourbon
1494–1583

Matthew Stewart
Earl of Lennox
1516–1571

m. 1544

Margaret Douglas
1515–1571

James V
King of Scots
1512–1542
r.1513–1542

m. 1538

Marie de Guise
1515–1560

François, Duke of Guise
1519–1563

Charles, Cardinal of Lorraine
1525–1574

Charles Stuart
Earl of Lennox
ca.1556–1576

Henry Stuart
Lord Darnley
1546–1567

m.1565
(2)

Mary I
Queen of Scots
1542–1587
r.1542–1567

m.1567
(3)

James Hepburn
Earl of Bothwell
ca.1534–1578

m.1558
(1)

MARY, QUEEN
OF SCOTS

James VI and I
King of Scots, 1567–1625
King of England & Ireland, 1603–1625
1566–1625

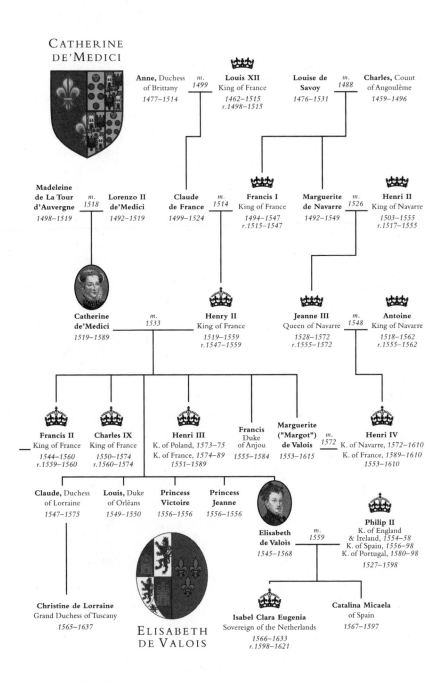

CATHERINE DE'MEDICI

Anne, Duchess of Brittany
1477–1514

m. 1499

Louis XII King of France
1462–1515
r.1498–1515

Louise de Savoy
1476–1531

m. 1488

Charles, Count of Angoulême
1459–1496

Madeleine de La Tour d'Auvergne
1498–1519

m. 1518

Lorenzo II de'Medici
1492–1519

Claude de France
1499–1524

m. 1514

Francis I King of France
1494–1547
r.1515–1547

Marguerite de Navarre
1492–1549

m. 1526

Henri II King of Navarre
1503–1555
r.1517–1555

Catherine de'Medici
1519–1589

m. 1533

Henry II King of France
1519–1559
r.1547–1559

Jeanne III Queen of Navarre
1528–1572
r.1555–1572

m. 1548

Antoine King of Navarre
1518–1562
r.1555–1562

Francis II King of France
1544–1560
r.1559–1560

Charles IX King of France
1550–1574
r.1560–1574

Henri III K. of Poland, *1573–75* K. of France, *1574–89*
1551–1589

Francis Duke of Anjou
1555–1584

Marguerite ("Margot") de Valois
1553–1615

m. 1572

Henri IV K. of Navarre, *1572–1610* K. of France, *1589–1610*
1553–1610

Claude, Duchess of Lorraine
1547–1575

Louis, Duke of Orléans
1549–1550

Princess Victoire
1556–1556

Princess Jeanne
1556–1556

Elisabeth de Valois
1545–1568

m. 1559

Philip II K. of England & Ireland, *1554–58* K. of Spain, *1556–98* K. of Portugal, *1580–98*
1527–1598

Christine de Lorraine Grand Duchess of Tuscany
1565–1637

ELISABETH DE VALOIS

Isabel Clara Eugenia Sovereign of the Netherlands
1566–1633
r.1598–1621

Catalina Micaela of Spain
1567–1597

PROLOGUE

The young girl lay tucked in her bed, her small body wrapped in the black habit of a Benedictine nun. Under her cap, her hair was clipped short in a quick and rough job. In the distance, there was a swelling commotion. Footsteps approached.

She waited in the room where she slept every night, in the belly of a stone-walled convent of nuns known as Le Murate, situated on the Via Ghibellina at the northern edge of Florence. The convent's massive wooden door separated the cloistered nuns and novices from the bustle and disorder of secular Florentine life. Le Murate was supposed to be a haven of pious female devotion, of spiritual stillness. But in the small hours of July 20, 1530, eleven-year-old Caterina de' Medici felt only fear.[1]

Caterina was not a nun; nor was she a novice. She was a guest at Le Murate, a hostage of the Republican Council that ruled Florence. Earlier that evening, soldiers and magistrates from the Council had arrived at the convent's door, torches lighting their way. The men were agitated. Three years earlier, in 1527, the Council had wrested control of the city from the Medici family. Now, however, they had lost their grip. The Medici pope, Clement VII, was besieging Florence with the help of the Spanish king and Holy Roman Emperor Charles V. Food and supplies were dwindling, citizens were revolting, and the Council had exhausted their options—all but one. On that July night, the councillors descended upon the Via Ghibellina to retrieve their young hostage, hoping to compel the pope to call off his troops.

But the Council hadn't counted on the resistance of the nuns of Le Murate. Gutsy and stubborn, the sisters refused to open the convent door.[2]

As the night wore on, the magistrates grew impatient. Someone signaled to the soldiers. Moments later, in an explosion of gunfire, the wooden door splintered open.

Stepping through it, the Council secretary, Silvestro Aldobrandini, and his men were met with a whorl of habits and veils. Trying to block the men from penetrating deeper into the convent, the nuns sank to their knees, then threw themselves to the ground, crying, praying, pleading, and arguing. At dawn, Aldobrandini pushed past the women and began to search the halls. Finally, in that small chamber, he found what he was looking for.

Aldobrandini got Caterina out of bed. She must have made for a sight, a tired and terrified little girl in a rumpled nun's habit. But if he expected meekness, Aldobrandini was disappointed. Caterina stood her ground. Even then, she showed the grit and tenacity that would define her later years, what one nun described as an "undefeated and generous spirit." And well before the men burst into her room, the child Caterina had decided to put up a fight.[3]

For decades afterward, the nuns of Le Murate told the story of that terrible night, passing it down from nun to nun, the stuff of convent legend. Only at the close of the century, in 1598, did Sister Giustina Niccolini decide to write it down. As she recorded this history, Giustina knew what eventually became of that scared little girl. Born in Florence, Caterina had died a French queen, the power behind France's throne, one of the most formidable women in Europe.

Caterina lived an extraordinary life in extraordinary times. She married a man who, quite unexpectedly, became king of France. She witnessed the Protestant Reformation take root in Europe and watched as France was torn apart by religious and political strife. She made both peace and war. She gave birth to children, some of whom lived and some of whom died. She saw her sons made into kings as boys and stood beside them as they bore the immeasurable weight of the crown. She wept tears of sorrow when her daughters left her side to be married. When they, too, became mothers, she wept tears of joy.

Caterina changed the face of France, sculpting its gardens, constructing its châteaus, building its monuments. Clad perpetually in black, she became an emblematic figure of the realm, known across Europe simply as "the Queen Mother." France had changed her, too. By her teens, Caterina had taken on France's language and customs as her own. Even her name changed, from the Italianate *Caterina* to the Gallic *Caterine*. She had come to revere the nobility of France and to prize her own ancient French aristocratic bloodlines, although she would never quite shed her Italian commoner roots—not entirely.

The girl who would become Catherine de' Medici, Queen Mother of France, came to her crown almost by accident in an astounding ascent. More astounding still was the breadth of her power. Catherine held on to that power through deliberate choices, a steadfast belief in her own authority, and a determination to protect her children and her adopted realm. She fought to stay relevant, to steer France out of the morass of war. She persevered in the face of profound challenges. For almost thirty years, she ruled France in all but name.

For the duration of her reign as Queen Mother, her enemies wanted to send her back to the fold of domesticity, her chief task to care for her children. But Catherine decided her place was next to the king, her son.

———

Before she became Queen Mother, Catherine de' Medici was the queen consort of France, the dutiful wife of King Henry II. Their marriage endured over twenty-five years, until a summer day in 1559 when Henry suffered the horrific accident that would take his life. Deep in mourning, Catherine swathed herself in black, and kept close by her side her eldest daughter, Elisabeth de Valois, only recently married to Philip II, King of Spain. Mourning with her, too, was Mary Stuart, the beguiling Queen of Scots, Catherine's daughter-in-law. They were three queens together in one court: Catherine, now the French queen mother, Elisabeth, the queen of Spain, and Mary, the new queen consort of France. Faced with the uncertainty and fear that always surrounded a king's death, they gave each other comfort—two teenaged girls and a woman touching middle age, united in sorrow.

For Catherine, Elisabeth, and Mary, the death of King Henry would prove the end of an era. For over a decade, they had lived together in France, bound to each other through blood and marriage, through alliance, friendship, love, and filial piety. The king's death would thrust them into new roles, vesting them with new political burdens and pushing them toward new alliances and identities. Soon enough, they would part ways: Elisabeth leaving her childhood home to venture into life as the queen of Spain in late 1559; Mary returning to govern her kingdom of Scotland soon thereafter in 1561; Catherine remaining in France to shepherd her young son, ten-year-old King Charles IX. This parting—from France, from each other, from the comforts of childhood for Elisabeth and Mary, from young motherhood for Catherine—would profoundly alter their friendships and family bonds for the rest of their lives.

Catherine, Elisabeth, and Mary were family, and knew each other intimately as sisters, daughters, and mothers. For a time, they loved and respected each other—at least until political pressures frayed their relationships. Even then, they never forgot their ties of kinship and duty: Mary would always refer to Elisabeth as her "sister," and think of her fondly as one of her dearest childhood friends, a memory Elisabeth shared. And well after she left France, Mary would call herself Catherine's "daughter." Catherine would respond in kind.

Young Queens follows the interlaced lives of Catherine, Elisabeth, and Mary over the course of two decades. Telling their stories as one reveals patterns about women and power that we may miss or discount when assessing any of them in isolation. Catherine, Elisabeth, and Mary reigned in disparate kingdoms, and were forced to navigate distinct customs, cultures, languages, religions, and expectations. They had drastically different personalities and grappled with different pressures. But their experience on the throne was shaped more by their femaleness than by any cultural contingency. And in this thematic symmetry, they tell each other's stories.

The documents charting their lives—a tapestry of letters, diplomatic dispatches, ambassadorial reports, memoirs, poems, essays, notebooks, chronicles, and portraits—reveal the women behind the queens. They allow us to discover their friendships and jealousies, follow their schoolwork and favorite pastimes, glimpse their childhood quirks and proclivities—a tendency toward bossiness, for instance, or a penchant for mischief. We learn of their eagerness for marriage and their anxieties about it, the turbulence of their puberties, their love for their husbands and mothers, and sometimes their resentment. In these documents we can see their divided loyalties and private fears. We come to know them as they knew each other—as complex and flawed human beings, their potential coexisting alongside their faults and frailties.

Catherine, Elisabeth, and Mary were queens of kingdoms bound together in the political web of Renaissance Europe. Their reigns were shaped by the sea changes that transformed Europe in the second half of the sixteenth century, as war raged between Protestants and Catholics, and marriages, births, and loyalty to kin moved the pieces on the political chessboard. The threat of war and the fear of rebellion forced them in girlhood to shoulder political responsibilities that would have intimidated women twice their age. Barely pubescent, they uttered their wedding vows and left home for foreign lands, knowing they might never see their families again. Their bodies suffered in pregnancy and childbirth, the burdens of dynastic marriage imprinting themselves onto their very flesh. They grappled with anxiety and depression, yet nonetheless played the public roles required of them.

They harbored hopes, dreams, desires, and regrets—desires and regrets that were as instrumental in shaping the Renaissance as any edict, battle, or birth of a king.

As it traces the intertwined stories of Catherine, Elisabeth, and Mary, *Young Queens* also tells a larger story about queenship. Together, these women represent every sort of queen in the Renaissance. A sovereign queen, or queen regnant—a queen who reigns supreme over her kingdom. A queen consort, or a queen by dint of marriage to a reigning king. And a queen mother, the widow of one king and the mother of the next. At different times, Mary would occupy each of these roles; Catherine, two of them; Elisabeth, just one.

Such were the many faces of a queen in sixteenth-century Europe. Unlike for a king, the role a queen could occupy, and the breadth of her authority, were contingent on circumstance. In medieval and early modern Europe, sovereign kings were the norm; women ruled from the throne only infrequently. At least in theory, a king sat in the preeminent seat in the realm, and (barring a coup) his continued authority depended on his remaining alive; until he died, he answered to no master except God. Queenship was far more fluid: a woman could inhabit multiple roles, her power within those roles waxing and waning over the course of a lifetime.

Catherine, Elisabeth, and Mary were hardly the only powerful women in Renaissance Europe. On the contrary, they lived during a time when women governed many of Europe's kingdoms as sovereigns or regents, an unprecedented era of female rule. In part because of the religious and political strife of the mid-sixteenth century, women pushed the limits of their political power far beyond what was normally expected of them. A woman like Catherine de' Medici, for instance, practically invented the political role of the queen mother, infusing it with unprecedented authority. Even a young woman like Elisabeth de Valois, consigned to the childbearing role of the consort, discovered she could influence politics, often in secret and circuitous ways.

A queen's security on her throne, however, was inherently precarious. This was as true for a sovereign queen as for a consort. For although a sovereign like Mary, Queen of Scots, was vested with the same earthly authority as a king—an authority that, in theory, was sanctioned by God—in a culture of deeply entrenched misogyny she could not overcome her gender. In sixteenth-century monarchies, all loyal subjects were expected to commit themselves to the stability of the realm, the safety of the sovereign and the preservation of his authority. Sacrifice for the sake of the realm was not limited to women and girls. For the sovereign's welfare, a royal boy, too, could become a pawn; for the health of the kingdom, even a king could be forced to make painful choices.

Yet in a culture that considered women inferior to men both in body and mind, gender defined and compromised a sovereign queen's authority and even her value to the realm—and this rendered her experience on the throne closer to that of a consort than of a king.

No kingdom rejoiced at the notion of a woman wielding the power of the crown, either directly from the throne or from behind it. A woman's accession to the throne signaled the vulnerability of the kingdom at large to both foreign enemies and those from within. This gendered weakness became a particular liability in the sixteenth century as the Reformation questioned both the infallibility of the Roman Catholic Church and the sanctity of the sovereign, concepts that had previously composed the bedrock of society. Caught in the tumult of religious upheaval, could a kingdom helmed by either a child or a woman survive? Could monarchy itself survive? Women's rule was particularly anxiety-provoking. For whereas a boy king would grow into manhood, a woman on the throne could not outgrow her femaleness.

Indeed, gender determined the lives of Catherine, Elisabeth, and Mary from the moment of their birth. If they survived childhood, noble girls of their rank were expected to marry and bear children, a dynastic role they were reared to fulfill. The promise of fertility gave aristocratic girls their value and transformed young women into the currency of ambitious sovereigns and families who traded them in marriage. Catherine, Elisabeth, and Mary would live different iterations of this truth. Their bodies, passed across borders, became symbolic capital, the vector of peace, alliance, wealth, or empire.

A queen's foremost obligation to her realm was to give birth. A kingdom required heirs: no consort or sovereign queen could escape this reality.* A queen's very survival at court depended on her success in childbed. A consort like Catherine or Elisabeth who gave birth secured her place and earned her keep, especially if she produced a son; a queen who failed to do so risked repudiation. A sovereign queen like Mary who gave birth ensured the continuation of her dynasty for the realm. And yet, in pregnancy and childbirth, she jeopardized her life and thus the surety of her realm. As Mary would find in an ironic twist, even a successful birth could place a sovereign queen in peril and pave the way for her destruction.

It was precisely in the civil and religious disorder of sixteenth-century Europe that a queen's reproductive role became indispensable.

---

*Only Queen Elizabeth I of England managed to avoid this fate, although whether she did so willfully or by accident remains unclear. For decades, the question of her marriage remained the foremost concern of the realm, at tremendous emotional cost to Elizabeth.

For a queen's ability to produce children ensured the smooth continuation of dynasty and government, stabilizing world order as the Renaissance understood it.

Biology, more than bloodline, was destiny. This, then, was the queen's fundamental paradox: the source of both her strength and greatest weakness was rooted in her womb.

Catherine, Elisabeth, and Mary would each strive to steer their way as best they could within the confines prescribed for them. While marshaling law, and commanding councils and households, they also availed themselves of skills and assets acquired over years, honed out of necessity. Elisabeth leaned on her own gentle amiability, a gift for diplomacy, and the guidance of her mother. Mary relied on charm and beauty, alongside a deeply ingrained sense of her own blood right. Catherine made motherhood her strength. Canny and intelligent, she learned how to command and placate in equal measure. She drew heavily on the help of other women, a network built over years. She understood the power of theater and knew how to tell a story. Somewhere in her youth, she learned to read a room. She figured out what powerful men wished to hear.

Catherine began to learn these skills very young. Unlike her daughter and daughter-in-law, she was forced to navigate her way in the world from her earliest years, when she was still "Caterina," merely a "tender little virgin, pure and innocent of all her sins," as Sister Giustina wrote, recalling the July morning in 1530 when the secretary of the Florentine Republican Council came to take Caterina away.[4]

The child Caterina had wealth on her side; she had powerful connections, popes, kings, and dukes who were invested in her future. But as she faced Aldobrandini in the convent of Le Murate, however, Caterina was alone. She thought he had come to kill her. "She is small for her age," an envoy once noted. Aldobrandini must have towered over her.

She had attempted to hide, shearing her hair and scrambling into that nun's habit, a child's effort to trick a grown man. Aldobrandini wasn't fooled. And yet, in the moment, Caterina would discover that she wasn't entirely powerless.

"You tell those men, my 'fathers' the *Signori*," she shouted at Aldobrandini, "that I want to be a nun and stay here forever with my reverend mothers!"

Aldobrandini looked at her habit and ordered the sisters to put Caterina back into "her usual clothes." No one moved.[5]

Furious, Aldobrandini scooped Caterina up, plowed his way back to the street, and sat her on a horse. Still, Caterina refused to back down. As Aldobrandini led her through the streets of Florence, she wept and prayed aloud, crying out that she "was no more than eleven years old and did not understand why God and the heavens had made her so important and given her such good fortune if only to make her die so cruelly."[6] Somewhere along the way, Aldobrandini began to soften. Maybe it was the crying that tugged at his heartstrings. Perhaps he admired the bravery of this small girl, ready to resist him despite the guards and guns. She had shown an extraordinary presence of mind. Maybe it was the devotion of the nuns who had united against him for her sake—perhaps this was a sign that God was on Caterina's side. Somehow the actions of the nuns and of Caterina herself moved Aldobrandini. In the convent of Le Murate, he had witnessed real courage.

Aldobrandini told Caterina that no harm would come to her. He promised to return her to Le Murate within the month. He proved as good as his word, though events did not turn out in the Republican Council's favor. Just weeks later, on August 12, 1530, the Council surrendered to Pope Clement VII, and the Florentines escorted Caterina back to the reverend mothers, who welcomed her with open arms. She would never forget the nuns' kindness and bravery during that summer of 1530. They had loved her very much, Sister Giustina wrote. Caterina was deeply grateful for that love and sent gifts to Le Murate for the rest of her life. Years later, Giustina was proud of all the Queen Mother of France had given the sisters.[7]

Despite his name, Pope Clement VII would show the Republican Council no mercy. After the pope restored the Medici and their deputies to power, six of the councilmen were beheaded, while others were tortured before being banished from the city.[8]

Aldobrandini was spared. Though he, too, had been sentenced to die, Caterina intervened to commute his death into exile. She'd decided to forgive Aldobrandini.* He had been gentle with her, in the end. "I have never seen anyone of her age so quick to feel the goodness and the ill that are done to her," a French diplomat once wrote about the young girl. He sensed a strength in her character. Caterina never forgot a wrong, but she could repay even the smallest of kindnesses. At eleven years old, she had learned she had a voice. She'd learned that men would listen.[9]

And that with generosity, too, comes a certain kind of power.

---

*Aldobrandini's son, Ippolito, born years later in 1536, would go on to become Pope Clement VIII in 1592. Clement VIII still reigned as pontiff in 1598 as Sister Giustina composed her chronicle.

PART 1

I

THE ORPHAN
Italy, 1519–1533

In September 1533, fourteen-year-old Catherine de' Medici boarded a galley headed from Porto Venere on the northern shore of Italy toward the port city of Villefranche on the southern coast of France, not far from Nice. The weather was fair for sailing; she expected to arrive within days. She brought with her a wealth of treasure packed in trunks and crates and jewel boxes. She carried with her, too, a wealth of memories—of suffering, fear, even terror, along with memories of laughing cousins, the scent of rose pomanders, the sticky taste of sweet buns smeared with jam. In Nice, she would meet the French king, now her sovereign, the man who would soon become her father-in-law. She would also meet his son, her future husband, Henry, Duke of Orléans. Not yet betrothed, she already thought like a bride. She still signed her name *Caterina* but would soon switch to *Caterine*. She'd already tried out that signature once or twice, gripping the quill firmly in her fingers as the ink flowed onto the page.

In a way, Catherine de' Medici's story begins not at her birth but rather on those waters, under those Mediterranean skies, the sails of her ship whipping against a late summer breeze. This was the moment of her crossing from Italy to France, from maiden to bride, from the Medici family to a royal French one, from girlhood to young womanhood. Already, she had assumed a new importance as those who observed the pendulum of Renaissance politics now took note of her, measuring her looks, her bearing, her potential to give birth; from this moment forward, the traces of Catherine will appear more prominently in the archives. At fourteen, she was barely in her teens, ignorant of what the coming years would bring. And yet, to the sixteenth-century world, this part of her story was nothing new. A wealthy girl leaves her homeland to marry a prince, neither for love nor looks but for the dowry and value she brings? This had been the path charted for Catherine's mother, for countless girls of Catherine's time and place. A path that, to a girl like Catherine, must have seemed as ancient and predictable as the rising sun.

She left behind neither mother nor father in Italy. Catherine had been an orphan almost since birth. Her father had been Lorenzo di Piero de' Medici, Duke of Urbino and ruler of Florence. The scion of the Medici family's senior branch, Lorenzo was the grandson and namesake of the great fifteenth-century Florentine banker and patron Lorenzo de' Medici, known as *Il Magnifico*.

Her mother had been a teenaged French princess, Madeleine de La Tour d'Auvergne, Countess of Boulogne, a fact that her contemporaries, and many a historian since, would sometimes forget. Madeleine had been an orphan, too, by the time of her own wedding to the Italian Lorenzo, married on the orders of that same French sovereign, King Francis I. Even as a squalling infant in Florence, Catherine had commanded the attention of King Francis, who, from far-off France, began cogitating plans for the child, knowing she had the potential to bring new lands under French rule. Several years would pass before the king's projects for Catherine could unfold as he hoped. And long before those plans came to fruition, Madeleine de La Tour d'Auvergne had died.

When she set sail on that galley in September 1533, Catherine de' Medici was traveling to a land both unknown and strangely familiar, her mother's kingdom.

She was finishing her mother's story. And in a sense, Catherine was coming home.

Baptized Caterina Maria Romula in the Medici parish church of San Lorenzo, she was the great-granddaughter of *Il Magnifico*. Every important event in her childhood turned on this single fact. From her earliest years, Caterina was subject to the whims of princes and the ebb and flow of Italian and European politics. Even her conception had been political, her flesh and blood plotted by ambitious relatives who anticipated her birth with both delight and greed.

The marriage of her parents in 1518 was the pet project of the Medici pope, Leo X, and the young King Francis I of France. The scene of their wedding was Francis's magnificent royal château at Amboise. The backdrop was a series of bloody conflicts known as the "Italian Wars" that had hounded French kings for generations.

Just twenty years old when he ascended the French throne in 1515, Francis was a charismatic and athletic warrior prince, a slender version of the larger-than-life king he would become, as comfortable in battle armor as he was in silks. An English diplomat once called Francis "merry of cheere."[1] The king loved a good party, reveled in the hunt, and surrounded himself with beautiful and fawning ladies, but he was also ambitious, ready to lock horns with the other young kings of Europe. Both Henry VIII of England and Charles I of Spain had ascended their own thrones within a decade of Francis's accession. Henry VIII inherited his kingdom in 1509 just before his nineteenth birthday; Charles I was only sixteen when he took up his Spanish crown in 1516. Descended from Isabel of Castile and Ferdinand of Aragon on his mother's side, and the Hapsburg dukes of Burgundy on his father's, Charles joined most of the provinces of the Netherlands to the kingdom of Spain. By the time he was nineteen, Charles had added Hapsburg Austrian lands, along with several Italian territories, to his growing dominions. In 1519, their rivalry already heated, Charles successfully outbid Francis to become Charles V, Holy Roman Emperor. From that moment on, everyone called Charles simply "the emperor."

The contests among these young kings would define the age, each seeking to best the others both on the battlefield and at court. Francis, sleek and stylish, ushered the Renaissance into France, importing art, artists, and architecture from Italy into his palaces and gardens, and patronizing renowned scholars and writers. Charles V declared Spain the "empire on which the sun never sets," and relentlessly pushed the boundaries of his kingdom farther into Europe, over the Mediterranean into Africa, and past the Atlantic into the New World. Insecure on his throne as only the second Tudor to reign in England, Henry VIII yearned for a son. In the meantime, he sent marauding

English armies over the border into Scotland, desperate to expand his kingdom to cover the whole of Britain. Contemporary portraits of these kings could have been studies in boastful virility. Over the years, the beards on their faces grew thicker, their sleeves broader, codpieces larger, swords longer, stances wider as if to connote the swagger of their strides.

Francis hated that Henry VIII dared call himself "King of France," which English sovereigns had done ever since the English conquered Calais in the fourteenth century. But Francis saw Charles V as his chief nemesis. Their battlefield was the boot of Italy. Since the late fifteenth century, the kings of France and Spain had vied for supremacy over several provinces in Italy; taking up the mantle soon after his accession, King Francis set his sights on Milan, Genoa, and Naples. During the early years of his Italian Wars against Charles V, Francis garnered some wins but suffered more setbacks, depleting his coffers and watering Italian fields with French blood. Dissatisfied with his progress on the battlefield, Francis looked for ways to win papal support for his Italian enterprises from Pope Leo X.

In September 1517, he wrote to the young Lorenzo II de' Medici, scion of the Florentine banking clan and the pope's nephew. "I hope . . . to marry you to some beautiful and great lady," he ventured, "one who would be a relative of mine and of great lineage so that the love I bear you would grow and strengthen even more." "I would have no greater desire," replied a coy Lorenzo, "than to take this lady from Your Majesty's hand."[*2]

This was a quid pro quo. Pope Leo had the power to vest Francis with Milan. In exchange, the French king offered the Medici royal support and aristocratic prestige, which he knew the Medici had coveted for generations.

Despite their unfathomable wealth, the Medici were decidedly common-born. To be sure, no one could deny their importance. The family had learned to play a long game over hundreds of years as slowly, over generations, they'd made themselves the de facto

*This was not the first political French–Medici marriage. Months after his accession in 1515, his Italian ambitions already thrumming, King Francis offered his maternal aunt, Philiberte de Savoy, to Leo X's younger brother, Giuliano. She came with no dowry; marriage to a royal family was seen as prize enough. The union proved fruitless. Giuliano died within a year of the wedding, the marriage having produced no children. Without a child to reinforce it, the alliance faded away.

rulers of Florence and power brokers across Europe. The family first tasted affluence in the thirteenth century, and civic influence by the fourteenth. In Florence, their common birth became an asset as the Medici transformed themselves into populist leaders in contrast to the noble-blooded families like the Orsini and Visconti, who governed Rome and Milan. Slowly, the Medici infiltrated Florentine corporations, building their wealth and power, penetrating the College of Cardinals, and aspiring to the papal throne itself. They chiseled the Medici *palle*—the family insignia, comprised of six balls shaped like pills or cupping glasses, said to harken back to their origins as doctors—onto monuments and churches, painted them into frescoes, stamped them onto book covers and into the hearts and minds of Florentines.

By the early fifteenth century, the Medici served as the titular heads of the Florentine republic. By midcentury, they were underwriting kings and princes across Europe. Lorenzo I de' Medici, *Il Magnifico*, oversaw Florence's golden age. "Peace reigned in Florence," waxed the historian Guicciardini, a fervent Medici supporter. "The people revelled daily in spectacles, festivals, and new marvels." No one went hungry; art and learning flourished. "The city breathed health . . . elite and cultivated minds lived in prosperity."[3]

The Medici had faltered somewhat in the sixteenth century, their starry ascendance hampered by political rivals in Florence, weak leadership among the descendants of *Il Magnifico*, and the bald fact that the senior branch of the Medici was dying out. The family pinned its hopes on young Lorenzo, the only legitimate male heir of *Il Magnifico*. Pope Leo tried to fashion Lorenzo, a notorious profligate, into an aristocrat. In 1517, shortly before Francis I sent his marriage proposal, Leo named his nephew the Duke of Urbino. But as Francis well knew, the Medici were parvenus in a world that put more stake in bloodlines than wealth. The Medici were still commoners, not a single drop of blue blood coursing through their veins. That would change if Lorenzo de' Medici married the French noblewoman Francis offered, and if she bore a child. The Valois dynasty of France and the Medici of Florence would be united. The alliance would secure Medici control over Florence and put the force of the French crown behind Medici enterprises in Europe. The children of the marriage would be French aristocrats, the Medici now a hair's breadth from royalty.

Francis made good on his promise. The bride he chose was his distant cousin, Madeleine de La Tour d'Auvergne, a fantastically wealthy and pedigreed orphan. She was sixteen; Lorenzo de' Medici was twenty-six. The French king kept up his wooing of the pope, hosting the wedding the following spring, on April 28, 1518, at his favorite château of Amboise. Francis escorted the bride to the altar himself and arranged for ten days of candlelit ballets and balls, jousts and feasts. Soon after Lorenzo brought Madeleine back to Florence that summer, he wrote to both Pope Leo and King Francis announcing her pregnancy.[4] And on April 13, 1519, at precisely 11 o'clock in the morning, Madeleine gave birth to Caterina.[5]

Then Madeleine died two weeks after the baby's birth. The cause was likely puerperal fever, her womb having failed "to purge itself fully," as the doctors explained to the grieving household. The Medici's distress only mounted when Lorenzo followed his wife to the grave just days later, on May 4.[6] Shaking with his own fever, he had taken to his sickbed weeks earlier, suffering from an affliction (likely syphilis) that had plagued him since before his wedding. With Lorenzo's death, the French–Medici alliance lay in ruins. King Francis was unable to recuperate the good understanding he'd shared with the pope. By 1521, Leo X had abandoned Francis and agreed to a new treaty with Charles V, Francis's bitter enemy. Having decided that Spanish domination of Italy was inevitable, Leo X preferred to bet on the winner.

Leo X wept upon hearing of Lorenzo's death, then raced to shore up the Medici inheritance. He claimed the duchy of Urbino for the infant Caterina, and sent his cousin, Giulio de' Medici, to guarantee Medici stewardship of Florence. There remained the problem of what to do with the baby girl herself. King Francis had offered to raise Caterina at the French court, but Leo politely refused, unwilling to give the French control over his bargaining chip. Instead, the pope sent the baby to live with her Medici aunt Clarice, who lived with her Strozzi husband and growing clutch of Strozzi children in Rome.

Caterina would remain in Clarice Strozzi's household for the next several years. This was a waiting game. Pope Leo had hoped Madeleine would give birth to a boy—a son who could inherit his father's titles and properties, and push Medici good fortune into France and beyond. Instead, the Medici got a girl. Certainly, she could prove useful one day as a bride to seal other worthy political alliances. If, that is, she lived—and it was a big if, given that sixteenth-century parents half-expected their children to die before the age of seven, no matter how wealthy the family or how tenderly their babies were loved. In fact, at the age of three months, the infant Caterina fell so deathly ill that Pope Leo feared another imminent Medici tragedy.[7] The baby pulled through, yet everyone knew the next childhood illness was just around the corner.

As it turned out, death came for the pope first. Leo X expired suddenly on December 1, 1521, just weeks after endorsing Charles V's claim to Milan. The new pope, Hadrian VI, was a Dutchman with no interest in Medici affairs or their infant children. Slipping the Ring of the Fisherman on his finger, Hadrian left Catherine nestled in the bosom of the Strozzi household. For a brief but blissful few years, she was mostly forgotten.

From the time the infant Caterina disappeared into the Strozzi villa in Rome until her appearance at the gates of the Le Murate convent in 1527 when she was eight, there is hardly a trace of her in the archives. Clarice Strozzi was a kind and attentive foster mother, but she left no letter describing her young niece, no portrait of the girl, or at least none survives. We are left to imagine and wonder. These were formative years for Caterina, who, growing up among her cousins, developed lifelong attachments to her Strozzi kin. It was in Clarice's home that the tiny orphan enjoyed something of a family, and there that she learned what it meant to be a Medici.

The Strozzi household was a bustling place. Caterina lived surrounded by women and children, bound by the rules of the nursery, governed by the daily rhythms of eating, playing, sleeping, and, in a Catholic Europe still barely touched by Protestantism, praying in a Catholic way, a Latin way—the only way, as far as the Medici and the Strozzi were concerned. She learned to walk and run along sunbaked terraces and among the sculptures and chestnut trees inspired by fashionable Medici gardens, lush designs that Clarice had brought to Rome. Sweets and smells and color from a Renaissance garden formed her senses, teaching her the flavor of melon, the scent of rosemary, the perfume of roses, the touch of billowy hydrangea. Medici and Strozzi tastes began to train her child's eye. She learned about beauty yet didn't even realize it was happening.[8]

Scampering with her cousins, she romped through games of blindman's bluff and hide-and-seek and rolled polished stones on tiles like marbles. As the Strozzi boys rode hobby horses to learn what noblemen do, she played to learn, too, with *bambole* or dolls, dressing them in lace and satiny skirts. At Lent she played with tops; trinkets and knickknacks filled other days. She felt the bumps and scrapes of childhood, the bruised ego of bickering, the lightness of laughter.

She was too young for schooling and too young for the wafer and wine of Holy Communion. Both would come after she turned seven or eight, when children reached the age of reason according to the Catholic Church, and when adults became more confident a child might live. But a little girl like Caterina could begin to learn to stitch and to speak well, to chant her ABCs and to sing. Above all, she learned to pray: the Ave Maria, the Credo, the Pater Noster.[9] In the backdrop of her childhood, she saw rosaries swinging from girdles and heard the chorus of church bells. She learned the Hours of the Virgin, her place in Clarice's home, and her place before God.

Was it in Clarice's home, too, that she first learned something of her mother's family? The Medici were too starved for blue blood not to have relished Madeleine's vaunted ancestry, their link to the French royal family. Through her own mother, Madeleine sprang from a branch of the Bourbons. The second family in the kingdom of France, the Bourbons descended from the sainted crusading king, Louis IX. Known as the "princes of the blood," the Bourbons were poised to inherit the French throne if ever the current Valois dynasty died out. King Francis I and his fertile wife Claude had already produced enough sons to ensure a Valois king in the next generation, but the Bourbons were nonetheless powerful and beloved by French subjects, revered for their ancient bloodlines. King Francis had kept his promise to the Medici indeed when he delivered Madeleine, a Bourbon, to the altar at Amboise in 1518.[10]

When did the child Caterina learn of this exalted inheritance? What did she ask about her mother? An Italian diplomat once gushed that Madeleine was "beautiful and wise . . . gracious and very worthy," words that extol and yet say very little.[11] No doubt the young Caterina learned of Madeleine's wealth, of her vast, rolling estates in Auvergne. Perhaps she saw a portrait. As with so much of Madeleine's life, we can't be sure of what she looked like. One painting now hanging in the Uffizi is sometimes said to be of Madeleine. A slim girl, straight and stylish in her dark velvet bodice and opulent red sleeves, looks out from under a French hood. Her hair is auburn and her cheeks round. Her eyes are blue.

As a grown woman, Caterina would prize her French roots. She would hang a portrait of her mother, now lost, in her private gallery at Soissons; she would commission books, penned by the famous calligrapher Geoffroy Tory, tracing the history of her ancestors, the counts of Auvergne, and keep them carefully in her library.[12] She likely heard stories—of her parents' wedding reception in Florence, perhaps, where her Medici grandmother propped up a portrait of Leo X at the head table and ordered so much silk for the occasion that merchants in Florence ran out.[13] (Couriers galloped to nearby Lucca and Venice to fetch more.) But if stories and portraits gave Caterina a vague sense of her mother's origins, the reality of her French connections would shortly be driven home by the arrival in Rome of a Scottish-French soldier prince.

His name was John Stewart, Duke of Albany. He was Caterina's maternal uncle. Sent by King Francis to Rome, he arrived at the Strozzi villa sometime in 1525, when Caterina was just about six years old.

King Francis hadn't lost sight of the Medici orphan; through the years, he was kept apprised of her whereabouts and her health. Under the Dutch Pope Hadrian VI, the Medici lost some of their political leverage in the European theater. The setback proved short-lived. After Hadrian died in September 1523, the papal conclave elected Cardinal Giulio de' Medici as the new pope. Giulio took the name Clement VII. Whereas Hadrian had paid little mind to Caterina's existence, Clement took a renewed interest in the girl, and began to call himself her uncle (though he was in fact her second cousin once removed). Clement's accession also breathed new life into King Francis's hopes for a Medici alliance. Once again, the French king looked to the papacy as an ally in his never-ending conflict with Charles V.

By 1525, the Italian Wars had brought King Francis to new lows. In February of that year, Charles V's Imperial troops pummeled French battalions in the disastrous battle at Pavia, slaughtering the flower of French nobility and sending Francis himself into Spanish captivity. Although the exact timing remains unclear, it was likely from his Spanish prison that Francis wrote to his trusted counselor and general, John Stewart, Duke of Albany, urging him to visit the new pope. While in Rome, suggested Francis, Albany might make a little side trip to the Strozzi villa.

Tall and square-shouldered, John Stewart, Duke of Albany, was a Scotsman who was also a Frenchman. Born in France to a French duchess and a royal Scottish prince, Albany was a grandson of King James II of Scotland. He was also a cousin to Madeleine de La Tour d'Auvergne and her older sister Anne. Albany had been raised with them, spending a happy childhood hunting and hawking in the wooded hills of Auvergne. Although his birth placed him in line to the Scottish throne, Albany spent much of his adulthood in the service of King Francis, to whom he demonstrated an irreproachable fidelity. If Albany's title belonged to Scotland, his heart belonged to France. French was his first language, and for his entire life, he always preferred to sign his name the French way: *Jehan Stuart* instead of *John Stewart*.

Albany had married his cousin, Anne de La Tour d'Auvergne, and taken the younger Madeleine in as a ward after the death of her parents. Close to both cousins, Albany had loved Anne deeply, an unusual attachment in this age of arranged marriages. They had no surviving children, all three of their babies having died in early childhood. When Anne died in 1524, five years after Madeleine, she bequeathed her landholdings to her niece Caterina, making her the sole heir of the Auvergne fortune.[14] Albany hadn't met Caterina before he appeared at the Strozzi villa in 1525. Did he detect any traces of his beloved wife or her sister in the young girl's face?[*]

If love for his deceased wife bolstered Albany's attention to Caterina, his primary mission in Rome was to promote King Francis's political

---

[*]Albany never remarried, an unusual decision for a man of his rank. Although Anne bequeathed her property to Caterina, she made sure that Albany could use the estates during the remainder of his lifetime, and left him all her furniture, tapestries, and jewels.

interests. Though Caterina was still young, Francis already saw her as the key to future Italian conquests. Dutifully, Albany would keep watch over his niece from afar during the coming years.

They were turbulent years for Caterina, turned upside down as the Italian Wars sent shockwaves through Europe. The events that led Caterina to the convent of Le Murate began to unfold in 1527. By then, Clarice Strozzi had brought eight-year-old Caterina back to Florence. Although the exact reasons for the move remain unknown, it is likely that Clement wanted to establish a Medici presence in Florence now that he had moved to the Vatican.[15]

That same year, King Francis, now released from Spanish captivity, set his sights once again on ousting Charles V from the Italian peninsula with the help of the papacy. Roundly defeated in the spring, Francis retreated to France to regroup. Charles's Imperial troops lingered in Tuscany. A motley crew, they were hungry, bored, and disgruntled by the delay of their wages. As spring warmed up, the ragtag troops turned rowdy and restless. In late April, they began marching south, barely skirting Florence. On May 6, they breached Rome's city walls. The plunder began.

The Sack of Rome was brutal, the Roman militia no match for the slaughter, rape, and ransacking that unspooled over the coming weeks. Forced to flee the Vatican, Pope Clement escaped through a secret passage to the Castel Sant'Angelo but could go no farther.[16] He remained pinioned there, a hostage to the pillage of the Eternal City.*

Meanwhile, Florence had erupted in civil unrest. In April, anxious that the mutinous Imperial troops might overrun their city, Florentine citizens demanded the right to bear arms in self-defense. Angry citizens filled the Piazza Signoria, climbing to the roof of what is today the Palazzo Vecchio, shattering windows and raining broken bits of furniture onto the mobs in the streets below. Amid the

---

*Charles V did nothing to help the pope, nor did he call off his renegade troops. Angry at the pontiff for allying with France against the Empire in the 1526 League of Cognac, he was determined to make Pope Clement pay.

chaos, the beginnings of a new government formed, led by a group of magistrates calling themselves the Republican Council. When, in May, news arrived in Florence that Clement VII had been taken hostage in Rome, the Council decided to strike. Staging a coup, the Council's soldiers overwhelmed Clement's proxies in Florence. The Medici were out.[17]

It didn't take long for the Council to find Caterina. She was at Poggio a Caiano, the Medici country estate, where she and Clarice had retreated to escape the turmoil in Florence. At first, the Council placed Caterina in various dingy and dirty convents, riddled with plague. But after Clarice Strozzi and the Duke of Albany bombarded them with complaints about the conditions, the Council moved her to the Benedictine convent of Le Murate. According to Sister Giustina, writing long after the events in question, she arrived at the convent door wearing "a metal band" around her neck. She would stay with the nuns of Le Murate for three full years.[18]

The move turned out to be a saving grace. Though still a prisoner, Caterina found a measure of tranquility at Le Murate, as calm a spot as possible in the midst of the city's unrest. The convent was a luxurious place. The reverend mothers were Benedictine nuns, not Franciscans who took vows of poverty: Le Murate's gardens were bountiful, its tables full, its rooms well appointed. Generations of Medici women had taken their retirement there, and an abbess from the convent had stood as one of Caterina's godmothers at her baptism. Le Murate's coffers were filled with Medici gold, a fact that had given the Council pause before choosing the convent as the landing spot for their little hostage.

Her life was comfortable, even loving. Morning Mass and prayers structured her days. Activities distracted her. Expert needlewomen, the reverend mothers sewed everything from tablecloths to church mantles; perhaps it was in Le Murate that Caterina developed her lifelong love of embroidery. One of the convent's many scribes, women who could read, write, and illuminate pages with silver and gold ink, probably taught her to write. From those first forays with a pen would spring a lifetime of letters. Perhaps she passed time at the lute or the virginals, for the reverend mothers loved music and kept instruments of all kinds. For some unknown reason, the kings of Portugal sent the nuns cases of sugar every year. Caterina may have helped make preserves and jams to sweeten the bread the nuns liked to bake.[19]

Not all the nuns of Le Murate favored the Medici. One Florentine citizen noted how they often bickered, "each faction [speaking] out in favor of their side." The infighting could take mundane and passive-aggressive forms. Sometimes Caterina would awaken to find the nuns had kneaded buns in the shape of the Medici *palle.* At other times, she spied little clusters of flowers arranged into six tight little balls, placed artfully on windowsills and tables. Cloistered women though they were, the nuns felt no compunction in airing their political views. Words were powerful stuff but so too, it seems, were bread and bouquets.[20]

Despite their quarrels, all the nuns were kind to Caterina, as Sister Giustina recalled. She was, after all, "only eight years old." Plus, she was a good little girl, "never rude to anyone" and "very gracious" in her manners.[21]

Even so, the nuns' loving attention couldn't erase the stress of Caterina's situation. Frustrated by the city's continued support for the Medici, the Council found endless ways to make the child miserable. They made her pay taxes and return indemnities paid to her dead father. Hoping to quash the leaks that passed through diplomatic channels back to France and Rome, the Council sharply curtailed her visitors, until eventually, by 1529, she was allowed no visitors at all. Caterina knew she was a prisoner. From the moment of her arrival, explained Giustina, "anguish . . . fear and terror gripped her soul."[22] That anguish must have deepened when, in May 1528, word filtered to the convent that Clarice Strozzi had suddenly died. Clarice was the only mother Caterina had ever known.

She was almost alone—but not quite. Though Clarice was gone, Caterina grew more aware of the presence of allies just outside the city walls. French envoys found ways to sneak Italian contacts into the convent (no doubt through the offices of a Medici-friendly nun), where they told Caterina to take heart, that powerful friends like the French King Francis were asking after her. There were little French-fueled victories. French ambassadors cajoled the Republican

Council into granting the girl more money for her expenses. And the Duke of Albany continued to protest her treatment and to make his own inquiries on her behalf.

In December 1528, a French envoy reported grim news to Albany. "Your niece is still in a convent. She's doing well, but is hardly visited or esteemed by these Florentine *signori* who would prefer to see her already [dead]." Then the envoy mentioned something extraordinary about Caterina. "She expects you," he told Albany, "to send her some presents from France for the Duke of Ferrara."[23] Was she thanking the Duke of Ferrara for some unknown service? Was she soliciting his help? She was already learning to network. And she had learned she could count on her uncle, the Duke of Albany.

It is generally assumed that Caterina developed her attachment to France following her marriage and, later, after the birth of her children. But her bond to the realm may have been first forged when she was much younger. For her whole life, Caterina would reward those who showed her loyalty and kindness, and during those difficult years in Le Murate, it was the Duke of Albany and King Francis who sent their messengers and tried to ease her suffering. Caterina developed a strong attachment to Albany; at some point she began to call him "father." The very first of her letters to survive, written when she was fourteen, are addressed to Albany. "To my uncle and father," she wrote at the beginning of each one.[24]

Just as devoted to her were the nuns of Le Murate. Indeed, in some ways they proved more loyal to her than any French connection: even those nuns who favored the Republic would try to protect Caterina on that terror-filled night in July 1530 when the Council secretary, Silvestro Aldobrandini, and his soldiers stormed the convent looking for her. By then, Florence had been starving for weeks. Three years after the Sack of Rome, Clement VII at last made peace with Charles V. Together, they sent Imperial troops to besiege Florence, intent on restoring Medici rule. Outrageous rumors swirled through the city. In retaliation for the siege, the Council (it was said) planned to seize Caterina and send her to a brothel, thereby ruining her for Pope Clement's marital plots. Or they would drag her to the city walls where she would be shot by advancing Imperial troops.[25] On that summer morning when Aldobrandini stepped through her chamber door, Caterina had no idea what would become of her.

The French could do nothing for Caterina in that moment. The good reverend mothers of Le Murate did what they could, weeping and begging Aldobrandini not to take her "while the city remained entangled," praying for divine assistance to protect the little girl.[26] In the end, the nuns couldn't restrain Aldobrandini; the secretary led Caterina away. Yet she had survived that ordeal in part, Caterina believed, because the nuns had intervened.

Forever after, she put her trust in their prayers. "Just as in my youngest years I was protected in your monastery," she would write to the nuns of Le Murate in 1573, "I can now be kept in God's grace through your kind intercessions and prayers." Ten years later, in 1583, filled with nostalgia, she wrote again, wondering half to herself, half to the mother abbess whether "perhaps some of those nuns whom I saw as a little girl are still alive." It was a wistful thought, a longing. Fifty years had passed since she had left the convent; Caterina had become more powerful than that forlorn little girl could ever have imagined. Even then, she still counted on the nuns. "Reverend Mother, these few lines from my own hand will show you my goodwill toward your monastery," she wrote, "and my desire that you continue to pray for . . . me for as long as I shall live."[27]

When she wrote that letter, she was nearing her sixty-fifth birthday. Her aunt Clarice and the Duke of Albany were decades in the grave; her own mother was but a picture conjured in her mind, a name. Other protectors and allies had come and gone. But the good nuns of Le Murate were still with her.

———

It was the Duke of Albany's galley that carried Caterina from Porto Venere to Villefranche in September 1533. Pope Clement was to follow his niece soon afterward, and together they would travel to Marseille, there to meet King Francis and his son Henry, Duke of Orléans. In trunks secured tightly against the pitch and roll of the ship, Caterina's ladies had packed fine linen and gowns, pounds of golden and silver cloth, and sets of silk sheets sent from Mantua by the great Marquessa Isabella d'Este, Caterina's distant cousin. Pope Clement would bring with him still other riches: a gold belt studded with gemstones, an enormous diamond ring, a glistening brooch of emerald hung with a pear-shaped pendant. A long string of silvery pearls, the finest in Christendom.[28] These were part of Caterina's dowry, just a fraction of the goods and lands with which she would enrich Prince Henry.

As the ship hugged the shore in search of calm waters, the cliffs of Porto Venere faded into the distance. This was the last time Caterina would ever see Italy, the land of her Medici fathers. She was headed to France, a return to the homeland of her mother and of her protector the Duke of Albany.

Did Caterina understand that her own wedding was the last chapter in her mother's story? King Francis had married Madeleine de La Tour d'Auvergne to Lorenzo de' Medici in 1518 with the hope of realizing his Italian ambitions. Now he sought out Caterina for the same reason. Still in search of those elusive Italian prizes—Milan, Genoa, and the kingdom of Naples—Francis sent Albany in 1531 to tender a marriage proposal to Pope Clement. Caterina was twelve years old.

After a few months of haggling, the plans were set: Caterina would wed Henry, Francis's second son. The Medici could hardly have imagined a more prestigious arrangement. Only the heir to the French throne would have made a finer groom. This was the greatest match the Medici had ever made.

In exchange—the king's men transmitted this secretly—Pope Clement would acknowledge Francis's claims in northern Italy. The pope would give Pisa, Livorno, Reggio, Modena, Parma, and Piacenza to Caterina in joint possession with her young husband. Clement would help Francis reconquer Milan and take Genoa. He would annex the duchy of Urbino in the name of the young couple. The majority of Italy would belong to King Francis and his heirs.

As for the Medici's common blood, Francis was prepared to overlook that deficit. As one Italian envoy put it to snobbish French noblemen, weren't Milan, Genoa, and Naples "three jewels worthy of a king's daughter?" And yet, one wonders if King Francis would have proposed the marriage, if not for the Bourbon blood Caterina inherited from her mother.[29]

The pawn of a pope and a king, Caterina was following in Madeleine's footsteps, yet in reverse. This was the life a noble girl could expect; Caterina had no choice in the matter. After her departure from Le Murate in 1530, she had spent time in Rome before returning to Florence. For a short while, she likely harbored a crush on her older cousin, the illegitimate Ippolito de' Medici, who boasted dark, sultry looks and had recently been made a cardinal by his uncle Clement VII. Caterina wasn't especially pretty—"she has bulging eyes like most of the Medici," wrote one ambassador, unkindly—yet her value lay in her inheritance as the direct descendant of *Il Magnifico*. Ippolito flirted with her for a time, imagining that he could abandon his church appointment, marry Caterina, and one day rule Florence. But Clement had other plans for his niece. He nipped their adolescent romance in the bud.[30] Marriage offers from across Europe began to roll in soon afterward.

None of the other potential grooms compared to Henry de Valois, Duke of Orléans, royal prince of France. Somber, serious, and quite unlike his dashing father, Prince Henry showed no tendency toward decadence or flagrant womanizing. Caterina was likely relieved to learn that Henry was her age: both children would be fourteen by the time of their nuptials. Unlike so many girls of her time and place, she would not have to play the nubile bride in the hands of a withered old man.

Some wondered whether she was ready to be a bride. "She is small of stature and thin," the Venetian ambassador Michele Suriano wrote in 1532. Another envoy said, "this little girl does not look like she will become a woman for a year and a half yet," though he admitted that she possessed "great spirit and intelligence." The painter Giorgio Vasari would catch a glimpse of that "great spirit" when he painted Caterina's portrait sometime before her wedding. After returning from lunch one day, he found his half-done picture transformed into the portrait of "a Moorish woman." Caterina and her friends had slipped into the room while he was away, pulled out the paints and brushes, and added their own touches. Vasari guffawed at the prank, already won over by Caterina's charm. "I am so devoted to her," he later told a friend. "I adore her, if I may say so, as one adores the saints in Heaven."[31]

On her way to joining the Duke of Albany, Caterina had practiced being a French bride. She had started her French lessons shortly after Pope Clement began her marriage negotiations, and on the road to Porto Venere she tried out her new skills. Writing to Albany in French, she updated him on all that had happened since she had last written. The language is new for her, the French a little stilted, but her excitement leaps off the page, her sentences touched by a breathless wonder. King Francis had sent her beautiful presents, she wrote, as well as the "first letter to me by Monsieur d'Orléans, his son and my husband." He wasn't her husband quite yet, but she tried on the word for size. Royal marriages were made for diplomacy and dynasty, rarely for love. Yet perhaps, Caterina dared to dream. After Ippolito, she may have known what it meant to love a man.

Above all, she was grateful to all these men. "I greatly thank our lord the king and his son Monsieur d'Orléans, and I also thank you my uncle and father," she wrote. The Duke of Albany, too, had helped find her a future.[32]

Albany's ship approached the Bay of Villefranche. For fourteen years Caterina had been shuttled from city to city, from villas and palaces to convents, from the embrace of distant family to the hands of strangers, some kind, some hostile. In France, Caterina, a daughter of the Medici, would become Catherine, bride of France—*Caterine*, as she would sign it in French, her mother's tongue.

King Francis and Pope Clement had laid out a path before her. From her uncle's ship, Catherine de' Medici stepped out of her childhood and onto the shores of France.

2

THE SECOND SON
France, 1533–1536

Someone must have told Catherine about sex. Before she left for France, Catherine spent some time with her father's cousin Maria Salviati. Perhaps it was the older matron who made sure Catherine had her facts straight, if only to warn her of the dangers of men. For any girl, but especially one like Catherine who was groomed for political marriage, reputation and chastity were paramount. "Suffer no man to touch your body, no matter who he is, no holding of hands or pressing of feet," Anne of France, a fifteenth-century French royal princess, once told her daughter. Love, that most insidious of passions, was out of the question. "Control your bearing, your expressions, your words, your sentiments, your thoughts, your desires, your wishes, and your passions," Anne of France wrote.[1] A girl could trust no one, not even herself. Her own body harbored deceptions and temptations.

But once a girl married, her attitude needed to change. A wife owed her husband "perfect and complete obedience," wrote Anne of France. For a bride, obedience was more important than love.

On the night of her wedding, Catherine got into the bed that Pope Clement had sent as a wedding gift. Painted with gold and encrusted with jewels, it had cost a fortune, nearly 60,000 crowns, according to one diplomat. Pope Clement and King Francis were staging a spectacle and the bed served as a fitting backdrop. It disguised a crude reality: the foreign policy between France and the papacy hinged on sex between teenagers.[2]

What stories did Catherine hear before her wedding night? Did she expect pain? Did she think about pleasure? Perhaps she hoped to please Prince Henry, her new husband. Bound to each other by God, they would have to live with each other, those bodies, for the rest of their lives. Or perhaps she simply gritted her teeth against the pain and embarrassment. Sex was considered a husband's conjugal right in the sixteenth century, the bride's consent and her pleasure irrelevant. There was no such thing as rape in a marriage bed. There was, however, fear.

We cannot be sure what happened that night. According to an aghast Italian diplomat, King Francis stayed in the room to ensure that sex transpired. The king couldn't take any chances. A marriage was binding only if it were consummated and Francis refused to stake everything on the unreliable word of a teenaged girl.* Whatever he witnessed satisfied the king. Equally pleased, Pope Clement blessed the new couple and offered Catherine a piece of advice. "A spirited girl will always conceive children," he told her before departing for Rome.[3]

Was Catherine relieved the morning after her wedding? From Henry, she probably received little more than polite awkwardness. Henry was a taciturn prince and his bride a stranger. He'd had no more say in his marriage than Catherine. He certainly didn't love her.

Catherine likely had no idea that Henry had a secret. In many ways he respected his father, at times even adored him. But part of Henry hated King Francis, too. Eight years earlier, when Henry was a little boy, his father had used him to solve a political crisis of Francis's own making. The king had gambled and lost in his Italian Wars and, in exchange for his own freedom, traded his young sons to the Spanish. Henry had never forgiven his father. Now, at fourteen, he found himself once again his father's pawn, his new bride simply another tool in the king's grandiose plans.

---

*By 1533, all of Europe knew that Henry VIII of England's divorce from Katherine of Aragon turned on whether she had slept with her first husband, Henry's older brother, Arthur. Katherine and Arthur had married when she was sixteen. Henry VIII later claimed their wedding had been consummated, but Katherine insisted she had remained a virgin for the short duration of their marriage. For years, the fate of England hung in the balance over the sex life of two teens.

Born on March 31, 1519—just two weeks before Catherine—Henry was the fourth child and second son of King Francis and his wife, Claude of France.[4] From the beginning, Francis was an absent father: since Queen Claude had already successfully delivered several other children, Francis decided to go hunting rather than stick around for the birth of this baby. Still, the birth of a son was always a happy event, and Francis used the baby's arrival to cement an alliance with King Henry VIII of England, who agreed to serve as godfather to the child. A second son himself, Henry bestowed his own name upon the infant, which is how the French prince became "Henry," spelled in the English style. Henry VIII sent his ambassador, Thomas Boleyn, to hold the baby at the baptismal font. In a return gesture of magnanimity, Francis expressed his hopes that one day soon King Henry, too, would enjoy the blessing of a son. This was backhanded: Francis knew how much Henry VIII, who had only one daughter after ten years of marriage to Katherine of Aragon, wished for a son to secure the Tudor dynasty.[5]

With his own nursery now chock full of children, King Francis set his sights on other worthy goals, including the conquest of Italy. He'd already won some and lost some in the Italian Wars. In 1515, the same year as his accession, King Francis had taken Milan in the Battle of Marignano; six years later, however, in 1521, he lost the city to Charles V. Fueled by the memory of that first, stunning victory at Marignano, Francis left his wife and children in the summer of 1524, when Prince Henry was five, to take Milan again.

Only weeks after Francis's departure, tragedy struck the royal household: Henry's mother died on July 20, at the age of twenty-four. Francis learned of her death while pressing toward Italy. Though he mourned, he chose not to return for her funeral. With their mother dead and their father gone, the children were left at the château of Blois under the care of Francis's sister, Marguerite de Navarre. Henry had been close to his mother. Her death dealt him a cruel blow.

In Italy, King Francis's campaign against Charles V began well. French armies pursued Imperial battalions over the Alps, driving them back toward Milan. Then, French fortunes shifted abruptly.

On the morning of February 24, 1525, Imperial troops decimated French armies at the Battle of Pavia, a small town on the outskirts of Milan. Dozens of ranking French noblemen died, including some of Francis's closest friends. Francis's own horse was slaughtered beneath him; forced to fight on foot, he slashed and hacked at oncoming troops. When the French king eventually fell, Imperial soldiers hemmed him in, snatching at pieces of his armor. The battle was over by noon. It happened to be Charles V's birthday.[6]

It was one thing to defeat the enemy, quite another to hold a king at your mercy. Gleeful though he was, Charles V hewed to codes of honor. Treating his French captive with the utmost respect, he consented to Francis's request to be moved from Italy to Spain. But Charles soon learned his prisoner had a delicate constitution. As the reality of his situation set in, Francis grew depressed. He refused to eat; in short order, an old abscess that had long troubled him began to ooze pus. By September 1525, the French king had fallen dangerously ill.

Francis had designated his mother, Louise de Savoy, to act as regent in France during the campaign. Learning of her son's dire condition, Louise began to negotiate with Charles V in earnest. The emperor set harsh terms. In exchange for Francis's immediate release, the French would have to renounce sovereignty in Italy and Burgundy. Francis would have to agree to marry Charles's sister, Eleanor, to seal the peace. Most urgently, Charles required Francis to send hostages to Spain in his place until he met the terms of the treaty. The emperor laid out two options: either Francis could send his son and heir, the dauphin, along with twelve great noblemen of the realm. Or he could send two of his sons—the dauphin and his second son, Prince Henry.

Royal sons were currency. If the heir died, the spare would take his place. Charles V knew he was asking Francis to wager his legacy. In the end, Louise de Savoy convinced Francis to send Henry rather than the nobles. Louise was not a cold woman. She was devoted to her son Francis to the point of obsession; it is hard to believe she didn't love her grandsons.[7] But Louise was also a profoundly political creature and, in this decision, there could be no room for emotion. Guessing that King Francis would renege on any promises made to Charles V, Louise knew Francis would need his remaining generals at hand or else risk another military disaster like the Battle of Pavia. Plus, Francis had a *third* son, Charles, still at home. Louise calculated: if anything happened to the young princes in Spain, this third boy could serve as his father's heir.

On March 17, 1526, just beyond the French border town of Bayonne, a boat carrying the two boys steered to a precise spot in the middle of the Bidasoa River separating France from Castile. Soon another boat approached from the opposite shore, this one bearing King Francis. Over a year had passed since Francis had fallen at Pavia. The dauphin had just turned eight years old. Henry was a few weeks shy of his seventh birthday.

For a moment, the boys hugged their father as the boats met. Then, clambering aboard the French vessel, Francis and his men raced back to the French border. "Now I am king. I am king once again!" Francis shouted the minute his foot touched the shore. Mounting a horse, he galloped back to Bayonne, where his mother and sister were waiting.[8]

On the opposite shore of the Bidasoa, Henry and his brother followed their Spanish guards. Henry didn't understand their language. He didn't understand their customs. He probably didn't even understand why he was there. He barely knew Francis beyond flashes of memory or stories heard in the nursery. His aunt, Marguerite de Navarre, had explained to the boys at Blois why they needed to go to Spain—what could she have said? Henry had no choice but to trust his aunt, his grandmother, and the strange man who had embraced him in the middle of the river. He likely hoped he would see his home again within days. Instead, it would take years.

For four years, Henry and his older brother remained in Spanish custody. Although the Spanish treated the princes well at first, they grew hostile after Francis indeed reneged on the peace treaty and waged war on Spain again in 1527. Charles V ordered the boys to be isolated, dismissing their French attendants and moving them from Madrid to a remote fortress high in the Sierra de Guadarrama. There, he surrounded them with guards: eighty on the way to church, fifty when they went out to play.[9]

Had Henry's mother lived, would he have remained in that Spanish jail? Would he have gone to Spain at all? As it was, Louise de Savoy was able to cut a deal to release the princes only in August 1529.

Even then, faced with the obstinacy of both Francis and Charles V, she had to work behind the scenes with an old friend, Margaret of Austria (Charles V's aunt), to hammer out the treaty that became known as "the Peace of the Ladies." By that point, the boys' treatment in Spain had deteriorated entirely. Louise de Savoy's usher, a man by the name of Baudin, who traveled to Spain to inform the princes of their imminent freedom, found the boys looking disheveled and fatigued. They were held in a cold chamber. The one window was small, cut out from a stone wall that was about ten feet thick, and covered inside and out with iron bars. Mattresses were strewn about the floor and the only seats were stools made of stone. The room was dirty, the boys themselves dressed in skimpy clothes they had clearly outgrown. Worst of all, Baudin reported, the boys had forgotten how to speak French. "How could I possibly remember it," asked the dauphin in Spanish, "when there is no one here for me to speak it with?"

Soon enough, Baudin gained the boys' trust and loosened their tongues. But the usher was distressed.[10]

Louise de Savoy wept when she read Baudin's report, then quickly wrote to Margaret of Austria pleading for help. Fresh food and clothing soon arrived for the boys, but they were already traumatized.[11] They had missed their family desperately. According to Baudin, they hammered him with questions about everyone back home. For Henry, the politics that kept him imprisoned were an abstraction. For him, the calculus was far simpler: *I went to prison so my father could go free. He promised to come for me and still, here I am.* The sacrifice was too much to bear for a boy who, during most of his imprisonment, was no more than ten years old.

Francis would pay a high price for the bartering of his sons. Henry never recovered from his deep sense of abandonment. When he finally returned to court in the summer of 1530, at the age of eleven, he had grown quiet and moody.* He became competitive with his younger brother Charles, who, in Henry's absence, had become his father's favorite. "Bright, vivacious, and impetuous," Charles was the mirror of the gallant King Francis, who showered his youngest

---

*The princes did not return to France until July 1, 1530, almost a full year after the Peace of the Ladies was signed.

son with honors and titles. Henry closed himself off so his father wouldn't disapprove of his temper, already "quick" and "bold."[12] He poured himself into sports, escaping the subtler interactions between people that were more difficult for him. The world was simpler for Henry in the jousting lists and on the tennis court than in his father's sophisticated circles.

Love and resentment together sometimes brew more bitterness than hatred alone. Henry blamed Francis for his pain. Over the following years, little injustices, real or perceived, no doubt magnified that first, most painful injustice that sent him to Spain as a child. But evidence suggests that Henry also loved his father deeply. Years later, as Francis lay dying in 1547, Henry refused to leave his father's bedside. "You have been a good and obedient son," Francis told him. A witness remembered that, upon hearing his father's words, Henry wept, then fainted, overcome with grief.[13] In the following weeks, Henry's actions spoke the words he couldn't. He gave a magnificent funeral for Francis and brought the bodies of his deceased siblings to be buried alongside their father in the basilica of Saint-Denis. Perhaps he yearned for his father to love him in return, a love his father couldn't give. Perhaps Henry could never quite separate the actions of the king from those of the father. Or possibly he did understand. He just couldn't bring himself to forgive.

Caught in the currents of the Italian Wars, Catherine found herself locked away in Le Murate for three years. She emerged all the stronger for it. It was different for Henry. The boy Catherine slept with on her wedding night was a wounded soul: a boy seeking his father's respect and love.

After their wedding night, Henry largely ignored Catherine. At fourteen, he was a boys' boy who cared more about sports and his friends than about a foreign girl who still spoke stilted French. Then, too, maybe he was put off by the snide whispers that followed Catherine from the beginning. Chitchatters warbled that Catherine was "an Italian shopkeeper's daughter" who hardly merited a French royal prince. The gossip grew louder when, nine months after the wedding, Pope Clement suddenly died. For both Francis and Catherine this was a disaster.

With Clement's death, Francis lost the secret papal endorsement of his Italian claims. Moreover, the new pope, Paul III, refused to send the last installment of Catherine's dowry. "The girl has come to me stark naked," King Francis grumbled.[14] Perhaps Henry believed his own lackluster marriage to Catherine reflected his diminished status in Francis's eyes. At the time of Clement's death, Francis was negotiating a royal bride for his favorite son, Charles. He had never aimed so high for Henry—or at least so it seemed to the prince.[15]

In the meantime, well before Catherine arrived in France, someone else had caught his eye. No one knows for sure how Diane de Poitiers and Prince Henry first met; King Francis likely introduced them, sensing that his second son needed a woman's guiding touch after his years of captivity in Spain. Nineteen years older than Henry, Diane was a high-ranking noblewoman, a widow, and the mother of two daughters.* By all accounts ravishing, she was tall and slender with auburn-gold hair, brilliant blue eyes, and alabaster skin—a paragon of female beauty in Renaissance France. "She was so beautiful," remembered the gossipy courtier Pierre de Brantôme, "that she would have been beautiful even if she had lived to be 110 years old." Great artists like Cellini would portray her as the luminous and scantily clad Diana, goddess of the moon and the hunt. What preserved her legendary beauty? According to some, Diane used magic; others said she exercised daily and bathed in milk. In all likelihood, she indulged in several anti-aging treatments popular at the time, including a tonic laced with precious metals. In the twenty-first century, scientists disinterred her corpse and found her hair still contained traces of gold.[16]

Their relationship may have begun innocently enough. Eventually, sometime in Henry's teens, their affair would take a sexual turn, although Diane, fiercely protective of Henry and mindful of his reputation, behaved discreetly. Years into the affair, many foreign diplomats still saw nothing scandalous. "Their relationship is the same as between mother and son," protested the Venetian envoy Marino Cavalli. "There is nothing lascivious in it."[17] Cavalli probably

---

*Diane was in fact a second cousin to Catherine de' Medici, through their mothers.

saw what Diane wanted him to see. Then again, maybe she remained a mother figure to Henry, even as she became something else.

There was nothing strange in the idea of a royal mistress. King Francis enjoyed his own mistresses, and even made the royal mistress an official court role, as *maîtresse en titre*. Over the years, Henry would fall madly in love with Diane. In public, he seemed to play the part of the foolish bumbling knight to her fair damsel in some kind of fantastical reenactment of medieval courtly love. He would write her simpering love poetry, wear her colors of black and white, and adopt her emblem of the crescent moon paired with a motto: "when full, it emulates the sun."[18] Diane would eventually eclipse all other women in Henry's eyes. Unlike his father, she made him feel powerful, loved, and safe.

With little beauty or value to her person, there was no way Catherine could compete with Diane for Henry's attention. Diane likely didn't see Catherine as a competitor. The girl simply had a different role to play in Henry's life. Diane coddled and mentored him; Catherine furnished him with a political alliance and would bear his children. Supposedly, it was Diane who had explained to Henry the advantages of a Medici marriage. And, as Catherine would soon discover, when Diane spoke, Henry always listened.[19]

Those first years of marriage were difficult for Catherine. She had trouble finding her niche. After Pope Clement's death, she lived in a kind of limbo, no longer valuable to her father-in-law, unappreciated by a husband who fell further into Diane's thrall with each passing month. King Francis's court and its culture must have intimidated Catherine at first, though she appreciated its splendor. The French Renaissance was in full swing by the 1530s and Francis, a great lover of art and letters, was determined to put France on the map as the epitome of elegance. Francis's court became an enclave for the best artists and thinkers his patronage could buy. Leonardo da Vinci was the most famous artist to enjoy Francis's hospitality, spending his final years in a beautiful manor, the Clos Lucé, tucked next to the château of Amboise.

For all that she admired the art and architecture that blossomed under Francis, Catherine had to get used to the size of his court.

It was a city unto itself. Up to 10,000 people surrounded the king and maintained the palaces he called home. Peripatetic, Francis's sprawling court wandered the kingdom, traveling from château to château. Stewards and staff at each palace spent weeks preparing for the arrival of the king and his court. And each time the king left one palace for another, the castle was scrubbed clean, its floor rushes replaced, its kitchens scoured and stables aired, the stench of waste wiped away.

Yet nothing could wash away the ugly court politics that, under Francis, often reached a fever pitch. Factions formed easily between the most powerful players, like cliques in a school. The center of one faction was Francis's mistress, Anne de Pisseleu, who threw her support behind Francis's favorite son, Charles. Another faction would soon form around Diane de Poitiers, Henry's mistress. King Francis had created another popular crowd of sorts, beautiful ladies known as his *petite bande*, whom he placed around himself to please the eye. The court of France was a glittering place, but it also fostered ambition, scheming, and rivalry. It was an easy place for a fourteen-year-old foreign girl like Catherine to get lost.

But Catherine would earn a protector in King Francis. Despite her inauspicious beginnings, the king grew fond of the Medici girl, in part because she embodied the Italian style he was trying so hard to emulate.[20] King Francis viewed Italy as the birthplace of the Renaissance, the font of new ideas and the wellspring of artists like Leonardo. Upon her arrival in France, Catherine wore her Italian connections quite literally on her sleeve, writing away to relatives in Florence for perfumes, silks, and Italian sleeves of white "all covered in embroidery work in black silk and gold. And send me the bill for the work." The traces of her Italian childhood surfaced in other ways, too. She came to France just old enough for the Italian cadence of her speech to linger—a few years younger and she would have lost her accent entirely. Instead, she kept it for life. Francis wasn't bothered by it. On the contrary, "when he saw how she tried to be in his good company," Brantôme wrote, "he liked her even more."[21]

On fair-weather days, the horses were saddled, and Catherine joined Francis and the *petite bande* on the hunt, Francis's favorite pastime. They set falcons to catch herons and kites and chased wild boar and stag deep in the forest. "Here one thinks only of hunting," the Bishop of Saluzzo once complained, but Catherine found she loved hunting, too. She grew into a superb horsewoman, "an excellent equestrian, and brave, and very graceful." She joined the hunt to survive. French language and customs were still so new. Hunting was a way to speak with the body, the unspoken language of her father-in-law, her king. Catherine understood that she had to make Francis's world her own.[22]

She found yet another protector in the king's beloved sister, Marguerite de Navarre, who was possibly intrigued by the young woman's intelligence. A brilliant scholar and writer, Marguerite found tutors to teach Catherine mathematics, poetry, Latin, even some Greek, burnishing the young girl for King Francis's sophisticated court. The older woman enjoyed Catherine's company and included her in hours of storytelling.[23]

It may have been through Marguerite that Catherine first glimpsed the beginnings of the Protestant Reformation. The German Martin Luther had published his Ninety-Five Theses back in 1517, but in the early 1530s, true Protestantism had yet to arrive in France. There were no "Protestants" or "Huguenots," no organized movement in France to break entirely with Catholicism and start a separate church. There were only the faintest rumblings of "reform" and a "new religion." But this nascent idea of cleansing the Catholic Church of its corruption inspired Marguerite and her circle. They thought of themselves as students of the *evangile*—the gospel. The holy word was key to their endeavors. They read the Bible in Greek, translated it into French, looked within its pages for a path to a "true" church.[24] Like her brother, Marguerite thrived in the secular world of the court. But the New Testament was always her pilot.

The "Queen of Navarre was particularly fond of you," a courtier would tell Catherine many decades on.[25] Did Catherine feel the heat of Marguerite's radical ideas? Though she would never embrace Protestantism herself, perhaps Catherine's memories of Marguerite de Navarre inspired some of her tolerance for the new religion years later.

Catherine had protectors, companions, even friends.[26] Yet something was amiss for her at Francis's court. Tainted by Pope Clement's broken promises, her role was ill-defined and insecure. The burden of her low-born Medici connections still weighed on her. Henry was diffident and distant, which King Francis noticed. "The Duchess of Orléans is still treated as usual," wrote the Spanish ambassador in 1535. "Some of her maids had heard the king say that he had not been well-advised when he made his son marry her."[27] On top of everything else, Catherine was homesick.

She had written and written to her cousin Maria Salviati, and had received no reply. "I . . . have never had any answer, which surprises me even more," she complained in yet another letter, pining for a comforting word.[28] France was now her home. But Catherine didn't feel she quite belonged.

———

Catherine would never divest herself of her Italian roots. Sometimes they proved an asset, sometimes a burden. And at certain moments, those Italian roots placed her in a dangerous spotlight.

On August 6, 1536, after a vigorous game of tennis, Francis's oldest son and heir, the dauphin, suddenly fell ill. He died four days later. King Francis was inconsolable. Although an autopsy found disease in the dauphin's lungs, the king cast about for someone to blame. Sixteenth-century people always suspected poison when a death occurred suddenly. According to stereotypes of the time, no one was more adept at poisoning than Italians. Immediately, accusing eyes turned to the dauphin's Italian secretary, Sebastian Montecuculli, who had offered the dauphin a cold drink after the tennis match.[29]

Appraising minds soon decided that Montecuculli had no reason to act of his own accord. While some blamed Charles V, others began to whisper about Catherine. Montecuculli had come to court in Catherine's train when she arrived in France.[30] Surely, the neglected Italian wife of a second son had everything to gain from the dauphin's death? It was much easier to blame Catherine, a foreigner, than her husband, a French royal prince.

Luckily for Catherine, King Francis paid no heed to the scandal, but the smear campaign must have made her painfully aware of the dangers at court. When times were good, the French admired Italians. When times were bad, however, the French hated Italians. Despite her mother's ancient French blood, Catherine was apparently still a Medici to certain Frenchmen unwilling to look past the immigrant.

And somehow, she already had enemies ready to slander her. Why was it so easy to blame her? In France, Italians were seen as ambitious. Was this true of Catherine?

While most historians acquit Catherine of any wrongdoing, they rarely question that she stood to gain from her brother-in-law's death. Did Catherine desire the crown? A crown brought power, but it was also a tremendous burden—no one had learned this better than King Francis when he earned his freedom by trading his sons to Spain. Now that burden fell on the shoulders of Henry and Catherine. Francis understood the task now facing Henry, his new heir. "Surpass your brother in virtue," the grieving king told Henry, "so that those who now mourn his passing will have their sorrow eased. I command you to make this your aim with all your heart and soul."[31] Henry wept, overwhelmed. Catherine, too, may have looked to the crown ahead of her with confusion and fear.

Yet there was no stopping that crown from coming. In an instant, her world had changed. Status at court suddenly shifted. Henry was now dauphin and Catherine the future queen consort of France. Diane de Poitiers, as Henry's favorite, now grew more powerful, attracting courtiers eager to curry favor with the future king.

It may have been after his older brother's death that Henry first slept with Diane. Maybe she used sex to tighten her hold on Henry, or maybe Diane wished to teach Henry about sex, since he now needed an heir more than ever. Until Henry had a son, his younger brother and rival, Charles, was second-in-line to the throne.* The birth of a son would strengthen Henry's position as dauphin, but until that day arrived, Charles would angle for power at court, even for the crown itself.

Diane could not give Henry an heir. There were birth control methods available in the sixteenth century and if she was still fertile Diane no doubt used them.[32] Even if she did become pregnant, any child Diane bore with Henry would be illegitimate. Only a royal wife would make a future king. And yet, in Catherine's three years of marriage, she had shown no sign of pregnancy.

She was still young, just seventeen. Her barrenness had not yet sparked the gossip that would surge in the coming years. But in

---

*Their rivalry would end only with Charles's death in 1545.

1536, Catherine was already well aware that childbirth was a queen consort's most important task.

The last French queen to give birth to royal babies was Henry's own mother, Queen Claude. According to many, there had been no better queen. Humble and docile, she had kept her nose out of politics. She had ignored Francis's mistresses and fled the dazzling spectacle of his court. She endured childbearing stoically, despite being "badly lame in both hips," a painful condition that worsened with each pregnancy.[33] Above all, Claude gave birth to seven children in eight years, delighting both king and kingdom.

Never was there "a more honest princess on earth, nor one more beloved in all the world," gushed one courtier. "A pearl of a woman . . . goodness without sin," said another.[34] Self-sacrificing and meek, Claude had also been the daughter of a French king and a French duchess—a decidedly uncommon pedigree.

This was Catherine's predecessor, her model. Only with the birth of a son would Catherine, the Medici pope's niece, find a way to belong.

3

BARREN
France, 1536–1542

A woman in Catherine's world wouldn't always know if she were pregnant, especially during the earliest months. Once she felt the quickening—the movement of the fetus in the womb—then she could be sure. Until then, she had to rely on certain signs that boded well. She might feel a "little frisson" at the moment of fertilization, as one sixteenth-century doctor suggested. She might notice a "swelling of the breasts" or a change in the color of her nipples. She could be hopeful if her "monthly purgation" disappeared, although both doctors and midwives knew that periods could stop for many reasons, including sickness or hunger. "If you have no other way of knowing whether a woman is pregnant," wrote the eminent physician Jacques Guillemeau, "the eyes will show you." Still, appearances could be deceiving. Anxious wives probed and prodded, hoping the womb would divulge its secrets.[1]

For ten years, from 1533 until 1543, Catherine probed and prodded to no avail. The reasons for her long barrenness remain a mystery. Although canon law approved marriage for a girl as early as twelve, most families allowed a girl to mature before expecting her to have sex with her husband. Some historians have suggested Catherine came late to puberty, but nothing can be sure. If Pope Clement and King Francis doubted whether Catherine was physically ready, they did not spare her the marriage bed.[2] Yet after the wedding, seasons passed, months folded into years, and still the signs of pregnancy failed to show.

The nature of the young couple's sex life during the early years of their marriage remains unclear. Catherine adored Henry. "She loves the king her husband as much as anyone can imagine," one ambassador observed. The Venetian envoy Matteo Dandolo claimed Catherine was "beloved and cherished by the Dauphin her husband" in return, but Dandolo may have mistaken courtesy for tenderness.[3] Catherine's love went unrequited. Diane de Poitiers maintained her absolute hold on Henry.

The mistress and the bride offered Henry two different kinds of sex. Diane represented passionate sex, a sensuality celebrated in courtly poetry—the kind of sex that never results in burdensome children, which Diane took pains to ensure. For Catherine, however, sex with Henry was entirely procreative. Children were expected, indeed required. And in this, Catherine was failing miserably.

Soon enough, there was proof that it was Catherine and not Henry who was to blame for the couple's sterility.

In early October 1537, Henry left the court at Fontainebleau to join the nobleman Anne de Montmorency on the battlefield during the latest installment of the Italian Wars. Henry was eighteen years old. Montmorency, then forty-four, was a seasoned warrior and Grand Master of King Francis's household. Montmorency had taken a liking to the young prince and, sensing the advantages of befriending the heir, became his mentor, the affectionate father figure Henry didn't have.

The campaign was Henry's first real experience in the field. He was at an age where boys are rapidly becoming men, yet still prone to fooling around with their friends, a fact that Montmorency lamented when, on one unfortunate occasion, Henry pierced himself in the thigh with his dagger after a burst of roughhousing; luckily the injury did no permanent damage. The prince was surrounded by other hotheaded young men who reveled in their newfound sexual appetites. One of his friends had just fathered an illegitimate child with a lady at court, and Henry had begun to explore fresh territory with Diane.

The campaign was grueling. Henry and his friends languished in the field and waded through marshes, their stomachs knotting with hunger as rations grew slim. Then, on November 1, Montmorency and his squadrons successfully attacked the Italian fortress of Avigliana, where forty-odd Spanish soldiers were sheltering after the French scorched the lands around Piedmont. Henry and his companions slaughtered every enemy soldier within. Exhilarated after the battle and drunk on victory, they readily agreed when a Piedmontese squire offered to host Henry and his friends for the night.[4]

What happened that night in the squire's home? All sources from the period skirt this episode. Probably, Henry and Diane controlled the narrative. A few scattered facts remain. In the squire's house lived a young girl named Filippa Duci; she was either the squire's daughter or sister. Something transpired between Henry and Filippa but the tenor of their encounter has been lost. Although most historians refer to a "seduction," that word may simply be a byword for rape.[5]

Sexual assault was a fact of life in the sixteenth century, both at court and in the country. Noble boys were trained to be aggressive warriors and it was understood that princes enjoyed certain prerogatives. At court, King Francis's own voracious sexuality was on display and set the tone. Marguerite de Navarre, the king's sister, may have known at first hand the dangers a noble girl faced. Her stories are peppered with tales of rape and sexual violence and at least one historian has suggested she may have been assaulted as a girl by one of her brother's closest friends.[6]

Prince Henry lodged at the squire's house for a single night, leaving the next morning with Montmorency to continue the campaign. Shortly after he returned to Paris a few months later, however, he learned Filippa was pregnant. The young woman gave birth to a girl in July 1538. Henry had the child brought to France and placed in the care of Diane de Poitiers, who gave the child her own name. Eventually, in 1548, Henry would legitimize this daughter as "Diane of France." No effort was made to hide the baby's birth.[7] On the contrary, the infant proved Henry's virility. She also proved that if Catherine couldn't bear a child for Henry, another woman certainly could.*

---

*Catherine did not seem contemptuous of Filippa Duci, however, or of the baby. In a striking example that sixteenth-century mores are not our own, Catherine would welcome Filippa as a lady-in-waiting in 1582. Diane of France, the future Duchess of Angoulême, would grow up to become one of Catherine's favorite ladies-in-waiting. In her surviving letters, Diane of France never mentioned her mother. It is possible she didn't know who her mother was.

Catherine would never entirely recover from these barren years. They left an indelible stain. Even her most fervent supporters, decades later, felt compelled to apologize for her infertility, to weave barrenness into a narrative of Catherine's perseverance. According to Pierre de Brantôme, all Medici women were "late to conceive," while the Bishop of Bourges, speaking at Catherine's funeral, would claim that neither Prince Henry nor King Francis abandoned their affection for her "since she was piously patient and prayed continuously."[8] But Bourges whitewashed his history. For in 1542, the talk at court had turned to divorce.

"Many people advised the king and the Dauphin to repudiate her because it was necessary to continue the line of France," wrote Brantôme. Among those many people was Claude, Duke of Guise, a newly made man from the junior branch of the House of Lorraine. In 1538, shortly after the birth of Henry's illegitimate daughter, the Duke of Guise suggested his own daughter, Louise, would make a fitting bride for the dauphin. Young and pedigreed, Louise de Guise descended from a long line of fertile women. Suspecting that the Guises were more interested in cultivating their own ambition than in the welfare of France, Francis refused the offer.[9] Instead the king made his own secret inquiries abroad, seeking a suitable royal replacement for Catherine.

The king was genuinely worried. Concern for the "line of France" wasn't hollow. And in subtle ways Catherine's barrenness touched Francis's growing anxieties about his own sovereign authority.

As far back as the Middle Ages, the French had believed that a king's power came from God. Kings themselves were considered quasi-divine. The ritual of coronation was called le sacre—quite literally the "rendering sacred" of the king; the ceremony made the inviolability of the crown explicit. But ideas of absolute power and the "divine right of kings" did not gain great traction until the seventeenth century during the reigns of sovereigns like James I of England and the Sun King, Louis XIV of France. In the sixteenth century, kingship was still considered contractual, a tacit agreement between a king and his subjects. A king's authority was subject to the same body of law and custom that governed the realm. A king did not own his crown, in other words, he merely borrowed it. "Kingship is the dignity, not the property of the prince," declared one French nobleman in 1484.[10]

Some kings were nonetheless more prone to authoritarianism and King Francis was one of them. Francis obeyed the law but, whenever possible, he made the law work for him. His autocratic streak was likely born of insecurity. After his humiliating imprisonment in Spain, Francis found any encroachment on his authority difficult to abide.

Still, he knew certain laws were sacrosanct, including the laws of succession. French law decreed that the crown must pass from a king to his next male kin.* Preferably, a king passed his crown to his son; if he had no son, the crown would pass to a relative. Francis himself had inherited the French crown from his first cousin once removed, Louis XIII, whose wife had borne only daughters.† It was blood right and kinship, rather than a king's discretion, that determined the next sovereign in line. In theory, this kept rivalries for the crown to a minimum. It also protected the monarchy: everyone knew who was next in line, and the kingdom was never without a king. Indeed, it was upon Francis's own accession that heralds had called out for the first time, "The king is dead, long live the king!"—barely a breath to separate one sovereign from the next.[11]

Henry had never been Francis's favorite son. If permitted, Francis probably would have passed the crown to his youngest son, Charles. But the law was out of his hands. And Francis knew he owed Henry the chance at both a legacy and a strong reign. The ability to father a son and ensure the dynasty was a sign of virility, authority, and divine sanction. Siring sons was a show of strength. Francis knew that if Henry had no legitimate heirs of his body, if his wife was barren, his authority would be crippled. The nobility of the realm would look instead to the next in line as the rising power.

He also realized that, more than ever, France needed a strong king. Religious dissension was becoming a wedge issue, fracturing political friendships among kingdoms and threatening stability within his own realm. In his quest for an alliance against Charles V, Francis

---

*A medieval custom in France called Salic Law excluded women from inheriting the throne.
†Louis XII descended from the senior branch of the Valois family and Francis from the cadet. Francis's wife, Claude, was Louis XII's eldest daughter. Their marriage was arranged to unify the two branches of the Valois.

was having a hard time seeing the chessboard clearly. In the past, Francis had allied with the heretic Turks (who liked to make regular incursions up the Danube against the emperor, much to the French king's delight); now, however, he feared the Turkish alliance would alienate the pope. Yet if he allied with the pope, Francis might upset the German Protestant princes who made trouble for the Catholic emperor. And if he allied with Henry VIII of England, he risked again offending the papacy, which viewed the English king as an impudent heretic after he broke with Rome to marry Anne Boleyn in 1533.

As religion caused problems abroad, it also spurred battles on the home front. The new evangelical ideas that Francis's sister, Marguerite de Navarre, had explored with her friends in the 1520s had begun to germinate. Reformist ideas were catching fire.[12]

During his early years on the throne, Francis couldn't quite make up his mind about the Reform. He loved his sister and supported her. He liked to think of himself as a liberal thinker, a modern man. New waves in art, technology, and philosophy excited him; the printing press, still a newfangled invention, thrilled him. Francis sponsored printers who churned out books by the hundreds, and created university lectureships whose professors embraced "humanism," the passionate rediscovery of ancient learning and the rethinking of man's relationship to the cosmos.[13] Proud of his lectureships, King Francis protected them from the conservative Parlement of Paris (the chief law court of the realm) and the Faculty of Theology at the Sorbonne, who saw these courses as hotbeds of heresy. As a forward thinker, Francis could see the argument for Church reform. After all, the ecclesiastical courts were filled with cases of corrupt and drunken priests.

But Francis was liberal only to a point. He was in fact a deeply pious man. He attended Mass every day. He reveled in the title of "Most Christian King," given to French sovereigns by the pope. And Francis abhorred the "Lutherans" or "Sacrementarians," as the French called them, who seemed bent on dismantling the entire institution of the Church, beginning with the sacraments. Politics and religion were intertwined in sixteenth-century France. For a king like Francis whose coronation rendered him sacred in the eyes of the Church, the very idea of questioning the sacraments smacked of revolution.[14]

Francis couldn't see that revolt was slowly taking shape right under his nose. He was blind to how the new thinking he patronized was sowing seeds that would ultimately shatter the bedrock of the Church, how the printing press he loved would become the arm of radical dissension. Then, thanks to a single night in the autumn of 1534, Francis's view of the Reform changed forever.

Overnight on October 17, a small band of men, led by a French Reformer named Marcourt, slipped into the public squares of Paris. The next morning, Parisians discovered their streets had been plastered with placards, cheap broadsides printed in large Gothic type. "Genuine articles on the horrific, great, and unbearable abuses of the papal Mass, invented directly contrary to the Holy Supper of our Lord, sole mediator and sole savior Jesus Christ," read the opening lines.[15] The Reformers were attacking the Mass.

Hysteria gripped the city. Arrests were quickly made. Stories soon spread of placards that had appeared in Orléans, Tours, Blois, and Rouen. To Catholics, this was no longer dispassionate, theological debate. This was heresy. Marcourt's placards mocked priests and monks, calling them "miserable sacrificers" and "fat hooded ones," while lashing out at the heart of the Mass, the concept of the Real Presence. Catholics believed in the doctrine of transubstantiation, which held that the wafer and wine transformed into the actual flesh and blood of Christ during holy communion. Marcourt, however, thought this was hocus-pocus. The priesthood was playing at conjuring, the ignorant common folk at their mercy. To Reformers like Marcourt, holy communion was merely symbolic: the truth was in the Word of God alone. Yet Marcourt was no pacifist. "Truth is lacking" in those who followed the old ways, he wrote. But God's truth "menaces them, follows them, and chases them. In the end, truth will find them out. By it they shall be destroyed."

Certain French Reformers would come to regret the Affair of the Placards, including the theologian Théodore de Bèze, who wished that cooler heads had prevailed.[16] If Marcourt's language seemed to threaten violence, so did his actions. A rumor spread at court that a placard had appeared at Blois, pinned to the king's chamber door.* It

---

*Another rumor claimed the intruder had rolled up the placard and placed it in King Francis's cup.

didn't matter that Francis wasn't at Blois that day. That a heretic had dared to approach his person utterly rattled the king.[17]

To Francis, there was no better proof that heresy had slipped into the sedition and treason of lèse-majesté. The king now stood back and let the Parlement of Paris and the Sorbonne do their work. The burnings began shortly after the first arrests. Scholars and thinkers fled the kingdom. The king made a show of his renewed commitment to Catholicism, organizing spectacular Catholic processions throughout the kingdom. The most magnificent of these took place in Paris on January 21, 1535. The holiest of all French relics, the Crown of Thorns from the Sainte-Chapelle, was carried through the streets. At the heart of the procession, royal princes held aloft a canopy sheltering the Bishop of Paris, who cradled the wine and wafer of the Holy Sacrament on a cushion. King Francis followed the bishop. Dressed soberly in black, Francis clutched a single burning candle. Whenever the procession halted, Francis would lose himself in prayer. The people cried. The day ended with the burning of six heretics.[18]

The twinning of heresy and sedition would underpin religious unrest in France for the rest of the century. After the Affair of the Placards, King Francis grew intolerant and afraid. Despite his new repressive measures, religious dissension only worsened in France. By the early 1540s, it was clear to the king that the "Lutheran" problem wasn't going away.[19]

While preoccupied with the Italian Wars, Francis had lost sight of the battle for the soul of his kingdom. Now he was fighting on two fronts. And here was his barren daughter-in-law Catherine, the Medici girl. Francis hardly expected a miracle. No royal baby would make a heretic believe that God was somehow in the wafer and the wine. But unless it was remedied, Catherine's barrenness would point to the fragility of the monarchy, to his son's weakness, the crown's weakness. Catherine was a living and breathing reminder of a fruitless deal with a slippery Medici pope, a stain on Francis's own judgment. At best the marriage looked like a blunder.

A new wife would fix everything. A new bride for Henry could provide a new alliance, one that would help Francis maneuver against Charles V and shore up his own authority at home. The king needed only a good reason to move Catherine out of the way.

There were precedents across Europe for putting away a barren wife. When Louis XII of France wished to marry the rich heiress Anne of Brittany, he annulled his first marriage, to Joan of Valois, by claiming Joan was sterile. In a more complicated workaround, Henry VIII of England argued that his wife was as good as sterile. To be sure, she'd endured several pregnancies, miscarriages, and stillbirths; only one daughter, Mary Tudor, had survived. Henry VIII wanted a son to safeguard the Tudor dynasty. He declared his marriage to Katherine of Aragon illicit in the eyes of God, the miscarriages and stillbirths a sign of His displeasure. Pope Clement VII refused to grant him a divorce, but Henry did as he pleased, marrying Anne Boleyn in a secret ceremony in 1533.

A marriage vow was no match for a king's ambition. Catherine's barrenness gave King Francis an opening. If she had already given birth to children, Francis would have struggled to dissolve the marriage. But Catherine hadn't. That made all the difference.

For Francis, the decision to keep or repudiate Catherine turned on politics. For Catherine, the consequences were personal. It isn't clear when she first saw the storm clouds gathering. Nor is it clear that she perceived the thin line linking the workings of her body to the political and religious unrest in France. Certainly, she didn't recognize the first rumblings of the Reform for what they would become—no one really did. In 1534, during the Affair of the Placards, Catherine was still new to France, only a year into her marriage, still only the wife of a king's second son; though expected to bear a child, the stakes were lower. At fifteen years old, she busied herself with new routines and friendships, and likely gave only passing thought to the religious changes rocking Europe. The Catholic way of life was a habit for her, one she brought with her from Florence to France. The bells rang and she prayed. The priest intoned in the familiar Latin, and she bent her head, the wafer melting on her tongue. Her religion wasn't something she could choose: it was simply the way it was.

Yet with Henry now set to inherit the French crown, the stakes for Catherine had changed. As she neared her twenties, shedding the last traces of girlhood, Catherine faced the stark reality of her sterility. She had arrived in France vested with the political potential to bring Francis his prized lands in Italy. Once that promise disappeared, her only value to the French monarchy remained in the possibility of bearing a child for the Valois dynasty. Now even that possibility was slipping away. What then? She could not start again. Sterility cast the longest of shadows for a young woman. With no chance of a second marriage, her best hope would be a quiet life in a convent. Repudiation would bring only humiliation.

She needed to buy time, to stay in that space of the possible. Once again, Catherine needed to fight to survive.

In a strange historical twist, the same English king who inspired Francis to replace Catherine may have indirectly helped her keep her place in France.

In 1541, King Francis made secret inquiries in England about Henry VIII's daughter, Elizabeth Tudor. Might she make a fitting bride for his son the dauphin? For some reason, King Francis did not realize that Henry VIII had legally bastardized Elizabeth shortly before executing her mother, Anne Boleyn. An embarrassed Duke of Norfolk was forced to clarify. "The younger of the two [Tudor girls] was not to be spoken of," he told the French ambassador, "because, besides being only seven years old, the [poor] opinion of Queen Anne, her mother, was such that it was quite decided to consider her illegitimate as the Act of Parliament declared." King Francis balked. The following year, he inquired about Elizabeth's older half-sister, Mary Tudor, as a bride, but withdrew that offer, too, when he learned that Henry VIII had also refused to acknowledge his eldest daughter's legitimacy.

Surely, retorted the English Privy Council, Lady Mary's royal blood was preferable to that of Catherine, the Medici pope's niece?*

---

*As the daughter of both Henry VIII of England and Katherine of Aragon, Mary Tudor descended from royal blood on both sides of her family. The same could not be said of Elizabeth Tudor, whose mother, Anne Boleyn, was an English gentlewoman.

It was indeed, said Francis (a stunning admission of Catherine's diminished value in his eyes). Even so, it was "more honorable for the son of France to marry the poorest gentlewoman, being legitimate than a dame of the noblest parentage, being illegitimate."[20] Chivalrous almost to a fault and proud, Francis would keep his Medici daughter-in-law, barren and poor though she was—at least until a better option came along.

In the end, Francis was swayed as much by Catherine's own gumption as by politics. Almost ten years after the fact, in 1551, the Venetian ambassador Contarini would tell the story of how Catherine saved herself. As soon as she heard of her imminent repudiation, Catherine approached King Francis, tears streaming down her face. "She told him she had heard he intended to find another wife for her husband, since God had not graced her with children," Contarini wrote. "If His Majesty was no longer willing to wait, it was important to consider the succession for so great a kingdom. As for herself, she was so grateful to the king for having deigned to accept her as a daughter-in-law that she would much rather suffer the great pain [of repudiation] than displease him. And so, she was ready to enter a convent or rather, if it pleased the king, to remain in the service of the lady who would have the good luck of becoming her husband's bride."

Historians have long noticed Catherine's ability to read the personalities around her and to tell them what they wanted to hear. She also had a penchant for the theatrical. This wasn't the first time she had used words and tears to soften a heart. But her fear and shame were heartfelt.

King Francis melted. "My daughter," he replied, "have no further doubts. Since God has wished you to be my daughter-in-law and the dauphin's wife, I do not wish it otherwise. Perhaps it will please God to grace both of us with the son we desire."[21] For all his strength, Francis had a soft spot for Catherine. He granted her a reprieve. But Catherine knew time was running out.

A woman who wished for a child could take certain measures. She could pray to Saint Anthony of Padua to protect against infertility or to Saint Catherine of Siena to ward off a miscarriage. She could rub her navel with special stones, steep in a bath of medicinal herbs, or weave the leaves into a girdle to wear around her waist. Folk medicine prescribed a monthly dose of donkey's urine to promote fertility while warning against riding a mule, lest a woman catch the creature's legendary sterility.[22]

Catherine availed herself of every method in her arsenal. She prayed to the saints and pleaded with the nuns of Le Murate to keep her in their prayers. She swallowed fertility tonics and drafts daily, "any and all medicine that might help her," wrote the Venetian envoy Matteo Dandolo. He found her desperation heartbreaking. "I believe no one would not willingly give their own blood to give her a son," Dandolo wrote.

One of those tonics came from Anne de Montmorency, Henry's friend and mentor. Montmorency feared the family of a new bride would gain sway over the dauphin; if he wanted to keep the dauphin's favor, it was best to keep Catherine at court. "If, God willing, this works for me, it will be the greatest benefit I have ever known," Catherine wrote to Montmorency in reply, her gratitude cut with despair.[23]

More unexpectedly, Diane de Poitiers also tried to help Catherine. For almost ten years, Catherine had tolerated Diane's presence, but another bride might not be so forebearing. What was best for the wife, in this case, was also best for the mistress. It was likely Diane who persuaded Henry to seek the advice of Dr. Jean Fernel, the esteemed physician. In Catherine, Fernel found a dryness of the womb and vagina. But in Henry, he found hypospadias, a deformity of the penis that obstructed the flow of semen. Fernel administered pills of myrrh and recommended certain sexual positions to remedy the situation. Afterward, Diane duly sent Henry to sleep with his young wife more often.[24]

Possibly, the mistress guessed that the real reason for the couple's barrenness was simply a lack of trying.

4
MOTHERHOOD
France, 1543–1553

Just after her twenty-fourth birthday, Catherine sensed something had changed. In June 1543, she began to share her news. "My friend," she wrote to Anne de Montmorency, her ally on the long road to fertility, "since I know you want me to have children as much as I do, I want to tell you that I hope myself to be with child. I know no one would be happier about it than you." A harrowing path stretched before her; every pregnancy in the sixteenth century carried the chance of illness, miscarriage, or death for mother and child. Yet Catherine had never wanted anything more. "This would be the beginning of all my good fortune and happiness. So, I hope it comes to pass. I pray for it," she told Montmorency.[1]

Her prayers were answered. At sunset on January 19, 1544, Catherine at last gave birth to a son in the palace at Fontainebleau. The baby was named Francis after his grandfather the king, who sobbed with joy. The birth seemed nothing short of miraculous. "The dauphin has left the Abbey of Saint Victor!" teased one of Henry's friends, punning on *vit tord*, meaning "twisted cock." Henry was relieved, his honor restored. King Francis showered his son with baby gifts: a place on the council and a generalship in the army, now on campaign in 1544 against Henry VIII of England, who was besieging Boulogne on the northern tip of France. Diane de Poitiers also reaped the rewards. Throughout Catherine's pregnancy, the mistress had coddled the dauphine with every care and comfort. Now Diane reveled in Henry's newfound prestige. This was her victory, too.[2]

The nuns of Le Murate sent the new mother a present. "I knew I was right to ask you to pray to God and to Our Lady of Conception for me," replied a grateful Catherine. Recovering after a long but uneventful delivery, Catherine at last found solace. She was mother to a baby boy, the prized possession. Giving birth was transformative for Catherine. She no longer feared her repudiation. And she had a new identity etched in the collective mind of the court: she was mother to the future king of France.[3]

How did the once barren Catherine become so fertile? At Fontainebleau, King Francis poked through the afterbirth, consulted his astrologers, and predicted Catherine would give birth to at least six children, maybe more.[4] Sure enough, on April 2, 1546, a scant two years later, Catherine delivered a baby girl just before midnight. This second delivery was difficult, and Catherine was bedridden for weeks afterward.[5] She recovered in time, though, for the baptism in July, held at Fontainebleau.

More than a christening, this baptismal ceremony was a celebration of the recent reconciliation between King Francis and Henry VIII of England after the English king's assault on Boulogne two years earlier. At Fontainebleau, the guests ogled lavish banners sewn with English and French coats of arms that were hung throughout the palace and admired the French and English heralds who stood trumpeting side by side. At the baptismal font, Thomas Cheney, the English ambassador, cradled the baby in his arms, standing proxy for Henry VIII, who agreed to serve as godfather for this child, just as he had for her father. Henry chose a name for the new princess that was dear to his heart: Elisabeth, after his beloved mother and his own daughter, Elizabeth Tudor, who was twelve years old. Here, then, was a new Elisabeth, though since she was French and not English, they spelled her name with an "s" instead of a "z."[6]

Elisabeth would go by many names during her lifetime. As a child of the royal house of France, she was called "Elisabeth of France" or "Elisabeth de Valois." Eventually, when she lived in Spain, she would be known to her subjects by a Hispanicized version of her name, as "Isabel." While she was still an infant, her family gave her a nickname: "Elisabel" or "Ysabel," names that slipped off French tongues easily and chimed like music. Often, they called her simply "Madame," which was the usual title for the oldest sister to a future king. "Elisabel" was for family and friends; to everyone else, she was "Madame Elisabeth." At her baptism, Madame Elisabeth was brought into the Christian world, God's kingdom, a realm stretching beyond all terrestrial borders. Yet everyone present at Fontainebleau understood her little body also brokered peace between earthly kings. From the moment the heralds announced her name, Elisabeth became the symbol of friendship between France and England.[7]

Catherine had high hopes for her daughter. "This baby will be the tie that binds and guarantees all alliances with . . . greater firmness," she wrote to her cousin Cosimo de' Medici, Duke of Florence, "through which all those of our house [of Medici] will be more delighted and reassured."[8] One day, Elisabeth would marry a prince, raising the ranks of the Medici still higher, bringing good fortune to both the Medici and the Valois. Catherine's note may have been something of an excuse; perhaps she was trying to rationalize the birth of a girl instead of a boy, another heir. Still there was truth in what she said. Daughters brought great families together. They helped create empires.

That Catherine was so forthright about it didn't mean she loved Elisabeth any less.

Over the next eight years, Catherine gave birth to eight more children. Four more boys—Louis, Charles, Alexandre-Edouard, and Hercules— and four more girls—Claude, Marguerite (known affectionately as "Margot"), and the twins Jeanne and Victoire. It became a pattern of life for Catherine, an unending cycle. Conception and pregnancy, confinement, labor, birth, recovery; anticipation and discomfort, pain, relief, joy. The confinement room was shuttered and shaded, the straw to soak up the blood of birth was laid, the birthing stool prepared. Catherine entered, labored, gave birth, emerged. She proved strong in childbed. Only once did the midwives truly worry.

Change was inevitable, of course. King Francis would not live to see most of his grandchildren born. He died in March 1547 at the age of fifty-two, succumbing to an illness that had plagued him for the better part of the year. Of the trio of kings who dominated European politics in the first half of the sixteenth century, King Francis was the second to go. Henry VIII had died earlier in the year, having written to warn his rival Francis that he, too, was mortal. After reading the letter, Francis slipped into a profound depression that lasted until his death. King Charles V, Francis's archnemesis, would survive him by more than a decade, though he withdrew from secular life: worn out, Charles abdicated his Dutch lands in 1555 and his Spanish throne in 1556, and retreated to a monastery. Slowly, the old guard was fading away.

The new King Henry II of France did his duty by his father, commissioning magnificent memorials and ordering an effigy of Francis to be served his meals for eleven days straight. The table was set, the wine poured, and the napkin proffered, all as if King Francis were still alive. By custom, the new king didn't attend the obsequies of the former king, but Henry insisted on watching the funeral procession from a house along the route. Hiding himself behind a curtain, Henry peered out from a window. According to his friend Vieilleville, the young king's eyes welled "to the point of tears." But the moment was fleeting. Despite Henry's filial devotion during Francis's last days, the deep rift between father and son remained. At twenty-eight years old, Henry was determined to be his own man. Once the funeral rites were over, he cleaned house.[9]

"Grave and virtuous thoughts" would govern his court, Henry pledged. A strict Catholic, untouched by his father's liberal views, King Henry scattered Francis's *petite bande*, scaled back the decadent parties, and set up the "burning chamber," a new tribunal in the Parlement of Paris whose sole mission was to persecute heresy. He also made new political appointments. Old families like the Bourbons, who once commanded great power at court, were pushed back as Henry's mentor Anne de Montmorency, now Constable of France, became the dominant force on Henry's council. The Guises, a relatively new family to France and allies of Diane de Poitiers, also penetrated the king's inner circle: François and Charles, the two eldest sons of Claude, Duke of Guise, were handsome and intelligent young men in their twenties, and staunch Catholics. With Diane's approval, Henry made François the Grand Chamberlain of France, while Charles would first become Cardinal of Guise, then, in 1550, Cardinal of Lorraine.[10]

Others sensed the shift in the winds. Anne de Pisseleu, Francis's mistress, left court after surrendering the jewelry she'd received from the old king. Even Marguerite de Navarre, King Francis's evangelical sister, withdrew to her estates in the south. Many of the changes at court were likely the work of Diane, to whom Henry turned more than ever now that he had ascended the throne. Diane advised him on all state matters, secrets, and appointments, and even signed some official correspondence: "*HenriDiane*."

After his accession, Henry's initials, etched and engraved in stone and marble, and sewn into silks and taffetas, popped up all over the royal châteaus. At first glance, the initials seemed to intertwine Henry's "H" with two "C"s, one facing forward and the other backward—*HenriCaterine*. But one day in 1555, the Venetian diplomat Giovanni Capello squinted hard at the royal insignia. Didn't the letters look like two "D"s rather than two "C"s? Was it *HenriCaterine*? Or *HenriDiane*? Or could it be *HenriCaterineDiane*? Capello wasn't sure, and that was the point. The official duo was always, in fact, a trio, the mistress hiding in plain sight.[11]

Unlike Diane, Catherine stood on the margins of Henry's palace revolution, a political side note to all the upheaval. When King Francis died, she lost a protector and friend. A diplomat once observed that, more than anyone else in France, Francis had loved Catherine. Now that he was gone, the babies she put in the nursery were her best protection. Though, in theory, she was the highest-ranking woman at court, few were deceived. Catherine might be Henry's queen, but it was Diane who ruled.[12]

Without a doubt, Catherine loved her children. It is hard to know how much her own years as an orphan colored her fierce devotion to them, the hours she spent obsessing over the smallest details. She mothered them almost as if she were making up for something. Catherine had suffered through an insecure and violent childhood, but her own babies were the children of a king, the "children of France." Unlike her own mother, Catherine was still alive and well, ready to watch over them. She vowed to give them the very best.

Giving them the best meant giving them up, at least for a little while. All of Catherine's babies were fed at the breast of a wet nurse, although thinkers like the Spanish Juan Luis Vives advised royal mothers to breastfeed their own babies, especially daughters. Through suckling, through a mother's love, a daughter could become like her mother's second self, said Vives: "A mother thinks the daughter to be more truly her own when she has not only borne her in the womb and given birth to her, but carried her continually in her arms as an infant, nursed her, nourished her with her own blood."* A beautiful theory and, for Catherine, entirely impractical. Every woman knew breastfeeding hindered conception, and Catherine was expected back in the birthing chamber as soon as possible. So Catherine's infants went to the wet nurse and she returned to the birthing pallet and the birthing stool—again and again and again.[13]

Once the babies were born, there was the matter of keeping them alive, sheltered from the pestilence that struck fear into the hearts of every sixteenth-century parent. Childhood was a dangerous business. A sniffle might signal something insidious; an earache might herald a raging fever. The royal children were assets, as precious as the jewels in Queen Catherine's crown. They were also children beloved by their very human parents. Catherine and Henry did all they could to protect them.

Soon, the new parents came to a decision: what the children of France needed was a little court of their own, a *petite cour* away from the comings and goings of thousands of people at the *grande cour* where contagion was rife. The château at Saint-Germain-en-Laye offered an ideal location. Twelve miles northwest of Paris, a good day's journey, it was neither too close nor too far from the capital, within easy visiting distance. It also had plenty of room. The children's chambers were decorated, the walls covered with miles of cloth of Holland to keep them clean and warm. A staff of over three hundred souls was hired to fulfill the children's every need. The

---

*Renaissance doctors believed that, after childbirth, a mother's blood rushed from her womb to her breasts to make breast milk.

tiny princess Elisabeth even had her own litter-porter, a man named André Fuyart.[14]

Catherine was meticulous in her instructions and picky about her preferences. When Claude was born, one year after Elisabeth, she ordered the girls to be dressed in matching clothes, given the same toys, and bundled into the same baby carriage as if they were twins. Her attentiveness was matched only by King Henry's. An anxious father, Henry spent hours poring over plans, plotting the best routes by which to move the children at the first sign of plague. Never satisfied, he wrote continuously to Saint-Germain for details. Baby Elisabeth had been weaned early? He was glad she still thrived. Baby Claude had fallen in an accident? Thank God "it was just a small thing easily healed." "That is the best news you could have sent me," he wrote, elated, when he learned all the children were happy and healthy. Still, he missed them. For reasons now unknown, he developed a deep attachment to baby Claude in particular. After she was born, the king resisted sending her to Saint-Germain, keeping her near him for a month longer than usual.[15]

Once the children moved to the *petite cour*, Catherine saw them only occasionally, but she kept up to date on every milestone through regular reports from Monsieur and Madame d'Humières, the children's governor and governess. Distant kin to Diane de Poitiers, the Humières were handpicked by the mistress—for in the rearing of the royal children, as in everything else, Diane inserted herself. Still, on this score, Diane chose well: the Humières were parents to no fewer than eighteen children of their own. This certainly counted for something. "I trust your opinion," Diane once wrote to Madame d'Humières when one of the children had fallen ill, "more than that of the doctors, especially given how many children you have had."[16]

Diane's consistent presence in the nursery probably irked Catherine. For every report the Humières sent to Catherine and Henry, they would send another to Diane. In return for information, the mistress did the Humières little favors at court or warned them in advance if the parents were unduly upset. And sometimes Catherine *was* upset. She found that, on occasion, the Humières wouldn't listen. "I believe the nurse is virtuous as you say but she must be changed," Catherine insisted when Charles proved a fussy baby. The Humières stalled, believing, like many sixteenth-century people, that women of honest character make the best milk. "For all her prudence and wisdom, her milk isn't good," the pragmatic Catherine protested. "We can see this from experience." "I am shocked you didn't do as I told you," she fumed when the nurse didn't budge. A few weeks later, baby Charles had a new nurse. Diane de Poitiers had conceded: Catherine was right. "I am very happy that [Charles] is better," Diane wrote to Madame d'Humières, her tone faintly scolding. "It seems the other nurse should have been removed sooner, seeing her milk was no good."[17]

Catherine would grow to despise Diane's ubiquitous presence in Henry's life. Years later, Catherine's secretary would tell a correspondent a secret story about the extent of her jealousy. One day, Catherine found herself so angry at Diane that she considered throwing acid in the mistress's face, destroying Diane's beauty and, with it, her hold over Henry.[18] It turned out to be an empty threat, and Catherine soon thought better of her anger. But the queen clearly found Diane trying.

In public, Catherine succeeded in hiding her feelings. Indeed, foreigners were often perplexed by the seemingly friendly relationship between the queen and the mistress, remarking how "the queen . . . works continuously with her and in turn [Diane] speaks on her behalf to the king."[19] Perhaps, as a young mother, Catherine's feelings for Diane were complicated. Diane seems to have caught at least some of Henry's infectious love for his children. She worked hard to keep them well, sending nurses, medicines, and reams of advice. She also nursed Catherine through childbed and serious illnesses. A grateful King Henry rewarded his mistress with estates and titles, making her Duchess of Valentinois in 1548, "for all the good and admirable services" paid to his "beloved companion the queen."[20]

Theirs was a strange relationship, one that adapted to the circumstances. Catherine would eventually become a hovering, even controlling mother, perhaps because she'd once been forced to share that role with Henry's mistress. At the same time, when her babies were small, when she was constantly pregnant or confined or recovering from childbirth, Catherine might have appreciated Diane's interventions. There was a lot to worry about: the children were often ill; some were fussy, others accident-prone. An experienced mother herself, Diane gave thoughtful advice. She was also powerful. One word from Diane and the deed was done.

Catherine's children were precious to her. And there were so many of them, a new baby almost every year. If anything, King Henry now feared having *too* many children, one envoy noted, since then he would "not be able to leave them the inheritance each deserves."[21] It was a happy problem for a king, but Catherine had her hands full. Possibly, she may have needed Diane's help. So Catherine found a way to compromise—a strategy she would employ for the rest of her life.

———

So long deprived of status and security at court, so long the outsider, Catherine now reveled in motherhood. She spent most of the 1540s and '50s consumed with her children's lives. Later, after they came to court, she would often see them every day, especially the girls. When they were small, though, when nurses did all the tending, Catherine found creative ways to bridge the miles between herself and the *petite cour*. She tried her best to stay close to her children.

Before he died, a fatigued King Francis had delegated some of his tasks. To Catherine, he assigned the special duty of commissioning royal portraits, capturing the faces of the court. An art lover, Catherine wasted no time in ordering hundreds of pictures. She was especially fond of the court painter François Clouet, a modernist for his time. Clouet liked to sketch in simple but rich tones of red and blue, the colors jewel-bright yet elegant. He used energetic strokes of crayon and pencil, filling in with watercolor, not a stodgy oil paint in sight.

Catherine decided Clouet should draw the baby pictures. Getting the children to sit still for more than two seconds was probably the hardest part of the task. At two years old, baby Francis came to get his portrait done, wearing a toddler's gown and a cap on his tufty toddler hair. The boy was bright of eye, plump of cheek, and undoubtedly wriggly. Judging from the completed portrait, Clouet didn't mind the squirming. Francis's hands seem to play with each other, his little finger stretched over the tabletop, all the movement of his body captured in that single, tiny gesture. Someone gave Francis a flower, probably to distract him; its pink blush mirrors the rosy flush of his lips. And he grins—too young to know that a royal prince isn't supposed to smile in his picture.[22]

Clouet kept up as the children grew. He sketched Francis again at the age of four, now wearing a dignified expression along with doublet and hose, having announced that he no longer wished "to dress like a woman." Princess Elisabeth's face, pudgy at four, grew slender by thirteen, yet her eyes remained hooded like her mother's. Soon Clouet began to draw the other noble children who joined the *petite cour*. Louis de Gonzaga and the young Duke of Lorraine had their portraits made. So did Mary Stuart, the five-year-old Queen of Scots, after she came to the nursery in 1548.[23]

Elisabeth loved those sketches, and never forgot her sittings with Clouet. Later, as a teen, she would ask her mother for "pencils in all different colors," which Clouet "will know how to make." Catherine also admired the pictures but, in some ways, she found them lacking. Polished and refined, they were perfect for hanging in palace halls or sending abroad as diplomatic gifts. But Catherine didn't always want polish. She wanted authenticity, to see what the children *really* looked like. In Italy, aristocratic parents had long demanded quick sketches as updates on their children's growth and progress. Deciding she would do the same, Catherine hired another painter who could join the *petite cour*, a man named Germain Le Mannier.[24]

Le Mannier was a hit with all the children, especially young Francis. In addition to sketching, Le Mannier made costumes for them and helped them stage little plays. Catherine liked that Le Mannier usually delivered exactly what she wanted. "Don't leave out anything from their faces," she urged him. "Do [them] in pencil so they can be completed quickly. Send them as soon as you can, that would please me very much."[25] If she didn't approve of the drawings, Catherine demanded new versions, as she once did after he sent sketches of her sons who'd only recently recovered from illness. (Too unlike her boys, she had declared in alarm.) Sometimes, gazing at the portraits, Catherine must have caught her breath. "I see how much they have grown since I last saw them," she wrote in 1548.

She found the pictures reassuring. Once, Le Mannier sent her a quick penciling of one of her sons. He had been ill but was now getting better. The little boy rests his head on a beautifully embroidered pillow, his chubby face no worse for wear. His eyes are wide open. He looks alive and well.[26]

But sometimes the children didn't recover.

In October 1550, two-year-old Louis caught the measles. He deteriorated so quickly that the Humières couldn't notify his parents before he died. "I won't say anything about the sorrow that the loss of Monsieur the Duke of Orléans, their son, has brought to the king and queen," Montmorency wrote to Madame d'Humières. "I will leave it to your imagination how it goes for them." Louis's room sat furnished for several weeks. Eventually, Diane took it upon herself to send his things away.[27]

The month after Louis died in 1550, Catherine announced a new pregnancy. Born in September 1551, the baby was baptized Alexandre-Edouard; later, he would take the name "Henri" after his father and would eventually reign as Henri III. This little boy would became Catherine's favorite, perhaps because he was born so soon after Louis's devastating death. She clung to baby Alexandre; she needed him to live. After his birth, Catherine rarely traveled far from Saint-Germain-en-Laye.

Death was all too familiar in the sixteenth century; both young and old were vulnerable to illness and unforeseen accident. Brothers were playmates but also insurance in case the heir should die—and the next one, and the next. In the summer of 1556, death carried off two more royal children. On June 24, Catherine delivered twin girls after a labor so agonizing that it almost killed her. Finally, at eight in the morning, one little girl was born. But her twin lay dead in Catherine's womb for six hours before the midwives could get her out, which they were able to do only by first breaking the baby's leg.[28] They named the dead infant Jeanne and the surviving twin Victoire. Barely six weeks later, Victoire died.

After that, Catherine had no more children.

Much later, long after her surviving children were grown, Catherine would hang a picture of Louis, along with another painting of two infants, in her large gallery at the château of Soissons. And in the 1570s, Catherine would ask her artists to include the babies' picture in a book of hours she'd commissioned. The little boy and his sisters gaze upward, eyes open, even Jeanne, who had never opened her eyes at all. Louis clasps his hands in prayer. Their little faces are frozen, serene, not quite alive but not quite dead. The most innocent of ghosts. Somehow the painter has captured them between two worlds.[29]

On a crisp November day in 1548, Catherine rode to Saint-Germain-en-Laye to greet a new child who had just joined the royal nursery. Already, the *petite cour* was full to bursting with the offspring of European princely families who sent their children to France to educate them and to nurture friendships and alliances that would last a lifetime. On this day, Catherine prepared to meet a very young girl, a tiny queen. Mary, Queen of Scots, was five years old. She had arrived in France from Scotland in late August.

Mary was a refugee of sorts. Scotland and England were at war. Fearing the English would kidnap Mary, the girl's mother, Marie de Guise, Dowager Queen of Scotland, had sent her to France for her protection.

In 1548, Catherine was almost thirty years old. She had already given birth to three children, and more would soon be on their way. Her body was now a seemingly endless well of good fortune. It was a blissful time, if fleeting, though she didn't know it yet. In 1548, Catherine had already savored the joys of motherhood. She had yet to feel the loss.

The same could not be said of Marie de Guise. Catherine and Marie knew each other from the years before Marie had left France to marry the King of Scots. Marriage and motherhood, Catherine knew, had brought their own sorrows to Marie de Guise. By 1548, Marie had buried two husbands and three children. Now she was sending her youngest child, Mary, far from home.

One day, Catherine would share Marie's pain. But on the road that November, she likely couldn't quite imagine it. Not yet. Possibly, though, she already understood the nature of Marie's sacrifice. Catherine was a young mother herself: she knew the love, and she knew the fear.

5

THE PRICE

Scotland and France, 1537–1548

On August 18, 1548, Louis de Brézé picked up a quill to write to Marie de Guise, Dowager Queen of Scotland. A devoted servant to the dowager, Brézé had just survived one of the most harrowing journeys of his life. Along with his young charge, Mary, Queen of Scots, Brézé had set off from Dumbarton on the River Clyde in Scotland, bound for the port of Roscoff on the northern shore of Brittany. What should have taken a week instead took sixteen days. The weather was rough, and ropes of rain beat down on a swollen Irish Sea. The waves pounded, the boat shuddered, the rudder cracked. Most of the passengers were sick even when they anchored along the way, hoping to ride out the weather.

Not Mary, though. She was "less ill upon the sea than any one of her company such that she made fun of the others," Brézé told Marie de Guise. Mary was thriving, "as well as you ever saw her"; as for Brézé himself, he was glad to finally be back on terra firma. They had landed on the fifteenth and moved to the nearby town of Saint-Pol-de-Léon to await the arrival of Mary's grandmother, the Duchess of Guise.[1]

Five-year-old Mary, Queen of Scots, had been the sovereign monarch of Scotland for almost her entire life. Born at Linlithgow Palace during a glacial Scottish winter on December 8, 1542, she arrived less than two weeks before her father, James V, died miles away at Falkland Palace. As her father's only living legitimate child, Mary became the Queen of Scots at nine days old.

For the next five years, Mary's mother, Marie de Guise, struggled to protect her daughter's crown from the English Tudor monarchs. Despite the blood kinship that linked the Scottish Stuarts to the English Tudors, there was no love lost between the two realms, and Henry VIII of England had long sought to bring Scotland under English rule. Skirmishes at the border were frequent, and the Scots feared real invasions from the English. Time and again, the Scots repelled King Henry VIII, but although they often won the battle, they nevertheless seemed to be losing the war against the red-haired Tudor. In 1513, Henry defeated the Scots king, James IV, at the Battle of Flodden. Twenty-seven years later, James V died, depressed and defeated, after Henry's English armies trounced Scottish troops at the Battle of Solway Moss. That left young Queen Mary. And Henry VIII was determined to vanquish her, too.[2]

Since Queen Mary was a girl, however, Henry VIII turned to a soft tactic. Instead of sending his armies to conduct their raids over the border, he offered a betrothal between Mary and his own son and heir Edward, in exchange for perpetual peace between the realms. Acquiring Scotland remained his goal. King Henry planned to raise young Mary at the English court to prepare for her future role as Edward's queen. Through his inviolable possession of Mary as his bride, Edward would procure Scotland's crown.

The Scots saw through the ploy. Although at first they signed the Treaty of Greenwich, agreeing to King Henry's terms, they soon broke it. A livid Henry VIII turned once again to war, this time instructing his generals to show no mercy. Raping, pillaging, and plundering quickly ensued. English soldiers burned entire villages around Edinburgh to the ground.[3] In fact, Henry VIII's goal hadn't changed: though the slaughter was meant to punish the Scots, he also hoped to coerce them, through sheer terror, into handing over their young queen.

Historians call these dangerous years the "rough wooing"—indeed, they were the most violent of seductions. After Henry VIII died in 1547, the carnage continued under his son, the Protestant boy king Edward VI. A devout Catholic, Marie de Guise could not abide the notion of her daughter falling into Protestant hands; nor could she stand the idea of Mary surrendering her sovereign crown to the English. As English armies drew ever closer to Edinburgh in the winter of 1548, Marie de Guise began to plot Mary's escape from Scotland.

She looked to France. Forged through a shared hatred of the English, the "Auld Alliance" between Scotland and France had endured for generations.[4] Marie de Guise had married James V in recognition of that friendship; now, she asked King Henry II of France to protect her daughter. The terms the French proposed were remarkably similar to the English ones: in exchange for French military action against King Edward, Mary would be raised at the French court. In time, she would marry Henry II's son and heir, the dauphin, Francis.

Clearly, Henry II of France was conducting some coercive wooing of his own. Yet the terms he proposed satisfied Marie de Guise. The French, for one, were Catholics. Unlike the English, the French promised to respect young Mary's sovereignty over Scotland: the child would keep her sovereign crown. Most importantly for Marie de Guise, France was home. She knew that her own parents, the Duke and Duchess of Guise, would look after Mary. More than any political alliance, Marie de Guise trusted her family.

She signed the agreement with France. By July 31, Mary had boarded a boat in the company of Louis de Brézé, her Scottish nursemaids and governess, a bundle of Scottish courtiers, and a gaggle of little girl friends, ready to brave the stormy seas.

In Saint-Pol-de-Léon, Mary played with her friends while nurses kept her warm against the chill that always lingered in a Breton summer. At five years old, Mary spoke hardly a word of French. Though her mother had brought French tastes to Scotland when she'd married King James V, Mary had lived in the care of her Scottish nurses and spoke only their language.

The Scotland she remembered was a land of upheaval, of endless travel through wooded lowlands and rocky highlands. She had spent the previous months trying desperately to outrun the marauding English, moving first from Stirling Castle to the island of Inchmahome in the Lake of Menteith, then back to Stirling, then on again to Dumbarton Castle on the western coast.

Now, she was safe in France. For weeks, her French relatives had prepared for her arrival. No one had prepared as much as Mary's grandmother, Antoinette de Bourbon, the Duchess of Guise. No one understood quite like Antoinette what it had cost her own daughter, Marie de Guise, to send young Mary away. "I am sorry for the pain you must have felt during her voyage," Antoinette wrote to Marie, "and before you could have known she had landed safely. And for what you must have surely felt when she left."[5]

Antoinette signed and sealed the letter, then sent it on to Scotland. There, Marie de Guise was waiting, still unsure whether her daughter had survived the voyage, if she had found a safe harbor at last.

The Guises were a tight-knit clan. Ambitious and fiercely loyal to each other, they would eventually become one of the most powerful families in Europe. In the first half of the sixteenth century, however, they were still considered a new family in France. Their patriarch, Claude de Guise, was the second son of René, Duke of Lorraine. Although it shared a language and many customs with its Gallic neighbor, Lorraine was technically an independent duchy outside the realm of France. This gave the Guises a certain panache and rank. When they arrived in France, they were given due esteem as foreign princes.

René endowed his sons with a healthy view of their own importance, a respect for their mother, and a strong sense of dynasty. A storyteller, he liked to vaunt the family's fearsome lineage, which stretched back to the great medieval crusader Godefroy de Bouillon, a man of great piety, which (René liked to tell his children) earned him the kingdom of Jerusalem in 1099. According to René, God had blessed the House of Lorraine ever since. A striver, René carefully plotted the careers of both his sons, seeking to weave the family's legacy into the firmament of European politics. To his eldest son, Anthony, René bequeathed the duchy of Lorraine. To Claude, his second son, he bequeathed all his landholdings in France. When young Claude turned nine years old, René dispatched him over the border to be raised in the home of a French aristocrat, with the hope that Claude's career would steer the family's fortunes into that great kingdom. Claude learned René's lessons well and inherited his ambition.

In adulthood, he adopted a personal motto, derived from his father's: *Toute pour une, là et non plus*. All for one, here and no further.* Family comes first. They were in it together.

As his father had hoped, Claude quickly fell in with the future King Francis I, who found much to admire in the prince from Lorraine. It was hard not to like Claude. He was blessed with charisma, stellar athleticism, a deep sense of chivalric honor, and striking good looks, with blond hair, blue eyes, and an enviable height—which prompted jealous rivals to point out that he looked more German than French. Despite Claude's foreign birth, the young man earned Francis's trust. Over the next twenty years he fought and won heroically on the battlefield during the Italian Wars and deployed his considerable political acumen in the council chamber. When Francis departed in 1524 to recapture Milan, he left Claude at court to advise his mother and regent, Louise de Savoy. Upon his return to France after the debacle of his Spanish imprisonment, Francis made Claude the Duke of Guise as a reward for his loyal service. This was an extraordinary move: until then, only princes of French royal extraction—never a foreign prince—had been granted the title of duke.

Francis had helped arrange Claude's wedding to Antoinette de Bourbon during their teenaged years. This was another step up for Claude and the House of Lorraine. Though hailing from a junior branch of the family, Antoinette was nonetheless one of the Bourbons, princes of the blood who descended from the medieval Capetians, the founding dynasty of France. This meant that, technically, Antoinette outranked Claude. Intimidated by her status, fearing her family would find his own rank wanting, yet nonetheless captivated by Antoinette's red hair and riveting conversation, Claude asked his friend Francis to intervene on his behalf. Francis readily obliged. The young couple married when Claude was sixteen and Antoinette seventeen. Once she became Claude's bride, Antoinette made herself into a Guise through and through.

Home for the couple was a magnificent estate at Joinville, a medieval fortress perched atop a rocky outcrop in the hills of Champagne not far from Lorraine. Joinville wasn't the only Guise

*In the nineteenth century, Alexandre Dumas would use a version of this same motto in his *Three Musketeers*.

château, but it was by far Antoinette's favorite. She loved its fairytale turrets, its roaming apple orchards, its marvelous view. Mountains peaked on the horizon and from grand windows in the main house you could look out over meandering streams and rolling woods in the valley of the Marne. Below the castle's walls, tucked next to the burbling river, the town of Joinville sheltered in the château shadow.

Since Claude was frequently away at court, Antoinette managed Joinville mostly herself with an expert eye and a deft hand. As in any great house, there were always people around: visiting guests, tenants of the duke's lands, and over a hundred servants. The patter of little footsteps, too, filled the halls in the wing where the nursery was set. Over twenty years, Antoinette gave birth to twelve children; ten survived into adulthood. Marie de Guise was the eldest, born in 1515. The youngest, named René, was born in 1536. At Joinville, as at any country estate, the food was local. The family feasted on fresh meat and fish, fruit and vegetables from the gardens, eggs, good country bread, and fine wine even on the "lean" days of Friday and Saturday.[6]

Like her husband, Claude, Antoinette cared mightily about the soul. Piety bound the Guises together, although they had yet to embrace the reactionary Catholicism that would define the family later in the century. Still, they were devout. Claude believed wholeheartedly in the God of his forebears and of the popes, eagerly chased Lutherans from Lorraine, and made doleful religious pilgrimages after disasters like the Battle of Pavia, endeavoring to right all wrongs. As for Antoinette, she was so pious that she installed her own coffin in the main hall of the château at Joinville as a reminder to herself of what was coming. Antoinette's sister was an abbess, two of her sons would become cardinals, and two daughters would become abbesses as well. At her mother's behest, Marie de Guise spent part of her own childhood in a convent and, had Marie's elegant features not pointed toward marriage as the more advantageous path, Antoinette might have considered the church for her eldest daughter, too.[7]

Church wasn't only about piety. For the Guises, the Catholic Church offered another path to power and career. A family teeming with children was expensive. Church appointments kept dowries to a minimum for daughters and provided a regular income for sons. Most importantly, careers in the Church kept rivalries among brothers to a minimum: the Guises did not suffer from the problem of "second sons" that so often troubled aristocratic families. Church benefices, moreover, consolidated the Guise patrimony, keeping money and estates in the family.[8] That was the thing about the Guises. Even God was, in a way, about family. And they were an ambitious family, pragmatic and savvy, proud of their bloodlines and eager to rise still higher. They coveted a royal crown—any crown. Their ambition was fierce and unified: the Guises leaned on each other with what seemed an unbreakable sense of devotion.

Marie de Guise's marriage to James V of Scotland in 1538 was a product of that family devotion. She married the King of Scots only reluctantly. In late 1537, when the marriage was first proposed, Marie was twenty-two years old, already the widow of the Duke of Longueville and the mother of a young son. There had been another son, an infant, but he had died only months after the sudden death of Marie's husband in June 1537.[9] The Scottish marriage proposal came before the year was out and, in Marie's mind, too soon. But when James V of Scotland requested a French bride in the name of the Auld Alliance, King Francis would not accept her refusal.*

In June 1538, family and friends gathered in Rouen to say a final goodbye. Before boarding a galley bound for Scotland, Marie gave her son, François, a final kiss. Just three years old, François was the new Duke of Longueville, having inherited the title upon his father's death. Though hardly more than a toddler, he was a peer of the realm, endowed with ceremonial positions that demanded his appearance at the French court. Moreover, if François left his Longueville estates, they would be vulnerable to theft and rival claims—a threat the Guises could not allow. When Marie accepted the Scottish marriage, the Guises decided together that she should leave little François behind.

Antoinette de Bourbon had agreed to manage François's estates, and to care for the boy in his mother's absence. At Joinville there would be children for François to play with, including René, Antoinette's two-year-old son, whom François charmingly nicknamed "Little

---

*James V's first wife was King Francis's daughter, the fragile Madeleine de France. She also died in 1537, at the age of sixteen, just months after arriving in Scotland.

Uncle." There would be aunts and uncles to coddle him, gardens to frolic in, ponies to ride. The little boy would be loved.

And so, Marie stepped up to her ship and departed. This was the price of a woman's fidelity to family, the price of ambition. "They say [Scotland] is not far by sea and even closer if you go through England," Antoinette had reassured Marie.[10] Their letters would travel quickly. To Marie, it must have been small comfort.

———

Like many a noblewoman sent abroad in marriage, Marie de Guise brought a touch of home with her to her new realm. This was expected, even desired. King James was an educated man, fond of fashion, and Scotland was a kingdom far more cultured than most Frenchmen believed. The Scots impressed Marie de Guise as she made her entry into Edinburgh. King James wanted Marie to elevate the status of his court, to bring the elegance of wealthier and chicer France to his realm. So Marie wrote away for French wine, fruit, and artists, even French masons to work on her Scottish castles at Falkland and Stirling. She brought over French ladies and gentlemen, marrying them off to Scottish courtiers. A dutiful queen, she made a good-faith effort to master Scots, though she never quite succeeded, finding some of the pronouns particularly difficult.[11] Committed though she was to her Scottish husband, French remained Marie de Guise's language and culture.

Letters from Antoinette served as French reminders, too. They came among bundles of French things, frequently arriving on the same ships that brought Marie her fruit and wine. People in the sixteenth century would often cut their letters short. "I will keep from writing you too long a letter," they would write if paper was scarce, the messenger hurried, or the reader potentially bored. But since Antoinette missed Marie, she indulged herself. She wrote letter after letter.

Fevers and bellyaches, births and baptisms, treaties and truces, dowries and deaths. In Antoinette's letters, politics slid easily into family news and back again, the one as vital as the other. Marie's young sister was feverish, so Antoinette wrote. The old governess had a new baby; Antoinette wrote. The Longueville estates were running well, King Francis and the emperor had reached a détente, Marie's brother was about to be married, and everyone was together at Joinville to celebrate their anniversary; Antoinette wrote yet again. "That's all the news here really," she wrote once when she had little to say—and still she bothered to put pen to paper. Antoinette loved writing to her daughter. Her only complaint was that Marie was a poor correspondent, just about as bad as her husband, Claude.[12]

Especially in the early years of Marie's marriage to King James, Antoinette wrote reams about François, Marie's son, "what I know you most want to hear about." Marie had made a beautiful baby, she said, a boy who grew so fast his gowns "didn't fit by three inches." At three years old, François was a chatterbox; at four, the apple of his grandfather's eye. Often, the boy fell ill—no doubt more frequently than Marie liked to hear. When healthy, though, he ate and slept well and grew "plump and round and so very pretty." As often as she could, Antoinette would send François's portrait. Once, Antoinette and François sent Marie a string the same length as the boy's height. She could see for herself how much he had grown.[13]

"Nostre petit filz," Antoinette liked to call François. *Our grandson—our little boy.* Soon enough, she had François writing his own notes to Marie. Too young to write them himself, he mostly dictated. His little missives are a marvel to behold. The handwriting is competent, the script of a grown-up. The scribe, a mystery man in the household named Jean, was a dedicated servant; listening to François, he changed not a word. The hand that writes is practiced and steady. But the voice that speaks is all boy.

There was so much to tell. There was eating and playing, sleeping and praying, the ponies, the chickens, the garden, Auntie and Little Uncle. There were games and day trips. There was feasting and fighting. He was a little boy in a grown-up world; sometimes sounds and situations confused him. "Desamoyre is the bride who slept next to my bedroom," he told his mother once. "She was crying *hec hec*, and her husband was hurting her."[14]

Then there was Grandpapa. Grandpapa was wonderful. Grandpapa took François for picnics, and they picked strawberries. Grandpapa went fishing and gave him a fish (sadly, Jean and Jousine ate it). Grandpapa hid in the closet while Auntie was putting him to bed. Grandpapa took him hawking and he caught two birds. "The heron was yelling *Qua! Qua!*" he said, "and the kite was saying *Let me go!*" François adored his Grandpapa. "I held his finger so tight," he explained, "and I didn't want to let go, because I love him so much and I am his darling." Grandpapa showed François how to hunt, and he wanted to show his mother, too. The hawks fly up, François told her, they catch the herons and the kites, and as for himself—"I run on my little horse, *fly! fly!*"[15]

He could barely contain himself. He dictated excited, rambling sentences that bounced from this to that, making hardly any sense at all—except to François and, perhaps, to his mother. He told her how Little Uncle sometimes teased him and threatened to steal his toys. He told how he had scurvy and "booboos" on his hands, how Grandmama fed him good black bread at bedtime, how he spent the day in the garden eating lots of cherries and feeding his pet chickens. He told her how he gave Auntie Louise little kisses, "the way I used to kiss you, Madame the Queen." He called his mother "Madame," "Madame the Queen," and sometimes simply "*Maman*." He told her he missed her. He was full of wishes. He wished she would send him a Scottish pony. He wished she would write more. He wished for a baby brother. He wished she would come to France to see him. She could bring King James, his stepfather, he said. He wished for that, too.[16]

Jean the scribe crossed the t's and dotted the i's. Then he handed the boy the pen. At the age of five, François had yet to learn how to handle a quill properly. He scratched and scribbled until, eventually, he produced something that passed for a signature.

Writing well takes practice, a skilled and nimble hand. Press the quill too hard and blots form, or the nib breaks; press too softly and the ink skips or fades away. Writing quickly was for secretaries and grandmothers, not for soldiers-in-training. For them, it took more time and attention. When he was old enough to write on his own, François would beg off now and again, though sometimes he had good reason. "Madame," he wrote in 1543, "please do not find it strange that I don't write in my own hand, but grandmother ordered me not to since I am still weak from a fever that I've had for three weeks." Everyone said the fever would make him grow, he explained, and then he could come to Scotland in her service.[17]

Over the years, François would send many notes in his own hand, both from home and from court once he had the chance to go. He was excited to travel to Fontainebleau, in 1546, for the baptism of the king's newest child, a little girl named Elisabeth. At his grandparents' side, François watched the English ambassador, Thomas Cheney, lift the infant to the baptismal font. But the boy's mind wandered toward his mother in Scotland. When he found paper, pen, and a little time during those festive days, he wrote to her. "I assure you, Madame, that I am marvelously happy about this peace treaty" with England, he told her, "because I hope it means I can now see you." A new portrait was on its way, he said, though it didn't really look like him. The artist had added a little something of his own. The boy was no doubt changing by the day; when François had last seen his mother, he was three. Now on that day at Fontainebleau, he was eleven years old. Almost a soldier. "Almost a man."[18]

———

Marie kept those letters from home. They brought her news from the Continent, and they comforted her during the darker years in Scotland. By 1542, four years after her wedding to James V, Marie had buried two more baby boys. Both children died inexplicably within hours of each other, though the boys were miles apart, in separate nurseries.* Then, just eighteen months later, James V was dead.

Letters in the sixteenth century often went astray. When Marie's infant sons died in April 1541, Antoinette didn't receive word until July 22. "The news is devastating for us," she wrote that same evening, "but since this is the will of God—who has power over all of us—to take them from this world and thus to make them fortunate in that way, let Him be praised for it." One day, Marie would surely have more children. "With patience, you will continue to live virtuously, so that you will live a life of joy in this world and the next. The surest way to arrive on the path to God is through tribulation and pain; if you've suffered, it is a good beginning." An oft-repeated message in a time of disease and war, when children so frequently died: *God loves those who suffer most.*

---

*Both Marie de Guise and James V suspected poison. Antoinette told Marie it was best not to consider that cruel and terrible possibility.

"God willing," Antoinette continued, "I will be at your side for the next child, for I would be the first to come help you."[19]

In fact, Antoinette couldn't come to Scotland for the birth of Mary, Queen of Scots. She was present for a rebirth of sorts, however, when five-year-old Mary crossed the Irish Sea to France. In this era of dynastic marriages, mothers and daughters often traveled remarkably similar paths. Catherine de' Medici followed her own mother's trail; so, too, did Mary, Queen of Scots, tracing her mother's path back to France. To Antoinette, the child's journey was a homecoming of sorts, a chance for Mary to find a new life, a safer life. Mary delighted everyone, Antoinette said, "the prettiest and best girl of her age that you've ever seen." "Nostre petite reyne," Antoinette called her granddaughter. *Our little queen.*[20]

Shortly after meeting Mary at Saint-Germain-en-Laye, Catherine de' Medici penned her own note to Marie de Guise, her words filled with a quiet compassion. "I cannot have the pleasure of seeing you and speaking with you which I would greatly desire to do, not only for my own pleasure but also to see the happiness I know you must feel knowing your daughter the Queen is so beautiful, well-behaved, and virtuous. She is such a pleasure, not only for you but for me, too, and for all those who see her." Catherine could imagine young Mary at her side, long into the future. "I am all the more fortunate since God has put her in my path," she continued. "For I think that she will be the sustenance of my old age, to have her with me. I praise God for this and pray that he gives you as much good fortune as you might wish in all things as he has given you in her."[21] Catherine saw what everyone else saw. A beautiful child. A marvel.

Of all the letters that flooded Marie after her daughter arrived in France, the most meaningful one likely came from her own mother. Fresh from leaving Mary in the royal nursery, Antoinette promised to care for her in the years to come, to "hold our little queen's hand." Then, for a moment, Antoinette's thoughts turned to Marie.

"You have had so little happiness in this world, and are so accustomed to suffering and worry, that I fear you no longer know what pleasure is. At least, I hope that through your daughter's absence, you might find some peace for this little creature. God willing, she will find honor here and every good fortune. More than anything, I hope to see you again sometime before I die. For if, God willing, things go well there and everything is recovered and if all the trouble ends and peace is restored . . . then, one day, you can leave that place with an easy conscience for as long as you like and come here to see your children and everyone else who is close to you. Everyone wishes for it, and you can enjoy yourself a little with your friends."[22]

Once the French had rid Scotland of the English menace, Marie could return. Antoinette wrote with a special tenderness, a matchless empathy. She had once walked Marie's same path herself, sending a daughter across the sea, living a loss that played out among aristocratic mothers and daughters time and again.

6

EMPIRES

France, 1547–1553

About a week before Catherine arrived at Saint-Germain-en-Laye to meet Mary Stuart, King Henry sat astride his own horse, headed from Moulins in Auvergne toward the *petite cour*. The weather had been fine during these last days in October, and Henry traveled quickly. Apart from a small retinue, the king came almost alone, hoping to steal some time with his children all to himself. He was also curious about the nursery's newest arrival. "There is no one who doesn't praise her as a marvel," the king wrote to Mary Stuart's uncle, François de Guise. "This doubles my desire to see her. I hope to do so soon."[1]

On the road, Henry brimmed with anticipation, a thousand thoughts already spent on Scotland and its young queen. Just under thirty, Henry had never mastered the finer manners of the courtier. But long days of exercise and time spent in the field had sculpted his body and honed his sense of strategy.

Henry dreamed of empire. A warrior king, he aspired from the early months of his accession to reverse the military gaffes of his forebears. Hoping to recapture the city of Boulogne, which the French had lost to England in 1544, Henry also sought to recover Calais, which France had surrendered two centuries earlier to the English in 1347. And his ambition didn't end there. He still yearned to step out from under his father's shadow and aspired to larger territorial gains. From Francis I, Henry had inherited the old Valois–Hapsburg battles over Italy. He also had a personal score to settle with Emperor Charles V. "As for the emperor the king hates him and

73

declares openly his hatred," a Venetian envoy would write. "He wishes him every evil that is possible to desire for one's mortal enemy. This virulence is so deep that death alone or the total ruin of his enemy can cure it." The memory of a gloomy Spanish cell still haunted the French king.[2]

Charles V was a formidable foe, however: his domains expansive, his armies legion. Already, the emperor controlled parcels of Italy and all the German states. He was also pushing into Northern Africa and sending fleets to the New World. On all sides, France was hemmed in by Spanish Hapsburgs or their allies. To the north lay the Hapsburg Netherlands. To the east and southeast sat the German principalities and feudalities, including Lorraine and Savoy. Spain, Charles V's principal seat, loomed large on France's southern border, abutting the mountainous kingdom of Navarre, half of which had been conquered by Ferdinand of Aragon in 1512 and annexed to Castile; the northern half of Navarre still honored an old feudal allegiance to France, a tiny buffer. To the west, an ocean away, the Hapsburg empire grew larger still as Spanish ships braved stormy seas, carving thoroughfares in the Atlantic.

Neither the New World nor Africa much interested Henry. Europe was Henry's world, the theater of conquest and reconquest. He imagined a Franco-European realm, including all the lands once ruled by Frankish kings such as Charlemagne, plus new conquests in Germany and Italy. So consumed was Henry by his own imperial projects that he named his younger sons after the emperor-heroes of old: Charles-Maximilian after Charlemagne, Alexandre after Alexander the Great and, for the youngest boy, Hercules.[3]

King Henry had youth on his side. While Charles V was growing gray and stiff, the French king sat tall in his saddle. Still fresh on his throne and somewhat intimidated, however, Henry preferred to avoid open conflict with the Empire, at least for the moment. Instead, he looked for other ways to nettle his enemy. He believed the answer lay not to the east but to the north.

England wasn't Hapsburg, but it was no friend of France. In the ongoing conflict between the Valois and the Hapsburgs, England was something of an interloper. More than once, England had taken advantage of French military vulnerabilities, most recently when Henry VIII successfully captured Boulogne in 1544 just as

Charles V's imperial troops set about attacking Paris. Time and again, France and England would make peace only to make war again a few years later. France's antipathy to England was ancient, old claims that undergirded the Hundred Years' War in the fourteenth century never entirely jettisoned. Plus, English sovereigns paraded an obnoxious sense of entitlement: because England held Calais, its monarchs styled themselves "Kings of England, Ireland, and France," a title they had used for almost two hundred years.

Scotland was a different story, an "auld" ally, if a poor one—a frigid rock compared to lush France. Yet, like Henry VIII of England, Henry II of France coveted Scotland. The French king calculated: impoverished Scotland would determine the balance of power in Europe. If Henry II could save Scotland from the English, he would showcase French military strength, put Charles V on his guard, and keep England from dominating the entirety of the British Isles, a situation he was eager to avoid if England was going to cozy up to the Empire. If Scotland became a French outpost, then France would both cripple Tudor ambitions and prove its mettle to the detested emperor. On the other hand, if France lost Scotland to England, Henry VIII of England would be emboldened. Charles V, too, would see weakness and an opening for war with France.[4]

The child Mary, Queen of Scots, was the embodiment of her kingdom. Whoever held her in his possession also held Scotland in his grasp. Yet this was not the end of Henry II's complicated calculus. He saw, too, that England itself might be in play. For the Scottish-French Queen of Scots was also a Tudor.

Mary's paternal grandmother—mother of James V—was Margaret Tudor, the older sister of Henry VIII. As a Tudor, Mary possessed her own powerful claim to the English throne. That claim wasn't incontestable. After the Scottish broke the Treaty of Greenwich in 1543, an irate Henry VIII legally excluded Margaret Tudor's descendants from the English succession. But no English law could deny the Tudor blood coursing through Mary's veins. Most European monarchs believed that blood right, more than law, put sovereigns on their thrones.

Three of Henry VIII's six wives had given birth to children who, according to English law, could inherit the English throne. The law notwithstanding, their claims were weak. Henry VIII's daughters,

Mary and Elizabeth Tudor, were illegitimate, the children of wives Henry VIII had cast aside. To many, this illegitimacy rendered their claims to the throne null and void. Even the legitimacy of Henry VIII's son, who now reigned as King Edward VI, could be questioned. Henry VIII's marriage to Edward's mother, Jane Seymour, was sanctioned by the new Church of England—Henry's English invention—rather than by the Roman Catholic Church. This one seed of doubt left an opening. Many English Catholics backed the claim of Mary, Queen of Scots, assuming that if she inherited the English throne, England would return to the papacy. That she was already a sovereign queen of her own realm made her claim to England all the stronger.

King Henry of France calculated: if Mary wed his son Francis, the French could push her onto England's throne. Then, England would fall under French control. Francis, the dauphin, would become first King of Scots through marriage, then King of England by dint of Mary Stuart's claim; in time, his Valois children by Mary would inherit England's throne. If the French controlled England, they would also control the English Channel. They could cut off the waterways connecting Hapsburg Spain to the Hapsburg Netherlands, scupper Spanish ships launched in Flanders and headed for the New World.

Young Mary was the key to empires. And now, safely settled in the French royal nursery, she belonged to Henry II of France. A war had raged over the girl's body and crown, a war against England that, for now, the French had won. It wasn't hard for Henry II to imagine a day not too far in the distance when he or his son wore the triple crowns of France, Scotland, and England.

Arriving at Saint-Germain-en-Laye, Henry at last beheld Scotland's little queen. There was something glorious about her, even at five. Blue-eyed, pink-cheeked, and silver-tongued, she seemed already to possess the charm that would soften hearts from her earliest girlhood until the end of her days.

But to King Henry, Mary's real beauty lay in the kingdoms she promised to bestow. She was, he wrote to his friend Constable Montmorency, "the most perfect child I have ever seen."[5]

During the sixteen days of Mary's voyage to France, the Guises held their breath. Was she as pretty as reported? As robust? Fair appraisals had flown across the sea from Scotland to France, along with conflicting rumors. Just after Mary's birth, stories circulated in Scotland that she was sickly and sure to die. But the English envoy Ralph Sadler, gazing at Mary a year later, saw "as goodly a child as I have seen of her age." She was healthy and big, built like the Guises themselves.[6]

So the Guises were hopeful. Still, the child who disembarked at Roscoff in August 1548 likely exceeded even Guise expectations. Early portraits made during childhood show something of her fabled beauty: a wide-open expression, high cheekbones, and eyes so clear they look like glass. They were blue when she was young. As she grew older, they deepened to a color closer to amber.[7]

"This little lady is very pretty and seems quite bright," hawk-eyed Antoinette de Bourbon told her son after meeting her granddaughter. "She has light brown hair and I think when she is older she will be a beautiful girl for she has a smooth complexion and white skin. The lower half of her face is attractive, her eyes are small and somewhat deep set. Her face is a little long. When all is said she is very graceful and confident."[8] She was pretty enough, but something beyond physical beauty probably rendered Mary so astonishing. Charisma was a Guise family trait, along with striking features, more handsome than delicate. Mary had grace and confidence even at five. What was it about her? All observers noted an ineffable quality in her that left them awestruck.

Perhaps being an anomaly added to Mary's allure. Girl queens were few and far between; boy kings were the more usual fare. Queen at nine days old, crowned before she was one, Mary was a phenomenon of birth, happenstance, and political capital, magnificent in her oddity, a curiosity as much as a keystone to power.[9]

After Mary landed, excited Guise letters flew. The Guises, too, dreamed of empire, their fortunes at the French court growing alongside the family. Antoinette still reigned as the matriarch of the clan, the heart and soul of the family. The younger generation had made their mark, led by the two eldest Guise brothers. François, who would become Duke of Guise upon his father's death in 1550, was handsome, gallant, and courtly, a fierce field commander and a friend to Henry II.* Charles, the second son and Cardinal of Lorraine, was the family statesman. Man of letters, patron of towering intellects like Rabelais and Erasmus, fluent himself in Latin, Greek, and Italian, the cardinal was a gifted orator. Such were his powers of persuasion that he soon became King Henry's trusted advisor; that same soaring eloquence would also earn him a reputation for cunning and deceit among his enemies. The flashy Guise presence at court and their sway over Henry grew so formidable that Constable Montmorency began to resent them. Even Diane de Poitiers feared for her own influence over the king.[10]

Like the Hapsburgs, the Guises knew women were instrumental to building empires, a process that took generations. Burgundy, Bohemia, Hungary, and Spain had all fallen to the Hapsburgs through the marriage of Hapsburg women to foreign crowns.[11] If they desired stature and influence, the Guises knew they needed to marry strategically.

In December 1548, shortly after Mary's arrival in France, François de Guise wed the chic and shrewd Anne d'Este, daughter of the Italian Duke of Ferrara and, through her mother, granddaughter of King Louis XII of France—bringing the Guises a step closer to the French royal family. Anne's French mother followed the teachings of the Reformist Jean Calvin and had raised her daughter in the new religion. Yet like Antoinette de Bourbon, Anne d'Este dedicated herself to the Guises as soon as her husband slipped the wedding band on her finger. From that point on, her loyalty to the family never wavered, a fact that endeared her to Antoinette. At court, Anne kept her ears pricked for news of Mary and visited her often in the nursery, as committed to the young queen as Antoinette.[12]

Toute pour une, all for one. Family feeling fueled the great Guise corporate machine as year after year they amassed clients, connections, marriages. Mary, Queen of Scots, embodied the next phase in the Guise plan to consistently marry up. However, certain doubts about her betrothal to the dauphin still lingered, which made the Guises wary.

---

*Claude, Duke of Guise, would die in 1550 after a deterioration so acute and inexplicable that the Guises suspected poison, which in the sixteenth century was often blamed for any mysterious illness.

Henry II's deal with Marie de Guise was more a promise than a firm contract. No binding agreement to join the children in matrimony yet existed, and Henry avoided giving away too much too soon. It was never a good idea to hand a noble family too much prestige, lest they draw influence and loyalty toward themselves and away from the crown. Henry also seemed to be stalling in case a more advantageous arrangement for his son presented itself.

The Guises banked a lot on one little girl who would not be betrothed to the dauphin for several years yet, not until both children reached their teens. Until then, the Guises counted on Mary maintaining a star position front and center within the French royal family. They were leveraging her Scottish crown. If all went as planned, a Valois–Guise son would one day reign on the French throne.

More than Queen of Scots, the Guises envisioned Mary as queen consort of France. They would teach her to think of that crown as her own, to feel it, to want it. If she played that part well, perhaps everyone else would come to see it as natural.

———

First, though, she would have to grow up, an enterprise that required a good deal of attention and careful planning. King Henry wanted Mary to think of herself as his daughter, loyal to the Valois and to France.[13] As Henry saw it, Mary would become French not only through food, clothes, or language. Frenchness was in the friendships Mary would make, in the people she would come to love.

Henry believed those bonds could be nurtured. From the first, he sought to cut the cord tying Mary to Scotland. In truth, the French found all the Scots boorish and tedious, their wardrobes outdated and manners uncouth. (Antoinette said they were even a bit dirty. Mary, of course, was an exception.)* Mary's Scottish companions included an entourage of friends who had traveled with her, four small girls almost exactly her age. All were the daughters of Scottish noble families and, like their young mistress, all of them were named

*Brantôme would write that the Scots language trilled on Mary's tongue whereas it rasped in the throats of most Scotsmen.

Mary: Mary Beaton, Mary Seton, Mary Livingston, and Mary Fleming, the daughter of Mary Stuart's Scottish governess, Janet Fleming. During long, arduous months of travel as they fled the English, the band of tiny Marys had clung together. Yet, once they arrived in France, Henry decided the little posse was best broken up.[14]

King Henry sent the four Marys to a convent school in Poissy, four miles northwest of Saint-Germain-en-Laye, where they would receive a sound education in French language and customs. He dismissed most of Mary's Scottish servants. In an unprecedented move, the king merged the households of the dauphin and the royal princesses so Mary and Prince Francis would come to know each other well. His plan worked. "I've learned," the king told François de Guise, "that from the first day, she and my son were as gentle together as if they had known each other for a long time." As for sleeping arrangements, the Queen of Scots would share a bedchamber with the oldest royal princess, Elisabeth, who was then two-and-a-half years old.[15]

The Scottish queen thrived in Henry's immersion school, soaking up her new language and making fast friends among the children in the petite cour. She radiated confidence. At her uncle's wedding in December 1548, Mary took center stage in a dance with the four-year-old dauphin, her steps already practiced, his hand in hers, both dolled up in silks, two children rehearsing their grown-up roles. At the end of the dance, as was customary, the tiny couple kissed. King Henry beamed and toasted the little queen.[16]

Like any child, she studied the faces of grown-ups and responded to their attention. Very early, Mary learned she was charming. The Guises were thrilled, the signs boding well that an official betrothal would soon be in hand. "She could not possibly be more highly honored," Antoinette gushed to Marie de Guise in Scotland. Mary and "Madame Elisabeth" were sharing the best room, she continued, "and this seems to me a very good thing. For this way they will be brought up to love each other as sisters."[17]

Everything conspired to teach Mary about her own importance, that her comfort mattered as much or more than any other child's. Lavish praise from grown-ups taught her she excelled. From the furnishings decorating her chambers, the splendid gowns bursting from her coffers, the ornate tapestries draping the walls, and the dishes perfuming her table, she learned she was magnificent. Her jewels tumbled from large brass chests and her dressing tables spilled over with sparkling pins and finely wrought hairbrushes. On grand feast days, she walked in clouds of silk, satin, taffeta, and velvet, her frocks stitched with silvered thread and festooned with lace, ribbon, and gemstones.[18]

With the other children of the *petite cour*, she dined on a daily cornucopia, dozens of servants toiling from dawn to dusk preparing platters of savory meats, pastries, sweetmeats, and fruit, stewed with leeks and saffron, steeped in nutmeg and cinnamon, and served in impossible quantities. "Twenty-three dozen breads," listed one household account, "18 pieces of beef, 8 sheep, 4 calves, 20 capons, 120 chickens, 3 goats, 6 goslings, and 4 hares," on hand to feed the children and their enormous staff on any given day. If Mary caught glimpses of the world outside the rarefied air of the nursery, it was as she peeked through the hangings of her litter when she traveled from one palace to another with the royal children, sometimes as often as every few days. In each palace, more splendor awaited her.[19]

As she grew older, she joined her playmates for classes in rhetoric and history, and lessons to make her a lady. An Italian dance master was hired, a guitar was procured; she spent hours learning to sing. There was still plenty of time to play with the dozens of lapdogs that ruled the palaces, or to gape at the exotic animals kept by King Henry in the royal zoo. The children delighted in their visits to Diane de Poitiers' château at Anet, where Diane gave them special rooms. Once, assigned to his father's chamber, the dauphin woke up wide-eyed, swimming in the sheets. "I never slept better than in a big bed where I lay in the room of my King," he wrote. At Anet, Mary discovered she liked to gamble—and never more than when she beat the dauphin for his pocket money.[20]

Outdoors, seated upon her favorite pony "Madame Royale," a gift from King Henry, she learned to canter and trot, and longed to follow the queen, Catherine de' Medici, one of the best riders she knew. On quieter afternoons with her little "sisters," Elisabeth and Claude, she would make sweet jam boiled with cinnamon and dried violets ground to powder. Her studies grew more rigorous by the year, and Mary attended Mass daily. For the Guises, play came only after piety—an orthodox piety. "You can be sure," the Cardinal of Lorraine promised his sister, Marie de Guise, "that God is well served [in Mary's house] and in the old style."[21]

In their letters, the Guises always implied that Mary could do no wrong. Mary's good behavior, however, demanded careful management. Behind the scenes, Antoinette kept watch over Mary, tracking her progress and scanning for mishaps. If Antoinette couldn't visit her granddaughter in person, she demanded reports from her children and friends. Letter after letter attest to Mary's virtue and obedience alongside her loveliness; without these, a girl's beauty counted for nothing. Her betrothal to the dauphin still only a promise, Mary could not afford to err. Antoinette adored her children and grandchildren, though like many Renaissance parents, she believed in tough love and was not above a spanking, as one of Anne d'Este's mischievous young sons learned the hard way. Mary was no different. Somehow, Antoinette taught Mary she was loved. She also made it clear that the Guises expected nothing less than Mary's complete obedience and immaculate virtue.[22]

Mary learned that lesson quickly. Of the earliest notes sent between Mary and her grandmother, only one survives, dating from 1550. Mary was eight years old. "Madame," she wrote to Antoinette, "I have been very glad to write this note so I could tell you the joyful news I have received from the Queen my mother. She has promised me by her letters dated 23 April that she will be here very soon to see you and me, which is the greatest happiness I could wish for in this world." "I am so happy," she went on, "that I am thinking only about doing what I must, and to work hard so I can behave very well so she will be happy, seeing that I am as good a girl as both of you want me to be."[23]

Marie de Guise came to France in the autumn of 1550 for both political and personal reasons. The previous spring, the French had successfully attacked English garrisons in Boulogne. The two kingdoms negotiated a cease-fire; peace in Scotland was part of the treaty. The rough wooing had ended at last, and the waterways were now clear for safe travel.

For years, Marie de Guise had wished to become Scotland's official regent, ruling until Mary came of age. In 1550, she came back to France hoping to win Henry II's endorsement for her bid. Currently, the role of Lord Governor of Scotland belonged to the Earl of Arran, an illegitimate son of James IV of Scotland.* As young Mary's closest kinsman, Arran was, in theory, the heir to Scotland's throne. In Marie de Guise's mind, this made Arran eminently untrustworthy, but the man was also profligate and self-interested, dipping freely into the royal treasury for himself and his friends. There was no one else that Marie trusted; it was best to steer the government herself.† It had become clear to her, moreover, that a firm hand was necessary in Scotland. Protestantism had gained traction among the nobility, and religious hostilities were surging.[24]

But her trip also gave Marie de Guise the chance to reunite with family and friends. Two years had passed since she'd last seen Mary, and twelve since she'd left her son, François de Longueville, with Antoinette. Now fifteen years old, François had never stopped writing to his mother. Marie kept him with her for much of the twelve months she spent in France, during what was, for the most part, a joyful and productive trip. One episode, however, filled the Guises with terror. In April 1551, seven months into Marie de Guise's stay, a pro-English Scots fugitive attempted to poison nine-year-old Mary. Discovered before he could execute his plan, the perpetrator fled to England, but the Guises were rattled. The threat of assassination was real, a sign of Mary's value.[25]

Tragedy unfolded during the final weeks of Marie de Guise's journey. In September 1551, while traveling with his mother from Joinville to Amiens, François de Longueville fell ill. Though he'd struggled with illness as a little boy, he'd seemed to grow stronger during adolescence. Whatever he caught on the road in 1551, however, overcame him quickly. He died within a few days.[26]

---

*At the time her husband died in 1542, Marie de Guise was still recovering from giving birth to Mary, and so the Lord Governorship had fallen to Arran. Had she been stronger at the time, Marie might have negotiated for the role herself.
†King Henry II would support Marie's bid, though it took her years to secure power. Eventually the French bribed Arran to step down with the promise of a French duchy. He became the Duke of Châtellerault and Marie de Guise assumed the Scottish regency in 1554.

Fond as she was of her older brother, Mary, Queen of Scots, was too young to attend the funeral. Marie de Guise stayed in France just long enough to see him buried, having resolved to return to Scotland. Though she lived at a time when almost no parent was spared, Marie's trial was especially cruel. Before her departure she wrote a letter to Antoinette, her faith straining against bitter sorrow. "I know, Madame, that you need comforting as much as I do, but your virtue overcomes all things. God wills us to think about the eternal life when we will all rest in peace. I believe, Madame, as you told me, that Our Lord wants me among His own, since He has visited me so often and in such extreme ways. But let Him be praised in all things!"[27]

Mary would never see her mother again. The Guises assumed Marie de Guise would return to France at some point, perhaps for Mary's wedding, but circumstances intervened, keeping her in Scotland. This time, Marie de Guise stayed by choice, not in response to the demands of her family. As regent, facing an increasingly hostile Protestant Scottish nobility, she felt her presence was required to stabilize the kingdom for her daughter.

As for so many aristocratic women in Europe, love and politics intertwined for Marie de Guise, making the one difficult to distinguish from the other. She stayed in Scotland in part because she loved her daughter and family. For the remaining years of her life, her relationship with Mary was confined to letters, a fierce correspondence touching on everything from early lessons in state secrets to how the young Queen of Scots should dispose of her dresses (charitably, said Marie de Guise, and preferably to a church).[28] Mary would always cherish her mother. She strived to please her, and she learned to fear her mother's displeasure.

In her mother's absence, Mary would turn to other women for emotional tenderness, to Antoinette and Anne d'Este, and to Catherine de' Medici. Catherine also regretted Marie de Guise's departure. Having lost baby Louis less than a year earlier, Catherine grieved with Marie over the death of François de Longueville. "You must take comfort in the queen your daughter, from whom in time you will take so much happiness, love, and obedience, that she will make up for all your misfortunes," she wrote.[29] She considered Marie a friend and, on many occasions over the next several years, would ask for Marie's portrait.

Catherine was drawn to many of the Guise women. She kept up an intimate correspondence with Antoinette and instilled a deep respect for the older woman in her own daughters. Catherine felt especially close to Anne d'Este, perhaps because they shared similar backgrounds. Born to a French mother and an Italian father, like Catherine, Anne had spent her childhood in Italy. Whenever Anne spent too much time away from court, Catherine would ask for her news, "which you couldn't send to anyone who loves you more than I do." There is almost a neediness in some of Catherine's letters to Anne, a yearning. It is difficult to know how much politics infused the friendship between Catherine and the Guise women. The Guises certainly understood the advantages to pleasing King Henry's queen. Still, whatever they shared was more than mere courtesy. Their letters breathe real tenderness.[30]

And Catherine may have learned a thing or two from the Guise women. In Marie de Guise, she found a model of patience, endurance, and self-sacrificing motherhood, a woman willing to wrangle power for the sake of her child—a position Catherine would find herself in years later. She also couldn't miss how the Guises fawned over Mary, how Guise aunts and uncles smothered the girl with attention, finding themselves "absolutely delighted with her."[31] What the Guises felt for each other was powerful. Catherine would seek to forge those same bonds of love and loyalty among her own children.

Perhaps Catherine's affection for the Guise women colored her own tenderness toward Mary. She showed that fondness in quiet ways, ordering portraits of Mary, and spending devoted hours at her bedside when the little girl was ill. She passed long afternoons teaching Mary and her own daughter Elisabeth to embroider, weaving gauzy webs of silk and filet lace—needlework skills Catherine had learned as a girl in Le Murate. In her letters, Catherine's voice softens whenever she writes of Mary. Catherine might have seen in the young queen an investment in her own future. From the moment her own daughters were born, Catherine knew they would one day leave her. Mary, though, would stay at the French court as Catherine's daughter-in-law, if all went as planned: as Catherine once told Marie de Guise, Mary would be the solace of her old age. Antoinette remarked that Catherine kept Mary with her often.[32]

Yet Catherine's feelings may have been more complex. Years later, she would grow to dislike Mary for reasons both political and personal. One has to wonder if the seeds of that antipathy took root sometime during Mary's childhood. Beautiful though she was, Mary was something of a disruptive presence in the delicate fabric Catherine had woven over the years at court and in the royal nursery. It was hard to miss how Mary enjoyed the spotlight and fueled the Guises' rising star, how she outshone all the French royal children. Even the dauphin, despite the eminence of his status, walked a little in her shadow. A year younger than Mary, he was small and frail, a wan prince compared to Mary's radiance.

Quite possibly, Mary could have exhibited a certain haughtiness. On one striking occasion, well into Mary's teens, her French governess caused a serious misunderstanding between Queen Catherine and the adolescent Queen Mary, though the details remain vague. Some historians suspect the governess repeated a snide reference by Mary to Catherine's Medici origins. If true, the story speaks both to the jockeying for rank and prestige even among queens—perhaps especially among queens—as well as the teenaged Mary's aggrandized sense of self. Whatever transpired between them made Mary sick with anxiety. Catherine never mentioned the episode in her letters, though later she would come to despise that arrogance in both Mary and the Guises.[33]

From years of living with Diane de Poitiers, Catherine was practiced at hiding her feelings. Still, not a single letter by Catherine betrays even a hint of reproach toward the child Mary Stuart. On the contrary, the Guises believed everything was falling into place. As the Cardinal of Lorraine put it in a letter to his sister, Mary "rules the king and queen."[34]

———

Soon after Marie de Guise returned to Scotland, the Cardinal of Lorraine began to oversee his niece's education, supervising every aspect of Mary's lessons and upbringing. Now that she was nearing adolescence, her schooling needed rigorous attention. The cardinal visited Mary's chambers at least once a month, rifling through drawers, interrogating the staff, inspecting wardrobes. Then he would send a report to Marie de Guise. Always mindful of his sister's nerves, the cardinal tried to convey the good news. Only rarely did he report the bad.[35]

In 1553, when Mary was eleven, the cardinal pushed an inky pen over several pages, writing about a matter of some urgency. Once again, France was at war with Charles V. Henry II's early timidity in the face of Imperial troops had long since evaporated. In this newest clash, Lutheran German princes had called upon Henry's assistance against the Catholic Charles V's ruthless religious persecution. Though fiercely opposed to Protestantism, Henry never relinquished the chance to chip away at the Empire. The front lines moved to the German territories around Metz.

The conflict was pushing the French treasury to the brink. Economies were necessary. King Henry decided the *petite cour* would have to go. The king ordered the dauphin to new quarters in the care of his tutors. As for the royal daughters, Elisabeth, now eight, and Claude, one year younger, Queen Catherine planned to bring them to live with her at court.

This was a cost-saving measure, but to save face, Catherine offered a different reason for the move. In previous generations, she claimed, French royal princesses lived in their own households because their mothers had died. But Catherine wished to supervise her daughters herself. This was the proper way to instill them with obedience and *la crainte*, as she put it—with fear. Catherine seems to have assumed that Mary, Queen of Scots, would live with her, too.

The cardinal admired Catherine's philosophy about mothers and obedient daughters. "It seems to me that, in this, she speaks the truth," he wrote. However, he had reached a different conclusion about the appropriate living arrangements. "I'm of the opinion that you ought to do the same," he told his sister, "and allow only yourself or those you trust to take charge of your daughter. I beg you to keep a strong hand in this so you will always exercise the most power over her. Although, knowing her virtues, I can assure you that you will receive nothing from her but complete obedience." As a solution, he proposed giving Mary her own household and offered a list of ladies and gentlemen worthy of Marie de Guise's "trust."[36]

Did the Guises distrust Catherine? In fact, there were manifold reasons to worry about moving Mary to court. At eleven, Mary was rapidly maturing. "You can hardly treat her as a child," wrote Anne d'Este; she said such grown-up things, had such grown-up ways.[37] Precociousness and charisma had won Mary many admirers, but in adolescence these skills made her vulnerable to predatory adults. As one English courtier would note over a decade later, she tended to talk a lot, sometimes with striking friendliness—even too much friendliness.[38] Perhaps the preteen Mary was already given to a certain flirtatious style. The court of France was filled with slick courtiers. The Guises may have sensed Mary needed protection or, possibly, careful watching.

But the cardinal's chief concern was with rank. Mary was a crowned queen. As long as she lived with the dauphin at the *petite cour*, the Guises tolerated a shared household. It made sense for a five-year-old child since Mary needed to learn the language and make friends, and the Guises were keen not to offend King Henry. Once the dauphin moved into his own household, though, the Guises scrambled for options that suited Mary's rank. That did not include living with Queen Catherine, apparently.

This may have reflected more Guise strategy than Guise snobbery. The betrothal between Mary and the dauphin was still only an informal agreement. The Guises worried that anything diminishing Mary's stature in King Henry's eyes—such as a shared household— could jeopardize the marriage. Mary had already internalized certain lessons about her worth. According to the cardinal, the girl resisted the move to Queen Catherine's household. "Believe me, Madame," he wrote to Marie, "she already possesses such a great and noble heart that she made a great show of being annoyed, finding herself treated so lowly. For this reason, she desires to see herself beyond such juvenile supervision."

It was expensive to set up a separate household, but by the end of the year Mary lived as her own mistress. On the first night in her new home, she celebrated by inviting the cardinal to supper. The time of the *petite cour* was past.[39]

The Guises were sending a message to the French court and teaching Mary yet another lesson. True, Queen Catherine might love her like a daughter, but Mary wasn't Catherine's daughter. She owed obedience first and foremost to her own mother and to the Guises. Mary might love Elisabeth and Claude like sisters, but Mary was different from the daughters of France. She was a sovereign queen, endowed with the blood of the Tudors, the Stuarts, and the Guises. She stood apart from the French princesses. She deserved better.

It was a lesson Mary would cling to for the rest of her life.

7

BRIDES

France, 1558–1559

On Tuesday, April 19, 1558, Mary, Queen of Scots, held out her hand to the dauphin Francis as they stood before her uncle, the Cardinal of Lorraine, in the Great Hall of the Louvre. Around them gathered King Henry, Queen Catherine, and the dauphin's brothers and sisters. Antoinette de Bourbon, Mary's grandmother, was there, too, serving as Mary's guardian for this, the week of her wedding. This was the handfasting ceremony, in which a bride passed into her future husband's keeping, her body and possessions now his own. "Of her own free will and consent, and by the advice of her lady grandmother, the Duchess Dowager of Guise, and the deputies of the three Estates of Scotland," Mary solemnly accepted Francis "for her lord and husband, and promised to espouse him . . . in the face of Holy Church."[1] At last, after eleven long years of promises, Mary and the dauphin were officially betrothed, a knot no mortal could break without the Church's permission. The wedding itself was scheduled for the following Sunday.

Mary was lucky. Unlike so many royal girls, she was marrying a boy she'd known for almost her entire life. Francis still worshipped her. "The dauphin adores the little Queen of Scots," the Venetian ambassador had written back in 1555. "Sometimes they embrace each other, and they like to stand together in a corner of the room, away from others, so no one can hear their little secrets."[2]

In April 1558, Mary was fifteen and Francis was fourteen. Like many adolescent girls, she had matured early, filling out the body of a full-grown woman by the time she was twelve or thirteen. The twinkling prettiness of her early childhood had blossomed into an almost sublime beauty, at least according to her many admirers. The poet Joachim du Bellay said no one who saw Mary would ever behold anything more beautiful. Her eyes, wrote the great courtier-poet Pierre de Ronsard, were like Cupid himself, his bow strung taut, his arrows primed.[3]

They were flattering her, the praise growing louder as the Guises consolidated their influence at court. Still, Mary was lovely and charismatic indeed, especially compared to the awkward and boyish dauphin. In one portrait, Mary is positioned behind the dauphin, her open face and strong features hinting at her commanding height. Francis, by contrast, peers out from the frame, round-faced and weak-jawed, nose just emerging from its button, cheeks rosy smooth, puberty still in the distance.[4]

The wedding had been arranged quickly, the Guises striking while King Henry was amenable. In recent years, the king's commitment to the marriage had wavered, and the Guises feared he might change his mind. The dauphin himself might have presented a challenge. As the Venetian ambassador remarked in 1557, the French king thought his son wasn't quite old enough to marry, since he was "still of a very weak constitution." King Henry likely suspected the dauphin couldn't yet consummate the marriage.[5]

The other obstacle was Constable Montmorency, who wasted no effort to block the Guises' ascension at court and in the council chamber. Where the Guises wanted war against the Hapsburgs—particularly in Italy, where they hoped the Duke of Guise could shine on the battlefield—Montmorency argued for conciliation with Spain. The tension eventually became personal. As princes from Lorraine, the Guises scoffed at the shabbier lineage of Montmorency, who was the son of a mere baron. Montmorency, a red-blooded Frenchman, mocked the Guises as foreigners.[6]

It was an old court story: rival factions competing over the king for their own personal gain and to raise the fortunes of their families. Constable Montmorency held one advantage over the Guises. Despite the Guises' youth, their panache, and their princely status, King Henry tended to favor Montmorency. Though prone to strategic gaffes on the battlefield, the old warrior nonetheless remained the closest thing to a beloved father figure Henry had ever known. As long as Montmorency presided at court, the Guises found it hard to persuade Henry to ignore the Constable's counsel for their own. And Montmorency worked assiduously to block Mary's marriage.

Then fortune turned in the Guises' favor.

By the late 1550s, the actors and alliances in the theater of war had changed. In 1556, Charles V abdicated his Spanish throne in favor of his son, King Philip II (though the emperor, finding it hard to retire, still managed to direct Spanish affairs with a heavy hand).* Married to Mary Tudor, Queen of England, Philip II had both Spanish troops and English battalions at his disposal. War surged anew, with Naples—long the holy grail of French kings—once again in play. King Henry II sent the Cardinal of Lorraine to negotiate a secret French alliance with Pope Paul IV, a native Neapolitan who harbored his own deep-seated hatred of the colonizing Spanish; he sent the Duke of Guise and French regiments to Italy. But even the Duke of Guise struggled to outmaneuver the Spanish Duke of Alba. The war was slow going.[7]

July 1557 saw English and Spanish troops—about 40,000 commanded by the Hapsburg Duke of Savoy—massing along the northern French border with Flanders, eyeing Picardy, the province north of Paris. The following month, at Philip II's command, the Duke of Savoy turned his armies toward the Picard town of Saint-Quentin.

Montmorency led the French defense but, badly outmanned and stymied by disorganization, he soon lost the town. The battle was a catastrophe. At least 2,500 French soldiers were killed, 7,000 were taken prisoner, and France's finest captains were captured, Montmorency among them. Messengers rode hard to the château of Compiègne, forty miles to the south, bringing the news to the French king within hours of the defeat. Only one hundred miles south of Saint-Quentin, Paris was suddenly vulnerable to the enemy. The court panicked. "I have such terrible news," wrote Mary Stuart to Antoinette de Bourbon, who was at Joinville. "It's

---

*Charles V could not legally bequeath the Imperial crown to Philip, however. The Holy Roman Emperor was chosen by an electorate, and in 1556 the Imperial crown passed to Charles's younger brother, Ferdinand.

that Saint-Quentin has fallen, and I don't know how we will appease God's anger, which He is showing us every day in the worst ways."[8]

The fall of Saint-Quentin seemed to replay the crushing defeat at Pavia thirty years earlier that had led to King Henry's captivity in Spain as a boy. Only now, it was Henry's mentor Montmorency who found himself a Spanish prisoner.

For the Guises, however, the fall of Saint-Quentin proved a shining opportunity. Quickly regrouping, King Henry decided that only the recapture of Calais, still held by the English, could restore French honor. He commanded the Duke of Guise to lead the charge. The Guise brothers went to work in the winter months of 1557, the Duke of Guise plotting strategy, the Cardinal of Lorraine wringing every last coin from taxpayers and lenders to pay for the campaign. On January 1 the Duke of Guise attacked, and on January 8 Calais fell into French hands. It was a stunning victory. For the first time since the Hundred Years' War, Calais belonged to the French. Both Mary Tudor and Philip II, as England's sovereigns, were humiliated; with one strike, the Duke of Guise had bested two enemies of the French.

What better time for the Guises to push for the marriage of their niece to the dauphin? Basking in victory, King Henry agreed. The wedding was scheduled for April, just a few months away. The Venetian ambassador, however, guessed the reason for the rush. "By the hastening of this marriage," he wrote to the Doge in secret code, the Queen of Scots' uncles "chose to secure themselves against any other matrimonial alliance which might be proposed to his most Christian Majesty in some negotiation for peace, the entire establishment of [Guise] greatness having to depend on this [marriage]; for which reason the Constable by all means in his power continually sought to prevent it."[9]

Just days before Mary's official betrothal, the Guises gave King Henry a gift. At the palace of Fontainebleau, on April 4, under the steady gaze of Henry, the dauphin, and her Guise uncles, Mary dipped a quill in ink and carefully signed her name on three documents.

The first document granted King Henry and his successors the entire kingdom of Scotland, along with any claim Mary had to the crown of England if she should die without "heirs of her body."

The second document agreed to repay Scotland's debt to France. The language suggested that without French protection, Scotland "would be in evident peril of total ruin." In gratitude, Mary ceded all Scottish crown revenues to the French until Scotland reimbursed its debt—about one million gold pieces.

Most underhanded of all, the third document ensured that Mary's gifts to France would take precedence over any efforts made by the Estates of Scotland to circumvent her God-given "right and freedom." As the "true Queen" of Scotland, she had the right to dispose of her kingdom as she saw fit.[10] In other words, using a notion of absolute sovereign authority, this document excised Scottish subjects and Scottish law from any discussion of Scotland's future.

Mary signed the three documents in secret, with not a single Scotsman in the room. Witnessed, signed, and notarized by French secretaries of the crown and the keeper of the seals, all three documents were binding. On the last one, the dauphin Francis affixed his own signature. Effectively, King Henry was securing Scotland's dependence on France. He was also securing the inheritance of the Scottish throne for his own Valois descendants. The dauphin would become King of Scotland and, if Mary died without children, the Scottish crown could pass to Francis's descendants by another wife.*

It is impossible to know whether Mary understood what she was signing. From earliest childhood, Mary was taught to follow Guise counsel. During her minority, a rhythm of ruling had established itself: she played the part of the queen, and the Guises did the thinking for her. This pattern continued even after Mary declared her majority as queen in 1554, when she was almost thirteen, and her mother took over as regent for so long as Mary lived in France. Mary sent her mother crisp sheets of white paper, embellished only with her signature: "Fourteen blank ones, signed 'Mary,' fifteen others signed 'Yours, Mary,' and six more signed 'Your good sister,

---

*By excluding Scottish representatives, the Guises and King Henry were deliberately duplicitous. The Estates of Scotland had already sent their own deputies to France, seeking French acknowledgment of Scotland's sovereign independence, and confirming the Earl of Arran as the heir to the throne.

Mary'"—these last intended specially for corresponding with other sovereigns.* Thus could her mother conduct state and diplomatic business in her name.[11]

Still, the documents she signed in April 1558 read as if Mary had made the grants of her own free will. She'd consulted with friends and family; she merely acknowledged the decades of generosity King Henry had shown her "during her childhood and youth," at his own expense. No doubt this is what the Guises told Mary herself. Perhaps, having been raised a Frenchwoman, Mary believed Scotland belonged in the hands of the French. As it was, from the day of her betrothal, Mary began to call the dauphin "King of Scots."[12]

The Guises were trying to purchase King Henry's continued favor and place him in their debt. They treated Scotland, a sovereign kingdom, as if it were part of Mary's dowry. Yet they created a loophole. According to the terms of the first document, the crown of Scotland would pass to King Henry and his heirs *only* if Mary failed to give birth to her own children. What were the chances of that? The fecundity of the Guise women was practically legendary. Antoinette de Bourbon had given birth to twelve children; Mary's own mother to four. Fifteen years young, Mary would surely produce the heir who would join the crowns of Scotland and France. Only a wedding was necessary for the work of begetting that future king to begin.†

Once he committed to going forward with it, King Henry decided Mary's wedding would be spectacular, determined to dazzle envoys and stifle the diplomatic gossip about Saint-Quentin. For weeks, Paris hummed with excitement. The king made the Duke of Guise master of ceremonies, a post that had previously belonged to Constable Montmorency, still in his Spanish jail. The meticulous duke organized every detail, down to the last embroidered stitch and piece of silver plate.

---

*Mary signed her letters using the French spelling of her name: "Marie," or often "Mari."
†If the Guises doubted Mary's ability to bear children with Francis, then they were truly leveraging Mary and her crown, trading it while it was in their possession for greater stature and favor with King Henry—an unsettling possibility.

The bride wore a stunning gown, "white as lilies," that shone in the sun. The color defied custom: white was the color of mourning in France, but perhaps Mary knew which colors suited her best and she never shied away from a choice that might garner attention.[13] From her shoulders flowed a velvet cloak of purple, the color of royalty. Her crown blazed with gemstones, including an enormous red carbuncle known as the "Egg of Naples," one of the prized French crown jewels.

Shortly after dawn on April 24, people began to line the roads on the Île de la Cité, the heart of the city. At ten in the morning, under a field of cerulean silk, the wedding party processed on a wooden pathway stretching from the palace of the Bishop of Paris to the nearby Cathedral of Notre Dame. To accommodate as many spectators as possible, the ceremony took place in the open air on a scaffold in front of the cathedral. Trebles from dozens of woodwind instruments, violins, and violas hung in the air. "Delectable!" declared the chronicler hired to record the day's sights and sounds.[14]

As the bride and groom approached the cathedral, the Duke of Guise began frantically waving his marshal's baton, ordering the heralds to scatter the crowds and clear the view. Once the wedding blessing was pronounced, Francis and Mary, trailing white, stepped into the cathedral for the wedding Mass. Seconds later, as heralds cried "Largesse!" handfuls of gold and silver coins rained down upon the throngs, who screamed in delight and dived in to grab what they could. In the roaring rush, several people fainted while cloaks were torn from shoulders and hats trampled underfoot.[15]

Earlier that day, Mary had written a rapturous letter to Marie de Guise. No thought for spelling hindered her racing pen; her words danced with unbounded excitement. Her uncles had shown her every kindness and the king had showered her with gifts. But Queen Catherine's generosity touched Mary the most. What did Catherine give her? The relevant part of Mary's letter is obscured, but Brantôme wrote later of a long string of fat pearls that Mary would cherish for years—perhaps the very same pearls Pope Clement brought from Italy as part of Catherine's own trousseau twenty-five years earlier.[16]

"I believe I am the happiest woman in the world," Mary gushed to her mother. There is a dissonance to the letter, as if Mary couldn't fully comprehend the Guise victory her wedding represented. She wrote like the teenager she was, giddy with joy, blissfully unaware that, for her Guise kin, the day offered a sweet release to the endless years of waiting for a betrothal. Or perhaps Mary understood perfectly well, and it was her own Guise pride that sent her hand rushing across the page.[17]

That afternoon there was a banquet and a ball. That evening, there was feasting and dancing, mummeries and masques. The guests were treated to a lavish spectacle, complete with six mechanical ships, sailors stationed at their helms. The symbolism was hard to miss. On the threshold of King Henry's Franco-British empire, the French were conquering Britain "without murder and war." Through Mary, Queen of Scots, the dauphin would command Scottish forces against the English enemy. Through Mary, even the English throne would one day fall to France. More than any ship wrought in wood and papier-mâché, it was Mary, body and crown, who served as the vessel of empire.[18]

Never far from the bride on that spring Sunday was Mary's little "sister," the royal princess Elisabeth de Valois. She had just passed her twelfth birthday. That evening, Elisabeth shared the spotlight with Mary, the trains of their skirts sweeping the floor as the two girls led the first dance. Mary had left her hair long and her head bare; that afternoon, she had insisted on removing the crown, "glittering with pearls, diamonds, rubies, sapphires, and emeralds," complaining that it was much too heavy. At the wedding supper, Elisabeth sat just two seats to Mary's left at the massive marble table, a place of honor. Peering past the head of her six-year-old brother, Charles, Elisabeth could easily admire her friend, the new *reine dauphine*, as the French called her—the "queen dauphine," future consort of France.[19]

Writing later in the century, Brantôme would say of Elisabeth de Valois that "in her childhood years, this princess promised great things." "She even shone," a nineteenth-century biographer wrote, "when compared with the graceful and versatile Mary Stuart."[20] It is hard to know the truth. In the sixteenth century, descriptions of royal women were usually penned either by fierce loyalists or rabid haters, and Brantôme, whose accounts furnished so much material for later scholars, was particularly fond of Elisabeth. Mary's wedding was Elisabeth's own debut: before then, she rarely appeared in public. Fiercely protected by Catherine, she moved in the smallest of circles, even after she came to live with her mother at court. Only select ladies and trusted friends knew the child Elisabeth well. Catherine believed she knew her daughter best.

Petite during childhood, like Catherine had been, Elisabeth may have been less robust. The Humières' letters discuss the usual round of childhood challenges, some more concerning than others: Elisabeth battling measles when she was two; Elisabeth weaned early after her wet nurse fell ill; Elisabeth struggling with teething, her cheeks swollen. Yet she couldn't have been so very frail. She survived the dangers of a Renaissance childhood, growing up in the shelter of a strict but doting mother who fussed over the smallest details and cherished her daughters.

Shortly before Elisabeth turned thirteen, François Clouet once again drew her portrait, tracing Elisabeth's almond eyes and full mouth. She looks remarkably like her brothers in Clouet's rendering, her features softened by dangling earrings and curls twirling around her forehead. Her complexion is smooth, unmarred by adolescent blemishes, though Clouet would hardly have tarnished the skin of his royal subject in a portrait. Still, with her snub nose and round cheeks, Elisabeth looks very young.[21]

When her own wedding preparations began in the spring of 1559, not long after Clouet put away his pencils, Elisabeth was still very much a child.

In a culture obsessed with rank, there were differences in stature among sisters, just as there were among sons. The oldest daughter of a king was more valuable than a younger one, and deployed accordingly. When, at the turn of the sixteenth century, the first Tudor king of England, Henry VII, sought a Spanish bride for his oldest son, Queen Isabel of Castile and King Ferdinand of Aragon sent their youngest girl, Katherine, to England. Their choice spoke volumes: the Spanish sovereigns were content to forge an alliance with England, yet the Tudors were too new and untested to risk sending an older girl, one of greater value on the dynastic marriage market.

What hopes and expectations did the child Elisabeth harbor for her own marriage? In 1551, when she was five, Elisabeth was promised to the boy king of England, Edward VI, son of Henry VIII, in a treaty that temporarily united the French and English against the Hapsburg Empire. But Edward died of a wasting illness in 1553, before Elisabeth was old enough to marry. King Henry II and Queen Catherine then kept her in reserve. Elisabeth's younger sister Claude was married first, to the Duke of Lorraine in January 1559, when Claude was eleven. "My daughter Elisabeth is such that a mere duchy is not worthy of her," King Henry is said to have quipped, explaining why he passed Elisabeth over. "She needs a kingdom."[22]

Soon enough, that kingdom appeared. Elisabeth de Valois's marriage was a final point in the accord between France and Spain known as the Treaty of Cateau-Cambrésis, signed in April 1559. At long last, King Henry had decided to end the Italian Wars with Spain once and for all.

King Henry itched for peace. He missed his friend Montmorency, still captive in Spain. The wars had dragged on for generations, taxing the royal treasury and exhausting French subjects. And with increasing urgency, Henry felt pressed to focus on domestic affairs. Heresy was catching fire in France.

The repressive measures Henry established early in his reign had proven ineffective. Protestant thinking had seeped from the universities into the law courts, even into the Parlement of Paris itself. Teeming with moderate judges and lawyers, many courts were loath to punish Reformers, fearing that oppression only aggravated the heresy problem and encouraged sedition. Henry thought the courts were too lenient, and suspected many jurists were heretics themselves.

Henry imposed more authoritarian measures. He created anti-heresy tribunals, separate from the courts and vested with special powers, and instituted programs to target heresy among lawyers. He pushed for an Inquisition in France, although most judges balked at such draconian measures. In July 1557, he managed to pass the most ruthless law to date. The Edict of Compiègne imposed the death penalty for any "Sacramentarian," meaning anyone who denied the Real Presence in the Mass. It also prescribed execution for any person who assembled with others illegally; any person who preached in public or private; anyone who insulted the sacraments, sacred images, the blessed Mother Mary, or the saints; any person who communicated with Geneva or traveled to that profane city; and anyone who owned or sold heretical books.

The new law was deliberately vague on details. How could anyone know if someone preached in private? What constituted illegal assembly? How would you decide if a book was heretical? Accusations could fly freely, exactly as Henry intended. He wanted trials; even more, he wanted convictions. The new edict also allowed infractions to be punished "by arms as well as by justice." If he wished, Henry could take up weapons against his own subjects.[23]

And still heresy continued to spread. In the streets of Paris, fights broke out. Catholics murdered Protestants. Protestants attacked Catholics in return. Even worse to Catholics, they sacked churches, destroyed relics, and desecrated images of the saints. Pro-Catholic authorities soon reported that it wasn't only commoners who were infected with heresy. The nobility was tainted, too—a worrisome development. In September 1557, as anxiety mounted in the kingdom after the disaster at Saint-Quentin, royal authorities raided a house in the Latin Quarter of Paris where dozens of people had gathered to hear a prayer service. Among the one hundred people arrested, two were noble ladies in the circle of Catherine de' Medici. Heresy, it seemed, had seeped into the royal court.

Henry hated the idea of persecuting aristocrats. As he hesitated, however, the number of converts among the nobility swelled, and French Protestants grew bolder.[24]

As tensions roiled Paris in the spring and autumn of 1558, negotiations for peace between the kingdoms began in the town of Cateau-Cambrésis, on the border between France and Spanish Flanders. Like Henry II, Philip II was ready to call a truce. His father, Charles V, who had directed affairs even after his abdication, died in September. Weary of fighting his father's war, Philip felt free to negotiate his own terms.

Henry II did not feel the same animosity toward Philip II as he did toward Charles V. The chemistry between the kings changed, too, after the death of Mary Tudor. As long as Mary Tudor lived,

Henry feared she and Philip would produce a child who would supplant Mary Stuart's claim to England. But when Mary Tudor died childless in November 1558, those fears melted away. Henry sued for peace in earnest.

He gave almost everything away. With the Treaty of Cateau-Cambrésis Henry renounced his claims to Milan and Naples, acknowledged Philip's rights to those territories, and promised to return Burgundian lands that had been in dispute between the Valois and the Hapsburgs since the fifteenth century.

He also settled with England. Because Philip II had waged much of the latest war while married to Mary Tudor, using English troops and finances to bolster Hapsburg resources, a second part of the Treaty of Cateau-Cambrésis negotiated peace terms with the new Queen of England, Elizabeth Tudor. Eager to repair her sister's errors, Queen Elizabeth angled for the return of Calais. Henry met her halfway: the French would keep Calais for eight years, then return it to England or pay a hefty fine.[25]

The Guises were livid; with a few signatures, the king had surrendered everything they had won for the French crown with blood, sweat, and high-handed diplomacy. The concession of Naples and the promise to return Calais stung especially. It seemed a betrayal of both kingdom and family now that the Guises were joined to Henry through marriage.

But Henry was determined to secure his borders and replenish his coffers. Most importantly, Montmorency would come home. When Henry at last saw the old Constable again, the king was so moved he struggled to speak. "My heart was clenched so tight that I found it impossible to find the words," he explained later to Montmorency in a letter. "I beg you to know that you are the person in this world whom I love most and, for this reason, I don't know what more to give you. For, since my heart belongs to you, I believe you already understand that I will spare nothing in my possession, nor anything else in my power, to have this good fortune of seeing you again."[26]

The Italian Wars had come to an end. Now there were celebrations to plan, including a double royal wedding. To seal the truce, King Henry proposed marrying his sister Marguerite to Philip's Hapsburg cousin, the Duke of Savoy. Elisabeth, eldest daughter of King Henry and Queen Catherine, would marry a prince of Spain.

But which prince? For several months, this remained an open question. At first, Philip proposed his son and heir apparent, Carlos. Born in 1545, Don Carlos was thirteen years old in the autumn of 1558 when negotiations began, the same age as Elisabeth de Valois. In March 1559, however, Philip altered the terms of the treaty.

After Mary Tudor's death, Philip proposed marriage to her younger sister and England's new queen, Elizabeth Tudor, hoping to keep the Spanish–English alliance alive. When Queen Elizabeth refused him, Philip changed tack. Withdrawing his son's name from the peace negotiations with France, Philip proposed himself as Elisabeth de Valois's groom. For their wedding, set for June in Paris, Philip would send as a proxy his ranking general, the deeply blue-blooded and notoriously haughty Duke of Alba. In Paris, Alba would also swear to the terms of the truce.

King Henry was disappointed; he'd hoped to meet Philip himself. But he caved to the terms, and on April 3, 1559, French, Spanish, and English deputies in Cateau-Cambrésis signed the treaty. It was the day after Elisabeth de Valois's thirteenth birthday. Philip II was almost thirty-two years old. Elisabeth would become his third wife.

———

No sixteenth-century document records either Elisabeth's excitement or apprehension as her wedding day approached. For months she believed she would marry the prince Don Carlos; it may have been unsettling to learn she would instead wed his father. But the honor was unparalleled. Though France's ancient enemy, Spain was a worthy rival, a formidable military power and an expanding empire. Spain paraded its allegiance to old Catholic ways and Philip II's piety was already legendary. In the fifteenth century, under the reigns of Isabel of Castile and Ferdinand of Aragon, the pope had named the Spanish king and queen *Los reyes católicos*—the Catholic monarchs—to honor Spain's expulsion of Muslims and Jews from the Peninsula. Elisabeth de Valois would be known as "the Catholic Queen," a venerable title. She would be the highest-ranking woman in Spain.[27]

First, however, there were endless details to settle. Just days before the ceremony, French secretaries were still tabulating the components of her extensive dowry, her armory of a trousseau. She would travel to Spain with dozens of elaborate gowns crafted from lush fabrics hand-picked by Catherine. There were bolts of silk, taffeta, and satin, rolls of lace, plush velvets for trimmings and bed hangings, yards of linen for shifts and underwear. There were tablecloths and sheets, petticoats and surcoats, furs and feathers. Elisabeth would bring coffers of jewels, mounds of plate for her table, wagonloads of furniture and musical instruments, and ponies and palfreys for riding. She would also bring people: hundreds of French courtiers, attendants, and staff. French secretaries itemized each entry, and Spanish envoys wondered how they were going to move the new queen's belongings through the winding mountain passes into Spain. At least until she arrived at the border, King Henry would pay for the transportation.

King Henry and Queen Catherine also agreed to settle 4,000 *écus* on their daughter: one third payable upon the consummation of the marriage, another third upon the first anniversary of their wedding, and the final portion six months later. In the event of Philip's death—it was important to prepare—Elisabeth would return to France post haste, along with all the French officers and servants, furnishings, clothing, and jewelry she brought with her to Spain. It was as if Elisabeth were on loan for the duration of Philip's lifetime, the best in a slew of French prizes. Indeed, upon his arrival in Paris, the Duke of Alba would declare that, of all the treasures he saw in the Louvre, Elisabeth was "the masterpiece."[28]

At the official betrothal ceremony, Elisabeth sat next to her parents in Queen Catherine's chambers as notaries read the marriage articles aloud. She would marry Philip, they stipulated, "of her own accord and consent."[29] On the morning of June 22, 1559, Elisabeth mounted a platform inside the Cathedral of Notre Dame, taking her place alongside the grizzled Duke of Alba. Over her dark curls, Elisabeth wore a crown encrusted with gems, a mantle of blue velvet swirling around a dress flashing with jewels. From her neck swung a cameo portrait of Philip hung with a pearl, a gift from Alba. Her outfit was a metaphor, a picture of the joint majesty of Spain and France. But the robes must have been heavy for the thirteen-year-old girl.

Turning toward the Duke of Alba, Elisabeth began her vows. "I, Elisabeth, take for husband and loyal spouse, Philip, the Catholic

King, and in his name Don Fernando de Toledo, the Duke of Alba, his special procurer to this effect."[30] With the wedding blessing, Elisabeth was *procured*.

That evening, after the nuptial feast, she was put to bed, one final ritual yet to perform. As witnesses crowded the room, the Duke of Alba entered and slipped a discreet foot between the sheets next to the new Catholic Queen. The foot was enough. The marriage was as good as consummated, the wedding sealed.

The real consummation would occur after Elisabeth met her husband, Philip. He was currently in Flanders, set to sail to Spain in a few weeks' time. Once the wedding celebrations concluded, King Henry would bring Elisabeth to the border. Philip planned to greet his bride in Guadalajara.

8

ACCIDENTS

France, 1559

It was late afternoon on Friday, June 30, eight days after Elisabeth's wedding. The days had unspooled in a string of elaborate parties, banquets, and dances, all aimed at impressing King Henry's new Spanish allies. To Henry, Elisabeth's wedding was a welcome distraction from the kingdom's dizzying array of problems. Religion was rupturing and debt was mounting. The Italian Wars had cost a fortune, paid with cash borrowed from lenders at exorbitant interest rates. Somehow the royal bookkeepers had managed to displace millions of francs. But in July 1559, Henry decided his debts were a problem for another day. Never one to economize at war or at play, he spent one million more for Elisabeth's wedding festivities, determined to show off Paris and his court at their finest.[1]

Henry had always loved a festival. Ever the athlete, he insisted on a tournament as part of the fanfare. He too would take part, of course. Henry had just turned forty years old, his beard shot through with silver. He still cut a formidable figure astride his horse, a new Turkish stallion given to him by the Hapsburg Duke of Savoy in honor of the peace of Cateau-Cambrésis. The years were catching up with Henry, though he tried to ignore new aches and pains, and dismissed the bouts of vertigo that had bothered him in recent months. Given the chance, the king never refused to run the tilt. And he didn't want the Duke of Alba to think he'd aged out.

The jousting lists were built on the rue Saint-Antoine in front of the Hôtel de Tournelles, a royal palace on the site of what is now the Place des Vosges. Workers chipped the paving stones off the streets to expose smooth ground for the horses and constructed a large wooden amphitheater with seats. Pennants and banners boasting the arms of France, Spain, and Savoy disguised the hinges and joists. The tournament was scheduled to take place over five days. The dauphin would run the tilt on the first day. Henry wouldn't appear until the third.[2]

The sun still burned hot at five in the afternoon that Friday as Henry spurred his new stallion to the edge of the yard, his armor trimmed as usual in black and white. The crowd was jittery. In the stands, Catherine de' Medici, seated between Diane de Poitiers and Mary, Queen of Scots, waited anxiously. The king's squire later remembered how the woodwinds rang loud enough to "split the head and blow out the ears." Then, as Henry and his opponent— the Count of Montgomery, captain of the Scottish Guard—entered the lists, an eerie stillness settled over the stands. The tournament was supposed to be over by now. But Henry had demanded one last run.

According to witnesses, the king already sagged with heat and fatigue. This was, in fact, Henry's fourth turn in the lists that day. He'd won his first two rounds, but on the third run, also against the strapping Montgomery, Henry took a hard blow and almost fell from his saddle. Embarrassed, the king ordered Montgomery to take up his lance again. Witnesses would report after the fact that Catherine de' Medici, the Duke of Savoy, Henry's squire, and even Montgomery himself begged the king to reconsider. Yet Henry refused.

"You cannot flee or avoid your destiny," the squire would later say.[3]

———

Henry entered the lists, and the crowd fell silent. In the void, everything else was magnified. A clash of wood on metal and then—a strange crack. Only seconds had passed. The horses reared. Montgomery recovered his balance, still clutching his shattered lance, the stub of it mangled and raw. Young and inexperienced, he'd forgotten to drop it, which he should have done the moment he felt the blow. That was his error. As Montgomery turned, he saw the king lurching forward in his saddle over the neck of his stallion, struggling not to fall against the lists. From the stands, women were screaming. Men were already running.[4]

In the ensuing chaos, everyone saw something different. Some accounts said Henry was lucid, others that he collapsed in a daze, unable to move his limbs. Even before he reached the king, Constable Montmorency could see the slivers of wood jutting from Henry's helmet, above the right eyebrow. "A splint . . . of good bigness," reported the English envoy Nicholas Throckmorton.[5] When the king's men removed the helmet, they found blood sheeting down the king's face. In the stands the dauphin swooned while Mary, Queen of Scots, and Catherine both fainted away, their ladies shrieking. Hoisting the king from under his shoulders, Montmorency and the Guises dragged him to the Hôtel de Tournelles, followed by guardsmen carrying the dauphin, still in a faint. Once the king and his heir crossed the threshold, the gates of the Tournelles slammed shut.

Inside, the frantic Montmorency and Duke of Guise laid Henry on a bed and began sprinkling his face with vinegar and rosewater, trying to revive him. Henry came to his senses long enough to whisper "fourteen or fifteen words of prayer" before falling, once again, into a stupor. That night, Catherine, the Duke of Savoy, and the Cardinal of Lorraine kept watch over the king until three in the morning; the Duke of Guise took their place until dawn. Though the Guises tried to keep Montmorency, their rival, away, the Constable insisted on serving his beloved king. Apart from a few foreign dignitaries, everyone else was kept out of the Tournelles.

Diane de Poitiers came to the gates of the palace but, at Catherine's command, the guards turned her away.[6]

That night a grim cloud descended over Paris. Riders barreled in all directions, searching for doctors and bringing word to foreign courts. In Paris, the papal nuncio prayed that God would spare the king, champion of Catholics. At his own desk, the dauphin's page Louis de Gonzaga was so shaken by the wood splinters he'd seen protruding from the king's forehead that he drew them to size in a letter he was writing to Italy—proving to his incredulous correspondent just how large they were.[7]

The next day, the cloud lifted. After the first ghastly night in the Tournelles, Henry rallied. The king was in no danger, Montmorency told Throckmorton, though he'd likely lose an eye.[8] Learning of the mishap, Philip II, in Flanders, immediately dispatched his best Flemish physician, the famous Andreas Vesalius, who rode overnight to Paris. After experimenting on the decapitated head of a criminal, Vesalius concurred with French doctors that the splinters had spared the king's brain. Henry sat propped up in bed, swallowed the rhubarb purge prescribed by his doctors, even attended to some of the kingdom's affairs. He instructed Catherine to move forward with his sister's wedding to the Duke of Savoy so the peace of Cateau-Cambrésis would hold. He commanded officers to find the Count of Montgomery, who'd fled the city in panic. The young man wasn't to blame, Henry said.[9]

From England, Queen Elizabeth sent a sympathetic note to the Constable Montmorency. She had harbored something of a grudge against Henry since he supported Mary Stuart's claim to the English throne ahead of her own. Even so, she could hardly wish the fallen king further ill. Elizabeth, too, had signed the Treaty of Cateau-Cambrésis. She needed Henry to live. "Great monarchs are subject to great misfortune," she wrote to Montmorency. She wished the king a speedy recovery.[10]

Yet all hope for that recovery vanished on July 4 when the king fell into a feverish delirium. During a moment of faint lucidity, Henry sensed the end was near, and blessed his son. Wild with grief, the dauphin wandered the palace, banging his head against the wall and wailing, "How will I live if my father dies?" He was tormented, witnesses said; a terrible sight to behold.[11]

As twilight settled over the Tournelles that evening, the doctors discussed trepanning the patient—boring a hole in his skull to ease the swelling of his brain. But after pulling back the sheets and finding Henry bathed in the "sweat of death," the physicians knew it was all over.[12]

Henry died at one o'clock in the afternoon of July 10, just hours after receiving the last rites. At the autopsy, the French physician Amboise Paré found the smallest of wooden slivers lodged in the king's brain.[13] Sepsis had been inevitable. God had shown His hand, wrote Throckmorton to the English Privy Council after the accident. "Among all these triumphs . . . [He] suffers such mischance and heaviness to happen."[14]

Catherine sat by Henry's bedside as he died. In the strangest of marriages, she had genuinely loved her husband. After they closed the king's eyes, Catherine adopted a broken lance as her emblem: Henry's lance and perhaps also her own—the heavy lance of a good wife, of complete devotion to a husband who had never loved her as much as she wished. Shattered though it was, she would carry it still. Catherine put on her mourning clothes—not the white usually worn in France, but hues of jet black, like widows wore in Italy. Except on two occasions—the weddings of her sons—for the rest of her life she wore no other color.[15]

In the sixteenth century, people often would search the mists of chaos for signs and patterns, if only to explain the unfathomable and make sense of the senseless. The king's squire Vieilleville later claimed an odd sense of foreboding came over him while he was helping Henry suit up for his final run. Decades later, Catherine's youngest daughter, Margot, would describe her mother's ghastly nightmare: "The very night before the tournament which proved so fatal to the King my father . . . she saw him wounded in the eyes, as it really happened; upon which she awoke, and begged him not to run a course that day." Others said Nostradamus, the famed French astrologer, had long predicted Henry's downfall. Protestants said God had taken revenge for the king's ruthless persecutions. According to an apocryphal story, the king's new Turkish stallion bore the name "Malheureux"—the unlucky one.[16]

Some Protestants cheered, but most French subjects were shaken by the death of their sovereign. Henry had been young and healthy, and he left behind a kingdom in far more turmoil than the one he'd inherited. The Duke of Guise and the Cardinal of Lorraine had begun to prepare as soon as they heard the physicians' dire predictions; as Henry breathed his last, they were ready. On July 11, the day after Henry's death, the Guises stepped out of the Tournelles and headed for the Louvre, along with the new King Francis, his wife Mary Stuart, the younger royal siblings, and Catherine in tow. Montmorency was not with them.

This was a shake-up, yet the exact intentions of the Guises remain unclear. To some historians, the Guises mounted nothing short of a coup; others suggest they filled a real and serious power vacuum, albeit opportunistically. Inexperienced, immature, and prone to illness, fifteen-year-old Francis was entirely unprepared to rule on his own, a fact everyone recognized; he turned desperately to the calm counsel of his wife's capable uncles. The other contenders to take charge of the government were notably absent. Constable Montmorency, stricken with grief, stayed behind in the Tournelles, keeping vigil over the corpse of his beloved king. By the time Montmorency emerged to offer his services, King Francis had learned his lines. Surely, the Constable must be weary from his sorrow and the draining years on the king's council. Perhaps he would prefer to retire to his estates. Within weeks, Montmorency withdrew to his lands in Chantilly.

He wouldn't disappear entirely, though. One of the richest men in France, and the patriarch of a networked and noble family, Montmorency would be a force to contend with for many years yet. In the country, the Constable bided his time.

Antoine de Bourbon, King of Navarre, might have wrested power from the Guises. Descended from the sainted King Louis IX, Antoine was the first prince of the blood and the ranking member of the Bourbons. This made him the most obvious choice to guide the new king. But while King Henry succumbed to his infection in Paris, Antoine de Bourbon tarried on his lands in Béarn near the kingdom's southern border. When he finally appeared at court weeks later, the Guises stroked his fragile ego, heaping upon him tokens of esteem, including the place of honor at the new king's coronation in September. Antoine decided Guise rule might suit him well enough.

If the Guises staged a coup, it was a soft coup. Doubtless, all power lay in their hands. The changes they made at court were subtle, however, and often practical, hard to dispute; in most ways, they appeared to support the smooth passage of the crown from father to son. The cardinal, especially, was a born politician, skilled at soothing egos. By September, shortly before the king's coronation, the cardinal concluded that the kingdom had settled down. Everyone knew their place. "Things couldn't be quieter and calmer than they are now," he wrote, "with everyone showing every sign of fidelity, obedience, and devotion toward the new king."[17]

Only one other dismissal was unavoidable.

Mary Stuart, the new queen consort, was sent to retrieve all the jewelry Henry had given to Diane de Poitiers. The request wasn't unusual: whenever a king died, anyone who'd received royal jewels was required to return them so the new king could dispose of them at his discretion. Still, Mary's appearance in Diane's chambers signaled the end of the mistress's reign. Catherine sent word to Diane that "she no longer wanted to see her," and that, from this point on, Diane should be content with "the gifts given to her by the former king." The Guises allowed Diane to retreat gracefully from court, an acknowledgment of the alliances they had built together over the years. However wrathful she may have felt, Catherine managed to check her actions, if not her emotions. Before she left the capital, the mistress surrendered her beautiful château at Chenonceau to Catherine but, in return, Catherine granted Diane the château of Chaumont.

Diane stayed in Paris until August 13, the end of the customary forty-day vigil over the king's corpse. That day, the funeral cortège snaked through the capital, carrying Henry's body to the Cathedral of Saint-Denis, the burial site of French kings. The king's effigy lumbered through the streets, the face of Diane's lover sculpted to perfection by that eminent artist of kings, François Clouet. No black or white adorned the effigy; instead ribbons of purple, the color of royalty, were draped over the funeral chariot. Yet, clearly visible on the chariot, the "H" of Henry's initial still embraced the "D." After the funeral, Diane retreated to her favorite château at Anet. She died there in 1566.[18]

"The House of Guise rules and does all about the French king," wrote Throckmorton to Queen Elizabeth, three days after King Henry's death.[19] The Duke of Guise installed himself in Montmorency's apartments in the Louvre and took command of the armies. The Cardinal of Lorraine seized Diane de Poitiers' rooms, next to the king's chambers, and began tackling matters tied to diplomacy, finance, and religion. Catherine moved into the Louvre as well.

Why was she there? Custom called for her to isolate in mourning for forty days after the death of her husband. But Catherine delayed her withdrawal. Some historians believe she wanted to share in the Guises' new power. Just as likely, however, the Guises looked to Catherine as a stabilizing force; her presence at the Louvre communicated to the kingdom a continuity between King Henry and King Francis his son.

Still reeling from Henry's death, Catherine may have taken refuge in the Guises' comforting strength. Though she had no choice but to trust them, she had no reason not to. Except for one moment back in 1542—when the old Duke Claude de Guise offered to replace her with his own daughter—the Guises had shown her almost flawless respect.[20] Catherine was close to the Guise women. More importantly, the Guises had become family through a suite of marriages: her son Francis to Mary, Queen of Scots, her daughter Claude to the Duke of Lorraine, a Guise cousin. She'd seen proof of the Guises' impeccable loyalty to their kin. And Catherine worried for her children. Four of them were still in the care of nurses and tutors, all of them small. Charles, Duke of Orléans, had just turned nine; Alexandre-Edouard (the future Henri III) was not quite eight. Margot, Catherine's third and youngest daughter, was six years old, while the littlest child, Hercules, was only four.

Who would protect these children now that their father was gone? Who would guarantee their inheritance, ensure their rights to the throne if something should happen to King Francis? What would keep the Bourbons, or even Montmorency, from using the younger children to leverage their own power? From personal experience Catherine knew royal children were vulnerable to exploitation, even abduction. Hadn't Henry II also lived that fear? Hadn't Mary Stuart? Sheltered in the Louvre with her children, Catherine could protect them. From there, she could also monitor Guise intentions.

And her son, the new King Francis, insisted she stay. "As he is but a youth . . . and therefore has need of support and counsel," the Venetian ambassador wrote on July 12, "he wills it that . . . the Queen his mother shall not only participate in, but superintend everything, and that all matters be referred and addressed to her."* Now more

---

*One story relates that, on his first night at the Louvre, Francis insisted on serving his mother supper. When counselors asked to consult with him, he turned to Catherine. She could speak for him.

than ever, he noted, Francis revered his mother. Catherine took the apartments directly under those of Francis; connected to her son by a private staircase, she could communicate with him "at all hours and without being perceived by anyone." Until she felt her son's throne was secure, Catherine would not leave the Louvre. Only at the end of July did she withdraw, briefly, to honor her forty days of mourning at Saint-Germain-en-Laye, bringing her daughter Elisabeth with her.

Francis followed her there.[21]

———

Shortly after the king's death, diplomats and courtiers began to call Catherine by a new name. Usually, a widowed queen was known as Queen Dowager. Yet Catherine preferred a different title: *Reine-mère*. Queen Mother.[22]

Once Catherine had settled in at the Louvre, the Duke of Alba paid her a visit to offer his condolences. Afterward, Alba wrote a letter to Philip II describing what he saw. Catherine's rooms had been converted into a chapel of sorrow. Not only were the walls draped with black fabric, but the floor, too, was covered in thick black cloth. The windows were sealed shut and shrouded with heavy black curtains, such that no fresh air or sunlight could penetrate. Even the stale August air within the chamber seemed bleak and murky. The only light came from the thin glow of two burning candles.

Sheaths of black cascaded over everything. "The Queen Mother's bed was covered in the same way," Alba continued. "Her Majesty was dressed in the most austere clothes." Catherine wore a heavy black dress, its black train curled around her feet, with no jewels or ornament except "a collar trimmed with ermine." A jarring touch, that stark flash of white at Catherine's neck. Then Alba saw another point of light. Mary, Queen of Scots, sat with her mother-in-law, wearing a mourning gown of pure white.

Alba greeted the two queens. Catherine could hardly answer, so feeble was her voice, he wrote. Instead, Mary piped up. Praising her uncles lavishly to the Spaniard, she invited the Duke of Alba to come to court often. And, she added, he must send her best regards to his master, King Philip II.

For the moment, Catherine had lost her voice. But Mary found hers.[23]

Catherine's youngest daughter, Margot, would later write that her father's death was "the appalling accident that deprived France of peace, and our family of its good fortune."[24] In retrospect, it is easy to see how this single event—tied to something as careless as a missing visor or as inexorable as a faulty screw—marked a watershed moment for both her family and the entire kingdom of France. History turns on accidents. Had Henry lived, might he have staved off the religious dissension that would plunge France into decades of bloody civil war? Already during his lifetime, the specter of war had loomed. Yet Margot, mired in her own loss, saw the accident—those horrendous few seconds—as the moment separating a lost golden age from an age of war.

Catherine's days as queen consort of France were over. And yet, her husband's death would thrust her into a far more powerful role at court, one that in July 1559 was still unimaginable. Elisabeth de Valois's life also changed irrevocably. Her father's accident profoundly altered the significance of her marriage, casting Elisabeth into a political role that, at thirteen years old, she could scarcely have asked for.[25]

Through July and all of August, Elisabeth stayed at her mother's side. She wouldn't leave for Spain until November 1559, almost five months after her wedding. This was not the original plan. Her father, King Henry, was supposed to have escorted her to the border in August, as Philip II set sail from Flanders for Spain. What kept her?

Confusion, for one, and political distrust. In the aftermath of Henry's accident, no one was sure whether the treaty of Cateau-Cambrésis would hold. Learning of Henry's injury, a fearful Philip sent his favorite courtier, Ruy Gómez da Silva, Prince of Éboli, from Flanders to Paris to sniff out the French intentions. Arriving in Paris, Ruy Gómez headed straight to the Tournelles and Henry's bedside, still wearing his riding boots and spurs. Since the doors to the chamber were sealed shut, however, no one was sure what, exactly, they discussed.

Similar misgivings hounded Catherine after Henry died. Would the Spanish now nullify the treaty? Or worse, might they attack now that the crown was in King Francis's fifteen-year-old hands? The peace treaty was only days old, Alba having just sworn to the terms while in Paris, but the hostility between the realms was ancient. Though Philip quickly reassured Catherine, both kingdoms remained guarded. And Alba and Ruy Gómez were loath to broach the topic of Elisabeth's departure when the Queen Mother already seemed so distraught.

But when, after the official forty days of mourning had passed and the Spanish envoys finally posed the question, Catherine stalled.[26]

First, in August, she explained that Elisabeth was ill. Chantonnay, the new Spanish ambassador at the French court, confirmed to Philip that Elisabeth indeed suffered from some sort of "stomach flux." Next, Catherine said Elisabeth's presence was required at her brother's coronation at Reims in September. The trouble didn't seem to lie with the girl herself, Chantonnay reported. She appeared eager to meet her husband: when Chantonnay told her Philip had set sail for Spain from Flanders, she cried, "Let it be a happy wind!" She seemed to grow more beautiful by the day, no doubt "the effect of her happiness" at the marriage, Chantonnay wrote, trying to appease his frustrated king.[27] Philip sent letters and gifts betokening his good intentions but to no avail. Catherine still refused to set a date for Elisabeth's departure.

Finally, the Bishop of Limoges, who was serving as the French ambassador in Spain, hinted that Philip was losing patience. "I understand the desire of the King my lord to see me," Elisabeth wrote in reply. "This has made me decide, with less regret, to leave to meet him . . . which, God willing, will be very soon." It was October 22. Catherine had conceded. Elisabeth had to go.[28]

The delay had bought both mother and daughter a little time. Catherine clearly dreaded sending Elisabeth to Spain. What might have been bittersweet under different circumstances—a blend of pride and sorrow at Elisabeth's parting for a splendid marriage—was now simply another loss to cap a spate of heart-wrenching losses. In the space of a few weeks that summer, Catherine's world had turned upside down. She had lost Henry, her beloved husband. The kingdom had lost its king. The France she knew as a young bride from Italy—a vigorous France that shone under the reign of her father-in-law, Francis I—was gone. In its place was a France mired in debt, fractured by religion, and factionalized by politics, in the shaky hands of her son, who quaked with fear on his throne. Tension and anxiety now reigned in the kingdom. The shadows accompanying Elisabeth's departure were dark and foreboding.

And Elisabeth was the first of her children to truly leave home. Claude, Catherine's second daughter, had married but remained a fixture at the French court. Elisabeth's marriage would take her deep into Spain. As Catherine knew, the Spanish hewed to protocol and were extraordinarily protective of their royal women; as Philip's consort, Elisabeth could not readily leave her kingdom. When, if ever, would Catherine see her again? Elisabeth was Catherine's "good girl," Brantôme would write decades later, "whom she loved above all her other daughters."[29]

Catherine likely had another reason to delay. The consummation of Elisabeth's marriage in July had been a mere formality, but that would soon change. Once her departure was set, servants frantically packed her trousseau, porters heaved furniture into wagons, and dozens of her French attendants tended to their own affairs, preparing for a long absence. In the fuss, it was easy to overlook the details. And yet, all along, the Queen Mother knew Elisabeth wasn't quite ready to be a bride: at thirteen years old, she had yet to begin her period.

PART 2

9
MARY'S BOOK
France, 1548–1554

The child Elisabeth de Valois probably knew Mary Stuart's back better than she knew her own. For every occasion requiring even a hint of ceremony—a banquet, a holiday, a visit from the king her father or the queen her mother—Elisabeth was freshly scrubbed and combed, laced into her frock and sewn into her sleeves. Then she took her place behind Mary, as rank demanded. Elisabeth loved art and had an eye for detail; she would have noticed certain things. She must have realized early that her own dresses, though splendid, were not quite as fine as Mary's.[1]

Before Mary first set foot in the *petite cour* at Saint-Germain-en-Laye, King Henry II of France determined the precedence among the children. The dauphin, Francis, would always walk in front of all the other children because he was the heir. But Mary, said King Henry, "would walk ahead of my daughters because her marriage to my son is decided. Besides that, she is a crowned queen and I want her honored and served as such."[2] No matter that, as a crowned queen, Mary outranked Francis so long as he remained dauphin. She was a girl and he was a boy. Scotland was second to France, and Scotland was "there" while France was "here." Elisabeth came only after Mary. It was hierarchy with purpose. Rank and its rituals gave order to court and country, and taught children their place from the first.

Elisabeth likely didn't question that Mary stood ahead of her, nor that rank would always separate them. At most, Elisabeth would become a queen consort, the helpmeet to a king. Almost like the sovereign

Queen Mary, yet not quite. This was a distinction that, in later years, would have important consequences for them both. Nothing could ever change that difference in rank. Elisabeth would never reign as sovereign: if her brother Francis died without children, she would never inherit the French throne, even though she was second-born. In France, Salic Law barred a girl from the succession by dint of her sex. Renée de France, daughter of the late French king Louis XII, is said to have quipped that all Frenchmen would be her subjects, "were I not so constrained by this hateful Salic Law." But there was nothing Renée could do: Salic Law was an ancient French custom, the "law" of the land. Though clearly Renée dared to dream of a different possibility.[3]

When they were small, Elisabeth and Mary shared a room and learned each other's habits. If one woke up grumpy or the other shirked her prayers, whether one preferred to sew and the other to draw. What made one giggle, what drove the other into a temper. These were the intimacies of friendship and sisterhood, the secret stuff of girlhood histories that go unrecorded. Even after Henry broke up the *petite cour* in 1553, the girls spent much of their time together, enjoying and enduring the trials of growing up royal and female. There was much to enjoy: riding, at which they both shone, or dance lessons, at which each apparently excelled—was there ever any rivalry on either score? There was much to endure, too: tight-laced frocks and tighter shoes, tiresome lessons, endless rules of etiquette, demanding tutors, rigid hours, watchful eyes.[4]

Mary would later say that Elisabeth was at the heart of her fondest childhood memories, "the best sister and friend that I had in this world." Yet Mary was hardly Elisabeth's only companion. With at least thirty-seven noble girls and boys in the *petite cour*, they didn't lack for friends. There was Clarice Strozzi, for one, the same age as Mary Stuart, and a distant cousin to the royal Valois daughters, the granddaughter of the Clarice Strozzi who had cared for Catherine de' Medici in her youth. Elisabeth was exceptionally fond of Clarice, just as she was of Mary, but while Clarice was a frequent playmate, Mary seems to have occupied a slightly different place, something closer to that of a wiser big sister.[5]

In the royal nursery, Mary ruled the throngs of tiny princes, princesses, and courtiers, equipped with natural advantages over Elisabeth and her siblings. Mary was older. She was clever, witty, and so very tall. Mary learned to write and to read first. At least in the beginning, she was quicker on her mount, more dextrous on her lute. Her penmanship was superior to everyone else's, elegant and smooth. Though Elisabeth cared about her sketching pencils, she was more impatient with her pen. Competent though it was, her handwriting lacked a certain grace.[6]

A spirited child, sometimes bored in the classroom, Elisabeth was always ready for a game. One envoy called her "sanguine," meaning she was vivacious; others referred to Elisabeth's natural gentleness.[7] Despite the accolades trailing both girls, one senses Elisabeth couldn't quite compare to Mary, whose coquettish charm and sovereign crown won her the adulation of countless adults. And Mary had plenty of opportunities to show off. While Catherine shielded her daughters from public view until they were older, the Guises pushed Mary to the fore. Mary, a pleaser, always did what she was told, and was usually rewarded for it with exclamations and hyperbole. "She was brighter even than a Scottish sun," Brantôme wrote, rhapsodic, "for sometimes the sun burns bright for only five hours in her country; whereas she was so radiant that her rays of light illuminated her country and her people."[8] Mary loved the limelight.

Mary embodied a kind of exceptionalism, like a beautiful novelty. She was possessed of an uncanny elegance, even though she hailed from impoverished Scotland. In French eyes, the crowns multiplied within her: Scotland, France, and one day England. Elisabeth de Valois's value was of a different ilk. A child of France, she was but one of a group: *Mesdames*, the brown-haired, brown-eyed daughters of King Henry, whom the court poet Pierre de Ronsard compared to the brown-haired, brown-eyed Muses, each blessed with her own special grace but who, together, find their real strength in numbers.[9]

Mary would always upstage Elisabeth. In private, did those gaps in rank, age, and ability matter to their friendship? While rank distinguished everyone, adults as well as children, Elisabeth was special to Mary. When Mary first came to the nursery, separated from her mother and from the "four Marys," Elisabeth's presence probably comforted the little Scottish queen. In those early days, in the bedchamber they shared, Elisabeth must have taught Mary some of her first French words. At what point did Mary begin to call Elisabeth "sister?" The Guises encouraged it, as did King Henry and Queen Catherine. "Sisters" is what the Guises envisioned—if uttered often enough, especially before Mary's betrothal to the dauphin was official, perhaps everyone might see its inevitability. To call Elisabeth "sister" was a political act. But more than anyone, Mary herself seems to have believed it.

Soon after Elisabeth turned five, her parents ordered her a special desk carved from walnut. Princesses were born but they were also made. Riding and hunting made the body strong while dancing taught a girl to be graceful. A young girl's mind also required careful tending. King Henry and Queen Catherine believed in the precepts of the humanists: more than an ornament, education sculpted character, a mind fit to rule.[10]

So Elisabeth had to sit at her walnut desk and parse her sentences. She learned from the finest teachers in France, including Jacques Amyot, the famous humanist Latinist who came to court in 1554. While Amyot spent most of his time with the royal princes, he taught the girls as well. Often Mary joined Amyot and Elisabeth in the classroom, too.

In July 1554, when Mary was eleven, Amyot gave her a book filled with creamy white pages. It was an exercise book, schoolwork for the budding queen. On the recto of every leaf—the right-hand side, or the front of each page—Mary was to write short essays in Latin to her "sister" Elisabeth. The essays were Latin practice for Mary, but also lessons to teach Elisabeth how to write and behave. There were rules, of course. Her letters should be as grammatically correct as possible. She shouldn't waste paper or ink. Her script should be neat. Above all, she should say something of substance. Think of Erasmus, Amyot instructed Mary. Think of Plutarch and Cicero.

Over the next six months, from July 1555 to January 1556, Mary wrote fifty-six letters to Elisabeth in her little book. She lectured, scolded, and praised. *Pay attention. Work hard. Don't give up.* "We must never lose courage, my sister," Mary wrote, "if virtue and knowledge take a long time to learn. For all things easily made are also easily undone." *Don't misbehave. Study, like me.* "I heard, sister, that yesterday you were very stubborn at your lessons. You had promised not to be like that anymore; please, stop this bad habit. Think instead: a princess takes a book in her hands not only to enjoy it but to understand the lesson better." *Be a good girl.* "I heard from our teacher, my dearest sister, that now you're studying very well. I am so happy to hear it." Still, it could be hard for little girls to behave. "It's for a good reason," Mary explained, "that the queen told us yesterday to obey our governess; Cicero says in the beginning of his second book of *Laws*: that those who know how to rule have once obeyed, and whoever obeys humbly is worthy to command." *Obedience and virtue, Elisabeth.* Obey the grown-ups, and you will learn how to rule.[11]

Were these Mary's own words, cloaked in Latin? If so, she may have had some help. Still, Mary's voice—sometimes prudish and bossy, yet affectionate—shines through. She shared her afternoon plans with Elisabeth (a stroll in the park), and she worried when Elisabeth fell ill: "The queen has forbidden me to visit you because she thinks you might have the measles. I am so upset about it. Please tell me how you are feeling."

Mostly, Mary loved Elisabeth. Over and over again, she professed that love. "My sweet," "my dearest," "my beloved sister," Mary called Elisabeth. "The true friendship with which I love you more than myself," she wrote, "tells me that anything good I ever have will be shared between us, my sister."

At eleven years old, Mary was bright but no prodigy. Her intelligence would later be compared to that of a different Elizabeth, the Queen of England, Elizabeth Tudor. In fact, the young Mary could not boast the same brilliance. At age eleven, the young Elizabeth Tudor translated a long poem by Marguerite de Navarre, an evangelical meditation on the soul.* She intended the book as a gift for her new stepmother; in fact, Elizabeth hoped to impress her father. In her fine italic hand, the young girl translated 1,450 lines of rhyming couplets

---

*Marguerite de Navarre's *Mirror of the Sinful Soul* was published in 1531 and condemned by the Sorbonne (although King Francis protected both the work and his sister). Scholars aren't sure how a copy landed in young Elizabeth Tudor's hands. Some have speculated that Marguerite de Navarre sent a copy to Anne Boleyn as a gift to acknowledge their shared interest in the Reform.

into flowing prose, only a few errors marring the script. Then she embroidered a cover for the book, weaving silk thread into ropes of Celtic braid and colorful heartseases. Mary's own schoolbook hardly measures up to Elizabeth Tudor's handiwork. The young Scots queen left some of her phrases rough; she made beginner's mistakes. Sometimes her margins wobbled, and sentences trailed onto the back of the page. And her notebook remained unfinished, no silk-stitched cover decorating the pages, despite Mary's love of embroidery.

But Mary never intended her book as a present. Nor did she feel a need to show off her genius. Whereas the child Elizabeth Tudor longed to prove herself to the father who had bastardized her, young Mary had never known a day without her family's love.

The Guises believed even her errors were worth preserving. They kept Mary's notebook. It was a record of her progress and proof of the singular friendship she shared with her little "sister," the French Elisabeth, the beloved daughter of the Most Christian King.

Mary did all the speaking in her little book. Elisabeth de Valois had no voice, although Mary's prose gives us a glimpse of her. What was she like, the child Elisabeth? A little stubborn, perhaps, somewhat impish. Not always keen on lessons about virtue and obedience. Possibly she was a little frail and somewhat sickly. At times, the doctors fretted over Elisabeth, as did both Catherine and Mary.

If Elisabeth ever had a book of her own, it hasn't survived. There is no record of her early feelings for Mary, no childish missives remaining in the archives. Perhaps, since the two girls were so often together, there was no need to write. Or perhaps their notes were easily discarded, the frivolous ephemera of a girlish friendship.

More surprising is the almost complete absence of surviving letters between Mary and Elisabeth once they had married and parted ways. Still, letters *did* pass between them, although how often they were exchanged remains a mystery. At least one survives, and it alludes to a steady correspondence between the two young women after Elisabeth arrived in Spain.[12]

What did those letters contain? Were they perfunctory and polite? Did they confide hopes and fears? What remained of their friendship after political circumstances intervened? In the first years of Elisabeth's marriage to Philip II, their friendship would be tested, struggling under the weight of rank and politics. As queen consort of Spain, an older Elisabeth would find that loyalty to blood and kingdom trumped any love for a friend. She would watch her own star rise while Mary's would plummet.

That was later. In childhood, friendship was simpler.

Even so, there were differences between them that Elisabeth might have felt in her bones. On the verso of each leaf in Mary's blank book—the left-hand side, the backside of the page—someone wrote the French translation of each of Mary's Latin essays. Who was this mysterious scribe? The handwriting is fluid and no-nonsense, likely the work of a teacher. But the sentences suffer from awkward constructions and grammatical errors, like the work of a child just learning to decipher her Latin. Perhaps Amyot or some other tutor finished the project, transcribing the student's translations into Mary's book. Were these Elisabeth's words? This is what historians suspect. As Mary learned to write her Latin, Elisabeth was learning to read it, translating the work of her "sister." Perhaps Mary's notebook was shared after all, an album of friendship and a mirror for their life together: Mary, confident and striving in Latin, blazing a trail on the front of the page; the younger Elisabeth, an echo of the older girl, following her friend at the back.

10

JOURNEYS
France and Spain, 1559

The last time Elisabeth de Valois saw Mary Stuart was in late November 1559, outside the palace at Châtelleraut, on the northern edge of Poitou, southwest of the Loire. Elisabeth was about to depart for Spain, and the court had gathered to see her off. She had hoped Catherine could accompany her as far south as Lusignan but King Francis, nervous about being apart from his mother, ordered Catherine to stay at his side.[1]

An early winter had descended on Châtelleraut. Snow dusted the ground. By the day of Elisabeth's departure, an enormous convoy had convened, some 160 people in all. The new Spanish ambassador to France, Thomas Perrenot de Granvelle, Sieur de Chantonnay, was in a panic. The sheer number of people in the convoy and their endless carts of baggage made for a secretary's nightmare. The bridal trousseau itself—heaps of plate and linen, piles of jewels, mounds of carpets, paintings, and furniture—filled dozens of carts, and Catherine had added untold numbers of gifts for Elisabeth to distribute en route. Everything was packed in ungainly "baskets, bullock wagons, and in coffers twice as long, deep, and wide" as any Chantonnay had ever seen in Spain. There was little hope of repacking. The new queen's clothes were so ornate that smaller trunks would damage them. "Best to send most of it by sea from the port at Bayonne," Chantonnay suggested to King Philip, unless His Majesty was willing to clear a new road over the mountains from Bayonne to Pamplona.[2]

The mood was somber, a strange brew of grief, anxiety, and impatience. Many in the convoy were honored to accompany the new queen to Spain. Others felt something closer to obligation and looked forward to returning to France in a few months' time. Elisabeth didn't know if she would ever return home. A childhood of lessons, both in the classroom and out, had sought to prepare her for what lay ahead. Every adage imparted by her tutors, every handoff of every ribbon to every little prince, every Latin phrase parsed and step danced had endeavored to shape Elisabeth into a consort who could order her court, command the love of her subjects, elicit the respect of her husband, and serve her own family. Elisabeth had far more education in the ways of queenly conduct than her mother, Catherine, ever had.

Later letters suggest the lessons Catherine may have taught Elisabeth in the months before her departure. Be mindful of your clothes and dress the part. Be wary of jealousy among your ladies, lest they disobey you. Keep yourself clean and neat, free of blemishes and odors, for King Philip's sake. Above all, obey your husband, honor him, and strive to please him. This last lesson was the most important. Now that King Henry II had died, the strength of the foundling alliance between France and Spain hinged on Elisabeth's success as Philip's queen.

Still, even a mother as vigilant as Catherine couldn't prepare her daughter for everything. We don't really know how mothers instructed their daughters about the marriage bed or childbirth. Conduct books were full of advice on guarding a girl's chastity but, prudish and discreet, they refrained from speaking about sex. Elisabeth probably wasn't completely naive. Yet what any mother might have shared with her daughter in private remained too shameful to consign to paper. Elisabeth's husband was a man of thirty-two, a widower twice over. This was a very different arrangement from the wedding of Mary Stuart, who married a boy she'd known from the nursery. Possibly, the situation being what it was, Catherine thought experience alone was the best teacher.

The Spanish would later balk at the number of courtiers Elisabeth brought with her, but Catherine was anxious to showcase French majesty. She also wanted sufficient Frenchmen and Frenchwomen on the ground in Spain to help Elisabeth in her new duties. Already, Sébastien de l'Aubespine, Bishop of Limoges and French ambassador to Spain, waited to greet the new queen in Guadalajara.

Catherine also chose Elisabeth's French attendants with special care. Eleven-year-old Mademoiselle de Montpensier, Elisabeth's distant Bourbon cousin and one of the richest heiresses in France, came as a companion, accompanied by her aunt Madame de Rieux. For Elisabeth's retinue, Catherine selected as chief lady-in-waiting her own close friend, the matronly Louise de Clermont. Part governess, part substitute mother, Madame de Clermont would advise and protect Elisabeth, and update Catherine on her daughter's progress. Madame de Clermont had already served Elisabeth for years, ever since the girl came to live at court. As Catherine once put it, apart from herself, Madame de Clermont knew Elisabeth best.[3]

Catherine also charged Madame de Clermont with another task. As a high-ranking French noblewoman, Madame de Clermont would enjoy a place of honor at the Spanish court. Catherine expected her to send regular letters on the political happenings in Spain, to decipher tricky diplomatic situations that Elisabeth, still young, could not. No secrets: Madame de Clermont must tell Catherine everything she heard and saw.

In other words, Madame de Clermont would serve as something of a spy.

There was a delay. When Elisabeth learned her mother couldn't come farther south, she asked for three more days at Châtelleraut. But she couldn't put off leaving forever. When it was time for the final farewells, even the Spanish ambassador, Chantonnay, was moved by the weeping.[4]

Sometime during those last days, Mary, Queen of Scots, handed Elisabeth a letter for Philip.

"Monsieur my good brother," she began. "If the Queen, Madame my sister, were going somewhere I didn't think she'd be as lucky and happy, I would not be able to keep from mourning infinitely the loss of her company, because it is so personal to me. This is a great loss for me and I fear I will never find anything like [her friendship] again. But since I know how lucky she is, I will try to forget my own sorrow so I can rejoice that she has the good fortune of being with you. And you, I believe, will be so delighted with her that you will pity the king, my lord and husband, for having lost her. Her virtues, as well as the friendship you show her, already commend her enough. Nevertheless, to show her the good friendship I feel for her, I couldn't help but add my own praise. I ask you to receive it, as it comes from the person who loves her most in the world."

Mary had worked over the draft carefully. At first, she signed it, "Your good sister." Then, thinking better of it, she crossed out what she wrote and signed instead: "Your *very* good sister, Mary." She had always walked in front of Elisabeth. Was she trying to precede her now, commending her to Philip like a bossy big sister—like the ranking queen she was—jockeying for a place in the eyes of the Spanish king?

Then again, perhaps her intentions were entirely innocent and wistful—as if, by underscoring her own goodwill toward Philip, Mary could soften his heart toward the "sister" she so loved.[5]

The enormous convoy lumbered south, first to Bordeaux and Béarn, up the treacherous mountain passes through the Pyrenees, down into Bayonne, then veering toward Pamplona in Spanish Navarre. The terrain gradually changed. Rolling hills and meadows gave way to bare sheets of rock jutting from plains of winter white. The faces of the people changed, too, as did the dialects and the local fare. Between bouts of tears, Elisabeth grew curious. "Do they have houses like this in Spain?" she is said to have asked. "Do they wear clothes like that?"[6]

In Bordeaux, Antoine de Bourbon, King of Navarre, would join the convoy. The marriage contract called for an escort of the highest birth for the new queen, as befitted her rank; at the time of the wedding, everyone had assumed that Elisabeth's father would accompany her. As first prince of the blood, Antoine de Bourbon now stepped in. It was an appropriate choice, but the Guises selected Antoine mostly to keep him out of Paris and King Francis's council. The Guises felt little respect for Antoine; nonetheless, they feared him. They knew the French people revered the ancient royal blood of the Bourbons and looked to them to furnish the next line of French kings if the house of Valois should falter.

Even more than Antoine's royal blood, the Guises feared his religion. Antoine clearly sympathized with the French Reform. Though he was somewhat indecisive about his own beliefs, Antoine's wife, Jeanne d'Albret, embraced Protestantism, as did his younger brother, Louis, known as the Prince de Condé. Protestants pressed Antoine to demand a stronger role in the government for the Bourbons while his fiery brother urged him to restore the Bourbons' rightful place at court.[7] The clannish rivalries at court now entwined themselves with questions of religion. Sending Antoine south allowed the Catholic Guises to tighten their hold on the government without either Protestant or Bourbon interference.

Antoine de Bourbon knew the Guises were shunting him aside. "Time has wrought many changes," he wrote to the Bishop of Limoges, Catherine's ambassador in Spain. Nevertheless, he had found an upside to the trip. Much to the consternation of French Protestants, Antoine cared more about his own lands in Navarre than about the new government in Paris. Antoine began his reign as King of Navarre after marrying Jeanne, the only child of Marguerite de Navarre.* An ancient kingdom with old feudal alliances to the French, Navarre straddled the Pyrenees. In 1512, the Spanish had seized half of Navarre; now, in 1559, Antoine de Bourbon hoped to persuade Philip II to return at least a portion of it. Young Elisabeth made an excellent pretext for his own political forays. At her age, Antoine rationalized, "the length of the journey and the poor weather will have improved rather than damaged her health." He jumped at the chance to go.[8]

As Christmas approached, the caravan inched its way into the Pyrenees. Snow fell "as if spiteful." Sometimes mounted in the saddle, sometimes snuggled under furs in her litter, Elisabeth felt the swaying of the horses, the crushing fatigue of the trip. She was never alone, constantly in the company of her Bourbon cousins, Mademoiselle de Montpensier and Madame de Rieux, or supervised by Madame de Clermont. Privacy, as we conceive it, is a modern concept. Elisabeth, having never known it, probably didn't miss it. Her caravan was a theater and Elisabeth its first player, every smile and tear noted by

---

*The kingdom of Navarre passed to Jeanne from her own father, and Marguerite's husband, Henry of Navarre. After marrying Jeanne, Antoine became King of Navarre in juris uxoris.

her companions. Daily, her beloved nurse, Claude de Nau, felt the heat of her skin while Madame de Clermont took the pulse of her mood. Catherine's messengers came and went, collecting letters alongside dispatches penned by Elisabeth's interpreter, Monsieur de Lansac (for Spain's new queen spoke almost no Spanish), or her secretary, Monsieur de L'Huillier, who wrote dutiful reports to both the Queen Mother and the Cardinal of Lorraine describing the journey.[9]

During those long weeks, Elisabeth must have wondered about Philip. Before her wedding, she'd seen a portrait, part of the standard fare in dynastic marriage negotiations. It probably resembled the famous picture of Philip painted around 1558 by Antonis Mor, Philip's favorite Flemish portraitist. In Mor's picture, Philip stands with legs askew and calf muscles flexing, as if caught in mid-saunter, the perfect pose to show off his codpiece. His chest rises under a cuirass flashing with gold, trimmed with the Hapsburg crosses of Burgundy. From his neck dangles a tiny, bejeweled sheep's pelt, the symbol of the Catholic Order of the Golden Fleece, founded by Philip's Burgundian ancestors. Mor captured a sensual tension between the king's courtly grace and a fierce, regal authority, the embodiment of Catholic Hapsburg supremacy.[10]

He was in his prime, the sovereign of an empire. Not quite handsome, Philip was still young and virile, with a thick beard softening the famous protruding Hapsburg chin, chestnut hair receding slightly from his temples. What might Elisabeth have seen in Philip's blue eyes when she gazed at his portrait? She would have known his reputation for austerity and hoped, at least, for kindness.

She belonged to Spain now, the ogre of her father's boyhood. Perhaps her naivety offered its own protection. Writing to a kinswoman from the road, Elisabeth said she still grieved for her father, whose loss "was almost intolerable to me." Yet she was comforted by "the assurances of friendship I have received from my lord the king, whom I hope will be a father and a husband to me, both."[11]

In Valladolid, the medieval seat of the kings and queens of Castile, Philip II waited for word from his messengers. Once the French convoy neared the border, he would travel to Guadalajara to meet Elisabeth. From there, they would proceed together to Toledo, the capital.

Philip had seen a portrait of Elisabeth, too, a painting based on the drawing Clouet made of her in 1558, just before the wedding of Mary Stuart.[12] Elisabeth was the first bride Philip had married of his own accord. His previous two marriages—the first to his Hapsburg-Spanish-Portuguese cousin Maria-Manuela of Portugal, the second to another Spanish-blooded cousin, Mary Tudor of England—had been arranged by his father, Charles V, to further Hapsburg interests. Philip had loved, respected, and obeyed his father, usually with only faint grumblings. But when Charles V died in 1558, Philip felt free to make his own decisions. In a marked departure from Philip's other wives, Elisabeth descended from neither a Hapsburg nor a Hapsburg ally.

Philip was not unlike Henry II of France. Reserved like Henry, and prone to shyness, Philip also struggled to emerge from under the thumb of his extroverted father, Charles V, who exerted an immense influence on his son from the time of Philip's birth until Charles's death in 1558. Like Henry II of France, Philip yearned for his father's approval; unlike Henry, he usually received it. Nevertheless, Philip did not share quite the same worldview as his father. Born and raised in Flanders, Charles V always felt more Flemish than Spanish. Born and raised in Castile, Philip preferred Spain—its sun, its soil, its religion. Charles V saw France as his ancient and avowed enemy. For the sake of his finances, Philip agreed to a lasting peace with that enemy—though Philip had inherited his father's thirst for empire and would never embrace France entirely as a friend.

Philip showed a deep respect for some women, if not all. He'd loved his mother, Isabella of Portugal, who died when he was twelve. He adored his blond-haired and blue-eyed sisters, Maria and Juana, whom he believed capable and competent, and frequently treated more like colleagues than underlings. He did not feel quite the same about his first two wives, although, as Spanish etiquette dictated, he remained courteous with them in words, if not in deeds. His feelings for them may have been complicated by the need to procreate, which caused the younger Philip undue anxiety. Charles V likely taught him to fear sex. At several points during Philip's teenaged years, Charles had written him long memos on "how to be king" in the event of his own death. In one of them, Charles preached that immoderate sex could kill a prince. "It is very important that you restrain your desires and do not make excessive efforts at this early stage, which could lead to physical damage because . . . [sex] can lead to such weakness that it interferes with conceiving children and even causes death." In fact, Charles said, too much sex had killed Prince Juan of Trastámara, his maternal uncle—this is how Charles V himself had eventually inherited the crown of Spain.* One self-indulgent tryst too many, it seems, could shift the course of kingdoms.[13]

Philip already knew that sex could kill women. His own mother had died in childbirth when he was twelve, a trauma from which he never recovered.

Married at sixteen to Maria-Manuela, Philip appeared embarrassed by his first wife, though he wept when she died just four days after giving birth to their son, Don Carlos—a stark and painful reminder of his own mother's demise. He barely mourned Mary Tudor, whom he'd wed only reluctantly, put off by the difference in their ages: Mary was thirty-seven at the time of their wedding and Philip twenty-seven. He'd been not-so-secretly relieved that his former sister-in-law, Queen Elizabeth of England, refused his marriage proposal in the wake of Mary Tudor's death. He'd had reservations from the beginning, although he liked the idea of keeping his hand in English politics and, after all the strides he'd made to bring Catholicism back to England, he hated to see his hard work undone. Plus—and this was most important—since Philip still considered France his rival, he needed Elizabeth Tudor comfortably on the English throne to keep the French and their pawn Mary Stuart off it. Married to Elizabeth, he could protect her. (Philip did not know his former sister-in-law very well: he assumed Elizabeth could not protect herself.)

Still, the idea of marriage to a heretic made Philip sick to his stomach. So when Elizabeth demurred, Philip exhaled his relief. He would secretly support the bastard Protestant English queen for

*Don Juan of Trastámara, Prince of Asturias, was the only son of Isabel of Castile and Ferdinand of Aragon to survive into adulthood. When he died in 1497, the crowns of Spain passed to his younger sister, Juana, mother of Charles V.

the sake of his own empire. But at least they wouldn't share the conjugal bed.

Now that he'd switched to Elisabeth de Valois, Philip seemed to look forward to his bride's arrival. Unlike Mary Tudor, who to Philip's mind had seemed almost decrepit, Elisabeth de Valois was a young teen, presumably nubile. And Philip needed more heirs. As one minister summed it up, with Elisabeth de Valois, "His Majesty will have no cause to complain that he has been forced to marry an ugly old woman."[14]

Philip was a workhorse, accustomed to clocking up to sixteen hours a day shut up with his advisors and papers. He nursed boundless imperial ambitions: he aspired to conquer Europe and return England, Scotland, Flanders, and Germany to the Catholic fold. He greedily eyed the New World and hungered to dominate north Africa. While Charles V liked to say that Spain was the "empire on which the sun never sets," Philip would eventually adopt a different motto: *Non sufficit orbis*. Indeed, to Philip II, even the whole world was not enough.

But Philip wasn't heartless. Well aware of his newest bride's youth and the trauma she had just endured, Philip had written gentle letters assuring Elisabeth of his goodwill. He'd graciously agreed to a large French household for his new queen so she would feel at home in Spain. He sent the bluest of his blue-blooded noblemen, the Mendozas, to fetch her in the Pyrenees—a show of honor and deep respect. Philip also gave strict instructions not to make any changes in Elisabeth's French retinue before she arrived in Guadalajara. Not a single French feather was to be ruffled.[15]

And he'd had another thought. Before the Duke of Alba left for the wedding in Paris, Philip asked him to find out more about the bride. Upon learning that Elisabeth liked to draw, Alba remembered a young Italian noblewoman he'd heard about during his days as governor of Milan. Sofonisba Anguissola hailed originally from Cremona and had studied in Rome under Michelangelo. Word of her talents had traveled throughout Italy. The Florentine painter Giorgio Vasari raved about her. "Sofonisba of Cremona," he would write, ". . . has done more in design and more gracefully than any other lady of our day, for not only has she designed, colored and drawn from life and copied the works of others most excellently, but she has produced rare and beautiful paintings of her own."[16] She was an artistic genius, Vasari believed—some said she surpassed even Leonardo himself.

Philip made inquiries; Sofonisba agreed to join Elisabeth's retinue in Spain as a lady-in-waiting.

Sofonisba's journey to Spain mirrored Elisabeth's own voyage, following the path of so many young women obliged to leave home. In his letter to Philip, Sofonisba's father, Amilcare Anguissola, echoed the note Mary Stuart wrote upon Elisabeth's departure, a similar lament lacing the sentences. "As a faithful subject, which I am, of both the late emperor and Your Majesty," he said, "I willingly give her with much affection to enter the Queen's service . . . Owing to your outstanding qualities, I am greatly consoled so that this, in part, diminishes the sorrow which my family and I feel due to the departure of our dearest daughter."[17]

Sofonisba left only "to obey Your Majesty," noted the Duke of Sessa, who organized her trip, his words carrying the faintest trace of reproval. "She has come here with the same goodwill, going so far away and leaving her parents, her siblings, her relatives, her home, and her country."[18] Too old to make the trip himself, Sofonisba's father asked two kinsmen to deliver his daughter to Spain. In January 1560, as Elisabeth and her sprawling convoy climbed into the Pyrenees, Sofonisba and her humble retinue braved the Ligurian Sea to Barcelona. From there, she traveled three hundred miles west into Castile, joining the Spanish court in Guadalajara in time to meet Elisabeth. There would be no need for the services of Monsieur de Lansac, the interpreter: Elisabeth already spoke Italian, her mother's language, which Elisabeth had polished in the classroom and honed in the company of the young Clarice Strozzi.

Settled in the queen's household, Sofonisba would teach the young queen to draw and paint. Not quite a wedding gift, she was nonetheless something of an acknowledgment of what Elisabeth had left behind.

All through Elisabeth's journey the snow continued to fall. Icy gales gusted over the mountains. Christmas gave Elisabeth and her attendants a short reprieve, spent comfortably at the palace at Pau, the seat of the king and queen of Navarre. For a week they played games, cast lots, and spent hours in conversation.[19] Too soon, they saddled the horses and started out again.

At Saint-Jean-de-Luz, near Bayonne, they found reinforcements sent by Philip to relieve the tired horses and replace carts that were too cumbersome to hazard the winding mountain passes. Under a "glacial sky" swirling with storm clouds, the roads grew steeper, slick with ice. On one pass, half the baggage belonging to the ladies-in-waiting tumbled over a cliff, the sodden and soiled contents recovered only days later by a search party. At times, the snow fell so thick and fast the riders had trouble steering their mounts.[20]

By the time they reached Roncesvalles high in the Pyrenees, the entire French convoy was chilled to the bone, exhausted after six weeks on the road. When the horses could go no further, they trudged on foot through deep snow to the abbey. Camped in the nearby village of Espinal, in Spanish Navarre, the Mendoza Duke of Infantado and the Mendoza Cardinal of Burgos awaited their arrival.

For Elisabeth, the long weeks of travel had imparted their own lessons in patience and diplomacy. Despite years of training at court, she still sometimes found the subtleties of rank and status perplexing. As they neared the Spanish border, Elisabeth wrote to her mother with a query. The Queen of Navarre was still in their company but so was Madame de Rieux, the Bourbon princess. Should there be one litter, then, or two? "They told me that, with you, there were never any litters except yours," she told Catherine. She feared breaking an unknown and unspoken rule. "I didn't want to do anything different from what you told me to do."[21]

Antoine de Bourbon had also caused problems. Trying to impress the Spanish representatives in the convoy, he was demanding and buffoonish, commanding befuddled French locals in every town to kneel before the new Spanish queen. (City magistrates were forced to explain that such behavior was normally reserved for the French king.) Crossing into French Navarre, Antoine grew pompous. He paraded his rights as the King of Navarre, insisting on the finest lodgings for himself while giving Elisabeth only second best. The Spaniards in the caravan bristled but, to all evidence, Elisabeth never complained.

In Roncesvalles, the handover to the Spanish was awkward. The delivery of the queen was supposed to take place in an open field near the abbey—a neutral space between the realms of France and Spain—but Antoine thought the weather too inclement to keep Elisabeth outdoors for the compulsory ceremonies. He insisted the Cardinal of Burgos and the Duke of Infantado come to the abbey. The Spanish balked. Coming to the French would defy the neutrality between the realms and alter the requisite rituals. It would mean desisting to the King of Navarre, an inferior sovereign! A standoff ensued, lasting several days. Afraid of displeasing Philip, Elisabeth begged Antoine de Bourbon to stick to the original plan. They had packed the baggage and harnessed the horses when messengers appeared announcing the arrival of the Spanish after all.[22]

The King of Navarre hustled Elisabeth back inside as her ladies raced to change their gowns and the porters scrambled to unpack Elisabeth's canopy of estate. When the Mendozas entered the abbey, they found Elisabeth perched on a chair of crimson velvet, her ladies and the Bourbon princesses arranged artfully to her left, the King of Navarre to Elisabeth's right. He, too, had a chair. As a concession to Antoine's kingly ego, the French had agreed he could sit.

The rest of the afternoon ensued in barely contained chaos. After the obligatory greetings, dozens of Spanish noblemen crammed into the room, pushing the ladies aside in their rush to kiss Elisabeth's hand. "We learned," grumbled one Frenchman, "that temerity, importunity, and indiscretion reigns not just in France but mostly in Spain." Elisabeth performed well. Catherine must have been anxious about what the Mendozas would think of her daughter. One French witness was quick to confirm the Spanish were charmed to find "such a beautiful, rare, and virtuous princess who, for her part . . . behaved so soberly and assuredly, coupled with her natural gentleness." Though clearly nervous in the beginning, another witness reported, Elisabeth soon relaxed.

Her gentleness, though, could not prevent some uncomfortable jockeying among the men, a sideshow to all the ceremony. Ever mindful of his own sovereignty, Antoine surprised everyone with an impromptu speech, warning that although the Spaniards had crossed into French Navarre to retrieve their queen, he ceded no territory to Spain. To this, the embarrassed Spaniards could only respond, "It's fine, it's fine." Antoine writhed with humiliation when a vengeful Duke of Infantado covered his head with his hat before the King of Navarre could cover his own—payback after Antoine dared place a patronizing hand on the Spaniard's shoulder. In the end, Antoine's preening was all for naught: the Spanish treated him like a pauperish upstart.[23]

At last, the long-winded tributes, aching smiles, and endless bowing came to an end. Once again, it was time to say goodbye. Before the final parting, Elisabeth gave Antoine de Bourbon a kiss. Her mother "ordered her to do so," she explained to the startled Spanish noblemen, because the Bourbons "were kinsmen and princes of the blood. And it is the custom in France." It was the last French custom she would follow. As trumpets and woodwinds sounded, Elisabeth stepped out of the abbey and into a Spanish litter, escorted by the Cardinal of Burgos and the Duke of Infantado.[24]

The convoy, now in Spanish hands, moved on through the snowfall. In the great hall of the abbey, Antoine de Bourbon lingered for a few moments, according to one witness, "happy to have accomplished the mission, but greatly saddened at having to leave the queen."[25]

The French crown's official account, which was published the following year, hailed Elisabeth's delivery to Spain as a victory, a balm to a kingdom still suspicious of Spain and reeling from the sudden death of Henry II. Paying little attention to Elisabeth herself, the pamphlet made no mention of the fear she must have felt. Yet those present at Roncesvalles probably sensed her anxiety. Stories later spread about Elisabeth's grief, and they likely capture something of the truth. According to one, when Elisabeth realized it was time to leave with the Spanish, she gripped Antoine de Bourbon's arm and burst into tears. The Cardinal of Burgos told her, "Oblivisce populum tuum et domum patris tui." *Forget your people and your father's home.*[26]

It was perhaps good advice. But Elisabeth could never bring herself to follow it entirely. Already, her mother's letters were arriving almost daily, each and every one a reminder.

11

LETTERS
France and Spain, 1559–1560

Catherine had no intention of letting Elisabeth forget where she came from. She expected Elisabeth to bridge the divide between kingdoms, and between her old family and her new one. "Remember that whatever great alliance you achieve," Anne of France taught her own daughter in the late fifteenth century, "you must never, out of some foolish pride, fail to value highly your own ancestors, those from whom *you* are descended—to fail in that would be against right and reason."[1] To women of rank this was simply common sense. A wife should serve her husband's family, yet never forget her own.

As Catherine conceived it, mother and daughter would make a team: Elisabeth would aim to make Philip fall in love with her—or at least to respect her—while the Queen Mother would try to forge a political alliance based on the "natural" connection between wedded kingdoms. They were family now, after all. Catherine threw around the vocabulary of family as if Spain and France had loved each other for generations. "The Catholic King, my good son," she called Philip whenever she chatted with Ambassador Chantonnay about her plans to visit Spain.[2] She would come to Philip, of course: an act of loving deference from a queen mother to a sovereign king, a woman to her son-in-law. This wasn't just talk—Catherine had several good reasons to travel to Spain, reasons as personal as they were political. Despite the charade, the alliance was fragile. With religion threatening peace in France, she could not afford any Spanish hostility. But she also wanted to see Elisabeth again soon. Her daughter had scarcely left and already Catherine missed her.

Letters to Elisabeth were in the messenger's saddlebag long before Catherine reached Amboise from Châtelleraut. It says something about Catherine's deep anguish, apparent to all, that her separation from Elisabeth became a popular theme among artists and writers over the coming centuries. Well into the nineteenth century the Romantic French painter Eugène Isabey caught the moment of their parting: Elisabeth dressed in white mourning, sobbing as courtiers pull her to a waiting coach, their own expressions dark and mournful; Catherine swooning in her regal black gown, her arms reaching toward her daughter. In the sixteenth century, a poem began to circulate, written to Elisabeth in Catherine's voice. "I am praying to God," she says, that Philip "will be mother and father to you, both husband and friend." It is unlikely that Catherine actually composed this poem herself. As happened often in the Renaissance, someone else probably wrote it, trying to capture what everyone knew Catherine felt.[3]

During Elisabeth's first weeks in Spain, letters from Catherine's envoys streamed back to France. Catherine tracked Elisabeth's progress closely, scanning the dispatches as they arrived, grilling messengers for details. For years Catherine had lived with Elisabeth at court, and had grown comfortable with having her daughter near. Now it was like a return to the early days of the *petite cour* when they lived apart, Catherine always a little anxious about her daughter's whereabouts; wondering whether those who sent their reports were merely trying to flatter her (as Clouet and the Humières had done), or if Catherine could trust them (as she had the painter Le Mannier) to tell her the truth, the bad alongside the good.

There were fixes for such doubts: many dispatches from many different people so you could test the facts. Otherwise, whom do you trust? Even unbiased witnesses were influenced by others, distracted or absent when some key detail unfolded. But when all reports agreed, then Catherine could relax—or worry.

Happily, most of the letters brought good news. People from all walks of Spanish life gathered on the roadside as Elisabeth and her convoy wound their way through Saragossa. They called her "Isabel de la paz," and cheered for "la reyna de la paz y la bondad!"—*the queen of peace and goodwill*. Catherine must have been thrilled to hear the description of Elisabeth's stunning entries into the towns of

Pamplona and Guadalajara, where the new queen enjoyed countless feasts, masques, balls, and bullfights—the first Elisabeth had ever seen. The scene was breathtaking and militaristic. In Pamplona thousands of soldiers lined the streets while hundreds of dancers, knights in armor, and toreadors performed along the procession route. Triumphal arches loomed over the crowds. The air thrummed with the ring of trumpets and tambourines. Banners sewn with Philip's initials, intertwined with Elisabeth's, fluttered from the windows of every house.[4]

The dispatches followed Elisabeth's every step. These first days were critical, the extension of the anxiety-ridden handover to the Spanish in Roncesvalles. Elisabeth needed to perform well. In Pamplona, Catherine learned, her daughter met the staid and ceremonious Countess of Ureigna, who would serve as her *camarera mayor*, officially her chief lady of the household. In Guadalajara, Elisabeth was greeted by a much warmer personality. Philip's youngest sister, Doña Juana, had returned to Spain from Portugal in 1558. Married to João Manuel, the heir apparent to the Portuguese throne, Juana was widowed just two years after their wedding. Forever after, she was known as "the Princess," more a reference to her venerated title in Portugal than to her rank in Spain. Thirteen years older than her new sister-in-law, the Princess took an instant liking to Elisabeth. In the evening of their first meeting, on January 28, Juana insisted Elisabeth share her supper, served by her own officers and ladies-in-waiting, a sure sign of the Princess's goodwill.[5]

All this was wonderful news to Catherine.

The Queen Mother had instructed Elisabeth to pay attention to the prime movers at the Spanish court, especially to the Duke of Alba and Ruy Gómez da Silva. Elisabeth had already met both men at the time of her wedding. Like her mother, she knew the two men despised each other with a stinging rancor.[6]

Spain, like France, was a jealous court, but no rivalry simmered hotter than the one between Ruy Gómez da Silva and the Duke of Alba.* Ruy Gómez had come to Spain in the household of Charles V's wife, Isabel of Portugal. Eventually he served as a page to the

---

*By convention, historians often refer to Ruy Gómez da Silva by his given name, "Ruy Gómez," rather than by his patronym.

young Prince Philip, and soon became the prince's loyal friend and companion, the older brother Philip never had.[7] Philip leaned heavily on Ruy Gómez's counsel, especially during the first years of his reign. Eventually, diplomats took to calling the Portuguese gentleman "Rey Gómes"—King Gómez.[8]

Ruy Gómez had soft brown eyes and a calculating mind. A consummate courtier, he was blessed with a remarkable ability to read the faces in the room and the moods of his master. What we might today call "emotional intelligence," Ruy Gómez possessed in spades. As a second son of a foreign country gentleman, with nothing to his name, Ruy Gómez's currency was charisma and bald-faced flattery. By the late 1540s, the courtier's star began its meteoric rise. In 1553, Philip helped arrange Ruy Gómez's marriage to the beautiful, supremely wealthy, and deeply blue-blooded Ana Mendoza, whose distinctive eye patch (she may have been blind in one eye) only added to her allure. When Philip returned to Flanders from England in 1558, he made Ruy Gómez his first gentleman of the bedchamber. And just before his wedding to Elisabeth in July 1559, Philip made his friend the Prince of Éboli.

Ferdinand Álvarez de Toledo, third Duke of Alba, was an entirely different story. He was "presumptuous, swollen with pride, consumed with ambition, given to flattery and very envious," one Venetian envoy griped.[9] A vestige of the old guard under Charles V, Alba was fifty-two years old in February 1560. If Ruy Gómez was the consummate courtier, Alba was the consummate warrior. Hailing from the ancient noble house of Toledo, he believed social status was forged in bloodlines and on the battlefield and had little patience for the foppery of the grasping courtier focused on favors and "career." He hated that King Philip preferred a self-made, low-born man like Ruy Gómez, ignoring all the rules of rank and status that should have made Alba the king's closest advisor. Warrior and courtier vied for precedence, each afraid to leave the king for long lest the other rise in favor. Whenever Philip took Ruy Gómez's advice over Alba's (which frequently happened), the ornery duke would retreat to his estates to mope.[10]

On Spanish policy toward France, the two men occupied opposite poles for entirely selfish reasons. Ruy Gómez preferred peace, a time when the art of the courtier flourished. He advocated alliance with

France. The Duke of Alba, however, thrived in the theater of war, where bellicose chest-beating earned reputation and reward. He believed Spain should dominate both the old world and the new. And despite his decorous courtesy at Elisabeth's wedding, Alba still saw France as the enemy.

To Catherine, a canny reader of men, the strategy was clear: Ruy Gómez's friendship required cultivating while the Duke of Alba needed placating. Elisabeth must strive to please them both.

In Guadalajara the festivities ramped up. The most important event occurred on January 30, two days after Elisabeth arrived in the city. That evening, Philip at last paid his first official visit to his bride, and appeared pleased by the young girl.[11] He did not spend the night. The next day, January 31, the Cardinal of Burgos married the couple once again in the Palace of El Infantado. That evening, after the celebratory ball and supper in Elisabeth's chambers, Philip went to change. "At ten o'clock," reported a witness, "he returned to sleep with her and stayed until seven o'clock the next morning." We do not know if the marriage was consummated that evening, but Philip made no complaint.[12]

Then Elisabeth was off again, now in Philip's company, headed first to Madrid, before turning toward Toledo, the end of the journey. There, the Bishop of Limoges—suffocating in the Spanish heat yet dutiful all the same—confirmed Elisabeth's safe arrival. Catherine exhaled. "I cannot express the pleasure that you give me," she wrote to Limoges, "by sending me all the news of the queen my daughter, discussing even the smallest details, as you do. You can believe how pleased I am to hear that she is so beloved by the king her husband and esteemed by his subjects. I am so pleased she is behaving in such a way as to give entire satisfaction to the king and his ministers."[13]

These were heady days, awash with relief at the end of the Italian Wars and with excitement over the new queen, even if the continued presence of Elisabeth's French retinue—dozens strong—caused some consternation among the Spaniards. Although it was common practice for a foreign queen to bring courtiers from her home country, Elisabeth's French entourage was unusually large. At King Philip's insistence, however, all the Spanish courtiers minded their manners. Elisabeth's first days in Toledo boded especially well. She was enjoying herself and dancing with her ladies, wrote a cheerful Limoges. Even the stuffy Countess of Ureigna made an effort. As another witness recounted, Elisabeth showed the countess how French ladies liked to dress. They were such darling and elegant outfits, cooed the countess. She hoped Elisabeth would wear them again soon.[14]

That tidbit no doubt reassured Catherine because, as every dispatch from Elisabeth's cortege confirmed, there had been friction between the French ladies and the countess as the convoy left Pamplona. As they readied the horses, Elisabeth invited the Countess of Ureigna to join her and Madame de Clermont in the first litter. Respectfully, the countess declined. Yet when the caravan set off, the countess's coach sprinted ahead, jostling the litter carrying the Bourbon princesses traveling just behind the queen, upsetting the order of precedence.

Reins were pulled; wheels ceased spinning. The caravan lurched to a halt. All eyes turned toward Elisabeth. Once again, she found herself perplexed by the delicate dance of status among noblewomen easily offended. True, the Countess of Ureigna was the highest-ranking noblewoman in *Spain*, but Mademoiselle de Montpensier and her aunt were princesses of the blood royal in *France*. Who outranked whom in this enormous convoy, on this endless trip? These were subtle questions for which there were no clear answers and few precedents. Now in a foreign kingdom—her new kingdom—what were the rules? Elisabeth, not quite fourteen, knew only that they mattered.

The situation was awkward, Monsieur de Lansac the interpreter translating tense words, the Countess of Ureigna willfully misunderstanding. In the end, Elisabeth settled the question in favor of the French ladies. The Bourbon princesses were royal guests, not Spanish subjects, she explained to the stone-faced countess. The Countess of Ureigna conceded but her displeasure was clear. At the first opportunity, Catherine's reporters sent agitated notes to France. As everyone knew, the Spanish were sticklers for ceremony. The countess belonged to a powerful Spanish family and was a fierce friend of the House of Toledo—the Duke of Alba's family. Elisabeth and her French retinue could not afford to make the countess, or Alba, an enemy.[15] It was an early test of diplomacy, and Elisabeth had not quite passed.

Such a serious social gaffe so early in her daughter's reign. A potential strain on the fragile Spanish friendship, and yet another thing for Catherine to worry about.

There was so much already for her to worry about. Catherine's son, King Francis, had inherited a kingdom racked by plague and beset by famine after a slew of poor harvests. The kingdom's debts, already crushing after twelve years of war with Spain, only mounted. The Guises rewarded friends, clients, and family with gifts of land and cash, yet insisted on curbing costs. They deferred the wages of royal troops, disbanded armies, and waived interest on royal debts. If anyone complained, soldier or nobleman, he could expect to be punished. Disgruntled rumblings surged. Was the boy king making his own decisions? Or were the Guises in control?

Under King Francis, persecution of French Protestants increased, the cardinal and the Duke of Guise intent on quashing the new religion before it could gain a foothold. They razed and burned as if heretical thinking might blow away like ashes on the wind. Believing heresy would lead to sedition—a real threat, said the Guises, since King Francis was so young—they destroyed houses reportedly used for Protestant gatherings and persuaded the courts to pass new laws requiring French subjects to denounce Protestant meetings on pain of death. All informants would be richly rewarded. Anyone harboring even the pettiest of grudges against their neighbors now had good reason to report them as heretics. The new laws fostered a climate of suspicion, vengeance, and fear. Bit by bit, the social fabric was fraying.[16]

As in England under Mary Tudor, burnings at the stake turned persecution into public theater. Back in December 1559, while Elisabeth de Valois sheltered from the Christmas snows in Pau with the King and Queen of Navarre, King Francis sent a young Parisian judge named Anne du Bourg to the pyre. Du Bourg had been arrested in the summer of 1559, shortly before Henry II's fatal accident. In the presence of King Henry, the young jurist dared suggest the courts should pursue "blasphemers, adulterers, perjurers, and horrible debauchers" rather than those who broke no laws but merely "call on the name of their prince in their prayers." Further interrogations proved that Du Bourg sympathized with heretics, but it was the remark about adulterers that sealed his fate: a furious Henry assumed the young man was alluding to his relationship with Diane de Poitiers.[17]

Henry II's death delayed Du Bourg's execution, but not for long. The Guises made an example of the young judge, sentencing him to be first hanged, then burned—a double execution for the double crime of heresy and treasonously insulting the king.

On the morning of December 23, carpenters hammered at the gallows in the Place de Grève, the large square abutting the Hôtel de Ville in Paris. Later that day, a two-wheeled tumbrel rolled into the square carrying Du Bourg. The young man stood erect, wearing only a tattered dressing gown. Witnesses could hear his voice rising as he sang the psalms. The reactions of the crowd must have been mixed: for French Protestants, singing psalms was both a demonstration of faith and an act of protest. Catholics considered such singing proof of heresy.

Soldiers, mounted on horseback and armed with pikes, restrained the press of the crowd. From the Hôtel de Ville, those lucky enough to secure a ringside seat crowded the upstairs windows. The square was mobbed, a sea of humanity.

The executioner placed a noose around Du Bourg's neck, the rope threaded through a pulley nailed to the gallows. The young man clasped his hands in prayer. The rope tightened, the pulley turned, and the body heaved into the air. Below his dangling limbs, bundles of brushwood caught flame, the crackle of the fire rising to a roar. Clouds of ash billowed into the crowd. In the Place de Grève was a large wooden cross, erected by Parisian magistrates as a monument to the piety of Paris, this most Catholic of French cities. A well-known engraving later captured the scene: as the tinder smoldered, a boy climbed the cross, seeking a better view. Du Bourg's corpse swayed in the smoke. The flames licked his heels.[18]

The rifts were deepening. Du Bourg's execution fanned emotions on both sides, Catholic and Protestant. Catherine found herself caught in the crosshairs. After Du Bourg's death, one embittered Protestant pastor wrote her a blistering letter. God would punish them all for Du Bourg's death, he wrote, just as he had wreaked vengeance on Henry II. God's "arm was still raised to visit His revenge upon her and her children. His justice will be clear; nothing will dissemble or disguise it."[19]

It was an appalling letter. Yet Catherine's response was measured. Though Catholic, she dealt in practicalities—of troops raised and funds procured—rather than in sweeping, fanatical pronouncements of piety and faith. Catherine could see that if the king was weak, the monarchy itself was weak. Power was already flowing into the hands of the great noble families surrounding the throne, the Guises and the Bourbons. With the crown in debt, noblemen flocked to the old and wealthy families of the realm for patronage.[20] Those loyalties and friendships formed factions at court and in the countryside, factions now hardened through religious hatred. Which side would prevail depended on its resources: men and money.

Catherine disliked the Guises' policies of persecution and refused to advocate drastic steps. What might Protestants do if pushed too far? There were several powerful noble families among them who, if riled, could threaten her son's crown. She knew Protestants were organizing to establish Antoine de Bourbon's place at court by dint of blood, custom, and law. Catherine began to fear a coup. She responded by informing herself, sending out queries, meeting with Protestant leaders. How much popular support did Protestants actually command? The answer would determine her next steps.[21]

She tried both to buy time and seek a resolution, to contain the problem before it threatened Francis's crown. Catherine's efforts were infused with hope that a compromise between factions could be reached. For the next ten years, she would continue to harbor that same hope.

In the meantime, her son depended on her. Though at fifteen he was legally too old for a regent, everyone recognized his inexperience and immaturity. Skinny and short, Francis was the ghost of his father, King Henry. Catherine became his de facto counselor, a figure of stability in a kingdom tottering under a frail king.

While the cardinal and duke hovered behind the throne, Catherine stood next to King Francis, his helpmeet and his conscience. In her ebony skirts she was an unwavering totem, her widow's weeds harkening back to a better time when strong French kings reigned— the forefathers of King Francis II, who would surely come into his own. In the meantime, Catherine served as the bridge. It was as if together, a matronly woman and an awkward boy, they forged sovereign strength where it was otherwise lacking. She appeared with Francis in person at every court function, every session of council. She even appeared with him on paper, at the head of official acts issued in the king's name. "This being the good pleasure of the Queen, my lady mother . . ." wrote the king's secretaries, "since I also approve of every opinion she holds."[22]

Historians usually look to later years, under King Charles IX, for the moment when Catherine seized the power behind the throne. But the seeds of her power were first sown in the time of Francis II. It was during Francis's reign that Catherine learned how to wield real authority. And it was under Francis II that courtiers and envoys became accustomed to the raven-clad sight of her, familiar and comforting, and always within eyeshot of the throne.

Once a forlorn girl at court, at forty Catherine became indispensable. But the work was grueling, and she still mourned her husband. She often fell ill. "If the King her son weren't so obedient to her," a worried Mary Stuart wrote to her own mother in Scotland, "I believe she would soon die." "And this," Mary went on, "would be the greatest misfortune that could befall all of us in this poor country."[23]

In Spain, the teenaged Elisabeth could hardly ease her mother's burdens. Or could she? Under different circumstances Catherine might have given Elisabeth years to mature and adapt to her new kingdom before requesting her help. But in the winter of 1560, Catherine did not feel that she had the luxury of time.

It was widely understood that a queen consort would intervene with her husband on behalf of those who enlisted her help, be they commoners, gentlefolk, or far-flung family. The role had ancient origins, modeled on the biblical stories of Esther from the Old Testament, or Mary, mother of Christ, who interceded with her son for those who prayed to her.

In the sixteenth century, it was also customary for women to play the part of neutral hostess in fraught situations. A woman's gentle touch, the thinking went, helped to cool hotheaded male tempers. Thus women often hosted peace negotiations—as happened in 1559 when, under the watchful gaze of Christine, Duchess of Lorraine, French and Spanish deputies hammered out the terms of Cateau-Cambrésis.[24]

Catherine held no illusions. Elisabeth was no Esther; she was a child. She might be hailed as *Isabel de la paz*, yet she barely spoke Spanish. It is a mark of Catherine's anxiety over escalating tensions in France that she turned to her daughter in 1560. Catherine knew Philip II would not tolerate the rising tide of Protestantism in France for long, not when heresy threatened to boil over into Hapsburg territories. She needed Elisabeth to appease her husband, to remind him that France was a friend.

No illusions: to help her mother, Elisabeth would herself need a lot of help. Catherine turned to her ambassador in Spain, the Bishop of Limoges, and enlisted the gentle guidance of Madame de Clermont. But Catherine considered herself Elisabeth's best teacher.* From the moment Elisabeth left France, Catherine started writing to her daughter. She wrote letter after letter, and for the rest of Elisabeth's life she never stopped writing.

———

Catherine had a gift: she knew what to say, how to say it and to whom. Her talent would infuriate partisans from both sides of the religious divide who saw her as dissimulative and manipulative; her admirers, however, considered her diplomatic. Catherine deployed that same persuasive skill in her letters, a voice in paper and ink. Sometimes her readers found a mother's voice, sometimes a friend's. Invariably, they found the voice of a queen—authoritative and usually (but not always) self-assured.

In her *cabinet*, a private chamber in each of the royal palaces, Catherine kept a desk; likely a small lady's desk meant for writing, the wood finely hewn and glistening with varnish, its top slanted at a graceful tilt, easy on the hand, the nib, the neck. If the need arose— and the need did arise—there were always bigger tables, too, shoved into the corners of rooms and halls. For traveling, there were small portable desks so there need never be a lapse in correspondence. Catherine had paper in reams. She owned quills by the hundreds. She probably possessed dozens of pen knives to scrape away mistakes,

*Catherine believed that only a queen could truly teach a fledgling queen, mother to daughter, just as Charles V believed that only a king could teach a future king, father to son.

but Catherine left the scraping to the secretaries. With no time to fix errors, she crossed out. Better yet, she let the mistake simply lie. Already she had moved on to the next thought, sometimes forgetting even to finish the first.*

Over the years, from her first writing lessons at the convent of Le Murate, Catherine had built a network through letters. She had hundreds of correspondents who recognized her seal, her inimitable signature. She wrote all kinds of letters: formal letters and casual ones, angry letters and affectionate ones, letters of commendation, letters of advice, letters to family and friends. She was not alone: countless aristocratic women wrote incessantly to keep in touch with family and allies across kingdoms. The Guise women, especially Antoinette de Bourbon, were copious letter writers, and perhaps in her own writing Catherine once again followed their example. But if other women wrote missives by the hundreds, Catherine wrote them by the thousands. We still have records of her letters in part because she was so prolific, in part because she was diligent. As Brantôme recalled, Catherine built a writing habit. She preferred to write after the dinner hour, and almost always she made copies.[25]

No person could write all those letters alone. Like any busy royal, Catherine relied on her secretaries. They would draft letters in her name, she would approve them; they would make a fair copy, she would affix her signature. For family, however, or if she needed the letter to really make its mark, Catherine would take the time to write in her own hand, a gesture of special affection—and sometimes a sign that the recipient should keep the contents a secret. Catherine's early schooling was erratic and so was her spelling, which, her whole life, retained the vestiges of her first years in Italy. As it was for many a sixteenth-century writer, punctuation was optional; Catherine's letters bore hardly a comma, nary a full stop. Her handwriting was a deep and slanting scrawl. Catherine usually wrote in her own hand to King Philip. She always wrote in her own hand to Elisabeth.[26]

Those letters to Elisabeth were filled with touches of tenderness. *Ma fille*, Catherine called her, or *m'amye*, a word with no real translation: "my love" or "my dearest" are perhaps closest. She loved Elisabeth, yet, as the situation grew more tense in France, that love

---

*Which can create certain challenges for the historian.

began to take on a second function. Simple, innocent love between a mother and a daughter was a luxury Catherine could not afford. She needed Elisabeth's help. All those letters, however sincere, were also reminders to Elisabeth of her family: of the people she loved and of what she owed them.

In the meantime, Catherine found other ways to nurture friendship between realms and remind Elisabeth of home. Once Elisabeth arrived in Toledo, the gift-giving began, not only between mother and daughter but among their servants and households. There were things you simply could not get in Spain and things you couldn't get in France. Usually, the presents were luxuries big and small: Spanish carpets, for instance, "perfect for Chenonceaux," as Elisabeth wrote when she sent them to Catherine. Madame de Clermont sent Catherine dozens of Spanish gloves. Mary Stuart implored one of Catherine's secretaries to ask Limoges for bloomers, detailing precisely what she hoped for: one pair in "dark azure" and another in crimson, "made of silks from Granada."

Sometimes the presents were people. There was the favorite gardener Catherine sent to build a terrace for the Spanish royal retreat at Aranjuez. (The poor man died en route. In her next letter to Elisabeth, Catherine promised to send another.) Several months later, Elisabeth packed off a young Spanish maidservant to serve her mother, who professed herself quite pleased by the young woman's competence. On still another occasion, Elisabeth wrote on behalf of a lute player who came to her in Toledo via the Duchess of Savoy. Though the details remain unclear, the man had committed some sort of mischief in France, which had compelled his hasty departure from the kingdom. But he missed French food and wished one day to return, as Elisabeth explained to Catherine while recommending the good gentleman's services. Please pardon him "out of love for me," she wrote, perhaps a little homesick herself.[27]

There were French bedspreads Catherine wanted embroidered with Spanish silks, which—Elisabeth warned—would take time to sew properly. In Spain, Catherine's beauty balms were in high demand once it became clear to Madame de Clermont that the Spanish had nothing like them. Catherine's concoctions were soothing and complexion-perfecting, whipped with beaten egg whites and redolent with herbs.[28] A French woman through and through, Madame de Clermont didn't trust Spanish methods at all and was especially finicky about skincare.

Elisabeth's favorite gifts were the bust-sized portraits by Clouet that Catherine sent of herself and the younger children. "In the evenings, after her prayers," wrote one of Elisabeth's ladies to Catherine, "she never fails to curtsey first before your portrait, then before that of the king her brother and the others." Once, Catherine sent Elisabeth a psalter. "Your brother," she told her (it was likely nine-year-old Charles), "wanted to send you this rosary and to write in the psalter." When Elisabeth opened the covers a familiar scribble scrabble greeted her. "I couldn't let this letter leave," he wrote in another note, "without sending you my blessings and telling you that I am well." "You will recognize this handwriting," was all Catherine needed to say.[29]

No gift could quite match her mother's letters. Most of what we understand about the relationship between Catherine and Elisabeth comes from those missives. Nevertheless, much has been lost, if only because it is indecipherable to us. Although she never used it for Elisabeth, Catherine and her secretaries often wrote in code, especially if the topic concerned state secrets. But cipher was cumbersome even for the best cryptologists. "Write no more than is needful [when] writing the cipher," the English William Cecil once told an envoy, after finding decryption codes particularly laborious.[30] Women had other ways of veiling their meaning when writing about sensitive topics, like dropping hints and lacing their letters with sly allusions among more innocuous subjects.

Then, too, much of what passed between mother and daughter was oral, rather than written. For affairs both public and private, especially if they didn't concern the most secret of state secrets, the real message wasn't even in the letter. The letter was merely a placeholder: the real message was in the mind of the messenger.

Catherine scrawled, signed, folded, and sealed. Then, handing the letter to her messenger, she told him what she really meant to say. No shortage of spies lurked in royal courts, no dearth of courtiers or kitchen staff who might pilfer a letter for a favor or a handful of coins. One fix was a good porter: a trusty gentleman, skilled with a dagger, sword, or musket, and equipped with a strong memory and a good horse. Catherine often wrote barely the minimum, relying on the messenger himself to bring the real news. "Madame my daughter," Catherine wrote to Elisabeth, "I have charged this messenger with telling you many things, which will keep me from having to write you a longer letter." This "Sieur de Pasquier," this "Sieur de Saint Sulpice," or simply "this porter," "this courier," "this gentleman." These were the men Catherine trusted. Elisabeth knew that if a messenger carried a letter written in Catherine's hand, then she could believe what he told her.[31]

Yet in other letters Catherine spilled all her thoughts, no cipher or messenger required. Her pen scratched the surface of the paper, laying down a treasury of mother's advice and commands. *Do this, don't do that; eat this, not that; say this, not that; trust him, not her.* Her messengers barreled down the well-worn routes to Valladolid, Toledo, and Madrid with strict instructions to return with Elisabeth's replies.

Catherine's letters inspired mixed feelings in Elisabeth. Once, the Bishop of Limoges told Catherine that a homesick Elisabeth scolded him when too many days had passed without word from her mother. But Brantôme would say later that, whenever Elisabeth received a letter from Catherine, she would tremble in fear.[32]

In May 1560, Catherine wrote to Elisabeth for a political favor, the first she had explicitly asked of her daughter. Three months had passed since Elisabeth had arrived in Toledo. She had just celebrated her fourteenth birthday.

There was trouble in Scotland. The Dowager Queen, Marie de Guise, faced a rebellion. For years, unrest in Scotland had brewed beneath the surface. The Scots despised their "auld enemy" England, but they didn't much like their French allies, either. They yearned for independence, and resented that France treated Scotland like an inferior outpost.

Although the Scottish nobility admired Marie de Guise as regent—her temperance, intelligence, and tolerance of a growing Protestantism—lately they'd grown wary. During the last gasp of the Italian Wars, Marie de Guise had raised an army of Scots to fight for the French—a deeply unpopular move. Powerful Scottish nobles disliked how the regent packed her council with French officers; they began to see Marie de Guise as an operative for a French agenda and their young queen, Mary Stuart, as a tool for French ambition. Women were weak rulers, and foreign husbands to be feared. With Queen Mary wedded to the dauphin, would Scotland fall entirely to the French? After word leaked of the secret donations to France that Mary Stuart approved on the eve of her wedding in April 1558, Scottish nationalism flared anew.

If nationalism created fissures, religious differences cracked them wide open. By 1559, Protestantism had taken hold in Scotland, and a growing swathe of powerful Scottish nobles subscribed to the new faith. Whipped up by the fiery rhetoric of the Scottish Calvinist preacher John Knox—whose radical sermons transformed ambivalent lords into deeply believing converts—these noblemen saw Protestantism as key to Scottish independence. In 1557, several Scottish lords formed a faction known as the Lords of the Congregation that, in 1559, raised an army to oust Marie de Guise and install a Protestant government. Civil war soon exploded. Recognizing the strength of the French military, the Lords sent Knox to England seeking Queen Elizabeth's aid in the name of her coreligionists.

Elizabeth Tudor had both religious and political reasons to support the Protestant Scottish Lords. Committed to returning her own realm to the Reform after the disastrous Catholic reign of Mary Tudor, she relished the notion of a Protestant regime running her neighbor to the north. Her own northern provinces remained staunchly Catholic—Protestant allies in Scotland would hem them in. She looked forward to a new friendship between Scotland and England, reversing centuries of animosity and severing the Auld Alliance with France. Most important of all, a Catholic defeat in Scotland would deflate Mary Stuart's hereditary claims to England.

This was an especially sore point with Elizabeth Tudor. The daughter of Henry VIII and Anne Boleyn, Queen Elizabeth was widely considered by both English and foreign Catholics to be illegitimate, with no right to the throne. She hated that Francis II of France and Mary Stuart made a point of crossing the arms of France and Scotland with those of England at every opportunity—as if

Mary were already the legitimate Queen of England and Elizabeth a mere usurper. A Protestant victory in Scotland would nip that arrogance in the bud and reinforce Elizabeth's strength on her own throne.

Elizabeth hesitated for a few weeks—the expense of war, the cost in blood, the humiliation and political risk if defeated—then sent an army to Scotland.

The English queen waged a tough war. In his role as King of Scotland, Francis II vowed to crush the Scots rebels and their English allies, but lacked the necessary troops. Just across his southern border was Spain, France's newest friend, a stalwart Catholic kingdom. Surely Philip II could appreciate the need to punish a rebellious outpost.

Now, in May, Catherine took it in hand to ask her daughter for help. "Madame my daughter," she began, "you will hear from the Bishop of Limoges the trouble I am having. The Queen of England is ready to do something mad, unless the King, Monsieur my good son, your husband, puts a stop to it. For this reason, *m'amye*, I must ask you: if you have any influence with your husband, you must speak to him in such a way so that he makes his intentions clear to [Queen Elizabeth], so she finds it quite disagreeable to ignite such a fire in Scotland. As for my part, I can assure you that, for as long as I live, I will ensure that the King my son, your brother, will never start any trouble, and moreover will think it a great misfortune if we lose the peace . . ."

Ultimately, she found it simplest just to tell Elisabeth what to do. Show Philip my letter, she wrote, "where he will find my most affectionate commendations."[33]

It was a gamble. At fourteen years old, just three months a bride, what capital did Elisabeth have with her husband? "God be thanked," Catherine wrote to Limoges, "I always believed when she undertook any matter that she would perform it well; yet because she is young, she does not yet have sufficient experience or knowledge of the world. I know, then, how much your wise counsel has benefited her."[34] Unlike for a young king, there was no regent or council to make decisions on Elisabeth's behalf. Barely in her teens, Elisabeth found herself in the thick of the morass fulminating in Scotland and France. In time, Catherine hoped, she would learn to use charm and affection to shape Philip's thinking.

In the meantime, the Queen Mother kept writing, dictating, commanding, putting words into her daughter's mouth, sending her letters meant for Philip's eyes.

———

If Elisabeth de Valois followed her mother's instructions, she failed at her task: Philip would not agree to support the French in their Scottish forays. Though the treaty of Cateau-Cambrésis ended the Italian Wars, Philip was still fighting them—the conflict had simply become a cold war. He worried that, with Spanish help, the French might actually succeed in subduing Scotland, then turn around and invade England, ousting Elizabeth Tudor from the throne and replacing her with Mary Stuart. England would become a French territory and Philip would have handed them their victory.

Philip politely refused the French, holding to his tacit support of Elizabeth Tudor.[35]

In the end, the conflict in Scotland fizzled out. Discouraged by a few setbacks on the battlefield, Elizabeth decided to sue for peace, while the French, preoccupied by their own civil tensions, soured on the foreign war. The Treaty of Edinburgh, drafted in July 1560, required Queen Mary and King Francis to cease crossing English arms with Scottish and French ones and insisted Mary renounce her claims to the English throne. The French, moreover, would withdraw all troops from Scotland.

Lastly, and most pleasing to the Scots Lords of the Congregation, the treaty compelled Mary to form a new council for her government. It would consist of twelve members: six councillors of Mary's choosing, and six others approved by the Protestant Lords. All foreigners (meaning Frenchmen) were barred from holding posts as officers. It was a blow for the Auld Alliance.

The treaty satisfied the English, though Queen Elizabeth wondered irritably to her secretary William Cecil why the return of Calais hadn't been part of the negotiations. The Guises, eager to pull their regiments back to France and thankful not to have to surrender Calais, also consented to the terms.[36]

If anyone lost the war in Scotland, it was Mary, Queen of Scots. Forced to renounce her claims to England in favor of Queen

Elizabeth, Mary also gave ground on her authority with the formation of the Scottish council. It is tempting to wonder whether Marie de Guise might have secured more favorable terms for her daughter. But Marie died in Scotland in June 1560, just weeks before the end of the war, never having returned to France as she had hoped.

In theory, Elizabeth Tudor and the Protestant Scots emerged the victors: Protestants gained a foothold in the Scottish government and Elizabeth secured her throne against Mary's pretensions.

Mary and Francis, however, would not surrender quite so easily. As Queen Elizabeth would soon discover, the young Scottish queen kept one strategy in reserve: although Mary and Francis agreed to the terms, they refused to ratify the Treaty of Edinburgh.

12

KING'S HEART, QUEEN'S BODY
Spain, 1560

Elisabeth soon discovered that life as the Catholic Queen was tightly controlled. Audiences were choreographed, greetings were scripted, and outings orchestrated according to a strict protocol, from the ornamentation on the horses' saddles down to the rank and file of litters, ladies, and lackeys. Even within Elisabeth's own household, ceremony reigned, while appraising eyes, both French and Spanish, followed her through the day. Since she was so young, the adults around her were especially vigilant. Madame de Clermont stuck to her side. Hovering nearby, her *camarera mayor*, the stodgy Countess of Ureigna, supervised her ladies-in-waiting, all of whom slept and ate together under the wary eyes of chaperones. Then there was Elisabeth's majordomo, the Count of Alba. The frosty count turned out to be a keeper of queens. Every evening after Elisabeth retired to bed, the Count of Alba would lock the door to her chamber and hand the key to the Countess of Ureigna. During the day, her chamber door was opened only with his permission. At night, armed sentinels stood guard.[1]

Even Princess Juana served more as a supervisor than a true friend to the new queen, at least in the beginning. Ten years older than Elisabeth, Juana had grown up under the rigorous etiquette of the Spanish court imposed by her father, Charles V. Known to be a tad pretentious, Juana liked things just so, and expected the same of Elisabeth. And although she was gentle with her young sister-in-law, the Princess probably conveyed much of what she learned about Elisabeth to Philip.

In Toledo, Elisabeth's days unfurled in long innocent hours. Some hours were brighter than others. Elisabeth delighted in her art lessons with Sofonisba Anguissola and proved herself a talented student. She would "soon surpass even the lady who teaches her, who is a real master," Madame de Vineux prattled to Catherine, keen to flatter both the new queen and her mother. The Bishop of Limoges thought he detected flashes of real brilliance in the young queen. He sent Catherine a particularly impressive pencil drawing Elisabeth had made. "Do you recognize it?" he asked. She'd sketched a picture of the bishop himself.[2]

Sometime during their first year in Spain, Sofonisba painted Elisabeth's portrait, a large-format, three-quarter-length painting destined for the gallery of royal portraits in the country palace at El Pardo. She captured a picture of blooming royal youth: Elisabeth wears Spanish black with pink accents, her arms elegant in pendulous Spanish sleeves softened with lace. Over her right arm hangs a marten's pelt hung with jeweled chains. It was the perfect accessory—jewels for sparkle, fur to keep fleas at bay. Elisabeth's lips barely curve, but her eyes smile. By then, Sofonisba had become one of her favorites.[3]

Art was a joy, but Elisabeth couldn't draw all day. She passed her afternoons reading or redecorating her *cabinet*, spent hours answering correspondence, writing letters to her mother. Dutifully, she practiced her Spanish with her tutors, and sent a few notes in her new language to Catherine. But Elisabeth had never been given to rigorous hours of study. Even years later, her written Spanish was riddled with errors.[4] After a few Spanish letters, she went back to writing to Catherine in French.

Compliant by nature, Elisabeth followed Princess Juana every morning to Mass. Afterward, she chatted with her ladies, listened to the viola, or—her favorite—played cards, rolled dice, cast lots.

It was pleasant, it became habitual—and a little monotonous, although during the first few months Elisabeth had a lot to learn. Besides the new language, there were new customs and clothes. She paid meticulous attention to her outfits, following Catherine's strict warnings that if she wished to satisfy snobbish Spanish expectations, she should appear nothing less than majestic. Elisabeth arrived in Spain with dozens of dresses, and she often changed them once or twice a day, her figure molded, shaped, garnished, adorned. Already she was mastering new sartorial details, acquiring new frills and plumes. Like his Burgundian ancestors, King Philip preferred black, a pious yet regally chic color. Elisabeth ordered her own black gowns, heavy on the velvet and brocade. She added ornaments to her hair, and high cork-soled shoes. She cinched her frocks at the hips with wide jeweled girdles, having discovered the Spanish thought French ones were too skimpy. Elisabeth also learned what she could get away with. As Madame de Clermont explained to Catherine in one of her diligent descriptions of the young queen's daily outfits, if she wasn't going to see the king that day, Elisabeth sometimes wore the same gown both morning *and* afternoon—no doubt a welcome respite from the tedious hours required to stitch and pin her into her clothes.[5]

Not every gilded day was the same as the last. There were carnivals and banquets, new games and new faces. Elisabeth soon received visits from Don Carlos and his young uncle, Don Juan, an illegitimate son of Charles V whom Philip brought to court in the autumn of 1559; the two boys would become her friends. Still, it was a relief for Elisabeth to spend time at the royal hunting estate at Valsaín in the foothills of Segovia, where the woods teemed with ibises and wild boar. She especially enjoyed the summer palace at Aranjuez, just a few miles south of Madrid. It was a beautiful place, a hybrid place, marked by Spain's past and present. The palace still bore traces of Moorish architecture, remnants of the centuries before the Reconquista when Philip's great-grandparents, Isabel of Castile and Ferdinand of Aragon, united their Catholic crowns. Grand fountains, chiseled by Spanish sculptors, ornamented gardens flush with fruit and nuts—gardens soon to be transformed by one of the French gardeners Catherine was sending as a gift.[6]

At Aranjuez, away from eagle-eyed diplomats and ambassadors, Elisabeth and her companions could relax. Of course, Catherine kept close tabs on her daughter, thanks to Madame de Clermont, who maintained a diary of Elisabeth's activities even on holiday. One afternoon at Aranjuez (Madame de Clermont wrote), Elisabeth and Princess Juana went for a ride and discovered a field full of grazing goats and cows. Why not try to milk a cow? Finding themselves without a pail, they improvised. After milking the creature into Juana's hat, they tore up pieces of bread, dunked them into the warm froth, and gobbled them down. Philip seemed at ease at Aranjuez, Madame de Clermont said. He spent more time in Elisabeth's company, sometimes visiting her after his afternoon nap, or accompanying her and Juana on their promenades alongside the river—Philip on his mount, the ladies in a litter. Once, he even interrupted his lunch so he could join Elisabeth at her own. This was a marked breach of his usual protocol and surely a sign, thought Madame de Clermont, that Philip enjoyed Elisabeth's company.[7]

In Toledo, Elisabeth's days were more sedate. In Madrid—where the court moved in 1561 after building works finished on the royal *alcázar*—things were better but not by much. Elisabeth tried to spice things up for herself and the court, to bring a little French elegance to the capital. She spent mountains of cash on lavish entertainments, the kind she remembered from the courts of her father and brother. Many of the Spanish courtiers were glad to see a little more glitz. Those who had returned from Flanders to Spain with Philip in 1559 found their native country wanting, especially compared to the chic court of the Netherlands. The Count of Feria, who'd spent years abroad, found Spain rather tiresome. "Spain is the most backward province on the face of the earth," he complained, "and the devil take me if I do not round up half of all I have and return to Flanders."[8]

Even Elisabeth admitted she was sometimes bored. She missed the lighter air of the French court, the carefree conversations between girls and boys. Here in Spain, the Bishop of Limoges wrote, "visits . . . are not so much the fashion as in France." Thanks to the frigid Count of Alba and the hostile Countess of Ureigna, the queen's household could be tense, the atmosphere stifling. It was all a little gloomy.[9]

"I have to say, Madame," Elisabeth once wrote to Catherine, "if not for the kindness of my company here, and if I didn't have the good fortune of seeing my lord the king every day, I would find this place one of the dreariest in the world." Then, she thought better of her grumbling. "But I assure you, Madame," she rushed to say, "I have such a good husband and am so fortunate that, even if it were a hundred times worse, I wouldn't be upset at all."[10]

It was not for Elisabeth to complain. It was not about her happiness. Elisabeth understood the importance of her marriage to the Spanish–French alliance, but for a fourteen-year-old, the stakes must have felt more personal. More than anything, she wished to please her mother. And if she wanted to please Catherine, she had to please Philip.

Was she pleasing him? No one could say for sure. Madame de Clermont, Madame de Vineux, and the Bishop of Limoges duly reported what they believed were signs of real affection. Philip was respectful and attentive, they said. If Elisabeth fell ill, he sent his best physicians and came to her bedside every day. If she wanted to speak with him, he always obliged her. If she wished for spectacles and balls, he paid for them. At night, he frequently came to her chamber. On the surface, all seemed well.

Yet Catherine clearly believed that Philip had not yet taken Elisabeth into his confidence, because one or way or another, she kept asking the question and demanding an answer. "The queen your daughter and the king her husband have continued in good health," wrote Madame de Vineux in August 1560. "Their good understanding continues, and it seems to me that the queen has lately taken the courageous step to speak more intimately and openly about certain matters of state to her husband."[11] But Elisabeth's courage would achieve nothing for France if Philip wasn't listening to her.

So Elisabeth stood quietly day after day while her ladies laced her into elegant gowns. She kept putting herself in Philip's path, hoping to build on a word and a smile. She kept up her outings with Princess Juana and welcomed Philip into her bedchamber. The French ladies declared that these tactics were working, but from the tenor of their letters, Catherine must have suspected they were just guessing.

Others shared her suspicions. Diplomats noticed how Philip often traveled on state matters and left Elisabeth behind. One Venetian thought he saw nothing but frigid courtesy between husband and wife, noting that Philip gave Elisabeth no authority, not even "in the governing of her own household." And in an otherwise enthusiastic letter to Catherine, one lady carelessly let slip that, even at Aranjuez, Philip often retreated for long afternoons with his councillors, leaving Elisabeth to her own affairs.[12]

Catherine likely guessed the truth: when it came time to do the real work of the kingdom, Philip retreated to his papers, leaving Elisabeth to play with Princess Juana and their ladies.

It was a vulnerable time for Elisabeth. In many ways she was still a child. "After dinner, Her Majesty spent some time dressing her dolls in her *cabinet*," Madame de Clermont told Catherine. During her first year in Spain, she was still growing, quite literally. Madame de Clermont was happy to report in the autumn of 1560 that Elisabeth had now grown taller than Clermont herself. The girl had filled out, too, such that every dress in her wardrobe had to be taken out by the space of four fingers. Not to worry, Madame de Clermont reassured Catherine: in Spain "they do not have high regard for thin women." Slowly, Elisabeth was taking on the contours of a woman, growing so busty that the Spanish expressed surprise. "They find it quite remarkable at her age," Madame de Clermont noted.[13]

If Madame de Clermont was anxious to report the good news, it was likely because she so often had to account for the bad, at least when it came to Elisabeth's health. Although Elisabeth was growing taller and plumper, she had also fallen ill in worrisome ways.

To Catherine's alarm, Elisabeth had sickened within days of her arrival in Spain. On February 23, 1559, Catherine received a full report from the Bishop of Limoges. Elisabeth's illness had taken everyone by surprise. One evening, she was happily dancing with her ladies; by the next morning, she'd developed a raging fever with "pustules or blood blisters" dotting her forehead. The immediate fear was smallpox—at best a potentially disfiguring disease, at worst a deadly one. Fortunately, the fever waned and the blisters began to fade shortly after her team of physicians bled her from the arm.*

The scalpel had sliced her flesh, a thin stream of vermilion pooling in the basin. Elisabeth "tolerated the procedure virtuously and very bravely," Limoges assured Catherine, who hated the idea of phlebotomy but who, hundreds of miles away, found herself powerless to stop it. The disease turned out to be short lived and not the dreaded smallpox.

---

*Philip assigned a phalanx of physicians to his young queen, but Catherine had also sent several doctors of her own choosing with Elisabeth when she left for Spain. Catherine believed French doctors would understand Elisabeth's constitution better and, perhaps more importantly, tell Catherine the truth.

In the sixteenth century, people believed in the medical theory of the four humors, which held that a person's health depended on the proper balance of four liquids coursing through the body: blood, phlegm, yellow bile, and black bile. A mild predominance of any one liquid determined temperament. A person dominated by blood, for example, might be "sanguine" or cheerful. A person tending toward bile might anger easily. A more severe disequilibrium among the humors, however, was the cause of disease. An imbalance could occur for many reasons, including a change in environment or diet.

The Bishop of Limoges believed the change in climate had triggered Elisabeth's illness, "the heat of the country and this change in air: since the air of this country is like its meats, very subtle and sharp, such that few foreigners can escape such illnesses, especially during the spring which is coming on strong." He was sure she would soon adapt to her new country. In the meantime, the dry Spanish air had left her "excessively full," meaning she had too much blood. When Elisabeth's nose bled toward the end of her illness—a natural evacuation process according to Renaissance doctors—Limoges thought he had been proven right.[14]

As Limoges predicted, Elisabeth began to adapt to her new kingdom, but she was not out of the woods. Less than one year later, in early January 1561, both Elisabeth and her cousin Mademoiselle de Montpensier fell sick. This time, the doctors were sure it was smallpox. Ribbons of weeping blisters erupted across Elisabeth's face and body, and a high fever set in for over a week.[15] The Spanish physicians bled her once again. Philip sent a special messenger to inform Catherine and reassure her simultaneously that Elisabeth was already on the mend. Yet anything could transpire in the week it took for a letter to travel between realms. Only after Philip wrote again confirming Elisabeth's recovery did Catherine's concern abate.

Worried that Philip might find reason to repudiate Elisabeth, Catherine shifted her focus to the state of her daughter's face. "Take care to preserve her eyes and keep her from scarring," Catherine warned Limoges, as afraid of blindness as she was of pockmarks. She recommended a mixture of pigeon's blood and cream to heal the skin and sent a soothing balm to Madame de Clermont. For weeks thereafter, Madame de Clermont bathed Elisabeth daily in donkey's milk and rubbed ointment onto her face and hands where the scabs were particularly tenacious. She'd had so many pustules, Clermont said, "it was impossible to have more."[16]

As for Elisabeth herself, Catherine ordered her daughter to rest indoors for twenty days "because if you go out too soon, the stomach flux that can result is quite dangerous."[17]

Ensconced in her chambers, Elisabeth could gaze at the family portraits Catherine had sent. She had lined them up: her mother first, then her siblings from oldest to youngest. She tried to joke about her illness. Mademoiselle de Montpensier "had fewer blisters on her whole body than I had on one hand," she wrote to Catherine, "and she is so small, she really could be called 'small pox.'" As for herself, Elisabeth told her mother, she was healing well.[18]

But in truth, her recovery was slow and miserable. Well into February, she suffered from fevers, which caused her at one point to "vomit three full bowls of phlegm." The smallpox had triggered some old complaints. On top of the scars and indigestion, her head ached with migraines and her bowels throbbed with constipation. Madame de Clermont worried so much about hemorrhoids that she gave Elisabeth an enema of her own formulation. The migraines, however, were another matter. "She was doing much better than usual with her headaches," Madame de Clermont fretted to Catherine. "But I ran out of marjoram seeds, which is why I must ask you to send me some by the first messenger since the season for planting them here has passed and it is no longer possible to find any."[19] Evidently, the good matron had dipped into her supply more than once.

***

The headaches weren't new. Neither were the constipation, the churning stomach, nor the days in bed. Well before the first pustule swelled on Elisabeth's skin, Madame de Clermont was attending to the girl's fragile health. As Clermont's letters to Catherine disclosed, Elisabeth often felt nauseated and threw up, sometimes with little forewarning. She was prone to nosebleeds. Sometimes she fainted. The bouts of sickness came in waves; between them Elisabeth enjoyed sound health, even vigor. But when they appeared, the symptoms were as upsetting as they were chronic: in all of Elisabeth's years in Spain, they never really disappeared.[20]

We cannot know the exact nature of Elisabeth's illness, how a physician might diagnose her today. Witnesses from the distant past—both casual observers and medical professionals—are unreliable narrators, their description of symptoms hazy, colored through their own Renaissance views of medicine and anatomy. Most striking in the surviving letters is the oblique way in which Madame de Clermont, Catherine, and even the Bishop of Limoges refer to the symptoms of Elisabeth's condition. Their letters whisper. They seem to speak as if hinting at something they all know about, something that may have reared its head while Elisabeth was still in France. The letters sound as if Madame de Clermont was tasked with keeping something insidious under control. Was she also tasked with keeping it out of sight?

———

Elisabeth de Valois wasn't the only royal teen to fall seriously ill from vague and recurring complaints. In England, Elizabeth Tudor fought through several debilitating bouts of dropsy in her late teens and early twenties, particularly during the reign of her older sister. Beginning in her own teenaged years, Mary Tudor famously battled difficult periods and a tormenting malady made up of myriad symptoms; the sickness came upon her seasonally, so regularly that Mary called it her "old complaint" and others nicknamed it her "old guest." And despite the glowing health of her early childhood, the teenaged Mary, Queen of Scots, sometimes struggled with fever and gastric illness, along with a jabbing pain in her side. For the rest of her life, these symptoms would appear on and off, especially during moments of stress.[21]

In March 1559, a few months before Elisabeth de Valois's wedding, Mary was struck by some sort of fainting illness. The following May, Throckmorton noted the young Scots queen "looks very ill on it; very pale and green, and therewith all short-breathed." Rumors circulated that she didn't have long to live. Mary survived, but the stomach upsets continued, as did the swooning, such that she sometimes had to be revived with *acqua composite*—that is, smelling salts and spirits.[22]

One of these fainting spells occurred just after the death of Henry II, in the summer of 1559, sparking surprise among Spanish envoys in

France and alarm among the Guises and Catherine. In August, Mary was with Catherine when Ambassador Chantonnay and the Duke of Alba paid one of their visits of condolence to the bereaved Queen Mother. When the two men arrived, Chantonnay saw immediately that Mary was ill. She swooned from her "indisposition," he wrote later to King Philip, so weak that the cardinal was forced to escort her from the room. "She had all but lost her senses so they let her rest on the King's bed, as that was the nearest bedchamber," Chantonnay wrote. "Of course, it was such a shame to see her so ill and pale."

Chantonnay might have seen more than he should have before the cardinal whisked Mary away. The ambassador didn't dwell on the moment for long in his letter, but his keen ears had picked up on one more detail. "They call it 'her pale color,'" he wrote of Mary's illness. Whatever plagued her was chronic enough for the French to give it a name.[23]

While some scholars suggest Mary suffered from the blood ailment porphyria, others point to a disease that was attracting attention in the sixteenth century and was thought to affect teenaged girls and young women. In England, they called it "greensickness." In the Netherlands, they called it "white fever." Among physicians, its Latin name was "chlorosis." Many people knew it as the "disease of the virgins"—more a descriptor of age than of a patient's sexual status. Indeed, some historians believe the disease was called "greensickness" not because of the color of the skin (though Throckmorton described Mary as looking "pale and green") but because the patients were invariably "green"—meaning they were young.[24]

Renaissance doctors considered the bodies of women and young girls to be especially hot, moist and leaky, prone to excess blood, especially as they began to menstruate. In a healthy female, this excess blood left the body every month through a woman's period or, in a nursing mother, through mother's milk. Doctors believed menstrual blood could also leave the body through nosebleeds or vomiting. If a woman didn't bleed regularly, doctors could facilitate the process through phlebotomy: this was the procedure Elisabeth de Valois endured during her first weeks in Spain.

But what of greensick girls? Many sixteenth-century physicians believed a weak liver in a greensick body produced too much water and not enough good blood. All agreed on the symptoms: a

KING'S HEART, QUEEN'S BODY

greensick girl was usually in her teens. She suffered from headaches and faintness. She had trouble with digestion and would pick at her food or eat strange things. Two symptoms were particularly striking. A greensick girl often possessed an ashen face, a "pale color." And, filled with water instead of healthy blood, a greensick girl rarely, if ever, got her period.

Greensickness was a disease produced by a certain cultural moment, a way for doctors in the sixteenth century to classify a specific set of symptoms and behaviors. It had a long heyday nonetheless; physicians diagnosed it well into the nineteenth century. But historians have noted another curious detail about the disease, one that might tell us something about the kinds of symptoms doctors were observing: as a diagnosis, greensickness began to wane with the rise of other maladies that plagued adolescent girls and young women. The most important of these "new" diseases were anorexia nervosa and bulimia.[25]

Catherine de' Medici never gave a name to Elisabeth de Valois's ailments. There is no mention of anything like an "old guest" or "greensickness," not even a descriptive name like "her pale color." Catherine was secretive about her daughter's health. No document records anything unusual before Elisabeth left France, although her departure for Spain had been delayed in part by a "stomach flux," and she clearly suffered ongoing headaches, nosebleeds, and what Catherine and the Bishop of Limoges both described obscurely as "fullness." Catherine likely feared that Philip would see Elisabeth as damaged goods. When her daughter's infirmities persisted during Elisabeth's first year in Spain, Catherine's anxiety only mounted.

There were other signs of disorder, hints that Elisabeth's daily habits were less than healthful. Sometimes Catherine found Elisabeth self-indulgent, ready to "take to her bed as soon as she felt the least bit ill." She neglected to exercise. She had a particular fondness for meat and a bad habit of snacking too much, which Catherine believed brought on the dreaded vomiting. Others in Elisabeth's circle also noticed these bad habits. Soon after Elisabeth recovered from smallpox, the Bishop of Limoges felt compelled to mention the tiniest of concerns in one of his letters to Catherine.

"I wish she would govern herself in a slightly more orderly fashion," he wrote. "Not that she isn't restrained enough, but she gets up at uncertain hours and sometimes, since she is young and has a good appetite, she can't help but eat outside of regular hours. I've asked her doctor to write to you so that you might mention something about it to her."[26] Ever the diplomat, Limoges was careful not to put too poor a spin on things. Still, that he bothered to mention these habits to Catherine at all—and asked the physician to write—shows the level of his concern.

Of all the "symptoms" that afflicted Elisabeth, one was particularly worrisome to Catherine well beyond her daughter's first year in Spain: like many a greensick girl, the teenaged Elisabeth rarely if ever got her period.

———

Had Elisabeth menstruated at all before she left France? If Catherine was late to puberty, as some historians contend, perhaps her daughter followed suit. Then again, quite possibly Elisabeth had menstruated but only sporadically, as happens to young girls. Although custom called for a girl to begin her period before marriage, in the wake of Henry II's death, Catherine had focused solely on maintaining the French–Spanish agreement. Though she delayed sending Elisabeth to Spain, Catherine likely feared waiting too long would give Philip time to have second thoughts or an excuse to break the treaty, especially if he knew the reason.

Catherine charged Madame de Clermont with keeping track of Elisabeth's cycle. As first lady of the bedchamber, Madame de Vineux, too, claimed to know when Elisabeth bled and when she didn't. Both ladies counted the weeks between any sign of a period, and the days any bleeding lasted. Often, to Catherine's great disappointment, those weeks stretched to months.

The Queen Mother may have received conflicting reports. In September 1560, the Bishop of Limoges wrote a winking letter to France announcing that Elisabeth had fallen ill again. This time, however, the doctors believed "it would be a nine months' illness, though it's impossible to know for sure for a few days yet."[27] Catherine was skeptical. "I fear it may not be so, given the doctor's letters, that rather it is some fullness of humors that is making her nauseated or pale . . . I have great fear that it is all nothing." She followed up with

Madame de Clermont, but Catherine's doubts proved well founded. After that September, no one again mentioned a pregnancy, and soon Catherine was issuing, once more, a familiar command to Madame de Clermont: "Send me word the moment her period arrives."[28]

But Elisabeth's period didn't arrive, not the next month, or during the months thereafter. The following January, as Elisabeth recovered from smallpox, Clermont wrote that Elisabeth's doctors were bathing her "to make her periods come." Even after Elisabeth began menstruating more often (likely sometime in mid-1561), her cycle was unpredictable. "Her periods aren't as settled as we might wish," a disappointed Madame de Vineux would write as late as the autumn of 1561.[29]

There was little Catherine could do but wait, her daughter's affliction a painful reminder of her own years of barrenness, with even greater political consequences. And there were other mysteries. Were husband and wife even having sex? No one writing to Catherine could say for sure. Surprisingly, Madame de Clermont and Madame de Vineux were not privy to what went on, exactly, between the sheets. According to Madame de Vineux, the king usually spent the night with his wife unless Elisabeth was sick, or Philip was away on state affairs. But then the chamber doors snapped shut and the ladies-in-waiting were left to guess what happened, along with everyone else. True, they saw signs of affection between the couple—their shared lunches! Their pleasant conversations! Philip's graciousness!—but Catherine suspected Philip simply followed Spanish rules of etiquette. She does not seem to have posed the question directly to Elisabeth.

Someone knew what was happening in the bedroom. "A person who is in a position to know some of these things," Madame de Vineux would confess in early 1561, said that although King Philip "loved [Elisabeth] as much as possible," he hesitated to touch his young wife lest he "inconvenience her" and hurt her with his "strength"—a reference to the size of Philip's penis.[30]

How much did Philip know about Elisabeth's period? He seems to have understood something about menstruation. Before Philip married Maria-Mañuela of Portugal, a counselor had told him that "according to her ladies, [she] . . . has been very regular with her period since she began to have it, which is, they say, the most important thing for having children."[31] Whatever the case, it was becoming disastrously clear to Catherine that Philip visited his wife at night merely out of conjugal duty, to pay his respects. Perhaps he even crawled between the sheets. Yet he likely went no further. He sensed he was sleeping with a child.

———

It was an old story. Only if Elisabeth bore a child would her place at the Spanish court be assured. Until then, her security depended entirely on Philip's goodwill. A bride who didn't menstruate—who couldn't conceive—was easy to send away. A king's affection alone could save her, as Catherine herself had learned long ago.

Until Elisabeth gave birth, Catherine trusted Madame de Clermont to steer her daughter through the maze of Spanish court politics. Catherine and Clermont had an understanding: "I ask you to continue sending me news of my daughter," Catherine wrote, "and I will take care of your affairs as if they were my own."[32] And so, when she learned Madame de Vineux was threatening Madame de Clermont's place in Elisabeth's household, Catherine panicked. Then she grew enraged.

Rumblings of trouble first reached her in November 1560 when Don Antonio de Toledo, a loyal follower of the Duke of Alba, came to Paris.* The crafty Don Antonio let slip some salacious gossip: Queen Elisabeth paid undue attention to Madame de Vineux, preferring her to all other ladies, even to the blue-blooded Mademoiselle de Montpensier, a royal Bourbon princess and a guest of Spain. Elisabeth devoted all her attention to her maids of honor but precious little to the matrons. Bickering had erupted among the French ladies. The Spanish court buzzed with the scandal, and word of it had leaked to King Philip himself.

Whipping up letters frothing with rage, Catherine sent the Bishop of Limoges scurrying to inquire further. What he discovered was far worse than anything Don Antonio had reported. The trouble turned around a vacancy in Elisabeth's household. Her beloved nurse had

———

*His secret mission, endorsed by Philip II and apparently unbeknownst to Catherine, was to prevent the establishment of a Protestant church council in France.

returned to France, and Madame de Vineux wished to take her place. As the ranking French lady-in-waiting, however—and acutely aware that she was supposed to keep close watch over Elisabeth—Madame de Clermont wanted the role for herself. Madame de Vineux had said outrageous things about Madame de Clermont. The infighting got so ugly that Madame de Vineux accused Clermont of pilfering 10,000 crowns from Elisabeth.[33]

According to Limoges, Madame de Vineux felt no compunction. She deserved the promotion, Vineux said. She was popular with the Spanish ladies. As it was, she was already "the queen's intimate servant at night," and besides, she knew "all the queen's secrets."[34]

All the queen's secrets. It had the whiff of blackmail. "Everyone will try to procure his interest and advancement from his master," wrote a cynical Limoges. Catherine was dismayed. She issued a stern warning: by no means should Madame de Vineux threaten Madame de Clermont, nor "should she get involved in the affairs of the queen my daughter." She promptly commanded Limoges to fix the problem quickly, whatever it took—never mind displeasing the Spanish. And if he even dared *think* of lying to her about the state of affairs: "You should also know I have spies who will tell me everything that happens over there."[35]

Catherine had counted on Madame de Clermont as a steadying hand; now that steady hand had stirred the pot. As Catherine knew well, the Spanish already despised the presence of Elisabeth's bloated French retinue. The Countess of Ureigna had never warmed to the French ladies after the fiasco in Pamplona. She particularly resented Madame de Clermont, who stayed constantly at Elisabeth's side, and performed duties that the countess believed were rightfully hers. The spat among the French ladies would only cement the Spanish belief that the French should go home. But for Elisabeth's sake—for the sake of the marriage—Catherine desperately needed Madame de Clermont to stay.

The Bishop of Limoges understood the gravity of the situation. Clearly, Madame de Clermont was "essential during the young years of the queen, until God gives her children."[36]

He went to work. The first step was to win over the Countess of Ureigna. Rolling up his sleeves, Limoges raced back and forth between Elisabeth and the French-friendly Ruy Gómez, making acrobatic arrangements to get Madame de Clermont, the Countess of Ureigna, and King Philip all together in the same room. Then, as pre-scripted, Elisabeth took the spotlight. Playing her role as peacemaker, she deftly praised the devoted service of both ladies to the king. Philip nodded his approval. To all appearances, the French noblewoman and her Spanish counterpart called a truce. Limoges believed he'd salvaged Madame de Clermont's position in Elisabeth's household. As for Madame de Vineux, she would no doubt desist now that Philip had clearly given Madame de Clermont his blessing. For the first time in days, Limoges felt he could rest easy.

Limoges wrote a detailed letter to Catherine in late November, his tone faintly self-congratulatory.[37] In early December, however, the ambassador received an important visitor.

King Philip had a way of deploying his grandees and courtiers almost as if in code. Whenever the king wished to convey a friendly message to the French, he would send Ruy Gómez. But for a warning, he would send the Duke of Alba.

On this winter day, it was the Duke of Alba who appeared at Limoges' door.

The next day, a subdued Limoges wrote again to Catherine: Madame de Clermont would have to go. According to Alba, the grandees of Spain were "scandalized" to see their queen handled by a "foreigner." King Philip felt the need to make at least some concessions to his nobles. "They become so difficult in other serious matters," Alba had said, "if they are not appeased in such trivial ones."

More importantly, Alba explained, King Philip adored the culture of Spain. He wished for Elisabeth, whom he dearly loved, to become "entirely Spanish," which Madame de Clermont's presence prevented. If Elisabeth became a true Spanish woman she would "govern her husband all the better," Alba said, "because [Philip] never loved his previous wives as much as he loved her."[38] Surely Catherine could understand that Madame de Clermont's presence spoiled the good understanding between husband and wife. As both the Duke of Alba and King Philip knew, this good understanding was the very thing Catherine wanted most.

Catherine was caught. King Philip saw Madame de Clermont for what she was: Catherine's surrogate in Spain. He saw how Limoges had contrived to keep her there. Alba's warning was Philip's way of telling his mother-in-law to back off. Seeing they had no other choice, Limoges recommended sending Madame de Clermont home and replacing her with Madame de Vineux. He believed the young woman was loyal. And after all, she was already intimately familiar with Elisabeth.

Catherine had lost this battle. Relenting, she agreed to Madame de Clermont's departure. Yet the damage was done. Catherine was furious at Madame de Clermont for bringing scandal to Elisabeth's household. She was furious at the Bishop of Limoges for not doing more to protect Madame de Clermont. Her anger also fell upon Elisabeth. Obviously, there were lessons her daughter hadn't learned.

At the height of the affair, Elisabeth opened a letter to find the following:

"Madame my daughter, someone from Spain has told me that your ladies can't get along, and that Madame de Vineux is trying as hard as possible to get involved in your affairs. This is marvelously bad; you should look at the letters I am sending to Madame de Vineux and Madame de Clermont about this. You must do what I told you to do when you left, for you know of what great consequence it is if anyone found out what you have. If your husband knew it, you can be sure that he would never see you."

If anyone found out what you have. Was Catherine speaking of the quarrels among the ladies in her household? Or something else that plagued the young queen? Five centuries later, this phrase is still fraught with mystery. But Elisabeth no doubt understood what her mother meant. Catherine went on:

"Although I believe Madame de Vineux may be loyal to you, yet have I heard that she is quite fond of presents and favors. When this is the case, sometimes a lady like that forgets what she owes her mistress in order to please the master—and your husband has more ways to please her than you have.

"I've also heard from those who have seen your household that you favor Madame de Vineux more than any of your other ladies. Indeed, that you do not pay attention to anyone else as much as you do Madame de Vineux—not [Mademoiselle de Montpensier], or even her mother, or Madame de Clermont. And now all the Spanish and even your husband are talking about it and laughing at you.

"Truth be told, given the rank you hold and where you are, this looks quite bad, and shows too much that you are still a child, managing the ladies the way you do and in front of other people. When you are alone in your chamber, in private, enjoy yourself and play with Madame de Vineux and the other ladies. But in front of others, you must honor and pay attention to your cousin and Madame de Clermont. Listen to them carefully, for both are wise and want nothing more than your honor and happiness. As for these other little wenches,* you will learn nothing from them but foolishness and stupidity."

These were punishing words. Then at the end of the letter, Catherine brought out the whip.

"Do what I tell you if you want me to be content with you and love you, and if you want me to believe that you love me as you ought, being the good girl that I know you to be. For I desire nothing more in this world than to see you as happy as you are joyful, and to be content for your entire life. Your good mother, Catherine."

It was a brutal message, controlling and cruel. Yet Catherine would take no chances. There was no room for such childish mistakes.

The affair of the ladies was resolving just as Elisabeth came down with smallpox in January 1561. With hands slathered in lemon ointment, Elisabeth wrote to Catherine, praising both Madame de Vineux and Madame de Clermont for their devoted service during her illness. She was trying, once again, to make peace. Elisabeth was grateful to Philip, too, for visiting her so often while she was sick in bed. "He really is a good husband," she wrote.

And, in her own way, Elisabeth apologized to her mother for the mess she had made. "I will tell you that I am the happiest woman in the world, and I owe this happiness all to you. Madame, I cannot imagine anything better than to be honored with your commands. And I will try to serve you, as I am obliged to do."39

---

*The word Catherine uses is "garce." Though in the sixteenth century the word did not have quite the derogatory connotation it has today, Catherine meant nothing kind.

From the evidence of years to come, it seems Elisabeth meant what she said: she would always strive to serve and honor her mother. To honor Catherine, she had to succeed as Philip's wife. Was Elisabeth succeeding? When she rose from her sickbed, the routine would begin again: the endless efforts to win Philip's affection and respect, the day-in, day-out pinning and stitching of gowns heavy with fabric and jewels—all of it to project a portrait of magnificence that followed Spanish rules and appealed to the king. Yet underneath it all, Elisabeth's young body ached and writhed, heaved and hungered. It bled too much, or it bled too little. It was a body beyond her control.

Elisabeth understood the consequences if the alliance should fail. Already, she felt the cudgel of her mother's wrath. Perhaps the pressure of it all was enough to cause headaches and vomiting, nosebleeds and faints. To drain the blood from her face. Or to make her weep. "I think," wrote her French physician to Catherine, who wondered at the reports, "she might suffer from a touch of melancholy."[40]

13

SONS AND DAUGHTERS
France, 1560–1561

Sometime in early November 1560, just as Catherine was learning of Elisabeth de Valois's bickering ladies, King Francis noticed a strange twinge in his inner ear. The ear had bothered him on and off for several years, so at first few people paid this new ailment much mind. After a few days, however, the ear began to throb more than usual. Worse still, it oozed.

It oozed and oozed for ten days straight, according to the king's page Louis Gonzaga. Then, on November 17, while at table, King Francis was gripped by a horrible headache. Waves of nausea hit him soon afterward. Put to bed, he shivered with fever. For a few days, his symptoms waxed and waned, in an undulating cycle of fever, pain, and recovery. But by the end of the month, Francis was delirious, racked with the shakes, crying out from the pounding in his head whenever anyone raised a voice above a whisper. The physicians were confounded, their purges and cauterizing useless. When the pus ran the king seemed to improve; inevitably, when the abscess closed, he would worsen. As November passed into December, Catherine began to prepare herself for the worst.[1]

The state of the realm mirrored the suffering of the dying boy. During King Francis's short reign, tensions in the kingdom of France had festered. Edicts were violated, parleys broke down, and trust eroded entirely. Periods of healing between Protestants and Catholics gave way to episodes of strife, which were then followed by renewed hope for reconciliation between the factions. By the autumn of 1560, however, hope on both sides was faltering. There were no clear paths to religious resolution.

Goodwill had given way to rancor and a thirst for vengeance. Fights broke out in the streets and in the law courts. New insults emerged. "Papist" and "Huguenot"—a word of unknown origin— became epithets, to be spat in the faces of neighbors and strangers alike. The name-calling got so bad that the crown outlawed both terms, though "Huguenot" eventually became synonymous with "French Protestant" in everyday speech.[2]

Distrust turned into fear as false reports spread like wildfire. Back in early March 1560, word had reached court of a Huguenot plot that would take place sometime in the middle of the month. Stories swirled of an imminent coup, a conspiracy to kidnap the king and his family.[3]

Moving to crush the revolt before it could begin, and seizing the moment to showcase their own power, the Guises mobilized troops and gendarmes in the region of Tours where they believed the Huguenots planned to launch their attack. Royal soldiers lay in wait as Protestants gathered in the forests near the château of Amboise. The woods became the killing fields. Royal guards took cover behind trees, picking off the so-called conspirators with sniper-like precision. Other soldiers drowned men in the Loire, piling the bodies on the banks. Dragged to the castle, several prisoners died by the executioner's sword, their heads arrayed atop the gallows. Others, beaten and bloodied, were strung from the balconets in a macabre warning to all future plotters; when the balconets were full, they hung them from the turrets. Corpses dangled from the towers.[4]

The Tumult of Amboise became a beacon for Huguenots, their version of a "never forget" event. Though the Protestants blamed the Guises, they also blamed the young King Francis. Never again would French Protestants entirely trust the monarchy: at worst, the crown was willing to massacre its own subjects; at best, it had lost control. One of the Protestants at Amboise that day was a man named Aubigné, who barely escaped with his life. Decades later, his son, the Huguenot nobleman and poet Agrippa d'Aubigné, would remember how, months after the ambush, the fly-bitten heads still rotted on the gallows in front of the château. Just eight years old at the time, Aubigné was traveling with his father through Amboise on their way to Paris when they witnessed the grisly spectacle. As they rode past the château, the father turned to his son and swore him to vengeance. "If you try to spare yourself this vengeance," he told the boy, "I will curse you."

These were sights and sounds that clung to memory, emotions that sculpted identity. Like the boy who clambered up the cross in the Place de Grève to watch Anne du Bourg burn, from those decaying heads of the Huguenot martyrs the boy Aubigné learned there were no shades of gray. There was us and there was them. There was right and there was wrong. A fellow Frenchman could now be your foe. An entire generation of children, both Protestant and Catholic, hardened toward violence. Parents reared their sons for war.[5]

For the sake of her own son, Catherine was doing everything possible to avoid that war. The descriptions of the violence at Amboise revolted her. She believed that peaceful negotiation, the give and take of compromise, offered the only sure path to reknitting the fraying ties that bound the French nobility together. Five months after the Tumult of Amboise, in August 1560, Catherine hosted talks between the religious factions at Fontainebleau. For a short while the conference seemed promising; even the Cardinal of Lorraine was pliant, willing to accede to some Huguenot demands. Alas the talks ultimately failed, the victim of bristling intransigence among the warriors. The Bourbon brothers, Antoine de Bourbon and the younger Prince de Condé, refused to show up at the conference, while the Duke of Guise radiated petulance and hostility, mocking the new leader of the French Reformers, Gaspard de Coligny.*[6]

Historians tend to think Catherine underestimated the fervor fueling religious hatred in France, a fervor she did not share. While she looked for peace, Huguenots and Catholics already looked for war. She tried to remind both sides that all Frenchmen, despite their religion, owed allegiance first and foremost to King Francis her son. She hoped that, in time, Francis would grow into a strong king, like his father and grandfather before him. Under his hand, the

---

*Coligny was a nephew of the Constable Anne de Montmorency. The Reform divided families across the lower and upper classes.

kingdom would heal. But then, just three months after the talks at Fontainebleau, the young king was dead.

It took three weeks for King Francis to die. The end was excruciating, his body so tormented that "they almost wanted him to die," according to one historian.[7] On December 5 at noon, the priest administered Extreme Unction. By two in the afternoon the boy's limbs had gone cold. He died that evening, between ten and eleven o'clock at night.[8] He was seventeen years old, and his reign had lasted a mere seventeen months.

That night, the crown fell to Catherine's second son, Charles. He was ten and a half years old.

Even Henry II's horrific accident was likely not as traumatizing to Catherine as those few weeks surrounding the death of Francis II. It was only days later that the Queen Mother learned her daughter Elisabeth, in Spain, had fallen gravely ill with the smallpox. Knowing what the Queen Mother had just suffered, King Philip II quickly confirmed Elisabeth's imminent recovery in an unusually gentle note. Catherine still reeled. In the space of mere days she had come close to losing not just one, but two children—her king and her peacemaker—a disaster of unparalleled proportions. She would soon return to business, to her incomparable practicality. Yet at several moments, she wrestled with heart-wrenching anguish.

"I beg you," she wrote to Philip, "please tell [Elisabeth] to do everything she's told for her health . . . so that I may not endure still more misfortunes. And may Our Lord allow her to live so that she can serve and please you, and continue the friendship between you and this crown, which I will work to nourish and augment for as long as she lives."[9]

She wrote with both searing desperation and a renewed sense of purpose. For as King Philip knew, Catherine had taken charge of King Charles's government. Francis's death had left a power vacuum, a kingdom on the brink of war. It was up to Catherine now to pick up the shattered pieces and put them together again, one by one.

When did Catherine decide to seize the reins of government? From at least the first days of December, as Francis entered his final agony, she was putting the necessary steps in place. According to the Venetian ambassador, Catherine had suspected her son would die young. "She remembers all the prognostications made by the astrologers, all of them unanimously foretelling that His Majesty would have a brief life," he wrote.[10] Quite likely, she had prepared for Francis's death for a long time.

Over the course of her son's short reign, Catherine had soured on the Guises. While objecting to their politics, she also felt a more personal contempt. "They tried to take my husband from me," Catherine would write to Elisabeth de Valois, remembering that time long ago when King Francis I almost sent her back to Italy and Claude de Guise offered his own daughter as a replacement bride. "They tried to turn your brother away from me." Under the Guises, young Francis "was afraid," Catherine said. She could not allow the same to happen to Charles.[11]

It was a terrible time for the crown to fall to a child. French custom provided that a king could legally declare his majority at the age of thirteen, when he had "entered his fourteenth year." At only ten years old, Charles required a regent for at least three years. For a kingdom on the brink of civil war, three years was a long time to be in limbo.[12]

So who should govern for Charles? Even in peacetime, regencies were fragile and a little frightening. When a child reigned, rival claimants or kingdoms saw an opening to seize the throne. Ambitious courtiers and noblemen could take advantage of the child monarch. An unpopular regent, moreover, might incite rebellion among dissatisfied subjects. Although a regency was supposed to stabilize a monarchy in the event of a child's accession, in fact it exposed the monarchy's weakness.

The options for a regent were always dismal, whether a kingdom was at peace or at war. Sometimes kings specified who should take over in the event of their illness or death, yet Francis II had made no such provision. Without a direct royal order, nothing was codified. No single individual or governing body was in a position to choose a regent for King Charles in December 1560. There was only precedent and custom.

Catherine would have to make the case for herself and garner support for her regency. She knew what she was up against. For one, she faced a formidable adversary in the form of a centuries-old precedent known as Salic Law.[13]

Although they didn't much like the idea, the English, Spanish, and Scots accepted the concept of a sovereign queen. But the French were entirely against it. Even notions of a woman wielding power from *behind* the throne made Frenchmen nervous. More a custom than an actual law, Salic Law was the invention of a cunning fourteenth-century uncle who craved the throne. In 1316, Philip V (a second son) came to the French throne after the death of both his older brother, King Louis X, and the king's infant son. Only a daughter, Joan, survived the king, and Joan believed the crown belonged to her. Philip argued that Joan's mother had been unfaithful to her husband, leaving lingering doubts about Joan's paternity. After bribing key lawyers, noblemen, and counselors, Philip won support for his claim. "At that time," wrote one chronicler, "it was declared that a woman might not succeed to the crown of the monarchy of France."[14]

By 1340, Pope Benedict XII had agreed that the French practice of excluding daughters was acceptable, if only because the French seemed driven to continue doing it. By the end of the century, the custom had grown to exclude not only daughters from the throne but the children of daughters—even if those children were boys. "According to the reasonable custom of the French," wrote one papal jurist in 1377, "the daughter of the king may not succeed to the realm, nor in consequence may her son claim any right therein."[15]

In short order, Salic Law became a political convenience for the kingdom of France. Under Salic Law, the line of succession was clear—from king to son, or from the ruling king to the princes of the blood, from man to man—which kept conflicts over royal inheritance to a minimum. The practice also kept the French king French: there was no way a son of a French princess married to a foreigner could inherit the throne.

This line of reasoning became particularly useful in the fifteenth century during the Hundred Years' War between England and France. Salic Law had gone slightly cold in the intervening years for lack of need, but, faced with the English claim to the throne, French jurists trotted it out again. England had no right to the French throne, they said, because the English claim descended through a woman: Isabella of France, mother of Edward III of England.[16] To bolster their case, these same lawyers invented a long history for Salic Law. Ignoring its origins in the fourteenth century, one jurist, Jean de Montreuil, declared that Salic Law derived in fact from ancient Roman law. Another anonymously authored treatise traced it back to the time of Pope Boniface I, patron of Saint Augustine in the fifth century. Lest anyone mistake his message, this author titled his treatise *The Salic Law, First Law of the Franks.*[17]

By the sixteenth century, Salic Law carried more force than any decree. It had also adopted distinctly nationalist overtones. Once again, it was convenient. If not for Salic Law, King Francis I would never have inherited the throne. Instead, the crown would have passed to Louis XII's oldest daughter, Claude. As if to cover up how he came into his inheritance, King Francis married Claude, thereby joining the two branches of the Valois dynasty. He also ordered political theorists such as Claude de Seyssel to write books like *The Great Monarchy of France*, which explained just how "pernicious and dangerous" a foreign-born ruler could be. A foreign king honored different customs, spoke a different language, and came from an altogether "different way of life from the men of the lands he comes to rule."* Thanks to Salic Law, King Francis saved France for the French.[18]

Repeatedly, the French convinced themselves that Salic Law was only natural, even God-given, thanks to a certain circular logic. Women *couldn't* inherit the French throne, went the thinking, because they couldn't be anointed with the chrism of the Holy Ampulla, the holy oil by which French kings were rendered almost sacred at their coronations, their authority blessed by God. The chrism was reserved for men. Nor could a woman raise that other grand symbol of French monarchy, the Oriflamme: the war banner of the "golden flame" that, when it rippled over the heads of soldiers fighting

---

*Charles V of Spain encountered this very problem when he took up the throne of Spain at the age of sixteen. Born and raised in the Netherlands, Charles initially seemed too Flemish to native Spaniards. He never did entirely master Castilian Spanish.

hand-to-hand, meant the French would take no prisoners. Women didn't go to war. These were ancient and legendary symbols, the Oriflamme traced back to the twelfth century, the Holy Ampulla allegedly used in the baptism of Clovis, King of the Franks. To settle the crown on a woman meant breaking centuries of tradition— tradition that, to the French, made kings sacred and transformed mere soldiers into Christian warriors.[19]

Besides, weren't women unfit to rule? Didn't nature make them second to men? The custom held fast in part because its logic made sense to most sixteenth-century French people. The "laws of nature" said that women were inferior to men. What need was there for legal precedent in Roman or Church law when women were clearly made more for hearth and home than for the public sphere? Such language had wafted around questions of governance since at least the late fourteenth century. "Women are reputed false," read one text, meaning they were liars. They were, moreover, "uncertain, rash, and malicious; in all things they follow the dictates of their arbitrary desires." Above all, they were weak. For that reason alone, only men should govern: "The public sphere is better kept and defended by a man than a woman."[20]

Not only did Salic Law save the French from foreigners. It also saved France from women.

Salic Law governed the succession, but it did not dictate who should—or shouldn't—govern as regent. Even so, Salic Law made the French squeamish about any woman who dared come close to ruling. There were, of course, exceptions. In practice, kings across Europe often chose their wives to serve as regents in the event of their absence, such as when they left for war. The rationale for this practice sprang from the notion that a wife would be faithful to her husband and act in his interests. Plus, a king usually provided a council or a pair of noblemen to assist her in the task; it was to these men that the king entrusted the royal seals, leaving little doubt about who was really governing. Of course, during these short regencies, there was no chance of the queen remarrying and putting the crown in another prince's hands. Under such controlled conditions, Catherine de' Medici had served twice as regent while Henry II was away on campaign. It was assumed these temporary regencies would last maybe a few months at most, pending the king's return.[21]

The prolonged regency of a boy king presented a more disquieting situation since he required proxies and counseling for years. For this task, women—by nature weak-willed—were not ideal. In these cases, it was assumed, the regency would pass to a royal uncle or, in France, the ranking prince of the blood. But as precedent had shown time and again, uncles and princes were often much worse than the women.

Lawyers, counselors, and historians usually agreed: uncles were trouble. They tended to harbor aspirations for the throne. Would a greedy uncle use the crown to his own advantage? Would he renounce his authority once a young king came of age? Ironically, the very case that established the custom of Salic Law—King Philip V, uncle to Joan—showed just how perfidious an uncle could be.

In 1560, Catherine and her counselors didn't need to dig through medieval history to find examples of scheming royal uncles. They had only to look across the Channel. England crawled with them. According to the story then circulating, Richard III of England had killed his own nephews to usurp the throne in the late fifteenth century, only to fall to Henry Tudor at the Battle of Bosworth, thereby ushering in an entirely new dynasty. More recently, Edward Seymour, Duke of Somerset, had commandeered the regency, turning his nephew, King Edward VI, into a radical Protestant whose religious policies oppressed his Catholic subjects and whose warmongering ravaged Scotland. Another uncle to King Edward VI, Thomas Seymour, had conspired to grab power from the Duke of Somerset, his own brother, by using both the boy king and the king's sister, Elizabeth Tudor. Seymour lost his head on the block. Devious uncles could muster armies, bribe allies, rally foreign supporters. Too often, they put their own interests before those of king and kingdom. Their foibles destroyed dynasties.

By angling for the regency, Catherine was trying, in fact, to steer clear of a set of grasping uncles. Although related to King Francis only through marriage, the Guises had behaved like the nefarious uncles that jurists and noblemen so feared. They had appropriated the crown to advance their own religious agenda, inciting violence throughout the kingdom. Catherine felt they were hardly an apt choice as regent for the new king. The Guises themselves suspected their reign was over. As their nephew struggled on his deathbed, they prepared to return to Joinville.[22]

In theory, the princes of the blood—meaning the ranking princes descending from the family next in line to the throne—could serve as regents, yet they were hardly preferable to royal uncles. The very concept of princes of the blood ensured a smooth transition from one dynasty to the next. Yet these same rights of succession made princes of the blood inherently untrustworthy. By definition, they stood to inherit the throne if the current dynasty died out: putting these princes in charge was like giving them a taste of the crown they craved.

For religious reasons, French Huguenots endorsed the Bourbon princes of the blood as regents. But in December 1560, the Bourbon princes appeared blatantly seditious. Antoine de Bourbon and his brother, the Prince de Condé, were suspected plotters in the Tumult of Amboise. They had defied the crown by failing to appear at the assembly of Fontainebleau. Condé seemed particularly intent on sedition. Back in October 1560, two months before King Francis's death, word had reached court that Condé was raising a Protestant army. He was arrested, tried, and found guilty of lèse-majesté. Fearing Huguenot rage, Catherine stalled the execution by asking the chancellor, Michel de l'Hôpital, a political moderate and her devoted counselor, not to sign the death warrant. In the end, only King Francis's unfortunate death kept Condé from the gallows. On December 4, as the king breathed his last, Condé was still a prisoner.[23]

There were no perfect choices. But Catherine and her counselors would argue that a woman was the safest port in troubled waters. In an ironic twist, Catherine found her Italian birth could, in these circumstances, play in her favor. In theory, a foreign-born queen was isolated in the kingdom, tied to its blood and soil only through her sons. In theory, she had no stake in acquiring landholdings. She possessed, in theory, no web of clients to protect. The same "laws of nature" defining women as weak and unfit to rule also praised mothers as naturally affectionate: foreign-born queens were attached to the kingdom not through ambitious power networks but through a mother's love.

Sometime in the days leading up to Francis's death, Catherine's advisors discovered a valuable precedent. Poring through dusty archives, they unearthed the story of the Spanish-born Blanche de Castile, mother of the Crusader Louis IX, eventually canonized as Saint Louis. In 1226, Louis had inherited the French throne at the age of twelve. His mother, Blanche, ruled in his name for eight years, until 1234, protecting her son's kingdom against rebellious barons who refused to recognize his birthright. After Louis reigned on his own, his mother still served as a trusted advisor.

Catherine's counselors couldn't have found a more perfect story. Through a mother's love, Blanche de Castile had saved the kingdom of France for its most vaunted king. There were other advantages to this particular history lesson: Saint Louis was an ancestor of the Bourbons. The Bourbon princes of the blood, Catherine wagered, would see in Blanche's tale an acknowledgment of their own exalted ancestry.

And perhaps the story would remind them that Catherine herself was a descendant of Saint Louis through her own Bourbon mother, Madeleine de la Tour d'Auvergne. Catherine wasn't an enemy of the Bourbons. She was their kinswoman and ally. They could put their trust, and the French crown, into her hands.

If the naysayers had Salic Law and women's weakness on their side, Catherine had Blanche de Castile and mother's love. Love made a queen into a good mother, virtuous and benevolent, ready to protect her son and his interests. Were not his interests her own? The legal scholar Jean du Tillet had argued just this during the reign of Francis II, defending Catherine's place at the young king's side. "According to written and natural judgment, a mother loves her children with more piteous love, and with a sweeter heart and lovingly nourishes them more tenderly, and carefully guards their bodies and their possessions more than any other person whatsoever, no matter how close in lineage." A mother, he continued, "ought to be preferred over all others."[24] How apt du Tillet's reasoning seemed, now that little Charles would be king.

On December 5, the day Francis died, Catherine knew she would use mother's love to assert her right to govern. She was already shoring up her support. "I will take in hand the necessary duty that must be given to the administration," she wrote to the king's deputy in Burgundy, "using the good counsel of princes and great noblemen, of which we are not lacking, God be thanked . . ." Rest assured, she told him, the kingdom was safe—not in spite of Catherine's gender, but *because* Catherine had done her duty as queen. "Grace be to our Lord, He has not left this kingdom deprived of legitimate and true successors, of which I am the mother."[25]

In a different context, her gender, motherhood, and Florentine birth might have weakened her case.* Instead, Catherine made them her strength.

———

On the evening of December 6, the day after King Francis's death, the preeminent noblemen of the realm gathered at Orléans for the first meeting of King Charles IX's council. At Catherine's behest, both the Guises and their rival Antoine de Bourbon attended. The chancellor, Michel de l'Hôpital, also took a seat at the table. King Charles sat at the head, a stark reminder that everyone owed loyalty to him alone. Of the chief grandees in the kingdom, only Constable Montmorency was absent. He would arrive in Orléans the next day.[26]

Through canny negotiation, Catherine had successfully bought off both the Guises and Antoine de Bourbon. She easily persuaded the Guises: having despaired of their life at court, they grasped at the chance to play a role in the new government. Knowing the Guises commanded legions of loyal followers and sensing they would serve as a buffer against both the powerful Montmorency clan and the untrustworthy Bourbons, Catherine included them on the new king's council.

Winning over Antoine de Bourbon had proven more difficult. As first prince of the blood, Antoine believed the regency was his birthright.[27] He and the Queen Mother fell to haggling. Antoine protested his rights; Catherine wouldn't budge. She countered by declaring him a traitor, like his brother Condé. He offered to step down from the regency "to prove his loyalty." He fell right into

---

*Indeed, Marie de Guise's gender, motherhood, and foreign birth had stalled her efforts to seize the regency of Scotland for years.

her trap. Catherine demanded confirmation of his renunciation in writing.

Still, Catherine sought to assuage the King of Navarre's ego. As part of the deal, she agreed to release Condé from prison. Moreover, she would make Antoine lieutenant-general of the kingdom, giving him control over the armies. Most importantly to Antoine, she also promised to appeal to Philip II on his behalf regarding the lost lands in Navarre. (From that moment on, Catherine would flood Elisabeth de Valois with anxious letters asking for her help.)

Officially, they agreed that Antoine would appear to play a role in the regency. But Catherine made it clear who was really in charge.*

Candles lit the faces in King Charles's council chamber; the doors were shut and guarded. To the noblemen assembled, Michel de l'Hôpital made the case for Catherine. His speech was merely a performance. The deals had already been cut. The moment Catherine walked into the council room, she had the government in hand. By appearing together at the table, the Guises and the Bourbons merely acknowledged the authority they had already granted her.

She never called herself regent. Nor did she ask the Parlement of Paris to grant her that name. Catherine knew that, as a woman, modesty could play to her advantage. Few could argue that she sought power for herself if she never asked for the title. Instead, she worked as "governor of the kingdom" only for the preservation of France and her son's authority—the selfless act of a loving mother.[28] Yet, from Charles IX's first day as king, Catherine was regent in all but name.

As the council closed their first meeting, the Cardinal of Lorraine picked up the seal of King Francis and broke it in two, symbolizing the end of Francis's reign. Turning to Catherine, he placed Charles's new seal in her hands. The new king's seal would appear on every royal document, every edict, every set of letters patent.

Whoever possessed the seal held the key to the kingdom. Now it belonged to Catherine.

---

*To appease Montmorency, who also might have opposed her rule, Catherine immediately placed him on the king's council after he arrived at court on December 7.

If she believed the transition would be smooth once the king's council sanctioned her authority, Catherine was wrong. For months, disorder reigned.

In late December, deputies at the Estates-General at Orléans reluctantly approved Catherine's government.* But when the Estates-General met in Paris in March, three months after Francis's death, they moved to quash it. Dominated by Huguenots and political moderates, the Estates wanted the Guises banished from court, the council reorganized, and Catherine's role reduced to the "guardianship of the person of the king and of her other sons," like a mere nursemaid. They wanted Antoine de Bourbon placed in charge of the regency. At the prospect of a Protestant regent, rebellion rose within the ranks of the new king's council. In an ironic twist, the Duke of Guise joined with his old nemesis Anne de Montmorency, the rivals now mounting a united front in the name of the Catholic religion.† In theory, they opposed the growing threat of Protestantism in the government, but they also sought to curb Catherine's power. Guise and his followers began to circulate rumors that Catherine was "changing religion."

More than ever, Catherine sought out her daughter's emotional support. "Madame my daughter, you have seen from my previous letter how they are tormenting me," she wrote to Elisabeth in a tortured letter, her thoughts scattered, her spelling undone by despair.[29] Though Catherine tried to project an image of cool conciliation, inside she was a wreck. While wrangling the government, she was also in deep mourning. Francis II had been king, but he had also been her son, her first born.

"God took your father from me," she'd scribbled in another letter, on December 7, just two days after Francis died. "And not content with that, he took your brother, whom I loved as you know, and left me with three little boys in a completely divided kingdom. I do not have a single person whom I can trust at all who does not have some particular

---

*The Estates-General was an advisory assembly, called and dismissed by the French king, including representatives from the three estates—the nobility, clergy, and commoners. Although the Estates-General did not have the power to pass laws, it could be summoned to advise the crown on matters of state.
†Guise and Montmorency joined with a third privy councillor, Marshal Saint-André, to form a Catholic triad that came to be known as "The Triumvirate."

agenda. Let me be an example to you, my love . . . lest you forget to commend yourself to God. For whenever God pleases, he could put you in the same position in which I find myself. And I would rather die than see you there, for fear that you could not withstand the pain I am suffering, which I could not endure without God's help."

Heartbroken and terrified for Charles, she was haunted by memories. "Commend yourself to God," Catherine told Elisabeth, "for you once saw me as content as you are now, with not a single care other than not being loved by the King your father as much as I would have liked."[30] Once, she was almost happy. But fortune—or God—had changed all of that now.

Catherine fought through her grief—she almost always did. Twelve days later, she recovered enough composure to write a second, more measured letter to Elisabeth, obscuring some of the backroom dealings for the sake of her story.

"Madame my daughter, I was so troubled when I wrote to you the other day . . . that I was unable to tell you what I greatly desire you to do for your brother, who is now the king, and for this kingdom. I am sending this messenger to the ambassador to tell you, my daughter, *m'amye*, that because you love us, you must try to encourage the King your husband to keep the same goodwill he felt toward your father and [older] brother, as well as the goodwill he has shown me in particular. Reassure him that so long as I live, he will receive nothing but friendship and good intelligence from us, and that I will nourish the King my son in this same friendship. He should also know that at this point I hold the authority and government of this kingdom . . . And even though I have the King of Navarre at my side (because the laws of this kingdom specify that when the King is young, the princes of the blood must be at the mother's side), [your husband] should harbor no doubts, for the King of Navarre is quite obedient to me and follows no other order than what I command."[31]

Once again Catherine enrobed politics with maternal love: if Elisabeth loved her mother, she would spread Catherine's story of mother's love.

No doubt Elisabeth spoke to Philip just as she was told. And after receiving her mother's note, Elisabeth sent her own to King Charles. "I should not fail to tell you," she wrote, one child to another, "since we are both so fortunate, how much we should pray to God for the Queen Mother. Let Him keep her safe for us. I know that you will always obey her, but I will remind you anyway how much you should love and honor her." "Because," she explained, "you are beholden to her for everything honorable and good that you possess."[32]

PART 3

14

HOME

France, 1560

The morning after King Francis died, Mary pinned on a gauzy white veil that fell over her shoulders and down the back of her black dress. It was the third time she had worn the *deuil blanc* in eighteen months—the first for Henry II in 1559, the second for her mother in June 1560, and now, just six months later, for Francis.

For the entire day, Mary refused to see anyone but her grandmother, Antoinette de Bourbon. As she grieved, a stark reality closed in. Her future was uncertain, the kingdom of France no longer her own. Watching Mary in the days following Francis's death, the Venetian ambassador Micheli Suriano felt only pity. "Little by little," he wrote in a dispatch of December 8, "everyone will forget the death of the former king, except for the little queen, his wife, who is as noble a lady as she is beautiful and graceful." She was so young, wrote Suriano. "She refuses any consolation, but always remembering one or the other of her misfortunes, through her incessant tears and her lamentations, full of pain and crying, she inspires great compassion in everyone."[1]

As Suriano predicted, King Francis was soon forgotten. Whispers of a hasty burial, devoid of the pomp normally given to deceased kings, filtered into Spain. It was said the Guises gave Francis's body short shrift, leaving him in the hands of negligent secretaries while they raced back to King Charles's council. The Spanish—such sticklers for etiquette—sniggered, using the gossip to embarrass the despised French courtiers who still hung about Elisabeth de Valois.[2]

Yet Spain would have found no fault with Mary Stuart's behavior. As her uncles gathered around the new king's council table, the young woman surrendered to her grief. "Immediately upon her husband's death,"Throckmorton wrote to the English Privy Council, "she changed her lodging, withdrew herself from all company, and became so solitary and exempt of all worldliness that she does not to this day see daylight, and so will continue out forty days." She passed most of that time with Antoinette. At dinner they ate together, and at night they slept in the same room.[3]

What would she do now, where would she go? A clause in Mary's marriage contract stipulated that, in the event of Francis's death, she could choose to stay in France. A baby might have given her an excuse to remain, especially if that baby was a son. Her own mother had stayed in Scotland after the death of James V to protect Mary's crown, and Mary might have done the same. But there was no baby. At eighteen she'd become a dowager queen but not the queen mother.[4]

During the two-and-a half years of her marriage to Francis, only once had rumors of a pregnancy circulated. "They say the Queen of France is pregnant," Chantonnay wrote to Philip II in September 1560, adding that "it is not certain." *They say*. Chantonnay was probably not the only skeptic. There is a startling lack of excitement in the archives at the prospect of a baby; Chantonnay's letter is the only source to mention a possible pregnancy. Perhaps, like her uncles, Mary wished so badly for a pregnancy to seal the Guise hold on the throne that she tricked herself into believing it. The rumor was short lived. After September, Chantonnay never mentioned a pregnancy in his dispatches again.[5]

Some observers doubted from the beginning that the marriage would ever bear fruit. Almost a full year earlier, in December 1559, the Count of Feria, then at the Hapsburg court in Flanders, had heard "the Scottish Queen is not likely to have any children." Decades later, the French memoirist Louis Régnier de la Planche described how certain doctors—alarmed by King Francis's puffy and pale face, by the putrid liquid that sometimes flowed from his infected ear out through his nose—had warned the Guises of a poor outcome."They advised them secretly to settle their affairs since this prince was not long for this world. And what is more, they should not expect their niece the queen to bear children, unless they are fathered by someone else, as much for the above reasons as because his genitals were completely malformed and stopped up."[6]

Both Feria and La Planche believed the fault lay with Francis, not Mary. Francis was frail and immature. The Venetian ambassador claimed the couple consummated the marriage on their wedding night, though one wonders whether that was true—or whether they ever had sex at all.[7] Without sex, the marriage was vulnerable to dissolution, which the Guises could not risk. Is it possible they spread rumors of Mary's pregnancy precisely to quash any doubts?

With no baby tying her to France, the widowed Mary considered Scotland. She found ways to procrastinate. On January 12, just before finishing her forty days of mourning, Mary told her Scottish deputies she intended "to return to her kingdom [of Scotland] as soon as her affairs in this kingdom allowed her to do so."[8] Only the expense of the trip kept her from leaving immediately.

The prospect of returning filled her with ambivalence. Scotland was a far-off and potentially hostile kingdom, where the Scots Protestant lords dominated her council and still threatened to rebel. France was Mary's home. France had schooled Mary's religion, cultivated her mind, sculpted her tongue. France defined her, in details great and small, from the towering châteaus of the Loire to the taste of violet petals simmered into jam, the poets she read, the fashions she followed, the face of her beloved grandmother. Barely more than a distant memory to her, Scotland was foreign and threatening, filled with roiling politics and heretical lords. Her crown tied her to Scotland, but in her heart, Mary belonged to France.

She wished "a hundred times more to reside in France a simple dowager, and to be content with Touraine and Poitou that were given to her as her dowry, than to go reign" in Scotland, wrote Brantôme.[9]

More than most, Catherine de' Medici might have been able to empathize with Mary. Both women had loved Francis. And like Mary, Catherine had come to France from a distant realm. Like Mary, she was the daughter of a French noblewoman and a foreigner—Catherine might have understood her daughter-in-law's vexed relationship to Scotland, the sense that she belonged more to the kingdom into which she married than the kingdom of her birth. Over the years, however, Catherine had woven herself fully into the fabric of France. Motherhood had won her a place at the helm of Charles's kingdom, in the heart of his council. Moreover, unlike Mary, Catherine did not wear the sovereign crown of a different kingdom. Catherine stood at the center of the French court, whereas Mary now lived between kingdoms, an outsider at the margins.

At least on paper, Mary claimed her bond to Catherine remained as strong as ever. The Queen Mother gave her "as much love and friendship . . . as a daughter might receive from her own mother," she wrote to her Scottish deputies.[10] Under Charles IX, she assured them, the Scottish–French Auld Alliance would hold fast. In the first weeks after Francis's death, Catherine gave Mary little reason to doubt those words. Though she demanded the return of Mary's crown jewels, as required, Catherine showed Mary due respect, even kindness. But, as Mary must have noticed, Catherine did not encourage her to stay in France.

Catherine distrusted Mary. A bitterness had welled within her, though it is hard to say when it began, exactly, or why. Some of Catherine's dislike may have been personal. There was a smugness about Mary, an arrogance. According to the papal nuncio Saint-Croix, Mary Stuart once declared her mother-in-law "would never be anything more than a merchant's daughter." It is difficult to prove Saint-Croix's reliability—his dispatch is the only source to report a statement of this kind.

Then again, much of Catherine's distrust was political in nature. If La Planche can be believed, Catherine had good reason to be on her guard: on at least one occasion, Mary had clearly demonstrated her loyalty to the Guises at Catherine's expense. In May 1560, eight months before Francis's death, Mary stumbled upon her mother-in-law just as Catherine was reading a report by a delegation of leading French Protestants. The memo demanded the removal of the Guises from power, the drafting of a new council for the king, and the establishment of a national council on religion. The young queen "followed every action of the Queen Mother as if on watch," said La Planche. Mary demanded to know who sent the memo. Catherine named the messenger. Immediately, the Guises arrested the man while Catherine was forced to explain why she was consorting with heretics.[11]

If it happened, this incident revealed a dawning truth: more than she was queen consort of France or even Queen of Scots, Mary was foremost a Guise. Her obedience to family eclipsed all other obligations, including any tenderness she once felt for Catherine. As she'd been taught since childhood, Mary followed her uncles' lead. Although with age she would come to assert herself, time would not diminish that fierce devotion to the Guises—or Mary's conviction that the Guise view of politics and religion was usually right.

Mary's early devotion was innocent, like that of any child to her family. And Mary was especially obedient to the Guises. Filial fidelity was not inherently blameworthy. Catherine, after all, expected no less from her own children—a parental expectation that she may have learned from the Guises themselves, a family she had long admired.

Yet the shifting fortunes of the realm had altered Catherine's view of the Guises. By the last months of Francis's rule, she feared their maneuvering. She was willing to keep the duke and cardinal on King Charles's council for the sake of politics, but increasingly, she saw the Guises as personal adversaries. Her spite could border on hatred. "They are so angry to be no longer in control of the government," she would write in early 1561 to Elisabeth de Valois. "They are trying to make everyone hate me . . . they think that if we have war then I will be forced to throw myself into their hands and follow their advice: but I promise you, by my faith, I will never do any such thing, for they have been too ungrateful toward me. They spoiled this kingdom with all their spending, such that everything fell into ruin."[12]

Still, Catherine's feelings for the Guise family were complicated. She could not summarily dismiss them; they were a force within the realm, wealthy and networked. Keeping them close meant she could watch them—and Catherine was not above using the Guises when necessary. At times, she seemed genuinely to appreciate the duke's patrician sense of honor and the cardinal's crafty politicking. Catherine would always feel a sincere affection for Anne d'Este and Antoinette de Bourbon.

Mary, Queen of Scots, however, was a different story. The girl's arrogance rankled, but politics, more than personal reasons, fueled the Queen Mother's growing antipathy toward her. Catherine realized the Guises would use the widowed Mary as a weapon, deploying her to further Guise agendas—agendas that ran counter to Catherine's. Mary's youth, her Scottish crown, her blood right to the English throne made her once again a prime pick for another marriage to suit Guise ambitions. And to Catherine, that fact alone made Mary dangerous.

———

Mary ended her mourning on January 15, 1561. Folding away her *deuil blanc,* she made no immediate plans to return to Scotland. After idling at court for a few months, she wandered about the kingdom visiting her Guise relatives as if unmoored, searching for comfort. Her first stop was the Guise château in Nanteuil, fourteen leagues to the west of Paris. From there, she headed northeast to Reims, the diocese of the Cardinal of Lorraine, where she spent time with her Guise aunt, Renée, who was abbess at the convent of Saint-Pierre.

Not long afterward, in March 1561, the body of Mary's mother was secreted out of Edinburgh Castle and transported to France. Eventually, Marie de Guise came to rest in the crypt of her sister's convent, a bittersweet homecoming at last. By the time of her mother's reburial, however, Mary had already gone.[13]

Slowly she inched her way southeast, moving closer to the Guise family seat at Joinville. In Nancy, on the eastern edge of the kingdom, she visited her distant cousin the Duke of Lorraine and his young wife, Mary's sister-in-law, Claude de Valois. Mary found Claude had changed. Now "presumptuous and haughty," the girl paraded her marriage to the exalted House of Lorraine. Somehow, Claude felt superior to Mary. "Her Highness intended to upstage and outshine her Majesty the Queen of Scots," remembered Brantôme, who witnessed the tension. Years of childhood friendship evaporated almost overnight. Had Claude always entertained such uncharitable feelings toward her sister-in-law? Or perhaps, like Elisabeth de Valois, Claude was her mother's child and knew where her loyalties should lie. "She hoped to accommodate herself somewhat to the Queen Mother for the next time they saw each other," Brantôme concluded. He couldn't help but notice that if Claude was a proud young lady, Catherine was "proud and a half."[14]

Where did Mary's loyalties lie? Many people wanted to know. In March, during her travels, Mary received two separate emissaries from Scotland. The first to arrive was the Catholic John Leslie, Bishop of Ross, who encouraged her to return home and assured her that 20,000 Catholic troops would help her wrest Scotland from the Protestant lords by force. Mary welcomed his enthusiasm but shied away from another civil war in Scotland.

The second Scottish envoy to arrive came on behalf of the Protestant lords. An illegitimate child of King James V of Scotland, Lord James Stewart was Mary's half-brother, twelve years older. Mary knew him but not well. As a teenager, James had accompanied the five-year-old Mary when she first arrived in France in 1548, returning to Scotland soon thereafter; he'd also attended her wedding to the dauphin. During the War in Scotland of 1559 and 1560, James's influence grew among the Scottish lords. An able politician and committed Reformist, he had fostered close ties with English Protestants, garnering fans among statesmen such as William Cecil, Nicholas Throckmorton, and Thomas Randolph.

John Knox's sermons had spoken to Lord James and over the years his faith had deepened into an authentic fervor. Throckmorton described him as "one of the most virtuous noblemen, in whom religion, sincerity and magnanimity as much reign as ever he knew in any man in any nation."[15]

James hoped to persuade his sister to continue the religious tolerance shown by Marie de Guise or, even better, to embrace the Protestant faith herself.* To this, Mary could not agree. However, like her mother, she was willing to accept her subjects' Protestant beliefs, Mary said, even if she didn't surrender her own.

Mary was relieved when James appeared amenable to her point of view. She thanked him for his counsel; he thanked her for the audience and departed. Naively, Mary believed she'd landed upon a way forward with her Scottish subjects. She also mistakenly saw Lord James as a trustworthy and faithful kinsman, like her Guise uncles, his loyalty assured by blood bonds. Mary did not realize the depths of her half-brother's fervor for the Reform or his distrust of the Auld Alliance. He had long concluded that an alliance with Protestant England was far preferable to the old friendship with Catholic France. Unbeknownst to Mary, after their meeting in Paris,

---

*William Cecil, a true believer himself, wanted to ensure Mary's commitment to Protestantism in case she inherited the English throne, though he prayed this would never be the case. Among the English councillors who hounded Elizabeth Tudor to marry and bear an heir, Cecil was the fiercest.

James returned to Edinburgh by way of London, where he conveyed every word of his meeting with Mary to Nicholas Throckmorton.[16]

Although Mary listened patiently to both the Bishop of Ross and Lord James, in truth, she still hoped never to return to Scotland at all. She tarried in France for another reason: talks were already underway about a second marriage for her. Even as King Francis had sickened, the court had whispered about future husbands. "Some say the Prince of Spain, some the Duke of Austria, others the Earl of Arran," Throckmorton wrote in November, while the physicians still hoped that Francis might live. By the following March, while Mary wandered the kingdom, other proposals were flowing in from Sweden, Denmark, and Ferrara.[17]

At least publicly, Mary was no virgin bride. But if, in theory, widowhood dimmed her appeal on the marriage market, in reality, she was a catch. The sovereign queen of Scotland, in line for the throne of England, she was also very young, just eighteen years old, motherhood still a possibility.

Mary was no innocent bystander in the discussion of these proposals. She believed she deserved a stellar second marriage. As far as Throckmorton could tell, she wasn't interested in a union just to "please her fancy" or obtain the "small benefit" of a temporary alliance. No, what Mary really desired was "the continuation of her honor, and to marry [a husband who] may uphold her to be great."[18] Having already married a king once, she looked for no less than a king for her future.

Unlike Catherine de' Medici, Mary would not embrace a lifetime of black gowns and veils; unlike her cousin the English Elizabeth Tudor, she would make no declaration of avowed singlehood. As all of Europe knew, Queen Elizabeth was already wreaking havoc in her Parliament and Privy Council by refusing matrimony. No one in England or abroad could understand the persnickety English queen. Surely a young queen, especially one as insecure on her throne as Queen Elizabeth, required a husband for protection and guidance.[19]

The teenaged Queen of Scots did not possess the grit of either Catherine de' Medici or Elizabeth Tudor. Mary believed marriage was the only path to a woman's strength and stability on the throne. She had practical reasons to remarry, of course: Scotland needed an heir, and a strong husband could support her against rebellions like the one that triggered the War in Scotland, the memories of which were still fresh. More importantly, Mary doubted her own capacities: raised to think of herself as a consort, she couldn't conceive of ruling Scotland without a man.

And for the young Queen of Scots, the prospect of another crown—the crown of a consort—touched a deeper sense of self. Her family had taught her from childhood that she would one day reign in three kingdoms. She had reveled in that unparalleled rank and the flattery that accompanied it. The prospect of those three crowns had defined her value for others and for herself. Yet now she reigned only in impoverished Scotland—a stinging demotion. Another crown, as great as that of the Most Christian Kings of France, could restore what she'd lost: that priceless exaltation, that sense of her own greatness—an acclaim as familiar to Mary as the taste of sweet violets, the vistas of Joinville, the blue skies vaulting over the Loire.

Before Mary left the French court, Throckmorton hired several spies to track her movements. It proved to be difficult work. Mary darted from estate to estate, disappearing for weeks at a time into Guise-friendly castles and convents where no one could follow. Throckmorton wanted to know whom Mary dealt with, what kind of advice she received—what kind of marriage she plotted. The Queen of Scots still hesitated to ratify the Treaty of Edinburgh, which infuriated Elizabeth Tudor. To both Throckmorton and Queen Elizabeth, Mary's dithering seemed an ominous sign. Obviously, she still coveted England's throne.[20]

Until Mary ratified the Treaty of Edinburgh, Queen Elizabeth wanted her isolated from any foreign support. Mary's marriage proposals were of deep concern; the husband she chose would reveal what position Mary planned to take toward England.

Throckmorton wasn't the only person interested in the Scottish queen's second marriage. Sometime in the opening days of January 1561, while Mary still pined away in her mourning chambers, Catherine de' Medici confronted the Cardinal of Lorraine about certain matrimonial chitchat. Ambassador Chantonnay, hearing of the conversation (probably from the cardinal himself), recounted it to Philip II.

Negotiating for Mary's hand already? Catherine asked. And "the corpse of her own son barely cold in the grave?"

He knew nothing about it, replied the cardinal coolly. But surely it was no surprise. "One would do the exact same for the paltriest lady at court, let alone a queen."[21]

A few weeks later, in early February, Elisabeth de Valois wrote an urgent letter to her mother. "Beware not to let my sister go to Joinville," she warned. "We have known for more than three weeks that she is planning a trip there, even before your letters about it arrived, which makes me believe that they are well acquainted with Joinville's news."[22] By *sister*, she meant Mary Stuart. By *they*, Elisabeth meant Philip II and his counselors.

Set high in the cliffs of the Haute-Marne, Joinville was just a stone's throw from Hapsburg Flanders. Away from the curious eyes of the French court, it was an easy place from which to send surreptitious messages to Spanish deputies in Flanders, and in which to receive their replies.

Elisabeth's letter only confirmed what Catherine already feared. The Cardinal of Lorraine and the Guises had opened talks with Philip II about a marriage for Mary. The proposed groom was the Prince of Asturias: Philip's only son and the heir apparent to Spain, Don Carlos.

15

DON CARLOS

France and Spain, 1561

In the winter of 1561, Catherine was almost forty-two years old. Childbirth, grief, and worry had taken a toll, yet no portrait bears witness to any silvery hair or wrinkled skin. No envoy writes of Catherine's weariness or resignation. Instead, her majesty captivated every comer. Clothed in regal black, Catherine was the picture of devout motherhood: plump, solid, stable, yet nimble on her feet, rushing everywhere she went. To all observers she seemed a ballast for young Charles, an image she promoted. In one painting commissioned shortly after Charles's accession, Catherine gathers around her the three sons and one daughter remaining at home. All the children resemble one another, as if to show off the abundance of Henry II's legacy, the fruit of Catherine's boundless fertility. These were *her* children, the children of France. Catherine pulls the young Charles close, her fingers resting lightly on his shoulder. She cradles his hand in her own.[1]

She was the king's mother. As his mother, she would protect her son from threats to his sovereignty. And some of those threats sat at Charles's council table.

Shortly after the death of Francis II, the Guises had briefly made noises about a possible marriage between the new King Charles and Mary. Catherine quickly struck down that possibility, citing closeness in kinship and the boy's youth. In truth, she looked to block the Guises from acquiring the kind of power they had enjoyed under Francis II. Catherine guessed the Guises planned to marry Don Carlos to Mary with the same goal: they sought a back-channel way to salvage their control over council and country. French Catholics would see no need to compromise with Huguenots if they enjoyed Spanish support in the form of troops and coin. They would rally around the Guises. Through Elisabeth, Catherine was trying to convince Philip that her policies of conciliation were working. If the Guises allied with Philip II, she feared her authority would crumble.

More than Catherine, the Guises were a natural ally for Spain. The Spanish ambassador, Chantonnay, made sure to broadcast Philip's distaste for the Reform. Philip especially despised the notion of a French national council of religion, one of the Huguenots' chief demands. The idea of compromise with Protestants repulsed Philip. He believed the Guise policies of eradication were the only way to proceed.[2]

This was a war for Philip's heart: would he follow his Catholic instincts? Or would he respect his brother-in-law King Charles and his mother-in-law Queen Catherine? For the sake of peace, Catherine needed to strengthen those family ties through marriage. And now the Guises were interfering with her marital plots.

More than anything, Catherine wanted Don Carlos to wed, not Mary Stuart, but her own youngest daughter, Margot. She'd been pushing the match ever since Elisabeth married Philip in 1559. At the time, the cardinal had advocated the marriage himself. "If there was hope for the Prince of Spain," the cardinal wrote to Ambassador Limoges, "we would prefer that to any other party that might present itself." As if to underscore the point, Catherine took the pen and appended her own note at the bottom of the letter. "It is one of the things that I most desire in this world, to see [Margot] by her sister's side."[3]

In early 1561, with a boy king on the throne of France, that second Spanish–Valois marriage seemed more urgent than ever. But rather than a collaborator, the cardinal had now become Catherine's nemesis. Mary, Queen of Scots, had got in the way.

And Catherine wrestled with yet another concern. "If Don Carlos hasn't married a woman who would be entirely loyal to you, like your sister Margot," Catherine wrote to Elisabeth de Valois in January, "and if your husband should die, and Don Carlos became king, you would be in the greatest danger of becoming the most unfortunate woman in the world."[4] Once again, the thorny problem of rank reared its head. Don Carlos was the heir to Spain. If Philip were to die, Don Carlos would hold Elisabeth's fate—and those of her children, once they were born—in his hands. Margot would ensure their well-being. Would Mary Stuart prove as trustworthy?

With that one letter, Catherine tried to plant the seeds of doubt in Elisabeth's mind, to make the problem personal. For a queen, the personal was always political. As the bride of Don Carlos, Mary would threaten Elisabeth's standing at the Spanish court. A sovereign queen, Mary would outrank Elisabeth, as she always had. Once she married the heir, Spanish subjects would look to Mary as the mother of their future kings. Mary outshone everyone at the court of France; she would outshine everyone at the court of Spain.

Elisabeth—still grappling with her health, still struggling to gain her husband's affections and, worst of all, still childless—could not afford a competitor who would whip up support for Guise agendas among fawning Spanish courtiers. Neither could she afford a competitor for Philip II's admiration. Mary was armed with rank, charisma, and exquisite beauty. But Catherine needed Elisabeth to remain first lady of Spain.

She would fight beauty with beauty; she would find a way to entice Don Carlos. In mid-January, hearing rumors of the Spanish–Guise match, Catherine quietly sent a pretty portrait of little Margot to Elisabeth in Spain. As the painting made its way over the Pyrenees, the Queen Mother plotted. Margot was just seven years old. How could a little girl compare to the Queen of Scots, whom Ronsard once praised as "more beautiful than Dawn itself?" This would take all Catherine's ingenuity. She assumed the Guises had already sent a portrait of Mary Stuart, too.[5]

———

Catherine might have been even more concerned had she known the extent of Don Carlos's ambition. Desperate to prove himself to his father, the boy yearned for an exalted marriage. Yet it is unclear how much Catherine, the Guises, or Mary knew about Don Carlos. Nothing in Elisabeth de Valois's surviving letters betrays anything unusual about the prince, though she must have realized soon after meeting him that Don Carlos was different. Philip, too, tried to control the flow of information about his son. He likely hoped Don Carlos would eventually grow out of his strange ways.

They were indeed strange ways, though when, exactly, the boy's behavior began to cause concern remains unknown. His earliest years passed smoothly, if not happily. Born in July 1545 and named after his grandfather, Don Carlos lost his mother four days after his birth. He lived for a time with his aunt, Princess Juana, who coddled him. Shortly after Don Carlos turned seven, Philip removed him from Juana's care, and placed him with governors and preceptors who kept him tied to a strict daily regimen. Both Philip II and Charles V organized Don Carlos's schooling and activities, yet these same domineering men remained largely absent from the boy's life. From 1548 until 1551, Philip resided in Brussels; he left Spain again in 1554, first to live in England with Mary Tudor, then, once more, to travel to Flanders, where he stayed until 1559. Whenever he was in Spain, Philip spent most of his time with his papers and counselors. As for Charles V, he had retired by 1556 to the monastery at Yuste, about 150 miles southwest of Madrid. There, the emperor lived closer to his grandson and received regular reports, but the weary Charles had little interest in seeing Don Carlos in the flesh. Before his death in 1558, Charles visited his grandson only once—on his way from Flanders to his sanctuary at Yuste.

While his father traveled and his grandfather prayed, young Carlos spent his preteen years under the careful watch of his preceptors. On the surface, his days were serene and wholesome. He ate three square meals and a snack at midafternoon, according to his governor, Don García de Toledo. He attended Mass daily. He slept exceptionally well and spent regular time at his books and exercise. He enjoyed a social life, too, passing several hours each day in pleasant conversation with friends.

During those same preteen years, however, family and teachers began to notice something amiss. Don García believed Don Carlos suffered from "bile," meaning he was given to fits of excessive anger. Moreover, he'd grown lazy about his studies, unwilling to apply himself. So frustrated was Don García that he dared suggest, ever so discreetly, that Charles V might consult doctors. Perhaps they might choose to medicate the boy.[6]

One year later, in 1558, Don García's exasperation was replaced by genuine alarm. Don Carlos wasn't learning. "As for his studies and physical exercises," he wrote once again to Charles V, "he is not advancing as much as I'd like. However, I don't think it's possible to bring more care and energy than we have to the task of teaching him all the things he should know. I would greatly desire Your Majesty to bring him for a time to Yuste so you can see him. Perhaps you might discern the obstacles to his education and decide that something could be changed in the way in which I am fulfilling my task. As for me, for the moment I don't see what I could change. However, I must note that, even though His Highness is as respectful and obedient as possible, neither my words nor any form of discipline—to which he is however quite sensitive—produce the desired effect."

Princess Juana implored her father to bring Don Carlos to Yuste as soon as possible. "Your Majesty cannot understand how important it is that you do this for us," she begged.[7] Yet Charles demurred.

Stories spread about Don Carlos's odd behavior. Around the same time that Don García penned his worries to the Emperor, the Venetian ambassador described what he'd heard while stationed in Flanders. "Prince Don Carlos is twelve years old," he wrote to the Doge in Venice. "His head is disproportionate to the rest of his body. His hair is black. Feeble in complexion, he already possesses the beginnings of a cruel character. One of the peculiarities they cite about him is that, when someone brings him hares captured in hunting . . . he wants to see them roasted alive. Someone gave him the present of a large turtle: one day, the animal bit him on the finger. Immediately, he bit off its head. He seems to be quite rash and extremely inclined toward women . . . His preceptor tries to teach him the *Offices* of Cicero, in order to moderate the impetuousness of his character; but Don Carlos only wants to talk about war and read books that have to do with war."[8]

What ailed the boy? No one knew. As the years passed, Philip's delight at a son and heir turned into apprehension as Don Carlos grew more difficult to control. The sixteenth century did not understand disability or development in the same way we do today. Instead, Philip saw Don Carlos as God's handiwork, a punishment for his own failings. The boy suffered from "defects of understanding that God, for my sins, has allowed in my son," Philip would later say.[9]

Where Philip saw God's work, we might see the mechanisms of biology. The prince's troubles likely stemmed in part from his genetic makeup. As one biographer points out, Don Carlos was the product of generations of inbreeding, not only by the Hapsburgs but by his Burgundian, Aragonese, and Castilian ancestors as well. His own parents were first cousins; their parents, in turn, were also first cousins. And these first cousins were more closely related, genetically, than most.

"Instead of eight great-grandparents," writes the historian Geoffrey Parker, "Don Carlos had only four, and instead of sixteen great-great-grandparents he had only six."[10] Even those distant forebears shared bloodlines, thanks to webs of intermarriage. In theory, the Catholic Church prohibited such consanguinous alliances, but royal families like the Hapsburgs and the Trastámarans (Don Carlos's Spanish ancestors) found it easy to obtain dispensations from popes whose permission they could purchase. Mental instability was inevitable. A strain of "madness" may have already cropped up in the Spanish side of the family. Charles V kept his own mother, known as *Juana la loca* (Juana the Mad), locked away in the palace at Tordesillas.[11]

Marriages among family solidified bonds of alliance and built empires. They had also produced a little boy whose body and mind suffered cruelly. Don Carlos was supposed to be purebred, the scion of the great Hapsburg dynastic machine. Instead, by adolescence, he seemed broken.

His head was too big, his shoulders uneven, his back hunched. His chest caved and he limped from a left leg that was shorter than his right. He was frighteningly pale (a fact every envoy noticed, and that contemporary portraits register), and so delicate that his preceptor refused to let him mount a horse. A severe case of "quartan fever," likely malaria, in 1560 left him constantly ill, beset by chills and sweats. Disease alone did not account for his feebleness, however. "In his nature," the Venetian ambassador explained, "he has neither great health nor vigor."[12]

Such details peppered diplomatic dispatches, some of which relied on hearsay; it is unclear if envoys exaggerated Don Carlos's physical characteristics to paint a more convincing portrait of his purported villainy.

By Carlos's midteen years, ambassadors treated the boy as if he bordered on the monstrous. His body was lopsided, his voice rasped, his tongue stuttered. He was given to gluttony and to cruelty. Some said he was ugly. His comprehension seemed no better than a seven-year-old's, and though he asked questions incessantly, rarely could he understand the answers. He was obsessive; war remained his favorite topic. Not everyone was entirely unkind. The Imperial ambassador noted that the young man demonstrated exemplary piety and possessed an excellent memory, though he admitted that Don Carlos lacked any sort of filter, simply saying whatever was on his mind.[13] The boy was excessively literal. As many observers reported, he hated liars and, unlike his father, loathed jesters and fools—perhaps because he could not understand their jokes and quips.

It was Don Carlos's temper, bouts of uncontrollable rage, that caused the most distress at court. His tantrums were episodic. "This is something that has phases," Philip explained, "so that at times there is more serenity than at others."[14] He could go weeks, even months, with little disquiet. Then, suddenly, the storm would grip him.

"He likes no one as far as I can tell," reported a Venetian, "but there are many people whom he hates unto death." If Don Carlos disliked a person, he pursued them with a vengeance. Brantôme would later recount an especially sinister story. "Once, his shoemaker made him a pair of boots, done very badly. Don Carlos had them chopped up into little pieces and fried like beef tripe. Then, as he watched, he made the shoemaker eat them that way, piece by piece."[15] The young man reserved a special hatred for Ruy Gómez, whom Philip appointed grand master of his son's household. From Ruy Gómez's first day on the job, Carlos was bent on driving the courtier into a state of desperation. Don Carlos suspected Ruy Gómez spied on him. He also despised how Philip lavished favors upon the man, despite Ruy Gómez's slight pedigree, yet paid only scant attention to his own son.

In his teens, Don Carlos noticed a troublesome trend. As of 1559, Philip had stipulated that, in the event of his own death, Carlos would reign over both the Netherlands and Spain, as soon as he was married. Strangely, though, his father gave him no official responsibilities—assignments a boy of his age and rank should already have received to prepare him for the role. Carlos couldn't understand it. Others noticed, too. Philip pushed Carlos aside, wrote the Imperial ambassador, employing "him in no affairs, which greatly humiliates him."[16]

Carlos believed Philip kept him down, a frustration he hoped a brilliant marriage would resolve, if only his father would allow it.

The Venetian envoy was wrong: there were a few people Don Carlos liked, even loved. One was his young uncle, Don Juan, the illegitimate son of Charles V, whom Philip brought to Spain in 1559. Two years younger than Don Carlos, Don Juan was the prince's ever-present companion, "the best friend that I have in this world."[17]

The other person he cherished was Elisabeth de Valois. More a peer than a stepmother, Elisabeth met Don Carlos in Toledo when she first arrived from France in early 1560. Bowing low before her, Don Carlos looked hardly a day over twelve, and was as pale and frail as ever, having just recovered from his first serious bout of quartan fever. She was gentle by nature; he was vulnerable. They soon became friends, as close as they could be in a court where strict codes of conduct governed the behavior of men in the presence of the young queen. Don Carlos seems to have visited Elisabeth as often as he could.

Beginning later in the century, a story blossomed that Don Carlos fell in love with Elisabeth, that he reproached his father "for having stolen his wife, the lady Elisabeth of France, who had been promised to him by the peace accord [of Cateau-Cambrésis] and who should have been his; and this greatly displeased him, for he loved her always and honored her until his death. And certainly, she was among the kindest and loveliest princesses in the world. It greatly angered him that she was taken from him."[18] This story would dominate romantic literature and opera in ensuing centuries. Yet nothing among mid-sixteenth-century sources suggests it was true.

Instead, they were companions. Loneliness likely drew them together, especially in the first years after Elisabeth's arrival in Spain, when Philip traveled often or holed himself up with his councillors. "She tried as hard as possible to give [Don Carlos] some kind of pleasure during the evenings," the Bishop of Limoges told Catherine in March 1560, "whether by dancing and other honest amusements, of which he is in great need."[19] They shared a love of art; Don Carlos had already gathered an impressive collection of paintings, and he too admired Sofonisba's skill with brush and oils. Elisabeth had every political reason to foster a friendship with the prince, if only to please her mother, who wanted him to marry Margot. Even so, Elisabeth's attempts to befriend the boy were heartfelt. She liked him, and he liked her. "He shows the queen a singular attachment," wrote Madame de Vineux.[20]

Not once in her letters to Catherine does Elisabeth mention a limp or hunched back, or dwell on unsavory aspects of Carlos's character. Rather, she worried for him. After Don Carlos suffered a life-threatening fall at Alcalá in 1562, Elisabeth and Princess Juana spent several sleepless nights on their knees, weeping and praying for his recovery, and Elisabeth wrote Catherine letters full of despair.* Don Carlos repaid her with gifts of jewelry and with kindness.[21] "He had an evil opinion of all women, and especially for great ladies, more than others, believing them to be hypocrites and traitors in love who, behind the curtains, are even more whorish than others," said Brantôme.[22] But Don Carlos never voiced any such thing about Elisabeth.

The friends were not always entirely forthcoming with each other, however.

The picture of Margot that Catherine sent to Elisabeth came with one other portrait. Historians do not know the identity of the person in this second picture; the letters between mother and daughter betray no hints. The portraits arrived in Spain in the first days of

---

*In 1561, after a particularly bad spell of quartan fever, Philip sent Don Carlos to recover in Alcalá de Henares, a picturesque little village on the banks of the Henares River, about twenty miles outside of Madrid. There, Philip believed, his son could recover in the fresh air and commit himself, at last, to his studies. For several months, the boy diligently set about his books. But the following year he tripped down a flight of stairs and slammed the back of his head into a wooden door. The gash quickly became inflamed. By the end of the week, Carlos babbled deliriously, the infection spreading over his head, sealing his eyes with pus, and seeping into his neck and down his torso, paralyzing one arm. The physicians—including the famed Vesalius—tried cupping, washing, massaging, diuretics, and bleeding. They called in a Moorish doctor who was popular with the locals, but to no avail.

Twenty-one days later, the doctors gave him up for lost. But by some miracle, natural or divine, Don Carlos began to recover after the townspeople disinterred the dessicated body of Fray Diego de Alcalá, a fifteenth-century Franciscan monk widely considered a saint. Hauling the corpse to the palace, the townspeople lifted it onto the boy's bed. Flitting in and out of consciousness and blinded by pus, Don Carlos groped with his one healthy hand to touch the holy relic. He would later credit the saint with saving his life. But Fray Diego couldn't heal his soul. After Carlos's fall, the bouts of rage grew only worse.

February 1561 as Elisabeth was still convalescing from her bout with smallpox. She displayed them in her chambers. While paying her friend a visit one afternoon, Princess Juana declared them "the most beautiful in the world." She especially admired the one of young Margot. Then, as if on cue, the prince Don Carlos was announced.

"He looked at the portraits too," Elisabeth wrote a few days later to her mother, "and told me three or four times while laughing: *Mas hermosa es la pequegna*"—the little one is prettier. "And it is a very pretty painting indeed, and I agreed with him that it was quite well done. Madame de Clermont told him that she would make a very good wife for him. He began to laugh and didn't answer."[23]

What those giggles signified, Elisabeth couldn't say. Maybe his laughter boded well; maybe the awkward prince really did admire Margot and simply didn't know how to answer. But perhaps, as Elisabeth secretly knew, there was another reason for Don Carlos's mirth. Quite possibly, the joke was on her and Catherine, because the prince's thoughts had already turned toward a certain Scottish queen.

16

THE TEST

France and Spain, 1561

That spring, a mysterious figure began to inhabit the letters exchanged between Catherine and the Bishop of Limoges, her ambassador in Spain. They called him *le gentilhomme*: the gentleman. "Madame, I received Your Majesty's orders," wrote Limoges, "and . . . because it is a thing of such great importance and such consequence to the king and to the future of our entire kingdom . . . with every care I am employing my friends and others, both here and there, to obey the king and shed some light, Madame, on the affair of the *gentleman* who so aggrieves you."[1] The gentleman in question was tall, willowy, and graced with amber eyes—*he* was none other than Mary Stuart herself.

From her conversations with the cardinal, it was clear to Catherine that she was not supposed to know about Mary's marriage plans. For her part, Elisabeth de Valois gleaned what she could from furtive looks and indiscreet remarks, but learned nothing substantive. Foiling the marriage plans meant undercutting men who were, at least outwardly, Catherine's allies: the Duke of Guise and the Cardinal of Lorraine, who sat on the king's council, and Philip II, her own son-in-law. Catherine needed to proceed with the utmost secrecy, coordinating carefully with the Bishop of Limoges. Sending letters was risky. Vulnerable and porous, letters passed through multiple hands as they traveled between realms and could easily land under spying eyes. Cipher offered one solution. Catherine's secretaries wrote enciphered letters, sending decryption keys in separate dispatches to the Bishop of Limoges.* In Spain, Limoges' eyes flitted back and forth from the decryption papers to the letters as he painstakingly deciphered each symbol. Catherine worried, however, that even code was not secure enough. Hence *le gentilhomme*.

The so-called gentleman was proving sneaky in her dealings, so Catherine doubled down on her own deviousness. Cornering Don Juan Manrique de Lara—the Spanish nobleman sent to mourn officially with the French court after the death of Francis II— Catherine gushed about her plans to one day arrange a brilliant match for young King Charles, all the while poking and prodding (as she confessed in a coded letter to Limoges). Alas, Catherine learned nothing from the sly Don Juan about "that other marriage." She remained determined, however. "I am doing and will continue to do everything in my power to stop it," she vowed to Limoges.[2]

She faced a formidable enemy. The Guises were clearly in cahoots with the Spanish ambassador, Chantonnay, whom Catherine detested. Who else had they bought off in Spain? Catherine's own resources there were scant, only a few select agents who could divulge anything useful. "They are saying that the match would be a fine one for *them*," Madame de Clermont wrote, using a veiled term for Don Carlos. "And using Scotland, *they* will get to rule Flanders. And since the kingdom of England belongs to *her*, as is claimed, soon Spain, Flanders and Scotland will be in *their* possession." But Madame de Clermont was good only for nuggets of Spanish gossip and could do nothing to influence Spanish policy. Only the Bishop of Limoges and Elisabeth might sway Philip.[3] Yet so far, Elisabeth had succeeded in persuading Philip of almost nothing.

The Queen Mother didn't use either cipher or cryptic references to *le gentilhomme* when she wrote to Elisabeth. Decryption was, of course, a confounding task and Catherine still explained concepts to her daughter in simple language appropriate for a fifteen-year-old, reserving nuance for her savvier ambassador. More importantly, writing to Elisabeth in cipher would have been dangerous. The Bishop of Limoges resided in his own house, but Elisabeth lived in the lion's den. Spanish ladies-in-waiting flocked about her, and

---

*One of Catherine's most trusted secretaries was Claude de l'Aubespine, older brother of the Bishop of Limoges.

Philip and Don Carlos paid her regular visits. How would it look if a Spaniard discovered an encrypted letter in the young Catholic Queen's apartments? (Snooping eyes worried kings and queens. On at least one occasion Charles V warned Philip to keep his papers "under lock and key where neither your wife nor any other living person can see" them.)[4]

It was best to use evasion and obfuscation. Catherine's missives to Elisabeth—and Elisabeth's replies—made only glancing references to Mary, never naming the Queen of Scots outright. Instead, they wove innuendo among innocuous topics like Elisabeth's gift to Catherine of four dozen gloves, "some perfumed white ones, some perfumed black ones, and some without any perfume but well washed." Catherine would let the Bishop of Limoges spell out details to Elisabeth during their private conversations.[5]

"You know what I wrote to you about . . . regarding the marriage that was brewing here," read one of Catherine's late-December messages to Limoges. "I have since discovered that it is going forward. Watch over this matter to discover what is involved."

Catherine had a way of dictating exactly what her correspondents were supposed to say. Now she ordered Limoges to paint the rosiest picture possible about the state of affairs in France for King Philip. Catherine was so beloved by the people, she claimed, that French subjects "believe it greatly fortunate that Our Lord, though he wished to take their prince, has left me here to govern the next one [King Charles], who is so well born and of such good character that the people hope much good and relief will come from him."

In the meantime, the ambassador must do everything in his power to steer Philip away from approving the marriage to Mary Stuart. "You know how important this is," she implored. "Warn me immediately of everything you learn about this matter. Use this messenger, whom you will send back without any dispatch other than your response to this letter." Above all else: "Keep my daughter well informed of the role she must play."[6]

———

Catherine plotted and schemed. On the one hand, she desperately wanted to thwart Mary Stuart and the Guises. On the other, she desired with equal desperation for Don Carlos to marry her own Margot. Achieving the second goal would accomplish the first—so Catherine set her mind on advancing Margot's candidacy. She used every ploy she could think of, hoping at least one would work. She sent sugared notes to King Philip asking for a meeting face-to-face, at Monzón. She flattered Ruy Gómez, feeding his partiality to France. She sent the portrait of Margot. And she urged Elisabeth to drop hints at court about her little sister's fetching character.

Philip was one of Catherine's targets. The other target was Princess Juana. Catherine believed Juana could be coaxed into supporting Margot. Of course, Elisabeth would have to do the coaxing.

Through Madame de Clermont's skillful reporting, Catherine had learned of the blossoming attachment between Juana and Elisabeth. The news delighted the Queen Mother. Everyone knew Philip adored his youngest sister. A woman beloved by the Princess might more easily maneuver her way into Philip's affections. Now, in 1560, could Catherine use that friendship to get what she wanted?

Juana doted upon Elisabeth from the moment they first met in Guadalajara. A born nurturer, Juana loved her nephew Don Carlos despite his frequent rude behavior and took pains to ensure his health. She spread those maternal feelings around widely. Stridently pious, she had founded a convent of Poor Clares in Madrid in 1557, housed in the palace where she had been born. The convent was known as *Las Descalzas reales* ("the royal barefoot ones"), in recognition of the vow of poverty taken by the women who lived there. It was a place where Juana and her female relatives could withdraw whenever court life became a burden—though Juana, exceptionally proud of her rank, sometimes found it difficult to give up court life and instead brought it with her to the convent. Her main goal, however, was to raise nuns for the Franciscan order. In one portrait, possibly painted by Sofonisba in 1561, Juana stands with a young novice who looks no more than seven or eight years old. The child leans into the Princess's skirts. Anyone who didn't know better would think this was a portrait of a mother and daughter.[7]

Juana was, in fact, a mother. She had married her first cousin, the Portuguese heir João Manuel, in 1552, at the age of seventeen. Their marriage lasted less than two years, with João Manuel dying in 1554, one week before Juana gave birth to their son. The infant, Sebastian, was four months old when Juana received Philip's call to return to Spain, there to take up the regency while he lived in Flanders. Obediently, she packed up her household, leaving her son in the care of his paternal grandmother. She always hoped to return to Portugal as regent for her child, but the opportunity never arrived. Though she received regular portraits of Sebastian, and papered the Portuguese court with letters, Juana would never see her son in person again.

With no child of her own at the Spanish court, Juana focused her maternal attentions on the new queen. Elisabeth may have seen faint traces of her own mother in the Princess, who, like Catherine de' Medici, dressed perpetually in austere black after the death of her husband. Yet Juana wasn't so very austere. Her father, Charles V, often found fault in his youngest child, complaining that Juana was "very haughty" and that she "led a disorderly life."[8] That youthful disorderliness, a dash of spontaneity in Juana's nature, matched well with Elisabeth's vivaciousness, though physically they were opposites: Elisabeth raven-haired, Juana blond and blue-eyed. Juana's "haughtiness," too, probably made Elisabeth—the only woman at court to outrank her—one of the few companions Juana deigned to accept.

Their friendship was real and deeply felt. At Aranjuez, Madame de Clermont noticed that not a single day elapsed without a visit or message passed between Juana and Elisabeth. Sometimes they spent every minute of the day together. They attended Mass each morning, picnicked and danced, planned masques and ballets, chatted idly, visited convents, and attended vespers at nearby monasteries. Juana, a music lover, invited Elisabeth to spend hours in her chambers, listening to the viola and the harp, or the winsome notes of the flautist Elisabeth brought with her from France. Elisabeth taught Juana to ride *à la française*. That was a trial. More accustomed to a litter and a mule, Juana fell from her horse on her first attempts. Determined to please Elisabeth, Juana dusted herself off for another round until she had more or less mastered her new skill.[9]

Juana tended to Elisabeth in her most vulnerable moments. "On Friday morning her migraine seized her," wrote Madame de Clermont about yet another of Elisabeth's chronic headaches. "She didn't get up, but instead heard Mass, and dined and supped from her bed. Madame the Princess came to visit her that night." Elisabeth had likely never enjoyed a closer friendship—not even with Mary Stuart as a child. Certainly, with Juana there was nothing like the "fear"—*la crainte*—governing Elisabeth's relationship to Catherine.[10]

Catherine, though, believed that Elisabeth owed allegiance to her mother first, and to Juana only second. The Princess was simply another tool to achieve Catherine's objective, one she assumed Elisabeth shared. "Lose no occasion to prevent the prince from marrying any woman other than your sister [Margot]," she told her daughter. "I've heard that the Princess loves you infinitely. To accomplish your goal, you need to ask her to help you."[11]

Meanwhile, Catherine assigned Elisabeth yet another task. The Guises were making the Queen Mother's life miserable. They pushed an unforgiving Catholic agenda and set about undermining Catherine's authority. Buttering up the vainglorious King of Navarre, they tried to persuade him to break his agreement with Catherine and take over the regency himself. The Guises had an inkling that, given the right enticement, Antoine de Bourbon would abandon his support for the Huguenots and support the Catholic cause in France, undercutting Catherine's efforts at compromise. They convinced Antoine that he would regain Navarre from Spain if he alone ruled France as regent and controlled its armies—only then would he earn Philip II's respect. As February 1561 rolled into March, Antoine began to chafe at Catherine's control over the regency, grumbling about his rights in Navarre. He played right into Guise hands.

A shaken Catherine wrote once again to Elisabeth, her letter so fractured and rambling that it barely made sense. But from the garbled prose, Elisabeth gathered the following request. "If you wish for me to have peace, and if you love me, make it so your husband [King Philip] gives [the King of Navarre] some sort of resolution." Perhaps Philip could return a portion of Spanish Navarre, or even offer up a different Spanish holding, such as Sardinia. Surely, with some small gift, the King of Navarre would be subdued, his good understanding with Catherine restored.

These were dangerous requests to make of anyone, let alone a teenager. Not only should Elisabeth meddle in the marriage of Mary Stuart—she should now attempt to sway her husband's relations with a fellow king. Such was the measure of Catherine's desperation.

Catherine never seemed to doubt Elisabeth's obedience, the strength of her allegiance. During her first years in Spain, Elisabeth gave her no reason to do so. "Your very humble and obedient daughter," the girl signed at the end of every letter, and Elisabeth's actions during these months proved her words, however rote. Indeed, in her blind adherence to her mother's wishes, Elisabeth had developed her own duplicitous streak, even against her close companions.

In March, as the plotting against Mary Stuart intensified, Catherine finally settled on a departure date for Madame de Clermont. The lady-in-waiting seems not to have realized the extent of Spanish hostility toward her, nor that Catherine planned to bring her home. Catherine instructed Elisabeth to pretend as if she knew nothing. "Madame de Clermont came to me the other day," a guilt-ridden Elisabeth confessed to Limoges. "She made me swear that I knew nothing of her parting, nor you either. And since I feared she might fall ill if I did otherwise . . . I did swear to it, at least that you hadn't said anything to me and promised you knew nothing . . . I promised her that I would ask you, like someone who was completely innocent."* Later, Elisabeth may have regretted lying. After Madame de Clermont left Spain for good, Elisabeth missed her terribly. "I cannot tell you how sad I feel to lose such good company," she told Catherine. Catherine gently explained why Madame de Clermont had to leave: "lest your husband believe I am using her as a spy." Still, she always expected Elisabeth's complete acquiescence.[12]

In Catherine's mind, the dynamic was straightforward. The Queen Mother banked on her daughter's absolute, almost mechanical compliance, and on Elisabeth's boundless trust. Not once did she give her daughter room to question her decisions, to ask, for instance, whether a marriage between Mary Stuart and Don Carlos might benefit Spain, the kingdom of which Elisabeth was now queen. Or whether the marriage could, in fact, promote religious reconciliation

---

*Madame de Clermont was anguished to learn of her departure, believing she had failed Catherine. The Bishop of Limoges asked Catherine to assure Clermont of her goodwill; Elisabeth also asked Catherine to treat Madame de Clermont gently. Clearly, all three worried that Catherine would punish Madame de Clermont once she returned to France.

in France. Catherine behaved as if Elisabeth were merely an extension of her own will: there to serve Catherine as Catherine saw fit.

Nor did Catherine ever seem to consider how her plotting might compromise Elisabeth's security in Spain. She voiced no concerns about asking Elisabeth to maneuver against her husband, no misgivings about exploiting the friendship with Juana that was surely part and parcel of Elisabeth's happiness in Spain.

Likewise, Catherine felt no pangs of conscience at asking Elisabeth to obstruct a marriage that would serve both Don Carlos, Elisabeth's new friend and son-in-law, and Mary Stuart, Elisabeth's old friend—a girl Elisabeth still called "sister," a girl whom Catherine once treated like a daughter. Whenever Catherine wrote openly (and not in code) about Mary during this period, she betrayed not a trace of pity for the grieving young woman. For Catherine, the lines were clearly drawn: if Elisabeth was an extension of Catherine's own self, Mary belonged heart and soul to the Guises.

"She shows me as much obsequiousness as ever," a spiteful Catherine wrote to Elisabeth that March about Mary. "But I have no doubts about her true intentions."[13]

To Catherine, friendship could be sacrificed when politics intervened. As soon as Francis II died, Catherine's bond with Mary was severed. But blood ties—the ties binding mother to child, or at least child to mother—remained unbreakable, stronger even than a marriage vow.

Over the previous eighteen months, Catherine had sent Elisabeth countless letters and gifts. Now, that deep love she felt for Elisabeth, the unsevered cord to France and family, would serve Catherine politically when she needed it most. Elisabeth was a princess of France: wasn't it her duty to help the kingdom of her birth? As Catherine's panic mounted, however, her letters also told a slightly different story. Elisabeth must act for her *mother's* sake: this was the message Catherine hammered home. Possibly, she believed only this message would inspire Elisabeth to do what was necessary. Or perhaps, to Catherine, her own authority and the well-being of France had become one and the same thing.

Had France been at peace, Catherine might not have clutched at Elisabeth so desperately. But the circumstances being what they were, in her own mind Catherine could not afford to let Elisabeth go.

The spring of 1561 arrived. Catherine received disheartening and worrisome reports: Elisabeth was making little progress, and Mary Stuart's marriage plans appeared to be proceeding apace. Limoges busied himself decoding encrypted letters intercepted from a French monk who (the ambassador suspected) had come to Spain on behalf of the Guises "to break off some marriages and make others." The letters touched upon "the said *gentleman*," he told Catherine.[14] Even worse, Elisabeth reported that Philip seemed frosty about Margot. Though he had initially praised the little girl's portrait, in the ensuing months he'd taken little interest in the youngest Valois daughter.

In May, Catherine laid a piece of cream-colored paper on her writing desk and dipped her pen. In her panic, she had concocted yet another marriage scheme to cut off Mary Stuart's prospects: if Princess Juana would not support Margot, perhaps Elisabeth should persuade the Princess, her new friend and sister-in-law, to marry Don Carlos herself.

Once again, Catherine dictated exactly what Elisabeth was to say.

"Madame my daughter, I've read your letter regarding the marriage of the queen your sister and the prince.* Seeing that this continues, and that the matter has taken on new life, I think that if you believe it impossible for your little sister [Margot] to marry the prince, then you should help the Princess [Juana] to marry the prince, using everything you have in your power . . . Tell her that nothing would comfort you more than to see her married to the prince [Carlos], that because you are friends, you wish her to rise to the greatest rank possible. And, if she does so, the two of you will be able to spend your entire lives together. Ask her to tell you how she feels about this honestly so that you can serve her well in this affair. You must make it clear that you love her and wish to satisfy both her peace of mind and her dignity. I counsel you, my daughter, because you love us, to help her and do everything possible so that she marries him."

The prospect of endogamy hardly fazed Catherine. She was all too apprised of the Hapsburgs' fondness for marrying each other.

---

*Catherine also persisted in calling Mary Stuart Elisabeth's "sister."

Then Catherine turned to the topic of the petulant King of Navarre, Elisabeth's second charge. Sensing a reluctance on Elisabeth's part to intervene, Catherine changed her tack. "I've already written to you about speaking to your husband regarding some sort of remuneration for the King of Navarre . . . so I won't repeat my thoughts to you here. I will only entreat you to follow the instructions I've sent to the Bishop of Limoges. If you wish to help me, you must help him as much as you can. This, my daughter, will satisfy the King of Navarre and so it will achieve what your husband wishes to see happen in France.

"My daughter," Catherine continued, "think about all the good you will be doing if you achieve what [Philip] wants . . . Then I will be able to arrange everything here to your husband's satisfaction." Catherine conflated Elisabeth's obligations: to serve Catherine and to serve Philip had become one and the same thing.

Catherine closed with a pointed reminder about family. "I won't lecture you any longer, since I am sure you will do all that you can to follow the ambassador's advice. I am doing well here, as are your brothers and sisters. I pray to God that you are also well and that He continues your happiness and contentment for as long as you desire."[15]

Because you love us. If you wish to help me. A daughter's duty boiled down to love and obedience, distilled with "fear," as Catherine herself had once put it. This was the alchemy of attachment.

She held out love as bait. Elisabeth did love her mother. Her love for Catherine—and her deep yearning for her mother's approval— had been a presiding constant in her life. Now, Catherine put that affection to the test. If Elisabeth loved her mother, she would do exactly as she was told. From that would come everything Elisabeth ever wished for. Peace at home. Philip's approval. God's blessing. And, of course, her mother's abiding love in return.

No more and no less, the Queen Mother said, than what Catherine wished for too.

17

THE RETURN

France, Spain, Scotland, and England, 1561

"I find myself at peace thanks to the love and obedience the King of Navarre now shows me," a relieved Catherine crowed to Elisabeth at the end of May 1561. "I assure you he could not be more obedient if he were my own son." When she realized Elisabeth wasn't making headway in Spain, Catherine took certain steps of her own in France. At the Queen Mother's behest, her Bourbon friend and kinswoman, the infinitely diplomatic Madame de Montpensier, stepped in. It had been Madame de Montpensier who helped convince Antoine de Bourbon to accept the lieutenant-governorship when Charles IX acceded to the throne, persuading him that it was better to work with Catherine than against her. Now, once again, the good matron wouldn't let Catherine down.

Of course, Catherine continued, Elisabeth should still try to persuade Philip II to compensate the King of Navarre. It was just that the goal had changed: Catherine now needed less to purchase the King of Navarre's favor than merely to keep him happy.[1]

Just days later, Elisabeth sent good news of her own, the best the Queen Mother could have received: after months of secret negotiations, the wedding of Mary Stuart and Don Carlos was off. Somehow, Philip had discovered that Catherine suspected the marriage plans. Eager to save face, he pretended not to have known anything about it. "He heard that you believe [the Guises] have been discussing the marriage of their niece to the prince. He assured me this was not the case. He has commanded me to tell you that he would really like to know the origin of this rumor . . . I told him that you've said nothing about it to me, and that I didn't think you suspected anything like it." For Elisabeth it was becoming easier to lie.[2]

If everyone pretended that they knew nothing, the two realms could move forward, their alliance steadfast. In truth, several doubts put Philip off the marriage. He hesitated to jeopardize the Guises' position on King Charles IX's council, for one. Then there was the English queen to contend with. Elizabeth Tudor had got wind of the plans and, boiling with rage, made it clear to Philip that she considered the marriage an open act of hostility on the part of Spain. Finally, there was the gentle prodding of his wife, who never stopped talking about her sister Margot—which, Philip no doubt suspected, she did at Catherine's instigation. Hounded by the three women— and still harboring private doubts about Don Carlos—Philip thought it best to lay the negotiations aside.[3]

These were only temporary resolutions, as both Catherine and Elisabeth de Valois knew. The King of Navarre could change his mind about working with Catherine. The Guise–Spanish marriage negotiations could yet go forward. And Catherine had no guarantee that Don Carlos would one day marry Margot. For now, though, she had won her battles.

Most of all, she was assured of Elisabeth's loyalty. Her daughter had played her part as well as she could, a small yet decided victory. "[Elisabeth] grows every day in authority and virtue," confirmed the Bishop of Limoges. "She hopes . . . you will use your letters to continue to support her as she meets with her husband, with the assuredness and boldness that she is beginning to show quite effectively." *Help me help you*, Elisabeth might have said. They would serve each other, mother and daughter. Catherine obliged, confident that her eldest daughter remained firmly in her corner.[4]

During Mary Stuart's final days in France, Catherine de' Medici put on a show. In July, Mary joined the court at Saint-Germain-en-Laye, once the home of the *petite cour*, the site of so many of her happy childhood memories. Catherine planned a sumptuous send-off, four days of festivities and spectacles fit for an honored dowager queen.

On the twenty-fourth, Mary said her goodbyes. In public, Catherine mourned the Queen of Scots' departure, yet in truth she was only too happy to see Mary go.

"She embarked eight days ago, and if she had a good wind, she's already in Scotland," was all Catherine scribbled to Elisabeth de Valois a few weeks later, relieved the problem child would at last be somewhere across the sea.[5]

To King Philip II, Ambassador Chantonnay furnished other details. "Queen Mary left [court] the day before yesterday," he wrote on July 26. The Queen of England had denied Mary a passport in case her ships were driven onto English shores, since she still refused to ratify the Treaty of Edinburgh. Elizabeth Tudor had also asked Mary to renounce "all her pretentions to the kingdom of England and demanded that she bring no more than one hundred Frenchmen with her" when she returned to Scotland. Mary ignored the English queen, putting "all of it off until she returns to Scotland. She is headed now to Calais where there are two galleys awaiting her," Chantonnay said. King Philip had already issued a safe conduct for Mary in case she needed to land in Flanders, but Elizabeth Tudor extended her no such goodwill.[6]

Mary had spent the previous weeks slowly winding her way toward the port at Calais, mourning and delaying her departure. Even during her final days, some courtiers wondered if she would change her mind and stay. At last, however, on August 14, Mary resigned herself to the inevitable and boarded her galley, a large ship painted a gleaming white. Most of her entourage piled into a second vessel—this one glowing crimson—on which two flags flew at the stern, a blue one sewn with the arms of France, and a white one "glistening like silver." Brushing aside Elizabeth Tudor's warnings, Mary brought with her scores of Frenchmen and Frenchwomen. Among the courtiers in her train were the four Marys, her little Scottish friends, now grown, and three of her younger Guise uncles. The Duke of Guise and the Cardinal of Lorraine remained behind in France.

During those last, ceremonious days at Saint-Germain-en-Laye, the French court had plied Mary with gifts. She brought those presents with her now, along with other mementos of her French childhood—pomanders, books of poems, embroidery, the thick strings of pearls Catherine had given her. Few gifts were quite as touching as the elegy Pierre de Ronsard composed in her honor. Without Mary, wrote Ronsard, France was like a portrait stripped of color, a ring robbed of "its precious pearl." Of all French poets, Ronsard was Mary's favorite. Whenever she was feeling homesick in the years to come, she would sift through his verses and weep.[7]

Her fleet weighed anchor at noon. On board, everyone strolled the deck for the rest of the afternoon as the ships struggled to reach open water. Among the French contingent sailing with Mary to Scotland was the courtier Brantôme. Later, he would recall watching Mary as she settled herself upon the deck, refusing to retire to her chambers below. As her galley slowly drifted from the shore, a weak wind filling its sails, she remained fixed at the helm. Propped up on her arms and peering over the sideboard, Mary gazed back at the coastline. Then she fell apart. "Goodbye France!" she wept. "Goodbye!" She stayed near the helm for nearly five hours.

That evening, she barely ate, and that night she barely slept. When she refused to retire to her rooms below, her ladies cobbled together a bed for her on deck. Crawling under the covers, Mary begged the helmsman to wake her early if the French coastline were still visible. The next morning, she awoke to a sliver of shoreline far in the distance. The wind had ceased, refusing to carry them out to sea. "Fortune had favored her," said Brantôme, but it was a cruel gift. When at last the wind picked up, driving the galley into open waters, she sobbed again. Her words are famous. "Adieu France! It is over. Adieu France! I think I shall never see you again."[8]

As she predicted, Mary would never see the kingdom of her childhood again. To return to France would remain her most fervent wish, one that colored her choices in all the years to come. For Mary, France wasn't merely a place. It was a state of mind. There, she had found shelter from childhood perils, a loving family who coddled her, courtiers who flattered her, kings who prized her as the capstone of their imperial dreams. Now all that had disappeared. Mary would hold on as best she could, maintaining a steady correspondence with her Guise uncles and grandmother, although almost all the letters to Antoinette have been lost. During the coming years, especially at times of profound crisis, Mary would say that she wished she could go and live with her grandmother in

France. She missed Antoinette terribly and wanted nothing more than to go home.*

Once the wind picked up, Mary's galleys set a course for Leith, just north of Edinburgh. Whereas thirteen years earlier, Mary had braved the Irish Sea, sixteen days of sickness and swells, the return required only a quick jaunt through the Channel, the ships briefly flanking the Netherlands before proceeding up the eastern coast of England—a mere five days. On August 19, at six o'clock in the morning, Mary's galley crept up to Leith just as a thick fog began to lift. Always looking for portents, the French on board thought the brume augured poorly. Years later, the Scottish Calvinist preacher John Knox echoed the sentiment, his words dripping with scorn for the young woman he would come to hate. "The sun was not seen to shine two days before, nor two days after" Mary landed, Knox wrote. "That forewarning gave God unto us; but alas, the most part were blind."[9]

The fog likely mirrored Mary's state of mind. She had not seen the kingdom of Scotland since she was five. Her heart sank when she saw the horses and hackneys awaiting her. Her galley had sailed too quickly; the reception at Leith was hastily arranged. "This is not the magnificence, these are not the provisions, these are not the fine horses of France that I am used to," she complained, according to Brantôme. That night, as she settled in at Holyrood Abbey, townspeople gathered under her window, playing fiddles and signing the Psalms, trying to pay their respects. John Knox said later that Mary enjoyed the musicians. But Brantôme complained they were woefully out of tune. Even decades later, the Catholic Brantôme couldn't hide his disdain for the Scots. Nor his sorrow for Mary, returning to her land of heretics and savages.[10]

―――――

A few years later, rumors would circulate that before Mary left France, Catherine de' Medici forced the Guises to make a choice.

―――――――――――――――――――――――――――――――――

*Brantôme's image of the eighteen-year-old Mary gazing back to France as the wind carried her to Scotland is such a perfect metaphor for the next chapter of her life that one wonders if he made it up. The ship of state had sailed indeed and, though stationed at its helm, Mary remained merely a passenger, always looking back to what she once had in France.

They could arrange Mary's marriage to a rival kingdom, or they could choose the interests of France. In the end, like good Frenchmen, they "preferred to seek the well-being of France over any advantage for their niece." According to one historian, during her last days in France, when Mary asked the Duke of Guise for advice regarding her next marriage, the duke gave no answer, saying only that "he was not able to tell her which steps suited her best."[11]

The Guises would continue to write, of course, and to counsel her. Still, Mary felt their distance. She returned to Scotland an orphan. Unlike Elisabeth de Valois, she had no mother to "hold her hand," as Antoinette had done all those years earlier, when Mary first arrived in France at the age of five. And her burdens were different from those of Elisabeth de Valois: what would Mary have given to be, like Elisabeth, the wife of a powerful king, unburdened by the responsibilities of ruling on her own? Had the politically astute Marie de Guise lived, perhaps Mary might never have returned to Scotland at all, choosing instead a dynastic marriage to a princely husband and the life of a consort—a life that had suited her well. Or, had Marie de Guise lived, she might have continued to advise her daughter, standing behind the throne until Mary grew into the role.

If affairs had gone differently in France, one other woman might have stepped in to guide Mary. Catherine de' Medici possessed the wherewithal to shepherd a young queen through the intricacies of a new kingdom and culture, as Elisabeth de Valois's experience had proven. In her mother-in-law, Mary might have found the guiding, maternal hand she had lost. Yet the Guises' ruthless policies, their raw striving for influence within the kingdom of France, had alienated Catherine and interfered in a relationship that had once been tender. Long ago Catherine had described Mary as the girl who would bring her comfort in old age. Now the Queen Mother saw her chiefly as the weak instrument of Guise ambition. The two queens would correspond, as appropriate, though almost all of Catherine's letters to Mary have disappeared.* Mary's communications to Catherine during this time were polite enough, and she never failed to sign dutifully, "Your humble and most obedient daughter." But her letters

---

*However, Mary would repeatedly refer to Catherine's letters in her own correspondence.

showed few traces of real warmth. Only later, when Mary believed she had much greater need of Catherine, did that reserve melt away.

As it happened, Mary returned to Scotland bereft of a mother's advice. She had no real political friends, no supervisor, no Princess Juana to chaperone her through the ways of the strange land she was entering. In truth, she was still a political child, in need of a regent. But at eighteen, no regent was legally necessary. She was on her own.

There was one other woman whose aid Mary would try to enlist. As the scholar Susan Doran has suggested, possibly it was Mary's overwhelming sense of solitude that pushed her to seek Elizabeth Tudor's friendship so ardently, to secure Queen Elizabeth's endorsement of her place in the English succession: this friendship, this inheritance, would become Mary's most famous obsession. Even before she departed France for Scotland, Mary had met with the English ambassador, Nicholas Throckmorton, and assured him of her goodwill toward her cousin, the queen.[12] Perhaps she believed Elizabeth could help her navigate the dark waters of Scottish religion and politics, serving as a friend and guide, the kind of older relative on whom Mary always relied. Perhaps, if Mary became England's heir, Elizabeth would invest in their alliance and lend her the assistance she needed. Perhaps then, Mary's Protestant Scottish lords would be appeased—or so Mary hoped.[13]

Then again, Mary's desire to secure the English succession was complex. Like the crown of the French consort, the English sovereign crown had defined her while she lived in France. It was the promise of the English crown that brought her to France in the first place as a child under Henry II's protection, the crown that had purchased her refuge. We can never know the hidden workings of Mary's mind. Perhaps she couldn't decipher them herself. Possibly, though, she wished to prove to the Guises, to her fellow sovereigns, even to herself, that her value still held. With the English succession in her possession, she could recover what she had lost: unparalleled status, a royal husband, a home.

Years afterward, Brantôme wrote, the Guises came to realize their miscalculation in sending Mary back to Scotland and "repented of their mistake."[14]

Soon after the fog cleared at Leith, messengers galloped south, bringing word to the English court of Mary's landing in Scotland. If Catherine de' Medici felt elated about Mary's departure, Elizabeth Tudor felt something closer to distress at her return. Before she left France, Mary had made it clear to the English envoy, Nicholas Throckmorton, that she hoped Queen Elizabeth would soon acknowledge her right to the English succession. Now Mary brought the succession question back to Elizabeth's side of the Channel, adding to an already anxiety-ridden slate of problems. The War in Scotland in 1560 had taxed the English queen's finances, and the Treaty of Edinburgh still dangled unratified. Her own subjects fretted over the English succession, too, and clamored for her to marry and produce an heir. This Elizabeth was loath to do.

"This shall be for me sufficient, that a marble stone shall declare that a queen, having reigned such a time, lived and died a virgin," she had announced to her House of Commons shortly after accession. That answer satisfied no one. Though Elizabeth shouted her opposition, her counselors and Parliament continued to urge her to wed. Mary's return would only make them push her harder to marry and bear an heir to secure her throne against the Catholic Queen of Scots.[15]

In the late summer of 1561, Queen Elizabeth was almost twenty-eight years old and had reigned for nearly three years. Beneath her bold facade—a haughty demeanor, a fondness for flattery, a propensity to swear in the council chamber, and that bewildering refusal to marry—she hid a gnawing insecurity. The daughter of Anne Boleyn and Henry VIII, Elizabeth had been bastardized by her father at the age of three. Though he eventually restored her place in the English succession, Elizabeth never recovered her legitimacy. She'd lived an isolated childhood, largely friendless, her mother's adultery and execution a dark shadow she could never shake. Until she was nine years old, her father refused to see her. She had almost no relationship with any of her stepmothers except the last one, Katherine Parr, to whom she grew close. Their friendship did not last long, however. Shortly after her father's death, the thirteen-year-old Elizabeth joined the household of Katherine and her new husband, Thomas Seymour, who was uncle to Elizabeth's younger half-brother, Edward, the new king. Soon Katherine caught the young girl in Seymour's arms and sent Elizabeth to live elsewhere.

Elizabeth likely had fallen in love with the older man and submitted to his touching and fondling, too young to recognize that he was grooming her in pursuit of his own political ambitions.

In her early twenties, Elizabeth lived through the terrifying reign of her older half-sister, the Catholic Mary Tudor, who detested her Protestantism and held that Elizabeth, a bastard, possessed no right to the throne. To become her sister's heir, Elizabeth endured the persecution of her coreligionists, hid her own beliefs, and fought for the succession. She bought off supporters, mounted secret campaigns, plotted to force her sister's hand. It worked, but just barely: Mary Tudor acknowledged Elizabeth's rights only on her deathbed.

Elizabeth had suffered for her birthright, clawed her way to the English throne. A swathe of her Parliament still doubted her legitimacy, but Elizabeth meant to stay where she was. She feared any action that might undermine her own power and could ill afford to take it lightly. She scorned anyone who did.

Still, Elizabeth felt ambivalent about the Queen of Scots. She had reason to admire Mary: the Scottish queen seemed a virtuous young woman in deep mourning for a husband she'd cherished. Dutifully, she had returned to her kingdom and subjects. Even Mary's claim to the English throne wasn't entirely offensive to Elizabeth. In theory, Mary had no legal rights: Henry VIII of England had barred his Scottish relatives in both the 1544 Act of Succession and his last will and testament. Mary based her claim on blood right, as the descendant of Henry VIII's oldest sister, Margaret Tudor. Elizabeth could accept this, believing it was blood right, more than law, that justified her own crown.*

All the same, Mary seemed too eager to claim a crown that did not yet belong to her. Under Kings Henry II and Francis II, she had dared cross the arms of Scotland with those of England as if she were already England's queen—much to Elizabeth Tudor's annoyance. What made Mary more trustworthy now? To Throckmorton in Paris just that summer, the Scottish queen had promised Queen Elizabeth only friendship. Everything up to that point had been the work

---

*In fact, none of the potential candidates had a clear legal path to the English throne. Henry VIII's marital foibles, followed by the religious tensions in the kingdom, had mired England in succession woes.

of her husband or father-in-law, Mary said.[16] Her pledges seemed earnest enough.

And yet. To Elizabeth's great chagrin, Mary still wouldn't ratify the Treaty of Edinburgh. Her hesitation nurtured the English queen's suspicions. With a single signature, Mary could prove her goodwill. She could put the hostility to bed. Why, then, did she refuse?

About the Guises, Queen Elizabeth felt something akin to wrath. The austerity of their Catholicism repelled her. She also believed the Guises saw her as a usurper and suspected they had long coveted England's throne for themselves. She was sure the Guises stoked Mary's refusal to ratify the Treaty of Edinburgh. Now that Mary had returned to Scotland, were the Guises, in spirit, there, too?

In September, Mary's new ambassador to England, William Maitland, Laird of Lethington, rode to the English court to present his official papers, deliver Queen Mary's good tidings, and ask Queen Elizabeth once again about the succession. Maitland found the redheaded English queen to be a regal woman, if not quite as beautiful as his Queen Mary; poised like Mary, but not nearly as tall. Queen Elizabeth's tongue, though, was even quicker than Mary's, as Maitland would shortly discover. As for her mind, that was sharp as a tack.

Queen Elizabeth asked Maitland a pointed question of her own. Why did Mary, Queen of Scots, still refuse to ratify the Treaty of Edinburgh? Oh, but Queen Mary was busy greeting her nobles, Maitland lamely explained.[17] Elizabeth grew visibly annoyed. If Mary was going to dally on the treaty, then Elizabeth could dawdle, too, tit for tat. Over a series of conversations that September, Maitland would learn Elizabeth had gathered her thoughts about the English succession. Her answer did not bode well for Mary.

Elizabeth spoke plainly to the Scottish ambassador: to be honest, she feared for her own security on the English throne. But the threat didn't come from Mary, or at least not Mary alone. Instead, it came from her own subjects. The people were greedy, ready to turn at any moment to the prince they believed would serve them best. Elizabeth had witnessed this phenomenon when, under the reign of her sister Mary Tudor, she had played the part that Mary Stuart now played. Then, men had flocked to Elizabeth in droves, leaving Mary Tudor isolated and alone. Fickleness, Elizabeth explained, was a particularly English trait.

"I know the inconstancy of the people of England, how they ever mislike the present government and [have] their eyes fixed upon that person that is next to succeed; and naturally men be so disposed: *Plures adorant solem orientem quam occidentem*." This was Plutarch. *More do adore the rising than the setting sun.* "I have good experience of myself in my sister's [reign] how desirous men were that I should be in place, and earnest to set me up [on the throne]." But now that Elizabeth was queen, men no doubt looked beyond her. Such was the way of men and women, always looking for the next thing, the better thing. "As children dream in their sleep after apples, and in the morning when as they awake and find not the apples they weep, so every man that bore me goodwill when I was Lady Elizabeth, or to whom I show a good visage, imagines with himself that immediately after my coming to the crown every man should be rewarded according to his own fantasy." No prince was ever so rich as to satisfy everyone, and Elizabeth was no exception. When men realized she would not fulfill their dreams, they would turn to the next in line.

As for so-called political friendship, wasn't that merely a fiction? Behind every expression of goodwill lay a threat. Mary promised alliance, but how could Queen Elizabeth be sure that the Queen of Scots wouldn't conspire with Catholic English subjects once she was named heir? How could she know that Mary wouldn't try to push her from the English throne? Maitland tried every which way to reassure her that some guarantee could be put in place. Elizabeth, however, understood human nature. "It is hard to bind princes by any security where hope is offered of a kingdom."

No, Elizabeth preferred to remain the rising sun. "Once I [was] married already to the realm of England when I was crowned with this ring, which I bear continually in token thereof," she said. "So long as I live, I shall be queen of England: when I am dead, they shall succeed that has most right." She would not say who that future sovereign might be.

Queen Elizabeth punted the succession question into the future. If Mary, Queen of Scots, was certain she deserved the throne of England—an inheritance only God could bestow—then the throne would eventually come to her. But if someone else possessed a better claim, then Elizabeth had no right to name a different successor. Patience, she counseled. Mary would get what was coming to her—if it was deserved.

Of course, they could still be friends. "I could never find in my heart to hate her," Elizabeth told Maitland. "She is of the blood of England, my cousin and next kinswoman, so that nature must bind me to love her duly."[18] Maitland could extract nothing more from the English queen. The Scottish ambassador left his audience, disappointed.

———

In those conversations with Maitland, Elizabeth had planted the seeds of a strategy. Over the coming years, the English queen would never crush Mary's hopes for the English throne. On the contrary, she would keep those hopes alive. She would never deny that Mary might possess the most legitimate claim to the English throne. Elizabeth simply refrained from acknowledging that claim *now*. In the meantime, Elizabeth always agreed that England and Scotland should work toward alliance and friendship.

This was no game. For Elizabeth Tudor, this was a matter of survival on her throne. She needed Mary to ratify the Treaty of Edinburgh. Until then, she held out the succession as leverage (and Elizabeth suspected that Mary held back the treaty as leverage of her own). Elizabeth knew that Catholic enemies both in her kingdom and abroad plotted against her, using Mary's claim to rival her own. If she lost her throne, Elisabeth would suffer the fate of a usurper. At best, imprisonment. At worst, the scaffold.

For years Mary did not perceive the ploy. She believed Elizabeth would eventually come around, just as the English queen's councillors thought that one day she would surely agree to marry. And each time that Elizabeth sent her the gift of a poem or letter, a portrait for her chambers or a jewel for her hand, Mary convinced herself that she could nudge Elizabeth further in her favor. Yet each nudge, ultimately, would meet with Elizabeth's stonewalling.

They should have been friends. So much pointed toward a tight alliance. Lord James could see how much they shared. They were cousins, both women and thus natural peacekeepers, he told Queen Elizabeth, "both queens in the flower of your ages, much resembling each other in most excellent and goodly qualities, on whom God hath bestowed most liberally the gifts of nature and fortune."[19] But if gender should have united them, it was gender that kept them apart. Both weak on their thrones in part because they were surrounded by men hostile to female rule, Elizabeth and Mary each employed tactics they thought would protect their crowns—tactics that put them at cross purposes.

Mary pursued the same goal as Elizabeth. She, too, wished to play the part of the rising sun—indeed, she'd spent her entire childhood as the heir apparent. She'd tasted the power of future promise, of being the next in line, whether that was to the throne of France as a consort or the throne of England as its sovereign. That light had once burned brilliantly for Mary. How she yearned to step into it once more.

As it turned out, though, the English succession would prove a zero-sum game. Mary believed she needed the succession to appease her Protestant subjects, to earn the respect of her fellow sovereigns, and to fulfill her own sense of self-worth. In England, Elizabeth felt compelled to hold the succession question hostage, if only to control her own subjects. And as Mary would come to realize, Elizabeth held all the power. She was the reigning queen of England, Mary only an aspirant. Until Elizabeth's death, the choice of heir was Elizabeth's alone.

Elizabeth would make Mary wait, indeed. The Queen of Scots would wait and wait for almost thirty years. She would wait until the end of her days.

PART 4

18

QUEEN OF FAITH
Scotland, France, and Spain, 1561–1563

For the first time since she was five years old, Mary, Queen of Scots, found herself in a strange and uncomfortable spotlight. She had worn the crown of a queen regnant for almost her entire life, yet her mettle as a ruler remained untested. In childhood she'd handed the thinking and governing over to her mother, merely affixing her signature to plain sheets of white paper. Mary's bookish learning unfolded in the isolated and theoretical space of the class-room, touching upon practical matters of policy only occasionally. "Queen of Scotland" had been an abstract title, more like a jewel she proudly displayed than a kingdom she ruled, the place and its people a lifetime and an ocean away. The court life of France made up the tangible world she could see and touch, and the Guises prompted her to stay at its center. Mary never questioned whether she should do otherwise.

She wore her education like another polished bauble. In childhood her fingers had learned to flit over the virginals, though with little art.[1] Wielding a graceful pen, she'd spent dutiful hours at her desk, pulling ink into fine italic letters and reciting Cicero's flowery lessons, before gliding off to her dance master and ponies. Coached by tutors, she could recite a Latin discourse reasonably well. But now real life beckoned, and councillors awaited her command. Her mother had tried to equip Mary to rule, sending her a book on the chief nobles in the kingdom, describing which of them had been loyal to the crown and which seditious.[2] Had she lived longer, perhaps Marie de

Guise would have invested even more in Mary's political education. Or perhaps Marie had tried, but the lessons didn't quite take.

In France, the cardinal gave Mary cues and whispered instructions in her ear. In Scotland, faced with the appraising gaze of her lords, Mary could only guess what her uncle might advise. She dispatched messages to France and waited on tenterhooks for his replies. But the cardinal now lived far away, his focus more on the mounting civil tensions in France than on the fortunes of his niece in Scotland. For the first time, Mary was forced to use her own judgment—a skill she had yet to hone.

At least, she could bring the Scottish court up a notch. This she knew how to do, and this her Scottish subjects encouraged; they were as eager for majesty and splendor as the French and Spanish. Like her mother before her, Mary happily obliged, adding touches of France wherever she could. She'd loaded her galleys with furniture, plump cushions, soft linens, and elaborate tapestries, along with three French upholsterers and her favorite French embroiderer. Pierre Oudry's deft fingers worked magic with a needle. He sewed and sewed, draping beds and walls with hangings worked in fine silk thread, fringed with braid and lined with thick wool to shut out the frigid Scottish winters.

As for her own outfits, Mary's ladies covered her in blue satin and cloth of gold, trimmed her with green velvet, sewed on sleeves threaded with purple, white, gray, and gold silk. They balanced jaunty hats of taffeta on her head and layered cloaks of blue and black frieze over her shoulders. She liked the brightness of yellow, orange, and carnation, the soft decadence of linen, gauze, and gossamer tulle. The Channel wouldn't stop her; Mary resolved to keep up with French fashion. On at least one occasion, she sent her French chamberlain, Servais de Condé, to Paris to take stock of the latest looks and make purchases as required. He dutifully returned, bearing trunks of trinkets and accessories, including scores of butter-soft gloves and perfumes to scent them.[3]

The primping worked like a disguise, making up for Mary's youth and obvious inexperience. "Indeed, I confess, I . . . do want [for] experience," she'd told Throckmorton just that summer in what was, perhaps, an earnest moment. On the dance floor, in the polite exchanges of the audience chamber or amid the breezy repartee of supper parties, her companions smiled upon Mary's French habits. In the council chamber, less so. Sitting among her councillors, burly Scots lords, Mary felt her foreignness and her ignorance. Sometimes, she would take her place, eyes cast down and hands clutching her embroidery, a trick she'd learned from Catherine de' Medici, who spent her afternoons weaving silk into lace, all the while chatting with her ladies. Now, seated at council, Mary kept her ears pricked and needle flashing, the picture of female virtue and modesty, as her advisors inveighed and debated.[4]

She had much to learn about the web of noble families who dominated Scottish politics, and the seemingly never-ending contest among them for her approval, for influence, for power. The Scots revered their kings, but power was not yet entirely centralized in the kingdom. Scottish kings depended on the lords for security, and, in return, their nobles expected favors. Above all, they coveted titles and estates—the land that furnished their revenue. Feuds were common. Lords jockeyed for position in Parliament and Privy Council. Family feeling was strong and often dictated allegiances. In the Highlands, the Gordons and Campbells reigned; in the Borderlands, the Hepburns and Humes. The Stewarts, Hamiltons, and Douglases controlled the Lowlands. Marie de Guise had studied these dynamics assiduously during her years as queen consort before becoming regent. She had successfully played to the interests of the factions, placating tempers. But she was gone by the time Mary returned.[5]

Scottish clan politics were confounding enough, even aside from the morass of religion. As in France, Protestants still made up a minority in Scotland, but the new religion was growing fast, sweeping the cities and countryside. A powerful contingent of Protestant noblemen had greeted Mary upon her return, the old Lords of the Congregation. Following her uncles, Mary thought of French Protestants as heretics and rebels; the Protestant Scots lords, she knew, also had a penchant for rebellion. Yet they seemed willing to work with her, and she had no choice but to work with them. She'd already agreed to uphold the Protestant Kirk at the conclusion of the War in Scotland, and she renewed this promise before her return to the kingdom. She respected many of these Protestants, especially her ambassador to England, William Maitland,

and Lord James, her older half-brother. Lord James spoke for these men and understood the jealousies and rivalries that brewed among them. His counsel seemed sound. And, in truth, she had no one else to trust.

———

On the day of her official procession into Edinburgh—September 2—Mary stepped out of Edinburgh Castle to find herself surrounded by fifty young men dressed as Moors, their limbs and faces smeared with black paint. For this festive day, the weather cooperated. Under a pale September sun, Mary rode down the long road (now known as the Royal Mile) from Edinburgh Castle to Holyroodhouse. Music thrummed, mixing with the voices from pageant plays staged all down the route. Here, the people stopped her to make a little speech. There, her subjects paused the procession again to present her with the keys to the town. The trip was slow going, but Mary enjoyed the scenes, the good wishes of her people. Her subjects had worked hard to devise plays for her. About halfway down the road, Mary met with four young "virgins" who in fact were prepubescent boys. They wore dresses, and represented prudence, temperance, fortitude, and justice. These were the cardinal virtues that befitted a ruling queen.

She did not need reminding. Already, Mary strived for prudence and temperance in the face of subjects whose audacity surprised her. Even on that festive day, she sensed a tension in the air that mingled with the cheery notes of the woodwinds and rebecs. Against the music echoed the faint tones of Scottish voices singing the Psalms. In one play, a child spoke loudly of "putting away the Mass." Halfway down Castle Hill, a little angel handed Mary the gift of a Bible and psalter wrapped in purple, and sang a ballad instructing her to read them to find "God his due command" and the "perfect way unto heavens high." Clearly, her Protestant subjects were sending a message, and it wasn't exactly a message of peace. They despised the Church of Rome. They detested the Mass. Catholics were "papists" and Protestants "the godly." They welcomed their queen but found her religion appalling. Most shocking to Mary, they were not afraid of telling her so.[6]

Her subjects had already made their feelings plainly known, just days after she landed at Leith. On her first Sunday in Edinburgh, August 24, the feast of Saint Bartholomew, Mary attended Mass in a private chapel in Holyroodhouse, joined only by a few household companions and the younger Guise uncles who had accompanied her on the trip from France. Someone leaked word of the Mass, and a scuffle ensued in the courtyard outside the chapel doors, led by friends of the Calvinist preacher John Knox. From within the chapel, Mary could hear the shouting: "The idolater priest should die the death!" At the altar, that selfsame priest—a Frenchman, no less— began to quake. Only the presence of Lord James, who stationed himself outside the chapel, kept the angry Scotsmen out while the shaken priest was escorted to safety.[7]

The incident frightened Mary, and she rushed to quell the unrest. The next day, she issued a proclamation promising to find a resolution to the divisive question of religion. For the moment, she forbade her lords to make any alteration to the state of religion as she had found it upon her arrival in Scotland, "on pain of death." The Protestant Kirk, in other words, would stay. She also agreed to recognize the other reforms made by the Lords of the Congregation. The Mass would continue to be banned and papal authority rejected. Protestantism, she acknowledged, was the official faith of the realm. Yet she also asked her subjects to show forbearance to the French guests still on Scottish shores. All Scotsmen were forbidden from hassling her French servants and companions, again "under pain of death."[8]

She wished merely to keep the peace temporarily while she figured out what next to do. No one knew for sure how to handle the upswell of Protestantism, everyone merely guessing which strategy would best contain the situation. Even the Cardinal of Lorraine was of two minds. To be sure, he abhorred heresy in France, and still hoped to coax French souls back from the brink. But the cardinal, a practical man, had started to wonder if rigorous punishments did more harm than good.[9] Scotland, moreover, was not France. The Lords of the Congregation had waged a successful rebellion against Marie de Guise. With the Protestant Kirk officially recognized, in effect they had won, and Protestantism had taken a firm hold in the kingdom. The cardinal expected Mary to remain Catholic; anything else was unfathomable. Nevertheless he may have counseled her to find some way to mollify her Protestant lords, at least for the time being, to win their trust and support. With her proclamation, Mary made a first attempt.

The entire situation perplexed her. Shouldn't her subjects be afraid of her? True, sovereigns were supposed to cultivate an attitude of benevolence. A king was thus a loving father to his subjects and a queen a loving mother. Yet, as in every mother–child relationship, should there not be an element of fear? Of course, that fear had to be cultivated. Her own mother had scolded her in letters; Antoinette, moreover, knew how to deploy a slap and a spank. As for rebellious subjects, Henry II had crushed religious insurgency among his people with the scaffold and the pyre. In the fracas outside her chapel door, Mary had heard nothing like submission. Instead, the people bristled with violent defiance. It seemed that in Scotland the people did not answer to their queen, at least not in matters of religion.

At eighteen years old, Mary found herself grappling with a populism now streaking across Scotland and the whole of Europe, one that put two systems of authority at cross purposes. On the one hand, there was the obedience that any subject owed his sovereign. "With the whole subjects' due obedience," announced the Lord Provost of Edinburgh as he handed Mary the keys to the city.[10] On the other, there was obedience to God's command, set above any mortal prince. Rituals like the French *sacre*, or coronation, explicitly fused those systems into one: God's blessing imbued a king with his right to rule, symbolized by the anointing with the holy chrism. The French king answered both to law and to God. But the rise of Protestantism, which set subjects ideologically against the belief systems of their Catholic sovereigns, threatened to cleave God from the sovereign, pitting the first against the second.

The Cardinal of Lorraine believed that the heretical teachings of Calvin or Luther naturally led to insubordination, which, when accompanied by gunpowder, crossed the line into sedition. To a Calvinist preacher like John Knox, however, disobeying God's commands, even at the expense of obedience to the prince, was the greater crime. "If, Madame, the true knowledge of God, and his right worshipping be the chief causes [of rebellion]," Knox told Queen

Mary, "wherein can I be reprehended?"[11] The faithful did not want to choose between their God and their prince but, if forced, they would always choose God.

Knox met Mary on a Thursday, September 4, after railing the previous Sunday against Mary's Mass at Holyroodhouse. Mary knew Knox by reputation. The preacher had put his misogyny on ample display in 1558 with *The First Blast of the Trumpet Against the Monstrous Regiment of Women*: "Nature, I say, paints [women] to be weak, frail, impatient, feeble and foolish; and experience has declared them to be unconstant, variable, cruel and lacking the spirit of counsel and regiment," read one choice morsel. Women's rule, moreover, was "contumely" to God. Thus did the people have every right to thrust a ruling queen from her throne.[12]

Knox intimidated Mary. For one, he looked old for his forty-five years. A steely intensity and an absolute conviction in his own beliefs had etched furrows into his brow and streaked his waist-long beard with white. He was also a firebrand, immensely popular with the people and almost single-handedly responsible for the conversion of many of her noblemen. Though a simple merchant's son, he clearly felt no compunction about criticizing Mary, his queen. She would have to win him over or beat him in the fight—and this Mary wasn't sure she could do.

The preacher proved initially meek—somewhat. Obliged to show some measure of respect to his young queen, Knox calmly admitted he'd written every word of the *Monstrous Regiment* but claimed to have been targeting the murderous Catholic Mary Tudor of England, rather than either Mary Stuart or her mother, Marie de Guise. Mary blinked with skepticism. His display of good manners over with, Knox tried a different tack. True, he avowed, Mary had done nothing unduly offensive to her Scottish subjects, at least not yet. So long as she didn't "defile [her] hands with the blood" of the faithful, said Knox, he would remain content to live under her rule, much as Saint Paul had patiently endured the reign of the Roman Emperor Nero.

It was an unpromising beginning to a difficult conversation. Even so, Mary hoped they might come to an understanding. The preacher enjoyed unquestionable popularity among her subjects. She could not afford to alienate him.

Mary moved quickly beyond the man's misogyny. Wasn't gender beside the point? She believed sovereignty was conferred by God. To her, the equation was simple: subjects were supposed to obey their rulers by divine decree. Yet Knox taught the Scottish people a new religion that opposed the one that had always been practiced by Scottish kings and that Mary practiced now. His sermons eroded her sovereign authority.

"How can that doctrine be of God, seeing that God commands subjects to obey their Princes?" she asked.

To Knox, the answer was simple. Religion didn't come from earthly princes; it came from God. "So are not subjects bound to frame their religion according to the appetites"—petty, changeable and entirely human appetites—"of their princes."

But she had read the Scriptures, too, protested Mary, and she interpreted them differently. "I will defend the Kirk of Rome, for I think it is the true Kirk of God."

Knox shrugged his indifference. Mary was wrong. Though a queen, her rank gave her no authority over scriptural affairs. "Your will, Madame, is no reason; neither does your thought make that Roman harlot [the Catholic Church] to be the true and immaculate spouse of Jesus Christ." Nothing like a relative truth existed between one church and another. There was only one true church, one Word of God, and that Word spoke plainly, at least to John Knox and "the godly." "The word of God is plain in the self; and if there appear any obscurity in one place, the Holy Ghost . . . explains the same more clearly in other places."[13]

As for subjects who might resist their princes, Knox had something to say about that, too. The people had every right to rebel if a sovereign abused her people, as had Knox's nemesis Mary Tudor, who had sent hundreds of her English subjects to the pyre. "If their Princes exceed their bounds," he said, "and do against that wherefore that should be obeyed, it is no doubt but they may be resisted, even by power."

Mary was speechless. For once, her silver tongue failed her and, for at least fifteen minutes, she stood quietly "amazed." Knox's words conjured visions of revolt and revolution. In the end, she could think of nothing to say.

Mary would meet Knox several times over the coming years. Each time, Knox carried the conversation. Yet Mary, raised to believe in the righteousness of Guise convictions, proved as stubborn as Knox. "I will be plain with you," she had told Throckmorton in the summer of 1561, ". . . the religion that I profess I take to be most acceptable to God, and, indeed, neither do I know, nor desire to know, any other . . . I have been brought up in this religion, and who might credit me in anything if I should show myself light in this case?"[14] How could any subject trust her if she were changeable?

This was a morsel of crafty rhetoric on Mary's part, a glib way to rationalize what worked best for her. Like her Guise uncles, she could be stubborn and strident, and was determined to have her way. She would never change religions, though it is unclear how deeply she felt her confessional convictions. Mary had thrived by obeying the old ways endorsed by the Guises. She did not possess the intellectual mind of the evangelical Marguerite de Navarre or Elizabeth Tudor of England, the kind of inquisitiveness that might have prompted her to hear out, at least, the new religious ideas energizing her subjects. Her Catholicism was one of her last ties to France, to the people she'd left behind. For this reason alone, she would never let it go.

Perhaps, though, she could agree to something of a middle ground: surely her subjects might follow their beliefs while she followed her own? Mary didn't see that to a preacher like Knox, the notion of compromise was inconceivable, even more so for a ruling queen who was supposed to be the earthly representative of her people. Knox believed that, more than a man, a woman like Mary depended on the people's acquiescence to keep her throne. Mary didn't impress Knox. "If there be not in her a proud mind, a crafty wit, and an indurate heart against God and His truth, my judgment fails me," he said.[15]

Mary would, in fact, strive to compromise with her Protestant subjects for the next several years, often saying one thing yet doing another. She would allow the Protestant Kirk to flourish, all the while in her private chapels patiently watching the priest raise the host. As she wrote to prelates and the pope pledging her eternal commitment to Catholicism, she allowed Protestantism to remain the official religion of Scotland. Pious Catholic kings like Philip II were flabbergasted. They kept waiting for the hammer to fall. But it never did.[16]

For Mary harbored entirely worldly and self-centered reasons to tolerate the Protestant church in her kingdom.[17] Powerful Protestant noblemen like her brother Lord James worked steadily to try to win her the English succession. In the council room, he advocated a new friendship with England, one to unite the realms. Mary's succession to the English throne was part of that new friendship, as Lord James envisioned it. Mary didn't see the part she played in James's plan: he hoped that by winning Mary the succession, he could secure her protection of Scottish Protestants in perpetuity. All she knew was that she couldn't afford to alienate a powerful nobleman like her brother. She needed him for her council table and for the English succession—a crown she wanted so badly that part of her was willing to sacrifice even God to get it.

———

Since the midwinter of 1561, as Catherine de' Medici set about thwarting the nuptial projects of a certain *gentleman*, she'd also fielded Spanish accusations that she was too soft on heresy. Philip II could not understand why Catherine made so many concessions to French Protestants. In his mind, she spent too much time talking to heretics; instead of supporting rigorous punishments, she passed laws to protect Protestants. In January, by royal edict, she moved heresy trials from the royal courts to local church courts, effectively ending royal supervision of persecutions. This newest edict suspended all heresy cases entirely and ordered the release of all subjects imprisoned for religious reasons, including those who had taken up arms against the crown. Even prisoners caught up in the Tumult of Amboise were let go.[18]

Catherine's leniency appeared to extend beyond politics into the very heart of her home. Of particular Spanish concern, wrote Madame de Clermont, was the little princess Margot, whom Catherine so desperately wanted to marry Don Carlos. "They are quite worried here about the education of Madame your little daughter, and about the kind of people who are in her company," a worried Madame de Clermont told Catherine. "They wonder whether she is well nourished in the proper views of God."[19] Was this the behavior of a good mother? In Spain, tongues wagged.

The Queen Mother denied every accusation. Such "beautiful news . . . from Spain," she declared sarcastically to Limoges, "as untruthful as it is malicious." She would never waver from the old beliefs; she wished simply to find a way forward out of the hostilities threatening to drag the kingdom into civil war. The crown had ceased the burnings "for fear of the great emotion" they triggered among the people. Such swells of anger were dangerous. "Every day, as new circumstances arise, we are constrained to find new remedies, sometimes using clemency and gentleness; other times rigor and severity, according to the occasion," Catherine explained. One of those remedies, Catherine believed, was an assembly of Frenchmen—a council on religion—to help reunify the French Church.[20]

French Protestants had been clamoring for a council for months, and Catherine was inclined to agree with them, if only to solve French problems within French borders. This was not the approach endorsed by Rome. The previous year, in November 1560, Pope Pius IV had called for the reconvening of the Council of Trent, the ecclesiastical council organized to discuss the Catholic response to the heresy sweeping Europe.* But Catherine feared unilateral action by the papal Council could worsen religious hatred in France; she hoped to resolve the tensions within the kingdom first, before sending French representatives to Trent. The solution was to get French Catholics and Protestants together in the same room.

In June 1561, Catherine announced that a French national council would meet to discuss ecclesiastical questions. French Catholic prelates would be joined by representatives from Rome. The talks would take place in September at Poissy, a convent just three miles to the north of the château of Saint-Germain-en-Laye, the former home of the *petite cour*. Only the following month, in July, did Catherine spring her surprise. It was not only Catholic clerics who would be in attendance, she declared. "All subjects" who wished to explain their views would be allowed to attend part of the proceedings. While Catholics bristled, the Huguenot

---

*This was the third summoning of the Council of Trent, which had met earlier, in multiple sessions, during the years 1545–47 and 1551–52. The Council was active for a third period between 1561 and 1562.

leadership began to strategize. Who best to send? Jean Calvin was too inflammatory. Instead, they selected Théodore de Bèze, Calvin's second-in-command.

On August 24, Saint Bartholomew's Day, just as Mary Stuart cowered in her chapel from the angry mob protesting her Mass in Scotland, Catherine prepared herself to meet the Protestant Bèze at Saint-Germain-en-Laye. Tall, handsome, aristocratic, and smooth as glass, he arrived to a warm welcome from the Queen Mother and two dozen Protestant ministers and noblemen, including the Prince de Condé and Gaspard de Coligny. A nephew of Constable Anne de Montmorency, Coligny was one of the new leaders among French Protestant nobles. Catholics griped that Bèze was better received than if he'd been the pope himself.[21]

Catherine had high hopes for her parley. After all, there were precedents for reconciliation between religious factions. Thirty years earlier, Charles V had managed to hammer out an agreement with the German Lutheran princes in Augsburg; surely Catherine could do the same in Poissy. What the Queen Mother didn't appreciate is that, by the 1560s, Protestantism had splintered. Unlike Charles V, she wasn't dealing with Lutherans. She was working with the far more radical Calvinists.

The talks at Poissy began well enough. Before the proceedings officially opened, Bèze met privately with the Cardinal of Lorraine at Catherine's behest. With Catherine skillfully managing the conversation, the men tried to iron out their differences. After Bèze assured the cardinal that he sought only peace in the realm, the two turned to the sticking point of the Real Presence in the Mass. Bèze was unwilling to concede that the "body and blood of Christ are truly present, and are distributed to those who eat the Supper of the Lord," which Lutherans believed. (Here, Bèze held true to his beliefs: the question of the Real Presence was one of the fundamental issues separating Calvinists from Lutherans.) Yet the cardinal carried on, desperately searching for some common ground with his Protestant counterpart.

"Do you confess," asked the cardinal, putting the question differently, "that we communicate truly and substantially the body and blood of Jesus Christ" in the Mass?

Indeed we do, answered Bèze, "spiritually and by faith."

Gratified, the cardinal didn't bother to tempt fate by analyzing the nuances of that reply. Catherine too was visibly relieved. "Do you hear, Lord Cardinal?" she asked. "He says that the Sacramentarians have no other opinion than this, with which you agree."[22] The cardinal, feeling conciliatory, embraced Bèze as the two men left the chamber. "You will find," he said, "that I am not as black as they make me out to be."[23]

So both Catherine and the cardinal were wholly unprepared for what happened next. On September 9, during the first day's proceedings and in the presence of the royal family, the princes of the blood, six cardinals, forty-six bishops, and scores of theologians and canon lawyers, Bèze stood tall, dazzled them with eloquence, then announced that, to be sure, Calvinists believed in the Real Presence. Yet—*yet*—"we say that His body is as far removed from the bread and wine as is heaven from earth."[24] Jesus was present in spirit, but not in body.

Howls of "Blasphemy!" punctuated the hissing that rose from the bishops. In a corner of the room, Gaspard de Coligny buried his head in his hands. Shriveled, feeble, and now shaking in horror, the seventy-year-old Cardinal of Tournon began to cry. How could the Queen Mother permit "these horrible blasphemies in the presence of the King?" Catherine raced to reassure him that both she and her son would live and die in the Catholic faith.[25]

It was a misstep on the part of the Calvinists, as grave as the error leading to the Affair of the Placards almost thirty years earlier under King Francis I. Bèze's gaffe doomed the Colloquy at Poissy. Catherine tried reducing the number of debaters, first to twelve on each side, Protestant and Catholic, then to five. The Cardinal of Lorraine, striving to move past the issue of the Real Presence, made a fiery speech emphasizing the ecumenical elements in Catholicism, Lutheranism, and Greek Orthodoxy (pointedly leaving out Calvinism), to insist that compromise was still possible. He tried meeting Bèze halfway, urging him to endorse the Lutheran view of the Real Presence in the Eucharist. Couldn't Bèze agree at least to this interpretation? But Bèze disappointed the cardinal. A staunch defender of his creed, he refused to compromise on the issue of the Real Presence.[26]

The weeks dragged on. On October 13, 1561, after a full month of debate, the Colloquy disbanded, not a single issue on the Reform in France settled. A demoralized Cardinal of Lorraine adjourned to his estates and spent the rest of the year preparing for the Council of Trent. In September 1562, he left for Italy. In Trent, against the backdrop of the Italian Alps, the cardinal tried once again to counsel caution and compromise but faced only hostility from the Italian and Spanish clerics in attendance. Isolated, he saw no way forward other than to reconcile his beliefs with the Church of Rome. When the cardinal returned to France, his views had hardened, all thoughts of conciliation wiped away.[27]

Catherine soldiered on, unwilling to concede that both Protestants and Catholics had dug in, not simply because of personal rivalries and pride but because each side believed wholeheartedly that their way was the only way. The alternative to compromise horrified Catherine: that civil war might erupt under her watch while King Charles was a still a minor was impossible for her to accept.

In truth, a war of sorts had already arrived in the kingdom. The tension was searing. Vigilantism reigned. Reports of Catholic brutality and Protestant iconoclasm abounded. The south, where Protestantism held a particularly firm grip, was especially volatile. In November, one month after the close of Poissy, several Catholic priests in the southern city of Cahors orchestrated an attack on the home of a local nobleman where dozens of Protestants had gathered for a sermon. In the melee, fifty Huguenots were massacred. After the slaughter, the Catholic perpetrators set fire to the house and dragged the corpses out onto the street, the blood still flowing.[28]

Catholics recounted their own stories of Huguenot wickedness, complaining to the crown and publishing tales of violence and iconoclasm in pamphlets. Not only did Huguenots kill Catholics but they also defaced churches and defiled the sacraments—to Catholics, these were crimes tantamount to murder. One Catholic account described how Huguenots assaulted a priest at a church at Christmastime, stamped upon the bread of the Holy Sacrament, smashed the church windows and altars, and pilfered ornaments and relics. Afterward, brandishing their swords, the Huguenots marched through the city streets crying out, "The Gospel, the Gospel; where are the idolatrous papists?" The accused Protestants protested, claiming they'd been provoked. During their prayer meeting, neighborhood Catholics had thrown stones at them and clanged church bells incessantly to disturb their worship.

Protestant violence only galvanized Catholics. And Catholic violence did nothing to deter the growth of the Reform. On the contrary, French aristocrats converted to the new faith in droves, even those who had dutifully served the old kings Henry II and Francis II.[29] Only through conciliation, Catherine believed, could the crown quell the unrest. Toleration alone would bring the temperature down and restore the crown's authority.

Toleration in the sixteenth century did not mean approval. It did not mean one person's conviction was as true as another's. Toleration meant simply that you accepted someone's beliefs or practice because you could not change them—so long as those differing beliefs didn't fundamentally defy and limit your own. Toleration was endorsed by French political moderates who sought to eschew the fury of partisanship. Catherine turned to many such moderates during the summer and autumn of 1561, especially her chancellor, Michel de l'Hôpital, who helped organize the Colloquy at Poissy.

But resolute defenders of Catholicism saw any form of moderation as just one more concession to the Protestants. In the wake of Poissy, they excoriated Catherine's permissiveness: How dare she give the Protestants a pulpit? To conservative Catholics, the signs suggested that Catherine either failed to recognize the seriousness of the problem or actually supported the Protestants—or, worse, that she had turned Protestant herself.

Among other stories, lurid reports (some of which may have been true) circulated that the Queen Mother's Protestant ladies-in-waiting organized Huguenot sermons in Catherine's chambers while the queen turned a blind eye. An aghast papal nuncio spotted King Charles sporting a bishop's miter during a masquerade with his playmates, which reportedly caused Catherine to burst out laughing. The boy king also reputedly confided to the Protestant Jeanne d'Albret, wife of the King of Navarre, that he went to Mass only to please his mother. Jeanne d'Albret told the whole story to Throckmorton, who noted it with glee.[30]

This was scandalous and, to orthodox Catholics, heretical behavior. Yet Catherine spoke of toleration. So disgusted was the Duke of Guise by Catherine's laxity that he left court and retreated to his estates. Even French Protestants began to believe that Catherine not-so-secretly supported them. "I assure you," wrote Bèze to Calvin in December, "that this Queen, *our Queen*, seems more disposed toward us than she has ever been before."[31]

Catherine brushed off the critics. "Madame my daughter, I assure you they are lying to you about your brother," she scoffed to Elisabeth de Valois when stories of King Charles's delinquency trickled down to Spain. "They are telling you so many lies. It upsets me, the pain they are causing you. But do as I do, for I laugh at their wickedness."[32]

In January 1562, the Queen Mother would issue what would come to be known as the Edict of Toleration. The law was the most forgiving of any of the French edicts to date. Though it recognized the Catholic Church as the preeminent church in France, the edict granted Huguenots the right to worship freely, a privilege they had long sought. Catherine insisted on certain constraints. Huguenots were allowed to gather for worship, but not within town walls. Nor could they gather at night without special permission. Despite such limitations, both Huguenots and Catholics saw the edict for what it was: a victory for French Protestants.[33]

No other kingdom in Europe had ever passed anything like the Edict of Toleration. No other kingdom had yet officially recognized, let alone permitted, the coexistence of more than one strain of Christianity. France was the realm where *one God, one king, one law* once reigned supreme. Now, Catherine not only recognized the Reformed religion—she also appeared to give it room to thrive.

Shortly before the Colloquy at Poissy collapsed, Catherine sent Monsieur d'Ossance, one of her regular couriers, to Philip II's court, where he was to deliver the Queen Mother's carefully scripted view of the proceedings. But the Spanish ambassador, Chantonnay, beat him to it. By the time Ossance arrived, Philip was already well apprised of the goings-on at Poissy. As Elisabeth de Valois explained to her mother, a furious Philip almost slammed the door in the French envoy's face. Only his respect for Catherine, Elisabeth said, and his innate sense of generosity had compelled Philip to grant the hapless Ossance an audience.

The Colloquy at Poissy seemed to support some crazed notion of equivalence between the two religions. To Philip's mind, there was only orthodoxy and heresy. Differences among the strands of Reformed thinking were beyond his caring. It didn't matter if you followed Calvin or Luther, or if you dabbled in the teachings of the Swiss Reformer Zwingli. Invariably you were a "Lutheran." The word carried the same negative connotation in Spain as "Sacramentarian" or "Huguenot" did in France.

As it turned out, Philip needn't have worried about Poissy, though he certainly didn't know it at the time. For reasons historians still struggle to understand, the Reformation never really took off in Spain. Some elements of Reformed thinking had burbled in fits and starts since the 1520s, when many Spanish intellectuals, ready to see reform in a Spanish Church dogged with corruption, welcomed the biting criticism of ecclesiastical vice and venality in books like Erasmus's *Praise of Folly*. But neither Erasmus's thinking nor Luther's ever morphed into organized Protestant action. Their teachings made headway only in small intellectual circles—a minor threat, easily managed.

In 1557 and 1558, just before the death of Charles V, authorities discovered a few Protestant circles in Seville, deep in Andalusia, and in the Castilian city of Valladolid. Officials quickly scrubbed those cities, and from his cocoon at Yuste, the old emperor advised his daughter Juana (who then ruled as regent) to adopt a kingdom-wide policy of utter ruthlessness and complete eradication. Juana turned to Inquisition tribunals established by Isabel and Ferdinand in the late fifteenth century to root out and punish the unorthodox thinking of *moriscos* and *conversos*, Muslims and Jews who had converted to Christianity. As King Philip would come to believe much later, thanks to the Inquisition, heresy in Spain never stood a chance.[34]

One weapon of the Inquisition was the auto-da-fé, a days-long spectacle complete with trials, declarations of repentance, and burnings. In May 1559, Princess Juana presided over the first grand-scale auto-da-fé in Valladolid. There, twenty-nine prisoners repented of heresy and fourteen were burned. Most of the accused were strangled first; only the most unrepentant were burned alive. The scenes were grisly, nonetheless. Even the dead weren't spared. One woman, who had died of natural causes before she and her family were accused, was disinterred for sentencing and her corpse immolated.

The *autos* achieved their purpose. Within three years, all traces of native Spanish Protestantism had disappeared almost entirely.[35]

Still, in 1561, the growing popularity of the Reform among France's highest-ranking nobles fanned Philip II's fears. A foreign revolution, he knew, could seed itself in Spanish villages and universities, take root and grow. As it was, Spanish religious orthodoxy was like an iron lid clamped down on a simmering pot. Isabel and Ferdinand had expelled the Jews and persecuted *moriscos* and *conversos*, but rebellions by *moriscos* still flared up now and again, especially in the south. Could waves of Protestant heresy trigger other revolts?

Of greatest concern to Philip were the Spanish lands abutting France. What was to prevent French heresy from spilling over its southern borders into northern Spain, or moving east, bolstering the uprisings that already racked Spanish Flanders? The King of Navarre's religious equivocating—not to mention his fiercely Protestant wife, Jeanne d'Albret—troubled Philip especially. Béarn, the King of Navarre's realm, straddled the Pyrenees, abutting Spain's northern border.[36] Philip's fear of a French "Lutheran" contagion likely explains why he eventually pushed French nobles to leave Elisabeth de Valois's retinue, lest they import heretical ideas into his queen's household.

To most Spaniards, the news issuing from France was scandalous. Bewildered French courtiers in Spain felt compelled to defend their homeland. They often found it difficult to distinguish fact from fiction. The Spanish "always represent things worse than they are," Madame de Clermont had written back in the spring of 1561, as if to ask whether things were in fact as bad as they seemed. "I always affect to believe that they speak in jest," she said, hopefully. Elisabeth, too, couldn't tell what to believe when her mother's letters said one thing and Chantonnay's another. Some reports were too loathsome to accept. When Elisabeth learned that Huguenots had destroyed the tomb of her great-grandfather King Louis XII, she recoiled in horror. After she heard of a French bishop who had married his mistress (as Protestant ministers were wont to do), Elisabeth claimed not to believe it—then wrote a furtive note to the Bishop of Limoges asking if it were true.[37]

Well before the disaster at Poissy, Madame de Clermont and Elisabeth both worried that war would soon erupt between Spain and France if Catherine didn't act quickly to punish the heretics. "Madame, would it not be more politic for Your Majesty to establish greater devotion and chastise some of the culprits," Madame de Clermont ventured to suggest, "if only to demonstrate that you do not support them?" Even the devoted Clermont could not understand why Catherine didn't do more.[38]

The Colloquy at Poissy threatened to become a tipping point. At the time, the Queen Mother still sought some sort of Spanish territorial restitution to keep the King of Navarre happy. In October 1561, after word of the colloquy reached Spain, Elisabeth explained to her mother: until Catherine proved her devotion to the Catholic cause, Philip would do her no favors.

The letter Elisabeth wrote covered both sides of four large sheets of paper and trailed onto a fifth—her longest extant letter. She began in her best handwriting.

Philip had begun to question Catherine's judgment, Elisabeth warned. He believed Catherine should think less about appeasing the King of Navarre and more about crushing the rebels. If Catherine felt outnumbered, "Your Majesty should ask [Philip] for help; as we would willingly lend you our wealth, our armies, and all that we possess to maintain the cause of religion. If you cannot do this, the king asks that you not take offense if His Majesty grants his favor and protection to [Catholics] who suffer for the sake of their faith. This concerns His Majesty very nearly; for if France becomes Lutheran, Flanders and Spain will not be far behind."[39]

Catherine's promises were empty; only stern action would prove her commitment. "For we in Spain," Elisabeth continued, "believe only in what we see."

Our wealth. Our armies. We in Spain believe only in what we see. Philip spoke through Elisabeth. Perhaps he dictated this portion of the letter. Or maybe Princess Juana, so often in Elisabeth's company, helped her compose her thoughts. Still, nothing Elisabeth wrote suggested she saw things differently from her husband. At fifteen years old, after not quite two years in Spain, had she already begun to look back at France through Spanish eyes?

Toward the middle of the letter, Elisabeth's handwriting began to deteriorate. Blobs of ink formed, and the letters lost their shape. She wrote quickly, with new urgency. Catherine's hesitation threatened to tarnish Elisabeth's own reputation in Spain.

"Madame, if you do not begin immediately to punish the Lutherans, I shall no longer know what to say to everyone here. The Duke of Alba has told me that since you now reign supreme in the government, I no longer have any excuse for why you're not doing what I had promised them you would do. I beg you, please do not make me a liar . . . Now, since the King my husband offers you all his armies, you can put them down. If you wait any longer, there will only be more of them. They say here that the late king my father [Henry II] punished them until there were gone; and that under the late king my brother [Francis II], very little more was heard from them once the punishments began. Which proves that if they are punished, they will not dare make trouble. But they will have every reason to act boldly if you allow them."

Schooled by Catherine in realpolitik, Elisabeth conveyed a simple answer to what was, in King Philip's view, a simple problem. If Catherine wanted to preserve the alliance with Spain, marriages between the Hapsburgs and the Valois would not suffice. She needed to destroy French Protestantism.

Did Elisabeth believe this, too? Nothing suggests she was anything but a Catholic. As a queen consort, rather than a ruling queen, she passed her days with her ladies, unexposed to the nuanced discussions of the council room. And she was still little more than a child. Elisabeth had passed her early years immersed in Catholicism's tenets. She left France before Reformist thinking touched the lives of her younger siblings and began to flourish at the French court. As she grew older and accustomed to her life in Spain, she saw that early faith mirrored at the Spanish court and in Philip's own orthodoxy, more than in the wild stories of prayer meetings and married priests flying in from France. Spanish Catholic ritual structured her days, from the Mass she attended every morning to the vespers closing her evenings. In her friend Princess Juana, Elisabeth found an embodiment of Spanish Catholic devotion: a woman so pious that, at the age of twenty-one, she secretly took Jesuit vows to become one of the few women ever allowed to join the Society of Jesus.[40*]

As a younger man in 1551, Philip had spent almost a year with his father in Augsburg, where he spent much time in the company of German Lutherans with whom he "got on very well," by his own admission.[41] But Philip was a man and a future king, obliged to adjust his convictions for political reasons. Elisabeth de Valois was a young woman, her mind fragile and impressionable, according to theories then in sway. She lived a sheltered life in Spain, under the scrupulous supervision of Princess Juana and the Countess of Ureigna; Philip would never permit even a hint of heterodoxy to sully and confuse his young queen.

"She lives according to Spanish desires," Madame de Clermont once wrote of Elisabeth. Those Spanish desires would come to shape her thinking. Much later, in 1567, Elisabeth would describe French Protestants as "wicked traitors," exhorting her brother King Charles to "take vengeance" upon them and "show them no mercy."[42] Like Philip, she saw Protestants mostly as the enemy.

She would always love her mother. All the heresy and scandal in the world couldn't alter Elisabeth's abiding affection for Catherine. After Poissy, Elisabeth warned Catherine *because* she loved and feared for her. "I have presumed, Madame, to write this to you . . . since you know the affection that I feel for you. And besides having the honor of being your daughter, I owe you so much, which I can never repay." Still, Elisabeth could no longer make excuses for her mother. And quite possibly, she could no longer understand her.

In the end, Catherine's laborious efforts to reconcile Catholics and Protestants could not calm the eddies of hatred. Religious intolerance had hardened; every insult, assault, and violation was collected, catalogued, and remembered, the mountains of evidence

---

*Juana may have used her vows to the Jesuits to avoid a second marriage that would take her far from Spain. If so, Juana landed upon an ingenious strategy to exercise some degree of control over her own marital future—a remarkable feat from a young Hapsburg woman of her rank. Impeccably pious, Juana knew her equally pious brother Philip would not force her to break her vows.

that justified the righteousness of each side piling up like tinder. War had threatened to explode for years. In March 1562, all the Duke of Guise had to do was strike the match.

That month, the duke rode from his manor at Dommartin-le-Franc near Joinville to his estates at Eclaron, accompanied by his family and about two hundred armed men. He'd plotted a slightly circuitous route in the hope of avoiding Wassy, a town that had exhibited a bullish Protestantism in recent months, such that, on his latest trip home to Joinville, the duke had suffered a tongue-lashing from his mother warning him either to clean up the area or risk losing his reputation forever. The whole region had turned Protestant, which unnerved the duke, prompting him to travel with scores of soldiers. Wassy was a particularly sensitive topic for him. The château there belonged to his niece, Mary Stuart, and before she departed for Scotland, she'd assigned its administration over to the duke himself.

When it came time to stop for breakfast on that March morning, the duke halted his convoy in Brousseval, a small village about a mile from Wassy. He planned to hear Mass, then gather his troops and head through Wassy as quickly and quietly as possible.

As they were breakfasting, the convoy heard a faint chiming. Church bells, ringing from within the walls of Wassy. But it wasn't the usual time for church bells to ring. At least not if you were Catholic.

The duke sent several scouts toward Wassy to investigate. Mounting his horse, he followed them soon after.[43]

Two hours later, fifty Protestants were dead and over two hundred wounded. The Duke's scouts had discovered about five hundred Protestants, men, women, and children, packed into a barn not far from the local church. There were no pews: the people stood shoulder to shoulder, listening to the sermon. When the soldiers tried to push their way inside, the Huguenots blocked them. Inside the barn, within the crowd of agitated congregants, a Protestant reached down and picked up a stone.

By the time the duke arrived at the scene, frantic men clogged the narrow street. Muskets fired. Voices shouted, "Kill! Kill! By God's death, kill these Huguenots!" In the barn, the duke's soldiers slashed their way through the panicked crowd. As fleeing Protestants tore up the stairs to the roof, sharpshooters outside picked them off one by one. Ducking behind the pulpit, the preacher tried to shelter from the ricocheting bullets. When the killing spree was over, "the posts and walls of the barn were splattered with blood."[44]

Called to explain himself before King Charles and Queen Catherine, the Duke of Guise protested his innocence. The situation had got out of hand. "If I had intended such a thing, why would I have brought . . . my wife, who was following in a litter with our own seven-year-old? I never thought something like this could happen. Most of the people were my subjects. They knew me well."[45]

Yet few Protestants believed the massacre at Wassy was an accident. Word of the killings spread through Protestant networks within France and beyond. Within weeks, pamphlets decrying the massacre flooded the streets of London. When he learned of the killings, the Protestant Prince de Condé, then in Paris, demanded a full account. Then, in April, after refusing to meet the king and his mother at Fontainebleau, Condé withdrew to Orléans in the Loire Valley, and began to raise an army. On behalf of the crown, the Duke of Guise raised his own.[46]

Both sides held back for a few months. Hostilities sputtered throughout the spring, summer, and autumn of 1562. Finally, Protestant and Catholic armies met just south of the town of Dreux on December 19. For a few hours, nothing happened. The two armies simply faced each other, waiting.

They had fought together in the Italian Wars. How had they become enemies? Years afterward, a Huguenot captain named François de La Noue recalled: "Each one braced himself for battle, contemplating that the men he saw coming were neither Spanish, English, nor Italian, but French, indeed the bravest of them, among whom could be found his own comrades, relatives and friends, and that within the hour it would be necessary to start killing one another."[47] To kill each other for the sake of the wafer and the wine, or for the right to cradle the Bible in your hands and read it in your own tongue.

By the time the Battle of Dreux was over, 10,000 men had died.

War had arrived, a war that Catherine had tried to prevent at all costs. Time and again during this first conflict, she begged each side to compromise and make peace. What Catherine couldn't have known was that the clashes of 1562 were only the first of what would come to be called the French Wars of Religion. These civil wars would rock the kingdom during the second half of the century. Before Catherine's death in 1589, she would witness no fewer than eight such conflicts in France. The violence tore apart families and inspired vendettas that lasted well into the seventeenth century. Historians estimate that the wars, coupled with the disease and famine that accompanied them, killed somewhere between two and four million people.[48] The French called these civil wars "the troubles."

In 1562, Catherine could hardly foresee the carnage. She hoped this first war would be the last. Already the fighting had exacted a high toll. Antoine de Bourbon, King of Navarre, was killed during the Siege of Rouen, not long before the Battle of Dreux.* And in February 1563, almost one year after Wassy, as Catholics prepared to seize the city of Orléans, the Duke of Guise was shot in the back in his own camp, bleeding out on a surgeon's table six days later. Under torture, the assassin claimed to work for the admiral Gaspard Coligny, the Protestant leader and nephew of Constable Montmorency—the Guises' old enemy.[49]

The rivalries waxed and waned, taking on a new face yet never disappearing entirely. Following the duke's death, the Guises grew more righteous in their Catholicism. The family's vendetta against the Protestant Coligny would last until the end of Coligny's life.

The assassination of the Duke of Guise shook Catherine to her core. But his death gave her the chance to call for peace. In March 1563, the war ended with the issuing of a new edict, the Peace of Amboise. The edict permitted freedom of conscience yet placed new restrictions on Protestant worship, limiting Protestant gatherings to select districts within the suburbs of certain towns. Protestant worship was banned entirely in and around Paris, officially to protect King Charles although, in reality, the restriction catered to the increasingly rabid Catholic sentiments of the capital.[50]

---

*Antoine de Bourbon ultimately turned against his brother Condé and joined the Duke of Guise, thereby confirming his reputation as a political aspirant and religious lightweight.

Neither side emerged victorious from the first War of Religion. Catherine's strategy hadn't wavered: she still sought to strike a balance, giving concessions to both Catholics and Protestants. Because of these concessions, the Peace of Amboise satisfied almost no one.

Catherine was blinded by hope. Others, however, could see from the start that something ominous was upon them. Riding through the streets of Paris in the spring of 1562, on the eve of the first civil war, the lawyer Etienne Pasquier, a moderate Catholic, watched troops assemble in all quarters of the city. He was seized with apprehension. "Now, all one talks about is war," he mused to a friend. "There is nothing to fear more in a state than civil war, especially civil war waged under the pretext of religion, particularly when a king, because he is young, does not have the power to command absolutely.

"If I could assess these events," Pasquier wrote, "I would say it was the beginning of a tragedy that will play itself out among us, at our expense."[51]

CATHOLIC KINGS
Scotland, 1562–1565

Soon after the Duke of Guise's death, Catherine sent an envoy, Philibert du Croc, to condole with Mary, Queen of Scots. Writing to thank the Queen Mother, Mary begged her to look after the duke's children, and most of all to bring justice to "the traitors who have so wickedly pursued this great treason against the most faithful servant that you have had and will ever have." To have shot such a worthy man in the back. Her Guise pride churned with grief. "My trust in you," she wrote, "consoles me a little."[1] She knew the Queen Mother disliked the Guises. Now, she hoped Catherine would do the right thing.

News of the duke's death crushed Mary. Already, she'd suffered through a difficult year. The previous summer, Elizabeth Tudor had postponed a much-anticipated summit between the queens. Mary had lobbied hard for the meeting, believing that, in the flesh, Elizabeth would find it impossible to resist her charms; surely then, she would grant Mary the succession. Gifts of jewelry and poems made their way south, along with requests for Elizabeth's portrait and fluttery little notes that sounded more like love letters than diplomatic missives. The wooing worked. In July 1562, the English queen caved and formally invited Mary to meet later that summer, perhaps in Nottingham, perhaps in York. With the invitation, Queen Elizabeth at last sent the longed-for portrait of herself.

Does it look like her? Mary asked Thomas Randolph, the English envoy, as she admired the picture.

Very much so, he answered, though in real life Queen Elizabeth was even prettier. "I trust," he told Mary, "Her Grace would shortly be judge thereof herself."

"That is the thing that I have most desired ever since I was in hope thereof," Mary answered. "I honor her in my heart and love her as my dear and natural sister."[2]

Just two days later, Mary received word that Elizabeth had rescinded her invitation, putting it off for at least a year. The recent escalation of tensions in France made the summit impossible: Queen Elizabeth could hardly meet with the Scottish queen when the Guises and French Catholics were slaughtering her coreligionists so mercilessly. Of course, she promised, they could still be friends.[3]

Mary cried for a full day. The canceled summit was her first personal casualty of the French civil war, the Duke of Guise's assassination the second.[*]

Death had by now become a regular and devastating visitor, but the duke's murder hit Mary hard. She'd sought his advice almost as much as the cardinal's, and her letters overflowed with pledges of love and loyalty in return. Earlier that year, she'd fretted over the Guises' diminished status at the French court, and wrote urgently to the cardinal, her words tight with worry. "You must know how many honest offers of assistance she gave us," the cardinal told Catherine. "You know her heart and good understanding . . . and besides our shared blood and our services to her, she can hardly forget how well we served the king her husband, and the late king her father-in-law."[4] Mary grieved deeply for the duke. The only thing worse would have been the death of her grandmother Antoinette, or her uncle the Cardinal of Lorraine.

A few years later, Mary's fears almost came to pass. In 1565, she learned the cardinal had barely escaped an assassin's bullet. "Forgive me if I seem passionate about this," she wrote Catherine hastily, once again demanding punishment for the perpetrators, "but I've already lost one uncle and now almost have lost another."[5] And that, Mary knew, she could ill afford.

---

[*]Mary would continue to press Elizabeth for a summit and forever hold out hope but, as was her habit, Elizabeth kept Mary waiting. Despite the Queen of Scots' fervent desire, the two queens would never meet.

Sometime during those trying months of 1562–63, Mary began to consider remarrying. Elizabeth's postponement of the summit was likely one inducement. Friendship and wooing hadn't worked: Mary now wanted a husband—one equipped with armies, and ships, and treasure, and threats—to push Queen Elizabeth into acknowledging her place in the English succession. As her obsession hardened, so too did her need to find some way to actualize it. According to William Maitland (who confided in the Spanish ambassador De Quadra in London, who then told Philip II in the usual string of diplomatic communications), the Queen of Scots resolved to marry "as would enable her to assert her rights" in England "by force, if they could not be obtained by fair means." She thought, especially, that France might provide the "remedy."[6]

The Duke of Guise's death may have given the marriage question fresh urgency for Mary. The warrior duke had fiercely advocated her rights in England, yet, more importantly, he'd served as something of a father figure. With his death, another of the stronger hearts and minds Mary trusted had disappeared. Perhaps a husband could fill the void. She was twenty years old. Francis had died two years earlier. She was sovereign queen of a kingdom that demanded an heir. She had every reason to marry again.

To Mary's surprise, however, the groom she'd imagined for herself failed to materialize. She had hoped, almost beyond hope, that a proposal from Charles IX might still be forthcoming, despite Catherine de' Medici's loud declarations that only a Hapsburg princess would do for her son. A return to France as consort to the king would have put Mary right back where she left off. For several years, she clung to a fantasy that Catherine would change her mind, that Charles himself would insist. In the meantime, the cardinal threw out other options. Mary received them patiently but with little enthusiasm.

To be sure, there was no shortage of possible grooms, and several presented their suits. Certainly, they were all honorable men, as Mary would affirm to a kinswoman.[7] The difficulty was Mary herself. Not one of the contenders was good enough for her. When the French Sieur de Mauvissière paid her a visit in 1564, he found she could catalog from memory the candidates for her hand, along with their faults. There were the dukes of Nemours and Ferrara, the Hapsburg Archduke Charles of Austria. For a short time, Prince Erik of Sweden bobbed among the flotsam of names though, to Mary's embarrassment, he would politely bow out, uninterested. Eventually the young King of Navarre and the young Duke of Guise, Mary's cousin, would join the list. Even the Prince of Condé proposed marriage, thinking his own Reformist beliefs would satisfy Mary's Protestant subjects. None sufficed.

She stiffened her resolve and resented anyone who suggested she aim lower. "I hope you agree that I should follow the counsel of Monsieur the Cardinal on matters [of marriage]," she wrote to Catherine, tepidly, when the Queen Mother ventured her own opinion, unsolicited. "I thank you very humbly for your concern, the same you would show to your most obedient of daughters."[8]

But Mary wasn't following her uncle's advice. The cardinal placed Charles of Austria at the top of his list. Mary flinched at the thought: the hapless archduke was the youngest of three brothers and poor, without the clout to "advance her interests in Scotland or in England, in which I have some right." The Scottish Catholic Hamiltons pushed their own Earl of Arran, but the young man had suffered a mental breakdown in 1562, and now lived locked away in his bedroom. Other candidates were simply beneath her, the sovereigns of insignificant duchies and realms. Even the Duke of Orléans, younger brother of King Charles IX and Catherine's favorite son—whose candidacy Mauvissière had presented—was deemed insufficient. Mauvissière tried to sweeten the deal: if she married Orléans, he astutely pointed out, Mary could return to France. The savvy envoy touched on one of Mary's deepest desires. Mary remained unmoved. To the young Queen of Scots, even a homecoming wasn't worth compromising her rank. She longed for a king.[9]

If not Charles IX, then only one other boy could hold Mary's attention. In 1563, she turned again to Don Carlos, Prince of Asturias. And once again, she beseeched the cardinal to negotiate on her behalf.*

---

*The cardinal rather begrudgingly agreed to assist Mary. Yet he may have calculated that, unlike a more powerful prince, Archduke Charles would not threaten the Auld Alliance with France or compromise the cardinal's own standing with Catherine. As a third son, the archduke could rule as King of Scotland

We do not know what Mary understood about Don Carlos's incapacities, though it is unlikely she held any illusions. Scotland did not enjoy official diplomatic ties with Spain, so no Spanish ambassador resided at Mary's court. Spanish news filtered to Mary, however, through Flanders and France, or through gossip sent by her envoys in London; likewise, news from Spain frequently reached Thomas Randolph's ears, funneled to him from the Spanish ambassador at Queen Elizabeth's court. It seems impossible that Mary hadn't heard reports about Don Carlos's volatile episodes, which had only worsened since his tragic fall at Alcalá nearly two years earlier. Though she dismissed the Earl of Arran's suit on the pretext of his insanity, nothing she heard about Don Carlos put Mary off.

Don Carlos's infirmities didn't matter. Mary looked beyond the boy to the father. Possibly, given Mary's propensity to imagine and fantasize, Philip II had acquired in her mind's eye the combined paternalistic features of the strong men in her life: Henry II, the Duke of Guise, the cardinal. It was Philip, not Don Carlos, whose crown rivaled that of France, and who boasted the armies, treasure, and willpower to win her the English succession; Philip who possessed the sovereign strength to quell any hint of rebellion by her Protestant subjects. Married to Don Carlos, she could live in Spain at the prince's side, while Philip helped run Scotland from afar. With Philip's approval, his blessing, she could return to her life exactly as she had once lived it in France, only this time transplanted onto the Peninsula, under an Iberian sun.

It does not seem to have occurred to Mary that, if Don Carlos should die—as would indeed happen within four years—she would be right back where she was, the reluctant ruler of Scotland in search of a husband to help govern her kingdom. Perhaps she thought that, this time, there might be a child who would keep her attached to Spain. She would be embraced as a Spanish dowager, Scotland forever ruled as a Spanish protectorate.

She'd tried to write Philip whenever the proper occasion presented itself, sometimes merely polite notes, at other times heartfelt letters. She sought to please him, even when he was trying to please her.

without overly intimidating Scottish subjects worried about a takeover by a foreign power. Alas, the cardinal could not get his niece to agree.

After the death of her mother: "Monsieur my good brother, I cannot describe the comfort it brings me to read of [your regret] at the death of the late Queen my mother. I don't know how to thank you enough. I feel so indebted to you, that I desire more than anything to have some opportunity to do something to please you in return." When Francis II died, Mary's pen wept on the page. "Your letters have consoled the most afflicted woman who ever existed on earth," she told Philip. "I beg you, in my misfortune, to remain my good brother and keep me in your good graces."[10]

Undeterred by Philip's reluctance two years earlier, in 1563 Mary remained determined to marry his son.

This time, Philip again insisted on the strictest secrecy until the marriage was "settled," deputizing agents in Flanders—the Cardinal of Granvelle and Mary's distant kinswoman the Duchess of Aarschot—to handle the correspondence. Mary dispatched her messages in cipher, putting as little on paper as possible, instructing her secretary for French affairs, Monsieur Raulet, to use the utmost discretion. Of course, the secret soon leaked.

Elizabeth Tudor responded by showering insults on Don Carlos. No Hapsburg princes for Mary, Queen Elizabeth declared. And no French princes, either. The Queen of Scots should marry a red-blooded Englishman if she had any hope for the English succession. Yet Queen Elizabeth offered Mary no peers of her realm. Instead, she suggested her best friend and favorite, Lord Robert Dudley, who served as her Master of the Horse, and was reputedly her former lover. In 1563, Mary brushed off the proposal as preposterous, sure that Elizabeth was merely joking.*

In France, Catherine remained relatively calm, her strategy for undoing Mary's Spanish plans now firmly in place. Convinced the Cardinal of Lorraine was up to his usual tricks, angling "one way or another to return to running this kingdom [of France]," Catherine ordered Elisabeth de Valois to employ "all possible means to see this does not go forward." She rattled on about the Guises and their usual

---

*Queen Elizabeth would offer Lord Robert Dudley to Mary once again in 1564. This time she was quite serious and raised Dudley to the peerage as Earl of Leicester so he might appeal to the haughty Scottish queen. Mary eventually concluded, however, that the proposal was a sham: Elizabeth appeared reluctant to send her favorite up north. Dudley himself seemed unwilling to leave Elizabeth's side, even for a crown. Mary bristled at the insult.

grandiose claims: the English queen would be declared a heretic and a usurper! Don Carlos and Mary would rule all of Britain! Catherine dismissed such talk. "The Queen of England thinks little of all this, since they have nothing but words to depose her with," and certainly no armies. An excellent judge of character, Catherine couldn't help but admire Elizabeth's acuity.[11]

Philip stretched out the talks longer and longer. Mary persisted, dispatching nervous letters to the Cardinal of Granvelle and the Duchess of Aarschot. She could not fathom why Philip delayed. Begging the duchess to press her case, a desperate Mary promised her everlasting devotion and reverence, "as if you were my own mother."[12] Her pushing achieved nothing: after almost two years of secret negotiations, Philip ended the talks abruptly in October 1564. Mary would not wed Don Carlos, not now, not ever. Delays beset the Duchess of Aarschot's letter bearing the bad news. Mary received it only in late December.

If she hoped that Philip II, like Henry II, would see in her a beautiful Scottish prize, Mary was deceived. Philip had doubts about his own son, but unbeknownst to Mary, he also harbored concerns about her. In Mary's supposed commitment to Catholicism, Philip detected a certain speciousness. Mary talked a good game. "I wish to live as [the Church's] most obedient daughter, sparing nothing in my power for this cause, even my own life if necessary," she wrote to Pope Pius IV in 1563. She would force her subjects to "recognize in all dignity the Holy Roman Catholic Church," and would send her uncle the cardinal to kiss the pope's feet. Nonetheless, she neglected to send representatives to the Council of Trent and instead asked the Cardinal of Lorraine to act on her behalf, offering only feeble excuses.[13]

That wasn't all. She allowed that heretical villain John Knox to bully and berate her and responded (Philip had heard) by crying. Protestantism showed no signs of abating in her kingdom, moreover. On the contrary, the Scottish Kirk held fast as the official church of the land. Mary seemed distracted, focused on the English succession when she should have been concentrating on fixing Scotland. Despite Mary's avowed Catholic devotion, Philip saw little evidence of actual rigor. He had drawn out the marriage talks just long enough to ensure the Queen of Scots would not marry a French prince, which may have been his goal all along.[14]

"I am glad to know the matter is decided," Mary wrote to the Duchess of Aarschot about Don Carlos, masking her distress. She still needed a husband: "my affairs and my subjects press me to make some decision."[15]

All through the Spanish-marriage talks, she'd suffered bouts of anxiety. In late 1563, she fell ill with a pain in her right side, which made her weepy and morose. Mary thought she had a cold. The physicians diagnosed "melancholy," which was more an assessment of the humors coursing through her body than of her state of mind. Medicine did nothing. Randolph found himself delivering his messages from the foot of her bed while Mary sat propped up on pillows. She felt shackled by the capriciousness of her subjects, who rejected all foreign princes, and by the reticence of the powers abroad, none of whom seemed eager to rush with her to the altar. "Some think that the cause of the Queen's sickness is that she utterly despairs of the marriage of any of those she looked for," Randolph reported to Cecil, "as well that neither they abroad are very hasty, nor her subjects at home very willing [to] those ways."

Sometimes, struggling to get purchase on her next steps, she wondered aloud whether marriage was the right choice. "Sometimes [Queen Mary] likes to hear of marriage," reported Randolph. "Many times the widow's life is best."[16] The single life never appealed to Mary for long. Far more at ease in the role of a consort, she yearned for a husband.

Most of all, Mary wished someone would tell her what to do. In January 1564, while the Don Carlos discussions dragged on and on, Mary sent her secretary, Raulet, to Joinville. He carried with him an enciphered letter for the cardinal and a note for her grandmother. "I have ordered Rollet [sic] to tell you the details of all my affairs," she wrote to Antoinette. "Please hear him out and tell me what you wish me to do. I will always follow your wishes more than anything else in the world, because I now have no one to serve and obey other than you, my good mother, for you have taken the place of all my relatives, both my father's and my mother's. I beg of you to keep me always in your good graces."[17]

Most likely, Antoinette endorsed the cardinal's view: Mary should wed the Hapsburg Archduke Charles. But this, despite all her filial devotion, Mary could not bring herself to do.

Within the year, any despair she felt in the autumn of 1564 turned to steely determination to marry again when, in the winter of 1565, her cousin Henry Stewart, Lord Darnley, appeared on the scene. Eighteen years old, Darnley was decidedly handsome: sandy blond hair, blue eyes, white-and-rose skin. An athletic and poised young man, his legs were so long that he stood taller than Mary herself, a rare thing since Mary reached almost six feet. Darnley was not the king she desired, though Mary would convince herself that he could be, one day. After all, royal English and Scottish blood flowed through his veins.

Like Mary, Lord Darnley was a grandchild of Margaret Tudor, eldest sister of Henry VIII of England. Though he descended from the Scottish Tudors, whom Henry VIII had excised from the English succession, Darnley had been born in England, as had his mother, which bolstered his claim to the English throne. Darnley was Catholic. His mother, Margaret Douglas, the Countess of Lennox, was famous for her zealotry. Seeing in Darnley the return of Catholicism to an England besmirched by a heretic queen, English Catholics supported his claim to the English throne almost as much as they did Mary's.[18]

So Mary envisioned Darnley as a future king, her path to England's throne. Foreign envoys would say she fell in love with him in the spring of 1565. This was probably true. She admired his flaxen looks and towering height, his Continental manners and his beautiful French, honed by tutors and a good deal of time spent with his French cousins in Aubigny back in 1562. He was an ace at cards and an avid gambler; he relished music, spoke Latin, boasted beautiful handwriting, and high-stepped a fine *galliard*. He probably reminded her of the French noblemen she'd grown up with. Darnley could be lovable when he wished—and during his wooing of the Scottish queen, Darnley was extraordinarily lovable. Soon he would develop an endearing habit of calling her "*Ma Marie*."[19] In April, foreign dispatches began twittering about the smitten Scottish queen. But love wasn't the only emotion agitating Mary. The spring and summer found her simmering with a resentment she had nurtured for years.[20]

In March 1565, news had drifted up from England that Elizabeth Tudor would postpone investigating the legality of Mary's claim to the English throne until "she herself had married or notified her intention of never marrying, one or other of which she meant shortly to do." Wait for Queen Elizabeth to decide to marry! The Queen of Scots prickled with humiliation at the mockery.[21] Still worse news arrived in April. Mary learned of a new marriage proposal, but not for her own hand: Catherine de' Medici had offered her son, King Charles IX, in marriage to Elizabeth Tudor—and despite her protestations of the previous month, the English queen now seemed to be considering the offer.[22]

It was one thing to be rebuffed by King Philip and spurned by Queen Elizabeth. Mary had never met the English queen: having seen only a portrait, Mary's sense of her was abstract, the signature Elizabeth affixed to the page the sole tangible mark of the flesh-and-blood woman. While Elizabeth was her cousin, Catherine was *family*: she was the mother-in-law who had taught the young Mary to embroider, who had cared for Mary in her childhood sickbed, the mother of Mary's dear friends and "sisters," and the intimate friend of Mary's beloved aunt Anne d'Este. Mary had once admired Catherine, perhaps even loved her. Yet now Catherine—a mere Medici—offered her son the king to the usurping heretic queen who had supported Mary's Protestant subjects and refused to give Mary the English succession—the thing to which Mary believed she was entitled.

To Mary herself, Catherine offered only the hand of the Duke of Orléans, her second son. The Queen Mother had revealed her pecking order.

As Mary confided to Lady Lennox, Lord Darnley's mother, "The Queen Mother of France was very much against her."[23] That spring, Mary surrendered to a whorl of emotions, her passion fueling anger and anger fueling passion. Mary no doubt fell in love with the comely Darnley, but more than love, it may have been spite toward both Catherine de' Medici and Elizabeth Tudor that spurred her to act.

Sometime later, in an undated memo, Mary would explain, defensively, why she married Darnley, a young man who turned out to be such a poor choice, weak-willed and profligate, prone to violence; a boy whose Catholic convictions proved shallow, and whom her lords despised. She had always wished to marry Don Carlos, Mary pointed out, but her "relations in France" thwarted her efforts "against her will." She went on to blame everyone but herself.

Among her reasons—her subjects' ceaseless calls for her to marry, her lack of funds and military support to induce her Protestant nobles to behave, the complete absence of any counsel she could trust— Mary would also name Lady Lennox. "The Countess of Lennox . . . entreated me to marry her son, of the blood of England and Scotland, and the nearest after me in succession, Stuart by name, in order always to preserve that surname so agreeable to the Scotch, of the same religion as myself, and who would respect me according to the honor conferred upon him."[24] Lady Lennox's reasoning seemed logical. Darnley fulfilled all her needs. Perhaps most importantly of all to Mary, at last someone had told her what to do.

During the first half of 1565, Mary had received a stream of messages from the Countess of Lennox pushing her to marry Darnley. This was a project the countess had been formulating for years. In the spring of 1565, Mary was especially fragile, the wounds inflicted by King Philip, Queen Elizabeth, and Queen Catherine still fresh, the cast of available grooms dwindling, the list of counselors whom Mary consulted reduced to almost no one. Mary had lost trust even in the cardinal, who was still stuck on the Archduke Charles. She looked for others who would tell her what she wished to hear.

So when, in the winter of 1565, Lady Lennox sent her couriers from London, laden with secret missives, parcels, and portraits, Mary eagerly received them. That February, the boy himself arrived in Fife, having picked his way through snow-choked roads during the coldest winter in recent memory. Mary had prepared to meet a good-looking young man. The Darnley she saw that February positively glowed: a beautiful boy worthy of a beautiful queen.

Soon, she would learn that Lady Lennox had opened another secret channel of communication, using the Spanish ambassador to England, Diego Guzmán de Silva, to correspond with Philip II. In the winter of 1565, Silva confirmed to Philip that "this [Lady Lennox] and her son are Catholics and profess attachment to your

Majesty." For the next few months, the countess applied slow and steady pressure on the Spanish king.

We don't know in any detail how Lady Lennox and Mary communicated. Any paper evidence was destroyed, and with good reason: in London, Lady Lennox worked her cunning right under the English queen's nose. Elizabeth Tudor had no liking for a marriage that would weave together the claims of Darnley and Mary to the English throne, a double threat. Though their messages have been lost, we know the countess and the queen corresponded from oblique references in third-party letters that do survive. Anything Mary said to Lady Lennox traveled through the Spanish ambassador in London. And sooner or later, Philip II's replies always reached Mary's ears.

By June, word of Mary's betrothal to Darnley landed in Spain. In London, Lady Lennox met again with Guzmán de Silva, who had heard from King Philip: "You may convey to Lady Margaret Lennox the sympathy and goodwill I bear toward her son and the successful accomplishment of the project [marriage], in order that they may be satisfied and may know that they can depend upon me in matters concerning this business, and so be able to entertain and encourage the Catholics and their party in England . . . You will make Lady [Lennox] understand this . . . Not only shall I be glad for her son to be king of Scotland and will help him thereto, but also to be king of England if this marriage is carried through."[25]

The next month, on July 29, Mary and Darnley were married at Holyroodhouse. She entered her private chapel just before dawn, on the arm of Darnley's father, the Earl of Lennox. Two priests officiated, following Catholic ritual to the letter. At her first wedding, Mary wore white, an unusual choice. This time, she wore all black apart from her *deuil blanc*, a Catholic custom. Smugly satisfied that she now enjoyed Philip's support, she donned the clothing of a virtuous Catholic widow about to leave mourning behind.

———

Like her mother-in-law, Catherine, Mary had a knack for the theatrical; unlike Catherine, she sometimes fantasized. As a young girl in France, she eagerly sported Scottish attire for feasts and banquets, soaking up the attention of French courtiers amused by her "outlandish" costumes. Soon after arriving in Scotland, still acting much like the child she was, Mary would sometimes don men's breeches and wander the streets of Edinburgh with her four Marys. Her imagination could roam. Just that winter, while she enjoyed a short holiday near St. Andrews, Randolph found her settled in a merchant's house, gathered with a few friends beside a roaring fire. No queen lodged there, she joked with Randolph. No, for the moment, she played at "being a bourgeois-wife" with her "little troop" of friends, divesting herself of the trappings of a queen and with them the burdens—at least for a time.[26]

She would play again that Easter in 1565, just as her love for Darnley began to bloom. On a spring day, Mary's ladies laced her into the gown of a "burgess"—an ordinary townswoman. Laughing, she strolled the city with her friends, "up and down the town, and of every man they met they took some pledge of money toward the banquet" planned for later that day. Soon thereafter, she celebrated this holiest of Catholic holidays by dining at a merchant's home while townspeople crowded around the table to stare. Here was their laughing queen dressed as a commoner, the tallest and prettiest young woman most of them had ever seen.[27]

Her levity that holiday belied a calcifying heart. That same Easter, to the dismay of her Protestant lords, Mary insisted only the traditional organ be played at Mass and forbade any "Scottish instrument," especially the fife or the drums.[28] And unbeknownst to her Protestant nobles, on July 24, five days before her wedding to Darnley, Mary painted herself as the most pious of Catholic queens in a letter to Philip II. A page had turned: with her new marriage, Mary discovered a fresh commitment to her Catholic faith. A commitment that, she hoped, would win her Philip's admiration. She could not have Don Carlos, yet she still yearned for the Catholic King's approval.

"Monsieur my good brother, as I know well the virtues God has given Your Majesty, I see that he has entrusted you not only with the fate of so many subjects of whom you are the King, but also that he seems to have charged you, above all others in this world, to be the defender of the holy Catholic faith. As I am also one of those queens to whom God has granted a kingdom, I have always resisted, with everything in my power, those who espouse a faith contrary to mine. To have greater means to achieve that resistance, I have resolved, taking the advice of my subjects, to marry the son of the Earl of Lennox. I have been assured that your ambassador [in London], who was forced to intervene in all of this, if only to halt the progress of the new sect, has shared with Your Majesty all the reasons that brought me to this decision.

"[My subjects] have tried to force me to abstain from the Mass. I have refused to do so and, having resolved to resist them or die trying, I have warned your ambassador of all that has occurred here. I am certain Your Majesty will grant me your help and assistance, given my great need of it, to maintain the faith, as you already do by sending so many armed forces against the Turks."

Gone was the Mary who made concessions to Protestants and failed to send envoys to Trent, or so it seemed. Here was a sovereign resolved to embark on a war of religion. A queen eager to take up a crusade of her own, not with weapons, but with matrimony. Was she performing again? Was this the queen Mary believed she already was? The queen she wished to become? Or the queen she knew Philip wanted to see? It was easy for Mary to sketch a portrait of Catholic piety with paper and ink. Mary had no Elisabeth de Valois to tell her that "we in Spain" paid more tribute to actions than to words.

Mary had good reason to solicit Philip's help. Her lords disliked the marriage for sundry reasons. The Protestants among them worried that Darnley heralded the return of Catholicism to Scotland—a concern Mary's letter to Philip would surely have confirmed, had they known about it. All the lords mistrusted the power Mary vested in Darnley: she had showered him with titles and estates, including the earldom of Ross and duchy of Albany, the latter normally reserved for Scottish royalty. The coming days would stoke their fears further: on the eve of their wedding, Mary would bestow upon Darnley the title of "King."

Lord James had already retreated from court to register his opposition to the marriage; he began to amass allies and troops. Refusing to negotiate, Mary rushed to shore up her own supporters. To dithering Protestant noblemen unsure whether to support their kirk or their queen, she sent reassurances: there would be no attempt to "impede or molest any [of] our subjects in the using of their religion and conscience freely." This was a vow Mary wasn't sure she could keep. She said nothing of such promises, of course, to Philip.[29]

Civil war seemed imminent; Mary looked for Spanish support yet, as always, her gaze skipped ahead to the thing she wanted most. In the second half of her letter to Philip, Mary asked the Spanish king for a favor. She was unaware of how transparent she'd become.

"I am certain there is no other war more dangerous for Christendom and more pernicious to the obedience due to princes than this war of the 'new evangelists' (and let it please God that Your Majesty will never feel their effects in his kingdom!). So, in light of these [religious] reasons as well as the sincere wish I have always had (and will always have for the rest of my life) to be allied with Your Majesty in all things, I beg Your Majesty to consider recommending to your ambassador to support the rights that the son of the Earl of Lennox and I have in England, and to command him to tell the Queen of England that Your Majesty will never allow anything to be done to prejudice [our claim]. I hope that we can one day repay the debt we owe you for this service. In the meantime, I commend myself to your good graces, praying God, Monsieur my good brother, to give Your Majesty a long life and all the prosperity you desire. From Edinburgh, this 24th of July, 1565. Your good sister, Marie, R."[30]

20

FAMILY AFFAIRS
France, on the border with Spain, 1565

The portrait Elisabeth de Valois posed for in 1565 was not so different from the one Sofonisba Anguissola had painted of her four years earlier. Full-length, with a three-quarter profile, it showed all of Elisabeth from the jewels of her tiara to the edges of her ruby-studded black skirts. A train of black velvet spilled from her shoulders. All down the front of her bodice and skirt glistened silver ornaments that snapped together like buckles. These ornaments were the Spanish *puntas*, and they were Elisabeth's favorite accessory. A heavy golden belt hung about her hips, exactly the type of belt the Spanish preferred, as Madame de Clermont noted so many years earlier. Tall, cork-soled shoes known as "chopines," which required tiny, mincing steps, likely graced Elisabeth's feet, too, though they disappeared under her skirts. Elisabeth adored Spanish footwear. As one French emissary wryly noted after presenting her with a pair of French slippers, a gift from her mother, Elisabeth admired French fashion but "when it comes to chopines, she is entirely a Spanish woman."[1]

About twenty years old in the portrait, Elisabeth looks every inch a Spanish woman indeed. Lest anyone doubt, however, she holds a miniature portrait in her hand, unmistakably a picture of Philip II. This, the artist is saying, is King Philip's queen.

The painter of this portrait remains uncertain. Some experts believe it was Alonso Sánchez Coello; others that it was Sofonisba Anguissola herself. Some think the portrait was intended as a gift for Catherine de' Medici, which Elisabeth was supposed to give to her mother in person.[2]

In the late spring of 1565, Elisabeth was preparing to meet her mother and younger siblings on the French–Spanish border. She had longed for such a visit since her arrival in Guadalajara in the winter of 1560. Now, in 1565, she looked forward to a family reunion at last.

The meeting, planned for June of that year, would take place in the French border town of Bayonne, just north of the Spanish Pyrenees, where the kingdom of France touched Basque country. In 1526, Bayonne had been the site of Valois sorrow when, as a young boy, the future King Henry II had crossed into Spain to serve as a prisoner in his father's stead. Now, Bayonne would become the scene of Spanish and French rejoicing.

As soon as Elisabeth learned she would see her mother, the packing began. Sofonisba Anguissola and a few select ladies would accompany her. But if Elisabeth meant to take the new painting, it didn't make the trip. Perhaps there hadn't been time to finish it. When Elisabeth traveled north from Madrid in April of that year, the portrait remained behind in Spain.

The meeting at Bayonne was the brainchild of Catherine de' Medici, who sought an alternative path to peace in France. Although the Edict of Amboise of 1563 had restored a fragile calm to France after the first War of Religion, Catherine sensed the law would not fend off fresh hostilities. What she needed was a show of strength: it was time for young King Charles to claim his authority. On August 17, 1563, in the Parlement of Rouen, surrounded by his mother, the princes of the blood, and his councillors, Charles declared his majority. The boy was barely thirteen—the minimum age at which a French king could reign without a regent. An exception would be made, of course, for his mother, "to whom he reserved the right to command." That day in Rouen, Charles stood, hat in hand, and stepped toward Catherine. Saying anything more was almost unnecessary. There was no greater show of deference.

If Catherine believed ending her regency would bring the religious factions together around the figure of a young king, she hoped in vain. Tensions still reigned in the kingdom. Bouts of violence sputtered and sizzled. Jurists railed in the provincial courts, refusing to register the edicts of toleration. Parisian lawyers, especially, objected to the new laws, sensing that although Charles now reigned in theory, in fact Catherine still ruled.[3]

Catherine itched to see the situation in the provinces for herself. She also believed that, more than ever, the kingdom of France needed a display of majesty the likes of which had not been seen in years. A show in which young King Charles would be the star. A parade of pageantry to stun all Frenchmen, Protestant and Catholic, into submission. In the autumn of 1563, she began planning.

Catherine had become a storyteller. Each time she commissioned a painting, erected a monument, landscaped a garden, or renovated a palace, she added to the chapters, telling the story of the Valois dynasty built through her labor, flesh, and blood. It was a visual story, told without words, for an age when fewer could read than couldn't (although, thanks to Protestantism's insistence on reading the Bible, that was slowly changing). Catherine's lexicon consisted of sights and sounds, smells, even tastes: of banquets and spectacles, waterworks and fireworks, parades and show-stopping pageants. In 1563, Catherine sought to tell a tale of bright potential embodied in the person of King Charles. Her message was simple and powerful: all Frenchmen and Frenchwomen, whatever their rank or birth, owed their allegiance to the king, her son.

By the closing weeks of the year, Catherine had choreographed an enormous tour of the realm. She would bring with her Charles, most of her younger children, and almost the entire court of France. The royal tour, as it came to be called, would take her and Charles to over thirty French towns and cities and countless villages. Their path would wind east from Fontainebleau to Champagne and down the border through Burgundy, follow the twin rivers of the Saône and the Rhône south beyond Lyon, then dip further into Provence. From there, the tour turned west toward Languedoc, traveling through Bordeaux and dropping into the southernmost tip of the kingdom at Bayonne before wending north again into the heart of the Loire Valley.

All told, the trip would last over two years. Charles would come of age on the road. When they set off in the winter of 1564, he was a thirteen-year-old boy. When the court returned to Fontainebleau in the spring of 1566, he was a handsome young man of sixteen, the whisper of a beard sweeping his chin.[4]

The concept of a royal tour was not radical. Sovereigns often traveled through their kingdoms, showing themselves to their people, assessing the state of affairs, giving their popularity a boost. Catherine herself had accompanied Francis I as his court wandered the kingdom, as well as Henry II during splendid official entries into towns like Rouen and Lyon. Now, Catherine banked on the people remembering those trips, that dazzle of long ago. When the people saw young Charles, tall and hale upon his stallion, in the company of splendidly dressed soldiers and peers of the realm, they would recall those bygone days of Francis I and Henry II. Catherine would trade in dreams and memories, triggering the people's nostalgia. She would show them Charles not as he was, but as she wanted him to be, the image of his forefathers. For Charles, she planned a spectacle to eclipse even the majesty of those great warrior kings. Or so she hoped.

The tour kicked off near Fontainebleau in mid-February 1564. On Sunday, February 13, Catherine hosted her own send-off at a small manor farm in the forest just beyond the château.[5] There, against a backdrop of thicketed evergreens, Catherine's guests feasted as actors performed and musicians played. Everyone reveled in the florid lines of a poem by Ronsard. Shepherds and shepherdesses frolicked through the poet's stanzas, among meadows bursting with flowers and flowing with milk. Ronsard cheered Catherine's efforts to unify the kingdom. "She restored to us our fields and woods," he wrote. "She returned us to our former pastures, gave us back our homes, and drove out our fear." Catherine was like the Roman goddess Cybele, the earth mother. At the dairy farm that Sunday, the royal children recited Ronsard's verses.[6]

It was only the first variation on a theme played out during countless occasions over the next two years. Her son, King Charles, was the star of this show. But Catherine bridged France's great past and its future. Her motherly touch would nurture peace and prosperity.

It was an exhausting trip, a working trip, requiring Herculean logistics to lodge and feed thousands of bodies; advance teams to scout safe traveling routes for the slow-rolling convoy; specialized gear for looking after the beasts of the royal zoo, which Charles, who loved his pets, insisted on bringing along. Charles learned patience as he sat idle in law courts, listening to his chancellor, Michel de l'Hôpital, lecture obdurate jurists who still refused to register the peacekeeping edicts. He greeted villagers who flocked around him, seeking his healing touch, and stood with his mother as godparent at dozens of baptisms along the way—all for baby girls, it turned out, which produced scores of infants named "Charlotte Catherine."* Catherine honed her already excellent skills of organization, managing affairs and diplomacy, responding to complaints by Protestants and Catholics alike, all on the road. She brought with her, of course, her secretaries and their quills. She was far from Paris, but the letter-writing never stopped.[7]

There was plenty of playing, too, on the royal tour, many moments of exquisite joy. None was quite as poignant as those few days early in the trip, at Bar-le-Duc in the province of Champagne. There, Catherine proudly hosted the baptism of her first grandchild, the son of her daughter Claude. Like the adolescents they were, Charles and his younger brother, the Duke of Orléans, jumped at the chance to gorge themselves at the endless banquets and to cheer their favorites at the dozens of tournaments. Charles wanted to ride in the tournaments, too, but his mother wouldn't allow it. Since the brutal day in July 1559 that took Henry II's life, jousts made Catherine jittery. Even the *course de bagues*—a kind of faux joust, where the goal was to skewer rings suspended from a stake in the ground—seemed too dangerous to her. Though a superior rider, a grumpy Charles had to settle for combat on foot, using fake weapons with blunted edges, humiliated that his mother babied him like his younger brother.[8]

Catherine conceived the idea of meeting Philip II sometime in the early months of the trip. She had longed to meet Philip ever since he had married Elisabeth in 1559. Somehow, Philip had always found a way to avoid her. But now, with Catherine so close to the southern border, he had little excuse. Why not meet, she proposed to her Spanish son-in-law, somewhere near Fuenterrabía, Saint-Jean-de-Luz, or Bayonne? It would be the perfect occasion to bring along his wife.

---

*The touch of French kings was famous for healing the ragged lesions of scrofula.

To further entice Philip, Catherine decided to rechristen her two youngest sons after the kings she most admired. On a spring day in Toulouse, 1565, mid-trip, the Duke of Orléans, Alexandre-Edouard, became "Henri," after his father. Catherine also announced that her youngest son, Hercules, would become "Francis," after his late older brother and grandfather. Catherine suspected King Philip would find "Alexandre" too reminiscent of Greek myth, "Edouard" too English and too Protestant; "Hercules" was outright pagan. The new names evoked the memory of valiant French Catholic kings—Catherine was certain they could not offend.[9]

Catherine's proposed conference with Philip was hardly a new idea. Monarchs had met in person before, their rivalries nominally set aside during weeks of conviviality. Borders between kingdoms were the perfect places for such conferences. Meeting at the border meant neither sovereign had a home advantage. And lands near the border were less constrained by the authority radiating from a kingdom's capital. This made them fluid and dangerous: it was no accident, for example, that King Henry VIII of England feared rebellion in the northern lands abutting Scotland, or that those lands remained defiantly Catholic in the face of his new English church. It was also no accident that French Huguenot strongholds flourished in the south of France, far from conservative Paris. Yet this same marginal nature also made a kingdom's borders a space to cast aside old ideas and suspend, at least temporarily, ancient hostilities. They could become a place to explore what was possible without ceding any ground.

The most famous of these summits-at-the-border took place in 1520 between Francis I of France and Henry VIII of England in a vast field in Picardy, halfway between Ardres on the northernmost tip of France and then-English-held Calais. The kings were young men: Katherine of Aragon was still Henry VIII's adoring wife, Anne Boleyn nowhere on the horizon; Claude, Francis I's fertile queen, still lived. Their friendly smiles masked fierce competition and outsized egos. Workers had landscaped the valley floor so that neither king's camp would sit higher than the other. (The English

Cardinal Wolsey, who organized the event, almost literally moved mountains.) So much golden cloth glittered on every surface that the event was dubbed "The Field of Cloth of Gold." The opulence astonished everyone. In fact, behind the scenes, little diplomacy was achieved.

Not every wished-for meeting between monarchs succeeded, especially on the island of Great Britain. Back in 1562, the talks between Mary, Queen of Scots, and Elizabeth Tudor, on which Mary set her heart and soul, foundered before they could even begin.

Despite her disappointment—or perhaps because of it—Mary had embarked on a progress of her own. Since her return to Scotland, she had focused almost entirely on her halting friendship with Queen Elizabeth and had yet to see her own country. She set forth, winding her way up toward the northern lochs near Inverness. It was a terrible journey, noted Randolph, who rode in her train: "cumbersome" and "painful." In Old Aberdeen, he scratched out a complaining note to William Cecil. The trip was taking forever, and the weather was wet and cold. Food was expensive and in short supply. Even the ears of corn in the fields looked stunted, soaked with rain. Randolph was sure they would "never like to come to ripeness."[10]

Ignoring the aching pace of the trip, Mary pushed on, determined to show herself to her people. In Aberdeen, her disappointment at the canceled summit smoldered again. Not three miles along the route was the home of the Earl of Huntly, one of the "fairest in the country," a fine place to lodge. Mary was wary. Huntly, though a Catholic, had never shown much support for her mother, Marie de Guise, and, to Mary's vexation, he'd also disapproved of her meeting with the Protestant Queen Elizabeth. Now, he showed other signs of imminent revolt. When she summoned him to Aberdeen, he appeared with 1,500 soldiers instead of the 100 she'd commanded. Soon she received word that Huntly's son had defied an order to report to Stirling Castle. And when she arrived at Inverness, intending to stay at Huntly's castle, the warden refused to admit her without Huntly's permission. The disobedience bordered on treason.

Mary was enraged. Whipping up the local loyal countryfolk, she forced the castle to surrender and ordered the captain hanged. As his body swung from its rope, Randolph watched the Scottish queen: she had behaved with a remarkable sangfroid, even relished the confrontation. "I assure you I never saw her merrier, never dismayed," he wrote to Cecil, "nor never thought that so much to be in her that I find." Randolph was accustomed to seeing Mary sitting in her presence chamber, sewing "some work or another"; he hadn't realized she could stomach such violence.[11] The pretty queen was more than he'd bargained for, capable of ruthlessness, and just possibly the slightest bit volatile.

Mary had confirmed her sovereignty and proven she'd tolerate no hint of rebellion, not even from a fellow Catholic like Huntly. But if she rejoiced at the proof of her power, Elizabeth Tudor soon put her back in her place. Mary returned to Edinburgh in October, to a letter written in the English queen's own hand. Elizabeth explained at length why she had deferred their conference. She described French brutalities, the "burials in water," "men cut in pieces," pregnant women strangled while holding their wailing babies. As everyone knew, the Duke of Guise's abominable actions at Wassy were the cause of the troubles. "What hope is left for strangers when cruelty so much abounds among the household?" Elizabeth asked. What friendship could blossom among masters when servants were at war?[12]

The English queen's doubts would persist. No matter how often Mary pledged sisterhood and friendship, Elizabeth remained reserved. And though she had promised to postpone the summit only for a year, Elizabeth never delivered. Over the years, Mary would try several times more to arrange a parley between them, but Elizabeth never agreed to meet. Each time Elizabeth refused, Mary felt her own powerlessness.

Where Mary Stuart had failed, Catherine de' Medici endeavored to succeed. Hoping her own royal tour of France would build up excitement for her proposed conference with Philip II, she nonetheless hedged her bets in case he proved stubborn.

In the winter of 1565, while still on tour, Catherine struck up a shaky alliance with Elizabeth Tudor. The enmity between England and France had softened the previous year when Elizabeth signed the

Treaty of Troyes, renouncing English rights to Calais in exchange for a payment of 120,000 French crowns. Never one to hold a political grudge for very long, Catherine brushed aside the English queen's open support of Condé and French Reformers during the religious war of 1562–63. Now, in February 1565, she put forward a marriage proposal: Elizabeth, age thirty-two, would marry King Charles, age fourteen.

This was a case of the enemy of your enemy becoming your friend—or even your family. Who, here, was the enemy? The Spanish ambassador De Quadra guessed they were both trying to unsettle Mary Stuart.[13] This was true, to a point. While Elizabeth thought mostly about Mary, Catherine's chief target was Philip II himself. If Philip refused to meet with her or made too many demands, Catherine was not above turning to Protestants like Elizabeth Tudor: this was the message embedded in the English marriage proposal.

In Madrid, Philip had no wish to meet with Catherine. In fact, the idea filled him with dread. Meeting Catherine might send a message to the world that he tacitly approved of the heresy in France. Nor did Philip wish to meet any French heretics, and he was certain that Protestant nobles would be in attendance.

Nevertheless, five years of his mother-in-law's ceaseless demands for a meeting had worn him down. Clearly, Catherine would never stop asking. Moreover, Ruy Gómez's tactful counsel had convinced Philip to maintain the alliance with France, if only to demand Catherine implement the persecution of heresy he'd so readily applied in England, when he was married to Mary Tudor. Philip also wanted Catherine to adopt the decrees issued by the Council of Trent when it had adjourned in 1563. The Council had revised some of the Catholic Church's basic tenets, hoping to shepherd souls back to the fold. But it had given no ground on the Mass, however, declaring in no uncertain terms that Christ resided in the consecrated bread and wine of the Eucharist. The papacy demanded adoption of the decrees by all Catholic kingdoms. Yet Catherine had resisted doing so.

Philip decided to meet Catherine halfway. Unwilling to grant her the satisfaction of meeting him in person, Philip sent his regrets. But knowing how avidly mother and daughter wished to see each other again, he decided to be gracious: "To satisfy both of them in their desire, I have responded to the Most Christian Queen that I am very pleased to send the Queen, my wife, to see her at Fuenterrabía."[14] He warned Catherine that Elisabeth's attendance was conditional. Should any French heretics attend, Elisabeth would refuse to show up. "I would refuse to allow her," wrote Philip, "and she would not wish to either."

Catherine protested, fearing the Protestants would take their exclusion badly, which would then trouble France's fragile peace; as she explained to Philip, the Prince de Condé, especially, hoped to pay his respects to the Queen of Spain. Philip held firm, nonetheless—and the Queen Mother was forced to send the Prince de Condé and Jeanne d'Albret, Queen of Navarre, home from the tour.[15]

Philip ordered his envoys in foreign courts to alleviate any Protestant doubts: the reunion was "simply a family meeting of affection," they were to explain, if anyone grew suspicious.[16]

A few weeks after Elisabeth de Valois left Madrid for Bayonne, Philip thought twice about it. Through diplomatic channels, he'd discovered that Charles planned on meeting with the Turkish ambassador while in Bayonne. The Turks were old enemies of the Hapsburgs; Catherine seemed intent on showing Philip she had other allies. Would Elisabeth take a hard line with her mother? Philip dispatched the Duke of Alba to follow the queen, just in case.

———

The town of Irún, nestled at the Spanish border where the Bidasoa River meets the sea, welcomed Elisabeth de Valois and her slim retinue in June. Her trip had taken two months. There'd been changes of itinerary. An outbreak of plague in Burgos forced Elisabeth northeast instead to Soria, leaving a planned banquet at Burgos untouched, much to the regret of the city's inhabitants. Happily, she'd lost only four days.

Near Irún, Elisabeth at last met up with her younger brother, the newly christened Henri, Duke of Orléans. He arrived on June 9, dressed splendidly in crimson, galloping at the head of a hundred men all head-to-toe in red like their prince—a sea of scarlet. Young

Henri had been nine when he last saw Elisabeth; now he was just shy of fourteen. "Monsieur, I have met with the queen our sister and we are making merry," he wrote to Charles later that evening. The family resemblance was unmistakable. "She really looks a lot like you," Henri wrote.[17]

She *did* look like Charles, but there was now something Spanish in the mix, and it wasn't only the clothes. Brantôme—who had an uncanny knack for attending young queens as they moved from kingdom to kingdom—had arrived in Spain as a French envoy in the months before Elisabeth left for the border and joined her retinue. Elisabeth fascinated Brantôme. He saw something hybrid in her, a grace that "mixed Spanish with French in gravity and gentleness." Spanish now came as easily to her as French, the latter reserved for speaking with her French ladies and foreign envoys like Brantôme, the former for all other occasions. Carpets were best when Spanish, books when French, and musical instruments, too. She often liked to soften her black Spanish gowns with colored bows and ribbon. There was a cheekiness to that ribbon, a droll French smile. Elisabeth melded two worlds.[18]

It was exceptionally hot in Basque country that summer. In the early afternoon swelter of June 14, Elisabeth arrived on the left bank of the Bidasoa, which sat within the kingdom of Spain. On the right bank, which belonged to France, Catherine waited anxiously with King Charles.

The Queen Mother's impatience to see her daughter again had been mounting for months. Catherine had written to Elisabeth assiduously from the road, keeping track of her journey to Bayonne. When the Queen of Spain arrived at Irún earlier that June, Catherine had hoped to travel there and spend the night as Elisabeth's guest. She was disappointed: the wary Spanish had dissuaded Elisabeth from agreeing to Catherine's request. Catherine was forced to wait until the middle of the month. Now, at last, the moment of their reunion had arrived.[19]

In the end, it was Catherine who crossed the river. To prevent any appearance of aggression toward Spain, King Charles remained on French soil, but Catherine as queen—especially the shape-shifting yet formidable Queen Mother—had the power to intercede and traverse borders. Her presence would set the tone: this was a meeting between queens, natural peacemakers. Besides, Catherine was Elisabeth's mother. She would bring her daughter home.

Disembarking on the left bank of the Bidasoa, Catherine stepped toward her daughter. Elisabeth—now taller than her mother—sank into a deep curtsey, "so low," wrote one witness, "that she made as if to kiss her mother's knee." Catherine wouldn't allow it. Raising Elisabeth up, Catherine kissed her three times. Then, "both fell to weeping so tenderly and shed so many tears that, when they arrived back at the river's edge, their eyes still weren't dry."

The two women sailed back to the French bank, Spaniards and Frenchmen now mingling on the decks of the barge. After the boat dropped anchor, King Charles raced up to the deck. Even in his excitement, he managed to check himself. He wouldn't kiss Elisabeth; he dared not offend the Spanish. Instead, he hugged his sister—twice. But the fifteen-year-old Charles was a sensitive boy. Later, he too found it difficult to hold back the tears.[20]

———

From the moment the young Duke of Orléans fetched Elisabeth with his army of crimson-clad attendants until the final days of the interview, Catherine wanted the Spanish in her thrall. French elegance, French ingenuity, French wealth, French taste. Spain would cower in France's majestic shadow. This was Catherine's message, crafted not only for the Spanish but for the other nations who had sent envoys, like the Venetians, the English, and the papacy. Bayonne was Catherine's stage; all of Europe her audience.[21]

With each spectacle—what the French called a *magnificence*—Catherine aimed bigger and brighter. At the tournament of "Diverse Nations," scores of soldiers representing Trojans and Amazons, French and Spanish, Moors, Romans, Greeks, and Albanians waged a mock battle under the blazing sun. During the indoor masquerade, soldiers mounted an assault on an enchanted castle. On a day trip to an island on the river, a flotilla of thirty boats ferried guests past wondrous marvels. Midriver, six Tritons played their woodwinds while astride an enormous tortoise. A Neptune spouted verses while seated in a shell drawn by giant seahorses. For the pièce de résistance, spectators turned to see an enormous breaching whale. Within half an hour,

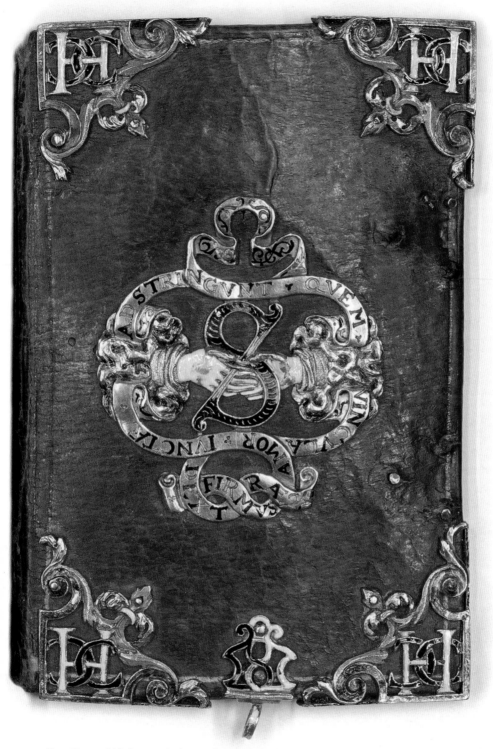

King Francis I likely gave Catherine this prayer book, known as a book of hours. Her initials, intertwined with those of her husband, Henry II, grace the corners. Later in life, Catherine would paste several portraits of her extended family into the book.

A Spanish noblewoman's dress, made of silk and linen.

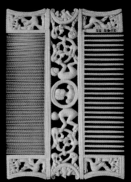

French comb in ivory, dating from about 1550. Elisabeth and Mary likely brought several such combs with them when they respectively traveled to Spain and Scotland.

A sixteenth-century version of the wedge heel. These fashionable Spanish-made *chapins*, or chopines, are made of silk with cork soles. Though not nearly as high as the ones that were all the rage in Venice, they still forced the wearer to take mincing steps. Elisabeth adored her *chapins*.

A sample of Italian filet lace, the kind Catherine learned to make in the convent of Le Murate. Catherine taught both Elisabeth and Mary, Queen of Scots, to embroider and weave. Elisabeth preferred to paint and draw, but Mary's love of embroidery lasted her entire life.

Catherine de' Medici's bedroom at Chenonceau, her favourite chateau. The decor is a nineteenth-century re-creation of how the room might have looked during Catherine's lifetime.

Aristocratic women wore decorative girdles around their hips, like low-slung belts. The Spanish thought French girdles—like this one, made in Paris—were too skinny, and preferred wider ones.

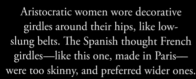

A music lover, Elisabeth de Valois brought French musicians and instruments to her new kingdom. A gift to Philip II, the "Kurtz violin" is believed to have traveled from France to Spain with the young queen.

A new mother recovers in bed while the women of the household bathe the newborn. There is cause for celebration: both mother and child have survived the ordeal of childbirth.

Charles IX at sixteen, c. 1566. The young man looks serious and vibrant—a promising start to what Catherine hoped would be a prosperous reign.

Mary, Queen of Scots, at twelve or thirteen years old. The Guises banked on her beauty and charisma.

Elisabeth de Valois at twelve or thirteen, shortly before her marriage to Philip II of Spain.

Catherine's baby pictures. Clockwise from top left: Mary, Queen of Scots, age five; one of Catherine's sons recovering from illness; toddler Francis laughing for the artist; Catherine's lost children, two-year-old Louis and the infant twins, Jeanne and Victoire. Catherine had this portrait pasted into her book of hours.

Catherine with four of her children. From left to right: Hercules (later Francis, Duke of Alençon), King Charles IX, Marguerite (Margot), and Alexandre-Edouard (later Henri III). A protective mother, the guardian of her children and kingdom, Catherine holds King Charles's hand.

Elisabeth as Sofonisba Anguissola remembered her twenty years after the queen's death. Based on an earlier portrait made in 1561, when Elisabeth was fifteen, this painting captures an ethereal beauty not often associated with the Spanish queen—testament, perhaps, to Sofonisba's loving memories of her

King Francis I's resplendent armor.

Miniature of Catherine's husband, Henry II of France.

Henry II wore parade helmets like this one during magnificent royal pageants.

The joust that would lead to the death of Henry II. The lance has just broken, and the splinters are flying.

Jean Clouet painted this portrait of Francis I between 1527 and 1530, when the king was in his prime.

Charles of Guise, Cardinal of Lorraine, here painted by El Greco, was Mary Stuart's favorite uncle.

Joinville, the seat of the Guise family in Champagne, as imagined by a nineteenth-century artist.

The burning of the Protestant jurist Anne du Bourg. A boy climbs
the cross in the Place de Grève to catch a better view.

A sixteenth-century depiction of the massacre at Wassy, which sparked the first French War of
Religion. Protestant parishioners flee to the roof of the barn where they had been worshipping.

The Tumult of Amboise. Some prisoners were executed in front of
the chateau while others were hung from the turrets.

A nineteenth-century painting of the Colloquy at Poissy conveys Charles IX's youth. His feet
barely touch the floor pillow and, as the Protestant Bèze speaks, Charles's gaze wanders.

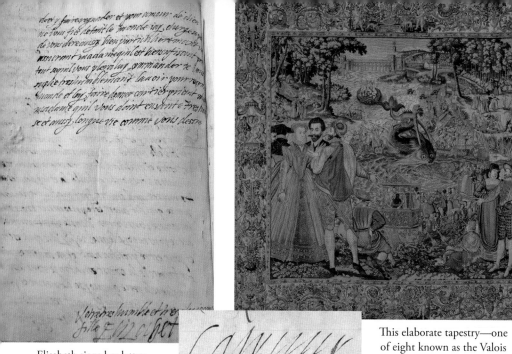

Elisabeth signs her letter to Catherine: "Your very humble and most obedient daughter."

"Caterine": Catherine's inimitable, scrawling signature.

This elaborate tapestry—one of eight known as the Valois Tapestries—shows the Festival of the Whale, one of the many sumptuous spectacles Catherine arranged for her meeting at Bayonne with Elisabeth.

A sixteenth-century Italian writing box. Suited to both travel and everyday use, the box was handy for storing writing implements and paper. The sloped lid made writing with a quill easier.

After her imprisonment in England, Mary turned frequently to embroidery for comfort. She made this osprey, likely with the help of the Countess of Shrewsbury, around 1570, two years after her flight to England.

The mermaid and the hare, 1567. After Darnley's death, satirical pamphlets appeared all over Edinburgh, showing Mary as a seductive siren and Bothwell as a hare—a creature symbolizing lust.

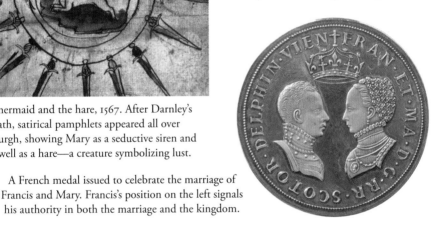

A French medal issued to celebrate the marriage of Francis and Mary. Francis's position on the left signals his authority in both the marriage and the kingdom.

The island fortress of Lochleven Castle, where Mary was imprisoned by her lords in 1567–1568.

The royal palace of Aranjuez, the holiday spot of Spanish kings, was one of Elisabeth de Valois's favorites.

A self-portrait of Sofonisba Anguissola, eminent artist of the Renaissance, and one of Elisabeth's favorite ladies-in-waiting.

The nineteenth-century painter Eugène Isabey captured the trauma of Elisabeth de Valois's departure from France. Catherine

Juana of Austria, Princess of Portugal,
Philip II's youngest sister.

Philip II by the Flemish artist Antonis
Mor. The Spanish king was so pleased
by this portrait that he had several
copies made and sent to foreign courts.

The "Bayonne Portrait." Elisabeth, about nineteen, has
mastered Spanish fashion: her black gown is decorated
with silver puntas and she wears a wide girdle. In
her right hand, she holds a miniature of Philip.

Philip commissioned these gold statues of his family
for the Escorial. Don Carlos, tall and strong, looks
over Philip's right shoulder. Elisabeth, the mother
of Philip's beloved daughters, kneels behind him.

This is the first known Clouet portrait of Catherine, c. 1550. She is pregnant, probably with either Louis or Charles, as the high-necked gown and Mona Lisa smile suggest. Now the mother of several royal children, Catherine has settled into her place at court. She is about thirty years old.

courageous whale hunters, drawing their spears, had vanquished the fearsome beast.*

There were waterworks and fireworks, comedies and tragedies, jousts on horseback, naval battles, sonnet-singing castrati and dancing shepherds galore. Politics wove itself into the spectacle. On June 21, the Duke of Alba honored Charles by inducting him into the Order of the Golden Fleece. And on June 26, as the summit drew to a close, the papal nuncio presented Elisabeth with the Golden Rose, celebrating her as *Isabel de la paz*. Like the rose, Elisabeth was the epitome of virtue. The queen of peace would heal all wounds.

Years later, young Margot, who was eleven years old at Bayonne, would still remember something of those glorious days. Most of all, she recalled the splendid feast hosted by her mother on an island in the Bidasoa. In a meadow edged with trees, tables were laid for twelve. Under a silk canopy sat her mother, Queen Catherine, her brother King Charles, and her older sister Queen Elisabeth. As dancers dressed like shepherds circled the tables, barges floated on the water, their decks filled with musicians "singing and playing the entire time." "The Poitevins played on bagpipes," Margot remembered, "the Provençales on the viol and cymbal; the Burgundians and Champagners on the hautboy, bass viol, and tambourin, the Bretons danced the *passepied* and the *branle gai*, and so it went for all the other provinces." It was a celebration of France. A France unified, as it should be.

As the banquet ended, satyrs sashayed from behind large boulders as dozens of dancing nymphs poured over the top of the rocks and onto the grass, delighting the dinner guests. Suddenly, thunder clapped, and rain fell; everyone ran laughing for the boats. For the young Margot, the weather couldn't spoil the memory.[22]

Behind the magic, however, the atmosphere was more strained. Catherine had two objectives for the summit. First, she wanted

*The whale appears to have been mechanized. This particular spectacle honored Bayonne, a seafaring, whale-hunting town.

King Philip to support her policies of toleration. Second, as always, she hoped to arrange more marriages between the Valois and the Hapsburgs. Charles was off the table, his marriage negotiations with Elizabeth Tudor still ongoing. Instead, Catherine proposed a marriage between Princess Juana and her son Henri, Duke of Orléans. And she still held out hope of marrying Margot to Don Carlos. Philip, of course, had charged Elisabeth and Alba with a far different agenda.

Secrecy whirled around their discussions. We can piece together some sense of the talks from letters by Alba and the Spanish envoy to France, Francés de Alava, as well as from Philip's own accounts after the fact, but much has been lost. One thing is clear: if Catherine expected Elisabeth to bow to her wishes, she was sorely disappointed. Nor did Catherine give any ground herself. According to Alba, Catherine had fixated on the marriages; Elisabeth replied only that Philip might consider them. Elisabeth pushed the decrees of the Council of Trent; Catherine said they weren't necessary. The royal tour had pacified the people, the Queen Mother insisted, and now that King Charles had declared his majority, order would soon be restored.

Alba saw no hope. As the end of June approached, he grew almost despondent. Charles simply parroted his mother, Alba reported to Philip. "It is impossible for us to augur something good from it . . . Each day [France] is led toward destruction without a remedy being applied."[23]

Then, at the eleventh hour, the mood shifted. The queens reached some sort of agreement. What happened exactly remains murky but, in some way, Catherine capitulated to her daughter. Elisabeth's inflexibility surprised Catherine. "How Spanish you've become!" she protested, according to Alava.* "I am Spanish, as is my duty," Elisabeth agreed. "But I am still your daughter, the same as when you first sent me to Spain."[24]

What did they decide? We will never know. Only Alba, Catherine, Elisabeth, and a few deputies were present; all kept their lips sealed. Suspicious Protestants would eventually claim that numerous

---

*Alava was now Spanish ambassador to France after Philip, bowing to pressure from Catherine, sent him to replace the detested Chantonnay.

Catholic atrocities were first hatched at the border, including the Duke of Alba's bloody suppression of the Dutch Revolt in 1566 and, in 1572, the ruthless slaughter of thousands of French Protestants during the Saint Bartholomew's Day Massacre in Paris. Protestants throughout Europe excoriated Philip, Alba, and Catherine for these appalling events. They spared Elisabeth de Valois.

As Philip himself reported it, however, Elisabeth actively participated in whatever unfolded at Bayonne. In August of that year, Philip wrote a letter to a Spanish cardinal then resident in Rome, Francisco Pacheco, explaining what had transpired at the border. According to Philip, Elisabeth made it clear to Catherine that toleration only incited French Protestants to take up weapons, that peace edicts led only to rebellion. It was Elisabeth, not Alba, who told Catherine that Philip insisted on "the regulation of religious affairs in the kingdom," and that Charles must "enjoy absolute obedience." It was Elisabeth, said Philip, who strenuously pressured her mother to adopt the Tridentine decrees; Elisabeth who "destroyed" the idea of yet another French religious council "so skillfully" that Catherine agreed to give the decrees due consideration. When she saw no other way out, it was to Elisabeth, not Alba, that Catherine offered "to bring about a remedy as quickly as possible and that she would delay no longer once she finished" the royal tour.

And once Catherine capitulated, it was Elisabeth who sent the Duke of Alba scurrying off to report the good news. Philip's wife had taken a hard line after all.

Affection and love, combined with persistence, rigor, and insistent demands—weren't these Catherine's own weapons? Elisabeth was her mother's first and most important student. Elisabeth believed her mother would apply a "remedy" to the disease of French Protestantism, Philip concluded. "The Queen, my wife, was happy with such a resolution because it is clearly understood, without a smidgen of doubt, that the day when such a remedy is necessary, the thing will be done," he wrote. Philip swore Cardinal Pacheco to secrecy; even the pope, he said, should keep mum, lest the French back out to save face.[25] Whether that "remedy" entailed any specific action against French Protestants or simply a course correction, vaguely conceived, remains a mystery.

During the final celebratory days at Bayonne, the queens managed to put their differences aside. Nothing could shake their love for each other. The goodbyes in July were heart-wrenching. "The tears flowed like waves," wrote Alava. Charles was so upset that Constable Montmorency was forced to remind him that "a king must never cry."[26] The boy wept anyway.

The Catholic Queen left Bayonne on Monday, July 1. Her party traveled by night to avoid the heat of the midday sun, so the trip took almost six weeks.* Despite the drudgery of the journey, Elisabeth remained in fantastic spirits, the French ambassador assured Catherine. The whole way back, her entire entourage reminisced about the marvels they had seen, the food they had tasted, the people they had met. Elisabeth was still beaming when she finally arrived back in Madrid on a Saturday, August 27, to a King Philip who likely had never been so pleased to see her.[27]

Before she quit Bayonne herself, Catherine wrote to Philip. "Monsieur my son," she scrawled, "I cannot thank you affectionately enough for the honor and good you've done me by giving me the joy of seeing the Queen my daughter. I have found her so well that the King my son and I, along with this entire kingdom, are in debt to you for the good treatment she receives from you. This should assure you even more of the good friendship that [King Charles] your brother feels for Your Majesty, a friendship this meeting will only strengthen, as the Queen your wife will tell Your Majesty in fuller detail." She signed, as always, "Your good mother and sister, Catherine."[28]

In truth, the meeting at Bayonne had disappointed her. Though she had seen Elisabeth again, a worthy prize, not a single one of the Valois–Hapsburg marriages Catherine had proposed would go forward. Philip, moreover, had refused to endorse her edicts of toleration. Perhaps most disappointing of all, Elisabeth had stood by her husband's commands. She'd become very Spanish indeed.

---

*Catherine had instructed her envoy to keep her updated on Elisabeth's trip and her health, especially because it was so hot, and to inform her the minute the Catholic Queen was back in Madrid.

Never one to give up easily, Catherine readjusted her focus: she looked toward England. In August, after leaving Bayonne, she sent a messenger of her own to Elizabeth Tudor, who had decided to reject King Charles's marriage suit.* Trying to change Elizabeth's mind, Catherine sent a gift copy of Ronsard's *Elegies, Mascarades, et Bergerie*, newly printed. The book contained the same poem the French royal children had recited during Catherine's send-off party for the royal tour at her farm over two years earlier. Ronsard himself had offered a copy to his muse, Mary, Queen of Scots. But Catherine wanted the book dedicated to "Her Majesty, the Queen of England."[29]

"Madame," the dedication began, "the greatest fortune that our France could receive at this moment, after that of her own private repose, is the Peace solemnly sworn with Your Majesty, whose strength is such that you have . . . ruptured the bitterness and almost natural dissensions that the centuries have nourished and amplified, with so many disadvantages to these two flourishing kingdoms, each so near to the other."[30] Once again, Catherine tried her hand at illusion—as if, with a few printed words, she could wipe away generations of hostility.

Catherine also intended the book as a peace offering: like her fellow Protestants, Elizabeth Tudor wondered if some nefarious plotting had transpired at Bayonne. But by the end of the summit, news from Scotland distracted the English queen from events at the Spanish–French border. She learned her cousin Mary had married Henry Stewart, Lord Darnley—creating a double claim to the English throne.

---

*Elizabeth may have entertained the French proposal only long enough to rattle Mary Stuart. Whether Elizabeth meant to push Mary into her disastrous marriage with Darnley remains the subject of some debate.

21

THE QUEENS' TWO BODIES
Scotland and Spain, 1566

On January 30, 1566, Mary, Queen of Scots, wrote a letter of congratulation to Pope Pius V, who had ascended the Throne of St.
Peter just weeks earlier. She wished to assure the new pontiff of
her devotion to the Roman Catholic Church, though she admitted
neglecting "these most pious and holy requests" that Pius's predecessor had expected of her. She offered an excuse: the fault lay
with her subjects, still so prone to heresy and rebellion. "Everyone
knows how great have been the troubles to which our realm has
been exposed, and how cruel the agitations which have befallen
us personally. The enemies of our religion are many," Mary's clerk
wrote in a clean Latin. They were powerful enemies, Mary claimed,
and devious. Thus far, they had thwarted her every effort to return
Scotland to the old faith.[1]

Mary felt no need to name names. Everyone knew, indeed, that
Lord James and his Protestant allies had revolted just days after
her wedding the previous summer on July 29. The "Chaseabout
Raid"—so dubbed because the rebel and crown armies chased each
other around the kingdom of Scotland yet never actually met—had
continued through October. Despite the lack of armed combat, the
insurgency was real.

At the height of the conflict, in September, Mary had appealed to
France for aid, threatening to throw herself "into the arms of another
prince" should King Charles and Queen Catherine abandon her. At
the same time, she wrote to that other prince, seeking soldiers or,
failing that, cash. "Events have occurred in this kingdom that will

lead to the entire ruin of Catholics and to the establishment of these wicked errors [of belief]," she told Philip II of Spain. "We are resisting, yet the King my husband and I will risk losing our crown" and "the rights that we claim *elsewhere*, if we do not have the help of one of the great princes of Christendom."[2]

Her pleas landed well. Philip II, always eager to stamp out heresy, sent 20,000 gold crowns, which, alas, never arrived in Scotland.* Catherine, thinking compromise was always best when weak women or children had to deal with powerful Protestant lords, argued for diplomacy. She sent an envoy who did show up in Scotland, along with Catherine's stern warning that war "threatens to put [Mary's] entire kingdom in peril." The Sieur de Mauvissière found Mary unrelenting, set on crushing her enemies at all costs, unwilling to listen to reason. "Her Majesty . . . would rather abandon her scepter and crown than negotiate with those who are by nature her subjects, yet show no faith in her, and even worse, are ungrateful for the wealth and honors that Her Majesty has bestowed upon them," he wrote.[3]

Deploring the Scottish queen's recalcitrance, the Queen Mother sent Mauvissière to England to see if Elizabeth Tudor might be more flexible. She worried that Mary would pursue her half-brother to the bitter end and that the English queen, who also despised the Darnley marriage, would throw her weight behind Lord James. Above all, Catherine wanted to avoid a war. Mired in its own civil tensions, France could not afford to support Scotland against England, and besides, the Queen Mother was still trying to negotiate a marriage between Charles IX and Queen Elizabeth.

Despite the lost Spanish gold, despite her former mother-in-law's reluctance to lend material aid, Mary had prevailed, to a degree. In October, Lord James and the rebels fled to England, where they sought refuge with Elizabeth Tudor. In deference to her Scottish sister queen and to the French appeals for peace, Queen Elizabeth subjected a kneeling Lord James to an hours-long tongue-lashing in

---

*Mary sent an agent by the name of Yaxley to brief Philip further on the war. Philip put Yaxley and the gold on a ship back to Scotland. Unfortunately, the ship foundered, Yaxley drowned, and the gold washed up on the shores of England, where it was seized by the Duke of Northumberland, who, despite Mary's beseeching letters, refused to yield his booty.

French about the dangers of rebellious subjects. Then, in deference to her coreligionists, she granted the rebels refuge anyway.[4]

As Mary wrote to Pope Pius V in January, Lord James and his allies still bided their time in England. James's duplicity stung Mary personally. More than on anyone else, she had relied on him to forge relations with England, and on his protection from the fulminations of men like John Knox. And they were family, joined by blood—a bond that, raised by the Guises, Mary believed was unbreakable. Now, she wished only for vengeance. She had confiscated the rebels' estates and repealed their titles. She'd also summoned them to appear before the Scottish Parliament on March 12. There, they would learn of their attainder—the confiscation of their rights and estates—and answer to charges of treason.

All was not lost, as Mary assured Pius. "Things have not yet reached that extremity of ill which forbids us to hope for recovery by relying upon your advice and assistance as we are . . . bound to do." At that same Parliament called for March, Mary planned to introduce articles aimed at restoring the old faith to the kingdom. She was sure that, with the new pope's assistance, she would triumph.

Mary had another reason to hope, though she discreetly refrained from mentioning it to the Holy Father. She was now almost six months pregnant. Mary found comfort in her pregnancy: as she had told Randolph on her wedding day, she did not wish to leave the kingdom "destitute of an heir." This was her first duty as queen, the point of her marriage.* Perhaps the birth of an heir would quell the fractiousness of her Protestant subjects. Her ladies loosened her laces. Mary prayed for a son.[5]

If her marriage had spurred a new Catholic zeal, her pregnancy stiffened her religious resolve. Mary's message to Pius in January brimmed with piety. And yet Mary let slip the shadow of the young woman who always put her own interests first. "By granting what [my messenger] asks (or rather what we ask by him)," she wrote at the end of her letter, "we shall have cause to be more attached than ever to the Holy See." Piety, of course, should not be contingent on her getting her way. "To which, however, we have always been most

---

*Of course, Mary did not announce to Randolph that she was using Darnley to secure the English throne, though she didn't have to: Randolph, like Elizabeth Tudor, was already well aware of her intentions.

attached," she hastened to add, correcting her mistake. Then, to prove her point: "May God long preserve Your Holiness to ourselves and to the whole Christian world!" And finally, in her own hand: "Mary, the Queen. The most devoted daughter of His Holiness."

———

Only Mary signed the letter to the pope. She did not invite Darnley to append his signature. This was a marked alteration from a few months earlier, when Mary gave Darnley "her whole will to be ruled and guided," as Randolph noted in disgust, as if she were the consort and he the king.[6] By December 1565, Mary's passion for her husband had cooled considerably.

Her clerks struck Darnley's name from documents, a coin stamped "Henricus et Maria" was recalled, and although everyone previously referred to them as the "King and Queen, his Majesty and hers," now everyone called Darnley simply "the Queen's husband."[7] "I never knew so many alterations as are now in this government," wrote a wondering Randolph on Christmas Day 1565. The couple fought often and over everything. ("Lovers' quarrels," Randolph wrongly guessed.)[8]

The mask had slipped. The objections her noblemen had mounted even before the wedding had proved woefully true—a fact that must have galled Mary as much as Darnley's atrocious behavior. The golden boy of their courtship had become ornery, jealous, and, to Mary's horror, frequently drunk. He threw tantrums when he didn't get his way, which first occurred during the Chaseabout Raid after Mary refused to promote Darnley's father, the Earl of Lennox, to a lieutenant-generalship. Instead, she preferred the Earl of Bothwell.

Mary believed she had good reason. James Hepburn, fourth Earl of Bothwell, a young man of thirty, had already proven himself a stalwart defender of the crown's interests. Despite his Protestantism, Bothwell had never wavered in his loyalty to Mary and to her mother, Marie de Guise. When the Lords of the Congregation revolted against Marie de Guise in 1559–60, Bothwell had worked assiduously on behalf of the regent, pilfering funds sent secretly from England to the Scottish rebels. For disloyalty to his fellow Protestants, Bothwell had earned the everlasting hatred of the

English, of many Scots noblemen, and especially of Lord James, who never forgave him for his treachery.

Mary had spent years trying to reconcile Lord James and Bothwell, but now she believed the discord between them could be of service. And Bothwell was a skilled commander, valiant on the battlefield. Moreover, Bothwell detested the English; Mary could be sure that Bothwell wouldn't be swayed by English gold to join Lord James's cause. True, the earl had been mired in violent disputes with several other lords over the years, including with the Earl of Arran, who, in 1562, had accused Bothwell of trying to kidnap the Queen, an accusation that proved specious. Moreover, Bothwell had a reputation for vulgarity and impiety. Throckmorton called him "vainglorious, rash, and hazardous" and deplored his superficial commitment to Protestantism, while an aghast Thomas Randolph claimed Bothwell had once called Mary the Cardinal of Lorraine's whore.[9]

In 1565, Mary ignored the stories about Bothwell's character, however, seeing them as the result of petty Scottish jealousies and English spite. She looked instead at his record of devoted service— from personally arranging the transport of her baggage from France to Scotland, to couriering secret letters on her behalf to the continent—and decided she could trust him.*

In contrast, Darnley's father, the Earl of Lennox, had a track record of switching allegiances from Scotland to England as suited his interests. But Darnley thought Mary had snubbed his father—a blow to the ego of a boy who prized family as much as Mary did. From there, the marriage quickly spiraled downward.

Mary blushed hot at Darnley's churlishness and his penchant for insulting her. His lackadaisical commitment to Catholicism mortified her. While she wrote pious letters to Philip II and to the Holy Father, her husband could barely make it to Mass.[10] He seemed utterly ungrateful that she, a crowned sovereign queen, had honored him by raising him to the exalted status of king. He accused her of parsimony

---

*The historian John Guy has pointed out that a family connection might also explain Mary's trust in Bothwell. The earl's sister was married to one of Mary's illegitimate half-brothers, Lord John of Coldingham, which made Bothwell a close relation by marriage. Always ready to lean on family, Mary might have turned to Bothwell after Lord James, another kinsman, betrayed her.

and complained that she spent too much time with her secretary, David Rizzio. Most vexing of all, he kept hounding her to grant him the Crown Matrimonial, even though she'd repeatedly refused.

The Crown Matrimonial was Scottish law, an Act of Parliament that, if approved, would grant Darnley full sovereign rights as king of the realm. If Mary died without children, the crown would pass to Darnley's descendants. Mary had effectively signed these same rights over to Francis II before their betrothal when, under the gaze of Henry II and the Guises, she had affixed her name to the three secret "donations." Scottish dismay at the donations had fueled the war in Scotland of 1559–60 against Marie de Guise. That war had ended only with the sticky Treaty of Edinburgh, which curtailed Mary's authority over her own council and weakened the Auld Alliance between Scotland and France.

Maybe she'd learned her lesson from 1560, or maybe she perceived early hints of Darnley's immaturity. Whatever her reasons, the newlywed Mary in 1565 hesitated to grant her new husband the Crown Matrimonial. Remarkably, the young woman who wished above all to be a queen consort wisely took the one step that would protect her sovereign authority as queen regnant. When Darnley persisted and grew belligerent, she walked back his privileges and kept him from her bed—which her pregnancy easily excused. The boy brooded and sulked. Mary dismissed him as a nuisance. She thought her austerity might curb his obstinacy.

In France, Catherine fretted about Mary Stuart, though not so much because of concern about the personal welfare of the Queen of Scots. Mary represented something of a political wild card. So long as she had been married to Francis II, Mary's value as the Queen of Scots and the potential heir to the English throne advanced French imperial aims. Now, however, Mary was a free agent, able to make her own decisions about marriage and to pursue her own interests—some of which ran contrary to Catherine's. Luckily, the Queen Mother had managed to thwart the match with Don Carlos, ensuring Mary's Scottish crown and English claim did not go to the Spanish—for, although Catherine wrote endearing letters to "The

Catholic King, my son," she knew France and Spain remained rivals at heart.

Yet with Mary, trouble always seemed to come from many corners. The Queen Mother disliked Mary's persistent quest for the English succession, which proved to be another liability once Francis had died. Catherine still saw Scotland as something like a French conservatorship, to be deployed as needed in rivalries against England or Spain. But Catherine was no longer certain of Mary's feelings. Mary's Protestant lords despised the ancient French–Scottish ties, and preferred a new alliance with England. As for Mary, everyone knew she was obsessed with the English crown. Would Mary break her ties with France to satisfy her lords and win the succession?

On the other hand, if war exploded between England and Scotland, England might win, and France would lose its tenuous hold on Scotland entirely. Catherine would not sacrifice King Charles's welfare for Mary Stuart's wild ambitions.

Always sly, Catherine helped mediate the Chaseabout debacle in part to remind Mary that her political survival depended on her French connections. If she wished to remain friends with England, if only for the sake of the English succession, Mary would need France's help. Catherine's envoy Mauvissière would make several trips to Scotland in the coming years.

Catherine kept Mary in the recesses of her mind, but in January 1566, her attention turned mostly toward Spain. While the pregnant Mary wrote obsequious letters to the pope, Elisabeth de Valois awaited a baby of her own. Catherine oscillated between joy and anxiety, her interests as a queen melding with those of a mother and grandmother. That a baby might at last bind the two crowns thrilled Catherine; fear that Elisabeth's pregnancy might fail, or worse, terrified her.

At the end of January 1566, Elisabeth had just entered her fourth month. Six years had passed since she had left France for Spain, and she had yet to carry any baby close to term. Thus far, this pregnancy had proceeded smoothly, though it was early yet, and Catherine agonized over possible complications and the dangers of the birth itself, still months away. Her daughter had always suffered from fragile health. As Catherine would shortly tell the new ambassador to Spain—Raymond de Rouer, Sieur de Fourquevaux—she felt like she was sitting "on thorns" waiting for the child to be born.[11]

Square-shouldered and strong-nosed, Fourquevaux was a seasoned diplomat, about sixty years old. Catherine trusted him entirely. For every letter he wrote to Charles IX, Fourquevaux wrote another for Catherine, including all the intimate details he knew she craved. Staid though he was with the grandees at Philip II's court, Fourquevaux couldn't help but soften toward Elisabeth. The young queen and the weathered envoy became fast friends—Elisabeth never knew a more devoted servant.

Fourquevaux shared some of Catherine's anxiety about the birth. He knew the road to this pregnancy had been arduous, sometimes alarming, and painfully long. For many years, the Queen Mother and everyone in Elisabeth's entourage in Spain had feared the young queen would never conceive at all.

The trouble began with Elisabeth's period, slow to appear after she arrived in Spain, then visiting her only occasionally. When her menstrual cycle finally stabilized in 1562, everyone hoped she would soon become pregnant. All the pieces seemed to be in place. Her periods came at regular intervals, according to her ladies: about three to four weeks between, and three to four days of bleeding each time. Madame de Vineux claimed that she usually enjoyed a healthy complexion, as did Philip. Moreover, Elisabeth's French ladies reported that Philip came to sleep with Elisabeth often. Each month, Catherine waited expectantly for the letter that would finally bear good news. Yet each month brought only fresh disappointment.

By all accounts Elisabeth had earned the respect of her husband and the love of her subjects. She'd even won over the peevish Countess of Ureigna. "She is so well adjusted . . . to make everyone happy, she needs only to bear a child," wrote a plaintive Madame de Vineux to Catherine.[12]

As the years passed, Catherine's concern mounted. Philip had married a barren woman once, Mary Tudor. For how long would he tolerate another? With Don Carlos still volatile, Philip needed more children to protect his legacy and kingdom. Then, too, Elisabeth's struggles must have reminded Catherine of her own long and distressing infertility. The Queen Mother was sure Philip would not wait ten years for Elisabeth to bear children.

Surely with "God's grace," Catherine told Fourquevaux, Elisabeth could conceive and bring a baby to term. Of course, Catherine was ready to assist if God required a helping hand. The Queen Mother wrote out recipes for dozens of tonics, shipping them off to Elisabeth, to her ambassador, and to Madame de Vineux, adding a dose of maternal pressure to the lists of ingredients. "I found these very useful for having children," she mentioned in one note, "and hope they will do the same for her because it is the thing I most desire in the world." Catherine paid off women whom she suspected were sleeping with Philip (Ana Mendoza, the jaunty wife of Philip's pliable right-hand man Ruy Gómez, received a large diamond), and fed suggestions to Vincenzo Mugnoni, an Italian physician on Catherine's payroll, who had come to Spain in Elisabeth's train as her personal doctor. Mugnoni joined a bevy of Spanish doctors whom Philip appointed to Elisabeth's household. If she had her way, Catherine would have dismissed all the Spaniards, for she disliked their methods and especially their penchant for bloodletting. True, medical approaches varied in different kingdoms. But Catherine trusted only Dr. Mugnoni.[13]

Elisabeth hardly understood her own body, its rhythms incomprehensible, its aches and pains a mystery. Over the years, her fluctuating periods, migraines, and waves of nausea had made her body difficult to read. She was almost afraid to hope. "Madame, I cannot hide from you that I don't know if I could be pregnant," Elisabeth wrote to Catherine in 1562 when her ladies were certain of good news. "My ladies say I show all the signs of a pregnant woman but I don't know if I am. I never feel sick except at night. If there are any sure signs I will be sure to write to you immediately." In this, as in so many things, Elisabeth feared disappointing Catherine: "I wouldn't want to lose your good opinion of me if I am mistaken." Later that month, the so-called signs faded to nothing.[14]

Such false alarms unnerved Catherine. In the spring of 1564, however, Elisabeth did conceive and this time she was sure. Soon she received a warm note of congratulation from her aunt the Duchess of Savoy, one of Catherine's dearest friends.

"I can promise you, Madame," wrote the duchess, "that I have never seen the queen, Madame your mother, so happy. Clearly, she now has almost everything she could wish for—this will certainly be true, Madame, when she has the good fortune of seeing you again. When this good fortune comes to pass for you both, if God will grant me this grace, I can die happy afterward."[15]

The pregnancy proceeded for about five months, enough time for Catherine to offer Philip the services of two French midwives: good and proper Catholic women, she assured him. "Since I can't have the pleasure of being there myself while she is in this condition, as a mother I only desire that she be well served and cared for."[16] Philip and Elisabeth refused the midwives, although, as it turned out, their services would have been pointless. Just weeks after Catherine sent her letter, Elisabeth miscarried while suffering from a fever so unrelenting it almost killed her.

The ordeal had been horrendous. As Catherine traveled the first leg of the royal tour with King Charles in August 1564, letters from her ambassador (at the time, the Sieur de Saint-Sulpice) began flying in, reporting that Elisabeth lay near death. Days later, other missives arrived, reassuring her that Elisabeth was recovering. Only after she received a lengthy report from Dr. Mugnoni at the end of the month did Catherine learn the extent of Elisabeth's illness. Mugnoni spared the Queen Mother no gruesome detail.[17]

In truth, Mugnoni wrote, Elisabeth hadn't felt well since the previous April. By May she suspected a pregnancy. Her ladies chalked up certain symptoms—spates of fever, her usual headaches, some vomiting, and loss of appetite—to the discomforts of the early months. As her belly burgeoned, so did the kingdom's jubilation. Philip ordered banquets and celebratory jousts. It was during one of these parties, on August 5, in what Elisabeth guessed was her fifth month, that she took a chill after dinner and retired to bed. That night, her ladies mentioned nothing to the physicians, much to Mugnoni's regret.

But after the queen spent a sleepless night gripped by an unquenchable thirst, her ladies sent for help. The queen's doctors, both Spanish and French, promptly diagnosed a serious fever—a persistent and scorching one that plunged the queen into cycles of sweats and chills. More disturbing still, blood trickled from her nose.

The doctors discussed phlebotomy. "In Spain it was usual and customary, by long practice, to let blood from pregnant women without any obvious necessity, but just to preserve the fetus in the belly of the mother." Mugnoni argued, however, that this practice defied all the teachings of the ancient Greek and Roman medical authorities, Hippocrates and Galen. Those venerable doctors had shown how serious illnesses could develop in pregnant women between the third and seventh months. Bloodletting in such cases, Mugnoni warned, could *provoke* a miscarriage. The Spanish opinion nonetheless prevailed. A slice of the scalpel drew "seven ounces of blood . . . from her right arm." Yet the bleeding did nothing to soothe Elisabeth's fever, her pounding headaches, or the radiating pain that "tormented her day and night" over the next several days.

As her condition deteriorated, the Spanish and French doctors locked horns. Over Mugnoni's strenuous objections, the Spanish physicians insisted on bleeding the queen again, this time from her left arm. That night, wrote Mugnoni, Elisabeth miscarried, a lengthy process that continued over the course of the next two days. The doctor described the miscarriage in graphic fashion, as if the Queen Mother were as interested in the clinical details as himself—and, given Catherine's interest in both medicine and the state of Elisabeth's body, perhaps she was. Most importantly, Mugnoni realized, the flesh that emerged from Elisabeth's womb—"shaped like the heart of a ram"—proved "that there truly was a fetus," for until that moment, he had remained in some doubt.* However, the miscarriage brought Elisabeth no relief. The queen's fever only worsened.

As Mugnoni and the Spanish physicians worked on their patient, the grandees in attendance stood by helplessly. The Countess of

---

*Though Mugnoni does not mention the sex of the fetus or describe anything resembling a human form, the ambassador Saint-Sulpice would report that Elisabeth miscarried twin girls, although the envoy from Ferrara believed there was only one fetus, male in appearance.

Ureigna never ceased crying while the Duke of Alba, who insisted on attending every medical consultation, swung between anger and panic. Philip was called away but came when he could; the Duke of Alba, meanwhile, ran back and forth to the king with updates.

Assuming that retained fluids and pieces of afterbirth had inflamed the womb (Mugnoni continued in his report), the Spanish bled Elisabeth again, this time from the right foot. By the eleventh day of her illness, the physicians—now in a unified front—agreed to purge her but were confounded when the purge brought on a profound sleepiness that left Elisabeth limp and unresponsive, as if dead. In a frenzy, the doctors tried everything— cupping and rubbing, bindings, mustard wraps, whiffs of castoreum, and yet another bleeding, this time piercing the middle of her forehead. When Elisabeth's right arm began to quake with tremors, her mouth to writhe and twist, the doctors feared "apoplexy"—a stroke. Mugnoni advised a purge of agaric (a type of red-capped gilled mushroom), prompting yet another round of debate and disagreement. In the meantime, the queen was seized by a horrific swelling in her face and throat.

The Spanish doctors surrendered her to God. The Duke of Alba and the Duchess of Ureigna insisted on calling a priest to administer Extreme Unction, the last rites for the dying. They brought pen and ink so that, during a lucid moment, Elisabeth could sign her will.

Unbeknownst to Mugnoni, foreign envoys at the Spanish court had already raced to their writing desks. One of these was Thomas Challoner, the English envoy in Spain, who wrote to Elizabeth Tudor that the Catholic Queen had miscarried and now lay "at the mercy of God." A pall fell over the palace. "The gates are shut, and the lamentations of the Court, both men and women, are very tender and piteous. The chapel is filled with noblemen praying for her; and generally an unfeigned moan is made on all parts, as well for the favor her virtues and gentleness obtained of all, as for the hope they had she should have been the mother of many Princes." Everyone feared that if Elisabeth de Valois died the Spanish and French might find themselves enemies once again.

Challoner wove in one more worrying thread of gossip. This was the summer of 1564; Mary, Queen of Scots, had yet to meet Darnley and remained unwed. Challoner wrote, "Among the ambassadors and others of this Court, account was already made that the King would be a suitor" to Mary, Queen of Scots, if Elisabeth de Valois died. Challoner guessed the French would block the marriage but couldn't be sure. The fortunes of several kingdoms, and several sovereigns, hinged on the life or death of the young Spanish queen.[18]

In Elisabeth's bedchamber, Mugnoni refused to give up. A believer in science and observation, he insisted there was still life in the suffering queen. As the Archbishop of Santo Jacomo and Elisabeth's confessor arrived with the last sacraments, the physician hauled the Duke of Alba back into the bedchamber to look at Elisabeth. Peering into her face, Mugnoni was sure he still perceived a spark of "good energy" in her ashen complexion. The doctor convinced Alba to take his advice to King Philip, who "was doubtful and stuck . . . between fear and hope."[19] Hope won. Philip approved Mugnoni's purge.

As Alba and the sobbing Countess of Ureigna looked on, the doctors assembled around Elisabeth's bed. Mugnoni "put that agaric infusion with a little rosewater syrup in a silver bottle, and with one hand he put it up to the lips of the dying queen, while with the other he opened her teeth, and in the meantime the Countess came to help her." Not long after, Elisabeth began to improve. It happened so suddenly, wrote Mugnoni, that it was almost as if "a divine rather than human hand" was at work—a touch of modesty, perhaps, from the good doctor, who was clearly the man of the hour. Mugnoni happily concluded his letter on that victorious note. Strangely, he apologized for his brevity, though his letter stretched on for pages. "I know how busy you are," he told Catherine.

Elisabeth lived, but her recovery dragged on for months. She followed Catherine's advice to the letter, getting plenty of fresh air and exercise, much to the dismay of the Countess of Ureigna, who thought she was better off in bed. As Elisabeth grew stronger, the kingdom of Spain exhaled, as did both Catherine and Elizabeth Tudor, though the English queen soon panicked again after Mary Stuart went on to marry Lord Darnley the following summer of 1565, just as the French and Spanish contingents were assembling at Bayonne. Philip realized how fond he'd grown of his young wife. He gave up his mistresses and spent more time with Elisabeth, enjoying outings in the palace gardens, riverside strolls, leisurely picnics. A tentative optimism had taken hold of the king: as distressing as Elisabeth's miscarriage had been, it showed she *could* get pregnant—a small yet steady light. Once Elisabeth recovered, Philip's nocturnal visits increased.

We don't know for sure how Elisabeth felt about her miscarriage. Any sense of failure may have waned in the face of Philip's solicitous attention to her afterward, and her mother's tender instructions to look after her health. Elisabeth still sought her mother's approval, and Catherine was grateful her daughter had survived at all. Elisabeth was still healing that February when Philip approved her reunion with Catherine at Bayonne. In a way, he intended the trip as a gift to both women. Philip understood how much Catherine would have grieved, like himself, had they lost Elisabeth. And at the end of the trip, when Catherine wrote to tell Philip how well her daughter looked, she was thanking him for saving her life.

After Elisabeth returned from Bayonne in the midsummer of 1565, the royal couple focused once more on making an heir. By December 1565, Elisabeth could confidently confirm she was pregnant again, about two or three months along. What worked? Elisabeth, for her part, would credit Saint Eugene. As she explained to Ambassador Fourquevaux, she'd gone with Philip in November to watch the brittle remains of Saint Eugene—patron saint of suffering families—as they were transferred from Madrid to a new resting place at Alcalá de Henares. As the bier bearing the corpse of the saint lumbered by, Elisabeth made a promise "to give his name to the first fruit that God would send her." That afternoon she asked her doctors for a bath, and that evening she and Philip retired to bed together. Saint Eugene, she believed, heard her prayers.

For all Elisabeth's ailments, her pregnancy progressed well. The third month crept by without incident, then the fourth and fifth. Catherine sat on her thorns. Fourquevaux reported that Elisabeth had felt the baby kicking "two or three times" and, from the look of the queen, the Countess of Ureigna was sure Elisabeth carried a boy. Philip became more attentive with each month, deigning to visit his wife for two hours each day, after dinner. "This entire kingdom is ecstatic, from the greatest subject among them to the smallest," Fourquevaux wrote, his sentences popping with excitement. If Elisabeth guessed the date of conception correctly, the baby would be due in August.[20]

Only two things dampened Catherine's elation. The first was that Elisabeth clearly wished to keep her mother out of the delivery room. Once again, Catherine offered to send a trusted French midwife. Philip (whose nerves began to get the better of him as the birth approached) seemed inclined to agree, but Elisabeth refused, insisting she already had "a very experienced Spanish woman for such things." Fourquevaux kept pressing the matter, yet Elisabeth remained obstinate, promising that Catherine would receive word as soon as the baby was born. She also objected to her brother Henri, now Duke of Anjou, coming for the birth. The Spanish distrusted foreigners, she explained, casting about for an excuse. They wouldn't want the Duke meddling. At Catherine's insistence, Henri came anyway.[21]

Catherine was loath to tell Elisabeth her real reasons for sending Henri. In May 1566, when Elisabeth entered her seventh month, the Duke of Alba asked her to review and sign her last will and testament. The request alarmed Catherine. What did it signify? On the one hand, she wondered if Philip was pressuring Elisabeth to bequeath her dowry—those wagonloads of treasure transported over the Pyrenees with her in 1560—to Hapsburg heirs, rather than return it to France. To Catherine's consternation, Elisabeth wouldn't reveal the contents of the will, despite Fourquevaux's repeated hints. Her daughter's evasion was distressing. Catherine wanted Henri present to speak for French interests in case the worst should come to pass.

At the same time, the idea that Elisabeth might die in childbirth filled Catherine with terror. The will seemed ominous. Was her daughter ill? Elisabeth rushed to reassure her mother. Writing a will was merely Spanish custom, demanded of all expectant women. But the memory of Elisabeth's near-death in 1564 haunted Catherine. "If it's the custom of the country [to write a will], we should be less doubtful," she wrote to Fourquevaux. "Find out if it's true and tell me as soon as you know. In the meantime, do what you can to comfort her so that she can endure God's will with greater vigor and hope in Our Lord." Elisabeth's time drew near; both mother and daughter now had to be brave. "For every and all occasions, be sure to send me her news," Catherine added. She found it impossible not to worry.[22]

In early April, as Elisabeth began her sixth month, Catherine received a visit from Mary Stuart's ambassador to France, the Archbishop of Glasgow. Just a few days earlier Catherine and Charles IX had learned of the atrocious murder of Mary's secretary, the Italian David Rizzio, from the French ambassador in London. The Scottish archbishop now arrived to deliver Mary's version of events.[23]

On March 9, Mary had been hosting a small supper party in her upstairs privy apartments in Holyroodhouse. She had recently been ill, and the party was small. As they dined, hundreds of armed soldiers occupied the palace, led by the Protestant lords Ruthven and Morton. Bursting into her chambers, they'd seized Rizzio, dragged him into Mary's presence chamber, and stabbed him to death practically in front of the queen. Fifty-six stab wounds, reported the somber ambassador, with "whingers and swords."

The murder proved only the beginning of the horror. Mary remained a prisoner for two days in her own chambers, repeatedly terrorized by the rebels, before she managed to escape to Dunbar Castle with the help of the loyal lords Bothwell and Huntly. After five days at Dunbar, she had returned to Edinburgh "well accompanied with our subjects." Upon her escape, the rebels had fled south. Mary intended to pursue the fugitives "with all rigor," having already seized their "whole fortunes, strengths and houses . . . their goods and gear." In the meantime, order had been restored.

The coup had been planned for the days just before Parliament was scheduled to judge the Chaseabout rebels, explained the Archbishop of Glasgow. Measures for "restoring the old religion" had also been on the agenda. The plot was an act of treason by heretic lords intent on subverting the Queen's will.

The archbishop had learned all this from a letter Mary had written to him on April 2, her official account of the crisis. She'd commanded him to forestall "any rumors" that might have already traveled to the court of France.[24] To Catherine, the full extent of the tale must have sounded stranger than fiction. The murder itself was not the most horrifying piece of news. As the uncomfortable ambassador was forced to admit, the attempted coup had taken place at the behest of the King of Scots himself.

Darnley had agreed to bring Lord James and the Chaseabout rebels home from England, restoring their titles and estates. He'd promised to uphold the Protestant religion in the kingdom. In return, the Protestant rebels agreed to grant Darnley the Crown Matrimonial, thereby crowning him king. Mary suspected the plotters had planned to kill her and her unborn child. Once Darnley realized the lords had no intention of honoring their agreement, he confessed everything to Mary. The young man had stupidly believed the rebels' promises, "we suppose"—as Mary put it—"because of his facility." He'd been inconceivably gullible.

Darnley had escaped Holyroodhouse with Mary and returned at her side to Edinburgh. The couple appeared reconciled, Glasgow reported. As for the poor secretary, Rizzio, he seemed to have been the unfortunate victim of a much larger plot. Although Darnley admitted to enabling the coup, he swore to Mary that he'd never intended for her to be harmed or Rizzio murdered. On March 20, in Edinburgh, heralds formally proclaimed the young king's innocence at market crosses across the kingdom of Scotland. Mary claimed the proclamation was Darnley's idea.[25]

Even to a queen ill-disposed toward her former daughter-in-law, the news was horrendous. "So full of compassion" were King Charles and Queen Catherine, the Cardinal of Lorraine later wrote, "that they could scarcely restrain their tears."[26] Darnley's audacity horrified Catherine. The violence was appalling, exactly the kind of brutality Catherine feared from Protestants in France. As Mary described it, her captors threatened at one point to throw her "over the wall in pieces, in order to make steaks of us."[27]

Even more abominable, the rebels had threatened a pregnant woman, her unborn child seven months in the womb. "That these wicked men intended to kill not only the secretary, but also [the queen] herself and the child she carried," King Charles said, repulsed.[28]

Yet politics, too, underpinned the young king's reaction: Mary wasn't just any pregnant woman. She was not even a queen consort. The rebels had attacked the queen regnant and her heir, the next king, as if to wipe out the dynasty. If the threat to the suffering woman was sickening, the threat to sovereignty was terrifying.

Mary returned to Edinburgh relieved to be alive and still on her throne, determined to pursue the rebels at all costs, furious at her husband, yet unsure how to handle him. It took her several weeks to organize her thoughts before writing to the Archbishop of Glasgow on April 2. Her letter to France was only one in a cascade that she poured into foreign courts as she struggled to control the narrative.

Mary had a good idea of the kind of sordid story that might be circulating at the French court. The murder of her secretary looked like the vengeful act of a cuckolded husband. She knew her lords despised Rizzio—a Catholic, Italian, and commoner. She also knew Darnley had heard ugly stories about Rizzio and Mary that triggered his jealousy. They had fought. "Somewhat we are sure you have heard of divers discord and jars between this Queen and her husband," Randolph had secretly written to Cecil just days before the coup. "Partly for that she has refused him the crown matrimonial, partly for that he has assured knowledge of such usage of herself as altogether is intolerable to be borne, which if it were not over well known, we would . . . be very loath to think that it could be true . . . You have heard of the man whom we mean of."[29]

At the time, Mary had dismissed those salacious accusations, thinking them nothing but drivel fueled by petty jealousies. The consequences of her complacency had been deadly.* And the gossip now flowing was equally ruinous: the murder impugned both her honor and the integrity of the throne. It cast doubts on the legitimacy of the child she carried—and thus on the child's right to the crown both in Scotland and England. A king could indulge in public infidelity. A queen, of course, could not. Darnley had managed to turn her pregnant body—a sign of her virtuous duty as a queen—into a signifier of adultery.

---

*There has been much speculation that the Protestant lords planted these rumors to rile Darnley into initiating the plot. Randolph, the English envoy, is also suspected of having contributed to the rumormongering. Mary likely thought the lords were goading Darnley, but she had not anticipated that he would act on it.

Had this been Darnley's plan? To eliminate his unborn child, either through murder or the stain of illegitimacy, so he could rule as king? To compel her, by destroying her reputation and threatening their child, to grant him the Crown Matrimonial?

While Mary remained a prisoner in Holyroodhouse, she'd had no choice but to forgive Darnley, if only to enable her own escape. She'd absolved him publicly of the murder to protect the integrity of her marriage and stanch the tide of ugly rumors, her priority. She wrestled with the story on paper, with only words for weapons against the gossip percolating through France and Spain, the two great powers whose favor she desperately desired. Spain, especially, worried her. She had no envoy there. And she couldn't find the nerve to write to Philip directly.

At the end of her letter to the Archbishop of Glasgow, she'd added a personal note in her own hand: "I beg of you, as soon as you've read these letters, go to [the French] court, so you can keep them from believing these false rumors. And make sure you speak to the Spanish ambassador and other foreigners."

None of Europe's crowns believed that Mary had committed adultery with Rizzio, and most agreed that Darnley was guiltier than his public protestations suggested. The plot had backfired, in fact: Scottish subjects and the crowns of Europe applauded Mary's courage and sangfroid. She had displayed the heart of a true sovereign. So moved was Pope Pius V that he wrote her a personal letter and (perhaps sensing a certain reticence) exhorted Spain and France to come to her aid.[30]

In Edinburgh, Mary grappled with the precariousness of her situation. The perpetrators remained at large, no doubt plotting other attacks. The real danger lay far closer to home. Mary had only pretended to forgive Darnley. In her letter to the Archbishop of Glasgow, she did not tell the whole story. Darnley's duplicity had stunned her. He had stepped quietly into her private *cabinet* that night, stealing up the stairs that linked his chambers to hers during her supper. He had sat next to her, flinging a friendly arm over her shoulders. When Ruthven and his henchmen burst in, Darnley held

Mary tight, pinning her arms to her sides as Rizzio shrieked and clawed at her, the soldiers peeling back his fingers from her skirts one by one. Later, her lady-in-waiting found Rizzio's mauled body, stripped of jewels and clothes, at the bottom of a staircase, Darnley's dagger stuck in the corpse. Mary had heard what Ruthven shouted that night in the chaos: "all that was done was the king's own deed."[31]

Nor did Mary recount to Glasgow the coldness with which Darnley had treated her and their unborn child during their midnight escape from Holyroodhouse. Decades on, in England, she would share that story with her French secretary, Claude de Nau.

"He tried to make the queen's horse go faster," Nau wrote in his memoirs, "by flogging it on the hind quarters, crying out, 'Come on! Come on! By God's Blood, they will murder both you and me if they can catch us.' Worn out by the fatigue which she had already endured and in great suffering, the queen dreaded a miscarriage, and entreated him to have some regard to her condition. She said she would rather expose herself to any danger than deliberately imperil the life of their child. Hereupon the king put himself into a fury. 'Come on!' said he. 'In God's name, come on! If this baby dies we can have more.' At the last, however, the queen could bear the galloping of the horse no longer. She asked him to push on and take care of himself. And this he did, very thoughtlessly."[32]

She had showed Darnley unparalleled generosity, raising him to the rank of sovereign—and yet he betrayed her. Mary would focus on this fact several times in the coming months, as if unable to comprehend his ingratitude. If she felt any personal remorse, she never expressed it. Yet guilt may have needled her. No one had foisted Darnley on Mary. She had foolishly chosen him herself. "So this unhappy Princess has received this reward for giving her kingdom and herself to the King," wrote the Venetian ambassador Marc'Antonio Barbaro. "And preferring him to the many powerful Princes who sought her hand, as one of the most beautiful women in Europe."[33]

As a child, Mary had fled a foreign enemy in the "rough wooing." Now, the enemy was tethered to her by a marriage vow. She could not escape him, yet she feared him—a fact Mary was not ready to admit in any letter she wrote to foreign courts. Nor could any diplomatic letter truly convey the terror of that days-long ordeal, her exhaustion and pain. Mary, sick and pregnant, her belly swollen and her joints aching, had felt the attack in her bones.

To one sovereign, though, she did offer a glimpse of that embodied experience. On April 4, Mary wrote to Elizabeth Tudor, someone who shared her gender and rank but who would never know the burdens of marriage or pregnancy. Thanking Elizabeth for her kindness in the aftermath of the plot, Mary asked for a favor, queen to queen.* Invoking their "former friendship," she begged Elizabeth to secure the border and to arrest any Scottish rebels who had fled to England. To prove her goodwill, Mary asked Elizabeth to stand as godmother if "I recover well this month of July"—the month her baby would be born.

Then, at the end of the letter, Mary added: "Please forgive me if I write badly, for I am so pregnant, already far into my seventh month, that I cannot even bend over, and what I am able to do already leaves me in great pain." It was the slightest crack in Mary's composure—a request for Elizabeth's compassion. But in her suffering, Mary was, in fact, alone, pleading for Elizabeth to understand, which she never truly could.[34]

---

*Elizabeth Tudor was sincerely distressed by news of Rizzio's murder and the attempted coup. She'd already recalled Thomas Randolph before the plot unfolded, out of respect for Mary, who believed the English ambassador was trying to undermine her. Always fearful of her own overthrow, Elizabeth agreed with Catherine: all princes should beware lest a similar rebellion unfold in their own kingdoms. After the murder, Elizabeth took to wearing a small portrait of Mary affixed to her girdle, in solidarity. However, her renewed friendship with Mary did not last long.

22

THE BIRTH OF PRINCES
Scotland and Spain, 1566–1567

Mary believed in a certain cosmic order, a clear hierarchy. "God commands subjects to obey their princes," she had announced primly to Knox upon their first meeting. Her calculus was simple, even simplistic: first God, then the sovereign, then the Scots lords, her subjects. Didn't her nobles owe her uncompromising respect, whatever her will? In her mind, this was the way of things. It was also a puerile view of the world and an emotional one, a remnant of her coddled childhood and perhaps a misunderstanding of both the Scottish and French view of royalty: in Mary's mind, she was the queen and should get what she wanted. Randolph had noticed this facet of her character, at once tyrannical and childlike, although the envoy believed gender had something to do with it. "She is a woman," he put it pithily, "and in all things desires to have her will."[1]

Randolph's own Queen Elizabeth, woman though she was, showed no such naivety. Elizabeth believed her survival on the throne depended on a never-ending negotiation with her subjects. She invented her own strategy for keeping them in line. Her repeated promises to the English Parliament that she would one day marry—*maybe*—kept the prospect of resolution within reach. She would say neither "yes" nor "no": it was just enough to stave off her nobles' impatience until she made up her mind about matrimony. Forestalling marriage and childbirth, avoiding naming an heir, prevented her nobles from moving on. Elizabeth remained, as she wished, at the center, like the sun at the horizon, perpetually rising.

Catherine de' Medici, too, perceived how the grandees of her kingdom "loved her only with words."[2] Their loyalty was contingent, and the sooner she recognized it, the sooner she could get what she needed. She could purchase their devotion for a time (as she had done with the King of Navarre), but the work was never done; the ravenous wolves always demanded their feed. Elisabeth de Valois was learning this lesson, too: when she lost Madame de Clermont in deference to the Countess of Ureigna, she realized that sometimes a monarch must concede to powerful nobles, including female ones, lest they make trouble. Obtaining a crown was a matter of birth or marriage. Retaining sovereign authority came down to hard work and, sometimes, tactical concessions.

With every ounce of her being, Mary rejected this idea. "God has elected the kings and commanded the people to obey them," she wrote sometime in early 1566. "And the kings have made princes and noblemen to support them, not to fight them."[3] Raised in the kingdom of France, where coronation was practically a sacrament and kings were anointed with the holy chrism, Mary basked in the notion that sovereigns were touched by God, as if sovereign power was part and parcel of their flesh, blood, and soul. Wasn't this divine order? Wasn't this natural? As the teenaged queen consort of France, she hadn't witnessed the backroom dealings necessary to maintain that sovereign authority, the maneuverings behind the trappings, ritual, and ceremony.

Then again, overwhelmed by the demands of her kingdom, Mary might have clung to the idea that her subjects' obedience was a God-given right from a sense of desperation. What other recourse did she have to contain them? She had tried to win her nobles' loyalty with concessions and gifts, showering them with honors, estates, titles, and wealth. She had promised to maintain Protestantism in the kingdom; she had indulged her subjects' heresy; she had granted their Kirk. She had raised her bastard brother Lord James to the peerage as Earl of Moray as early as 1562, turning to him for advice. And still her lords betrayed her, as had Darnley. That was the problem with nobles, Mary believed. You bestow gifts upon them and yet, like greedy children, they always want more.

This was the conclusion Mary reached in an undated memo, scribbled on a piece of scrap paper, probably written around the time of Rizzio's murder. It is a curious document. Only a fragment remains, from "a wast[e] paper of the Queen of Scotts owne hande."[4] Mary had worked out her ideas, then thrown the draft away. She was answering a charge: why had she granted so much influence to Rizzio—foreigner, commoner, papist—instead of relying on the counsel of her own nobles, as generations of Scottish kings had done before her?

Mary scrawled a shrill response. Who were these so-called nobles? They were men who owed their rank not to some intrinsic valiance or wisdom but rather to the merit of men who lived long ago, their fathers and grandfathers, who'd been raised to the peerage by her own kingly ancestors. "The [sons] have inherited nothing from the father except to play the grandee and take what advantage they can, to order people about, disdaining all laws and even the king"—or the queen. So why shouldn't Mary, appointed by God, elevate a man like Rizzio, "of low estate, poor in wealth, but generous of spirit, faithful in his heart, and capable of doing what service we require?" Was this not her prerogative? But no, she remained shackled by her unworthy nobles, forbidden to grant Rizzio any influence at all, "because the grandees who already have so much [power] always hunger for more!"

She hated to concede to these grasping nobles, these men so unworthy of her gifts—men who had slaughtered her secretary and threatened her with death, subjects both insubordinate and treasonous. Nonetheless, in the days following Rizzio's murder, Mary found herself pardoning Lord James. Shortly after she escaped to Dunbar, James had sent "diverse messages to procure her favor." He claimed not to have known about the Rizzio plot and sought her forgiveness. After consulting her council, Mary concluded that she had no other choice. She had few forces at her disposal and her physical condition left her weakened. On the cusp of giving birth, she could not withstand another attack. It was "very difficult to have so many bent at once" against her, she explained in a letter to France.[5] Lord James had shown her his power. She would not risk seeing it again. And so, in spite of herself, Mary pardoned him.

Mary's forgiveness, however feigned, bought her a little time. She entered her confinement at Edinburgh Castle—practically a fortress, a citadel against any impending insurgency. The capital remained calm, placated by Lord James's return and excited by the prospect of a newborn prince. In the final weeks, Mary thought about both new life and death. Her own body had become a crucible. The shock of Rizzio's murder, the exhaustion of her overnight escape afterward, the strain of her anger at Darnley, Lord James and the Rizzio rebels and the fear of further plots had all sapped her strength. She suffered from abdominal cramps during her final weeks of pregnancy, perhaps the first signs of labor. The pope, taking pity on her after the Rizzio plot, had dispatched to Scotland a nuncio bearing a purse of gold to fund war against the heretics. But a war of weapons would have to wait. Mary thought of a different kind of battle, the one she would soon wage on the birthing pallet.

Even within Edinburgh Castle's thick walls, she could feel death encroaching. The danger did not come from insurgents, though. No sovereign authority, however powerful, could stop her own body's rhythms. The birth neared, whether she willed it or not. There was no outwitting a fundamental paradox: giving birth was a queen's greatest triumph, yet the ordeal might also kill her. The only thing Mary could do was prepare.

She spent late May and early June writing to supporters and family, easing her conscience and settling affairs. To her favorite Guise aunt, Anne d'Este, she sent her best wishes for Anne's upcoming second wedding, to the Duke of Nemours. Mary's words glow with warmth, though they were tinged with sorrow, perhaps, that she couldn't join Anne on that happy day. "It seems to me," she wrote, "that you can expect nothing of this marriage but every good fortune, and to become once again among the happiest women in the world. So I desire this marriage for you, and wish as much happiness to the gentleman you will marry." Perhaps she thought for a moment about the difficulties of her own marriage. She could not count herself among the "happiest women in the world." Mary told Anne she was about six weeks from delivering her baby. She didn't mention that additional soldiers now guarded the castle for fear of further insurrection.[6]

She grappled with the unthinkable possibility of her own death or that of her child. What, then, would become of the realm? A fracas would surely ensue, rival clans and religions fighting for the throne. A consort's death in childbed triggered a kingdom's grief before the search for a new bride. But a sovereign queen's death could spawn a revolution.

Sometime during her final weeks of pregnancy, Mary dictated her will, making three copies. She kept the first for herself and supposedly gave the second to those who would take the reins in the event of her death. She sent the third to the Guises in France. The copies, unfortunately, have all been lost and no one revealed their contents. We do not know the terms they contained, only that, if the newborn survived her, Mary assigned the regency to a council of lords. The men named in the will included the Earl of Argyll and the Earl of Mar, both hostile to Darnley. Whether Darnley himself was included remains unknown.[7]

After attending to the government, Mary turned to her personal belongings, her jewels, furniture, tapestries, and books. Too tired to handle the pages of inventory herself, she asked Mary Livingston, one of the four Marys, to help. Livingston read off the items and marked the beneficiaries in the margins. Mary had many friends and servants she cherished and whom she wished to acknowledge in the event of her death. Her Master of the Horse, Arthur Erskine, behind whom she'd sat in the saddle during the midnight ride after Rizzio's murder, would receive a sapphire. To each one of her serving women, Mary gave a golden ring. Mary Beaton, the most bookish of the four Marys, would receive all the queen's books in French, English, and Italian. Mary remembered a favorite set of enameled black-and-white buttons, decorated with the crescent moon of Henry II and Diane de Poitiers, which had delighted her as a little girl. Now she offered them to another child, her godson Francis Stewart.[8]

With her gifts, Mary also hoped to heal wounds, ease tensions, and purchase support for whomever she named as successor in her will. Mary rewarded all her councillors, including Lord James, now returned to her council table. She avoided any gift that might stir up rivalries or show favoritism. To her councillors the Earls of Bothwell and Huntly, who had bravely rescued her from Holyroodhouse after Rizzio's murder, she bequeathed rings and decorative jewels of diamond, enamel, and ruby. The gifts suited their rank, as appropriate.

If she had wished to reward Bothwell further for his years of stalwart service, Mary restrained herself.[9]

She thought of Darnley. The young man remained "boyish and unstable," according to a Spanish diplomat, but at least until the birth of her baby, Mary had decided to feign forgiveness. Perhaps she thought Darnley would assume power as regent, and wished to acknowledge his rights, if only to ensure he looked after their child's interests. Then, too, she remembered a time, not so long ago, when Darnley had made her smile, "so content in myself and entirely at ease." Mary bequeathed to him twenty-six items, including one of her wedding rings, a diamond enameled in red. She acknowledged his title, perhaps to satisfy her own pride. "This is the ring I was married with," she said. "I return it to the king who gave it to me."[10]

Of all her beneficiaries, she was kindest to the Guises, leaving them copious gifts of dazzling jewels. She thought carefully about what to send the Cardinal of Lorraine, the man she loved most. In the end, she settled on an emerald ring.

These bequests were contingent, of course. After Mary Livingston compiled the lists, Mary took the pen herself. "I intend for this to be executed in case the child does not survive me. If he lives, he shall inherit all." *He.* There may have been a kind of irrevocability to her thinking. And if her baby was a girl? Yet another sign of weakness, another opening for her restive lords to rebel, another female to overthrow. No, Mary was certain she would give birth to a boy.

Her writing was now little more than a scratch.[11] Those classroom lessons with Elisabeth de Valois had faded long ago. Or perhaps Mary was simply too fatigued by the late stages of pregnancy, by the tumult in her kingdom, to hold the nib steady.*

---

*There is a riddle that historians have never solved. After David Rizzio's murder, Mary was undeterred by the obvious revulsion of her lords. Incredibly, she promoted Rizzio's younger brother, the eighteen-year-old Joseph Rizzio, to the role of secretary in David's place. Now, in her bequests, Mary gave Joseph three jewels: one set with ten rubies and a pearl, an emerald ring, and a third jewel glittering with twenty-one diamonds. Upon her death, Joseph should carry these "to one whose name the Queen has spoken." The identity of that person remains a mystery.

Baby James arrived on June 19 between ten and eleven o'clock in the morning. The birthing room was tiny and wood-paneled, a fire roaring in the fireplace to keep the room warm for mother and child, even in midsummer. The midwives smiled at the thin caul shrouding the baby's face as he emerged from the womb—then as now, the membrane augured a lucky life.[12] Mary, however, would never see her son come into that good fortune, nor watch him grow into boyhood. He would remain, in her mind's eye, the chubby-cheeked infant he was at ten months, his age when she last saw him.

In James's early infancy, Mary paid loving attention to his health and safety, to his nurses and to the furnishings of his nursery. But she could not give her son the kind of assiduous care that Catherine had lavished on her own children at the *petite cour*. Mary did not enjoy the luxury of a peaceable kingdom, nor could she leave the governing to others. Nor did she have the luxury of time: events would soon unspool at a furious pace, separating mother and child. Later, with time to trace over her memories, her attachment to that lost child, forcibly taken from her along with crown and kingdom, could bloom. Peril connected them, she believed, stronger than any cord. "I have borne him," she wrote to Lady Lennox in 1570, when the little boy was four. "And God knows with what danger to him and me both."[13]

Until James was almost grown, Mary would fail to understand that for her he felt nothing like the warmth of filial affection. As a Guise, raised in the embrace of that fiercely attached family, and among the French royal children who basked in their own parents' love, Mary assumed her son's devotion was only natural. She did not recognize, perhaps, that her love for her own absent mother had been carefully shaped by her grandmother Antoinette and the Cardinal of Lorraine. No one fostered such family feeling in James. Raised by Mary's enemies, the little boy would rarely receive her gifts. He would seldom respond to her letters. His tutors would teach James to despise his mother. Only in adulthood, after Mary's death, did he come to form something resembling a detached respect for her. Even this remains unclear.

At his birth, however, Mary vested that plump and "goodly child" with all her dreams. "This is the son who, I hope, shall first unite the two kingdoms of Scotland and England!" she is said to have declared on the day of his birth. Bonfires blazed, Edinburgh Castle blasted its cannons, and "the lords, the nobles and the people gathered in St. Giles' Church to thank God for the honor of having an heir to their kingdom." In her chambers, Mary suffered. After an excruciating labor and delivery, she recovered slowly, keeping to her bed for fifteen days, the ache in her milk-filled breasts so severe that she canceled audiences with well-wishing envoys. But as she gazed at her infant, Mary felt a certain solace. The child would help repair her relationship with France; she expected Mauvissière to arrive soon to congratulate her. And her baby was a boy; God still looked kindly upon her. To Philip II, Mary wrote of having "found some consolation from her troubles, in the son that God has given me."[14]

Yet the baby's arrival solved few of her immediate problems. Although she had fulfilled a queen's greatest duty, her Protestant lords carried on with their obstruction. The papal nuncio and his Catholic gold tarried in France, their passage to Scotland impeded by Protestant noblemen who threatened to kill the man if he stepped foot in Scotland. Mary cringed with embarrassment and despaired of the funds. As for Darnley, Mary could not forget her husband's treachery. Already her anger had flashed on the day of James's birth, the pretense of any domestic peace falling away. "This is the son begotten by you and only by you!" she had announced bitterly to Darnley that afternoon when he came to see his baby for the first time. According to a witness, Darnley flushed red.[15]

The public scolding failed to humble him. Throughout the autumn, Darnley persisted in holding her reputation hostage. Erratic and impulsive, he had taken to plunging stark naked into nearby lochs for long swims, an alarming activity at a time when few people could swim, and one which her council deemed exceedingly dangerous. He boasted of bloated plans. He would invade England! Sail toward Cornwall and seize the Scilly Islands! Lay siege to Scarborough Castle! He became vengeful and menacing. In late September, complaining that she paid no attention to him, that he possessed no authority, and that all the nobles had abandoned him, Darnley threatened to leave her, to "see foreign lands." Effectively, he was announcing a separation. His announcement left Mary reeling at his ingratitude and distressed at the imminent scandal. His departure would surely spur ugly gossip across Scotland and Europe, resurrecting the Rizzio rumors, dishonoring the kingdom, her marriage—and Mary personally. Darnley had packed his trunks and readied his ship. "Adieu Madame," Darnley said, "you shall not see my face for a long space." Only the intervention of the French ambassador, who reminded Darnley that a departure would impugn his own honor, convinced the young man to stay.[16]

Sometime that autumn, Mary discovered her husband had written to both King Philip of Spain and King Charles of France, accusing her of slipping in her Catholic faith. Now the crowns of Europe had those letters in their possession. Philibert du Croc, the newly appointed French ambassador, overheard Mary several times saying, "I could wish to be dead."*[17]

She almost got her wish. Mary's health began to suffer, as it always did in times of stress, an all-too-familiar pain in her right flank flaring yet again. In October, while traveling to Jedburgh to attend the opening of a court of law, she fell violently ill with what was likely a bleeding ulcer. "The pain in her side was very sharp, and was accompanied by frequent vomiting of blood," wrote one witness. "She several times lost consciousness, so that she did not speak for three or four hours."[18] She raved with delirium, her limbs numbed and her vision dimmed. She would recover by the end of November, thanks to the ministrations of her French physician, who prescribed several purgatives. But for a few days, as she balanced on the precipice, everyone thought she would die—not least Mary herself.

During a lucid moment Mary asked to speak to the lords then present, and to Du Croc. She commended James to King Charles and the Queen Mother. She wished for the Auld Alliance to continue. She mentioned nothing about Spain.

The specter of death filled her with nostalgia and regret. She repented of her lapses from the Church of Rome; she wanted James reared in the old faith. Her thoughts drifted back again toward France. "Testify to [Charles IX] the king, my good brother, and to madame the queen [Catherine de' Medici] my good mother, and to

---

*Before this time, France did not maintain a resident ambassador in Scotland. In the interest of fostering the renewed Auld Alliance, especially given Scotland's recent troubles, Catherine decided to create a permanent post and, with it, a more direct line of communication. Du Croc would serve as an important witness to Mary's downfall.

madame my grandmother, to Monseigneur the Cardinal of Lorraine, and to all the lords my uncles, that I die in the Catholic faith, in which I have been instructed, and as I lived in France, and have continued to live since my returning in this realm." She asked her lords to respect her wishes. Never once had she pressed them to change their religions. She begged them to extend the same respect to Scottish Catholics and to Prince James.[19]

At every crucial step in this new life in Scotland—marriage, the birth of her child, and now her approaching death—Mary had tried to renew her Catholic faith. "May God grant that she may lay to heart this fatherly correction," wrote a Catholic Scotsman to a correspondent in Rome. "May [it] lead her to carry out with greater diligence the work which hitherto she has only begun, which all men hope and earnestly desire."[20] Perhaps Mary's intentions were always sincere. In the coming months, however, circumstances would intervene to foil, once again, this latest pledge to act on her piety.

Not even death's shadow could cure her loathing of Darnley. When he came to visit Mary in her sickbed at Jedburgh, she rebuffed him. Once recovered, Mary returned to Edinburgh and separated their lives—they were married still, but in name only. The more Mary snubbed him, the more Darnley wallowed in self-pity. Once again, the diplomatic circuits thrummed with stories of their rows. She wouldn't sleep with him, wrote an envoy, nor spend any time with him, "nor loveth such as him." She was certain "the king will never humble himself as he ought." She found him arrogant, irksome, and, above all, dangerously foolish. How easily the lords had taken advantage of him in the Rizzio plot! Mary's paranoia prickled every time she spied Darnley in the company of a nobleman. What plots might he be hatching now?[21]

Most of all, Mary worried he might harm Prince James. Darnley had dutifully dispatched cheery birth announcements to foreign courts, yet Mary wondered what her husband harbored in his heart. If their son was poised to succeed in both Scotland and England, as Mary declared, he also pushed Darnley down the line of succession in England and compromised his access to power in Scotland. Mary had given Scotland its future king. What point, then, was there in granting Darnley the elusive Crown Matrimonial? In the coming months, Mary would hear alarming rumors that her husband planned to kidnap and crown James and then set himself up as regent. As she told the Archbishop of Glasgow, she was certain Darnley spied on her.[22]*

Looking back years later, James Melville felt more pity for Darnley. He believed the young man's problem wasn't malice but rather inexperience and naivety. "He was misliked by the Queen, and by all such as secretly favored the late banished lords [the murderers of Rizzio]; so that it was a great pity to see that good young prince cast off who failed rather for want of good counsel and experience, than from any bad inclinations."[23] Pushed by his parents from an early age and prone to emotional outbursts, Darnley was not unlike Mary herself: he coveted a crown he couldn't have, one he believed he deserved, one he pursued at all costs.

In France, Catherine de' Medici took a harsher view of the young King of Scots. Writing to Anne d'Este shortly after James's birth, the Queen Mother oozed concern, though her words bore traces of the distinctive delight that accompanies good gossip. Catherine was thrilled for Mary, as happy as if the Scottish queen were her own daughter. The birth of a prince might finally allow Mary to "settle her affairs." But Catherine wondered what Darnley really thought of fatherhood. "He is so wicked that I don't know if he actually feels what he should!"[24]

Like Mary, Catherine balanced on the edge of fear, but her concerns were of a different order: in Spain, Elisabeth de Valois had entered her eighth month of pregnancy and was due to give birth soon. The Queen Mother found the last weeks of her daughter's pregnancy almost unbearable. She needn't have worried—Elisabeth's pregnancy ended as well as it began. The Spanish queen entered her confinement in the royal palace in the Bosque of Segovia. A false alarm on August 1 roused Philip from a deep slumber and created havoc in the queen's apartments, but turned out to be merely "cramps," Fourquevaux

*At least one historian has speculated that Darnley orchestrated the murder of Rizzio in front of Mary specifically to trigger a miscarriage.

reported, "only fear." A spate of fever and vomiting in the final week stoked alarm yet passed after forty-eight hours. Finally, at one o'clock in the morning on August 12, 1566, Elisabeth gave birth to a baby girl.

Philip proved to be an outstanding spouse in the birthing room, "the best and most affectionate husband one could desire," Fourquevaux wrote to Catherine. "He held the queen's hand during the entire night of labor and delivery, comforting and encouraging her as best he could. And just before the pains grew severe, he gave her with his own hand the medicine you prescribed, Madame." It worked so well that Elisabeth delivered soon thereafter with almost no pain. Catherine had insisted Elisabeth give birth lying down on a pallet rather than use a birthing stool, and Philip wholeheartedly agreed. His first wife, Maria-Mañuela of Portugal, had sat upright. Philip always wondered if it was the birthing stool that killed her and caused Don Carlos's troubles.[25]

Elisabeth had waged her war and emerged victorious: she'd given birth to a living child and survived. She earned her husband's beaming affection. After counting little fingers and toes, Philip ordered the baby shown to her mother, then retreated, bursting with gratitude and pride, to pray in his private chapel. Over the coming days, he visited Elisabeth and the new infanta often, and practiced for the baptism by walking up and down, cradling a doll in his arms. In the end, though, too afraid of dropping his newborn, Philip decided to let his half-brother, Don Juan, hold the baby at the baptismal font.[26]

If the birth was easy, the recovery was difficult. Elisabeth's breasts itched and throbbed with milk, and she developed more fevers, spurring the physicians to bleed her yet again. The Spanish doctors ignored Catherine's recipes for poultices, "fat beasts that they are," thundered Fourquevaux, "with nothing in them but arrogance and presumption." When, at last, the ambassador was permitted to visit the Spanish queen, however, he found she had "regained her usual smile."[27]

How long would it take for his letter to arrive in France? This was Elisabeth's first question to the ambassador.

One week, replied Fourquevaux. Then he reassured her. "Everyone in France would feel God's grace in giving her a beautiful daughter." Soon she would have a household of children. To Catherine,

Fourquevaux announced the same: "My lady the queen will make a boy or girl every year!"[28]

The new infanta had her own chamber five doors down from her mother. Fourquevaux padded down the hall and found her under a ruby-red canopy, a peacefully sleeping bundle. The ambassador gazed at her a for a long time. No flattery required, he told Catherine: this was a beautiful child. Her forehead was wide, her mouth full, her nose a little like her father's. She had emerged from the womb with a bloody splotch on her face, which caused some distress, but the blood turned out to be Elisabeth's and easily washed away. Nestled at the breast of her nurse, the baby suckled well.[29]

On the day of the baptism, a proud Don Carlos stood as godfather and Princess Juana as godmother. After the ceremony, Don Juan carried the baby back to Elisabeth's chambers, where the new mother, wearing pure white and still recovering in bed, waited anxiously. The room shone with golden cloth, swathes of the stuff hanging from Elisabeth's bedframe, which her ladies had decorated carefully that morning. Her ladies had gingerly dressed the queen, too, and though fever had left her weak, Elisabeth insisted they arrange her hair for the occasion. "They tormented her a little in doing it," a concerned Fourquevaux noted.

They named the baby Isabel Clara Eugenia—the first name after the great Isabel of Castile, the baby's great-great-grandmother; the second for Santa Clara, on whose name day the infanta was born; the third after Saint Eugene, to whom Elisabeth owed a debt. Elisabeth never seemed to equate "Isabel" and "Elisabeth," although the former was a Spanish version of the latter, and "Ysabel" had been Elisabeth's own childhood nickname. Fourquevaux, however, made the connection almost immediately. Within a few months he was calling the little girl "the infanta Madame Elisabeth," as if to recognize how much she was like her mother, the queen he adored.[30]

Baby Isabel was coddled, her coffers stuffed with expensive toys and baby clothes, her tiny hands given miniature instruments to clutch, her hair smoothed with little combs and brushes her mother ordered specially. Elisabeth purchased amulets by the dozen to ward off the evil eye, a superstitious practice she had learned, perhaps, from her own mother. Six months after the birth, Elisabeth had eyes only for baby Isabel. "I cannot tell you how happy I am to find myself a mother," she wrote to Anne d'Este, gushing with new-mother pride. Her baby girl was precocious. "You would be right to believe that I am silly about my daughter. She is doing so well. She is already like a little woman who understands everything when you speak to her. Now I will close my letter so I don't reveal myself to be the crazy mother that everyone says I am!"[31]

News of Isabel's birth spread throughout Europe. To her old friend, Mary Stuart, now a new mother herself, Elisabeth wrote a private and personal note. Though her letter has been lost, Mary would allude to it in the coming years.[32] Elisabeth appears to have ventured a thought: perhaps Mary could send baby James to Spain to be educated in the Catholic faith, just as Mary had come to France all those years before. And maybe one day their children might marry. How fitting for the children of two Catholic queens, two "sisters" from long ago.

A single trifling detail cast a shadow over Elisabeth's joy: Isabel was not the longed-for son. In Spain, royals and envoys alike hurried to rationalize this defect. Fourquevaux said that for most of her pregnancy Elisabeth insisted "she'd always wanted a girl as much as a boy." King Philip, moreover, was *happier* "to have a daughter than a son," which Elisabeth took pains to confirm to her mother. "Daughters build alliances and take nothing away from a kingdom," Philip had told her, "whereas sons always diminish them." He thought, no doubt, of Don Carlos.

For all her own relief and joy at the good tidings, Catherine couldn't help but feel a twinge of disappointment. "I am thrilled to receive the news of my daughter's safe delivery," she wrote to Fourquevaux. "Although we would have loved a boy just as much."[33]

There were precedents for kings who wished to rid themselves of queens. A king could easily dispense with a queen consort by claiming her barrenness—a fact that a woman like Catherine de' Medici knew well. Like Henry VIII of England, he could divorce. Even sovereign queens could be removed, as Philip II's great-grandfather Ferdinand of Aragon discovered. Conspiring with his son-in-law Philip the Fair, Ferdinand had his own daughter, Juana, Queen of Castile, deemed "mad." Locking her away in the palace at Tordesillas, he claimed Castile as his own.[34] Yet no model existed for a queen who wished to rid herself of a king.

One of the challenges Mary faced throughout her reign was a lack of precedent for each step along the way—few sovereign queens reigned at all, let alone sovereign queens who inherited their thrones young, married while on the throne, gave birth while on the throne, or separated from their husbands—as Mary now felt she must do. In November, she met with counselors at Craigmillar, just three miles outside of Edinburgh. Someone mentioned divorce. Mary disliked any action that might delegitimize Prince James. She ventured a different thought: maybe Darnley could remain in some distant province in Scotland, while she spent time in France. A flash of longing in those words; the hint of a wish. But Mary merely dreamed.[35]

On December 8, Mary celebrated her twenty-fourth birthday. One week later came the last straw: Darnley refused to attend Prince James's christening.

Mary fussed over the details of the baptism. She had to navigate tensions between Protestants and Catholics during what was supposed to be a celebration and reconciliation. In a show of "sisterhood," Queen Elizabeth had consented to serve as godmother and asked Mary's illegitimate half-sister, the Scots Protestant Lady Argyll, to stand in her stead at the baptismal font. Lady Argyll received Elizabeth's gift of a ruby and graciously agreed. The Protestant Earl of Bedford, however, sent by Queen Elizabeth as ambassador, politely refused to attend the ceremony on religious grounds, despite Mary's wishes. Trying to be amenable, though, Bedford agreed to stand outside the Chapel Royal, alongside Mary's Protestant Scottish lords.

Mary made her own concessions. Afraid of offending those same Protestant lords, she did not ask Philip II to stand as godfather. Then she worried about offending him. At the last minute, casting about for some sort of consolation prize, Mary asked the Duke of Savoy, thinking he made an anodyne Hapsburg substitute.[36]

She spared no expense. Guests arrived to overflowing banquet tables and outsized pageants. Fireworks of the kind Mary knew in France sparkled in the night sky. She ordered festive outfits for all her lords, wrapping them in so much silver and gold cloth that, as one snickered, they appeared almost as royal as she did. Mary still strived to please her lords, to show the "love" she felt for her nobility. How often had royal baptisms celebrated truces between warring kingdoms? Mary wished for nothing more than a truce with her own subjects. She paid for the lords' splendid outfits from her own accounts, an elaborate show of generosity. Lord James wore green. Lord Bothwell wore blue.[37]

All Catholic eyes were upon her. On December 17, in the Chapel Royal at Stirling, King Charles's envoy cradled the baby at the font. Mary had forbidden the priest to spit in the child's mouth (a long-standing Catholic practice that she found revolting), but otherwise "everything at this solemnity was done according to the form of the holy Roman Catholic Church," as Monsieur du Croc reported. As for the baby's Christian name, Mary looked again to France, seeing in her child a chance for renewed friendship and giving in to the traces of homesickness that never seemed to leave her. "It was the Queen's pleasure that [the infant] should bear the name James, together with that of Charles (the King of France's name)," wrote Du Croc, "because, said she, all the good Kings of Scotland his predecessors, who have been most devoted to the crown of France, were called by the name of James."[38]

Mary kept up the good cheer, but one absence stuck out. As Du Croc and every other envoy had anticipated, Darnley did not make an appearance.[39]

A week after the christening, Du Croc found Mary "laid on the bed weeping sore," suffering once again from a "grievous pain in her side." Her body had become the slate on which all her woes were etched. The French ambassador blamed Darnley. "His bad deportment is incurable, nor can there ever be any good expected of him," he wrote to Catherine de' Medici. Then he added, ominously: "I cannot pretend to tell how it may all turn out, but I will say that matters cannot subsist long as they are without being accompanied by many bad results." Du Croc proved prescient.[40] Darnley's end was very near. Mary's, as it turned out, was not far behind.

For a queen consort, a baby was a promise of future fertility, legacy, and dynasty, of security on her throne and in her husband's good graces. A baby provided her path to belonging. A queen could rejoice at the birth of a daughter so long as that baby presaged the imminent arrival of a son. In January 1567, just five months after Isabel's birth, Elisabeth de Valois announced a new pregnancy. "Let God bless her with a happy delivery and let it be a handsome prince!" wrote Fourquevaux to Catherine.[41]

There were fresh reasons for France to hope for a boy. Philip had lost trust in Don Carlos, confided Fourquevaux. "A little disobedient" and churlish, the boy inspired no confidence as a future leader. In fact, Fourquevaux understated the case. Irate that his father stalled on a promised marriage between the prince and the daughter of the Holy Roman Emperor, Don Carlos fell frequently into wild tantrums. Fourquevaux foresaw a French triumph: if Elisabeth bore a son, he guessed, Philip would rewrite the Spanish succession in favor of her child, a scion of the Valois.[42]

But the child born on October 10, 1567, after a second easy delivery, turned out to be another girl. Baptized Catalina Micaela, she was named after Catherine herself: "for the love of your Majesty," Fourquevaux wrote, adding that it was "impossible to imagine a prettier creature" than this baby, with her green eyes and black hair. Unlike after Isabel's birth, Elisabeth experienced no complications. On a diet of roast chicken and tisanes of maidenhair fern spiked with cinnamon, she quickly regained her strength. From poultices soaked in parsley juice, she found relief for her aching breasts.

No healing potion, though, could change the sex of her baby. A boy, a real heir for Spain, still eluded Elisabeth. Disappointed, Philip retired briefly from court. "The Catholic King is as joyful and happy to have this second infanta as if the baby had been a boy," Fourquevaux insisted to Catherine. It was a riff on a phrase he'd used merely fourteen months earlier, but now the words rang a little hollow.[43]

23

THE TURN

France and Scotland, 1567

In January 1567, Catherine believed that affairs were finally beginning to settle down in Scotland. To be sure, Mary still had much
to learn. Catherine found her former daughter-in-law too trusting
and, at the same time, too obstinate, too intent on victory. She
needed to make more concessions to her lords. Satisfied nobles were
obedient nobles. Compromise and conciliation were always the best
policies. At last, however, Mary seemed to be learning this difficult
lesson. She had forgiven Lord James and welcomed his return to the
council, a move of which Catherine could only approve. And just
that Christmas Eve, Mary had finally pardoned the lords Morton,
Atholl, and several other perpetrators of the Rizzio plot, restoring
their titles and estates. Catherine nodded her approval again. At last,
she told the Scottish ambassador, the Archbishop of Glasgow, Mary
could "hold herself at ease." "There was nothing more to fear."[1]

Catherine had good reason to warm to Mary. Thanks to the Auld
Alliance, the Queen Mother and the Queen of Scots were bound
to each other, each kingdom reaping the benefits of that oldest of
friendships. The alliance appeared to be thriving again. Baby James
had been baptized in the Catholic Church and blessed by her son
King Charles. Mary had requested that James be appointed captain
of the newly reinstated Scottish Guard, which had served French
kings for generations.[2] Only one thing troubled Catherine when
she considered Mary's affairs: her souring relationship with Darnley.
After all, the boy had shown himself thoroughly capable of treachery.

But in this, too, the Queen Mother thought Mary should think strategically rather than emotionally. Mary should consider her "designs and enterprises in England," Catherine told the Scottish ambassador, offering some unsolicited advice. If she patched up her marriage, Lady Lennox would surely rally English Catholics to support Mary's bid for the succession. Lady Lennox loved her son and resented anyone who displeased him—a sentiment Catherine could certainly understand.[3]

But just one month later, Darnley was dead, assassinated in the early hours of February 10. From the Cardinal of Lorraine, Ambassador Glasgow had heard rumors of nefarious plots underway. The ambassador wrote to Mary urgently, warning her to take heed. Before she could receive his letter, however, Mary wrote him one of her own, announcing the news of Darnley's death.[4]

Some of the bizarre details of the young man's murder flowed to France soon afterward. In late December, shortly after James's baptism, Darnley had sickened with a strange and disfiguring illness. As he traveled from Stirling to his father's house in Glasgow, he was seized with racking pains. Before long, "blisters broke out, of a bluish color" on his skin. The young man's physicians suspected poison, which seemed plausible, given the hostility Darnley faced from all corners.[5] In Glasgow, he remained in bed for almost all of January. When Mary visited him at the end of the month, the blisters still wept. So scarred was Darnley's face that he took to wearing a mask of black taffeta.*

Mary had arrived in Glasgow with a litter to transport Darnley closer to Edinburgh, where he could convalesce. Afraid of infecting Prince James, Mary hesitated to bring Darnley to Holyroodhouse. Instead, she settled on a spot close to the palace. Called the Old Provost Lodging, the house sat in a quadrangle then known as Kirk O'Field.

---

*Darnley may have suffered from smallpox, but historians now believe syphilis was a likely possibility. He had suffered a bout of "measles" during his courtship of Mary, which may have been a first iteration of the disease.

Did Mary know of the plot that was about to unfold? In the aftermath of Darnley's death, Mary's critics would contend that her concern for his health was feigned, that she lavished care and gifts upon him entirely in bad faith, knowing his murder was imminent. Her supporters, however, and Mary herself, claimed she'd had no idea. Instead, Mary insisted that she herself was the target. It was a reasonable assumption, especially after the Rizzio murder. Later, the earls of Huntly and Argyll would claim the lords had signed a bond to murder Darnley during the November conference at Craigmillar, but that Mary remained ignorant of the plan. Whether that was true remained an open question during Mary's lifetime, as it does to this day.[6]

For a few days, confusion reigned. Even Mary herself seemed unsure as to how exactly her husband had died. Eventually, through a mix of rumor and bits of testimony, envoys in London pieced together what had happened.

By Sunday, February 9, about two weeks after arriving at Kirk O'Field, Darnley's skin had mostly healed, and he prepared to depart the following day. That night he slept in a large wooden bed, a gift from Mary. Sometime after midnight, Darnley awoke to a scuffling outside his window. Fearing a plot afoot, he woke his servant, a man by the name of William Taylor. The two men attempted to escape through a window: Taylor lowered Darnley down in a chair using a rope of knotted bedsheets, then clambered down after his master. The assassins pounced. "They strangled [Darnley] with the sleeves of his own shirt," reported the Savoyard envoy Robertino Moretta, "under the very window from which he had descended."

Snatching up the bodies and the chair, the murderers hauled them away from the house and out of the city, setting them down again in an orchard just outside the town walls. Minutes after they left, a blast "as of a volley of twenty-five or thirty cannon" shattered the house. Darnley's killers had scrambled out of the garden with the bodies because they knew what was coming. Their plot, in fact, had gone amiss. Earlier in the evening, the assassins had filled the cellar with gunpowder, planning to kill Darnley in the explosion. Only after the king dropped unexpectedly from his window did they move to strangle him, lugging him away just before the house erupted.

After the smoke cleared, townspeople discovered the crushed bodies of several servants buried in the rubble but no king. In the morning, just after dawn, they found Darnley and his manservant Taylor in the orchard, the chair set carefully nearby. The king was lying under a fruit tree, clad only in his nightshift, his body strangely unscarred, his limbs arranged as if he were sleeping peacefully.[7]

No matter how repulsive most noblemen found Darnley, the nature of his horrific death began, incredibly, to turn popular sentiment in favor of the young king. As the visiting Englishman Henry Killigrew put it to William Cecil, Scottish subjects abhorred "the detestable murder of their King, a shame as they suppose to the whole nation." In the churches, preachers lambasted the murderers, and prayed "openly to God, that it will please Him both to reveal and revenge."[8]

Almost immediately, rumors accused several noblemen closest to the queen, chief among them her favorite, the Earl of Bothwell. Never popular among his fellow lords, especially Lord James, Bothwell now became the target of a fierce propaganda campaign. Two days after Darnley's death, in response to the crown's feeble offer to reward anyone who came forward to name the perpetrators, someone pinned a placard denouncing Bothwell on the Tolbooth in Edinburgh. In short order, dozens of similar bills and broadsides appeared throughout the city, nailed onto buildings and public pillories, even strung up on the gates of Holyroodhouse itself. Sketches of Bothwell lay scattered among the streets, bearing the inscription, "Here is the murderer of the King."[9]

Mary, too, was blamed. Within days of Darnley's death, Earl and Lady Lennox loudly accused the Queen of Scots, and the allegations quickly became vitriolic. The queen was an easy target: her hostility toward Darnley was well known, and Mary had visibly favored Bothwell since the murder of Rizzio, leaning on his strength and loyalty. Upon Darnley's death, a deep-seated antipathy among Mary's subjects was loosened.

Placards spread depicting Mary as a siren who seduced a lustful Bothwell. In the taverns, popular songs portrayed her as a bawd, a

Jezebel, and a husband-killing Clytemnestra. Mary's behavior was scrupulously studied for evidence of innocence or guilt. Did she behave like a mournful widow? Or like a woman besotted with her favorite, the treacherous Bothwell? Reports circulated that Mary covered her face with a black veil and swore to avenge the king's death, while other stories claimed she had traveled to Seton, where she took part in a shooting match with the earls of Bothwell and Huntly—hardly the actions of a grieving queen who should have isolated herself in mourning. As for Darnley himself, Mary ordered him quietly buried a week after the murder, with none of the expected pomp.[10]

We know hardly anything about Mary's state of mind during the weeks following Darnley's death. She made almost no effort to command the narrative, certainly nothing like the letter-writing campaign that followed the murder of Rizzio. Nor did she move quickly to hunt down the murderers, least of all Bothwell. On the contrary, she kept Bothwell close to her at Edinburgh Castle, made him her principal advisor, and made special arrangements to protect him, including—it was reported in London—a security detail of five hundred soldiers, taken from her own guards. Bothwell, meanwhile, had filled Edinburgh with his supporters. He vowed to discover whoever was pamphleting the city and to "wash his hands in their blood."[11]

Two weeks after the murder, the Spanish ambassador in London reported to Philip II that shameful rumors abounded. "Every day it becomes clearer that the Queen of Scotland must take steps to prove that she had no hand in the death of her husband."[12] Elizabeth Tudor pleaded with Mary: "I exhort you, I counsel you, and I beseech you," she wrote, "take this thing so much to heart that you will not fear to touch even him whom you have nearest to you if the thing touches him, and that no persuasion will prevent you from making an example out of this to the world: that you are both a noble princess and a loyal wife."[13]

But Mary would do no such thing. On April 12, she set up a trial of Bothwell, which was widely considered a sham: the jury heard scant evidence and unanimously acquitted the earl after a single day. Otherwise, Mary remained silent, almost as if she believed that if she ignored the problem long enough, it would eventually go away.

Catherine de' Medici was also markedly quiet in the wake of Darnley's death, although initially she displayed a certain nonchalance: "If he'd behaved better, I think he'd still be alive," she wrote to Montmorency at the end of February. After that, however, Catherine remained studiously silent, even as the rumors grew more scandalous with each passing week. Like every foreign sovereign who wondered at the noise coming from Scotland, Catherine likely had trouble parsing fact from fiction in the upswell of Scottish rage. And, like Elizabeth Tudor, she wondered why Mary did not pursue the allegations, hunt down her husband's murderers, and prosecute Bothwell if necessary.[14]

When the accusations against Bothwell and Mary grew tawdry, Catherine did feel the need to distance France from the scandal. By then she'd given Mary six weeks to clear her name. Finally, on March 29, Catherine unleashed an icy ultimatum: if Mary did not absolve herself and take steps to avenge her husband's death, she and King Charles would "not only think her dishonored but would be her enemies."[15]

Beyond that one remark, Catherine pulled back. She wrote no letters to Mary, or at least none have survived. She makes almost no mention of Mary or Scotland in any of her extant correspondence from that period. The silence is strange, yet it did not necessarily signify apathy. Perhaps Catherine wished to see how events would play out. Maybe she was consistently behind the news. No courier could ever ride fast enough, and events transpired so quickly in Scotland that even neighboring England had trouble keeping up. Then, too, like Queen Elizabeth in England, Catherine may have been at a loss. It was difficult to know how to help the Queen of Scots when she didn't seem to know how to help herself.

In the spring of 1567, Mary's ills in Scotland were the least of Catherine's mounting concerns; focused on more pressing matters, she looked in other directions. In Spain, Elisabeth de Valois was pregnant with her second child (the future Catalina Micaela), which kept Catherine on tenterhooks fretting about her daughter's health. In England, Elizabeth Tudor had begun to make pointed demands regarding the return of Calais, and Catherine was endeavoring to find a legal way to keep it permanently for France. There was looming trouble in the Mediterranean, too. According to Fourquevaux, reports had reached Philip II that France planned to seize Spanish-held Corsica with the aid of the Turks, who were long-standing Hapsburg enemies and heretics to boot. Spanish troops were mobilizing in Italy. That spring, as Mary, Queen of Scots, was sinking ever deeper into the mire, an anxious Catherine spent hours at her desk writing flurries of placating letters to Philip II and compiling packets of secret papers for Elisabeth de Valois to read, then burn. She worried a new chapter in the old Italian Wars was about to begin.[16]

And for several weeks, Catherine heard nothing from Mary herself. That, however, would soon change.

In late April, less than two weeks after Bothwell's trial, Mary rode to Stirling Castle to visit Prince James. She had moved her son there from Edinburgh shortly after Darnley's death, to protect him from the turmoil in the capital. On April 24, as Mary traveled back to Edinburgh, the Earl of Bothwell and scores of armed soldiers intercepted her on the road. Mary was surprised. She had not expected Bothwell; her traveling companions were few and Mary claimed no one else knew of her journey. But according to witnesses, when Bothwell insisted she come with him to his castle at Dunbar, Mary put up no resistance. News of her detainment at Dunbar traveled quickly to London, where the Spanish ambassador Silva wrote a dispatch to Philip II: "Some say she will marry him, and they are so informed direct by some of the highest men in the country who follow Bothwell. They are convinced of this both because of the favor the Queen has shown him and because he has the national forces in his hands."[17]

Sure enough, on May 15, barely three months after Darnley's death, Mary and Bothwell were married at Holyroodhouse. A Protestant preacher presided over the rites. Witnesses later confirmed that, shortly before the wedding, Bothwell had convened several lords for a supper at Ainsley Tavern, and there wrangled them into signing their consent to the marriage.

Bothwell was already married, a fact that did not deter the lords who signed the Ainsley Bond. By that point, the earl had initiated his divorce from his wife, the Lady Jean Gordon, who was the sister of the Earl of Huntly. Whether that divorce was legally concluded at the time of his wedding to Mary, however, wasn't clear, though Mary would later insist that it was. To foreign courts, Mary's third wedding was utterly shocking: the Protestant ceremony, the wedding following so soon after Darnley's unresolved death, Bothwell's suspected guilt in that same murder, and now the possibility that Mary was complicit in bigamy. None of this seemed in character for the Queen of Scots, unless the rumors were true—that Bothwell and Mary were lovers and had plotted Darnley's death to clear the way for their marriage.

Yet James Melville would later claim in his memoirs that Mary had no choice: "The Queen could not but marry him," Melville wrote, "seeing he had ravished her and lain with her against her will."[18]

———

In the last week of May, the Bishop of Dunblane brought Catherine a letter from the Queen of Scots. Mary wished to explain why she had married Bothwell without first informing her French relations of her intentions. Her letter was long. She spent pages detailing Bothwell's vaunted ancestry and his previous loyalty to the Scottish crown. She reminded them of his valor against Lord James in the Chaseabout Raid, and his heroic actions after Rizzio's murder—in short, Mary explained why she had trusted Bothwell when she had no one else to trust.

Then she explained why that trust had been misplaced. Mary did not use the word "rape," or its sixteenth-century counterpart, "ravish." There is a reticence to her words, a rambling circuitousness tinged with alarm, as if Mary was still in shock as she wrote her letter—as if she couldn't quite bring herself to say what had happened. Yet her meaning was clear. At Dunbar Castle, she explained, Bothwell confessed that he had fallen in love with her. Then, Bothwell implored her to marry him. After she repeatedly refused, he resorted to "force."

"In the end, when we saw no [hope] to be rid of him," Mary wrote, "never [a single] man in Scotland once making an attempt to procure our deliverance . . . so ceased he never till by persuasions and importune suit, accompanied not the less with force, he has finally driven us to end the work begun at such time and in such form as he thought might best serve his turn, wherein we cannot dissemble that he has used us otherwise than we would have wished or yet deserved at his hand.

"His behavior," Mary went on, ". . . may serve as an example of how cunningly men can cover their designs when they have any great enterprises in mind." She had favored Bothwell to show her gratitude for his service. His ardor and ambition caught her off guard. She had not realized he would seek "any extraordinary favor at our hands."[19]*

Writing his own letter from Scotland, Ambassador du Croc confirmed something terrible had happened, though what exactly, Du Croc couldn't say. Mary's clear distress alarmed him. "On Thursday the queen sent for me," he confided to Catherine. "She and her husband behaved strangely with each other. She tried to excuse it, saying that if she seemed sad, it was because she had no desire to be cheerful, and would never be, and that she desired nothing but death. Yesterday, when they were together in a *cabinet*— she and her husband—she called out for someone to give her a knife to kill herself . . . I believe that if God does not help her, she will fall entirely into despair."[20]

That despairing bride implored Catherine—along with King Charles, her uncle the cardinal, and her other "friends" in France—to help her "make the best of it." "It is past and cannot be brought back again," Mary explained.[21] She asked her French relatives to disregard the rumors of Bothwell's questionable divorce. She insisted their wedding had been conducted legally and in good

---

*This wasn't the first time Mary had been surprised by a man's infatuation with her. When Mary returned to Scotland in 1561, she brought with her a young poet named Pierre de Boscosel de Chastelard. Fond of the young man, and appreciative of his service, Mary offered him the gift of a horse. In 1563, Chastelard hid himself under her bed, planning to declare his love for her. Horrified, Mary banished him from Scotland, but just days later, Chastelard again surprised her in her bedchamber. The poet was tried and beheaded.

faith. She beseeched them to acknowledge the legitimacy of this newest marriage, for her sake.

Did Catherine consider it? Only a wedding could save the honor of a woman who had been "ravished" or raped. We do not know if Catherine believed what Mary had implied in her letter. Mary's critics would claim the kidnapping to Dunbar was a hoax, that Mary consented to it so she could marry Bothwell, the supposed rape a lie—an accusation that has persisted through the centuries, though most scholars now agree that some sort of assault or coercion likely occurred at Dunbar. Even at the time, many of Mary's own subjects believed "her Majesty [had been] ravished by the Earl of Bothwell against [her] will."[22] As for Mary's critics—Catherine understood the misogyny of her time. She knew from experience that a young woman in a position of power could fall victim to vicious rumors: long ago, Catherine herself had suffered accusations that she and her husband, Prince Henry, had poisoned his older brother, the dauphin. And Mary's explanation—that Bothwell had forced her— was plausible. Catherine surely recognized Mary's vulnerability to any ambitious man close to her who coveted power.*

Quite possibly, the Queen Mother believed Mary wished only to salvage her virtue by marrying Bothwell. Yet Catherine also knew that any pity she felt for Mary no longer mattered.

For the Queen Mother of France had no choice but to vehemently condemn the union. The situation looked scandalous. In the months leading to Darnley's death, Mary had lavished honors upon Bothwell, granting him undue power in her council. She had spurned Darnley before his grisly death, and now continued to favor the man who stood accused. The marriage, moreover, seemed nothing short of treason and lèse-majesté on Bothwell's part. Although Mary claimed to have wed Bothwell of her "own free will," to Catherine it seemed all too apparent that he had seized Mary's body to commandeer her sovereignty. Her daughter-in-law's suffering was unfortunate. But that suffering was secondary to the greater political crime of stealing the power of the crown.[23]

---

*So inflammatory was the Protestant propaganda against Mary in the coming decades that a sixteenth-century Scottish scholar, George Buchanan, could get away with holding both positions: admitting Mary was likely raped, or at least kidnapped, while also contending that she planned it for her own pleasure.

Still, Mary's letter stirred Catherine's compassion. The Queen Mother warily eyed the dangerous tides churning in Scotland. Du Croc reported that Bothwell was "hated" by all, and that the other lords had all withdrawn from court en masse. Catherine likely suspected Mary was not long for the throne. As Mary was a sister sovereign and family, Catherine felt obliged to assist, at least a little. With tensions brewing at home and on the Spanish horizon, Catherine could not afford to send an army to Scotland; nor is it clear that she would have sent one if she could. She did, however, send an envoy. On June 1, Catherine dispatched Monsieur de Villeroy to Scotland to see what could be done for Mary. The Queen Mother instructed him to pass through England on his way, to ask Queen Elizabeth for her help.[24]

At the end of June 1567, Catherine received urgent letters from Du Croc. The Queen of Scots had fallen. Edinburgh had surrendered to the Protestant lords.

On June 15, Mary and Bothwell had ridden to Carberry Hill, just east of Edinburgh, at the head of a mercenary army paid to fight for the crown. There they faced the defiant Protestant lords, who had mustered an army of their own, thousands strong. Earlier, the lords had assured Du Croc of their plans to liberate the queen from Bothwell's clutches. But when he arrived at the scene of the impending battle, Du Croc began to doubt their good intentions. He noticed their curious ensign: pure white, with the figure of "a dead man next to a tree (because the late King was discovered in a garden near a tree), and a child on his knees, representing the prince of this kingdom, holding a scroll on which was written: 'Revenge, O Lord, for My Just Cause!'" Nowhere on that banner was there a picture of the queen. It was as if Mary were already gone.

There was no fight, Du Croc told Catherine. After six hours of maneuvering, Bothwell fled and Mary surrendered to the lords, thinking they would free her. Instead, they marched her back to Edinburgh as people lined the streets to jeer at her. In the capital, they imprisoned her in the provost's house. Later that night, "her Majesty appeared at a window, crying and moaning in the most pitiful way imaginable," Du Croc reported, still rattled by what he'd seen. The next morning the lords marched her to Holyroodhouse, once again brandishing that terrible white banner. That evening, near midnight, the lords moved her north to the isolated fortress of Lochleven, near Perth.

Du Croc was exhausted and terrified. For weeks he'd been asking to leave Scotland, to let events "play themselves out." As France's official ambassador, he worried his presence might be seen to condone the turmoil. On Carberry Hill, he'd spent the entire day running back and forth between the two armies, trying not to compromise King Charles's official position. What was that position? Du Croc didn't know. Was he supposed to support the Queen of Scots or the rebel lords? He had received no specific instructions from the French crown and now Du Croc feared for his life. The bailiff of Edinburgh Castle had surrendered its arms and ammunition to the Protestant lords, the city had declared itself for the rebels, the streets roiled, and the mob ruled. Du Croc was out of cash; he had not received his wages in weeks. Panicked French men and women—numbering in the hundreds, appointed by Queen Mary to her household—clamored for his help. They were afraid, they wanted out of Scotland, and Du Croc wanted out, too.[25]

Catherine had other ideas. To be sure, she abhorred rebellious subjects and worried revolt would spread to other kingdoms. But the Queen Mother also weighed the consequences to the Auld Alliance. King Charles could not afford for Scotland to flip its allegiance from France to Protestant England, a shift that Spain might interpret as French weakness and a pretext for war. The Auld Alliance brokered friendship between kingdoms, not between sovereigns. Catherine would help Mary if she could. Mary was family, after all. More important than Mary to Catherine, though, was Scotland itself— and Catherine would endeavor to keep Scotland a friend. Ever practical, always expedient, the Queen Mother would deal with the winner.[26]

As for Du Croc? He owed his loyalty to France. Catherine sent instructions to her petrified envoy in Edinburgh. "The king wishes Monsieur Du Croc to know that His Majesty's desire and principal goal is to conserve the kingdom of Scotland's allegiance to him. He will not permit him to withdraw and thus lose this allegiance.

He wishes to bestow every favor and assistance to the Queen of Scots, but not at the cost of imperiling and ruining his own kingdom, or at the expense of service to the king and his affairs."[27] The Auld Alliance—King Charles's interests—must always come first.

24

THE PRISONER
Lochleven Castle, Scotland, 1567

The only way to access Lochleven Castle was by boat. Led by Lords Lindsay and Ruthven, Mary's captors paddled her across the dark waters in the predawn hours of June 17.* Mary was twenty-four years old. She hoped her imprisonment would last mere days, that Scottish loyalists would rally, that France would come, that she would soon regain her throne. No such rescue awaited her. On that summer night in 1567, however, Mary did not know that, apart from a brief reprieve, she would remain a prisoner for the rest of her life.

Set on an island in the middle of a loch, Lochleven Castle was an imposing medieval fortress owned by Lady Margaret Douglas, the mother of Mary's half-brother Lord James. The castle keep rose from the ground like a tribute to the strength of stone. A solitary turret—the Glassin Tower—crested at the southeast corner. Iron gates enfolded the grounds. "Strong," the Spanish ambassador described the fortress, "in the middle of so large a lake that not a single culverin in the country could even reach it, much less batter it." Nature had provided protection enough. The castle keepers required only a few soldiers to stand guard.[1]

What thoughts swept through Mary's mind as the boat drifted toward the castle? She recognized the lake, the keep, the stretches of grass flanking its walls. She'd once met John Knox at Lochleven, where she enjoyed one of their more agreeable conversations, and

*This Lord Ruthven was the son of the Lord Ruthven who orchestrated the Rizzio plot before dying of a liver ailment in May 1566, just months after the attempted coup.

had spent the night at the castle on several other occasions. Then, she was the queen; though still a queen, now she was also a captive of her own subjects. It isn't clear whether Mary knew her letter to the Bishop of Dunblane had arrived safely in France. She must have wondered if her French relatives believed what she'd told them. Or how it had all come to this.[2]

Mary harbored a secret: she was pregnant. We know almost nothing about this pregnancy or the conditions that engendered it. At the time, only a single dispatch by Nicholas Throckmorton mentioned Mary's pregnancy.[3]

Throckmorton arrived in Edinburgh on July 12, sent by Queen Elizabeth to try to negotiate Mary's release.* Forbidden to see the Scottish queen in person, he found a way to slip a message to Lochleven and to receive a reply. Throckmorton assured Mary that Queen Elizabeth was doing her utmost to procure her liberty. But why, he asked, did Mary still not repudiate Bothwell, as the lords had demanded for weeks? Throckmorton had heard chilling threats in Edinburgh: if Mary did not repudiate Bothwell, if she refused to renounce all forms of papacy in Scotland, the lords would charge her with tyranny, adultery, and the murder of her husband, of which they claimed to have certain proof. Upon Throckmorton's arrival he found the lords "so bent against" her that he feared her imminent death. He begged Mary: to save her own life, would she not renounce Bothwell?

Throckmorton's bewilderment echoed that of Mary's countrymen. In the weeks after Bothwell absconded with Mary to Dunbar, many of her subjects had assumed that Mary's behavior was compelled, that she wasn't "at liberty so long as she is in [Bothwell's] company." And yet, despite every opportunity to denounce Bothwell, if only to save herself, Mary refused. This, her lords couldn't understand.[4]

───────

It was to Throckmorton that Mary finally revealed her secret. She would "rather die," she explained, than repudiate her husband. "Taking

─────────────────

*Mary's captivity horrified Queen Elizabeth.

herself to be seven weeks gone with child, by renouncing Bothwell she should acknowledge herself to be with child of a bastard, and to have forfeited her honor, which she will not do to die for it," Throckmorton wrote to Queen Elizabeth. He had managed to save her life for the moment, he said, though he sensed Mary's days might be numbered.[5]

When did Mary first suspect this pregnancy? Her message to Throckmorton suggests she fell pregnant soon after marrying Bothwell, yet there is no way to know if Mary told the truth. Given the difficulty of ascertaining a pregnancy in the sixteenth century, it is possible that Mary couldn't say exactly when she had conceived. Perhaps it had occurred as early as April, when Bothwell took her to Dunbar, the pregnancy perhaps the result of rape. As one of Mary's biographers suggests, the dawning prospect of a pregnancy may explain why Mary agreed to marry Bothwell so quickly in May and publicly claimed to do so "of her own free will."[6]

If she hadn't become pregnant, Mary might have been able to denounce Bothwell. But she knew she had to protect her unborn child's dignity and recover what she could of her own. There was something else: Mary may have realized her pregnancy would condemn her in the eyes of critics eager to establish her guilt. In the sixteenth century, the prevailing view held that a woman fell pregnant more easily if she enjoyed the act of sex, whereas rape usually led to barrenness. As one Renaissance doctor wrote, "unwilling carnal copulation for the most part is vain and barren; for love causes conception and therefore loving women do conceive often." Lawyers echoed the view: "Rape is the forcible ravishment of a woman, but if she conceives it is not rape, for she cannot conceive unless she consents." It was commonly believed that a woman's pleasure in sex generated the right conditions for fertility, rendering the womb hot and moist. As Pope Clement VII had advised his newlywed niece, Catherine de' Medici, long ago: "A spirited girl will always conceive children."

Yet the inverse also held true. If a woman fell pregnant, however nonconsensual the intercourse, it meant she had probably enjoyed it. Anyone looking to establish Mary's desire for Bothwell—a murderous lust—could seize upon this line of thinking, if only for propaganda and slander. Her body issued its own verdict. Her pregnancy was a sign of complicity.[7]

Whenever it was that Mary realized she was pregnant, she knew she was a marked woman. She had every reason to fear for her unborn child. Though a king could beget bastards, no kingdom would tolerate bastards born of a queen. If born out of wedlock, the baby would embody Mary's willing and sinful capitulation to Bothwell. What would become of the infant, then? What of Mary herself, the adulterous mother of an illegitimate child by a man accused of regicide? Mary had no choice but to try to fix the situation. She would defend the legitimacy of her marriage vow. On that point, at least, she could redeem herself and her unborn child. And so even in Lochleven, Mary refused to renounce Bothwell, clinging to her story of wifely fidelity—perhaps because she so desperately needed to believe that story herself.[8]

As she told Throckmorton, her honor depended on it. What else did Mary have left? Her pregnancy kept her captive as much as any of her lords. But not for long. Sometime before the end of July, Mary miscarried. Nau would write later that she suffered terribly, and for days lay ill in bed, troubled "as much by the great sorrow she suffered, as by the great loss of blood . . . that came upon her such that she could scarcely move."[9] Whether Mary mourned the loss of the pregnancy, Nau didn't say.

She would remain in Lochleven for the better part of a year. She lived in limbo, trapped on an island, simply waiting. For months she remained hopeful that France would come to her aid and lived in terror lest they did not. Separated from the world, she was both a queen and yet not a queen. Mary would always hold herself to be Queen of Scotland. The Guises had soldered that crown to her sense of self; it was integral to her identity. Mary would cling to the idea of her sovereign dignity. As for the rest of it, the physical trappings of queenship, the lords would teach her how quickly it could all be stripped away.

Upon her arrival, Mary's keepers installed her in a first-floor chamber. No provisions had been made to accommodate a woman of her rank. At night, she clambered into a plain bed with modest hangings, the room furnished with whatever the governor of the castle had on hand. Never before had she encountered such a chamber, such meager living. The lords had allowed only two of her women to accompany her from Edinburgh. By August they replaced these women with two young girls, the daughters of the castle's governor, hardly attendants fit for a queen. Mary thought they spied on her, rifling through her things.

Not that she had much. She asked for paper and ink but was refused. She asked for more clothes, having only the gown on her back and a spare nightshift when she arrived. This too was denied, at least at first. Stinging with humiliation, and desperate to pull together some semblance of majesty, Mary begged to send for her gowns. When at last her captors consented, Mary's French chamberlain, Servais de Condé, rummaged through the royal wardrobes in Edinburgh, packing bodices and headpieces, cloaks and veils, skirts, sleeves, pins, and skeins of "sewing silk." But Condé was carefully watched and censored, the royal wardrobes half-pilfered. When the clothes arrived in Lochleven, Mary discovered a pittance of mismatched pieces. Furious, she would write again in August, again in September. Again in October. Condé sent what he could. Often, though, he sent nothing at all.[10]

She pleaded for the lords' compassion. If they would not respect her as their queen, would they at least treat her as "the King their sovereign's daughter, whom many of them knew, and as their Prince's mother?" Perhaps she could go to France, there to live in exile with her grandmother. Or at least be moved to Stirling Castle, where she could take comfort in her son, James.

Mary had almost no idea of what had become of her son and prayed for his safety. The French and English crowns would vie for James, each hoping to gain custody of the child—in theory for his protection, but in reality for their own political advantage. "She were rather herself and the prince were in [England] than elsewhere in Christendom," Mary said to Robert Melville, hoping that Queen Elizabeth might provide refuge for them both. Within days, that hope disappeared. Neither England nor France would prevail in their battle for James. The Scots lords would keep the baby in Scotland and raise him in the Protestant faith. As for her request to move to Stirling, her keepers refused this, too. Mary couldn't know that she would never see her son again.[11]

These were treacherous days. Mary walked the thinnest of lines between life and death. The crisis point arrived in the last days of July, when Lord Lindsay brought Mary her abdication papers and, according to Nau, terrorized her until she signed them. "It was the intention of the rebels, if she did not sign these letters," he wrote, "to take her from Lochleven, and as they were crossing the lake to throw her into it . . . [or] cut her throat, however unwilling they might be." Nau said she didn't read the papers, but he was likely rewriting the facts: Mary knew what she was signing.[12] At the time, Robert Melville said she was advised to act "with her own benevolence rather than to suffer rigor," which a great number of lords endorsed, "not only to make her incapable of governing, but also to pursue her both of life and honor." Mary would always maintain that her throne was taken from her by force. She told the truth: terror compelled her. Throckmorton suspected the lords would kill her anyway, after the prince was crowned.[13]

Despite Throckmorton's fears, the lords would not kill Mary, but they found a way to erase her nonetheless. At the end of July, the guards moved her to the Glassin Tower at the far end of the courtyard, into a chamber atop a winding staircase. If she could look through the window set high in the wall, Mary saw only a sea of forest leading to an expanse of blue. In winter, that water froze into desolate sheets of white. For several months, her visits were limited to her keepers and the girls who attended her. She spoke with almost no one.

Mary would stay there for most of the year. Her keepers would never permit her to write letters, though she did manage to smuggle a pen and paper into her room after several months. At least she had her embroidery: Servais de Condé sent her needles, netting, and silk thread. She whiled away the time, pushing her needle through squares of mesh, and grappling with the dawning realization that perhaps no one was coming for her.

On July 29, just days after Mary signed her abdication papers, thirteen-month-old James was crowned King of Scotland at Stirling. Lords Lindsay and Ruthven swore an oath that "the Queen their sovereign did resign willingly without compulsion, her estate and dignity to her son." Her abdication papers were read aloud, and Lords Lindsay and Dunn took the oath of fidelity to the realm on the baby's behalf. John Knox preached the sermon, expounding on the biblical story of Joash, the boy king of Judah crowned at the age of seven, after the massacre of his family. A temporary regency council was established for the new King James, the names of the Lords Atholl, Morton, Glencairn, and Mar read aloud at the ceremony.

Then the feasting began. Edinburgh was ecstatic. The city glowed with the blaze of a thousand bonfires. The castle fired its cannons while the people danced in the streets. They displayed more joy for their new king than sorrow for their queen, Throckmorton noted bitterly. The Scots nobility formally requested Lord James to serve as regent in August. In October, the Scottish Parliament would confirm his appointment.[14]

On the evening of James's coronation, far from Edinburgh, the governor of Lochleven Castle ordered bonfires lit and cannons discharged in fiery celebration. From her room in the castle, Mary could hear the commotion. When she inquired about the fuss, the governor mocked her. Celebrate with us, he said. "The bystanders made game of her Majesty, some in one fashion, some in another, telling her in their bravadoes that her authority was abolished, and that she no longer had the power to avenge herself upon them," Nau wrote. "Deposuit potentes," said the governor. *God has struck down the mighty*. Retreating into her chamber, Mary wept.[15]

25

THE DEATH OF A QUEEN
Scotland, England, France, and Spain, 1568

Apart from at suppertime, watchmen usually guarded the gates of Lochleven Castle around the clock. But at the appointed hour every evening, the guards twisted the key in the locks and handed it to the castle governor before heading to supper. Taking his own place at the table, the governor always laid the key next to his plate.

On the evening of May 2, 1568, a young page approached the governor's place with a dish, tossed a napkin over the key, and pocketed it as he picked up the cloth. Then, sneaking from the hall, the boy tiptoed up the stairs of the Glassin Tower to Mary's chambers.

There he found Mary dressed as a laundress and clutching the hand of a ten-year-old girl, one of the two maids her keepers had provided. The trio fled down the stairs and out of the castle gate, which the boy locked behind them. Clambering into a small boat, they steered it stealthily across the loch. On the opposite shore, a group of Mary's allies waited. Once in their safekeeping, Mary traveled south to Niddry Castle, according to the Venetian ambassador resident in France, who was at court when Mary's messenger arrived. This rescue-by-children had been concocted over weeks by George Douglas, the second son of Lady Douglas, the owner of Lochleven Castle. If the story spread soon after Mary's escape is true, the young man had fallen in love with her.[1]

During the long months of her imprisonment, Mary had despaired of her return to the throne. By March, she had smuggled a pen into her room and, in the middle of the night, scribbled imploring letters on scraps of paper, slipping them from the castle through the offices of the besotted George Douglas. She wrote one of her first to Catherine de' Medici. "I beseech you, have pity upon me," Mary begged, pledging her devotion. "I am now fully convinced that it is by force alone I can be delivered." If only Catherine would send French troops, "I am certain great numbers of my subjects will rise to join them; but without that they are overawed by the power of the rebels and dare attempt nothing of themselves."

Yet she suspected the French were ambivalent. However, in March, she'd heard that Charles IX and Catherine had made a deal with the French Protestants, again rebelling under the Prince de Condé and Gaspard de Coligny: in exchange for peace, the French crown would no longer pursue Mary's interests. "I can hardly believe this," Mary wrote at the time, "for apart from God, I place my hope entirely in the two of you." Now liberated at Niddry Castle in May 1568, Mary no longer counted on French help.[2]

For a short time, she believed she could prevail without it. For eleven glorious days after her escape, her Scottish supporters rallied, mustering an army 6,000 strong and vowing to overthrow the regent, Lord James. On May 13, Mary's army clashed with rebel forces at the Battle of Langside, just south of Glasgow. Though outnumbered, the tactically astute Lord James and his troops quickly gained the upper hand. From a nearby hill, Mary watched the carnage unfold. Fleeing before the battle was over, she galloped almost a hundred miles south. She stopped only after reaching the village of Dundrennan on the edge of the Solway Firth.

Now, Mary found herself in a quandary. Her companions at Dundrennan warned her not to trust England. Best to go to France, where Mary still had friends and family, the comfort of her grandmother, and the counsel of the cardinal. Or perhaps to Spain, where Philip II would fight for her crown.

To go to France: that had always been Mary's deepest wish. Yet she could not forget Queen Elizabeth's dismay at her imprisonment, the efforts Throckmorton had made to secure her release. While Mary was in Lochleven, Queen Elizabeth had sent Mary a jewel, a token of her promise to help and a remembrance of their friendship as sister queens. Mary had no choice but to believe those promises now.

In a reign filled with missteps, this misplaced trust would prove to be Mary's most fateful error.

In Dundrennan, she readied pen and paper. She appealed to the English queen's mercy, to their kinship and "sisterhood." It was May 15, less than two weeks since her flight from Lochleven Castle. "I am now forced out of my kingdom," Mary wrote to Elizabeth. "And driven to such straits that, next to God, I have no hope but in your goodness. I beseech you, therefore, my dearest sister, that I may be conducted to your presence, that I may acquaint you with all my affairs." More than ever, she wished to meet with the English queen, if only to explain herself.

Before handing the letter to a messenger, Mary wrote one last line. "To remind you of the reasons I have to depend on England, I send back to its Queen, this token, the jewel of her promised friendship and assistance." It was the same diamond Elizabeth had sent to Mary in Lochleven. Somehow, through the mayhem of escape and her preparations for war, Mary had kept that jewel with her.[3]

The following day, May 16, Mary and her companions boarded a small fishing boat and crossed the Solway Firth to Cumberland, in the northwest of England.

Mary was partially right: Elizabeth Tudor was willing to fight for her, to a point. So long as Mary was kept safely locked away in the Glassin Tower, Queen Elizabeth felt free to lambaste the Scottish rebellion. On principle she had good reason to object: Mary was her kinswoman and a sovereign queen, and like Philip II, Elizabeth Tudor believed rebellion had a way of metastasizing. As Elizabeth declared loudly to Catherine de' Medici, princes should support one another; the threat to Mary was a threat to sovereigns everywhere. Surely some sort of reconciliation between Mary and her subjects was possible.

Catherine received Queen Elizabeth's letter in October 1567, just a few months after Mary was first imprisoned in Lochleven. Catherine, however, read easily between the lines. Elizabeth wasn't writing merely to commiserate about Mary, but to gloat. Just the previous month Catherine de' Medici and Charles IX had narrowly escaped a coup of their own: in September, Protestants had tried to kidnap them while the court was at Meaux, a small city northeast of Paris. Catherine managed to foil the plan, and Charles demanded the Huguenots account for their actions in person. The Huguenots failed to show up. Another civil war seemed inevitable.*

Now Elizabeth crowed: if only Charles had subjects as well behaved as her own! They "are as faithful to me as I could desire . . . I never fail to condole with those princes who have cause to be angry," Elizabeth told the Queen Mother.[4] Those princes whose subjects disobey them—sovereigns like Queen Mary and King Charles.

It was a strange thing to say to the Queen Mother, dripping with irony. As Catherine knew—as all of Europe knew—Elizabeth Tudor had sustained French Protestants with both English troops and coin in the first French War of Religion, just as she'd funded the Scots Protestant lords and harbored them as fugitives during their various rebellions over the years. Catherine reeled at the audacity. Elizabeth's words would stay with her—perhaps Catherine even kept the letter. Soon enough, she would fling those same thoughts back across the Channel.

Catherine did not have to wait long. Mary's flight to England in May caught Elizabeth off guard. When Mary escaped from Lochleven Castle, Elizabeth cheered, thinking the Scottish queen would soon quell her unruly subjects, setting an example for all potential insurrectionists. She did not expect Lord James to defeat Mary at Langside. And she never expected Mary to breach the borders of England without her express permission.

Mary's surprise arrival presented Elizabeth with a different scenario entirely. It was one thing for her to play at diplomacy, to send Throckmorton to negotiate for the Queen of Scots, and quite

---

*The Surprise of Meaux, as it is called, resulted from layers of distrust both within France and between rival kingdoms. In the summer of 1567, King Philip II sent the Duke of Alba from Milan to Flanders to quash the Protestant rebellion in the Netherlands known as the Dutch Revolt. As Alba's troops marched north on the "Spanish Road," which bordered France, Charles IX and Catherine feared a Spanish invasion, and sent 6,000 Swiss mercenaries to the border, attempting to protect France from Spanish aggression. Huguenots, however, feared that the French crown planned to use the mercenaries to attack them. The Surprise of Meaux was their preemptive strike against the crown.

another to take action on Mary's behalf, and now actually help Mary. What would that entail? And at what cost? Elizabeth had no desire to wage a war against Scottish Protestants. As for her own subjects, the north of England teemed with Catholics who might rally around the Queen of Scots both to restore her Scottish crown and win her the English one. Elizabeth also suspected Mary might try to leave for France. If so, the Catholic crowns might launch a joint invasion of both Scotland and England. Why not quash a rebellion in Scotland and depose the usurper in England at one and the same time? England could not withstand such an onslaught, and no other foreign prince would come to Elizabeth's aid. It was best to detain Mary in England—Elizabeth decided—and prevent her departure for France.

As it happened, Catherine de' Medici had no wish to bring Mary to French shores. She had maintained relations with Scotland and was mired in ever-growing troubles at home. After the debacle at Meaux, civil war had broken out in France as anticipated—the second War of Religion. During the first battle of that conflict, the old Constable Montmorency was mortally wounded. This war had quickly concluded but now, in May 1568, France teetered on the brink of a third bloody installment. Two civil wars in less than a year and a third looming—meanwhile, Catherine de' Medici was convalescing from a grave illness.

We know almost nothing about this illness. We know only that it left Catherine so weak she could scarcely hold a pen. This is what Catherine explained to Elizabeth Tudor, at least, in a letter written on May 26, ten days after Mary's flight to England. Though her illness prevented her from writing in her own hand, Catherine felt obliged to plead with Elizabeth Tudor on Mary's behalf. But Catherine and Elizabeth were cut from the same cloth: now Catherine jumped at the chance to sting the English queen, quid pro quo. The wretched Queen of Scots had become a flashpoint in the fraught correspondence between the French and English queens.

"Madame my good sister," Catherine began, her words touched with irony. "As soon as the king, Monsieur my son, and I found out the state in which, at present, the Queen of Scots, my daughter-in-law, has been reduced, and how she was forced to flee into your lands, pursued by her subjects as you surely know, we immediately sent [our messenger] to your court. He will tell you how aggrieved we are to see her in such pain and affliction and how we are greatly contented that she has put herself into your hands. We assure ourselves that she will receive all the help, favor, succor and friendship that a princess so afflicted should hope for from you."

Then came the coup de grâce. What had Elizabeth written the previous October when she preached the importance of supporting Mary? "We are sure," Catherine wrote, "that you keep the same opinion you have always had"—and here she paraphrased Elizabeth herself—"*that princes must support each other to chastise and punish subjects that rise against them and rebel against their sovereigns.*" "I beg you," Catherine continued, turning the screw, "let all princes know, and particularly my son and myself, how much you desire the sovereign authority of princes to be conserved, and rebellious and disobedient subjects to be chastised and punished."[5]

How disingenuous of Elizabeth Tudor to preach to Catherine about sovereignty, "to condole" with Charles's troubles, all the while funding those same troubles! Years before, Catherine had rid herself of the beautiful and irksome Mary, Queen of Scots. Now the Mary problem belonged to Elizabeth Tudor.

———

If Mary's plight moved any hearts in Spain, neither the Catholic Queen nor the Catholic King would offer the Scottish queen any help. Trouble brewed at home. In May 1568, just as Mary fled the Glassin Tower, Elisabeth de Valois and Philip II had entered the darkest months of their lives.

Always volatile, Don Carlos had grown dangerous. Until the boy's late adolescence, Philip had found it easy to ignore his behavior. Don Carlos's bouts of violence were episodic, and since they would eventually give way to an even-tempered peace, sometimes lasting for months, Philip kept hoping the boy would one day grow into the son and heir he desired. Still, the king harbored secret doubts, and refrained from assigning Don Carlos any of the responsibilities normally due to a prince of his stature.[6]

Don Carlos boiled over with frustration and confusion. He noticed how Philip would trot him out at ceremonies yet refused to grant him the independence to act as his own agent. Worse, his father backpedaled and made empty promises. Since 1559, Philip had vowed to bring Don Carlos to Flanders, there to present the young man as the future ruler of the province. This thrilled Don Carlos; he imagined his father was grooming him to become the next Holy Roman Emperor, just like his grandfather Charles V. Another sign pointing to this exalted future appeared in 1564, when the Imperial ambassador arrived in Spain bearing a proposal to marry Don Carlos to Anna of Austria, Philip's niece and the oldest daughter of the Hapsburg Holy Roman Emperor, Maximilian II. Anna was blond and blue-eyed and extremely devout. So excited was Don Carlos that he hired a tutor to teach him German so he could impress the girl and her father.[7]

But no trip to Flanders ever materialized and the marriage negotiations stalled. Don Carlos began to suspect Philip would renege entirely, just as he had done with Mary Stuart. Incensed, the young man became obsessive, focusing single-mindedly on the wedding to Anna of Austria and on proof of his father's disfavor. He declared Philip's counselors his mortal enemies. When, in April 1566, Philip sent the Duke of Alba instead of Don Carlos to quash the Dutch Revolt, Don Carlos threated to kill Alba. Later that year, after Philip canceled yet another promised trip to the Netherlands, witnesses said Don Carlos threatened to kill Philip. From that point on, the relationship between father and son eroded quickly.

Don Carlos could not understand the roots of his father's contempt. Clearly, Philip had favorites: the Duke of Alba, for instance, or, worse, the lowborn Ruy Gómez. Desperate to leave the shackles of boyhood behind, he also despaired of ever gaining Philip's approval. Faced with his father's impassivity, Don Carlos sought out other, reckless paths to power. He forged friendships with sycophantic courtiers who eagerly exploited his desire for recognition. He wrote privately to grandees asking for their support. Philip grew suspicious.

"There is a marvelous indignation and evil satisfaction between the Catholic King and the prince his son," Fourquevaux warned Catherine de' Medici in September 1567. "If the father hates the son, the son hates the father no less, such that if God does not send a remedy, some great misfortune is bound to happen."[8] The betrayal occurred two months later, in December. Don Carlos plotted to flee Spain for Italy, travel up the Spanish Road to Flanders, and arrange to meet Anna of Austria. He revealed his secret plans to Don Juan, his young uncle and closest friend. Though Don Juan tried to persuade Don Carlos not to go, the prince persisted. Mounting his horse, Don Juan galloped to the Escorial. There, he divulged everything he knew to King Philip. It was December 25, 1567.

It took Philip three weeks to figure out his next steps.

On January 18, 1568, Philip slipped into Don Carlos's room in the palace, accompanied by several armed soldiers. It was shortly before midnight; the room was dark and still. Following the king's orders, the gentlemen attending Don Carlos had left the door unlocked and snuffed out the candles. They had dismissed the guards and locked away the weapons the prince normally kept in his room. As Don Carlos slept, Philip sidled up to the bed to remove the sword his son always placed at his bedside. Don Carlos would have noticed had the sword gone missing earlier.

The young man woke.

"Who is there?" Don Carlos was alarmed.

"The council of state."

Don Carlos rose from his bed to find his father standing before him. Philip wore his battle helmet. Chain mail hung from his shoulders.

"Has Your Majesty come to kill me?" the boy asked.

Philip reassured his son but ordered him back to bed. "What we are doing is for your own good." The king's men nailed the windows shut to prevent the young man from escaping, and ransacked the room, emptying coffers and desks. Before he left, Philip told Don Carlos that he would treat him as a king would, rather than as a father.[9]

Later, poring through the sheaves of paper discovered in Carlos's chamber, Philip found hundreds of letters from across the realm, requesting the prince's assistance or sending him bits of information Philip would have preferred to restrict. The letters dripped with groveling adulation. To Philip, the correspondence bore the hallmarks of a shadow government in the making, with Don Carlos as its figurehead.[10]

Philip ordered his son brought to a tower of the *alcazár* in Madrid, where he remained under constant guard. Don Carlos followed his captors meekly. Though Philip considered putting his son on trial, his clerks could unearth no hard evidence of any seditious intent. By then, Philip felt he had no choice but to find a "permanent remedy" to the problems his son posed. Just as Charles V had done with his own mother, Juana "the mad," Philip decided to lock up Don Carlos for life.[11]

Shut away in the *alcazár*, the boy was excised from the world. Philip permitted no visitors, no outside communications, not even from Princess Juana and Elisabeth de Valois. He questioned whether Don Carlos was fit to receive communion and, at first, prohibited him from hearing Mass. Don Carlos wept, but obeyed Philip's order to stay in his room. Eventually, a sympathetic priest worked out an arrangement through which he would say Mass in the antechamber while administering the wafer and wine through a screen to Don Carlos, who remained dutifully on the other side, in his room.[12]

Did Don Carlos understand the nature of his crime? If the young man hoped his father would forgive him, he hoped in vain. Philip refused to see his son, his rigor disguising his own cutting sense of guilt. The king grew curt with diplomats; Fourquevaux thought he looked gloomy and depressed. Philip issued an official announcement of Don Carlos's arrest yet provided few explanations to baffled foreign sovereigns. Only to his closest Hapsburg relatives would he write more candidly of his son's addled mind.

"At some times there is more serenity than at others" in his son, he explained to his sister Maria and her husband, Maximilian II. "It is one thing to deal with the prince's defects as they affect government and public affairs, and another as they affect personal actions and affairs, and private life—because it may well be that what could be disastrous in one could be excused and allowed in the other."[13] Now, Don Carlos's private affliction had encroached on public affairs.

Philip was learning the bitter lesson that had tormented generations of kings: the roles of father and king were always entangled in knotty cords of duty, honor, and affection. How do you choose between the boy in front of you and the kingdom at large? Philip could not separate the father from the king, the boy from the heir.

In the end, the king must always take precedence. "I have . . . made sacrifice to God of my own flesh and blood," Philip told Don Carlos's maternal grandmother. He would feed and shelter his son, but nothing more. And yet, he grieved. "With what sentiments of grief I have come to this decision, your Highness may judge . . ."[14]

Philip lived with his guilt for the remainder of his life. Years later, when constructing the majestic basilica at the Escorial, he commissioned giant memorial statues of his family, wrought in gold and placed high above the altar. Behind the kneeling statue of Philip stands Don Carlos. Dressed in stunning armor, he holds his head erect and chest high, his golden likeness showing none of the ailments of body and spirit that tortured him during life. The memorial reminded Philip of God's impenetrable will. The statue also honored Don Carlos as Philip wished to remember him. Here was the son and heir he should have had.

"I am not a madman, only desperate because of how Your Majesty treats me," Don Carlos cried out at his arrest.[15] In his seclusion, the young man fell into profound disorder. He looked for ways to kill himself. He swallowed a diamond ring to poison himself, slept naked on the tile floor, and doused his bed with ice, thinking he would freeze from the chill. He would refuse to eat, then binge until "he couldn't eat any more," all the while swilling buckets of water mixed with snow as if to drown himself. Finally, he ceased eating altogether. His fast lasted two weeks. Prying his jaws open with a metal prod, his doctors force-fed him some meat and soup. By the time a priest finally persuaded Don Carlos to eat, it was too late.

"The passages that convey our food had closed up so that he could scarcely take even a little broth," his jailer, the Count of Lerma, recounted.[16] Don Carlos had lived in his tower for six months. He had just passed his twenty-third birthday when he died, shortly after midnight, on July 24, 1568.

Philip had retreated to the Escorial. When he learned of Carlos's death, the king cried for three days and ordered the court into mourning for his "beloved son." Still, the duties of the king prevailed. Don Carlos was barely in his tomb before Philip wrote to the Emperor Maximilian proposing another wedding to unite their families. Now that Don Carlos had died, there would be no union with Anna of Austria, but perhaps Princess Juana could marry the Archduke Charles.

Others at the Spanish court breathed easier after the prince's passing. The boy's behavior had disturbed many comers. "The prince is just fine where he is," said the Count of Lerma after Don Carlos's death. "All of us who knew him give thanks to God for it."[17]

———

Elisabeth learned of Don Carlos's arrest the morning after it happened, in January. "She didn't stop crying for two days, until the King ordered her to stop," Fourquevaux told Catherine. "She wept both for the prince and for herself, because the prince loves her marvelously."[18]

At her husband's command, Elisabeth wrote to her brother, Charles IX, underscoring Philip's grief at imprisoning his son. She was either unable or unwilling to disclose any details about the nature of Don Carlos's crimes.[19] To her mother, Elisabeth probably dissembled the truth. "God let her believe what I told her," she told Fourquevaux.[20]

Despite centuries of myth, no romance existed between Elisabeth and Don Carlos. But in her own way, she loved him. "I cannot console myself under so great a misfortune, which I esteem my own, more than that of any person, because of the friendship which I bear the prince, and the many obligations I owe him," she wrote to Charles IX. From the moment she arrived in Spain when they were just children, Don Carlos had been kind to her, keeping her company even during those times when Philip was reserved— perhaps especially during those times. Both the queen and the prince lived at the mercy of their parents; both were used in the shifting and smothering demands of dynasty, alliance, and war. Perhaps Elisabeth understood something of the young man's resentment.

A week after Don Carlos died, Fourquevaux came to console Elisabeth on the evening of July 31 dressed head to toe in black, his head enveloped in a voluminous black hood, as Spanish protocol required. Though the ambassador chafed at the clothing, Elisabeth would hear of nothing less than proper mourning. She insisted Catherine show only compassion at the Spanish prince's passing, even to "do more rather than less" to show her sorrow.[21] She knew that Catherine had already made certain calculations. With Don Carlos's death, the kingdom of Spain would now pass to Elisabeth's child, especially if she gave birth to a boy. As it happened, Elisabeth was already pregnant again.

The pregnancies came fast and furious now to Elisabeth, just as they had to Catherine de' Medici. She was just twenty-two years old, her body now a wellspring of fertility. Elisabeth had announced this newest pregnancy in May 1568, only six months after the birth of Catalina Micaela. By July, she thought she was three or four months along.* Her pregnancy softened the blow of Don Carlos's death for Philip. He ordered the Spanish court to observe their mourning for an entire year *unless* Elisabeth gave birth to a son, in which case they would cast aside their grief to rejoice that the queen had fulfilled "their extreme desire" and "given them a prince."

Visions of a French triumph danced before Fourquevaux's eyes. "And if [Queen Elisabeth] is loved and respected now in the face of the death of Prince Carlos," he told Catherine, "she would from that point be loved and respected twice as much because, for better or worse, her descendants will reign over them. They also say that the friendship between your Majesties of France and Spain, your successors and kingdoms, will thus be unbreakable, since you will be at that point of one shared blood." Trust me, Fourquevaux said, as if Catherine dared not believe it, "what I am writing to you, Madame, they are saying in public."[22]

The pieces on the chessboard of royal marriages began to shift again, with new dynasties imagined and alliances contrived. Possibly Princess Juana would go to the Archduke Charles, strengthening the Hapsburgs. Anna of Austria perhaps to Charles IX of France, merging once again Hapsburgs and Valois. Or maybe Anna to the King of Portugal, impoverished prince though he was. Everything might change with the arrival of Elisabeth's baby. "We must wait and see what God gives to my lady the queen," Ruy Gómez confided to the French ambassador, "for many great things turn upon it."[23] As they always did.

---

*There had been another false pregnancy the previous March. Fourquevaux reported it but soon stood corrected. Even after bearing two children, Elisabeth, like many women of her time, had trouble knowing if she was pregnant. Catherine didn't receive confirmation of this latest pregnancy until late June.

Catherine dared to dream. "Tell my daughter that I beg her to take care of herself," she wrote to Fourquevaux, trying to encourage Elisabeth through the difficult early months. "Tell her to imagine how fortunate she will be if God blesses her with a son. And not only her, but all of Christendom, especially this kingdom [of France], and particularly her old mother who, before she dies, will have the happiness (once her brother the King of France has a son) of seeing herself the grandmother of the two greatest kings of Christendom." How exalted a future for that little Medici orphan, that barren girl, of long ago.[24]

The pressure of this pregnancy only added to the mounting tension Elisabeth felt during the summer of 1568. Shaken with grief at Don Carlos's death, she was racked with worry by the specter of a third civil war in France. Catherine's brush with death (the same unknown malady still consuming the Queen Mother as she wrote to Elizabeth Tudor about Mary Stuart) terrified Elisabeth. The news that Mary had fled to England must have seemed both remote and appalling, another crisis in a summer of incomprehensible disasters. And Elisabeth hadn't been well for months.[25]

Her latest pregnancy intensified strange symptoms she had experienced on and off ever since the birth of Catalina Micaela. Some of these, like the vomiting and fainting spells, or the occasional bouts of "melancholy," were familiar ailments. Others, like the tremor and distension in her left arm, were new. Like many a diplomat, Fourquevaux carefully avoided alarming his sovereign, knowing the Queen Mother hung on his every word. Elisabeth's ladies were sure these were the minor complaints of early pregnancy, he reassured Catherine. They would pass once Elisabeth progressed beyond the third or fourth month.

In truth, there were probably several symptoms the ambassador hesitated to share. Later, he would confess to Catherine that Elisabeth did not experience "more than eight days of good health" during the entire pregnancy.

In the last week of September, Elisabeth fell seriously ill, yet recovered quickly. Armed with that happy fact, Fourquevaux felt confident enough to describe certain details of Elisabeth's sickness to Catherine. Beyond her "infinite vomiting," he wrote on September 24, Elisabeth had developed a burning sensation across her stomach such that, for a few days, everyone feared a miscarriage. The trembling in her left arm morphed into pain, which radiated down her left flank and into her leg. Surely, wrote Fourquevaux, all of it was merely the result of "the cold, since she dressed only lightly for a few days this month while it was growing chillier in the area." He was thrilled to report her recovery. "All this ended, thank God, and she rose from her sickbed in good health." Fourquevaux still believed these were the passing infirmities of a pregnant woman.[26]

The ambassador wrote too soon. In the first days of October, Elisabeth's symptoms returned with a vengeance, the pain searing her entire left side, the vomiting now coupled with cramping diarrhea. The doctors found her urine had turned gritty. Her feces were mottled with yellow and black, and her back was seized by violent spasms—all signs of a disease of the kidneys.

Now it seemed crucial to intervene yet, afraid for the life of the unborn child, the physicians hesitated to purge her. As Elisabeth's condition worsened, they tried bleeding her from the foot. Before dawn on October 2, the doctors dispensed a tonic to expel the poisoning humors. When Elisabeth threw up the draft, they turned to pills of agaric, the medicine Dr. Mugnoni had administered so successfully four years earlier after her miscarriage. This time, however, the pills did nothing.

The sounds in the room, the looks on the faces gazing down upon her, and the slowing beat of her own body told Elisabeth she was dying. On the evening of October 2, she asked for her confessor. Bringing the wafer and the wine to her bedside, the priest heard her confession. It was not quite time for the last rites.

Philip sat at her bedside, hoping to catch her last words, tears streaming down his cheeks. According to an official narrative published by the crown, Elisabeth turned to her husband and apologized. She had never given birth to a son as he had wished, and as was her duty. She committed her daughters into his care, knowing he would be a good father to them. Her "swan song," as one account later called it, overwhelmed the king. Unable to bring himself to watch her die, Philip retreated from the room to pray.[27]

A few hours before dawn, a priest bent once again over Elisabeth's bed. Gently touching her forehead with oil, he murmured the prayer of Extreme Unction. Then, gathering a little strength, Elisabeth asked to speak to the French ambassador.

No one slept that night. In Elisabeth's chamber, the Duchess of Alba and the ranking nobles of her household kept watch over the dying queen.* The palace wept. Just before dawn, the Inquisitor General of the realm and the Bishop of Cuenca, who served as the king's personal confessor, arranged a procession of the court from the palace in Madrid to the parish church of Santa Maria. Streaming back to the royal chapel, the court sank to its knees. At ten o'clock in the morning, a messenger arrived at the chapel, bringing news that, in the throes of her illness, the queen had delivered a baby girl. The infant lived for a few minutes after the birth, Fourquevaux would assure Catherine de' Medici. There had been time to baptize her. Her soul would not remain in limbo—the smallest of consolations.[28]

In the chapel, the praying began anew. Voices whispered, keeping time with the intoning of the priests. Everyone simply waited for the end. They did not have to wait long. Less than two hours after her baby was born, shortly before noon on October 3, word reached the chapel that Elisabeth had died. She was twenty-two years old.

---

*The Countess of Ureigna had died in April 1566 after a two-week battle with "colic." The Duchess of Alba replaced her as Elisabeth's *camarera mayor.*

26

LAST LETTERS

Spain, France, and England, 1568

In life, Elisabeth de Valois's body defined her. A vessel of the state, her body was deployed in marriage by her father, employed as the instrument of dynasty by her husband. The future of two kingdoms hinged on her body's capriciousness, its potential to give birth, its failure to do so. Yet Elisabeth alone suffered her body's torments—the vertigo, faints, and headaches; the nausea, trembling, and bleeding. Even joyful moments came with pain, her body straining in labor, her breasts tender with unused milk, her bones aching with postpartum fever.

But as death approached, it was almost as if the sufferings of the flesh had ceased, as if Elisabeth's spirit began to divorce itself from her body—almost as if she had no body at all. Her mind's eye and the thoughts of all those who watched her die were trained entirely on the soul. To hear Fourquevaux tell it, Elisabeth died an exemplary death, filled with clarity and calm. In her final moments, "she listened devoutly to the exhortations of her confessor," Fourquevaux wrote, "remaining in full possession of her consciousness" so that she could willingly render her soul unto God. She raised a crucifix to her lips and kissed it. Then she prayed to God, to the Virgin Mary, and to Saint Francis, knowing that this, the day of her death, was also Saint Francis's feast day. She prayed to her ancestor, Saint Louis, and she prayed "to her guardian angel." The end was as easy as a breath of air. "She expired so gently," the ambassador said, "we knew not precisely the moment of her death."[1]

"The lamentations were incredible," he recalled. "There is not one person great or small who does not weep for Her Majesty's loss or affirm that she was the best and most gracious queen that had ever reigned in Spain." Fourquevaux struggled to write the words. Elisabeth's death gutted him. He was "more in need of consolation himself than he was able to give to the dying queen," he said later. Over his eighteen months at the Spanish court, his loyal devotion to Elisabeth had developed into a tender attachment. They began as partners navigating Catherine's demands in the labyrinth of Spanish politics; they ended as friends. Two weeks before she died, Elisabeth had congratulated Fourquevaux and his wife on the birth of their child, a baby girl. They had decided to name her Elisabeth.

"Please forgive me, Monsieur de Fourquevaux, if I haven't responded to your letters," she wrote. "I've been in such a state these past days because of vomiting, so I couldn't write to you. I am so pleased to hear that Madame de Fourquevaux is well and that she has given birth, and that she wants your daughter to take my name. For I will treat the baby like my own daughter—I ask you to allow me to do that."[2] It would be Elisabeth's last letter to the ambassador.

After she died, Fourquevaux returned home. Turning to his desk, he pulled out a sheet of paper to write an official announcement of the Catholic Queen's death to King Charles IX. He felt the need to apologize to the king. "Sire, I had the good fortune to write to you yesterday to say that there is only good news coming from this realm," he began. "But something terrible has occurred, so grave that I am forced to send you now the worst news you could receive, which is, Sire, that you have lost the Catholic Queen, your sister, today at noon."[3]

It was Fourquevaux's custom always to compose two letters whenever he sent dispatches to France: one to Charles IX and another to Catherine. Finishing the letter to Charles, Fourquevaux smoothed out another blank page. He dipped his quill. Then, brokenhearted, he began to write.

There was still the body to bury, the funeral to arrange. On the afternoon of Elisabeth's death, the Duchess of Alba oversaw the embalming of the corpse, then dressed Elisabeth in the coarse gray wool of a Franciscan habit to honor the saint on whose day she died. As Elisabeth's ladies pinned black cloth embroidered with French fleur-de-lis and the arms of Spain onto the walls of her chamber, noblemen lifted the queen into a coffin. For the rest of the afternoon, Spanish courtiers filed through Elisabeth's apartments, paying their respects. That night, a funeral procession snaked from Elisabeth's rooms to the royal chapel. Placing the queen's coffin on a large catafalque, the pallbearers covered it with a shroud of gold brocade. The requiem Mass began.

Outside the palace, the roads thronged with mourners. "Never was such grieving shown by any people," remembered one French witness. As Mass concluded in the royal chapel, only the Duchess of Alba stayed behind with the body of her mistress. Seated near the head of the coffin, her face shrouded in layers of black veils, the duchess would sit through the night during a long and silent vigil.[4]

Philip staggered under the blow. "To suffer so great a loss after that of the prince my son," he wrote to his envoy in France. "But I accept to the best of my ability the divine will which ordains as it pleases."[5] The following day, October 4, another procession accompanied Elisabeth's coffin to *Las Descalzas reales*, the convent founded by Princess Juana. There, Spanish subjects could visit their queen one last time. Peering into the open coffin, the people found Elisabeth cradled in velvet, the fabric lush against the stark drape of her gray robes. Next to the queen lay the tiny body of her baby girl. Philip had decided to bury mother and daughter together.

At the close of the visitation, the Duchess of Alba scattered herbs and flowers over the bodies, pressing balsam and other perfumes into the velvet. The pallbearers then carried the coffin to the tomb deep in the belly of the convent.

There, Elisabeth and her daughter would remain for a time. Philip planned to move the bodies to the Escorial but, in the days after Elisabeth's death, he had yet to decide when.

In the Cumbrian town of Workington, Mary Stuart busied herself writing letters, trying once again to tell her story. Soon after landing on English shores, she'd hastened to explain to Elizabeth Tudor why she was there, narrating her version of the previous months' events.

She reminded Queen Elizabeth of the Chaseabout Raid, the brutal stabbing of Rizzio, the murder of Darnley of which she stood "falsely" accused. She told Elizabeth that her subjects flouted due process, forbidding her to defend herself in council or Parliament. At length, Mary recounted the Battle of Langside and how she came to cross the Solway Firth. She portrayed her enemies as dishonest subjects who had conspired against their queen. Time and again, Mary had behaved like a beneficent sovereign, forgiving her rebellious lords, ready to receive them again "into favor." How generous she had been, Mary wrote. And yet they betrayed her.

Mary's letter also spoke through silence. Not once did she mention the Earl of Bothwell.[6]

Mary did not realize that evidence of her guilt had surfaced a full year earlier. The Earl of Morton later explained the circumstances in a deposition. In June 1567, just five days after the queen's fall at Carberry, three of Bothwell's men entered Edinburgh Castle and retrieved from under Mary's bed a small silver box, or casket. The lords subsequently arrested one of these men, who revealed the whereabouts of the casket. Inside, the lords discovered a treasury of documents, including two sheets on which Mary vowed to marry Bothwell, twelve love sonnets, and eight letters she composed to Bothwell before their marriage.

The Casket Letters, as they would be called, seemed to confirm both Mary's adultery with Bothwell and her complicity in Darnley's death. To this day, their authenticity remains unproven, but these were the lustiest of love letters. "I [am] . . . glad to write unto you when other folks be asleep, seeing that I cannot do as they do, according to my desire, that is between your arms by dear life," read one scandalous passage.

Most damning of all was the handwriting, which appeared to be Mary's own. The adolescent loops and scrolls of Mary's pen had long ago devolved into a hastier scrawl. Lord Morton swore, however, that the scribble was hers.[7] Her hand confirmed her collusion in the worst crimes imaginable for a woman, let alone a queen.

Although the minute details of this strange trove were not widely known until the autumn of 1568, over a year after the Scottish lords first discovered the Casket Letters, rumors of damning evidence began to circulate as early as the summer of 1567. In London, Lord

James (who was then passing through on his way back to Scotland from the Continent) told the Spanish ambassador that Mary knew of the murderous plot, as proven by "three sheets of paper written with her own hand and signed by her," in which she purportedly encouraged Bothwell to go forward with his plan.[8]

One year later, in the summer of 1568, Elizabeth Tudor wasn't quite ready to pass judgment on Mary. But her hands were tied. Guilty until proven innocent, the Queen of Scots shouldered the burden of acquitting herself. Until then, Queen Elizabeth declared, the two queens could not meet. Elizabeth was certain Mary's protestations of innocence were true. Yet for now, as Mary surely understood, Elizabeth must look after her own reputation. "You will see it would be *malaise* for me to receive you before your justification," Elizabeth wrote.[9]

Mary met this news with fits of humiliated tears, complaining of her "evil usage" and contrarious handling. How could Elizabeth, her sister queen, her kinswoman, decline to hear the petition of a woman so falsely traduced, a woman who wished only to recover her honor? How dare she receive Lord James, a known rebel, and not Mary herself? "I have chosen you from among all other Princes, as my nearest kinswoman and perfect friend, [and] hoped to receive this kindness from you, giving you the honor and the glory all my life, making you also thoroughly acquainted with my innocence and how falsely I have been led." Her pen splashed bitterness. "I see," Mary continued, "to my great regret, that I am mistaken."[10]

She was shocked to find herself still a prisoner. After she landed in Cumberland, an escort sent by Queen Elizabeth ushered Mary to nearby Carlisle Castle. She was assigned quarters in the Warden's Tower, there to await Elizabeth's pleasure. Her rooms were comfortable and well appointed; at Elizabeth's orders she received furniture, clothing, and servants as befit a queen. Elizabeth permitted Mary to ship her gowns from Scotland, and her favorite ladies to attend her. Mary Seton, one of the four Marys, still arranged her hair, pinning elaborate hairpieces swirling with color into the coiled locks.

Still, she was a marginal soul, ejected from the realm of Scotland, not quite a welcome guest in England. And that was Mary's own fault, Queen Elizabeth said. "You put in my hands the handling of this business," the English queen wrote, "which concerns all appertaining to you." Until this business was settled, Mary would live at Elizabeth's command. [11]

From the Warden's Tower, Mary cast about for help, sending letters to family and friends. "I have suffered injuries, calumnies, imprisonment, hunger, cold, heat, fleeing without knowing whereto, ninety-two miles across the country without stopping or dismounting," she wrote to the Cardinal of Lorraine. "Then, I have had to sleep upon the ground, and drink sour milk, and eat oatmeal without bread. I have been like the owls, without a single waiting woman, for three nights in this country, where now, to crown it all, I am hardly more than a prisoner." Also a wish: "God will soon take me from all these miseries." [12]

Mary sent a special messenger to Catherine de' Medici, not daring to put her thoughts on paper lest her letters fall into the hands of her enemies. She promised to place herself into French hands and serve Catherine like a dutiful child. [13] But her messenger was delayed. Elizabeth Tudor would not let him pass into France.

———

The twenty-fourth of September 1568. On that autumn day in Madrid, Fourquevaux wrote the dispatch to Catherine de' Medici explaining the alarming details of Elisabeth de Valois's most recent illness, the malady that would eventually kill her and her unborn child. That same day, in England, Mary, Queen of Scots, wrote her own letter to Elisabeth de Valois. Having lost faith in Elizabeth Tudor, Mary returned to the Elisabeth of her childhood, the young woman she once called "sister."*

She began by apologizing. Almost a year had elapsed since her last letter to Elisabeth, time lost to her confinement in Lochleven Castle where paper and reliable messengers were in short supply. Mary now thanked Elisabeth for the "loving and comforting letters" she had received from the Catholic Queen since her arrival in England. She'd

---

*Mary had been moved in July from Carlisle Castle to Bolton Castle, as the English deemed Carlisle too insecure.

heard from a courier that Elisabeth wept to hear of her misfortunes. "I must kiss your hands for it," Mary said.[14]

Mary wrote of their enduring friendship, composing a love letter to their youth. Frantic to recover her reputation with King Philip and King Charles, she hoped Elisabeth would intervene on her behalf. As agonizing to Mary as any accusations of adultery and murder were the rumors of her lapsed Catholic faith. She hadn't lived down the defamatory letters Darnley sent the Catholic crowns before his death, nor could she deny the scandal of her Protestant wedding to Bothwell. She looked to an old friendship for salvation.

She was still a good Catholic, Mary protested to Elisabeth. Determined to spin the shambles of her life into something purposeful, she insisted her arrival in Cumberland could save England for the papacy. She was oblivious to the absurdity of her claim: she had promised for almost a decade to return Scotland to Catholicism, but failed to act. Now she promised England?

Yet Mary wrote as much to convince herself as anyone else. "My disaster," she told Elisabeth, "could serve Christendom, for my coming to this country has made it clear to me that if I had just a little hope of foreign assistance, I could subjugate the religion here or die trying. This entire region [in the north of England] is dedicated to the Catholic faith." Queen Elizabeth of England was jealous, Mary continued. She was detested by her subjects, Catholic and Protestant alike. Mary, however, had already won over "many hearts" among Englishmen. With foreign help—Elisabeth de Valois's help—she could rally her English supporters for the Catholic cause.

This was dangerous language. That Mary eyed the English throne was exactly what Elizabeth Tudor feared. Years later, it would become clearer to the English queen that Mary was plotting just such a coup. But in September 1568, Mary wrote from desperation more than from any malicious intent. Elizabeth Tudor had betrayed her. Mary groped in the dark, looking to give Elisabeth de Valois and Spain a reason to rescue her.

As she wrote, Mary began to plead. She wished to return to France, but Elizabeth Tudor wouldn't allow it. She wished to hear Mass, but this too the English queen forbade. She begged Elisabeth de Valois to intercede with King Philip and with her brother, King Charles. In exchange, Mary offered Prince James to Spain: she would agree to James marrying the oldest of the infantas, Elisabeth's daughter Isabel, just as Elisabeth had suggested when the babies were first born. If Elisabeth had made the offer as a flight of fancy, now Mary hung onto it for dear life. The children could grow up together at the Spanish court, just as Mary had grown up with Francis before their own wedding. Elisabeth would mother James in Mary's stead. The little boy "would be too fortunate" indeed to find himself a Spanish ward instead of a pawn in the treacherous hands of either the Scottish lords or Elizabeth Tudor.*

"Keep this proposal a secret, for it will cost me my life," Mary warned. She promised to explain everything to Elisabeth in detail in a separate enciphered letter, "for to do otherwise would be dangerous." She closed by reminding Elisabeth of what they once shared. "I am obliged to praise God for the nourishing childhood we enjoyed together, to my good fortune. This is the source of our unbreakable friendship, as you have shown me. But alas! How will I repay your friendship, if not to love and honor you and, if ever I have the means, to serve you as I wish to do, and have always wished for my entire life?"

She signed her name, adding, "Your most humble sister, ready to obey you." She knew her letter would have to travel a stealthy and circuitous route toward Madrid. It would take a week to arrive, at least. Maybe even two.

———

Mary filled that letter to Elisabeth de Valois with hope, cloaking her despondency in religious righteousness and the language of friendship. *I too am a Catholic queen, your sister. I am your chance to rid England of heresy.* Trying to redeem herself, Mary resorted to the same tactics Catherine de' Medici often used with Elisabeth, scripting the words she wanted her friend to repeat to Philip II: *I have allies here; the English queen is unloved.* They were variations

---

*There is something tragic about this offer. As Mary wrote her letter, James lived under the regency of his uncle Lord James. Mary had no power to send the little boy to Spain yet nonetheless held on to this fantastical dream. As late as 1577, she expressed her wish for James to marry a Spanish princess, having completely lost touch with the reality of both James's Protestant upbringing and his lack of affection for her.

on a theme, a rondo she would play repeatedly for Spain in the coming months.

Her pleas would fall on deaf ears. Isolated in England, Mary possessed no leverage to persuade Spain to rescue her. She could only promise to restore Catholicism, and on that point her credibility was in doubt. King Philip would not antagonize Elizabeth Tudor for a disgraced queen—a fact that Mary might not have realized. The old politics still held fast. As much as Philip deplored the scourge of heresy, Elizabeth Tudor remained his bulwark against a French empire.

In the end, it didn't matter. Elisabeth de Valois died before Mary's letter could reach her. Had she lived, what might Elisabeth have done? The Catholic Queen had already betrayed the Queen of Scots once before. Much later, while still a prisoner in England, Mary would remember bitterly that "when the Cardinal of Lorraine . . . was negotiating my marriage with the late Prince of Spain," Catherine de' Medici tried to circumvent the match, "all the while protesting her goodwill." Dissimulative and untrustworthy, Catherine never wished "anything good for anyone unless there is some advantage or use in it for her."[15] Mary never mentioned Elisabeth's part in the mother–daughter ploy to prevent her marriage to Don Carlos. In all likelihood, she did not know. Or maybe she simply forgave. She, too, had once lived at the beck and call of her family.

The letters Elisabeth de Valois sent to Mary Stuart during her captivity likely expressed a sincere concern. Elisabeth cherished fond memories of her older "sister"; she no doubt grieved for her friend's suffering. Such friendships were born in the *petite cour*, bonds that were supposed to last a lifetime. Nothing, however, could compete with the stronger loyalties governing Elisabeth's life as queen consort. In the hierarchy and economy of attachment, Mary occupied a lower rung and lesser value. Elisabeth would never defy Spain or France, husband or mother, for the Queen of Scots. And, as Catherine herself came to realize, Elisabeth had come to embrace Spain and its policies. The Catholic Queen now embodied that name, heart and soul.

That is the real pathos of Mary's last letter to Elisabeth de Valois: not that Elisabeth died before she could read her friend's message but rather that, if she had received it, Elisabeth would have done very little for Mary. Probably, bending to the will of Catherine and Philip, to her own Catholic convictions, she would scarcely have tried.

———————

Autumn arrived. For over a year, the Earl of Lennox, intent on avenging his son Darnley, had painstakingly assembled witnesses. In October 1568, at Queen Elizabeth's command, an English commission assembled in York to investigate the evidence against Mary, Queen of Scots. There, the Earl of Morton and Lord James, Earl of Moray and Regent of Scotland, testified to the existence of the Casket Letters.

Now at Bolton Castle, Mary was writing yet another letter to the Spanish ambassador in France, Francés de Alava, when she learned of Elisabeth de Valois's death. It was November 3, six weeks after she'd written to the Queen of Spain.[16] The news devastated Mary. Who would save her now?

She had vested all her hopes in the Catholic Queen. "I had the greatest confidence in her," Mary said to Alava. "I have no doubt she would have stood up for me against such false accusations, and would have assured the King, her lord and husband, of my loyalty" to him and the old religion.[17] That hope died with Elisabeth.

Mary wrote her next letter to King Philip himself. "She was the best sister and friend that I had in the world. My heart weeps to think of her death. And yet, the love I bore her in my soul is ever present in my memory."[18]

Mary's letter had a political purpose: perhaps if Philip knew how much Mary had loved Elisabeth, he might take pity on her plight. In a way, she was still using Elisabeth, even in death. Still, Mary's grief rings with sincerity.

How could Mary not weep for Elisabeth as she waited in her English prison, bereft of crown, child, reputation, and of her beloved relatives in France? Elisabeth still lived at the heart of Mary's memories of better days—of the safety and splendor of France. Bittersweet visions that drifted toward her from long ago: memories that must have seemed from a different life, an entirely different world.

27

A DAUGHTER'S LOVE
Spain and France, 1568

It took over two weeks for Catherine to hear of Elisabeth de Valois's death. For reasons unknown, Fourquevaux's communications were delayed, both the letter of September 24 informing Catherine of Elisabeth's worsening health and the one he wrote on the day of her death in October. The autumn weather was still suitable for traveling, but the courier had to navigate a long and circuitous postal route from Madrid to Paris, over treacherous mountain passes. In the past, at least one of Fourquevaux's messengers had died on the road, resulting in missing dispatches. Usually, the ambassador expected his missives to arrive in France within a week. This time, neither Fourquevaux's letter of September 24 nor the letter of October 3 arrived in Paris until October 18.

Blissfully ignorant, Catherine sat at her desk that day, writing Elisabeth an update on the escalating tensions in France and abroad. French crown forces had defeated Protestants near Angoulême in the west, and razed Provençal villages supporting the Prince de Condé. King Charles and Catherine were sending French troops to Flanders, where the Duke of Alba struggled to defeat Protestant rebels. Catherine hoped the birth of a prince uniting the kingdoms of France and Spain would intimidate the rebels in both realms into surrendering. "God willing, you will send us your good news soon," she wrote in closing, "and you will make a beautiful baby boy."[1]

Catherine had wondered at the absence of news from Spain. Two days earlier, having received nothing from either Fourquevaux or her daughter, she sent a special courier to Spain to inquire. She knew the birth was imminent, maybe already past. Why hadn't her ambassador written? After finishing her letter to Elisabeth, Catherine whipped out another sheet of paper to compose, as usual, a twin missive to Fourquevaux.

Catherine had signed her name when a messenger arrived with Fourquevaux's delayed dispatch from September 24 describing Elisabeth's poor health. Catherine's alarm spiraled. "We are sending you this messenger immediately in all haste," she scrawled to Fourquevaux in a postscript. "I beg you to send me news of the health of the Queen my daughter." Even as she wrote, she tried to calm herself. "Your letter has assured me of her good health. However, as it displeases me to learn that she isn't feeling well, and because I now have some concerns, I would like you to clarify the situation. Use this very same courier to send me your answer."[2]

Minutes later, she wrote a terse note to Philip. "I have learned that the queen, your wife, is very indisposed," she said. "From what I've been told, I believe her illness comes from too much snacking and too much lying about with no exercise." She set down a flurry of advice. Meat only at supper. Two meals a day and only bread in between if Elisabeth grew hungry. No more indulgences; Catherine implored Philip to curb Elisabeth's excesses lest her daughter suffer a serious illness.[3] She told him she would write to Elisabeth herself.

No doubt she did intend to write to her daughter. If she sent the letter, however, it has been lost. Or perhaps she never had the chance to write at all. Because the following day, Catherine learned that Elisabeth was gone.

———

Fourquevaux had found the enormity of his task overwhelming. How does one tell the Queen Mother of France that her beloved daughter is dead? Pushing his pen across the page, he'd wished he were anywhere but at that desk. "Madame, how I wish Our Lord had not willed the terrible news that I must now write to you, even if it were at the cost of my own life. Or I wish that a servant other than myself were telling you this," he began.[4] Fourquevaux narrated the details of Elisabeth's last hours, explaining that she suffered, that death was a release. As best he could, he painted the deathbed scene for the Queen Mother. But he spared her the grittier details of the young woman's agony, describing only moments that might bring Catherine some measure of consolation.

After signing and sealing the letter, Fourquevaux placed it in a diplomatic pouch with other correspondence and reports destined for Paris. The Venetian ambassador in France recounted what happened next. The letter finally landed at the Louvre on October 18—coming not directly to Catherine but rather, as was customary, to one of her secretaries. The clerk broke the seal and scanned the sentences. Then he rose from his desk.

The hapless secretary could not bring himself to convey the message to Catherine. Instead, he informed the Cardinals of Bourbon and Lorraine, thinking that perhaps men of God, so close to the crown, should bring the doleful news to the Queen Mother. No one wanted to be the messenger. The French prelates kept the contents of Fourquevaux's letter to themselves for a full day while considering what to do.

The next morning, they paid a call on the Spanish ambassador, Alava, but the Spaniard respectfully declined the task, unwilling "to undertake an office which would probably ever after render his presence odious to their majesties."[5] In the end, the cardinals took it upon themselves to approach King Charles. It was October 19.

The young king came to Catherine with the two cardinals and several members of his council. As Charles spoke, wrote the Venetian envoy, Catherine's eyes welled with tears. Then, without saying a word, she retreated to her apartments alone.

A few hours later, she emerged again, appearing suddenly in the chamber where Charles and his councillors were deliberating. "God has taken to Himself all of my hopes," she said. "From only His hand do I await solace and assistance. I will wipe away my tears and commit myself alone to the defense and cause of the King my son and of God. Let each and every one of you do as I do so that the Huguenots don't rejoice too quickly over this death. Nor let them believe that the bonds uniting both crowns have broken because of this."

We cannot know what transpired in Catherine's heart during those few hours in seclusion. But, as it so often did, the political side of her would overtake the emotional in the face of unremitting despair. Work, her commitment to the realm, was Catherine's path forward.

Already, she had come to a decision. "The King of Spain cannot remain a widower forever," she announced to Charles and his councillors. "I have only one wish: for my daughter, Marguerite, to marry him and take her sister's place."[6]

In the coming weeks, Catherine seemed to make little room for private grieving. The death of a daughter, even a queen, didn't stop the business of a kingdom, especially not a kingdom at war. Catherine moved through her daily tasks, performing the rituals protocol required. She ordered the court into mourning and hid her tearstained cheeks behind black veils. She dispatched an official consoler to grieve with King Philip, as diplomacy required. From near and far, friends and envoys arrived to mourn with her. She read letters of condolence from Spanish noblemen and noblewomen, assuring her that Elisabeth had made a good end, the finest of Christian deaths. She had died, they said, as well as she had lived.

Still the depth of her grief was apparent to all. Catherine's daughter Claude worried about her mother's health and tried to comfort her, urging her mother to take the long view. Her surviving children and the kingdom needed her now more than ever. "You still have five children living," Claude wrote, "who, in losing you, would lose everything. And so would this poor kingdom, too, which is so afflicted. But with God's help and with yours, Madame, it will soon be at peace."[7]

Catherine wept for her granddaughters the infantas and implored Princess Juana to tend to them. During the coming weeks, the children were committed to the care of Sofonisba Anguissola, their mother's favorite artist and lady-in-waiting. Devastated by Elisabeth's death, Sofonisba said "she did not want to continue living," according to the envoy from the court of Urbino. She agreed to stay in Spain for the infantas, however, and became their first teacher. The little princesses would remain in her care for the next five years, until Sofonisba returned to Italy to marry.[8]

Only on November 13 could Catherine bring herself to write to Philip. "My grief at losing my daughter was so extreme that Your Majesty must excuse me for not writing to comfort you sooner, as would have been reasonable to expect," she told him.[9] To Pope Pius V, Catherine wrote that God works in mysterious ways. Wasn't suffering a mark of His love? Perhaps now God "would content Himself with so many sorrows and miseries as I have had in these past ten years, and most recently the most terrible loss of the queen my daughter." "I don't know how I will bear living without her help," Catherine added, "not only because of my own feelings, but also for the service I believe she paid to God and to all of Christendom." What a gift to have been the mother of such a child. "I count myself very fortunate to have given birth to such a princess. I take great comfort knowing she died a good Catholic. I thank God for giving her such grace."[10]

Catherine grieved as a mother. If, at times, her daughter had proven obstinate, testing her patience, those moments had been few and far between. Had Elisabeth lived longer—long enough to witness the toll the French civil wars would wreak on the kingdom of France— she might have fully endorsed her husband's rigorous policies over her mother's tactical approach to conciliation; what path might the civil wars in France have taken then? But Elisabeth never reached that point. Whether from circumstance or from a natural affinity between them, Elisabeth became Catherine's ally and confidante. Catherine was a controlling mother; she deployed mother's love— and sometimes withheld it—to ensure Elisabeth's obedience. At the same time, her love for her daughter was poignant and sincere. Catherine believed Elisabeth understood her. With Elisabeth's death, her burdens weighed heavier.

Catherine mourned as a queen. The political loss was incalculable. Her great regret, Catherine told Philip, came as much from knowing that Elisabeth had worked "for the conservation of peace and friendship" between the realms as from any personal grief. What would happen to their friendship now?

She would do her best to safeguard that alliance. Now a widower, Philip still needed a male heir. Surely, he would marry again soon. Though she held out hope for Margot, Catherine suspected Philip eyed his own niece, Anna of Austria, the young girl Catherine coveted for King Charles. Anna was now the most desirable bride in Europe. Just shy of eighteen in the autumn of 1568, she was a Hapsburg princess, daughter of the Holy Roman Emperor and a Spanish Hapsburg mother. Fresh-faced and flaxen-haired, Anna was untainted by the Protestantism that tarnished Elizabeth Tudor's appeal as a bride, uncrippled by the scandals that preceded Mary Stuart's fall from grace. Anna was born to be her husband's helpmeet, a queen consort unburdened by the pressures of a sovereign crown. If Philip married Anna, whom would that leave for Charles IX? Even in her mourning, Catherine couldn't abandon the needs of her son.

She wrote a kind but firm letter to Fourquevaux, her devoted servant waiting miserably in Madrid for her instructions. So distraught was the envoy at Elisabeth's death that he asked Catherine to end his commission early. "Having received so many honors and favors from the late queen your daughter in my embassy, it would cause me much grief to remain here any longer," he wrote.[11] But Catherine insisted Fourquevaux stay in Spain a little while yet. He understood the landscape; he was diplomatic and discreet. She needed Fourquevaux to find out Philip's thoughts on the matter of marriage so she could preserve the ties between the kingdoms. "You must take heart in the satisfaction you give to the King my son," she wrote.[12] Stay strong, she meant. There was still much work to do.

———

The tributes to Elisabeth didn't end with her burial. For nine days, requiem Masses were sung at every church in Madrid. Philip had retreated to the monastery of San Jerónimo, in the heart of the city, accompanied by his confessor and Ruy Gómez. There, he mourned mostly in solitude, hearing Mass twice daily.[13]

Writers sharpened their quills. Printers slathered the types with ink and pulled the press. Like a royal wedding, a queen's death was an occasion for state propaganda. Pamphlets narrating the official account of Elisabeth's funeral flooded bookstalls in Madrid. Translated into French, Italian, and Latin (the languages of good Catholics), the pamphlets flew across borders, spreading the story of the Catholic Queen's exemplary end.

France would produce its own memorials. Printed in Paris the year after her death, *The Tomb of the most high and mighty, the most*

Catholic princess Madame Elisabeth of France, Queen of Spain exalted Elisabeth in manifold languages—French and Spanish, as well as the venerated languages of Hebrew, Greek, and Latin, as if the Queen of Spain bridged all boundaries, both ancient and new. She was the "daughter, sister, and wife of kings," wrote the poet Antoine de Baif. "A balm of sweetness" and "a flower of piety," passed between realms as "a wager of peace and holy alliance." Another poet, taking a darker tack, wrote of how death had "ravished her in the spring of her age." Still other poems, composed in Elisabeth's voice—a common device in the sixteenth century—tried to understand why she had gone. "I wished to join my celestial husband," read one sonnet, as if Elisabeth spoke from the grave. Now she would intervene with another king, her Lord and Savior, on behalf of her mortal family on earth. "I plead with God Almighty to rain down Victory and Peace together" on the kingdoms of her husband and brother, racked by civil war and almost "deprived of all hope." She had departed to save them all.[14]

Other people grieved privately, grappling with their sorrow in bits of verse shared only with friends. Brantôme wrote one such epitaph. He'd always admired Elisabeth, noting how kind she was to him, how welcoming and generous during his assignments in Spain. Brantôme's poem was published only after his own death.

> Beneath this marble stone lies Elisabeth of France
> Who was once Queen of Spain and Queen of peace
> Christian and Catholic. In her beauty
> She served us all. Now, as her noble bones
> Lie withering beneath the earth,
> We have nothing but wickedness, troubles and war.[15]

He despaired of what her death portended.

———

On the day Elisabeth died, as he wrote his letter to Catherine, Fourquevaux understood the delicate task before him. The words he laid on the page would be of immeasurable importance. He tried to be gentle, knowing the cruelty of his message. But Fourquevaux remained Catherine's dutiful servant. Even when delivering the worst news imaginable, he wished to be of service.

Elisabeth's last words, the ambassador told Catherine, were not for her husband. Rather, they were for her mother. As Fourquevaux arrived at the bedside of the dying queen, Elisabeth opened her eyes. "She suddenly recognized me and said, 'Monsieur Ambassador, you see me about to leave this miserable world for a more pleasant kingdom where I hope to be with God in eternal glory. I beg you to ask the Queen, my mother, and the King, my brother, to endure my death patiently and to take solace in knowing that I am content—happier than from anything in this world—to go toward my Creator, where I hope to be able to serve them better. I will pray to God for them, and for my brothers and sister, that He keep them ever more in His holy protection.* Please, I ask you to beg them on my behalf to extinguish the heresy in their kingdom. I am praying now and will always pray to God to show them the way. Let them endure my death patiently and know that I am glad to die.'"[16]

In her final hour, Elisabeth remained bound to both kingdoms. Fourquevaux told a powerful story of a daughter's love and obedience. Here, then, were the last words of the queen of peace, the Catholic Queen of Spain who balanced devotion to her husband with loyalty to her mother.

Eventually, some of Fourquevaux's letter would filter into the world. Official eulogies borrowed snippets of his language to narrate the story of Elisabeth's exemplary end. But the ambassador had written his letter with only Catherine in mind. He told the story of Elisabeth that Catherine the queen would want everyone to know. And he told the story Catherine the mother needed to hear, so that she could continue to do the work of a queen. This was his last service to both mother and daughter—a parting gift.

---

*Elisabeth spoke of her "sister" in the singular. She was referring to Margot. Her sister Claude was alive and well but married and settled with her own children. Elisabeth was thinking of her younger siblings, still impressionable, in need of God's protection and Catherine's guidance.

EPILOGUE

In the end, Mary thought mostly of France.

In the small hours of February 8, 1587, Mary Stuart sat at her writing desk and pulled out a piece of fine French paper. She was forty-four years old and had spent half her life a prisoner. For almost twenty years she'd lived under house arrest in England, most of that time in the custody of the Earl of Shrewsbury and his wife, Bess of Hardwick. Her wardens had moved her the previous October to Fotheringay Castle in Northamptonshire for her trial. Now, still in Fotheringay on a cold winter's night, Mary couldn't sleep. It was around two o'clock in the morning. Her execution was scheduled for later that day.[1]

She had been caught in the Babington Plot of 1586. Supported by Spain, the conspirators, led by an English Catholic nobleman named Anthony Babington, had vowed to assassinate Elizabeth Tudor and set Mary Stuart on the English throne, the first of several acts intended to return England to the papacy. As part of the plan, and in tandem with the assassination, Spain would embark on a full-scale invasion of England. In the face of the Protestant onslaught sweeping the Continent, Philip's support of Elizabeth Tudor had faded away years before.

Was Mary an active participant in the plot? On July 17, the Queen of Scots wrote the letter to Anthony Babington that would seal her fate. Outlining three ways she could be rescued, Mary advised Babington to "set the six gentlemen to work"—a covert way of saying that the assassination should go forward. Mary didn't realize that Elizabeth Tudor's spymaster, the wily Sir Francis Walsingham, had contrived to intercept all of Mary's correspondence using an elaborate scheme involving several double agents and a brewer who supplied Mary's household with beer. Walsingham knew every detail of the Babington Plot as it unfolded, often before some of the plotters themselves. Mary's letter to the hapless Babington fell into the spymaster's hands. At last, Walsingham had what he needed to damn the Queen of Scots.

Of the thirty noblemen who comprised Mary's jury at Fotheringay Castle in October 1586, all but one found her guilty.

Seated at her desk, Mary set quill to page. She would write her last letter not to Queen Elizabeth, or to her son King James VI of Scotland, but rather to King Henri III of France, once her ally, friend, and brother-in-law. In clear script, she declared herself innocent of any treachery against Elizabeth Tudor. She insisted on her fidelity to the Catholic faith. She reminded King Henri that, as a child, he had loved her like a sister. She asked him to pray for her, she who had once been "the Most Christian Queen . . . who dies a Catholic, stripped of all her possessions."

Mostly, Mary wished to return home, an unlikely possibility. "I have been unable to have my body conveyed after my death, as I would wish, to your kingdom where I had the honor to be your queen, sister, and old ally," she wrote to Henri. She signed as she had since childhood: *Mari.*[2]

At about ten o'clock that morning, her head fell away upon a scaffold erected in the Great Hall of Fotheringay Castle, in front of three hundred witnesses. It took two full blows and another quick clip of the axe to finish the job.

Just a few hours after she wrote it, Mary's letter left her chambers in the careful keeping of her physician. One month later, the news arrived at the French court. "Among all the troubles that now plague me in this miserable time," Catherine de' Medici wrote to a correspondent, Monsieur de Bellièvre, on March 8, "the cruel treatment of the Queen of Scots, Madame my daughter-in-law, so augments the afflictions I suffer that, yesterday, when I learned the news I remained completely seized with shock." The offense of it stung. Her son, King Henri III, had sent special envoys to England the previous October on Mary's behalf, and Catherine herself wrote several letters in her own hand to Elizabeth Tudor, pleading Mary's case, to no avail.

Yet, as in so many things to do with Mary Stuart, Catherine feigned some of her dismay; the words she wrote to Bellièvre were ultimately intended for others. Rumors of Mary's death had in fact reached her a full week earlier. "You see what they are telling me about the Queen of Scots," she had confided to the same Monsieur de Bellièvre on March 1, the note scribbled in a postscript, her tone more calculating than shocked. "I am sending a note . . . to find out if it is true."[3]

———

Afflictions plagued Catherine, indeed. She reigned over a house with an uncertain future. After Charles IX died in 1574, her favorite son acceded to the French throne as King Henri III. Married since 1575, Henri and his wife, Louise de Lorraine, a Guise cousin, would wait in vain for a baby.

Catherine never ceased working toward marriages designed to benefit France. In 1579, the Queen Mother opened negotiations for a wedding between Queen Elizabeth of England and Catherine's youngest son, the twenty-four-year-old Francis, Duke of Alençon, heir presumptive to the French throne. In 1579, Elizabeth seriously considered the "French match," as it came to be called. Eager to encourage the Dutch Protestant rebellion against Catholic Spain (a revolt she happily funded) and to show off English strength, Elizabeth wagered that a French marriage would intimidate Philip II.

Catherine de' Medici, too, wished to intimidate her former son-in-law. By 1579, Spain had become France's enemy. Without the peacemaking of Elisabeth de Valois, the charade of an alliance had broken down. The Spanish barely concealed their support of reactionary French Catholics who battled both French Protestants and the conciliatory policies of the crown. As for the French, a swathe of the nobility still remembered the ancient rivalry between the kingdoms of France and Spain. Their hatred was hardwired, an easy habit to pick up again once Elisabeth de Valois was dead.

For Catherine, the rivalry with Spain had become almost personal. A decade earlier, in 1570, Philip had rejected her own daughter, Margot, and married his Hapsburg niece, Anna of Austria, the young woman Catherine coveted as a bride for her son Charles. In

June of that year, moreover, Catherine discovered that the Spanish envoy Chantonnay, now stationed in Germany, bragged openly that he had successfully stalled the marriage of Anna of Austria and Charles for five or six years, knowing that Elisabeth de Valois didn't have long to live.[4] Catherine had always despised Chantonnay; that he had predicted her daughter's death was almost more than she could bear. In retaliation, Catherine helped fuel stories that Philip had poisoned both Don Carlos and Elisabeth in a fit of jealous vengeance. The story only fanned French anti-Spanish feelings. Elisabeth de Valois's memory became a tool in the ever-bleaker war of slander.

Beyond politics, both Catherine de' Medici and Elizabeth Tudor harbored personal reasons to hope the French–English marriage might come to fruition. Ambitious for her sons, Catherine hoped to see Alençon crowned King of England. She also wanted to see him settled. A striving youngest son with a wild streak, Alençon longed to help the Dutch against the Spanish, despite his own Catholic beliefs. Worried about his troublemaking in the Netherlands, Catherine wanted the young man under Elizabeth's control.

As for Elizabeth Tudor, she had reached her midforties. If ever she'd hoped to marry and bear a child, Francis, Duke of Alençon, was her last chance.

He arrived on English shores in August 1579, the only suitor ever to meet Queen Elizabeth in person. Despite the twenty-year difference in their ages, Elizabeth found Alençon charming and set about charming him in return.

Would she really marry him? Judging by their fierce opposition, the English feared she might go through with it. To Elizabeth's surprise, xenophobia and religious hatred flared. Englishmen of all stripes hated the idea of a foreign match. English Protestants, especially, could not forgive the French crown for the Saint Bartholomew's Day massacre, an atrocity that had occurred seven years earlier in 1572 and had galvanized European Protestantism ever since.

Religious tensions had roiled Paris throughout the sweltering summer of 1572. That August was especially scorching. The capital—the most unwavering of French Catholic cities—was on edge as Protestants began arriving in droves for the wedding of the royal princess Margot to the first prince of the blood, Henri de Bourbon, King of Navarre—the son of Antoine de Bourbon and Jeanne d'Albret. Catherine de' Medici had devised the wedding to reconcile the French Protestant and Catholic factions after three civil wars: compromise and conciliation remained her strategy. The Parisians, however, did not share her vision. As the streets thronged with outsiders and the hostels teemed, the atmosphere on the streets grew tense.

The wedding took place on August 18. On the twenty-second, as Admiral Gaspard de Coligny returned to his lodgings after a meeting at the palace, he heard a shot ring out. A chance flick of his wrist deflected the bullet, and Coligny managed to return to his lodgings, wounded but alive. Most historians believe the Guises had hired the would-be assassin, pursuing their old vendetta against Coligny for the death of the Duke of Guise in 1561. But no one knows for sure who ordered the assassination.

Two days later, on August 24, the young Duke of Guise and his followers showed up at Coligny's rooms to finish the job. After throwing the slain Coligny from a window onto the street below, the young men dragged the body through the streets, dumped it in the Seine, then fished it out again. Decapitating the corpse, they skewered Coligny's head on a pike.

No one seems to have anticipated what happened next. The assassination triggered a mob reaction that surprised even the Duke of Guise. Over the coming days, thousands of Protestants died, by pike, sword, and dagger; they were pushed from rooftops and windows, suffocated in their beds, drowned in the Seine. Catholics killed Protestants. Frenchmen killed both compatriots and foreigners. Neighbors murdered neighbors, using religion to justify settling old grudges. Pregnant women were stabbed and strangled. Children were not spared. The killing began on the eve of the feast day of Saint Bartholomew. It lasted for at least four days before the crown could quell the violence.

Huguenots would blame the French crown for the massacre. They cited the long-ago family reunion at Bayonne between Catherine de' Medici and Elisabeth de Valois as the moment the nefarious plan began to take shape. Elizabeth Tudor took out her anger on Mary Stuart, at the time still her prisoner. In the wake of Saint Bartholomew's Day, the Queen of Scots' retinue was reduced to a mere nine servants.

And yet, in 1579, Queen Elizabeth pondered a marriage to a French Catholic prince, almost as if the brutal slaughter of her co-religionists had never taken place. The English wouldn't have it. Privy Councillor Christopher Hatton commissioned the famous portrait of Elizabeth holding a sieve—a symbol of the Roman vestal virgins—as if to remind his queen that she was supposed to remain immaculate. The celebrated poet-soldier-courtier Philip Sidney openly circulated a letter calling Catherine de' Medici the "Jezebel of our age." In his *Gaping Gulf*, the pamphleteer John Stubbs cast Catherine de' Medici as "the treacherous French Queen Mother" while pointing out that, at Elizabeth's advanced age, childbirth posed excessive risks to her health.[5] She was forty-six. Elizabeth exacted vengeance. On a scaffold, Stubbs lost his right hand.

But many English subjects agreed with Stubbs, and Elizabeth's own reluctance surged anew. Although the French match enjoyed one last gasp in 1581, and Alençon once again sailed to England, Queen Elizabeth packed him off with a ring, a kiss, and a promise to treat him as "a brother and a friend."[6] He was disappointed; she would think of him and sadden at the memory.

In 1584, Alençon sickened and died in Paris, his Dutch enterprises having ended in disaster. Elizabeth grieved sincerely and sent her written condolences to Catherine, painstakingly striking out words until the tone was just right. She shared Catherine's grief, though surely "your sorrow," she told the Queen Mother, ". . . cannot be greater than my own. For inasmuch as you are his mother, so it is that there remain to you several other children. But for me, I find no consolation except death, which I hope will soon reunite us."[7] Her wish was thwarted. Elizabeth would remain alive and mostly well for another nineteen years.

With her final refusal of the Duke of Alençon, Elizabeth had rejected marriage for good. She had avoided the fate of queens like Elisabeth de Valois and Mary Stuart, the pitfalls of a wife's obedience to a husband, the perils of childbirth. Unwed, she had consolidated her authority as queen, transforming herself into the mother exclusively of her people, an English sovereign devoted only to England. Her enduring reign turned on a certain irony: she had succeeded as queen by defying the demands made of royal women. But at what cost? Like her older sister Mary Tudor, Elizabeth would leave the kingdom without a clear legacy, without an heir of her body. The bloodline and dynasty of the Tudors, of her father Henry VIII, would end with her.

And like that same older sister, who lived her last years abandoned by her husband, Philip II, Elizabeth would remain alone.

———

They were two sides of the same coin, two survivors: Catherine de' Medici and Elizabeth Tudor, consort and sovereign, mother and virgin. Catherine, shrouded in her black veils; Elizabeth Tudor, enfolded in her billowing ruffs and the expanding cult of her virginity. For a decade after the collapse of the French match, Elizabeth promoted that virginity into almost mythic status in the eyes of her subjects. In the wake of Mary Stuart's execution and the defeat of the Spanish Armada the following year, English national pride swelled, launching what amounted to an industry of portraiture and propaganda around the queen. Paintings exalted Elizabeth, comparing her to the Roman virgin goddess Diana and to the Virgin Mary.

At the end of August 1588, sixty-seven ships had straggled back to Spain, scarcely more than half of the 130-strong fleet that had set off the previous May on what the Spanish called the "English Enterprise." Some of the returning vessels were so battle-weary, so damaged by stormy seas, that they had to be held together by cables. As many as 15,000 men had perished, 5,000 alone in the final leg of the journey as ships foundered off the coasts of Scotland and Ireland. Better English naval technology played some part in the Armada's defeat, as did the savvy deployment of fireships. But the most important factor was mere accident. In one of the worst sailing seasons in years, storms savaged the Spanish fleet, more destructive than any English naval savoir faire. To Queen Elizabeth and her elated subjects, the storms were a sure sign of God's favor.

Philip II recoiled at the thought. "I hope that God has not permitted so much evil," he scribbled on one particularly painful report of the disaster. "Because everything has been done for His service." But other excruciating reports soon arrived at his desk. "Very soon we shall find ourselves in such a state that we shall wish that we had never been born," Philip wrote.[8]

Painted sometime in 1588, the *Armada Portrait* celebrated Elizabeth as queen of the world. She appears larger than life, her mantle, overskirt, and bodice popping with large red ribbons, an elaborate lace ruff framing her face. The painting bursts with symbols of English supremacy. As waves pound Spanish ships in the background, in the calm serenity of the foreground Elizabeth caresses a globe: for Philip II the world was not enough, but now Elizabeth holds the world in her hand. In the lower right corner of the tableau there is a small mermaid statue—a reference, perhaps, to one of the pamphlets that had circulated in the wake of Darnley's death, depicting Mary, Queen of Scots, as an adulterous siren. The symbolism of the statue was powerful: now the siren sat, immobilized, in Elizabeth's possession.

And around her neck, Elizabeth wears rope after rope of glistening pearls, some "as large as nutmegs." Were these pearls yet another symbol of Elizabeth's dominance over Europe's sovereigns, over Europe's queens? Scholars have wondered if these were the same pearls that once belonged to Mary Stuart; if so, were they perhaps the pearls Catherine had given the Queen of Scots as a wedding gift, the ones Catherine brought with her from Italy? Elizabeth Tudor purchased the strands in 1568 when the Scottish regent Lord James, in need of cash, sold off much of the deposed Scottish queen's jewelry. Catherine de' Medici had tried to buy them herself, but Elizabeth outbid her in the end.[9]

Elizabeth Tudor would prevail in another way. The English queen outlived her rival Mary and her namesake Elisabeth de Valois, and she would outlive her French counterpart Catherine de' Medici, too. In January 1589, one year after the defeat of the Spanish Armada,

Catherine died at the age of sixty-nine. Elizabeth Tudor lived long enough to usher in the new century. She died in 1603, also at the age of sixty-nine, never having named an heir. Her Protestant councillors would work hard to ensure that the English crown passed to the Protestant James VI of Scotland. Mary Stuart's estranged son would become James I of England.

––––––

In the closing years of her life, Catherine struggled with grief, sickness, and an impending sense of doom. Almost all her children had died: her daughter Claude had succumbed to childbirth in 1575, and Alençon died nearly a decade later. Of Catherine's ten children, only Margot and Henri, her favorite son, still lived. Meanwhile, the kingdom of France was descending into a state of near-chaos.

The death of Alençon in 1584 provoked a succession crisis that spurred fresh hostilities in the kingdom. With King Henri III and his wife still barren, the throne was now slated to pass to the first prince of the blood: Catherine's Protestant son-in-law, Henri de Bourbon, King of Navarre. In response, ultra-Catholic Frenchmen formed an alliance known as the Catholic League, led by the newest generation of Guise men, chief among them Anne d'Este's eldest son, the Duke of Guise. In 1584, the League and the Guises secured the support of Philip II of Spain with the Treaty of Joinville.

The Catholic League quickly grew so powerful that King Henri III was forced to concede to their demands: in 1585, he agreed to the Peace of Nemours, which forbade Protestantism in France and deprived the Protestant King of Navarre of his right to the throne, paving the way for the Guises to install their own candidate. The concessions did nothing to subdue the League, however, or to repair King Henri's deep unpopularity with the people, or to stave off the menace of war. Instead, the threat of renewed violence only grew as the Huguenots panicked, reassembled their forces, and sought the assistance of Elizabeth Tudor.

In her final years, Catherine watched her son's authority slip away as Protestants rallied around the King of Navarre, and Catholics flocked to the magnetic Duke of Guise and his kin. On May 12, 1588, the king was utterly humiliated when Parisian Catholics erected barricades throughout the city in support of the Duke of Guise. As the duke strode through the streets, trying to calm the mob on behalf of the king, the people shouted rebelliously, "Vive Guise!" instead of "Vive le roi!" Though he admonished the people, the duke knew the hearts and minds of Parisians belonged to him. From that moment on, King Henri III plotted his revenge.[10]

Frequent illness during her final months kept Catherine from her son's council chamber, though she often worked from her sickbed while secretaries perched at its foot, scribbling letters and reports. She suffered from a panoply of ailments, her joints swollen from chronic rheumatism and gout, her lungs inflamed by a persistent cough, her teeth aching. She managed to rise from her bed on December 8 to attend the betrothal ceremony of her beloved granddaughter Christine de Lorraine—the child of Claude, Catherine's second daughter—to Catherine's far-distant cousin, Ferdinand de' Medici, Grand Duke of Tuscany. The Queen Mother rejoiced at the coming nuptials and hosted a ball for the new couple. But she may have found the celebrations bittersweet. Soon enough, the Queen Mother knew, Christine would leave with her new husband for Florence, retracing the path the teenaged Catherine had followed long ago.

Of all her granddaughters, Catherine was especially close to Christine. The Queen Mother had never met Elisabeth de Valois's children, Isabel Clara Eugenia and Catalina Micaela, though she kept up an energetic correspondence with them both. Unlike her Spanish cousins, Christine de Lorraine had grown up at the French court, frequently spending time in Catherine's company.* On December 15, Catherine returned to her bed. A diplomat noted that Christine's imminent departure would surely worsen the Queen Mother's condition.[11]

The final blow arrived in late December when King Henri orchestrated the brutal murders of the Duke of Guise and his younger brother, the Cardinal of Guise. The duke was assassinated in Henri's

---

*Christine was twenty-three when she married and had spent more time with Catherine than any of Catherine's own daughters, except perhaps for Margot. Following in her grandmother's footsteps, Christine would become a dominant force in Florentine politics, advising her grandson, the Grand Duke Ferdinand II, after the deaths of her husband and son. She also became an important patron of science and the arts. Her most notable beneficiary was Galileo.

presence on the twenty-third, while several other Guise family members were arrested. On the twenty-fourth, the cardinal was dragged from his prison and hacked to death, his body later burned alongside his brother's. Shortly after the murders, King Henri came to his mother's chambers and found her in bed, attended by a physician.

"Good day Madame. Please forgive me," he began. "Monsieur de Guise is dead. He will not be spoken of again. I have had him killed. I have done to him what he was going to do to me." "I want to be a king," he went on, "and no longer a prisoner and a slave." How Catherine responded to her son remains unknown.[12]

But on Christmas Day, she gave in to despair. "Oh, wretched man!" she is said to have confided to a priest. "What has he done? . . . Say your prayers for him, for he needs them more than ever. I see him rushing toward his ruin. I am afraid he may lose his body, soul and kingdom." Her health never recovered. Though she appeared to rally slightly for a few days, by January 4, 1589, she had a high fever. She signed her will on the fifth, asked for a confessor, and took communion. Soon after swallowing the host, at one thirty in the afternoon, she breathed her last.[13]

In the days after Catherine's death, Catholic magistrate Etienne Pasquier expressed his deep respect for the Queen Mother. "One cannot deny that she brought the greatest prudence to bear on the path of her fate," he told his son. "That a foreign princess, after the death of the king her husband, would know how to safeguard the state for her three [sons], all very young, even amid France's troubles, all the more so because of religion! These are no small things . . . It was she alone, finally, who orchestrated the pacifications between the king and his subjects." She had remained strong even in the face of great sorrow, including the deaths of most of her sons and of her daughters Claude and "Elisabeth, the Queen of Spain [who] . . . died a horrible death, if one is to believe what one hears."* So moved was Pasquier by Catherine's reign that he composed an epitaph for her. With her death, he saw little hope for France:

This lady armed with a great heart
Defending against the blows of hate and enmity

*This is a reference to the rumor that Philip II arranged for the death of both Elisabeth and Don Carlos.

She alone closed the door on our troubles.
At last, she has died on this Eve of the Epiphany
And through her death I fear, people of France,
That along with peace, royalty has also died.

Yet Pasquier knew that Catherine's critics disputed the merits of her reign and the brilliance of her legacy. "They claim that although she pretended to pacify everything when all of France was aflame," he wrote, "it was she who lit the fires and afterward pretended to extinguish them. For she had this proposition imprinted on her soul: that a princess, especially a foreign one, can only maintain her grandeur by sowing divisiveness among the princes and great lords, a lesson whose instruction and memory was imparted to the late Queen of Scots when she returned to her kingdom of Scotland after the death of her husband, King Francis II."[14]

Catherine died both beloved and hated. For the final fifteen years of her life, her critics had pummeled her with increasing vehemence, accusing her of duplicity and Machiavellian treachery. Her reputation never entirely recovered from the 1572 Saint Bartholomew's Day massacre. Were the killings planned? Did Catherine know? No one in the sixteenth century could answer these questions and no one can answer them now. King Charles and the Queen Mother probably knew of a plan, limited in scope, to eliminate the Huguenot leadership. If so, that plan went woefully awry. Afterward, Catherine bungled the narrative. The master storyteller could not account for the murder of thousands of French subjects. At first, Charles repudiated the violence. Just days later, he ordered his envoys to change their story and announce his triumph over French heretics. But how likely is it that Catherine, the queen of compromise, would approve the wholescale massacre?

In the aftermath of the killings, she was condemned both by Huguenots and by all those who detested her conciliatory policies. In Geneva, a self-exiled Huguenot named François Dubois made a painting of the Paris massacre, scattering bodies over a wood panel in a sixteenth-century version of the biblical Massacre of the Innocents. Like an angel of death, Catherine, arrayed in her black widow's weeds, looms over a pile of corpses stripped naked, the flesh already graying.

The pamphlet wars began. A particularly vicious tract known as the *Marvelous Discourse*, published across Europe in several languages between 1575 and 1576, dredged up an old accusation, long buried but never quite forgotten. Catherine's perfidy stemmed from her Florentine Medici origins, the pamphlet charged. Everyone knew Florentines were liars and thieves, the worst of all Italians. As for the Medici themselves, they descended from the "dregs of the people," mere tradesmen who had lifted themselves up through scheming and subterfuge. Catherine came "from very low stock . . . the French nobility should never expect from her anything but utter disgrace and destruction so long as she is allowed to govern."[15]

These were narratives that would endure. Yet Catherine herself refused defeat, dipping into her deep well of fortitude. She read the *Marvelous Discourse* in its entirety yet refused to seek out and punish its author. Instead, the French crown issued its own propaganda, hailing her as a "heroine." Descended from the esteemed "Medici family, so fecund in illustrious men," and from "Madeleine de Boulogne, born into the royal house of France," Catherine was the queen of queens, an "example to all princes."[16] She was a Bourbon. She was royal. She was French.

During solitary moments, Catherine may have looked back privately, too, telling herself a different story from the one given in the *Marvelous Discourse*. Sometime after the tragedy of Saint Bartholomew, she ordered artists to paint a series of exquisite, palm-sized portraits and paste them into a precious book of hours that King Francis I had given her long ago. There, amid the prayers, were pictures of King Francis II and Mary Stuart; King Charles and his wife Elisabeth of Austria; Catherine's husband, King Henry II, and her father-in-law, Francis I. There were her daughter Claude and her children, now scions of the House of Lorraine; there, too, were her own long-dead infants, Louis, Jeanne, and Victoire. Margot, crowned Queen of Navarre, appeared next to her husband, Henri of Navarre. There was Philip II, his hands clasped in prayer, Elisabeth de Valois beside him.[17]

Here was the family Catherine had built. Far from a mother-destroyer, she was a mother-creator, the tie binding great houses and kingdoms together, linking the old French nobility to the new.

And the kingdom of France still needed Catherine. Indeed, during the tumultuous reign of Henri III, France needed her more than ever. Catherine traveled the realm in the name of her son, negotiating parleys and truces, even forging a brief alliance between Henri and the King of Navarre, although it did not last. She felt the toll of work and the strain of age. Her muscles stiffened and her sciatica flared. She gave up her horse for a mule because its gait was gentler, though she would never settle for a sedan chair—as she told her friend the Duchess of Uzès, a litter would not suffice because she liked "to travel far."

Once, on one of her forays for King Henri, she crossed into a terrain so riddled with plague that birds dropped dead from the sky. She changed route, threading the roads "between the swamps and the sea," and made plans to spend two nights in a tent. "We will camp for the service of my king," Catherine declared.

She kept on, of course, anyhow.[18]

NOTES

PROLOGUE

1 The events of the night of July 20, 1530, are given in Niccolini 182–83, Nardi, Vol. 9, pp. 370–71, and Varchi 388–90, though the sources vary in some of their details. Niccolini errs in her dates; Cloulas clarifies, *Catherine de Médicis*, 42.
2 The history and practices of the convent are explained in Niccolini. For the significance of the wooden door, see Niccolini 87. Niccolini describes the guns as "harquebuses," which, in the sixteenth century, meant a long-barreled gun that was the precursor to the musket.
3 Niccolini 182.
4 Niccolini 183.
5 Nardi, Vol. 9, p. 371; Niccolini 183.
6 Varchi 389–90.
7 Niccolini 184.
8 Guicciardini, *Sack of Rome*, 432.
9 Varchi 559; Cloulas, *Catherine de Médicis*, 43; *Lettres*, Vol. 1, p. iv.

CHAPTER 1: THE ORPHAN

1 For quotations cited from non-English-language primary and secondary sources, all translations are mine unless otherwise noted. Quotations taken from English-language texts are given as translated in the source. I have modernized spelling for sixteenth-century English and Scottish citations.
   Knecht, *Renaissance Warrior*, 105.
2 Reumont and Baschet 251.
3 Guicciardini, *Storie fiorentine* (1509), cited in Reumont and Baschet 218.
4 Fleuranges 226; Mariéjol 17.
5 Reumont and Baschet 37, 256.

6 Marco Minio, the Venetian ambassador, reported to the *Signoria* on April 28; reproduced in Reumont and Baschet 257.

7 Reumont and Baschet 262.

8 On childhood in early modern Europe, see Ariès; Alexandre-Bidon and Lett; Orme. On the Renaissance garden, see Shepherd and Jellicoe; Lazzaro.

9 Orme 204–209.

10 On Madeleine's pedigree, see Brantôme, ed. Moland, 34–36; Baluze, Vol. 2, pp. 686–87.

11 "Cronica di Firenze dell'anno 1501 al 1546," appendix to *Archivio storico italiano* VII (1849), 133; cited in Mariéjol 20.

12 Cohen, ed., 28.

13 Reiss 137.

14 Stuart 22, 170; Baluze, Vol. 2, pp. 688–89.

15 The reasons for the move remain unclear. It seems likely, however, that Clement had ordered Clarice to return Caterina to Florence to ensure a continued Medici presence in the city, now that he had moved to the Vatican.

16 Guicciardini, *History of Italy*, 382–86; Guicciardini, *Sack of Rome*, passim.

17 Guicciardini, *History of Italy*, 376–77.

18 Cloulas, *Catherine de Médicis*, 39; Stephens 429; Niccolini 124–25.

19 Niccolini passim; Mariéjol 29.

20 Varchi, Vol. 2, p. 389.

21 Niccolini 181.

22 Niccolini 184.

23 La Ferrière-Percy and Bagenault de Puchesse, eds, *Lettres de Catherine de Médicis* (hereafter *Lettres*), Vol. 1, p. iv.

24 *Lettres*, Vol. 1, pp. 1–2.

25 Varchi, Vol. 2, p. 390; Cloulas, *Catherine de Médicis*, 42.

26 Niccolini 183.

27 *Lettres*, Vol. 10, pp. 112, 331.

28 Cloulas, *Catherine de Médicis*, 51.

29 Brantôme, ed. Lalanne, Vol. 7, p. 340; Reumont and Baschet 147–56, 182.

30 For a few months, Clement considered marrying Caterina to Alessandro de' Medici, whom Clement had named Duke of Florence. It seems likely that Alessandro was not an orphan, but rather Clement's illegitimate son.

31 Frieda 26; Knecht, *Catherine de' Medici*, 14–15. Unfortunately, Vasari's portrait has not survived.

32 *Lettres*, Vol. I, p. I. Shortly after writing this first letter in French, Catherine wrote two others in Italian to Albany—Caterina's first language was still easier for her.

CHAPTER 2: THE SECOND SON

1 Anne of France 39, 43; Vives 80–93.
2 Reumont and Baschet 323.
3 "Relation anonyme des ceremonies du mariage 1533," in Reumont and Baschet 323, n. I.
4 Claude was the eldest daughter of the previous French king, Louis XII.
5 Baumgartner 3–4.
6 Knecht, *Renaissance Warrior*, 218–22. Francis laid claim to Milan through his Italian paternal great-grandmother Valentina Visconti, the daughter of the first Duke of Milan.
7 Louise de Savoy 410–11.
8 Baumgartner 282, n. 9; Knecht, *Renaissance Warrior*, 248.
9 Baumgartner 16, 19.
10 Whether the boys refused to speak French out of suspicion, or whether they were in fact suffering from a version of Stockholm syndrome that made them identify more with their Spanish captors, remains a mystery. Baudin's account is included in the *Cabinet Historique*, 226–27.
11 In fact, before Margaret of Austria could mobilize her network in Spain, Charles V's wife, Isabella of Portugal, sent fresh supplies after she heard details of the boys' living conditions. At the time, her own son Philip, who would eventually rule as Philip II, was just three years old—a fact that may have inspired even greater pity in Isabella for the French princes.
12 Baumgartner 18, 34; Frieda 37.
13 Baumgartner 40–41; Knecht, *Renaissance Warrior*, 545–49.
14 Cloulas, *Catherine de Médicis*, 57; Knecht, *Catherine de' Medici*, 28.
15 Cloulas, *Catherine de Médicis*, 57; Knecht, *Catherine de' Medici*, 28. The arrangement—a marriage between the French prince Charles and the Spanish princess Maria or, alternatively, a niece of Charles V—was part of yet another peace treaty, known as the Peace of Crépy, between King Francis and Charles V of Spain. Francis's son Charles died suddenly, however, in 1545, before the terms of the treaty could be fulfilled.
16 Charlier et al., "Gold," 339; Wellman 186, 195–6; Cloulas, *Diane de Poitiers*, 78, n. 30.
17 Tommaseo, ed., Vol. I, p. 286.

18 Cloulas, *Diane de Poitiers*, 103.

19 Cloulas, *Diane de Poitiers*, 78–79.

20 Knecht, *Renaissance Warrior*, 125.

21 Brantôme, ed. Lalanne, Vol. 7, p. 345. Catherine's letter on the black-work sleeves cited in Frieda 51.

22 Brantôme claims Catherine invented the sidesaddle and was a skilled horsewoman, Vol. 7, pp. 344–45. Knecht, *Renaissance Warrior*, 111.

23 When Marguerite wrote her famous *Heptaméron*, a collection of spirited short stories, she claimed Catherine was one of the storytellers who inspired her.

24 Cholakian and Skemp, eds., 5; Wellman 151–58.

25 "Copy of Letters sent to the Queen Mother by one of her Servants after the Death of the Late King Henri II," in Cazauran, ed., 285.

26 See Dandolo in Alberi, *Caterina de'Medici*, 47–48.

27 *Calendar of State Papers* (hereafter *CSP*) *Spain*, Vol. 5:1, December 7, 1535, #232 n. 4.

28 Catherine to Maria Salviati, State Archive of Florence, Medici Aventi Principale (MAP), Dpc. 197, folio 197, 1534; cf. Frieda 51.

29 Baumgartner 32; Bourrilly 247.

30 Bourrilly 229, 233; Guiffrey 188–89; Knecht, *Renaissance Warrior*, 337.

31 Frieda 54.

32 Riddle, esp. 135–57.

33 Antonio de Beatis, *Travel Journal*, 107; cited in Wellmann 120.

34 Wellmann 120, 123; Knecht, *Renaissance Warrior*, 114.

CHAPTER 3: BARREN

1 Gélis 46–48, 59; Bourgeois 51; Guillemeau in Worth-Stylianou, ed., 7.

2 Parsons, "Mothers," in *Medieval Queenship*, 63–66. That Catherine "began her purgations late" comes from Mézéray 798. Many historians have followed this lead with no further proof.

3 Alberi, ed., *Caterina de'Medici*, 47; Tommaseo, ed., Vol. 1, p. 372.

4 Cloulas, *Henri II*, 97.

5 Cloulas says Filippa was the squire's sister: *Henri II*, 96–97; Baumgartner calls Filippa his daughter but, in general, glosses over this episode, 287. On rape versus seduction (or the avoidance of those terms), see Cloulas, *Henri II*; Seward 192.

6 Cholakian and Skemp 21; Cholakian and Cholakian, Chapter 2, passim.

7 Cloulas, *Henri II*, 102; Pébay-Clottes and Troquet 153 and passim.

8 Brantôme, ed. Lalanne, Vol. 7, p. 341; Bourges in *Lettres*, Vol. 9, p. 505.

9   Brantôme, ed. Lalanne,Vol. 7, p. 341; Cloulas, *Catherine*, 67.

10 Burgess 841; Knecht, *Renaissance Warrior*, 41.

11 Kantorowicz 409–13. The phrase was used for the first time upon the death of Louis XII.

12 Sutherland, *Huguenot*, 10 and passim; Gray, "Huguenot," 349–59.

13 Knecht, *Renaissance Warrior*, 306–7.

14 Sutherland, *Huguenot*, 10–39; Knecht, *Renaissance Warrior*, 142. On the revolutionary character of the Reform (against Sutherland's thesis), see Diefendorf, "Rites of Repair," 35.

15 The text of the placards is printed in Berthoud 287–89.

16 Bèze 10.

17 Holt 18; Sutherland, *Huguenot*, 28.

18 Berthoud 190–95; Sutherland, *Huguenot*, 41–61.

19 Knecht, *Renaissance Warrior*, 320; Kelley 13.

20 *Letters and Papers*, Vol. 16, p. 519; *Letters and Papers*, Vol. 17, pp. 65–66; cited in Doran, *Monarchy and Matrimony*, 14.

21 Alberi, *Caterina de'Medici*, 73.

22 Wellcome MS. 222 provides several recipes; Gélis 27–29; Defrance 35–37.

23 *Lettres*, Vol. 1, p. 6. n. 1.

24 Fernel's records have been lost, along with which sexual positions he recommended, to the disappointment of myriad historians. The accounts of his diagnoses come from seventeenth-century sources.

CHAPTER 4: MOTHERHOOD

1 *Lettres*, Vol. 1, p. 6. Catherine calls Montmorency her *compère*, a word that can mean "collaborator" or "ally."

2 Cloulas, *Diane de Poitiers*, 132; Genin, ed., Vol. 2, p. 228; Brantôme, ed. Lalanne, Vol. 7, p. 341; Cloulas, *Henri II*, 120.

3 *Lettres*, Vol. 1, p. 8.

4 Cloulas, *Catherine*, 132.

5 *Lettres*, Vol. 1, p. 10.

6 The births of the French royal children were later recorded by Claude de l'Aubespine, Catherine's secretary of state. See Paris, ed., *Négociations*, 892. The date of Elisabeth's birth is problematic. Many historians have cited the year as 1545, but as Edouard points out, common practice at the time usually placed the new year at Easter (rather than January 1). Elisabeth's birth date thus fell in the year 1546 according to modern dating practices. This date is corroborated by other correspondence. Edouard 17; *Lettres*, Vol. 1, p. 10. The description of the baptism comes

from Edouard 18–20; Godefroy 147; Archives nationales de France, MS. K 1715, no. 10.

7 See Diane de Poitiers's reference to the nickname in 1548 when Elisabeth was two, in Guiffrey, ed., 35 and n. 1.

8 *Lettres*, Vol. 1, p. 10.

9 Knecht, *Renaissance Warrior*, 543–44; Vieilleville cited in Baumgartner 41.

10 Monter 135–37; Sutherland, *Huguenot*, 42–44; Baschet, *Diplomatie*, 437, 441–44; Wellman 203; Knecht, *Renaissance Warrior*, 546–54.

11 Baschet, *Diplomatie*, 443.

12 Contarini in 1552, in Baschet, *Diplomatie*, 438–39. Dandolo in 1542, in Alberi, *Caterina de' Medici*, 47.

13 Vives, *Education*, 53. On breast milk, see the doctors Liebault and Guillemeau in Wourth-Stylianou, ed., 84, 216.

14 Edouard 22–23.

15 Guiffrey, ed., pp. 85–86, n. 2; pp. 19–20, n. 2.

16 Guiffrey, ed., 83.

17 Broomhall 195.

18 On the story of acid, disguised as "distilled water" or perfume, see Defrance 34.

19 Guiffrey, ed., lxiii.

20 Cloulas, *Diane de Poitiers*, 110.

21 Tommaseo, ed., Vol. 1, p. 372.

22 The royal portraits of the children are kept in the archival library of the Musée Condé at the Château de Chantilly, MN31–MN42.

23 BnF ms. français 3008, fol. 198; cf. Zvereva 106, n. 521; Zvereva 106.

24 Zvereva 142, 168.

25 Zvereva 107; *Lettres*, Vol. 1, p. 62.

26 *Lettres*, Vol. 1, p. 62; Musée Condé MN36; Zvereva 107, 109.

27 The measles had swept the nursery. Elisabeth also fell ill but recovered. See Catherine's reference to the illness in a letter to Anne d'Este, *Lettres*, Vol. 1, p. 39; Montmorency's letter, BnF ms. français 3116, f. 85; cf. Guiffrey, ed., 73 and n. 2.

28 Héritier 83–84.

29 Zvereva 122, fig. 36; BnF NAL 82, fol. 156v.

CHAPTER 5: THE PRICE

1 Stoddart 9, 405–11.

2 Guy, *My Heart*, 13; the Scots spelled the surname "Stewart" but both Marie de Guise and Mary, Queen of Scots, would spell it "Stuart" in

the French fashion. Mary's birthday has been disputed, but Mary herself claimed to be born on December 8. See Wormald 11.

3   The English privy council's instructions to the English captains were forthright in their brutality. See Merriman 144.

4   The Auld Alliance was given new energy when James V, encouraged by his regent, the Duke of Albany (uncle to Catherine de' Medici), married Francis I's daughter Madeleine in 1537. Unfortunately, she died that same year and James went on to marry Marie de Guise.

5   Stoddart 13; Wood, ed., Vol. VII, p. 7, V.

6   Pimodan 33, 105. Pimodan cites an account from the Joinville kitchens, BnF ms. français 8181.

7   Carroll 24; Marshall 31.

8   Carroll 46.

9   Marshall 36–39.

10 Wood, ed., Vol. IV, p. 4, III.

11 Pitscottie, Vol. 1., pp. 378–80; cf. Marshall 61–62.

12 See Wood, ed., Vols. IV and VI passim, and Vol. IV letters VII, X, XI, XLIV. We don't know, unfortunately, if Marie de Guise took the hint.

13 Wood, ed., Vol. IV, pp. 6 and 19–20, IV, XI, XIX.

14 Wood, ed., Vol. IV, p. 84, LVI.

15 François's letters are collected in NLS Adv. MS. 29.2.2. ff. 44–70; see also published versions in Wood, ed., Vol. IV, 85, LVI and following.

16 Wood, ed., Vol. IV, pp. 85–86, LVII. François and Little Uncle René were playing at hoops, one of the most common childhood games.

17 Wood, ed., Vol. IV, p. 97, LXVII.

18 Wood, ed., Vol. IV, pp. 144–45, CVII. Antoinette joked that François, growing quickly, was "almost a man" in 1541, when he was six; see Vol. IV, p. 73, XLIV.

19 Wood, ed., Vol. IV, pp. 60–61, XXXVII.

20 Wood, ed., Vol. VII, p. 14, XII; Carroll 45.

21 *Lettres*, Vol. 1, p. 556; Wood, ed., Vol. 7, p. 20, XIII.

22 Wood, ed., Vol. VII, p. 7.

CHAPTER 6: EMPIRES

1   Ruble, *Jeunesse*, 31; Letter of Henry II to Humières, BnF ms. français Vol. 3120, f. 72; cf. Guiffrey, ed., p. 44, n. 1.

2   Giovanni Capello in Tommaseo, ed., 383; translated in Baumgartner 133–35.

3   Baumgartner 133–48; Merriman 27.

4   Guy, *My Heart*, 36; Merriman 294.
5   Stoddart 68; Guy, *My Heart*, 45; Guiffrey, ed., pp. 45–46, n. 1.
6   Marshall 123; Arthur, ed., 84.
7   For reproductions of early portraits of Mary, see Zvereva 106, 300, 385. Originals are held at the Beinecke Library at Yale University, New Haven, CT; the Bibliothèque nationale de France; National Ossolinki Institute, Wrocław.
8   Pimodan 295.
9   Wood, ed., Vol. VII, pp. 29, 150.
10 On François de Guise and the Cardinal of Lorraine, see Constant 32–35.
11 Lee 21.
12 Pimodan 293; Anne's mother, Renée de France, was the daughter of Louis XII and the sister of Claude de France, first wife of Francis I. The crown passed to the junior branch of the Valois since Louis had only daughters by his wife, Anne of Brittany. Renée was an important follower of Jean Calvin. Her court at Ferrara became a refuge for French and Italian Protestants.
13 On the question of Mary's "Scottish temperament," see Stoddart 41. In 1548, a papal legate wrote to the Scottish Bishop of Orkney reporting that inquiries were being made in France about a doctor for Mary. There was some debate about whether a Frenchman or Scotsman was better suited to the position.
14 Janet Fleming was an illegitimate daughter of James IV, and therefore Mary's paternal aunt.
15 Brantôme, ed. Lalanne, Vol. 7, p. 407. Antoinette's letter in Pimodan 295; Henry's letter cited in Guiffrey, ed., 45–46; Bryce 49.
16 Guy, *My Heart*, 45; Wood, ed., Vol. VII, p. 18.
17 Wood, ed., Vol. VII, p. 25.
18 Ruble, *Jeunesse*, 37–40; Stoddart 36–37.
19 Ruble, *Jeunesse*, 40–41, accounts list fifty-seven kitchen staff for the *petite cour*; Stoddart 39.
20 Stoddart 36, 40.
21 Ruble, *Jeunesse*, 40–41, 57, 105–6; Wood, ed., Vol. VII, p. 146, CIII.
22 BnF français, 20468, fol. 157; cf. Pimodan 206. Her naughty grandson, she once wrote to his mother, Anne d'Este, trembled at the mere mention of "Grandmama" after Antoinette was forced to punish him. Conspiratorial words; Antoinette chuckles behind them. In the next sentence, she told Anne how pleased she would be with her boy, he was growing so well.
23 Labanoff, ed., Vol. 7, pp. 277–78; Pimodan 152; Labanoff notes that most of Mary's letters to her grandmother were destroyed, along

with the majority of the Joinville archives, during the French Revolution.

24 King Henry stopped short of assisting her financially. Marshall 102, 197.

25 On May 9, 1551, the boy king Edward VI of England noted in his diary, "One Stuart, a Scotsman, intending to poison the young Queen of Scotland and thereby thinking to get favor here [in England], was, after he had been held a while in the Tower and Newgate, delivered to my frontiers at Calais to the French in order to have him punished there as he deserved." In North, ed., 82.

26 Guy, *My Heart*, 52; Marshall 190–92; Pimodan 155.

27 Wood, ed., Vol. IV, pp. 176–77; Pimodan 380–81.

28 Which we can intuit from Mary's letter to her mother, Labanoff, ed., Vol. 1, pp. 29–32.

29 *Lettres*, Vol. 1, pp. 556–57; *Analecta Scotica*, 181–82.

30 *Lettres*, Vol. 1, p. 82.

31 Wood, ed., Vol. VII, p. 230.

32 Wood, ed., Vol. VII, p. 230.

33 King Henry would later recognize Janet Fleming's son legally and make him the Duke d'Angoulême. On the French governess and the misunderstanding between Mary and Catherine, see the Cardinal de Lorraine's 1556 letter to Marie de Guise, Wood, ed., Vol. VII, pp. 278–81.

34 Ruble, *Jeunesse*, 104; Labanoff, ed., Vol. 1, p. 36.

35 Wood, ed., Vol. VII, p. 29, XX, and pp. 109–110, LXXX.

36 For citations from the cardinal's letter to Marie de Guise, see Wood, ed., Vol. VII, p. 142, CIII.

37 Wood, ed., Vol. VII, p. 29, XX, p. 110, LXXX.

38 *CSP Scotland*, Vol. 2, June 11, 1568, p. 697.

39 Labanoff, ed., Vol. 1, pp. 17–18.

CHAPTER 7: BRIDES

1 Stoddart 142–43.

2 Baschet, ed., *Diplomatie*, 486.

3 Ruble, *Jeunesse*, 151; Cuisiat 243.

4 BnF NAL 82 f. 154 v°.

5 *CSP Foreign*, Vol. 6, November 9, 1557, #1079.

6 Carroll points out that, as of 1552, Henry had elevated the barony of Joinville to a principality, thus transforming the Guises into French princes rather than simply naturalized foreigners. Their elevation, however, did not erase the malevolent quips about their foreignness, p. 73.

7　Parker, *Emperor*, 462; Carroll 77–79.

8　Labanoff, ed.,Vol. 7, p. 279.

9　*CSP Foreign*,Vol. 6, November 9, 1557, #1079.

10　Labanoff, ed., includes all three donations inVol. 1, pp. 50–56.

11　Labanoff, ed.,Vol. 1, pp. 28, 53. "Your good sister" or "Your good brother" was the common signature from one monarch to another.

12　Labanoff, ed.,Vol. 1, p. 54. Mary's reference to Francis as "King of Scots" is evident from a letter Mary wrote to her mother after the betrothal but before the wedding, see below note #17.

13　On Mary's preference for white, see Fraser 71; on the silver-white gown, see Van Scoy et al. 45; *Discours du grand et magnifique triomphe* f. B.

14　*Discours du grand et magnifique triomphe* f. Aiv.

15　*Discours du grand et magnifique triomphe* f. Bii.

16　Brantôme, "Second Discourse," in Chang and Kong 185.

17　Hay Fleming 491–92.

18　*Discours du grand et magnifique triomphe* Cii v°.

19　*Discours du grand et magnifique triomphe* ff. Aiii-B; Godefroy,Vol. 2, p. 10.

20　Brantôme, ed. Lalanne,Vol. 8, p. 3; Freer,Vol. 1, p. 9.

21　For Elisabeth's portrait, see Zvereva 140, 301, and Musée Condé inv. MN 41; *Recueil de Plusieurs Secrets*, 9 v°.

22　The Guises were a junior branch of the House of Lorraine; the Duke of Lorraine was thus a Guise cousin. His marriage to Claude further entwined the Guises and the French royal family. Brantôme, ed. Lalanne,Vol. 8, p. 3.

23　"Sacramentarians" in the context of the edict included Calvinists but not Lutherans—Henry was unwilling to alienate the Lutheran German princes who remained his allies against Philip II.The text of the Edict of Compiègne is in Isambert, ed., 494–97.

24　On the affair of the rue Saint Jacques and assemblies at public sites like the Pré-aux-Clercs in Paris, see Roelker, *One King* 232–33; Sutherland, *Huguenot*, 344–45.

25　Knecht, *Catherine de' Medici*, 55; Ruble, *Cateau-Cambrésis*, 26; *CSP Elizabeth*,Vol. 1,April 2, 1559, #483.

26　Cloulas, *Henri II*, 301.

27　*Lettres*,Vol. 1, pp. 10–11.

28　Freer,Vol. 1, p. 42.

29　Paris, ed., *Négociations*, 201; cf. Freer,Vol. 1, pp. 42–48; Edouard 119–12.

30　Edouard 120 and n. 24.

CHAPTER 8: ACCIDENTS

1 Baumgartner 247–48.
2 Baumgartner 249. The account of the Bishop of Troyes, Antoine Caracciolo, is given in Williams 342–43.
3 Vieilleville 414–15.
4 Vieilleville 415. Caracciolo claims the stub of Montgomery's lance forced the king's visor open.
5 Forbes, ed., Vol. 1, p. 151.
6 Baumgartner 252.
7 The Bishop of Fermo to the Cardinal of Naples on July 1, 1559, cited in Romier, "La Mort," 141.
8 Throckmorton to the Privy Council, July 4, reporting on a conversation that took place on July 1; in Forbes, ed., Vol. 1, p. 154.
9 Baumgartner 251; Cloulas, *Henri II*, 591; Williams 343. Caracciolo reported that when Montgomery saw what had happened to the king, he raced to Henry's side, sobbing, and asked to have his hand and head cut off. Yet Henry refused to blame or punish him.
10 *CSP Foreign*, Vol. 1, July 1559, #965.
11 Romier, "La Mort," 149.
12 Romier, "La Mort," 150.
13 Baumgartner 252; Charlier et al., "Death," 5. Modern physicians believe Henry's death was not caused by the initial accident but rather by infection stemming from small fragments of the lance in the skull, which the physicians left because removing them caused the king too much pain. The infection then spread through veins in the face.
14 Throckmorton to the Privy Council, July 1; in Forbes, ed., Vol. 1, p. 151.
15 Her movements during the ten days between his accident and death are difficult to track. Most accounts, told well after the fact, do not focus on Catherine. She seems to have moved between Henry's chamber and other parts of the palace, conducting affairs and seeing to the king's last wishes. All sources, though, including the engraving of the death scene by Tortorel and Perrissin (ed. Benedict), put her at Henry's bedside when he died; Brantôme states that she wore black except for the weddings of her sons Charles and Henri (formerly Alexandre-Edouard).
16 Vieilleville 414–15; Marguerite de Valois 78; for Nostradamus's predictions of the king's death, all of which were understood as such well after the fact, see Crouzet 55–57.
17 Cuisiat, ed., 359.

18 Whether the exchange of Chenonceau for Chaumont was a generous trade or not is a question of some dispute. Ruble says it was generous; Cloulas and Mariéjol note that Chaumont was worth considerably less than Chenonceau. Still, there is little evidence, contrary to popular stories, that Catherine chased Diane from Paris. Cloulas, *Diane de Poitiers*, 304–306.

19 Forbes, ed., Vol. I, p. 157.

20 Although Montmorency had once been Catherine's "compère"— her friend or gossip—there is evidence of a falling out between Catherine and the Constable. Some stories suggest he derided her as a "merchant's daughter"; another conflict arose because Montmorency favored peace with Spain while Catherine, like the Guises, wanted to pursue French interests in Italy. The later relationship between the two is difficult to establish since sources rely upon the writings of Regnier de la Planche, a Protestant sympathizer who was an apologist for Montmorency and his clan. La Planche wrote his account years after the fact, and like any propagandist, he embroidered the truth to suit his agenda.

21 *CSP Venice*, Vol. 7, July 12 and 16, 1559, #85–86; Romier, *Conjuration*, 3, 9.

22 It is unclear who first began this practice. The Duke of Alba uses the term just a few days after Henry II's death.

23 AN K 1492, July 11, 115; cited in Ruble, *Jeunesse*, 173–74.

24 Marguerite de Valois 40–41.

25 Marguerite de Valois 40–41.

26 On Spanish and French confusion and Ruy Gómez's role after Henry's death, see Boyden, *Courtier*, 79–80, and Vandenesse, "Diario de los viajos de Felipe II," 1094.

27 AN K 1494, n. 65; cited in Ruble, *Cateau-Cambrésis*, 244, 246; Ruble, *Antoine de Bourbon*, Vol. 2, pp. 72–76; Freer, Vol. 1, pp. 66–69.

28 Paris, ed., *Négociations*, 131; Ruble, *Cateau-Cambrésis*, 216–17.

29 Brantôme, ed. Lalanne, Vol. 8, p. 13.

CHAPTER 9: MARY'S BOOK

1 On the differences between the wardrobes of Mary and the royal children, see Ruble, *Jeunesse*, 39–40.

2 Guiffrey, ed., 33–34, n. 1.

3 Brantôme, ed. Vaucheret, 174. My thanks to Dr. Kelly Peebles for this reference.

4 Freer, Vol. 1, pp. 9–10.

5 Labanoff, ed., Vol. 2, p. 243; Edouard 33.

6   The handwriting of both girls in the summer of 1559 is easily compared in BnF ms. français 3152, which contains short letters by each to Constable Montmorency.

7   Paris, ed., *Négociations*, 275.

8   Brantôme, ed. Lalanne, Vol. 8, p. 409; Fouquelin A3 r°; Wilkinson 41.

9   Ronsard, "A mes Dames filles du Roy Henry Deuxième," *Odes*, 751–52.

10 BnF ms. français 11207, ff. 208–14; cf. Edouard 29.

11 The text of Mary's notebook is given in Du Prat; see also Montaiglon, ed., *Latin Themes*, and BnF ms. latin 8660, "Mariae Stuart, Scotorum Reginae et Galliae Delphinae, epistolae variae, latinè et gallicè."

12 Labanoff, ed., Vol. 2, pp. 182–97.

CHAPTER 10: JOURNEYS

1   Ruble, *Cateau-Cambrésis*, 251; *Lettres*, Vol. 1, p. 128.

2   AN K1492 n.78; cf. Ruble, *Antoine de Bourbon*, Vol. 2, p. 77; Freer, Vol. 1, pp. 79–80.

3   The Bishop of Limoges was the younger brother of Claude de L'Aubespine, who was Secretary of State under Kings Francis I, Henry II, Francis II, and Charles IX and who would become one of Catherine's most important counselors. Madame de Rieux was Suzanne de Bourbon, married to Claude de Rieux, and the sister of the Duke of Montpensier. Broomhall 217.

4   Ruble, *Antoine de Bourbon*, Vol. 2, p. 77.

5   My italics underscore the addition of the word "very." BnF ms. Nouv. Acquis Fr. [NAF] 6007, f. 37.

6   Du Prat 80; Palma Cayet 176.

7   Mariéjol 61.

8   Paris, ed., *Négociations*, 161–62.

9   Unless otherwise noted, all relevant citations regarding Elisabeth's journey and her delivery to the Spanish come from the dispatches reproduced in Paris, ed., *Négociations*, 171–94. See also the account of the voyage in *Archives curieuses de l'histoire de France*, Vol. 4, p. 8. The attention of Madame de Clermont, and the constant presence of Mlle de Montpensier and Madame de Rieux, can be deduced from events at the end of the journey, and letters among Madame de Clermont, the Bishop of Limoges, and Catherine after Elisabeth's arrival in Spain.

10 Philip preferred Mor's painting to Titian's, made about seven years earlier when he was a much younger man and not yet King of Spain; Matthews 13–19.

11 Folger MS. Add 895.

12 Zvereva 301.

13 Ball and Parker, eds., 149–53.

14 BRMS II—2257; cf. Parker, *Imprudent King*, 46.

15 Edouard 49; "Instrucciones de Felipe II," in Amezúa y Mayo,Vol. 3:1, p. 90; García Barranco 94.

16 Vasari 328.

17 Perlingieri, *Sofonisba Anguissola*, 113.

18 Kusche 366; Ferino-Pagden and Kusche 54.

19 Ruble, *Antoine de Bourbon*,Vol. 2, pp. 84–85.

20 Lansac in Paris, ed., *Négociations*, 173–74.

21 Bnf ms. français 3902, f. 92.

22 Ruble, *Antoine de Bourbon*,Vol. 2, pp. 88–89.

23 L'Huillier in Paris, ed., *Negociations*, 181–83.

24 Lansac in Paris, ed., *Négociations*, 174.

25 Lansac in Paris, ed., *Négociations*, 174; *La Réception faicte par les députez du roi d'Espagne*, f. Dii v.

26 *La Recéption faicte par les députez du roi d'Espagne*, f. Dii v; Palma Cayet 176.

CHAPTER 11: LETTERS

1 Brantôme, ed. Lalanne,Vol. 8, p. 6; Anne of France 44.

2 *Lettres*,Vol. 1, p. 158.

3 Freer, Vol. 1, p. 95. Isabey's painting, *The Departure of Elisabeth of France for Spain*, now hangs in the Walters Art Museum in Baltimore, Maryland.

4 Lansac and the anonymous relation in Paris, ed., *Négociations*, 176, 194; Ruble, *Cateau-Cambrésis*, 263. The position of *camarera mayor* was an honorary but highly coveted role, usually given to a high-ranking widow or matron.

5 BnF ms. français 4815; cited in Ruble, *Cateau-Cambrésis*, 266.

6 Variously known as Da Silva or the Prince of Éboli, although biographers sometimes choose to refer to him by his first, double name of "Ruy Gómez," which practice I continue here.

7 Historians still aren't sure of Ruy Gómez's birthdate, though Boyden places it around 1516; Boyden 7.

8 Boyden 22, 46, 59–63, and passim.

9 Boyden 44.

10 Boyden 106; Kamen, *Alba*; on Alba's animosity toward France, see Limoges' letter in Paris, ed., *Négociations*, 271.

11 BnF ms. français 4815 recounts that Philip was already in the city, disguised, so that he could preview his new bride without her knowledge, but a letter from Philip to Chantonnay suggests that in fact he didn't arrive in Guadalajara until the thirtieth, the day he officially met Elisabeth; see also AN K 1493 n. 32, cited in Ruble, *Cateau-Cambrésis*, 266.

12 BnF ms. français 4815, cited in Ruble, *Cateau-Cambrésis*, 270.

13 Paris, ed., *Négociations*, 438.

14 Paris, ed., *Négociations*, 192, 272.

15 See the dispatches by Lansac, L'Huillier, and the anonymous source in Paris, ed., *Négociations*, 177, 185, 190.

16 A similar situation played out among Christians and *for conversos* during the Spanish Inquisition, beginning in the late fifteenth century and throughout the reign of Philip II. The denunciation of personal enemies was also widespread during the infamous Saint Bartholomew's Day Massacre in Paris in 1572. See Kamen, *Spanish Inquisition*; Perez; Heller; Carroll 109.

17 *Mémoires de Condé,* Vol. 1, p. 220; Cloulas, *Henri II*, 587.

18 Benedict reproduces the engraving of the execution by Tortorel and Perrissin, one of forty contemporary plates depicting episodes from the religious conflicts in France, 161. Protestant descriptions of the execution appear in *Mémoires de Condé,* Vol. 1, p. 220 and following.

19 La Planche 219.

20 Fraser 56.

21 Knecht, *Catherine de' Medici*, 66–67.

22 Frieda 126; *Mémoires de Condé,* Vol. 1, pp. 342, 344.

23 Labanoff, Vol. 1, p. 72; Roderer 169.

24 Silleras-Fernandez 11.

25 Brantôme, ed. Vaucheret, p. 56.

26 On early modern writing tools and letter-writing, including the significance of using one's own handwriting, see Daybell, especially 43–48, 86–87.

27 Paris, ed., *Négociations*, 461.

28 On the goods, gifts, and people sent between Spain and France, see Paris, ed., *Négociations*, 445–46, 509, 511, 521, 803, 854; Amezúa y Mayo ed., Vol. 3:2, p. 29.

29 Paris, ed., *Négociations*, 522, 807, 840.

30 Daybell 158.

31 *Lettres*, Vol. 1, p. 158; for mention of the messengers, see among others: Catherine to M. Nicot (1561, p. 30); Catherine to M. Maugiron

(1562, p. 55); Catherine to M. de Bellièvre (1567, p. 208), all in *Lettres*, Vol. 10. On the importance of the messenger in early modern letter-writing, see Gibson 617.

32 Brantôme, ed. Lalanne,Vol. 8, p. 13; Paris, ed., *Négociations*, 701.
33 Paris, ed., *Négociations*, 762–63.
34 Freer,Vol. 1, p. 185.
35 Ruble, *Première jeunesse*, 211–31.
36 Doran, *Elizabeth I*, 237.

CHAPTER 12: KING'S HEART, QUEEN'S BODY

1 Edouard 50–59.
2 Bnf ms. français 6614 fol. 58; Kusche and Pagden 56.
3 Perlingieri, "Lady-in-Waiting," 119; Kusche and Pagden, np (plate 14). The extant portrait is a copy of the original, but experts believe it is faithful. The portrait of Elisabeth that Sofonisba painted decades later from memory is also believed to approximate the original. See Cole 125, 143.
4 BnF ms. français 3902 f. 95 r.
5 *Rapport*, ed. Ferrière, p. 19. The preference for black at the Spanish court can be traced back to Philip's Hapsburg Burgundian ancestors. See Colomer 77–88; Brantôme, ed. Lalanne,Vol. 8, p. 19.
6 Philip only learned of Don Juan's existence in 1559, shortly before the wedding. On Aranjuez, see Edouard 192, 199; Philip acquired the estate in 1560 about the same time as he moved the capital to Madrid.
7 For Clermont's "diary," see *Rapport* and Amezúa y Mayo, Vol. 3, pp. 106–20.
8 Kamen, *Philip II*, 181.
9 Paris, ed., *Négociations*, 271.
10 Paris, ed., *Négociations*, 813.
11 Paris, ed., *Négociations*, 460.
12 Alberi, ed.,Vol. 5, p. 118; Edouard 217.
13 *Rapport*, ed. Ferrière, p. 17; Paris, ed., *Négociations*, 859.
14 Paris, ed., *Négociations*, 272–73.
15 Paris, ed., *Négociations*, 703, 808–12; On the length of the fever, see *Lettres*,Vol. 1, p. 162, n. 1.
16 Paris, ed., *Négociations*, 808.
17 *Lettres*,Vol. 1, p. 16; *Négociations*, 811.
18 Paris, ed., *Négociations*, 703, 807.
19 Paris, ed., *Négociations*, 808–809, 811.
20 Broomhall 214–31.

21 Chamberlin, *Private Character of Queen Elizabeth* 67, 218–23; Medvei 766–67; *Collected Works* 37; Francis I was considering a possible marriage between Mary and his favorite son, Charles d'Angoulême; he may also have been considering her as a replacement for Catherine de Médici. See Part II, Chapter IV. Catherine's barrenness may have made Francis hesitate at the possibility of Mary's infertility.

22 Armstrong Davison 306.

23 AN K 1492 #66.

24 The following discussion of greensickness and menstruation is drawn from King and Hindson.

25 King 2.

26 Paris, ed., *Négociations*, 551–52; On Elisabeth's preference for meat and her vomiting, see Catherine's letter to the Duchess of Alba in *Duquesa de Alba, Documentos escogidos de archive de la casa de Alba*, Madrid (1891), 174; cited in Edouard 223; *Lettres*, Vol. 1, p. 589, n. 2.

27 Paris, ed., *Négociations*, 549–50.

28 Paris, ed., *Négociations*, 701–702.

29 BnF ms. français 3902, f. 86; *Négociations*, 718–19.

30 Paris, ed., *Négociations*, 807; Edouard 226.

31 Silleras-Fernandez 4.

32 Paris, ed., *Négociations*, 702.

33 Freer, Vol. 1, pp. 206–10.

34 Paris, ed., *Négociations*, 708.

35 Paris, ed., *Négociations*, 705.

36 Paris, ed., *Négociations*, 713.

37 Limoges's detailed letter occupies ten full pages in Paris, ed., *Négociations*, 707–17. He warned Catherine to burn it after reading.

38 Paris, ed., *Négociations*, 724–25.

39 Paris, ed., *Négociations*, 724–25.

40 Edouard 216–17.

CHAPTER 13: SONS AND DAUGHTERS

1 Other accounts claim he fainted while attending vespers. Romier cites Gonzaga's letter to the Duke of Mantua in *Conjuration*, 277–78.

2 Sutherland, *Huguenot*, 10; Gray 349–59.

3 To this day, historians aren't sure what the Protestants planned. They may have wished to meet the king in peace to present a profession of their faith and ask for his protection.

4 Thompson 25–29.

5 Aubigné 52. My thanks to Professor Kathleen Perry Long for pointing out the effect these hostilities must have had on an entire generation of French children.

6 Knecht, *Catherine de' Medici*, 70. The Protestant and Catholic petitions, and a third separate petition made by the Reformers to Catherine, are included in *Mémoires de Condé*, Vol. 2, pp. 647–60.

7 Romier, *Conjuration*, 281.

8 Rait, ed., 10.

9 *Lettres*, Vol. 1, pp. 164–66.

10 Cloulas, *Catherine de Médicis*, 151.

11 Paris, ed., *Négociations*, 831.

12 The age of majority was not codified either. Kings, providing for their heirs in the event of their death, moved the age of majority around to suit their political purposes. They usually chose age thirteen—or a boy's fourteenth year—to avoid an overly long regency. A more realistic king like Louis XI, however, provided for a regency until his son, Charles VIII, turned twenty. Louis chose his oldest daughter, Anne of France, and her husband as regents. Much of what follows draws on Crawford's brilliant analysis of regency in *Perilous Performances*.

13 Mariéjol 61.

14 *Chroniques de Saint-Denis* in HGF, 20:699, cited in Crawford 16; Potter 236–37.

15 Potter 241.

16 Crawford 16.

17 An anonymously authored treatise written in 1464 as a justification against the English claim, *La loys salicque, première loys des français*, was printed in the 1541 edition of Claude Seyssel's *Grande monarchie de France*, leading many mistakenly to believe that Seyssel had penned it.

18 Louis XII and Francis I tried to thwart public dissatisfaction with the succession by marrying Claude to Francis, fusing the two branches of the Valois, and ensuring that Claude's children would inherit the throne; Seyssel, ed. Kelley, 48–49.

19 The coronation of a French king was called the *sacre*—literally the "sacralizing" of the king.

20 Potter 242, n. 1.

21 One exception to this was Louise de Savoy's regency after the disastrous battle of Pavia, though Louise and Marguerite de Navarre negotiated (at the expense of Francis's sons) to ensure his quick return.

22 Romier, *Conjuration*, 283.

23 La Planche 415–17.

24 Du Tillet, *Discours pour la majorité du roi très-Chrétien contre les écrits des rebelles* (1560), 9; cited in Crawford 31.

25 *Lettres*, Vol. 10, pp. 25–26.

26 The secretary of state, Claude de l'Aubespine, kept a record of attendance, including: Antoine de Bourbon; the cardinals of Bourbon, Lorraine, Tournon, Guise, and Chatillon; the Prince de la Roche-sur-yon; the dukes of Guise, d'Aumalle, and d'Estampes; the marshals Saint André and Brissac; the Admiral of France, and the bishops of Orléans, Valence, and Amiens. *Mémoires de Condé*, Vol. 2, p. 211.

27 Romier, *Conjuration*, 284.

28 Knecht, *Catherine de' Medici*, 72–73.

29 Paris, ed., *Négociations*, 831.

30 *Lettres*, Vol. 1, p. 568. Catherine refers to her "three little sons." She does not mention her youngest daughter, Marguerite, but the security of the realm did not depend on Marguerite's safety and well-being. The absence is notable—however sincere, Catherine was writing a political letter.

31 *Lettres*, Vol. 1, pp. 568–69.

32 Paris, ed., *Négociations*, 802.

CHAPTER 14: HOME

1 Ruble, *Jeunesse*, 208–209.

2 Clermont writes to Catherine reporting the malicious gossip in February 1561; Paris. ed., *Négociations*, 804.

3 Rait, ed., 11; Ruble, *Jeunesse*, 209.

4 Fraser 125.

5 AN K1493 #91.

6 La Planche, ed. Buchon, 74, 75.

7 *CSP Venice*, Vol. 6, April 25, 1558, #1216.

8 Labanoff, Vol. 1, p. 88.

9 Cited in Wilkinson 21.

10 Labanoff, Vol. 1, p. 86.

11 Mariéjol 76–77; La Planche 302.

12 Paris, ed., *Négociations*, 754.

13 Hay Fleming 244–45.

14 Brantôme, ed. Lalanne, Vol. 9, pp. 619–20.

15 Fraser 123.

16 Fraser 119–23.

17 *CSP Foreign*, Vol. 3, #738.

18 Hay Fleming 226 n. 4.

19 See, for instance, the assessment of Elizabeth's marital status among foreign envoys eager to present the suit of their princes. *CSP Spain (Simancas)*, Vol. 1, April 29, 1559, #29; *CSP Foreign*, Vol. 1, June 2, 1559, #813.

20 *CSP Foreign*, Vol. 4, March 22, 29, and 31, 1561, #61, #73, #77, #78.

21 Chantonnay reported to Philip II on January 12, Gachard 162.

22 Paris, ed., *Négociations*, 806.

CHAPTER 15: DON CARLOS

1 Zvereva 138.

2 Amezúa y Mayo, Vol. 3:1, p. 142.

3 Paris, ed., *Négociations*, 436, 440.

4 Paris, ed., *Négociations*, 814; *Lettres*, Vol. 1, p. 576.

5 Ronsard 72.

6 Gachard 23.

7 Gachard 28.

8 Gachard 29–30.

9 Parker, *Imprudent King*, 179.

10 Parker, *Imprudent King*, 180.

11 Whether Juana was actually "mad," or whether she was described as such to ensure that her father, husband, and son retained the power accorded the crown of Castile, remains the subject of dispute.

12 Gachard 140.

13 Parker, *Imprudent King*, 183–84.

14 Parker, *Imprudent King*, 179.

15 Gachard 140; Brantôme, ed. Lalanne, Vol. 2, p. 105.

16 Parker, *Imprudent King*, 181; Gachard 136.

17 Gachard 236.

18 Brantôme, ed. Lalanne, Vol. 2, p. 105. This story is at the origin of the play by Schiller, which then inspired Verdi's grand opera *Don Karlo*.

19 Gachard 233; Paris, ed., *Négociations*, 290.

20 Paris, ed., *Négociations*, 460. Sofonisba likely made several portraits of Don Carlos throughout the 1560s, though few of these survive. Cole discusses one document that refers to a Sofonisba painting of Don Carlos made in 1567, p. 126.

21 See letters by Elisabeth and the French ambassador to Catherine, Paris, ed., *Négociations*, 888–90; Gachard 147, 154.

22 Brantôme, ed. Lalanne, Vol. 2, p. 106.

23 Paris, ed., *Négociations*, 805. I've maintained the Spanish spelling as it appears in the original letter. On the mystery portrait, see Stoddart

323–24 and n. 2. Some historians have speculated that the second portrait was a poorly executed one of Mary Stuart, which Catherine sent on purpose to dissuade Don Carlos.

CHAPTER 16: THE TEST

1   Paris, ed., *Négociations*, 825.
2   *Lettres*,Vol. 10, pp. 26–28. Limoges kept the decryption papers, which allowed Catherine's nineteenth-century editors to decipher the letter.
3   Paris, ed., *Négociations*, 804. My italics.
4   Ball and Parker 154.
5   Amezúa y Mayo,Vol. 3:1, p. 29.
6   Catherine to Limoges, *Lettres*,Vol. 1, p. 571.
7   On Juana of Austria, see Cruz 105–22; on Juana's role in *Las Descalzas Reales*, see Sánchez 53–58; on the painting, see Cole 186, who notes the attribution is disputed.
8   Parker, *Imprudent King*, 159. He cites *Corpus Documental Carlos V*, ed. Fernádez Alvárez,Tomo 4 (Salamanca, 1974–81), p. 40, April 30, 1554.
9   Amazúa y Mayo,Vol. 3:1, p. 113.
10 Amazúa y Mayo,Vol. 3:1, p. 107.
11 Paris, ed., *Négociations*, 814; *Lettres*,Vol. 1, p. 576.
12 Paris, ed., *Négociations*, 840; Amezúa y Mayo,Vol. 3:1, pp. 27, 36.
13 Paris, ed., *Négociations*, 818–19.
14 Paris, ed., *Négociations*, 825.
15 *Lettres*,Vol. 1, pp. 593–94.

CHAPTER 17: THE RETURN

1   Paris, ed., *Négociations*, 851. On Madame de Montpensier, see *Négociations*, 860.
2   Paris, ed., *Négociations*, 853.
3   Paris, ed., *Négociations*, 871; Chéruel 27; Mignet 402–403.
4   Paris, ed., *Négociations*, 872.
5   *Lettres*,Vol. 1, p. 605.
6   Paris, ed., *Négociations*, 865.
7   Much of the contemporary reporting on Mary's departure is inconsistent. Hay Fleming describes the variants, along with the galleys, 249; Ruble, *Jeunesse*, 42; Brantôme, ed. Lalanne,Vol. 7, pp. 406.
8   Guy, *My Heart*, 127; Brantôme, ed. Lalanne,Vol. 7, pp. 415–17.
9   Brantôme, ed. Lalanne, Vol. 7, pp. 418–19; Hay Fleming 250–52; Dunn 182.
10 Brantôme, ed. Lalanne,Vol. 7, p. 417.

11 Gachard, *Don Carlos*, 162–63, n. 2.

12 Throckmorton's conversation with Mary, recorded and sent to Elizabeth, is in Mumby, *Beginning of the Feud*, 197–202.

13 Doran 72.

14 Brantôme, ed. Lalanne, Vol. 7, p. 413.

15 Elizabeth's famous speech exists in several versions; although the details vary, the substance remains the same in all of them. For versions and details of the delegation's appointment at Whitehall, see *Collected Works*, 56–58, and Holinshed, Vol. 1:23.3, pp. 1777–78.

16 Throckmorton's conversation with Mary, recorded and sent to Elizabeth, is in Mumby, *Beginning of the Feud*, 197–202.

17 *Collected Works* 61.

18 *Collected Works* 62–63.

19 Mumby, *Beginning of the Feud*, 191; Scottish Calendar, Vol. 1, August 6, 1561, #999.

CHAPTER 18: QUEEN OF FAITH

1 Melville 53.

2 Hay Fleming 65.

3 Swain 54.

4 Mumby, *Beginning of the Feud*, 199.

5 Lee 6–14.

6 Hay Fleming 45–46, n. 11; Rait, ed., 21; Knox, ed. Laing, Vol. 1, pp. 270–71; Guy, *My Heart*, 131–33. It is not clear if the city of Edinburgh endorsed the Protestant displays, though the town council was dominated by Reformers.

7 Knox, ed. Laing, Vol. 1, p. 271.

8 Rait, ed., 22–23; Goodare 56.

9 Carroll, *Martyrs*, 129.

10 Rait, ed., 22.

11 Knox, ed. Laing, Vol. 2, p. 278.

12 Knox, ed. Arber, pp. 11–12. Thus did Knox win the hatred of every woman on the throne, including his fellow Protestant Queen Elizabeth of England.

13 Knox, ed. Laing, Vol. 2, pp. 282–83. Guy determines the date of the meeting from a report by the English ambassador Randolph, p. 135.

14 *CSP Foreign*, Vol. 4, June 23, 1561, #265.

15 Rait, ed., 20.

16 Wormald 143.

17 Wormald 120 and passim.

18 This edict was, in fact, a resurrection of an earlier law known as the Edict of Romorantin. Knecht, *Catherine de' Medici*, 74.

19 Paris, ed., *Négociations*, 812.

20 Paris, ed., *Négociations*, 849–50.

21 Carroll, *Martyrs*, 149. With her colloquy, Catherine sought to imitate a meeting that had occurred thirty years earlier, in Augsburg, Germany. There, at the invitation of Emperor Charles V, German Lutheran princes had made a profession of their faith. The resulting document, known as the Augsburg Confession, revealed the shared threads of belief between Lutherans and Catholics, thus allowing the emperor to smooth over some of the religious rifts in the Empire (which were, at the time, threatening unified political support for his war against the Turks). With her own parley at Poissy, Catherine looked for a similar reunification among Frenchmen.

22 Knecht, *Catherine de' Medici*, 70.

23 Carroll, *Martyrs*, 150.

24 Carroll, *Martyrs*, 151.

25 Carroll, *Martyrs*, 151.

26 Carroll, *Martyrs*, 152. The cardinal, as Carroll points out, was being strategic: by establishing a middle way—endorsing conciliation among the factions—he hoped to appeal to the moderates of France, either to woo them back to Catholicism or to define a new and specifically French theological position that would lead to a unified French church.

27 See Carroll's fascinating analysis of the Cardinal of Lorraine's efforts to reach compromise, quite different from traditional views of his Catholic orthodoxy, in *Martyrs*, 127–59.

28 See the engraving by Tortorel and Perrissin of the massacre at Cahors in Benedict.

29 These Catholic and Protestant accounts are included in Diefendorf, *The Saint-Bartholomew's Day Massacre*, 61–67.

30 Mariéjol, *Catherine de Médicis*, 109–10. Diefendorf, *The Saint-Bartholomew's Day Massacre*, 62; *CSP Foreign*, Vol. 4, November 26, 1561, #682.

31 Knecht, *Catherine de' Medici*, 83; Mariéjol, *Catherine de Médicis*, 10. My italics.

32 Paris, ed., *Négociations*, 849.

33 Knecht, *Catherine de' Medici*, 85.

34 Kamen, *Spanish Inquisition*, 93–94; Perez 60, 69–70; AG Patronato Real leg. 28, f. 37, cited in Kamen, *Spanish Inquisition*, 94.

35 Kamen, *Spanish Inquisition*, 96; Perez 70.

36 Kamen, *Spanish Inquisition*, 100. The discovery of a Protestant circle in Valladolid in the late 1550s reinforced the Spanish xenophobic belief that heresy was mostly a foreign problem transported by immigrants into Spain. This same belief drove Philip's anti-French Protestant policy in the 1560s.

37 Freer, Vol. 1, pp. 274, 292, 297.

38 Freer 273–74.

39 All citations from Elisabeth's letter are from BnF ms. français 3902 ff. 76–80.

40 Cruz suggests Juana used her vows to avoid a second marriage, 107. The Princess hid her identity under the pseudonym "Mateo Sánchez."

41 Parker, *Imprudent King*, 40.

42 Paris, ed., *Négociations*, 812. Amezúa y Mayo ed., Vol. 3:1, p. 51.

43 Carroll gives a thorough account of the events at Wassy, 1–20. See also the Catholic and Huguenot accounts in *Mémoires-journaux de François de Lorraine* 471–76, 480; De Thou, Vol. 4, p. 167.

44 Carroll 18; *Mémoires-journaux*, 482.

45 *Mémoires-journaux*, 475–76.

46 *The Destruction and sacke cruelly committed by the Duke of Guyse and his company in the towne of Vassy, the fyrste of March in the year M.D.LXII* (London: Henry Sutton, May 1562); Knecht, *French Religious Wars*, 29; Holt 49.

47 Knecht, *French Religious Wars*, 32.

48 Knecht, *French Religious Wars*, 91.

49 Sutherland, "Assassination," 279–84; *Mémoires de Condé*, Vol. 2, pp. 133–37; Forneron, Vol. 2, pp. 18–20.

50 Forneron, Vol. 2, p. 20.

51 Pasquier 98–100; Holt 50.

CHAPTER 19: CATHOLIC KINGS

1 Labanoff, ed., Vol 7, p. 4.

2 *CSP Scotland*, Vol. 1, July 5 and 15, 1562, #1121 and #1125.

3 *CSP Scotland*, Vol. 1, June 17, 1562, #1116; Pollen, ed., 76.

4 Cuisiat 444; Chéruel 33.

5 Labanoff, ed., Vol. 1, p. 257.

6 Hay Fleming 86.

7 Labanoff, ed., Vol. 1, p. 249.

8 Labanoff, ed., Vol. 7, p. 5.

9 Labanoff, ed., Vol. 1, p. 249; Chéruel 37.

10 Labanoff, ed., Vol. 1, pp. 76, 90.

11 Cabié, ed., 150.

12 Labanoff, ed., Vol. 1, p. 205.

13 Labanoff, ed., Vol. 1, pp. 178–80.

14 On Philip's distrust of Mary's religious authenticity, see Wormald 143.

15 Labanoff, ed., Vol. 1, pp. 249–50.

16 *CSP Foreign*, Vol. 6, 13, 21, December 31, 1563, #1481, #1523, #1559; Rait, ed., 44.

17 Labanoff ed., Vol. 7, pp. 291–92.

18 On the debate surrounding Darnley's age, see Weir 131.

19 For example, see Nau in Stevenson, ed., 220. Darnley had gone to France in late 1561 because his parents, the Earl and Lady Lennox, had secretly sent him to Scotland to welcome Queen Mary upon her return. Already suspicious of Lennox ambitions, Elizabeth Tudor had the family arrested but Darnley managed to escape to France, where he found refuge with his French cousins. He remained in France until 1563. Bingham 76.

20 Dunn 236; *CSP Scotland*, Vol. 2, April 28, 1565, #171. Hay Fleming pp. 339, n. 92, 342, n. 97; *CSP Foreign*, Vol. 7, May 21, 1565, #1187; *CSP Foreign*, Vol. 7, June 3, 1565, #1221. On Darnley's education, see Bingham 54–61 and passim.

21 Hay Fleming 334–35, n. 83; Keith, Vol. 2, p. 266.

22 *CSP Spain*, Vol. 1, April 7, 1565, #293.

23 *CSP Simancas*, Vol. 1, #295.

24 Turnbull, ed., 147–49.

25 Weir 250, 259, 264; *CSP Simancas*, Vol. 1, #273, #292, #295, #300.

26 Fraser 54; Hay Fleming 332–33, n. 76; *CSP Foreign*, Vol. 7, February 5, 1565, #961.

27 Rait, ed., 60.

28 Rait, ed., 60.

29 Labanoff, ed., ed., Vol. 1, p. 275.

30 Labanoff, ed., Vol. 7, pp. 340–41.

CHAPTER 20: FAMILY AFFAIRS

1 Fourquevaux, Vol. 1, p. 57. Chopines took Europe by storm. In Spain, they were known as *chapins*.

2 Cole 194–95. During the fifteen years she spent at the Spanish court, Sofonisba Anguissola signed only a few of her works, likely because

it was considered inappropriate for a noblewoman in the queen's household to behave as if she were a working artist. Many current attributions thus remain conjectural. On the painting of Elisabeth known as the Bayonne portrait, see Perlingieri, *Sofonisba Anguissola*, 119.

3 Knecht, *Catherine De' Medici*, 97–98.

4 See the stunning drawing of Charles by Pierre Dumoustier (1565) in Knecht, *French Religious Wars*, 17; Holt provides a map of the tour, p. 61.

5 The farm was a kind of pleasure palace where Catherine could relax in rustic splendor and play at peasant (much as Marie Antoinette would do in the gardens of the Petit Trianon at Versailles over two hundred years later); Martin 30–35.

6 Scott and Sturm-Maddox 84.

7 Graham and Johnson collect the extant pamphlets that describe the tour; Holt 60; Weisner-Hanks 103–106.

8 Bordonove argues that Charles had every right to be disgruntled. Catherine treated him the same as she did the Duke of Anjou, who was both younger and of inferior rank, pp. 111–12.

9 Bordonove 119. The newly christened Francis was too young for the trip and had stayed behind in the nursery; Catherine announced plans during the royal tour to change his name, but the rechristening did not occur officially until after his return.

10 *CSP Foreign, Elizabeth*, Vol. 5, August 31, 1562, #554.

11 Hay Fleming 74–75.

12 Pollen, ed., 76. The word Elizabeth uses in French is "famille." In both English and French, the word "family" meant household, including servants or those who lived in the protection and pay of the master. But by using the word, Elizabeth seems intentionally to touch upon the kinship between Mary Stuart and the Guises.

13 *CSP Spain*, Vol. 1, April 7, 1565, #293.

14 Combes 23–25.

15 Combes 26–27, 29–31; Cabié 375–76.

16 *CSP Spain (Simancas)*, Vol. 1, February 3, 1565, #285.

17 Ribera 195.

18 Brantôme, ed. Lalanne, Vol. 8, pp. 18–19.

19 See the letter by Alba and Don Juan Manrique to Philip of June 15, 1565, in Amezúa y Mayo, Vol. 3:1, p. 296.

20 *Brief discours de l'arrivée de la royne d'Espaigne à Sainct Jehan de Luz*, Aiv r°; *Ample Discours de l'Arrivee*, Br°.

21 Graham and Johnson provide a thorough description and analysis of the events at Bayonne.

22 Marguerite de Valois 44–45; on the Spanish reaction, see Graham and Johnson 32.

23 *Papiers d'Etat [Granvelle]* IX, 312–14, cited in Weber 16, 18.

24 National Archives of Spain, Simancas, K 1504, cited in *Lettres*, Vol. 2, p. 76.

25 Combes 47–48.

26 NAS Simancas, K 1503, cited in *Lettres*, Vol. 2, pp. 300–302.

27 Cabié 395.

28 *Lettres*, Vol. 2, p. 297.

29 Scott and Sturm-Maddox 220.

30 Ronsard, *Elegies*, A2r°.

CHAPTER 21: THE QUEENS' TWO BODIES

1 Mary's letter in Stevenson, ed., 191–93.

2 Labanoff, ed., Vol. 1, p. 282. My italics. Teulet, ed., *Papiers d'état*, Vol. 2, p. 101.

3 *Lettres*, Vol. 2, p. 310; Chéruel 43; Teulet, ed., *Papiers d'etat*, Vol. 2, p. 96.

4 On Lord James's humiliation, see Guzmán de Silva's report to Philip II in *CSP Spain (Simancas)*, Vol. 1, November 5, 1565, #330.

5 Mumby, *Beginning of the Feud*, 389.

6 *CSP Scotland*, Vol. 2, December 25, 1565, #319.

7 *CSP Scotland*, Vol. 2, December 25, 1565, #319; Hay Fleming 342–43, n. 99; Keith, Vol. 2, pp. 299–300.

8 *CSP Scotland*, Vol. 2, December 25, 1565, #319.

9 Mumby, *Beginning of the Feud*, 347; Guy, *My Heart*, 211–16.

10 Labanoff, ed., Vol. 7, p. 340.

11 *Lettres*, Vol. 2, p. 379.

12 BnF ms. français 3902, f. 86r°; Edouard 226; Ferrière, *Rapport*, 28.

13 *Lettres*, Vol. 1, p. 320; Broomhall 224–26. For Philip's mistresses, see Alberi 63.

14 BnF ms. français 16958, f. 110r°.

15 Cabié, ed., 288.

16 *Lettres*, Vol. 2, p. 209.

17 The following comes from Mugnoni's letter in Amezúa y Mayo ed., Vol. 3:1, pp. 245–52; see also descriptions by Saint Sulpice in BnF ms. français 3162 f. 7 and 3163ff. 1–2.

18 *CSP Foreign*, Vol. 7, August 7, 1564, #635. Challoner mistakenly reported that she had miscarried twin girls.

19 Amazúa y Mayo ed., Vol. 3:1, p. 252.

20 Fourquevaux, Vol. 1, pp. 45, 58.

21 Fourquevaux, Vol. 1, pp. 65–66, 87, 100–101; Du Prat 455.

22 Du Prat 455.

23 In a letter to Fourquevaux, Charles IX explains that they learned of the murder at the end of March. *Lettres*, Vol. 2, p. 358, n. 1.

24 Mary's entire letter to the Archbishop of Glasgow is in Labanoff, Vol. 1, pp. 341–50. There is another letter in the *Calendar of State Papers Venice*, Vol. 7, April 2, 1566, #361, ostensibly to Queen Catherine and King Charles. This letter existed in an Italian copy in the Venetian State Archives, a translation from a letter that Mary likely wrote in French. Mary's letter to the Archibshop of Glasgow, in Scots, is also likely a translation (see Labanoff, ed., Vol. 1, p. 399). It is not clear whether these two copies are in fact two different translations of the same letter.

25 Hay Fleming 128; Labanoff, ed., Vol. 1, p. 349.

26 *CSP Spain (Simancas)*, Vol. 1, March 23, 1566, #344.

27 *CSP Venice*, Vol. 7, April 2, 1566, #361.

28 *Lettres*, Vol. 2, p. 358; *CSP Spain (Simancas)*, Vol. 1, March 23, 1566, #344.

29 Tytler, *History of Scotland*, Vol. 7, p. 30.

30 Stevenson, ed., 199–201.

31 The details of the murder can be derived from Ruthven's account, as reported later to Randolph and Bedford, in Keith, Vol. 3, pp. 260–76. See also Randolph and Bedford's own report in Mumby, *The Fall*, 48–56. Mary's letter to Charles and Catherine in *CSP Venice*, cited above, provides further details. *CSP Venice*, Vol. 7, April 8, 1566, #362.

32 Nau, ed. Stevenson, 17.

33 *CSP Venice*, Vol. 7, April 8, 1566, #362.

34 Labanoff, ed., Vol. 7, pp. 301–302.

CHAPTER 22: THE BIRTH OF PRINCES

1 Hay Fleming 335, n. 85; Keith's *History*, Vol. 2, p. 273.

2 Cabié, ed., 72.

3 Labanoff, ed., Vol. 7, pp. 297–99. The document is undated, but given its contents, Labanoff suggests it was written in 1566.

4 Labanoff, ed., Vol. 7, pp. 297–99.

5 Labanoff, ed., Vol. 1, p. 349.

6 Labanoff, ed., Vol. 1, pp. 354–55; *CSP Spain (Simancas)*, Vol. 1, May 1566, #355.

7 Guy, *My Heart*, 257.

8 See R. Johnson, ed., xxxi and bis for the inventories of Mary's bequests; Swait 58.

9   Guy, *My Heart*, 258.
10 *CSP Spain (Simancas)*,Vol. 1, May n.d., 1566, #355; Labanoff, ed.,Vol. 1, pp. 354; R. Johnson, ed., xxxiii.
11 R. Johnson, ed., xxxi.
12 Nau, ed. Stevenson, 27.
13 Strickland 424.
14 Herries 70;Teulet, ed., *Papiers d'état*,Vol. 2, p. 245; Melville 77; Nau, ed. Stevenson, 27. *CSP Scotland*,Vol. 2, June 24, 1566, #400.
15 Herries 79; Chéruel 48.
16 Teulet, ed., *Papiers d'Etat*,Vol. 2, pp. 139–46.
17 Hay Fleming 142.
18 Edmund Hay in Nau, ed. Stevenson, cxliii.
19 Nau, ed. Stevenson, cxxxvi–cxlii.
20 Hay in Nau, ed. Stevenson, cxlv.
21 Mumby, *The Fall*, 144.
22 Labanoff, ed.,Vol. 1, p. 398.
23 Melville 74.
24 *Lettres*,Vol. 2, p. 370.
25 Fourquevaux,Vol. 1, p. 111; Betegón Díez 31; Cabié, ed., 433.
26 Cabié, ed., 432–33.
27 Fourquevaux,Vol. 1, p. 110.
28 Fourquevaux,Vol. 1, p. 118.
29 Fourquevaux,Vol. 1, p. 112. Fourquevaux's curious mention of a spot of blood suggests he was in the room during the birth, potentially as a witness.
30 Fourquevaux,Vol. 1, pp. 117–18.
31 Amezúa y Mayo, ed.,Vol. 3:1, p. 48.
32 Labanoff, ed.,Vol. 2, pp. 182–97.
33 *Lettres*,Vol. 2, pp. 379; Cabié 433.
34 Bethany 231–33 and passim.
35 The "Protestation of the Earls of Huntley and Argyll, touching the murder of the King of Scots" recounts the events at Craigmillar. The document was composed in 1569 at Mary's command, so the objectivity of its contents is highly suspect. Goodall,Vol. 2, pp. 316–21; cf. Mumby, *The Fall*, pp. 138–41.
36 Stevenson, ed., *History* cxlv–cxlvii; Bingham 165; Hay-Fleming 425, n. 98.
37 Most of the cost of the ceremony itself was paid for through taxes, the first levied in years. Lee 8; Bingham 165.
38 Armstrong Davison 252.

39 Nau, ed. Stevenson, cxlvii.

40 Mumby, *The Fall*, 145. Might Du Croc have been aware of certain plots?

41 Du Prat 252.

42 Du Prat 256.

43 Fourquevaux, Vol. 1, pp. 281–82; Edouard 230.

CHAPTER 23: THE TURN

1 Keith, *History*, Vol. 1, p. ciii.

2 Labanoff, ed., Vol. 1, pp. 395–96.

3 Keith, *History*, Vol. 1, p. ciii.

4 Labanoff, ed., Vol. 2, pp. 2–4, 6–10.

5 Knox, ed. Dickinson, Vol. 2, p. 537.

6 The "Protestation of the Earls of Huntley and Argyll," in Goodall, Vol. 2, pp. 316–21.

7 Bingham 182–83; *CSP Venice*, Vol. 7, March 3, 1567, #384.

8 *CSP Scotland*, Vol. 2, March 8, 1567, #479.

9 Mumby, *The Fall*, 204.

10 Mumby, *The Fall*, 204; Hay Fleming 152.

11 *CSP Foreign*, Volume 8, February 28, 1567, #97.

12 *CSP Spain (Simancas)*, Vol. 1, May 3, 1567, #417; in fact, murmurs that Bothwell intended to marry the queen had circulated even in the days leading up to his trial.

13 Marcus et al., eds., 116–17.

14 *Lettres*, Vol. 2, p. 14; Mumby, *The Fall*, 204, 214; *CSP Foreign*, Vol. 8, February 28, 1567, #97; Bath and Jones 226–30.

15 *CSP Foreign*, Vol. 8, March 29, 1567, #1053.

16 *Lettres*, Vol. 3, pp. 25, 30–31, 33, 37, 40.

17 *CSP Spain (Simancas)*, Vol. 1, May 3, 1567, #417.

18 Melville 88.

19 Rait, ed., 118; Labanoff, ed., Vol. 2, pp. 36, 41.

20 Labanoff, ed., Vol. 7, pp. 110–11; Rait, ed., 121.

21 Labanoff, ed., Vol. 2, p. 42.

22 Mumby, *The Fall*, 234–35, 237; *CSP Scotland*, Vol. 2, May 7, 1567, #501.

23 Fraser 343. On the question, posed at the time, of whether Mary married Bothwell of her own "free will," see Mumby, *The Fall*, 234–35, 237; *CSP Scotland*, Vol. 2, May 7, 1567, #501. On the meaning of "ravishment" and its legal implications as "stealing" in addition to "rape" during the sixteenth century, see Palotti 215–16; Baines 72.

24 *Lettres*, Vol. 3, p. 37, n. 1.

25 Labanoff, ed., Vol. 7, pp. 111, 113–24.

26 Fourquevaux 80.

27 Chéruel 51; Teulet, ed., *Papiers d'état*, Vol. 2, p. 187.

CHAPTER 24: THE PRISONER

1 *CSP Spain (Simancas)*, Vol. 1, August 2, 1567, #434.

2 Hay Fleming 165.

3 In June, the Spanish Ambassador Silva in London reported: "Queen [Mary] is pregnant and they say five months gone." This, however, is impossible: there is no earlier mention of a pregnancy, and if she had indeed been "five months gone" Mary could have claimed Darnley was the father—and this she most certainly didn't do. Fraser gives a thorough discussion of Mary's pregnancy, and the difficulties of dating the time of conception, p. 343.

4 *CSP Scotland*, Vol. 2, May 7, 1575, #501.

5 Stevenson, ed., 221; *CSP Scotland*, Vol. 2, July 29, 1567, #578. Robert Melville, writing to Queen Elizabeth, shared Throckmorton's fears for Mary. One other hint at Mary's pregnancy may be taken from a letter by Bedford on July 17, reporting that Mary had calmed down enough both to rest and to take some leisure with her ladies, "much better than she was wont, so as (it is said) she is become fat." Bedford reported only what he had heard; he did not see Mary himself. Hay Fleming 468–69, n. 52.

6 Fraser 343.

7 Philip Barrow, *The Methode of Physicke* (1596), 201; cited in Levin 50; Sir Henry Finch, *Law, or a Discourse Thereof* (1627), 396, cited in Bashar 36.

8 Fraser 343.

9 Nau, ed. Stevenson, 264. Fraser gives a thorough discussion of the difficulties in dating Mary's pregnancy, p. 343.

10 Swain 55–56.

11 Stevenson, ed., 220; Mumby, *The Fall*, 270.

12 Mumby, *The Fall*, 287; Nau, ed. Stevenson, 60.

13 *CSP Scotland*, Vol. 2, July 29, 1567, #578.

14 Labanoff, ed., Vol. 2, p. 61; Hay Fleming 169; *CSP Scotland*, Vol. 2, July 31, 1566, #581.

15 Nau, ed. Stevenson, 64; Hay Fleming 477, n. 71.

CHAPTER 25: THE DEATH OF A QUEEN

1   *CSP Venice*,Vol. 7, May 26, 1568, #424–25.

2   Mumby, *The Fall*, 319–20; Labanoff, ed.,Vol. 2, pp. 64–69.

3   Mumby, *The Fall*, 329.

4   Mumby, *The Fall*, 316.

5   *Lettres*,Vol. 3, pp. 143–44. My italics.

6   Kamen, *Philip of Spain*, 120.

7   Parker, *Imprudent King*, 186; Gachard 164.

8   Fourquevaux,Vol. 1, 266.

9   Kamen, *Philip of Spain*, 121.

10 Parker, *Imprudent King*, 187; Kamen, *Philip of Spain*, 121; Fourquevaux, Vol. 1, p. 322.

11 Parker, *Imprudent King*, 189; Kamen, *Philip of Spain*, 122. Charles V maintained the "policy" toward his mother begun by his grandfather, Ferdinand of Aragon.

12 Gachard 449.

13 Gachard 437; Freer,Vol. 2, p. 300.

14 Freer,Vol. 2, p. 285.

15 Gachard 364.

16 Fourquevaux, Vol. 1, pp. 372–73; Count of Lerma cited in Parker, *Imprudent King*, 189.

17 Parker, *Imprudent King*, 190.

18 Gachard 401, n. 1.

19 Freer,Vol. 2, pp. 282–83.

20 Amazúa y Mayo, ed.,Vol. 3:1, p. 59.

21 Amazúa y Mayo, ed.,Vol. 3:1, pp. 64–65.

22 Fourquevaux, Vol. 1, p. 374; Catherine notes the confirmation of Elisabeth's pregnancy on June 23, 1568, *Lettres*,Vol. 3, p. 151.

23 Du Prat 306.

24 Du Prat 355.

25 Knecht, *French Religious Wars*, pp. 40–41.

26 Fourquevaux,Vol. 2, p. 382.

27 López de Hoyos, *Historia y relacion verdadera de la enfermedad, felicissimo transito, y suptuousas exequias funebres de la Serenissima Reyna de España Doña Ysabel de Valoys, nuestra Señora*, p. 11; Edouard 237.

28 Edouard 237; Fourquevaux,Vol. 1, p. 384; on the Countess of Ureigna's death, see Fourquevaux,Vol. 1, p. 83.

CHAPTER 26: LAST LETTERS

1 Freer,Vol. 2, p. 356; Fourquevaux,Vol. 1, p. 386.

2 Amézua y Mayo, ed.,Vol 3:1, pp. 67–68.

3 Fourquevaux,Vol. 1, p. 388.

4 Brantôme reports the words of Monsieur de Lignerolle, who was present in Madrid for Elisabeth's death; ed. Lalanne,Vol. 8, p. 8.

5 Rodriguez and Rodriguez, doc. 124; cf. Kamen, *Philip II*, 122.

6 Mumby, *The Fall*, 330–33.

7 The Casket Letters and their authenticity have inspired scores of studies over the centuries. An excellent summary, including the terms of debate, appears in Villius. The originals, now lost, appear to have been written in French; published versions were printed in Scottish, Latin, and English translations.

8 Mumby, *The Fall*, 286–87.

9 *CSP Scotland*,Vol. 2, June 8, 1568, #690; Mumby, *The Fall*, 342.

10 *CSP Scotland*,Vol. 2, June 14, 1568, #702; Mumby, *The Fall*, 344.

11 *CSP Scotland*,Vol. 2, June 8, 1568, #692.

12 Labanoff, ed.,Vol. 2, p. 116.

13 Labanoff, ed.,Vol. 2, p. 78.

14 Labanoff, ed.,Vol. 2, pp. 182–87. This is the sole surviving letter between the two queens.

15 Labanoff, ed.,Vol. 5, p. 23.

16 Labanoff, ed.,Vol. 2, p. 243.

17 Labanoff, ed.,Vol. 1, p. 243;Teulet, ed., *Lettres*, 295.

18 Teulet, ed., *Lettres*, 295.

CHAPTER 27: A DAUGHTER'S LOVE

1 Amezúa y Mayo, ed.,Vol. 3:2, p. 381.

2 *Lettres*,Vol. 3, p. 194.

3 *Lettres*,Vol. 3, p. 193.

4 Douais, ed.,Vol. 1, p. 388.

5 *Simancas*, K. 1394, n. 231, cited in Freer,Vol. 2, p. 369.

6 Amezúa y Mayo,Vol. 2:2, pp. 516–17.The Venetian's report, from BnF ms. français 3225, p. 57, is summarized in *Lettres*,Vol. 3, pp. xxxiii–xxxiv.

7 *Rapport*, ed. Ferriére, 30.

8 Cole 147; Kusche 100–101.

9 *Lettres*,Vol. 3, p. 204.

10 *Lettres*,Vol. 3, p. 201.

11 Fourquevaux,Vol. 1, p. 386.

12 *Lettres*, Vol. 3, p. 199.

13 Freer, Vol. 2, p. 367.

14 Amezúa y Mayo, ed., Vol. 3:2, np; *Tumbeau* f. Biv v°.

15 Amezúa y Mayo, ed., Vol. 3:2, p. 495.

16 Fourquevaux, Vol. 1, pp. 384–86.

EPILOGUE

1 On Mary's last night, see Guy, *My Heart*, 483–86, and Chantelauze 393–401.

2 Mary's letter is taken from the National Library of Scotland (NLS) Adv. MS. 54.1.1. Notes on the French watermark in NLS records, http://manuscripts.nls.uk/repositories/2/resources/16277.

3 *Lettres*, Vol. 9, pp. 189, 191. Monsieur de Bellièvre was one of the envoys Henri III had sent in October to plead the case of the Queen of Scots.

4 *Lettres*, Vol. 3, p. 318.

5 Sidney 50; Stubbs 25.

6 *CSP Spain (Simancas)*, Vol. 3, December 25, 1581, #186.

7 Marcus et al., eds., 260–61. Alençon may have died of malaria.

8 Parker, *Imprudent King*, 322.

9 Labanoff, ed., Vol. 7, pp. 129–30.

10 Knecht, *Catherine de' Medici*, 260–261.

11 Knecht, *Catherine de' Medici*, 267.

12 Estoile 581–82; Henri's words to Catherine given in Knecht, *Catherine de' Medici*, 266.

13 Mariéjol 405–406, translated in Knecht, *Catherine de' Medici*, 267.

14 Pasquier, *Oeuvres*, Vol. 2, pp. 379–80; Chang and Kong 250–53.

15 *Discours merveilleux*, pp. 131–32, translated in Chang and Kong 143. It is not clear whether the author of the *Discours merveilleux* was Protestant; he may have been a Catholic disgruntled with Catherine's policies of conciliation.

16 Pasquier, *Oeuvres*, Vol. 2, p. 378; Zampini f. 1, f. 11.

17 Bnf ms. NAL 82.

18 *Lettres*, Vol. 6, p. 360.

BIBLIOGRAPHY

Manuscript Sources

National Library of Scotland

Advocates MS. 29.2.2
Advocates MS. 54.1.1

Bibliothèque nationale de France

Fonds français 3008, 3120, 3152, 3162, 3163, 3902, 6614, 8181, 10751, 11207,
    15880, 16958, 20468, 23193
Fonds latin 8660
Nouvelle acquisition française [NAF] 607
Nouvelle acquisition latine [NAL] 82

National Archives of France

K 1492 nos. 66, 78; K 1493 no. 91; K 1715 no. 10

General Archives of Simancas

Patronato Real Leg 30, 28
Patronato Real Leg 30, 30

Wellcome Collection (London, UK)

MS. 222

Musée Condé, Château de Chantilly (Chantilly, France)

MN 31–MN 42

Folger Shakespeare Library, Washington, DC

MS. Add 895.
MS. Z.d.16.

Archives and Primary Printed Sources

Alberi, Eugenio. *Le Relazioni degli ambasciatori venetti al Senato.* Vol. 5. Florence: A Spese dell'Editore, 1861.

———. *Vita di Caterina de' Medici, saggio storico.* Florence: Batelli & Figli, 1838.

Amezúa y Mayo, Agustín G. De, ed. *Isabel de Valois, Reina de España (1546–1568).* Vol. 3. Madrid: Gráficas Ultra, 1949.

Ample discours de l'arrivée de la Rogne Catholique soeur du roy à Saint Jehan de Lus. Paris: J. Dallier, 1565.

Anne of France. *Lessons for My Daughter.* Edited and translated by Sharon L. Jansen. Cambridge: D.S. Brewer, 2004.

Archives curieuses de l'histoire de France, depuis Louis XI jusqu'à Louis XVIII. Edited by L. Cimber and F. Danjou. Series 1:4. Paris: Beauvais, 1835.

Ascham, Roger. *The Whole Works of Roger Ascham.* Edited by John Allen Giles. Vol. 1. London: J.R. Smith, 1864.

D'Aubigné, Théodore Agrippa. *Sa vie à ses enfants.* Edited by Gilbert Schrenck. Paris: Nizet, 1986.

Ball, Rachel, and Geoffrey Parker, eds. *Cómo ser rey: Instrucciones del emperador Carlos V a su hijo Felipe, mayo de 1543.* New York: Hispanic Society of America, 2014.

Baluze, Etienne. *Histoire généalogique de la maison d'Auvergne.* Vol. 2. Paris: Antoine Dezellier, 1708.

Baschet, Armand. *La Diplomatie vénitienne: Les princes de l'Europe au XVI siècle.* Paris: Plon, 1862.

Benedict, Philip, Jean Perrissin, and Jacques Tortorel. *Graphic History: The Wars, Massacres, and Troubles of Tortorel and Perrissin*. Geneva: Droz, 2007.

Bèze, Théodore. *Histoire ecclésiastique des églises réformées au royaume de France*. Edited by P. Vesson. Vol. 1. Toulouse: Société des livres religieux, 1882.

Bourgeois Boursier, Louise. *Observations diverses sur la sterilité, perte de fruit, fœcondité, accouchements, et maladies des femmes, et enfants nouveaux naiz*. Paris: Mechior Mondiere, 1651.

Brantôme, Pierre de Bourdeille, seigneur de. *Oeuvres complètes*. Edited by Ludovic Lalanne (1848). 11 vols. New York: Johnson Reprints, 1968.

———. *Recueil des dames, poésies, et tombeaux*. Edited by Etienne Vaucheret. Paris: Gallimard, 1991.

———. *Vies des dames illustres françaises et étrangères*. Edited by Louis Moland. Paris: Garnier Frères, 1868.

Brief discourse de l'arrivée de la royne d'Espagne à Sainct Jehan de Luz, de son entrée à Bayonne, & du magnifique recueil qui lui a esté fait par leurs Magestez. Paris: Guillaume de Nyvard, 1565.

Buchanan, George. *Ane Detectioun of the doings of Marie queen of Scottes*. London: John Day, 1571.

Buchon, J.A.C., ed. *Choix de chroniques et mémoires sur l'histoire de France*. Paris: A. Desrez, 1836.

Calendar of State Papers, Foreign: Elizabeth, Volume 1, 1558–1559. Edited by Joseph Stevenson. London: Her Majesty's Stationery Office, 1863. *British History Online*, accessed July 13, 2021, www.british-history.ac.uk /cal-state-papers/foreign/vol1.

Calendar of State Papers, Foreign: Elizabeth, Volume 8, 1566–1568. Edited by Allan James Crosby. London: Her Majesty's Stationery Office, 1871. *British History Online*, accessed July 13, 2021, www.british-history.ac.uk /cal-state-papers/foreign/vol8.

Calendar of State Papers, Scotland: Volume 1, 1547–63. Edited by Joseph Bain. London: Her Majesty's Stationery Office, 1898. *British History Online*, accessed July 13, 2021, www.british-history.ac.uk/cal-state-papers/ scotland/vol1.

Calendar of State Papers, Scotland: Volume 2, 1563–69. Edited by Joseph Bain. London: Her Majesty's Stationery Office, 1900. *British History Online*, accessed July 13, 2021, www.british-history.ac.uk/cal-state-papers/ scotland/vol2.

Calendar of State Papers, Spain (Simancas), Volume 1, 1558–1567. Edited by Martin A. S. Hume. London: Her Majesty's Stationery Office, 1892.

British History Online, accessed July 13, 2021, www.british-history.ac.uk
/cal-state-papers/simancas/vol1.

Calendar of State Papers, Spain (Simancas), Volume 2, 1568–1579. Edited by
Martin A. S. Hume. London: Her Majesty's Stationery Office, 1894.
British History Online, accessed July 13, 2021, www.british-history.ac.uk
/cal-state-papers/simancas/vol2.

*Calendar of State Papers Relating to English Affairs in the Archives of Venice,
Volume 7, 1558–1580.* Edited by Rawdon Brown and G. Cavendish
Bentinck. London: Her Majesty's Stationery Office, 1890. *British
History Online*, accessed July 13, 2021, www.british-history.ac.uk/cal
-state-papers/venice/vol7.

Carles, Lancelot de. *Epistre contenant le procès criminal fact à l'encontre de la
rogne Anne Boullant d'Angleterre.* Lyon: [N.p.], 1545.

Cazauran, Nicole, ed. *Discours merveilleux de la vie, actions et deportements
de Catherine de Médicis, royne-mère.* Geneva: Droz, 1995.

Chantelauze, Régis. *Marie Stuart, son procès et son exécution, d'après le
journal inédit de Bourgoing son médecin.* Paris: E. Plon, 1876.

Clifford, Arthur, ed. *The State Papers and Letters of Sir Ralph Sadler.*
Edinburgh: Archibald Constable, 1809.

Clouet, François, and De Mannier. Portraits of the French royal children.
MN31–MN42. Musée Condé, Château de Chantilly, France.

Cohen, Gustave, ed. *Geoffroy Tory and Catherine de Medici: An Unpublished
Manuscript of Geoffroy Tory of the Genealogy of the Counts of Boulogne.*
Translated by Samuel A. Ives. New York: H.P. Krauss, 1944.

Colleción de documentos inéditos para la historia de España. Vol. 87. Madrid:
Academia de la Historia, 1842–1895.

Colleción de documentos inéditos para la historia de España. 112 vols. Madrid:
Academia de la Historia, 1842–1895.

Condé, Louis de. *Recueil des choses mémorables faites et passées pour le faict de
la religion & estat de ce royaume, depuis la mort du roy Henry II. jusques au
commencement des troubles.* 3 vols. Strasbourg: Pierre Estiard, 1565–66.

De Thou, Jacques-Auguste. *Histoire Universelle.* Vol. 4. London, 1734.

d'Ewes, Simonds. "Journal of the House of Lords: January 1559." *British
History Online*, accessed April 24, 2020. www.british-history.ac.uk
/no-series/jrnl-parliament-eliz1/pp1-18.

*The Destruction and sacke cruelly committed by the Duke of Guyse and his
company in the towne of Vassy, the fyrste of March in the year M.D.LXII.*
London: Henry Sutton, 1562.

Diefendorf, Barbara, ed. *The St. Bartholomew's Day Massacre: A Brief
History with Documents.* Boston: Bedford/St. Martin's Press, 2008.

Discours du grand et magnifique triomphe fait au mariage du tresnoble [et] magnifique prince François de Valois [et] de tressaute [et] vertueuse princesse madame Marie d'Estruart roine d'Escosse. Paris: Annet Brière, 1558.

Du Bellay, Martin, and Guillaume Du Bellay. *Mémoires des messieurs Martin du Bellay, seigneur de Langey.* Paris: Olivier de P. L'Huillier, 1569.

Dupleix, Scipion. *Histoire générale de France.* Vol. 3. Paris: Denys Bechet, 1639.

Edward VI of England. *England's Boy King: The Diary of Edward VI, 1547–1553.* Edited by W.E.S. North. Welwyn Garden City: Ravenhall, 2005.

Elisabeth de Valois to Margherita Paleologa, 1559. MS. Add 895. Folger Shakespeare Library, Washington, DC.

Elizabeth I of England. *Autograph Compositions and Foreign Language Originals.* Edited by Leah S. Marcus, Janel Mueller, and Mary Beth Rose. Chicago: University of Chicago Press, 2003.

———. *Collected Works.* Edited by Leah S. Marcus, Janel Mueller, and Mary Beth Rose. Chicago: University of Chicago Press, 2002.

———. "The Mirror of the Sinful Soul." 1544. MS. Cherry 36. Bodleian, University of Oxford.

Ellis, Henry, ed. *Original Letters Illustrative of English History.* Vol. 3:2. London: Richard Bentley, 1846.

Estienne, Henri (?). *Le Discours merveilleux de la vie, actions, et déportement de Catherine de Médicis, Royne-mère.* Geneva [?], 1575.

———. *The Mervaylous Discourse upon the life, decides, and behaviors of Katherine de Medici, Queen Mother.* Heydelberge [London], 1575.

Fleuranges, Robert de la Marck, seigneur de. *Mémoires du maréchal de Florange: Dit le jeune aventureux.* Edited by Robert Goubaux and Paul-André Lemoine. Vol. 1. Paris: Renouard-Laurens, 1913–24.

Forbes, Patrick, ed. *A Full View of the Public Transactions in the Reign of Q[ueen] Elizabeth.* 2 vols. Paris: J. Bettenham, 1740–41.

Fourquevaux, Raimond de Beccarie de Pavie, sieur de. *Dépêches de M. de Fourquevaux, ambassadeur du roi Charles IX en Espagne.* Edited by M. L'abbé Douais. 3 vols. Paris: E. Leroux, 1896–1904.

Foxe, John. *Acts and Monuments of the Christian Church.* Edited by John Malham and T. Pratt. Philadelphia: Smith, 1858.

Gairdner, James, ed. *Letters and Papers, Foreign and Domestic, Henry VIII.* 21 vols. London: Her Majesty's Stationery Office, 1858.

Godefroy, Théodore. *Le Ceremonial françois.* Vol. 2. Paris: Sébastian Cramoisy, 1649.

Great Britain, comp. *Statutes of the Realm . . . From the Original and Authentic Manuscripts.* N.p., 1907.

Guicciardini, Francesco. *The History of Italy*. Edited and translated by Sidney Alexander. Princeton: Princeton University Press, 1969.

———. *The Sack of Rome*. Edited and translated by James H. McGregor. New York: Italica Press, 2008.

Guiffrey, Georges, ed. *Lettres inédites de Dianne de Poytiers (1866)*. Geneva: Slatkine Reprints, 1970.

Guise, François de Lorraine, duc de. *Mémoires-journaux de François de Lorraine*. Edited by Joseph-François Michaud et al. Paris: Nouvelle collection des mémoires pour servir à l'histoire de France, 1839.

Halliwell-Phillipps, John Orchard, ed. *Love Letters of Henry VIII to Anne Boleyn*. Boston: John W. Luce, 1906.

Hamy, Alfred. *Entrevue de François premier avec Henry VIII à Boulogne-sur-mer, en 1532*. Paris: Lucien Gougy, 1898.

Haynes, Samuel, ed. *A Collection of State Papers Relating to the Affairs in the Reigns of King Henry VIII, King Edward VI, Queen Mary, and Queen Elizabeth from the Year 1542–1570*. 2 vols. London: William Bowyer, 1740–59.

Herries, Lord John, comp. *Historical memories of the Reign of Mary Queen of Scotland and a Portion of the Reign of King James the Sixth*. Edinburgh: Abbotsford Club, 1836.

Holinshed, Raphael. *The First volume of the chronicles of England, Scotland, and Ireland . . . The last volume of the chronicles (1577)*, accessed April 24, 2020. http://english.nsms.ox.ac.uk/holinshed/texts.php?text1=1577_5332.

Isambert, F. A. et al., ed. *Recueil général des anciennes lois françaises depuis l'an 420 jusqu'à la révolution de 1789*. Vol. 13. Paris: Belin-Leprieur, 1828.

Johnson, Robert, ed. *Inventaires de la royne descosse douairiere de France. Catalogues of the Jewels, Dresses, Furniture, Books, and Paintings of Mary, Queen of Scots, 1556–1569*. Edinburgh: Bannatyne Club, 1863.

Klarwill, Victor Von. *Queen Elizabeth and Some Foreigners: Being a Series of Hitherto Unpublished Letters from the Archives of the Hapsburg Family*. London: J. Lane, 1928.

Knox, John. *The First Blast of the Trumpet Against the Monstrous Regiment of Women (1558)*. Edited by Edward Arber. Westminster: Archibald Constable, 1895.

———. *The Works of John Knox*. Edited by David Laing. Vols 1–2. Edinburgh: Bannatyne Club, 1846–88.

———. *History of the Reformation in Scotland*. Edited by William Croft Dickinson. Vol. 1. London: Thomas Nelson & Sons, 1949.

La Planche, Regnier de. *Choix de Chroniques et mémoires sur l'histoire de France.* Edited by J.A.C. Buchon. Paris: A. Desrez, 1836.

Labanoff, Alexandre, ed. *Lettres, instructions, et mémoires de Marie Stuart, Reine d'Ecosse.* 7 vols. London: Charles Dolman, 1844.

"Lettre de l'huissier Baudin à la reyne-mère Loyse de Savoie." In *Le Cabinet Historique,* edited by Louis Paris, 215–26. Vol. 2. Paris: Au Cabinet Historique, 1856.

López de Hoyos, Juan. *Historia y relacion verdadera de la enfermedad, felicissimo transito, y suptuousas exequias funebres de la Serenissima Reyna de España Doña Ysabel de Valoys, nuestra Señora.* Madrid: Pierre Cosin, 1569.

Louise de Savoy. *Mémoires, ou journal de Louise de Savoye, Duchesse d'Angoulesme, d'Anjou et de Valois, Mère du Grand Roi François I.* Edited by L'abbé Lambert (1786). Charleston, SC: Nabu Press, 2013.

Machyn, Henry. "November 1558." In *Diary of Henry Machyn 1550–1563, British History Online,* accessed August 31, 2021, www.british-history.ac.uk/Camden-record-soc/vol42/pp169–184.

Maidment, James, ed. *Analecta Scotica: Collections Illustrative of the Civil, Ecclesiastical, and Literary History of Scotland.* Edinburgh: T.G. Stevenson, 1834.

March, José Maria, ed. *Niñez y juventud de Felipe II: Documentos inéditos sobre su educación civil, literaria y religiosa y su iniciación al gobierno (1527–1547).* Vol. 1. Madrid: Ministerio de asuntos exteriors, 1941.

Marguerite de Navarre. *Lettres de Marguerite d'Angoulême.* Edited by François Génin. Paris: Jules Renouard, 1841.

———. *The Mirror of the Sinful Soul.* Edited by Percy W. Ames. Translated by Elizabeth I of England. London: Asher, 1897.

———. *Selected Writings, A Bilingual Edition.* Edited and translated by Rouben Cholakian and Mary Skemp. Chicago: University of Chicago Press, 2008.

Marguerite de Valois. *Mémoires de Marguerite de Valois.* Edited by Paul Bonnefon. Paris: Bossard, 1920.

Medici, Catherine de. *Lettres de Catherine de Médicis.* Edited by Hector de la Ferrière-Percy (vols 1–5) and Gustave Bagenault de Puchesse (vols 6–10). Paris: Imprimerie nationale, 1880–1943.

Melville, James. *Memoirs of His Own Life.* Edited by W. Mackay Mackenzie. Boston: Small Maynard, 1924.

Memoires de Condé, servant d'éclaircissement et de preuves à l'histoire de m. de Thous, contenant ce qui s'est passé de plus mémorable en Europe. 2 vols. Paris: Rollin Fils, 1743–45.

Mézéray, François. *Histoire de France, dupuis Faramond jusqu'au régime de Louis le Juste.* Vol. 2. Paris: Mathieu & Pierre Guillemot, 1646.

Michaud, Joseph-François, and Jean-Joseph Poujoulet, eds. *Mémoires-journaux de François de Lorraine, duc d'Aumale et de Guise, 1547–1563.* Vol. 6 of *Nouvelle collection des mémoires pour servir à l'histoire de France.* Paris: L'Editeur du Commentaire Analytique du Code Civil, 1839.

Montaiglon, Anatole, ed. *The Latin Themes of Mary Queen of Scots.* London: Warton Club, 1855.

Mumby, Frank Arthur. *Elizabeth and Mary Stuart: The Beginning of the Feud.* London: Constable, 1914.

———. *The Fall of Mary Stuart: A Narrative in Contemporary Letters.* London: Constable, 1921.

———. *The Girlhood of Queen Elizabeth: A Narrative in Contemporary Letters.* London: Constable, 1909.

Nardi, Jacopo. *Le storie della città de Firenze.* Vol. 9. Florence: Bartolomeo Sermartelli, 1584.

Nau, Claude de. *The History of Mary Stewart, from the Murder of Riccio Until Her Flight into England.* Edited and translated by Joseph Stevenson. Edinburgh: William Patterson, 1883.

New Year's gift roll of Elizabeth I, Queen of England, 1584/5 January 1. Folger Shakespeare Library Z.d.16.

Niccolini, Sister Giustina. *The Chronicle of Le Murate.* Edited and translated by Sandra Weddle. Toronto: Center for Reformation and Renaissance Studies, 2011.

Nichols, John Gough, ed. *The Chronicle of Queen Jane, and of Two Years of Queen Mary, and Especially of the Rebellion of Sir Thomas Wyat. Written by a Resident in the Tower of London.* London: Camden Society, 1850.

Palma Cayet, Pierre Victor, ed. *Chronologie novenaire: Choix de chroniques et mémoires sur l'histoire de France, XVIe siècle.* Vol. 1. Paris: A. Desrez, 1836.

Paris, Louis, ed. *Négociations, lettres, et pièces relatives au règne de François II.* Paris: Imprimerie Royale, 1841.

Parr, Katherine. *Complete Works and Correspondence.* Edited by Janel Mueller. Chicago: University of Chicago Press, 2011.

Pasquier, Etienne. *Lettres historiques pour les années 1554–1596.* Edited by Dorothy Thickett. Geneva: Droz, 1966.

Pitscottie, Robert Lindsay of. *The History and Chronicles of Scotland.* Vol. I. Edinburgh: Scottish Text Society, 1899.

Pollen, John Hungerford, ed. *A Letter from Mary Queen of Scots to the Duke of Guise, January 1562.* Edinburgh: Scottish History Society, 1904.

Rait, Robert S., comp. *Mary Queen of Scots, 1542–1587: Extracts from the English, Spanish, and Venetian State Papers, Buchanan, Knox, Lesley, Melville, The "Diurnal of Occurrents," Nau, etc.* London: David Nutt, 1900.

La Recéption faicte par les députez du roi d'Espagne, de la Royne leur souveraine dame à la délivrance qui leur en a été faite en la ville de Roncevaux. Paris: Abel l'Angelier, 1586.

La Reception faicte par les députez du roi d'Espagne, de la royne leur souveraine dame, à la deliverance que leur en a esté faicte en l'Abbaye de Rõcevaux. Paris: Vincent Sertenas, 1560.

Recueil de plusieurs secrets tresexcellents et admirables, pour l'ornent & embellissement de la face, & autres parties du corps. Paris: Vincent Norment & Jeanne Bruneau, 1566.

Recueil des choses notables qui ont esté faites à Bayonne, à l'entreveue du Roy très-chrestien Charles neuvième de ce nom & la roine sa treshonoree mere, avec la Roine Catholique sa soeur. Paris: Vascozan, 1566.

Le Reveille-matin des francois, et de leurs voisins. Edinburgh: Jacques James, 1574.

Robertson, Joseph, ed. *Inventaires de la rogne descosse douairière de France: Catalogues of the Jewels, Dresses, Furniture, Books, and Paintings of Mary Queen of Scots, 1556–1569.* Edinburgh: Bannatyne Club, 1863.

Rodríguez, Justina, and Pedro Rodríguez, eds. *Don Francés Alava y Beamonte. Correspondencia inédita de Felipe II con su embajador en Paris (1564–1570).* San Sebastian: Grubo Dr. Camino de Historia Donostiarra, 1991.

Ronsard, Pierre de. *Elegies, mascarades, et bergerie.* Paris: Gabriel Buon, 1565.

———. *Oeuvres Complètes.* Edited by Jean Céard, Daniel Ménager, and Michel Simonin. Paris: Gallimard, 1993.

Seyssel, Claude de. *The Monarchy of France.* Edited and translated by Donald R. Kelley. New Haven: Yale University Press, 1981.

Sidney, Philip. "A Letter Written by Sir Philip Sidney to Queen Elizabeth, Touching Her Marriage with Monsieur." In *Miscellaneous Prose of Sir Philip Sidney*, edited by Katherine Duncan-Jones and Jan Van Dorsten, 46–57. Oxford: Clarendon Press, 1973.

Stevenson, Joseph, ed. *Selections from Unpublished Manuscripts in the College of Arms and the British Museum Illustrating the Reign of Mary Queen of Scotland, MDXLIII–MDLXVIII.* Edinburgh: Maitland Club, 1837.

Stow, John. *A Survey of London (1603).* Edited by C. L. Kingsford. Oxford: Clarendon Press, 1908.

Stubbs, John. *Gaping Gulf with Letters and Other Relevant Documents.* Edited by Lloyd E. Berry. Charlottesville, VA: Folger Shakespeare Library, 1968.

Teulet, Alexandre, ed. *Lettres de Marie Stuart, publiées avec sommaires, traductions, notes et fac-similé.* Paris: Firmin Didot, 1859.

———, ed. *Papiers d'état, pièces et documents inédits ou peu connus relatifs à l'histoire de l'Ecosse au XVIe siècle.* Edinburgh: Bannatyne Club, 1851.

Thompson, Thomas, ed. *A Diurnal of Remarkable Occurrents that have Passed Within the Country of Scotland since the Death of King James the Fourth till the year M.D. LXXV: From a Manuscript of the Sixteenth Century in the Possession of Sir John Maxwell of Pollock, Baronet.* Edinburgh: Bannatyne Club, 1833.

Tommaseo, Niccolò, ed. and trans. *Relations des ambassadeurs vénitiens sur les affaires de France au XVIe siècle.* 2 vols. Paris: Imprimerie Royale, 1838.

Tumbeau de treshaulte, trespuissante et trescatholique princesse Madame Elisabeth de France, Royne d'Espagne. En plusieurs langues. Recuilli de plusieurs sçavans personnages de la France. Paris: Robert Estienne, 1569.

Turnbull, William, ed. and trans. *Letters of Mary Stuart, Queen of Scotland: Selected from the "Recueil des lettres de Marie Stuart": Together with the chronological summary of events during the reign of the Queen of Scotland, by Prince Alexander Labanoff.* London: C. Dolman, 1845.

Varchi, Benedetto. *Storia fiorentina.* Edited by Silvano Razzi. Vol. 2. Florence: Società editrice delle storie del Nardi e del Varchi, 1843.

Vasari, Giorgio. *The Lives of the Painters, Sculptors and Architects.* Vol. 2. London: J.M. Dent & Sons, 1950.

Vieilleville, François de Sceaux, sire de. "Mémoires de Vieilleville." In *Collection des mémoires relatifs à l'histoire de France.* Edited by Claude-Bernard Petitot. Vol. 27. Paris: Foucault, 1819–29.

Vives, Juan Luis. *The Education of a Christian Woman: A Sixteenth-Century Manual.* Edited and translated by Charles Fantazzi. Chicago: University of Chicago Press, 2000.

Weiss, Charles, ed. *Papiers d'Etat du Cardinal de Granvelle.* Vol. 5. Paris: Imprimerie Nationale, 1841–45.

Wood, Marguerite, ed. *Foreign Correspondence with Marie de Lorraine Queen of Scotland, From the Originals in the Balcarres Papers, 1537–1548.* Vol. IV. Edinburgh: Scottish Historical Society, 1923.

———, ed. *Foreign Correspondence with Marie de Lorraine, Queen of Scotland, From the Originals in the Balcarres Papers, 1548–1557.* Vol. VII. Edinburgh: Scottish Historical Society, 1925.

Worth-Stylianou, Valérie, ed. *Pregnancy and Birth in Early Modern France: Treatises by Caring Physicians and Surgeons (1581–1625)*. The Other Voice in Early Modern Europe, The Toronto Series 23. Toronto: Iter and the Center for Reformation and Renaissance Studies, 2013.

Zampini, Matteo. *Elogio della gran Caterina de Medici, reina di Francia madre del Re. Fatto in lingua italiana, & latina, per M. Matteo Zampini, et tradotto in francese, per M. Carlo Paschali, et in spagnuola per l'illustre signor Girolamo Gondi, gentiluomo ordinario della camera di S. Maesta Christianissimia*. Paris: Abel L' Angelier, 1586.

Secondary Sources

Ackroyd, Peter. *London: A Biography*. London: Anchor Books, 2000.

Alexandre-Bidon, Daniele, and Didier Lett. *Children in the Middle Ages*. South Bend, IN: University of Notre Dame Press, 2000.

Amezúa y Mayo, Agustín G. de. *Isabel de Valois, Reina de España (1546–1568)*. Vols 1–2. Madrid: Gráficas Ultra, 1949.

Aram, Bethany. "Juana 'the Mad's' Signature: The Problem of Invoking Royal Authority." *Sixteenth Century Journal* 29, no. 2 (1998): 331–58.

Ariès, Philippe. *Centuries of Childhood*. Translated by Robert Baldick. London: Jonathan Cape, 1962.

Armstrong Davison, Meredith Henry. *The Casket Letters: A Solution to the Mystery of Mary Queen of Scots and the Murder of Lord Darnley*. Washington, DC: University Press of Washington, DC, 1965.

Arnold, Janet. "The 'Coronation' Portrait of Queen Elizabeth I." *Burlington Magazine* 120, no. 908 (1978): 726–41.

Baines, Barbara J. "Effacing Rape in Early Modern Representation." *ELH* 65, no. 1 (Spring 1998): 69–98.

Balsamo, Jean. *Les Rencontres des muses: Italianisme et anti-italianisme dans les lettres françaises de la fin du XVIe siècle*. Geneva: Slatkine, 1992.

Bashar, Nazife. "Rape in England between 1550 and 1700." In *The Sexual Dynamics of History*, edited by London Feminist History Group, 28–46. London: Pluto Press, 1983.

Bath, Michael, and Malcolm Jones. "'Placardes and Billis and Ticquettis of Defamatioun': Queen Mary, the Mermaid and the Hare." *Journal of the Warburg and Courtauld Institutes* 78 (2015): 223–46.

Baumgartner, Frederic J. *Henry II, King of France: 1547–1559*. Durham, NC: Duke University Press, 1988.

Berthoud, Gabrielle. *Antoine Marcourt: Réformateur et pamphlétaire*. Geneva: Droz, 1973.

Betegón Díez, Ruth. *Isabel Clara Eugenia, Infanta de España y soberana de Flandes*. Barcelona: Plaza Janés, 2004.

Bingham, Caroline. *Darnley: A Life of Henry Stuart, Lord Darnley, Consort of Mary Queen of Scots*. London: Constable, 1995.

Bordonove, Georges. *Les Rois qui ont fait la France: Charles IX*. Paris: Pygmalion, 2002.

Borman, Tracy. *Elizabeth's Women: The Hidden Story of the Virgin Queen*. London: Jonathan Cape, 2009.

———. *Henry VIII and the Men Who Made Him*. London: Hodder & Stoughton, 2018.

Bourrilly, Victor-Louis. *Guillaume du Bellay: Seigneur de Lange, 1491–1543*. Paris: Société Nouvelle de Librairie et d'Edition, 1905.

Boutier, Jean, Alain Dewerp, and Daniel Nordman. *Un Tour de France Royal: Le voyage de Charles IX, 1564–1566*. Paris: Aubier, 1984.

Boyden, James M. *The Courtier and the King: Ruy Gómez de Silva, Philip II, and the Court of Spain*. Berkeley: University of California Press, 1995.

Broomhall, Susan. *Women's Medical Work in Early Modern France*. Manchester: Manchester University Press, 2004.

Bryce, Moir. "Mary Stuart's Voyage to France in 1558." *English Historical Review* 22, no. 85 (January 1907): 43–50.

Burgess, Glenn. "Divine Right of Kings Reconsidered." *English Historical Review* 107, no. 425 (October 1992): 837–61.

Cabié, Edmond, ed. *Ambassade en Espagne de Jean Ebrard, Seigneur de Saint-Sulpice de 1562 à 1565 et mission de ce diplomate dans le même pays en 1566*. Paris: Albi, 1903.

Carroll, Stuart. *Martyrs and Murderers: The Guise Family and the Making of Europe*. Oxford: Oxford University Press, 2009.

Chamberlin, Frederick. *The Private Character of Henry the Eighth*. London: John Lane, 1932.

———. *The Sayings of Queen Elizabeth*. London: John Lane, 1923.

Chang, Leah, and Katherine Kong. *Portraits of the Queen Mother: Polemics, Panegyrics, Letters*. The Other Voice in Early Modern Europe, The Toronto Series 35. Toronto: Iter and the Center for Reformation and Renaissance Studies, 2014.

Charlier, P., J. Poupon, I. Huynsh-Charlier, J. F. Saliège, C. Keyser, and B. Ludes. "A Gold Elixir of Youth in the 16th-Century French Court." *British Medical Journal* (2009): 339.

Chéruel, Adolphe. *Marie Stuart et Catherine de Médicis: Étude historique sur les relations de la France et de l'Ecosse dans la seconde moitié du XVIe siècle.* Paris: Hachette, 1858.

Cholakian, Patricia F. *Rape and Writing in the Heptameron.* Edwardsville: Southern Illinois University Press, 1991.

Cholakian, Patricia F., and Rouben C. Cholakian. *Marguerite de Navarre: Mother of the Renaissance.* New York: Columbia University Press, 2006.

Cioffari, Vincenzo. "The Function of Fortune in Dante, Boccaccio, and Machiavelli." *Italica* 24, no. 1 (1947): 1–13.

Cloulas, Ivan. *Catherine de Médicis.* Paris: Fayard, 1979.

———. *Diane de Poitiers.* Paris: Fayard, 1997.

———. *Henri II.* Paris: Fayard, 1985.

Cohen, Gustave, ed. *Geoffroy Tory and Catherine de Medici Queen of France.* Translated by Samuel A. Ives. New York: H.P. Kraus, 1944.

Cole, Michael Wayne. *Sofonisba's Lesson: A Renaissance Artist and Her Work.* Princeton, NJ: Princeton University Press, 2019.

Colomer, José Luis. "Black and the Royal Image." In *Spanish Fashion at the Courts of Early Modern Europe,* edited by José Luis Colomer and Amalia Descalzo. Vol. 1. N.p.: CEEH, 2014.

Combes, M. F. *L'Entrevue de Bayonne de 1565 et la question de la Saint-Barthélemy.* Paris: Librairie G. Fischbacher, 1882.

Constant, Jean-Marie. *Les Guises.* Paris: Hachette, 1984.

Crawford, Katherine. *Perilous Performances: Gender and Regency in Early Modern France.* Cambridge, MA: Harvard University Press, 2004.

Crouzet, Denis. *Nostradamus: Une médecine des âmes à la Renaissance.* Paris: Biographie Payot, 2011.

Croze, Josephe de. *Les Guise, Les Valois, et Philip II.* Vol. 1. Paris: Librairie d'amyotrophies, 1866.

Cruz, Anne J. "Juana of Austria: Patron of the Arts and Regent of Spain, 1554–59." In *The Rule of Women,* edited by Anne J. Cruz and Mihoko Suzuki. Urbana: University of Illinois Press, 2009.

Cuisiat, Daniel, ed. *Lettres du Cardinal Charles de Lorraine (1525–1574).* Geneva: Droz, 1998.

Davenport, Cyril. *English Embroidered Bindings.* London: Trübner and Company, 1899.

Daybell, James. *The Material Letter in Early Modern England: Manuscript Letters and the Culture and Practices of Letter-Writing, 1512–1635.* London: Palgrave Macmillan, 2012.

Dean, David. "Parliament." In *The Elizabethan World,* edited by Susan Doran and Norman Jones, 113–29. New York: Routledge, 2011.

Defrance, Eugène. *Catherine de Médicis, ses astrologues et ses magiciens-envoûteurs: Documents inédits sur la diplomatie et les sciences occultes du XVI siècle*. Paris: Mercure de France, 1911.

Diefendorf, Barbara. "Rites of Repair: Restoring Community in the French Religious Wars." *Past & Present* 214, no. 7 (2012): 30–51.

Doran, Susan. *Elizabeth I and Her Circle*. Oxford: Oxford University Press, 2015.

———. *Monarchy and Matrimony: The Courtships of Elizabeth I*. London: Routledge, 1996.

Du Prat, Théodore. *Histoire d'Elisabeth de Valois, Reine d'Espagne, 1545–1568*. Paris: Techner, 1859.

Dunn, Jane. *Elizabeth and Mary: Cousins, Rivals, Queens*. New York: HarperCollins, 2004.

Edouard, Sylvène. *Le Corps d'une reine: Histoire singulière d'Élisabeth de Valois, 1546–1568*. Rennes: Presses universitaires de Rennes, 2009.

ffolliott, Sheila. "The Italian 'Training' of Catherine de Medici: Portraits as Dynastic Narrative." *Court Historian* 10, no. 1 (2005): 36–54.

Fletcher, John. "The Date of the Portrait of Elizabeth I in Her Coronation Robes." *Burlington Magazine* 120, no. 908 (1978): 753.

Forneron, Henri. *Les Ducs de Guise et leur époque*. 2 vols. Paris: E. Plon, 1877.

Fox, Julia. *Sister Queens: The Noble, Tragic Lives of Katherine of Aragon and Juana, Queen of Castile*. New York: Ballantine Books, 2011.

Fraser, Antonia. *Mary, Queen of Scots*. New York: Delacorte Press, 1969.

Freer, Margaret Walker. *Elisabeth de Valois, Queen of Spain, and the Court of Philip II*. 2 vols. London: Hurst and Blackett, 1857.

Frieda, Leonie. *Catherine de Medici, Renaissance Queen of France*. New York: HarperCollins, 2003.

Frye, Susan. *Pens and Needles: Women's Textualities in Early Modern England*. Philadelphia: University of Pennsylvania Press, 2010.

Gachard, Louis Prosper. *Don Carlos et Philippe II*. 2nd ed. Paris: Michel Lévy Frères, 1867.

García Barranco, Margarita. "La Casa de la reina en tiempos de Isabel de Valois." *Chronica Nova* 29 (2002): 85–107.

Gélis, Jacques. *The History of Childbirth: Fertility, Pregnancy, and Birth in Early Modern Europe*. Translated by Rosemary Morris. Cambridge: Polity Press, 1991.

Gibson, Jonathan. "Letters." In *A Companion to English Renaissance Literature and Culture*. Edited by Michael Hattaway. 615–619. Oxford: Blackwell, 2000.

Goodall, Walter. *An Examination of the Letters, Said to Be Written by Mary Queen of Scots, to James Earl of Bothwell: Shewing by Intrinsick and Extrinsick Evidence, That They Are Forgeries. Also, an Inquiry into the Murder of King Henry.* Edinburgh: Printed by T. and W. Ruddimans, 1754.

Goodare, Julian. "The First Parliament of Mary, Queen of Scots." *Sixteenth Century Journal* 36, no. 1 (Spring 2005): 55–75.

Graham, Victor E., W. McAllister Johnson, and Abel Jouan, eds. *The Royal Tour of France by Charles IX and Catherine De' Medici: Festivals and Entries, 1564–6.* Toronto: University of Toronto Press, 1979.

Gray, Janet G. "The Origin of the Word Huguenot." *Sixteenth Century Journal* 14, no. 3 (1983): 349–59.

Gristwood, Sarah. *Elizabeth and Leicester.* New York: Viking, 2007.

Guy, J. A. *Elizabeth: The Forgotten Years.* New York: Viking, 2016.

———. *My Heart Is My Own: The Life of Mary Queen of Scots.* London: Fourth Estate, 2004.

Hay Fleming, David. *Mary Queen of Scots, From Her Birth to Her Flight into England.* London: Hodden & Stoughton, 1898.

Heller, Henry. *Anti-Italianism in Sixteenth-Century France.* Toronto: University of Toronto Press, 2003.

Héritier, Jean. *Catherine de Médicis.* Paris: Fayard, 1959.

Hindson, Beth. "Attitudes Toward Menstruation and Menstrual Blood in Early-Modern England." *Journal of Social History* 43, no. 1 (Fall 2009): 89–114.

Holt, Mack P. *The French Wars of Religion, 1562–1629.* 2nd ed. Cambridge: Cambridge University Press, 2005.

Ives, E. W. *The Life and Death of Anne Boleyn: "The Most Happy."* Hoboken: Wiley-Blackwell, 2005.

James, Susan. *Catherine Parr—Henry VIII's Last Love.* Cheltenham: History Press, 2009.

Jenkins, Elizabeth. *Elizabeth the Great.* London: Victor Gollancz, 1958.

Kamen, Henry. *The Duke of Alba.* New Haven: Yale University Press, 2004.

———. *Philip of Spain.* New Haven: Yale University Press, 1997.

———. *The Spanish Inquisition: A Historical Revision.* New Haven: Yale University Press, 1998.

Kantorowicz, Ernst. *The King's Two Bodies: A Study in Mediaeval Political Theology.* Princeton: Princeton University Press, 1957.

Keith, Robert. *History of the Affairs of Church and State in Scotland.* 3 vols. Edinburgh: Spottiswoode Society, 1544–50.

Kelley, Donald R. *The Beginning of Ideology: Consciousness and Society in the French Reformation*. Cambridge: Cambridge University Press, 1981.

King, Helen. *The Disease of Virgins: Green Sickness, Chlorosis and the Problems of Puberty*. London: Routledge, 2004.

Knecht, Robert. *Catherine de' Medici*. London: Longman, 1998.

———. *The French Religious Wars, 1562–1598*. Oxford: Osprey, 2002.

———. *Renaissance Warrior and Patron: The Reign of Francis I*. Cambridge: Cambridge University Press, 1994.

Kusche, Maria. "Sofonisba Anguissola al servizio dei re di Spagna." In *Sofonisba Anguissola e le sue sorelle*, edited by Leonardo Arte, 89–116. Cremona: Centro culturale Città di Cremona, 1994.

Kusche, Maria, and Sylvia Ferino-Pagden. *Sofonisba Anguissola: A Renaissance Woman*. Washington, DC: National Museum of Women in the Arts, 1995.

La Ferrière, Hector de. *Rapport sur les recherches faites à la Bibliothèque impériale de Saint-Pétersbourg*. Paris: Bibliothèque impériale, 1867.

Lazzaro, Claudia. *The Italian Renaissance Garden: From the Conventions of Planting, Design, and Ornament to the Grand Gardens of Sixteenth-Century Central Italy*. New Haven: Yale University Press, 1990.

Lee, Maurice. *James Stewart, Earl of Moray: A Political Study of the Reformation in Scotland*. New York: Columbia University Press, 1953.

Lettenhove, Baron Kervyn de. *Relations politiques des Pays-bas et de l'Angleterre sous la règne de Philip II*. Vol. 2. Brussels: Royal Academy of Belgium, 1883.

Levin, Carole. *The Heart and Stomach of a King: Elizabeth I and the Politics of Sex and Power*. Philadelphia: University of Pennsylvania Press, 1994.

Loach, Jennifer. *Edward VI*. New Haven: Yale University Press, 1999.

Loades, David. *Elizabeth I*. London: Hambledon and London, 2003.

———. *Mary Tudor*. 2nd ed. Stroud, Gloucestershire: Amberley, 2011.

Maltby, William S. *Alba: A Biography of Fernando Alvarez de Toledo, Third Duke of Alba, 1507–1582*. Berkeley: University of California Press, 1983.

Mariéjol, Jean-Hippolyte. *Catherine de Médicis: 1519–1589*. Paris: J. Tallandier, 1979.

Marshall, Rosalind K. *Mary of Guise*. London: Collins, 1977.

Martin, Meredith. *Dairy Queens: The Politics of Pastoral Architecture from Catherine De' Medici to Marie-Antoinette*. Cambridge, MA: Harvard University Press, 2011.

Matthews, P. G. "Portraits of Philip II of Spain as King of England." *Burlington Magazine* 142, no. 1162 (January 2000): 13–19.

Medvei, V. C. "The Illness and Death of Mary Tudor." *Journal of the Royal Society of Medicine* 80 (1987): 766–70.

Merriman, Marcus. *The Rough Wooings: Mary Queen of Scots, 1542–1551.* East Linton: Tuckwell Press, 2000.

Mignet, M. Review of *Lettres, Instructions, et Mémoires de Marie Stuart. Journal des savants,* 1847.

Monter, William. *Judging the French Reformation: Heresy Trials by Sixteenth-Century Parlements.* Cambridge, MA: Harvard University Press, 1999.

———. "Heresy Executions in Reformation Europe, 1520–1565." In *Tolerance and Intolerance in the European Reformation,* edited by Ole Peter Grell and Bob Scribner. Cambridge: Cambridge University Press, 1996.

Orme, Nicholas. *Medieval Children.* New Haven: Yale University Press, 2001.

Pallotti, Donatella. "Maps of Woe: Narratives of Rape in Early Modern England." *Journal of Early Modern Studies* 2 (2013): 211–39.

Parker, Geoffrey. *Emperor: A New Life of Charles V.* New Haven: Yale University Press, 2019.

———. *Imprudent King: A New Life of Philip II.* New Haven: Yale University Press, 2014.

———. "The Place of Tudor England in the Messianic Vision of Philip II of Spain." *Transactions of the Royal Historical Society* 12 (2002): 167–221.

Parsons, John Carmi. *Medieval Queenship.* New York: St. Martin's Press, 1993.

Pébay-Clottes, Isabelle, and Claude Troquet. "Philippe Desducs, Mère de Diane de France." *Bibliothèque de l'École de Chartes* 148, no. 1 (1990): 151–60.

Pérez, Joseph. *The Spanish Inquisition: A History.* Translated by Janet Lloyd. New Haven: Yale University Press, 2005.

Perlingieri, Ilya Sandra. "Lady-in-Waiting: Recovering a Lost Woman Painter of the Renaissance." *Arts and Antiques* (April 1988): 66–71.

———. *Sofonisba Anguissola: The First Great Woman Artist of the Renaissance.* New York: Rizzoli, 1992.

Picard, Liza. *Elizabeth's London: Everyday Life in Elizabethan London.* New York: St. Martin's Press, 2004.

Pimodan, Gabriel de. *La mère des Guises: Antoinette de Bourbon, 1494–1583.* Paris: Honoré Champion, 1889.

Porter, Roy. *London: A Social History.* Cambridge, MA: Harvard University Press, 1994.

Potter, John Milton. "The Development and Significance of the Salic Law of the French." *English Historical Review* 52, no. 206 (April 1973): 235–53.

Ray, Sid. "Rape and Violence Against Women." In *Women in the Renaissance: Italy, France, and England*, edited by Diana Robin, Anne R. Larsen, and Carole Levin, 313–15. Santa Barbara, CA: ABC-Clio, 2007.

Reese, M. M. *The Royal Office of Master of the Horse*. London: Threshold Books, 1976.

Reiss, Sheryl E. "Widow, Mother, Patron of Art: Alfonsina Orsini de' Medici." In *Beyond Isabella: Secular Women Patrons of Art in Renaissance Italy*, edited by Sheryl E. Reiss and David G. Wilkins, 125–37. Kirksville, MO: Truman State University Press, 2001.

Reumont, Alphonse de, and Armand Baschet, eds. *La Jeunesse de Catherine de Médicis*. Paris: Henri Plon, 1866.

Ribera, Jean-Michel. "L'entrevue royale de Bayonne (1565), d'après la correspondence de Jean Ébrard de Saint-Sulpice, ambassadeur du roi de France à Madrid." *Annales du Midi: Revue archéologique, historique et philologique de la France méridionale* 118, no. 254 (2006): 181–201.

Riddle, John M. *Contraception and Abortion from the Ancient World to the Renaissance*. Cambridge, MA: Harvard University Press, 1992.

Roelker, Nancy L. *One King, One Faith: The Parlement of Paris and the Religious Reformations of the Sixteenth Century*. Berkeley: University of California Press, 1996.

———. *Queen of Navarre: Jeanne d'Albret, 1528–1572*. Cambridge, MA: Harvard University Press, 1968.

Romier, Lucien. *La Conjuration d'Amboise*. Paris: Perrin, 1923.

———. "La Mort de Henri II." *Revue du seizième siècle* I (1913): 99–152.

Rowe, Katherine. "Dismembering and Forgetting in *Titus Andronicus*." *Shakespeare Quarterly* 45, no. 3 (Fall 1994): 279–303.

Rowse, A. L. *The England of Elizabeth*. 2nd ed. Madison: University of Wisconsin Press, 2003.

Ruble, Alphonse de. *Antoine de Bourbon et Jeanne d'Albret*. Vol. 2. Paris: A. Labitte, 1881–86.

———. *La Première jeunesse de Marie Stuart*. Paris: E. Paul, L. Huard et Guillemin, 1891.

———. *Le Traité de Cateau-Cambrésis (2 et 3 avril, 1559)*. Paris: Labitte, 1889.

Sánchez, Magdalena S. "Where Palace and Convent Met: The Descalzas Reales in Madrid." *Sixteenth-Century Journal* 46, no. 1 (2015): 53–82.

Scott, Virginia, and Sara Sturm-Maddox. *Performance, Poetry and Politics on the Queen's Day: Catherine de Médicis and Pierre de Ronsard at Fontainebleau.* Aldershot, UK: Ashgate, 2007.

Seward, Desmond. *Prince of the Renaissance: The Life of Francis I.* Edinburgh: Constable, 1973.

Shell, Marc. *Elizabeth's Glass: With "The Glass of the Sinful Soul" (1544) by Elizabeth I, and "Epistle Dedicatory" and "Conclusion" (1548) by John Bale.* Lincoln: University of Nebraska Press, 1993.

Shepherd, J. C., and Geoffrey Jellicoe. *Italian Gardens of the Renaissance.* London: Academy Editions, 1994.

Sheppard, Francis. *London: A History.* New York: Oxford University Press, 1998.

Silleras-Fernandez, Nuria. "Inside Perspectives: Catalina and João III of Portugal and a Speculum for a Queen-to-Be." In *Self-Fashioning and Assumptions of Identity in Medieval and Early Modern Iberia*, edited by Laura Delbrugge, 226–52. Leiden: Brill, 2015.

Smith, Helen. "'More sweet vnto thee are / than wholesome for ye mind': Embodying Early Modern Women's Reading." *Huntington Library Quarterly* 73, no. 3 (September 2010): 413–32.

Starkey, David. *Elizabeth: Apprenticeship.* London: Chatto & Windus, 2000.

Stephens, John. "L'infanzia fiorentina di Caterina de' Medici, regina di Francia." *Archivio storico italiano* 142 (1984): 421–36.

Stoddart, Jane T. *The Girlhood of Mary Queen of Scots from Her Landing in France in August 1548 to Her Departure from France in August 1561 [1908].* Charleston, SC: Nabu Press, 2010.

Strickland, Agnes. *Lives of the Queens of Scotland and English Princesses Connected with the Regla Succession of Great Britain.* Vol. 2. Edinburgh: W. Blackwood and Sons, 1851.

Stuart, Marie Wilson. *The Scot who was a Frenchman: Being the Life of John Stewart, Duke of Albany, in Scotland, France, and Italy.* London: W. Hodge, 1940.

Sutherland, N. M. *The Huguenot Struggle for Recognition.* New Haven: Yale University, 1980.

———. *The Massacre of St. Bartholomew and the European Conflict, 1559–1572.* New York: Barnes & Noble, 1973.

Sutherland, Nicola. "The Assassination of François Duc de Guise, February 1563." *Historical Journal* 24, no. 2 (June 1981): 279–95.

Swain, Margaret H. *The Needlework of Mary, Queen of Scots.* New York: Van Nostrand Reinhold, 1973.

Taylor, Craig. "The Salic Law and the Valois Succession to the French Crown." *French History* 15, no. 4 (December 2001): 358–77.

———. "The Salic Law, French Queenship, and the Defense of Women in the Late Middle Ages." *French Historical Studies* 29, no. 4 (Fall 2004): 543–64.

Thompson, James Westfall. *The Wars of Religion in France, 1559–1576: The Huguenots, Catherine De Medici and Philip II.* Chicago: University of Chicago Press, 1909.

Thurley, Simon. *Whitehall Palace: The Official Illustrated History.* London: Historic Royal Palaces in association with Merrell, 2008.

Tytler, Patrick Fraser. *History of Scotland.* Vol. 5. Edinburgh: William Tait, 1845.

Van Scoy, Herbert, Bernerd C. Weber, and Julio Alvarotto. "The Marriage of Mary Queen of Scots and the Dauphin." *Scottish Historical Review* 31, no. III (1952): 41–48.

Villalon, Andrew. "The 1562 Head Injury of Don Carlos: A Conflict of Medicine and Religion in 16th-Century Spain." *Mediterranean Studies* 22, no. 2 (2014): 95–134.

Villius, Hans. "The Casket Letters: A Famous Case Reopened." *Historical Journal* 28, no. 3 (1985): 517–34.

Warkentin, Germaine, ed. *The Queen's Majesty's Passage & Related Documents.* Toronto: Center for Reformation and Renaissance Studies, 2004.

Weber, Bernerd C. "The Conference of Bayonne, 1565: An Episode in Franco-Spanish Diplomacy." *Journal of Modern History* 11, no. 1 (March 1939): 1–22.

Wellman, Kathleen Anne. *Queens and Mistresses of Renaissance France.* New Haven: Yale University Press, 2013.

Whitelock, Anna. *Mary Tudor: England's First Queen.* New York: Penguin, 2016.

Wiesner, Louis. *The Youth of Queen Elizabeth.* Edited by Charlotte Yonge. London: Hurst & Blackett, 1879.

Wiesner, Merry E. *The Marvelous Hairy Girls: The Gonzales Sisters and Their Worlds.* New Haven: Yale University Press, 2009.

Williams, H. Noel. *Henri II: His Court and Times.* New York: Charles Scribner's Sons, 1910.

———. *The Brood of False Lorraine.* Vol. 1. London: Hutchinson, 1918.

Williams, Kate. *Rival Queens: The Betrayal of Mary, Queen of Scots.* London: Cornerstone, 2018.

Wormald, Jenny. *Mary Queen of Scots: A Study in Failure.* London: G. Philip, 1988.

Zanello, Marc, Philippe Charlier, Bertrand Devaux, Robert Corns, Patrick Berche, and Johan Pallud. "The Death of Henry II, King of France (1519–1559): From Myth to Medical and Historical Fact." *Acta Neurochirurgica* 157 (2015): 145–49.

Zvereva, Alexandra. *Portraits dessinés de la cour des Valois: Les Clouet de Catherine de Médicis.* Paris: Arthena, 2011.

ACKNOWLEDGMENTS

The book is never closed. There are always new ways to understand the history of women from long ago, new opportunities to retell their stories—even for women who have been objects of fascination for centuries.

In January 2023, just as this book was about to go to press, an international team of cryptologists revealed that they had cracked the code that Mary, Queen of Scots, used during the 1570s while she was imprisoned in England. For centuries, those enciphered letters had sat unreadable in the Bibliothèque nationale de France; no one even knew they were by Mary. Now, the cryptologists George Lasry, Norbert Biermann, and Satoshi Tomokiyo, along with other scholars from around the world, are collating, deciphering, and translating into clear French more than fifty of those letters, preparing them for further study.

While the cryptologists were poring over enciphered letters, a team of researchers at the Massachusetts Institute of Technology made another startling discovery. It turns out that Mary had spiral-locked her last letter, written to King Henri III on the morning of her execution, sealing its sensitive contents within by folding the letter in an elaborate pattern of pleats and slits. The spiral lock, the most complicated form of "letterlocking" known to scholars, ensured that a letter was virtually tamper-proof; no spy could read it without first breaking the paper seal. Where did Mary learn to spiral lock? Might it have been in France, where—as the same MIT researchers have revealed—Catherine de' Medici also spiral-locked her letters? Performing a spiral lock required great knowledge and concentration. I find it astounding that in those dark hours Mary had the presence of mind to lock that letter with the most intricate of techniques. What does that spiral lock tell us? In the face of death, Mary was calm and clearheaded. She cared what happened to her letter. She wanted to be sure the voice Henri read was truly her own.

Sometimes the "discovery" is a new trove of material; sometimes it's the reassessment of a single letter. What discoveries, rereadings, and rewritings of these women and others will the coming years bring?

In my own research, I have consulted sources produced over the course of five centuries, now housed in archives and libraries across Europe and the United States. Time and again, I have run up against what L. P. Hartley famously expressed: "The past is a foreign country; they do things differently there." It goes without saying, perhaps, that sixteenth-century people did not speak, write, or punctuate the way we do. To facilitate reading, I have modernized the spelling of quotes from sixteenth-century English-language sources and have added punctuation in my translations of foreign-language sources. Mid-sixteenth-century French people also dated their letters differently than we do; their custom was to change the year at Easter rather than on January 1. Most editors since the nineteenth century have adjusted the dates of French sixteenth-century correspondence to reflect modern dating practices, and I follow suit here.

Time passed both quickly and slowly during the years of researching and writing this book, but I was fortunate to be surrounded by many people who supported me through the thick of it, no matter the pace. My heartfelt thanks go to the colleagues, friends, and family who read parts of the manuscript at various different stages, helped me hash out ideas, gave me tips and translations, sent me sources, listened attentively or at least feigned interest, fed and watered me, and believed in this book before I did: Tyler and Lisa Anbinder, Giuseppe Bruno-Chomin, Surekha Davies, Meredith Francis, Michael Friedman, Peter and Lisa Glassman, Carissa Harris, Alli Hester-Haddad and Jeff Chang, Rita and Mike Hopper, Katherine Ibbett, Claudia Lahaie, Lisa Leff, Kathleen Perry Long, Anna Lucca and Mike Paley, Mary McKinley, Rachel Mesch, Tobie Meyer-Fong, Jacqi Mosselson and Scott Ardizzone, Danielle Naftulin and Colin McKee, Cindie and Scott Nemes, Kelly Digby Peebles, Carolyn Simpkins, Mihoko Suzuki, Sergio Waisman. My parents, Susan Redmond Chang and Robert Chang, and my in-laws, Gene and Karen Naftulin, are always delighted to talk about books and have been my unfailing cheerleaders.

A special thanks to Holly Dugan and Andrea Frisch for their friendship over the years, across oceans and through many life changes; thank you for staying with me through the many twists and turns in writing this book. And also to Lynn Westwater, brilliant scholar of early modern Italy, for her cheerful companionship on long walks and coffee dates, as well as her invaluable assistance on all matters of Italian translation.

To the generous librarians and archivists at numerous institutions across Europe and the States who gathered materials and pointed me toward sources—thank you. I am especially indebted to the staff at the London Library, who provided me with a home in which to read, think, and write. In the States, the Folger Shakespeare Library did the same, and I eagerly await its reopening. University College London in the UK and the George Washington University in the US both granted me research scholar status and much-appreciated library resources.

I was privileged to have worked with several industrious researchers. Veronica Lansberg provided critical assistance in the National Archives of France. From Oxford, Emily Di Dodo sifted through manuscripts and provided invaluable transcriptions. Dr. Emily MacLeod's tireless research helped me understand the English context; her enthusiasm for the project fueled mine. Dr. James Jewitt, an exceptional fact-checker and image-gatherer, saved me from myself on countless occasions. James is one of the most organized and painstaking people I have ever met. I am grateful for his corrections; any mistakes that remain in the text are entirely my own.

My editor at Farrar, Straus and Giroux, Eric Chinski, championed this book when it was just a prologue and a few chapters, and continued to do so with extraordinary kindness during several arduous years. At Bloomsbury, Alexis Kirschbaum and Jasmine Horsey knew exactly what the book needed and steered me down the right path with compassion and patience, while Lauren Whybrow made this book into a beautiful object and kept me chuckling with her good humor. To the teams at both Bloomsbury and Farrar, Straus and Giroux— David Atkinson, Mike Athanson, Carmen Balit, Phil Beresford, Hugh Davis, Debra Helfand, Martha Jay, Na Kim, Anna Massardi, Molly McCarthy, Bri Panzica, Lauren Roberts, Tara Sharma, Genista Tate-Alexander, Francisco Vilhena, Rima Weinberg—thank you for all the care you've given to the project.

Several years ago, my friend and colleague the historian Tyler Anbinder introduced me to the extraordinary Jill Grinberg. At the time, *Young Queens* was just the kernel of an idea. Thank you, Jill, for seeing what that idea could become and for encouraging me to think bigger. You are a queen among queens. To the entire team at JGLM, thank you for being such stalwart contributors and companions on this long road.

Much of this book was written during the Covid-19 lockdowns of 2020–2021. Although it is a truism that writing is often a solitary endeavor, in this case I was almost never alone. Like the *petite cour* at Saint-Germain of long ago, our house was teeming, or at least that's how it felt. And yet, I could not have imagined better writing companions. My husband kept me supplied with steady doses of coffee, did much of the heavy lifting during those years, read draft after draft, and—most importantly—offered gentle perspective during the darker moments of writing. Ryan, you make this writing life possible. My children played along, living with these queens and their entourages over several years. They drew pictures of queens with round eyes and curlicue hair; they memorized who was mother, sister, daughter, father, brother, son, to whom. They professed appropriate indignation on the part of a fellow child when Jean and Jousine ate François de Longueville's fish and mourned that young boy when he died. They wondered aloud if I would ever finish this book and tried to give me space so I could. They grew up alongside it, becoming artists, writers, thinkers, and translators in their own right, with an uncanny knack for finding the mot juste. They, too, helped shape *Young Queens*. I am grateful to live with such creative and courageous people. Ryan, Eli, Leo, and Paloma, this book is for you.

INDEX

Plate section image credits

Embellished cover, *Heures de Catherine de Médicis*, Image Copyright © Bibliothèque nationale de France, Paris, France; Comb, Image Copyright © Victoria and Albert Museum, London; Catherine de Medici's bedchamber, Château de Chenonceau, Photo by DeAgostini/Getty Images; Girdle, Image Copyright ©Victoria and Albert Museum, London; Postpartum scene, from Jacob Rueff, *De Conceptu, et Generatione Hominis*, Frankfurt, 1580; Andrea Amati, Kurtz violin, Purchase, Robert Alonzo Lehman Bequest, 1999. Image courtesy of the Metropolitan Museum of Art's Open Access program; Italian filet lace, Anonymous Gift, 1879. Image courtesy of the Metropolitan Museum of Art's Open Access program; Pair of chopines, Image Copyright ©Victoria and Albert Museum, London; François Clouet, Portrait of Charles IX, Photo by Fine Art Images/Heritage Images/Getty Images; Spanish dress, Fletcher Fund, 1925. Image courtesy of the Metropolitan Museum of Art's Open Access program; François Clouet, Mary Queen of Scots, Everett V. Meeks, B.A. 1901, Fund. Image courtesy of Yale University Art Gallery; François Clouet, Portrait of Catherine de Médici and her children, Accepted in lieu of Inheritance Tax by H M Government and allocated to Strawberry Hill, 2020 © Strawberry Hill House & Garden; François Clouet, Portrait of Mary Stuart, Anonymous Gift, 1907. Image courtesy of the Metropolitan Museum of Art's Open Access program; Germain Le Mannier, One of Catherine de' Medici and Henri II's sons © Bridgeman Images; François Clouet, Francis II as a baby © Bridgeman Images; François Clouet, Elisabeth de Valois © Musée Condé, Chantilly / Bridgeman Images; Sofonisba Anguissola, Portrait of Elisabeth de Valois, Photo by Fine Art Images/Heritage Images/Getty Images; François Clouet, Portrait of Mary Stuart; King Francis I's armor © Bridgeman Images; François Clouet, Portrait of Henri, Dauphin of France, future King Henri II, in armor and wearing a plumed hat, Photo © RMN-Grand Palais (musée du Louvre) / Michel Urtado; French burgonet, Rogers Fund, 1904. Image courtesy of the Metropolitan Museum of Art's Open

Access program; Jean Clouet, Francis I, King of France, Photo by Fine Art Images/Heritage Images/Getty Images; Portrait of Charles de Guise, Cardinal de Lorraine, Image courtesy of Kunsthaus Zürich, the Betty and David Koetser Foundation, 1986; Château de Joinville, from Eusèbe Girault de Saint-Fargeau, *Guide pittoresque du voyageur en France*, Paris: F. Didot Frères, 1838, volume 3; Injury of Henry II during a tournament, 1559, Photo by API/Gamma-Rapho via Getty Images; Franz Hogenberg, Execution of Anne du Bourg, Photo by DeAgostini/Getty Images; Credit: Executions of Huguenots after the Huguenot conspiracy of Amboise in 1560: Some conspirators are hung by the neck from a tower, others are beheaded. Woodcut by J. Perrissin, ca. 1570. Wellcome Collection. Public Domain Mark; Joseph Nicolas Robert-Fleury, Colloquy of Poissy 1561, Photo by: Universal History Archive/UIG via Getty Images; Jean Perrissin, Massacre of the Protestants at Wassy, 1562, Image courtesy of the Rijksmuseum, Amsterdam; Elisabeth de Valois letter © Bibliothèque nationale de France, Paris, France; Catherine de Medici's signature © Bibliothèque nationale de France, Paris, France; Festival of the Whale, Gallerie degli Uffizi, Palazzo Pitti, deposit, Florence; Placard of Mary Queen of Scots and James Hepburn, Earl of Bothwell, as mermaid and hare, image courtesy of the National Archives; Mary, Queen of Scots, The Ospray, Image © Victoria and Albert Museum, London; Guillaume Martin (design attr. to) Jean-Baptiste Salmson (struck by), Marriage of Francis II and Mary Queen of Scots, Anonymous Gift, 1907. Image courtesy of the Metropolitan Museum of Art's Open Access program; Lochleven Castle, Photo by Print Collector/Getty Images; Writing box, Robert Lehman Collection, 1975. Image courtesy of the Metropolitan Museum of Art's Open Access program; Royal Palace of Aranjuez, Photo by Cristina Arias/Cover/Getty Images; Alonso Sánchez Coello, Portrait of doña Juana de Austria, princess of Portugal, Image Copyright © Fine Art Images/Heritage Images/Getty Images; Antonis Mor, Portrait of Philip II of Spain, Image Copyright © Bridgeman Images; Sofonisba Anguissola, Portrait of Elisabeth de Valois, Photo by Fine Art Images/Heritage Images/Getty Images; Philip II memorial Image © Alamy Stock Photo; Eugène Isabey, The Departure of Elisabeth of France for Spain, Acquired by Henry Walters, 1892. Image courtesy of the Walters Art Museum; Sofonisba Anguissola, Self-Portrait at Easel, Photo by Ali Meyer/Corbis/VCG via Getty Images; François Clouet, Portrait of Catherine de Médici, Image Copyright © The Trustees of the British Museum